The State of Working America

12th Edition

The State of Working America

12th Edition

LAWRENCE MISHEL

JOSH BIVENS

ELISE GOULD

HEIDI SHIERHOLZ

Economic
Policy
Institute

ILR Press
an imprint of Cornell University Press
Ithaca and London

First published 2012 by Cornell University Press
First printing, Cornell Paperbacks, 2012

ISBN 978-0-8014-5170-6 (cloth: alk. paper)
ISBN 978-0-8014-7855-0 (paper: alk. paper)

Printed in the United States of America

Recommended citation for this book is as follows: Mishel, Lawrence, Josh Bivens,
Elise Gould, and Heidi Shierholz, *The State of Working America, 12th Edition*. An
Economic Policy Institute Book. Ithaca, N.Y.: Cornell University Press, 2012

Cornell University Press strives to use environmentally responsible suppliers and
materials to the fullest extent possible in the publishing of its books. Such materials include vegetable-based, low-VOC inks and acid-free papers that are recycled,
totally chlorine-free, or partly composed of nonwood fibers. For further information,
visit our website at www.cornellpress.cornell.edu.

Cloth printing   10 9 8 7 6 5 4 3 2 1
Paperback printing 10 9 8 7 6 5 4 3 2 1

For the newest generation in my family, grandson Oliver and great nephew Nathan, who won't hit the job market for two decades.

— LAWRENCE MISHEL

To Holley and Finn, as well as to my parents and in-laws, who sometimes must think that they're the only people in the world I'm not trying to flood with my views on how the economy is doing.

— JOSH BIVENS

To Alex for patience and understanding; Eli, Sarah, and Jess for inspiration and perspective; and mom and dad for everlasting support.

— ELISE GOULD

For my little sangha, Alan, Sal, and Iko.

— HEIDI SHIERHOLZ

Visit **StateofWorkingAmerica.org**

The StateofWorkingAmerica.org website presents up-to-date historical data series on incomes, wages, employment, poverty, and other topics. All data presented in this book can be viewed online or downloaded as spreadsheets.

Acknowledgments

The preparation of this publication requires the work of many people on EPI's staff as well as contributions from other researchers. At EPI, Nicholas Finio, Natalie Sabadish, and Hilary Wething provided valuable research assistance by collecting and organizing data and creating the tables and figures with diligence, dedication, and good humor. Jin Dai provided extensive and able computer programming and data analysis.

We thank all the co-authors of previous editions of *The State of Working America*—Sylvia Allegretto, Jared Bernstein, Heather Boushey, David Frankel, John Schmitt, and Jacqueline Simon—for their lasting contributions. Joe Procopio and Pat Watson, editors of previous editions of this volume, also deserve acknowledgment for their contributions.

We want to particularly recognize the contribution of Lora Engdahl, EPI's publications director. Lora directed the entire production process, coordinating with the authors, the publisher, the designer, and EPI staff to ensure the highest quality product possible. She spent many late nights and weekends editing every chapter, every table, and every endnote with intelligence, diligence, and precision, providing much-needed consistency throughout the chapters. The book is better for her efforts and we are grateful.

EPI's communications team, led by Jody Franklin, worked diligently, creatively, and around-the-clock to produce this publication, to make its information available on the Web, and to disseminate it to the media and many other audiences. We thank editors Michael McCarthy and Pat Watson. We thank the Web and design team led by Eric Shansby, our online and creative director, who devised a new, more efficient Web-based system for producing the tables and figures. Dan Essrow, EPI's graphic designer, designed the book cover as well as many collateral pieces associated with this project. Communications team members Arin Karimian and Yesica Zuniga also helped get text and figure files ready for the design firm Winking Fish, led by Kieran Daly, which once again laid out the entire book with dedication and great patience. EPI's media relations team—led by Phoebe Silag and including Karen Conner and Donté Donald—provided very creative work to communicate our findings to the media, in all its many incarnations, traditional, social, and new. We acknowledge the dedicated work of Karen Conner, who has recently left EPI—this is the sixth edition of *The State of Working America* she has been an integral part of, and we will miss her expertise the next time around.

Many experts were helpful in providing data or their research papers for our use. We are particularly grateful for the assistance of Ed Wolff, who provided special tabulations. Others who provided data, advice, or their analysis include David Autor, Jon Bakija, Michael Chernousov, Miles Corak, Dirk Jenter, Janelle Jones, Brooks Pierce, and John Schmitt. Colleagues at the Economic Policy Institute, particularly David Cooper and Monique Morrissey, provided guidance and data for particular sections of the book. Christian Dorsey was responsible for generating the fact sheets that make this information accessible to a broader audience who (though we can't imagine why) might not want to read the entire book.

We extend our gratitude to the many dedicated public servants who collect and produce economic data for the U.S. government, including those at the Bureau of Labor Statistics, the Census Bureau, the Bureau of Economic Analysis, the Congressional Budget Office, and the Federal Reserve. Without their work, we could not have written this book.

Last, we wish to thank the following funders for their support of the Economic Policy Institute: The Annie E. Casey Foundation; The Atlantic Philanthropies; The Bauman Foundation; Ford Foundation; W.K. Kellogg Foundation; Open Society Foundations; Public Welfare Foundation; The Rockefeller Foundation; and Anonymous.

—The authors

Table of contents

Chapter 4
Wages: The top, and very top, outpace the rest 173

Documentation and methodology

Documentation

This book's comprehensive portrait of changes over time in incomes, taxes, wages, employment, wealth, poverty, and other indicators of economic performance and well-being relies almost exclusively on data in the tables and figures. Each table and figure has an abbreviated source notation that corresponds with a full citation in the bibliography at the end of the book. More detailed documentation (as well as information on methodology) is contained in the table and figure notes found at the end of each chapter. This system of documentation allows us to omit distracting footnotes and long citations within the text and tables.

In instances where we directly reproduce other people's work, table and figure source lines provide an "author/year" reference to the bibliography. Where we present our own computations based on other people's work, the source line reads "Authors' analysis of (source)." In these instances we have made computations that do not appear in the original work and are thus responsible for our analyses and interpretations. We also use this source notation when presenting descriptive trends from government income, employment, or other data, since we have made judgments about the appropriate time periods or other matters for the analysis that the source agencies have not made. When we present our own analysis of survey data we list the name of the survey and cite as a source "Authors' analysis of [name of Survey]." The table or figure notes provide information on the data analysis.

Time periods

Economic indicators fluctuate considerably with short-term swings in the business cycle. For example, incomes tend to fall in recessions and rise during expansions. Therefore, economists usually compare business cycle peaks with other peaks and compare troughs with other troughs so as not to mix apples and oranges. In this book, we examine changes between business cycle peaks. The initial year for some tables is 1947, with intermediate years of 1967, 1973, 1979, 1989, 2000, and 2007, all of which were business cycle peaks (at least in terms of having low unemployment). We also present data for the latest full year for which data are available (2010 or 2011 when available). Whenever figures show recessionary periods we base these on the National Bureau of Economic Research dating of cycles (NBER 2010).

In some tables, we also separately present trends for the 1995–2000 period (referred to as the late 1990s) in order to highlight the differences between those years and those of the early 1990s (or, more precisely, 1989–1995) and the business cycle of 2000–2007. This departs from the convention of presenting only business cycle comparisons (e.g., comparing 1979–1989 with 1989–2000 trends) or comparisons of recoveries. We depart from the convention because there was a marked shift in a wide variety of trends after 1995, and it is important to understand and explain these trends. We frequently refer to the 1979–2007 period because it represents the long period of growing inequality that predated the recession that began at the end of 2007.

Growth rates and rounding

Since business cycles differ in length, to facilitate comparisons we often present the average annual growth rates in each period rather than the total growth. In some circumstances, as noted in the particular tables, we have used log annual growth rates. This is done to permit decompositions.

In presenting the data, we round the numbers, usually to one decimal place, but we use unrounded data to compute growth rates, percentage shares, and so on. Therefore, it is not always possible to exactly replicate our calculations by using the data in the table. In some circumstances, this leads to an appearance of errors in the tables. For instance, we frequently present shares of the population (or families) at different points in time and compute changes in these shares. Because our computations are based on the "unrounded" data, the change in shares presented in a table may not exactly match the difference in the actual shares. Such rounding discrepancies are always small, however, and never change the conclusions of the analysis.

Adjusting for inflation

In most popular discussions, the Consumer Price Index for All Urban Consumers (CPI-U), often called the consumer price index, is used to adjust dollar values for inflation. However, some analysts hold that the CPI-U overstated inflation in the late 1970s and early 1980s by measuring housing costs inappropriately. The methodology for the CPI-U from 1983 onward was revised to address these objections. Other changes were introduced into the CPI-U in the mid-1990s but not incorporated into the historical series. Not all agree that these revisions are appropriate. We choose not to use the CPI-U to avoid any impression that this book's analyses overstate the decline in wages and understate the growth in family incomes over the last few decades.

Instead of the CPI-U, we adjust dollar values for inflation using the Consumer Price Index Research Series Using Current Methods (CPI-U-RS). This index uses the post-1983 methodology for housing inflation over the entire 1967–2007 period and incorporates the 1990s changes into the historical series (though not before 1978, as doing so would make economic performance in the years after 1978 falsely look better than the earlier years). The CPI-U-RS is now used by the Census Bureau in its presentations of real income data. Because it is not available for years before 1978, we extrapolate the CPI-U-RS back to earlier years based on inflation as measured by the CPI-U.

In our analysis of poverty in Chapter 7, however, we generally use the CPI-U rather than the CPI-U-RS, since the chapter draws heavily from Census Bureau publications that use the CPI-U. Moreover, the net effect of all of the criticisms of the measurement of poverty is that current methods understate poverty. Switching to the CPI-U-RS without incorporating other revisions (i.e., revising the actual poverty standard) would lead to an even greater understatement and would be a very selective intervention to improve the poverty measurement. (A fuller discussion of these issues appears in Chapter 7.)

The Current Population Survey

Many tables and figures in the book are based on original analyses of survey data generated by the monthly Current Population Survey (CPS), which is best known for producing the monthly unemployment rate and for the annual data on poverty and incomes. There are three separate CPS sources of data employed in our analyses: the Annual Social and Economic Supplement (the ASEC, commonly referred to as the March Supplement), the full monthly public data series, and the Outgoing Rotation Group. We examine trends in annual household or family income and poverty, as well as employer-provided benefits (health and pension) and annual wages, using the March Supplement. The formal name for these data and the way the data are referred to in source notes is the "Current Population Survey Annual Social and Economic Supplement microdata" or "Current Population Survey Annual Social and Economic Supplement *Historical Income Tables*." Details of our use of the March microdata are presented in Appendix A. We employ the full samples of the monthly CPS in analyses of employment/unemployment trends, and this is referred to in source notes as "basic monthly Current Population Survey microdata." The CPS Outgoing Rotation Group (CPS-ORG) provides information on the wages of workers for one-fourth of each month's sample, and we use these data for analyses of wage trends. These data are referred to in source notes as "Current Population Survey Outgoing Rotation Group microdata." Details of our use of these wage data are provided in Appendix B.

Household heads and families

We often categorize families by the age or the racial/ethnic group of the "household head," that is, the person in whose name the home is owned or rented. If the home is owned jointly by a married couple, either spouse may be designated the household head. Every family has a single household head. A "household head" may sometimes be referred to as the "householder."

Black, Hispanic, and white designations

Unless otherwise noted, races/ethnicities are presented in the following mutually exclusive categories: White refers to non-Hispanic whites, black refers to non-Hispanic blacks, and Hispanic refers to Hispanics of any race.

However, we sometimes use data from published sources that employ the U.S. Census Bureau's convention of including Hispanics in racial counts (e.g., with blacks and whites) as well as in a separate category. For instance, in Table 2.5 a white person of Hispanic origin is included both in counts of whites and in counts of Hispanics. In these cases, we alert readers to the exception.

CHAPTER 1

Overview

Policy-driven inequality blocks living-standards growth for low- and middle-income Americans

Like its predecessors, this edition of *The State of Working America* digs deeply into a broad range of data to answer a basic question that headline numbers on gross domestic product, inflation, stock indices, productivity, and other metrics can't wholly answer: "How well has the American economy worked to provide acceptable growth in living standards for most households?"

According to the data, the short answer is, "not well at all." The past 10 years have been a "lost decade" of wage and income growth for most American families. A quarter century of wage stagnation and slow income growth preceded this lost decade, largely because rising wage, income, and wealth inequality funneled the rewards of economic growth to the top. The sweep of the research in this book shows that these trends are the result of inadequate, wrong, or absent policy responses. Ample economic growth in the past three-and-a-half decades provided the potential to substantially raise living standards across the board, but economic policies frequently served the interests of those with the most wealth, income, and political power and prevented broad-based prosperity.

America's vast middle class has suffered a 'lost decade' and faces the threat of another

Wages and incomes of typical Americans are lower today than in over a decade. This lost decade of no wage and income growth began well before the Great Recession battered wages and incomes. In the historically weak expansion following the 2001 recession, hourly wages and compensation failed to grow for either high school– or college-educated workers and, consequently, the median income of working-age families had not regained pre-2001 levels by the time the Great Recession hit in December 2007. Incomes failed to grow over the 2000–2007 business cycle despite substantial productivity growth during that period.

Although economic indicators as of mid-2012 are stronger than they were two or three years ago, protracted high unemployment in the wake of the Great Recession has left millions of Americans with lower incomes and in economic distress. This problem is actually quite solvable: Tackle the source of the problem— insufficient demand—with known levers of macroeconomic policy to generate demand. Unfortunately, the problem is not being solved.

Consensus forecasts predict that unemployment will remain high for many more years, suggesting that typical Americans are in for another lost decade of living standards growth as measured by key benchmarks such as median wages and incomes. For example, as a result of persistent high unemployment, we expect that the incomes of families in the middle fifth of the income distribution in 2018 will still be below their 2007 and 2000 levels.

Income and wage inequality have risen sharply over the last three-and-a-half decades

Income inequality in the United States has grown sharply over the last few decades. This is evident in nearly every data measure and is universally recognized by researchers. For example, if we look at cash "market-based incomes," which exclude the effects of taxes and transfers (benefits received through government programs such as Social Security) and employer-provided in-kind benefits such as health insurance, the top 1 percent of tax units claimed more than six times as much of the total income growth between 1979 and 2007 as the bottom 90 percent—59.8 percent to 8.6 percent. Similarly, there has been a tremendous disparity in the growth of wages earned by individual workers. Wages for the top 1 percent grew about 156 percent between 1979 and 2007, whereas wages for the bottom 90 percent rose by less than 17 percent.

Rising inequality is the major cause of wage stagnation for workers and of the failure of low- and middle-income families to appropriately benefit from growth

There has been sufficient economic growth since 1979 to provide a substantial across-the-board increase in living standards. However, because wage earners and households at the top reaped most of the benefits of this growth, wages were relatively stagnant for low- and middle-wage workers from 1979 to 2007 (except in the late 1990s), and incomes of lower- and middle-class households grew slowly. This pattern of income growth contrasts sharply with that of the postwar period up through the 1970s, when income growth was broadly shared.

The economy's failure to ensure that typical workers benefit from growth is evident in the widening gap between productivity and median wages. In the first few decades after World War II, productivity and median wages grew in tandem. But between 1979 and 2011, productivity—the ability to produce more goods and services per hour worked—grew 69.2 percent, while median hourly compensation (wages and benefits) grew just 7.0 percent.

Economic policies caused increased inequality of wages and incomes

Since the late 1970s, economic policy has increasingly served the interests of those with the most wealth, income, and political power and effectively shifted economic returns from typical American families to the already well-off. A range of economic policy choices—both actions and failures to act—in the last three decades have had the completely predictable effect of increasing income inequality. These choices include letting inflation consistently erode the purchasing power of the minimum wage, and allowing employer practices hostile to unionization efforts to tilt the playing field against workers. U.S. policies have also hastened integration of the U.S. economy and the much poorer global economy on terms harmful to U.S. workers, refused to manage clearly destructive international trade imbalances, and targeted rates of unemployment too high to provide reliably tight labor markets for low- and middle-wage workers.

Industry deregulation (of trucking, communications, airlines, and so on) and privatization have also put downward pressure on wages of middle-class workers. Meanwhile, deregulation of the financial sector—without a withdrawal of the government guarantees that allow private interests to take excessive risks—has provided the opportunity for well-placed economic actors to claim an ever-larger share of economic growth. An increasingly well-paid financial sector and policies regarding executive compensation fueled wage growth at the top and the rise of the top 1 percent's incomes. Large reductions in tax rates provided a motive for well-placed actors to take these risks and also fueled the after-tax income growth at the top.

Although these post-1979 economic policies predictably redistributed wages, income, and wealth upward, there was no corresponding benefit in the form of faster overall economic growth. In fact, economic growth from the 1970s onward was slower than the economic growth in the prior 30 years. Besides resulting in slower growth, economic policy decisions also contributed to the fragility of the U.S. economy in the run-up to the Great Recession. For example, otherwise-anemic economic growth in the mid-2000s was driven by a housing bubble made possible largely through a deregulated financial sector that was hiding, not managing, the growing risk that home prices would fall. This economic fragility proved catastrophic when confronted with the shock of plummeting demand after the housing bubble burst and destroyed families' housing wealth. More equitable and stable economic growth can only occur if there is a marked change in the direction of U.S. economic policy.

Claims that growing inequality has not hurt middle-income families are flawed

Despite the near-universal acknowledgement of growing income inequality as a fact of recent American economic history, a number of studies have claimed that it has not prevented middle-income families from achieving acceptable income growth since 1979. These studies argue that under a comprehensive measure of income that includes benefits from employers and government transfers, incomes of the middle fifth of households in the income distribution grew by 19.1 percent between 1979 and 2007. But this 19.1 percent cumulative (0.6 percent annual) growth rate does not mean that the private sector of the American economy is performing well for middle-income families. First, had the middle fifth's incomes grown at the same 51.4 percent cumulative rate as overall average incomes (i.e., had there been no growth in income disparities), their annual income in 2007 would have been far greater—$18,897 higher. Second, this 0.6 percent annual growth rate does not come close to the income growth between 1947 and 1979, when middle-fifth family income grew 2.4 percent annually.

Third, the large share of this 1979–2007 income growth coming from government transfers (53.6 percent) reflects the strength of American social insurance programs (Social Security, Medicare, and Medicaid) and is not evidence that the private U.S. economy is being managed effectively or fairly. Given the unnecessary push to cut these programs going forward, it is unlikely that this source of middle-class income growth can be relied on in future decades. Fourth, higher household labor earnings contributed a modest 6.1 percent to this middle-fifth income growth, and the impressive ability of American households to steadily increase their work hours over this period, in part by increasing the number of household members employed, will not be replicable in the years ahead.

Last, the data on comprehensive incomes are technically flawed because they count, as income, rapidly rising health expenditures made on behalf of households by employers and the government without accounting for the excessive health care inflation that has absorbed large portions of the increase in this particular source of income. If rising health care costs are properly accounted for, the 19.1 percent growth in comprehensive middle-fifth incomes is lowered by a third. If we strip out health care inflation, government transfers, and additional hours worked—elements that add to measured income growth but cannot be attributed to a well-performing private economy—middle-class incomes grew just 4.9 percent across the 28 years from 1979 to 2007, with most of that growth occurring just in the late 1990s.

Growing income inequality has not been offset by increased mobility

Growing income inequality in the United States is a trend made more disturbing by static, and perhaps declining, economic mobility. Despite the image of the nation as a place where people with initiative and skills can vault class barriers, America today is not a highly mobile society, compared with our international peers. In one study of 17 Organisation for Economic Co-Operation and Development (OECD) countries, the United States ranked 13th on a measure of mobility, ahead only of Slovenia, Chile, Italy, and the United Kingdom, and far behind Denmark, Norway, Finland, and Canada.

Americans largely end up where they started out on the economic ladder, and the same is true for their children. For example, one study showed that two-thirds (66.7 percent) of sons of low-earning fathers (in the bottom fifth of the earnings distribution) end up in the bottom two-fifths as adults, while only 18.1 percent make it to the top two-fifths. There is no evidence that mobility has increased to offset rising inequality, and in fact some research shows a decline.

Inequalities persist by race and gender

As this book, and our research in general, shows, there is actually no single economic "state of America" but rather an America that is experienced differently, and often unequally—not only by class, as discussed, but by race and gender. For example, a review of employment rates from 1979 to 2011 shows that black and Hispanic unemployment always far exceeded white unemployment. As this book was nearing completion in July 2012, the overall unemployment rate was 8.3 percent—roughly the same as the African American unemployment rate during all of 2007, the last year of economic expansion before the Great Recession.

Further, even in 1992, the peak of black/white equality in wealth holdings, median black household wealth was just 16.8 percent of median white household wealth. By 2010—after the housing bubble had burst and destroyed $7 trillion in equity in residential real estate (the most widely held type of wealth)—median African American wealth was just 5.0 percent of median white wealth.

And while gaps between labor market outcomes of men and women have closed in recent decades, progress has occurred not just because women gained ground, but also because men lost ground. Gaps in employer-provided pension coverage rates between men and women, for example, have rapidly closed in recent decades, but only because men's coverage rates have fallen while women's have stagnated.

Economic history and policy as seen from below the top rungs of the wage and income ladder

This chapter assesses U.S. economic performance over the last 30 years through the lens of this failure of the economy to deliver appropriate gains to the broad middle class and fuel greater social mobility. One could label this policy regime a "failure," but one could also say this was a "failure by design"—the policies worked as intended to boost the economic standing of those who already had the most income and wealth. Our discussion in this chapter begins with the Great Recession and its aftermath, moves to the lost decade period commencing with the 2001 recession, and concludes with the years between 1979 and the beginning of the Great Recession.

The Great Recession: The shock to demand and the need for continued stimulus. The key lesson to be learned from our current crisis is that full and meaningful recovery from the Great Recession that officially ended in June 2009 has not yet happened and is assuredly not guaranteed. As this book is being written in mid-2012, things are indeed better than they were two and three years ago, but the American economy remains far from healthy, and there is danger in prematurely declaring "mission accomplished." There is a clear continued need for fiscal stimulus such as aid to the states, infrastructure investments, and safety net supports such as unemployment insurance and food stamps, as well as expansionary monetary policy. But, just as patients prescribed antibiotics should not stop taking them as soon as their immediate symptoms fade, we must not remove economic supports before full economic health has been genuinely restored; doing so could come back to hurt us.

Economic lost decades: The threat of continued disappointing wage and income growth. Our examination of a broad range of living standards benchmarks argues strongly that recovery to the economic conditions that prevailed in 2007, immediately prior to the Great Recession, is too modest a goal. The 2000s expansion was the weakest on record and provided very little in terms of lasting gains for American families. As a result, we have had a lost decade where wages and benefits failed to grow for the vast majority of the workforce, including college-educated workers as well as the two-thirds of the workforce who lack a college degree. The typical working-age family had lower income in 2007 than before the early 2000s recession, and incomes fell further in the Great Recession. Using current projections of unemployment in coming years, we estimate that the average income of households in the middle fifth of the income distribution will remain below its 2000 level until at least 2018. This would lead to another lost decade for far too many American workers and the households and families they support.

Stagnating living standards before the lost decade: Rising inequality from 1979 to 2007 halts income and wage growth for most Americans. The stagnation of wages and incomes for low- and middle-income households during the 2000s was merely a continuation of longer-term trends. For most of the years between 1979 and 2007, living standards growth for most American households lagged far behind overall average growth because the vast majority of growth was claimed by a select sliver at the top of the income ladder. Without a brief period of strong across-the-board wage and income growth in the late 1990s, virtually the *entire* 28-year period before the Great Recession may well have been an era of lost growth for low- and middle-income families. The key to understanding the growing inequality of wages and benefits is the continued divergence between the growth of productivity and the hourly wages and benefits of a typical worker. Explaining this divergence is essential for understanding the failure of the U.S. economy to deliver for most Americans and their families.

Table notes and figure notes at the end of this chapter provide documentation for the data, as well as information on methodology, used in the tables and figures that follow.

The Great Recession: Causes and consequences

The State of Working America's analysis of economic data extends from the 1940s through 2011. In the context of recent history, there was good news for the American economy at the end of 2011: After peaking at 10.0 percent in October 2009, the unemployment rate had fallen by 1.5 percentage points, fully 1.3 of which had been shaved off just in the preceding 13 months.

Unfortunately, this decline in the unemployment rate from October 2009 to December 2011 was not driven primarily by a jobs boom. Rather, essentially all of the reduction was spurred by a sharp decrease in the labor force participation rate (the share of working-age people who are either employed or unemployed, i.e., jobless but actively seeking work), which dropped by a full percentage point. Most of this decline in labor force participation was due to the sluggish economy itself, rather than any long-term demographic trend (as demonstrated in Table 5.5 later in this book).

Even worse, the unemployment rate at the end of 2011 was 8.5 percent—higher than it had been since 1983 (except since the onset of the Great Recession). Further, there remained a huge gap between labor-market health at the end of 2011 and even that which prevailed in December 2007, which was hardly a high-water mark (as will be discussed later). The size of this gap in labor-market health is depicted in **Figure 1A**: In December 2011, the American economy needed roughly 10.3 million jobs to return to the unemployment and labor force participation rates of December 2007—5.8 million jobs to replace those still lost from

Figure 1A Payroll employment and the number of jobs needed to keep up
with the growth in the potential labor force, Jan. 2000–Dec. 2011

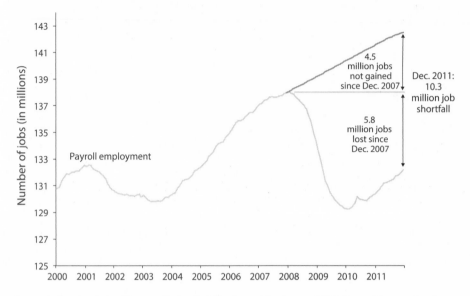

Source: Authors' analysis of Bureau of Labor Statistics Current Employment Statistics and Congressional
Budget Office (2012)

the recession and 4.5 million new jobs to absorb the growth in the working-age
population.

The source of this labor market distress is clear: the Great Recession, brought
on at the end of 2007 by the bursting of the housing bubble that had provided
the only real boost to the otherwise-anemic recovery from the 2001 recession.

A very condensed macroeconomic history of the Great Recession and its aftermath

Between June 2006 and June 2009, housing prices fell roughly 30 percent, which
erased roughly $7 trillion in U.S. household wealth. According to extensive re-
search literature on the housing "wealth effect," each $1 in housing wealth gener-
ates roughly 6 to 8 cents of annual consumer spending. Thus the $7 trillion in lost
housing wealth led to a roughly $500 billion contraction in consumer spending.
On top of this, as housing prices fell, activity in the overbuilt residential real estate
construction sector (i.e., building new homes and buildings) collapsed, leading to
roughly another $400 billion in lost demand. Then, the direct shock to demand
from this drop in consumer spending and residential construction quickly rippled
outward. As the supply of customers dried up, firms stopped investing in new

plants and equipment, depressing overall business investment. As tax revenues fell and social safety net expenditures increased, state and local governments reduced programs, cut jobs, and increased revenues, which further reduced overall demand for goods and services and exacerbated the recession. The relationships between home prices and wealth effects and residential investment are shown in **Figure 1B**.

In short, the Great Recession was a classic "Keynesian" downturn (one driven by deficient aggregate demand) that required, and still requires, Keynesian solutions (policy measures to restore this demand). The negative shock to private spending and demand that led to the Great Recession was enormous—greater in most estimates than the one that caused the Great Depression. Without sufficient spending to maintain demand for goods and services, the demand for labor fell, leading to massive job losses and a sharp rise in unemployment.

The proper policy response to this collapse in demand was analytically easy to design if daunting to implement: Use all the levers of macroeconomic policy that can spur spending in the near-term to restore the demand that was lost in the wake of housing price declines. Unfortunately, too many in the macroeconomic policymaking realm had grown accustomed to thinking that just one lever

Figure 1B Home prices and their impact on residential investment and housing wealth, 1995–2011

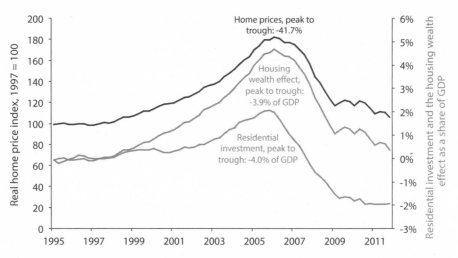

Note: The housing wealth effect is obtained by multiplying the change in housing wealth from its 1997 average by $.06 (the low-end estimate of annual consumer spending generated by each dollar in housing wealth) and expressing the resulting product as a share of overall GDP. Data are quarterly.

Source: Authors' analysis of Case, Quigley, and Shiller (2005); Shiller (2012); Bureau of Economic Analysis National Income and Product Accounts (Table 1.1.5); and Federal Reserve Board Flow of Funds Accounts

was ever needed to fight recessions. Specifically, a decades-in-the-making conventional wisdom argued that the U.S. economy could be revived simply by having the Federal Reserve lower short-term "policy" interest rates, putting downward pressure on the longer-term interest rates of housing and industrial loans. This, it was assumed, would spur households and businesses to sufficiently boost their borrowing and spending to buy new homes and new capital equipment. But in late 2008, these policy interest rates were buried at zero, even as job losses were reaching historic proportions, with roughly 740,000 jobs on average lost *each month* in the six months between November 2008 and April 2009.

This hemorrhaging of jobs was radically slowed and finally halted by the large boost to economic activity from the 2009 American Recovery and Reinvestment Act (ARRA), as well as by the federal budget's "automatic stabilizers"—progressive taxes and safety net programs that kept households' disposable incomes from falling as fast as market incomes fell.

However, as ARRA's support began fading in the second half of 2010, economic growth decelerated markedly. The policy response to the Great Recession had indeed arrested the outright economic contraction, but had not gone far enough to bring the economy back to full health. At the end of 2011, the unemployment rate remained at 8.5 percent and had matched or exceeded the highest rates of the recessions of the early 1990s and early 2000s for a full three years. As this book went to press, policymakers were *talking* about the need to reduce unemployment but were effectively blocking precisely those efforts that would provide more support to the flagging economy.

We should be very clear about the danger of this complacency in the face of elevated unemployment. It's not simply that full recovery to pre-recession health will come too slowly—though this delay alone does indeed inflict a considerable cost. Instead, the danger is that full recovery *does not come at all*. Nations have thrown away decades of growth because policymakers failed to ensure complete recovery. Japan has been forfeiting potential output—trillions of dollars' worth, cumulatively—for most of the past 20 years. Recent research (Schettkat and Sun 2008) has suggested that the German economy operated below potential in 23 of 30 years between 1973 and 2002 because monetary policymakers were excessively inflation-averse. Lastly, U.S. economic history provides the exemplar of what can happen to a depressed economy when policymakers fail to respond correctly: The level of industrial production in the United States was the same in 1940 as it was 11 years before.

While we cannot *guarantee* that the current policy path leads inevitably to stagnation, it is unwise to flirt with this possibility when there are clear solutions to our current unemployment crisis. It is in fact by far the most immediately solvable of the economic problems confronting the United States. Experts widely agree on the source of the problem (insufficient demand) and the levers of macroeconomic policy to pull to generate demand. Evaluations of ARRA and other interventions carried out so far overwhelmingly support this diagnosis and these cures.

If the U.S. political system cannot focus on and solve the joblessness crisis, prospects are dim indeed for solving the longer-term challenges documented throughout *The State of Working America* that have also been bred by policy choices made in recent decades.

Economic 'lost decades': Weak growth for most Americans' wages and incomes before and likely after the Great Recession

While a return to pre-recession unemployment and labor force participation rates is the most pressing U.S. policy priority, it is a far-too-modest goal for those committed to achieving broadly shared prosperity. To put it bluntly, the entire 2000–2007 business cycle was no Golden Age for most American workers and their families.

Even from a macroeconomic perspective, the economic recovery and expansion following the 2001 recession was historically weak. Gross domestic product, employment, compensation, and investment all turned in the weakest performance of any post–World War II business cycle, and consumption growth and unemployment performed far below average. This weak macroeconomic performance followed a decades-long policy trajectory that had deprived too many American workers of bargaining power they need to secure robust wage growth. As a result, on most measures of economic success, typical American families and households progressed little or not at all during this time. Layering the worst economic crisis in 80 years on top of this anemic growth produced a lost decade of prosperity for most American households.

We do not use the term "lost decade" lightly. It has a rich and sad history in economics, having first been used to describe the catastrophic performance of economies in the developing world (Latin America and Africa in particular) in the wake of international financial crises in the 1980s and 1990s. Later, the term was applied to Japan's experience during the 1990s and 2000s, when bursting asset market bubbles hobbled economic growth for over 10 years (in fact, Japan may have just been emerging from its own lost decade before the global Great Recession hit in 2007).

From the perspective of low, moderate, and middle-income American households, a lost decade *has already happened* here in the United States; key living-standards benchmarks such as median incomes and wages have posted either zero or negative growth since the early 2000s. Worse, given the dependence of incomes and wages on crucial labor market barometers such as unemployment and labor force participation rates, and given how long these barometers are expected to perform short of pre-recession levels, we may well undergo a full *two* decades of stagnation of many living-standard benchmarks.

Weak labor demand at the heart of the lost decade

Table 1.1 provides data on key labor market indicators and living-standards benchmarks over the full 2000s business cycle and through the Great Recession and its aftermath. Between 2000 and 2007, employment grew at an annualized rate of just 0.6 percent—only a third the rate of growth between the business cycle peaks of 1989 and 2000 and across all post–World War II business cycles. The stunning job losses inflicted by the Great Recession then followed this weak growth. By the end of 2011—two-and-a-half years after the official end of the Great Recession—payroll job levels had only returned to mid-2004 levels.

The last decade looks equally dismal as measured by the most widely cited barometer of labor market health—the unemployment rate. In 2000 the average annual unemployment rate was just 4.0 percent. This extraordinarily low rate was never regained. Even in 2006 and 2007, when unemployment was at its lowest point in the 2000–2007 business cycle, the average unemployment rate was 4.6 percent. The average annual unemployment rate spiked in the aftermath of the Great Recession, peaking at 9.6 percent in 2010. By 2011, it had fallen only to 8.9 percent, more than twice as high as in 2000. And, as high as it has been, the unemployment rate may well paint too-rosy a picture of the state of labor demand in the 2000s and today. When labor force participation falls, measured unemployment falls, all else equal—and by the end of 2011, the labor force participation rate was at its lowest point during either the recession or recovery.

Considerations such as these suggest going to other labor market indicators to better gauge labor market health over the 2000s and today. One of our preferred alternative measures of labor market health is the employment-to-population ratio (EPOP) of prime-age (25- to 54-year-old) workers. Because the unemployment rate examines only those who self-identify as actively looking for work, and because this active job search is likely curtailed when potential workers are unable to find jobs after long searches, the prime-age EPOP may better capture short-run changes in labor market health. Since the prime-age EPOP excludes many college students and retirees—population groups not expected to be actively searching for work—it is less affected by demographic shifts.

Changes in the prime-age EPOP—tracked in **Figure 1C**—tell an even darker story than changes in unemployment. The EPOP, which peaked at 81.8 percent in the first quarter of 2000, failed to approach that rate during the economic recovery and expansion preceding the Great Recession, instead peaking at 80.2 percent in the first quarter of 2007. Then the Great Recession hit and the prime-age EPOP fell, by a catastrophic 5.3 percentage points by the fourth

Table 1.1 Key labor market indicators and living-standards benchmarks, 2000–2011 (2011 dollars)

	Payroll employment	Unemployment rate	Labor force participation rate	Working-age employment-to-population ratio	Median household income*	Working-age median family income*	Worker hourly wages			Total economy productivity
							10th percentile	Median	95th percentile	
2000	131,785	4.0%	67.1%	81.5%	$54,851	$69,233	$8.24	$15.99	$45.44	$49.62
2007	137,598	4.6	66.0	79.9	54,499	68,893	8.45	16.40	49.39	57.22
2011	131,359	8.9	64.1	75.1	51,014**	63,967**	8.16	16.07	49.74	60.83
*Change***										
2000–2007	0.6%	0.6 ppts.	-1.1 ppts.	-1.6 ppts.	-0.1%	-0.1%	0.4%	0.4%	1.2%	2.1%
2000–2011	0.0	4.9	-3.0	-6.4	-0.7%**	-0.7%**	-0.1	0.0	0.8	1.9

* Data are for money income.
** Data are for 2010 (top panel) and 2000–2010 (bottom panel) due to data limitations.
*** Percent change numbers are annualized rates; percentage-point change numbers are cumulative change.

Source: Authors' analysis of Current Population Survey (CPS) public data series, CPS ASEC microdata and *Historical Income Tables* (Table H-5), CPS-ORG microdata, BLS Current Employment Statistics, and unpublished Total Economy Productivity data from BLS Labor Productivity and Costs program

Figure 1C Employment-to-population ratio, age 25–54, 1995–2011

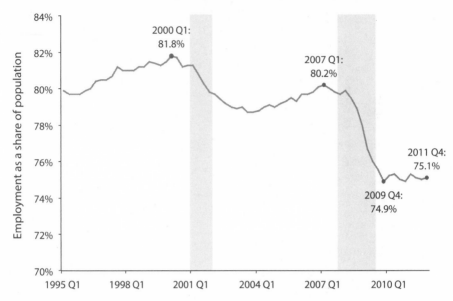

Note: Data are quarterly and extend from the first quarter of 1995 to the fourth quarter of 2011. Shaded areas denote recessions.

Source: Authors' analysis of Current Population Survey public data series

quarter of 2009—the largest cyclical fall in the history of this statistic. As of the last quarter of 2011, the prime-age employment-to-population ratio was 75.1 percent, which, except for during the Great Recession, was lower than at any point since 1983.

Weak labor demand devastates key living standards

The weak labor demand apparent in these trends in unemployment rates and employment-to-population ratios does not just damage those who cannot find work. Because a large pool of potential workers who are not currently employed provides extra competition for incumbent workers, employees' bargaining power is sharply reduced during times of weak labor demand. This reduced bargaining power results in depressed rates of growth of hourly wages. And because overall incomes for typical American households are so dependent on wage and salary income, overall income growth for these households tends to slow as well.

For example, a robust body of research has found that high rates of unemployment place downward pressure on wage growth. In our research, we find that a 1 percentage-point increase in the unemployment rate has been associated (all else equal) with a roughly 0.9 percent reduction in the annual growth of median wages for both men and women. Wages at the bottom end of the wage distribution are even more sensitive to changes in unemployment, while wages at the top end are a bit less sensitive. Recent history reflects this relationship. As the unemployment rate rose by 4.3 percentage points between 2007 and 2011, inflation-adjusted median wages for both men and women fell, and inflation-adjusted wages at the 10th percentile fell even more. While Chapter 4 examines this relationship between wage growth and unemployment in detail (particularly Figure 4W), it can be seen relatively well in the raw numbers, as in **Figure 1D**, which shows the decline in real (inflation-adjusted) median wages and lagged unemployment rates. High rates of unemployment lead to low (or even negative) annual rates of median wage growth.

Similarly, there is a clear empirical relationship between high levels of unemployment and slower income growth for families at the low and middle rungs of the income distribution. (In fact, there is a statistically and economically significant relationship between unemployment and income growth rates for all family income percentiles up to the 90th, though it tends to weaken as incomes rise.)

Figure 1D Unemployment rate and real median-wage decline, 1991–2011

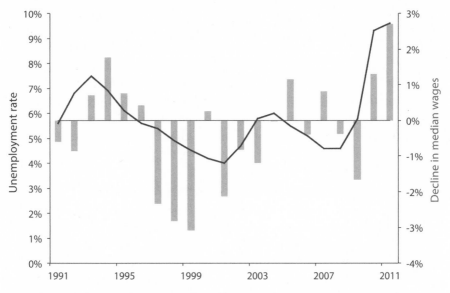

Note: In this graph, the unemployment rate is lagged by one year because its impact on unemployment is not immediate.

Source: Authors' analysis of Current Population Survey public data series and CPS Outgoing Rotation Group microdata

These historic relationships between wage and income growth and labor demand explain much of the lost decade of wage and income growth for typical American households. As the labor-market momentum of the late 1990s and early 2000s faded, higher rates of unemployment and lower employment-to-population ratios led to a marked slowdown in wage and income growth. As shown in Table 1.1, between 2000 and 2007, worker hourly wages at the 10th percentile and at the median grew only 0.4 percent a year, whereas wages at the 95th percentile grew 1.2 percent annually—three times as much.

Further, these rates probably understate just how weak labor demand was in the 2000s. Wage-growth momentum from the tight labor markets of the late 1990s carried into the early 2000s then faded, with wages for most American workers actually falling through most of the 2001 to 2007 recovery. For example, worker hourly wages at the 10th percentile peaked in 2002, then fell by 1.7 percent between 2002 and 2007. Median worker hourly wages peaked in 2003, then fell by 1.6 percent between 2003 and 2007. Then, as unemployment rose rapidly after the onset of the Great Recession (increasing 4.3 percentage points between 2007 and 2011), 10th-percentile and median wages fell rapidly. By 2011, after being battered by years of high unemployment, wages at the 10th percentile were down by 5 percent relative to their 2002 peak, and median wages were down by 3.5 percent relative to their 2003 peak.

Table 1.1 also shows data on median household income, another key barometer of typical living standards. This measure never recovered its pre-2001 peak during the subsequent business cycle. By 2010, median household income had fallen by 0.7 percent even relative to the level that prevailed a full decade before, in 2000.

The crucial role of tight labor markets in generating wage growth is highlighted by another finding in Table 1.1. The weak wage and employment performance for most American households occurred during a period of adequate economy-wide productivity growth: Between 2000 and 2007, productivity grew 2.1 percent annually, more than five times faster than median worker hourly wages.

Dim growth prospects forecast another lost decade

The crucial role of tight labor markets in generating wage and income growth is especially disquieting given the extreme economic weakness projected in coming years. Most near-term forecasts of unemployment do not project a return to even too-conservative official estimates of "full employment" (the absolutely lowest unemployment rate consistent with non-accelerating inflation) until 2017 or 2018. Further, if job growth continues at its 2011 pace, the U.S. economy would not return to December 2007 unemployment and labor force participation rates until 2021—assuming that the United States does not have another recession in this period. This would entail a 12-year stretch without a recession, a happy circumstance that has not blessed the United States since World War II, and almost certainly not before World War II either.

The consequences of recovery this slow are detailed in Chapter 2. Based on its historic relationship with unemployment, we can project income growth for middle-income families in coming years. For this exercise, we use two widely cited unemployment forecasts, one from the Congressional Budget Office (CBO) and another from Moody's Analytics Economy.com, both of which project that the U.S. economy will return to pre-recession labor market conditions for the first full year in 2018. As **Figure 1E** indicates, under both scenarios, in 2018 incomes of families in the middle fifth of the income distribution will still be below middle-fifth family income in 2000. This outcome would constitute two lost decades for family income growth, a likely scenario unless policymakers commit to ensuring a much more rapid decline in joblessness than is currently projected. This is an underappreciated economic catastrophe in the making.

Figure 1E Change in real family income of the middle fifth, actual and predicted, 2000–2018

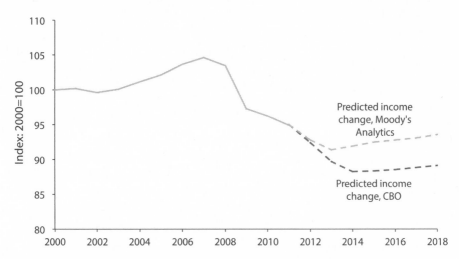

Note: The figure shows the paths of income growth projected by a model based on the relationship between income growth and the unemployment rate from 1948 to 2010, using forecasted unemployment rates from the Congressional Budget Office and Moody's Analytics. Data are for money income.

Source: Authors' analysis of Current Population Survey Annual Social and Economic Supplement *Historical Income Tables* (Tables F-2, F-3, F-5), Congressional Budget Office (2012), and Moody's Analytics (2012)

Two key lessons from the lost decade

This survey of evidence from both the Great Recession and the anemic economic expansion that preceded it imparts a clear lesson: Typical Americans' wages and incomes need tight labor markets in order to post gains that match economy-wide averages. And often what looks upon casual inspection to be a tight labor market (say, one with an overall unemployment rate below 5 percent, as was the case in 2006 and 2007) is not adequate to reliably spur across-the-board growth. (In the following section we detail the forces that have depressed wage and income growth for most Americans even in seemingly tight labor markets—forces driven by policy, such as declining unionization, eroding purchasing power of the minimum wage, and global integration.)

Given this, policymakers need not only to reverse the policy changes that have restricted wage and income growth but recommit to the goal of full employment. The pursuit of full employment should not be stymied by arguments (made often in contemporary debates) that it will lead to rising inflation. Purely *hypothetical* increases in inflation caused by excessively tight labor markets should be no excuse to abandon the effort to move the economy quickly back to full employment after a recession that has inflicted long-lasting damage on wages and incomes.

Another key lesson from our review of the lost decade can be found in the extent of wage declines across workers with different levels of education. Contrary to the conventional wisdom in certain policy circles, the wage problems of American workers are not driven by a lack of skills. The pattern of hourly wage declines as the late 1990s boom subsided affected high school and college graduates similarly. In the last four years of the recovery and expansion preceding the Great Recession, average compensation (wages plus benefits) for high school and college graduates shrank by 3.2 and 1.2 percent, respectively, even as overall productivity rose by 6.0 percent. **Figure 1F** shows the trends for high school and college graduates as well as for the median worker and overall productivity. The notable upward trend in compensation in the late 1990s and early 2000s had clearly flattened out well before the Great Recession, whereas productivity continued to climb.

This finding presages a key policy lesson from *The State of Working America*: Productivity growth—the increased overall ability of the economy to generate incomes—provides only the potential for, not a guarantee of, rising living standards for most American households. To make sure this *potential* growth translates into *actual* growth, policymakers must ensure that nothing drives a wedge between the two. The largest such wedge—the extremely large share of overall growth claimed by a narrow slice of already-affluent households at the very top—is discussed in the next section.

Figure 1F Cumulative change in total economy productivity and real hourly compensation of selected groups of workers, 1995–2011

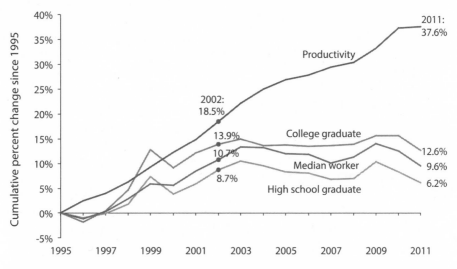

Source: Authors' analysis of unpublished Total Economy Productivity data from the Bureau of Labor Statistics Labor Productivity and Costs program, Bureau of Economic Analysis National Income and Product Accounts data, and Current Population Survey Outgoing Rotation Group microdata

Extraordinarily unequal growth *before* the lost decade: Rising inequality blocks income and wage growth from 1979 to 2007

Long before most Americans' wages and incomes were flattened by the lost decade, they endured a decades-long stretch when these wages and incomes lagged far behind overall economic growth. Living standards, which once advanced steadily and near-uniformly across successive generations of Americans, decelerated rapidly beginning roughly three decades ago. The primary source of the slowdown is easy to identify: A narrow slice of households at the top of the income distribution claimed a vast majority of the income generated from 1979 to 2007, leaving insufficient gains for everybody else.

Income inequality and stagnating living standards

The State of Working America documents the many ways in which the unequal distribution of economic growth affects the potential living standards of most of the population. Perhaps the clearest way to illustrate the top's disproportionate claim on economic growth is to calculate the share of overall income growth that is attributable to just the income growth of the top 1 percent. The results of this calculation are shown in **Figure 1G**.

Between 1979 and 2007, 38.3 percent of total income growth in the American economy was attributable to the income growth of the top 1 percent of households. This was a larger share than that attributable to the bottom *90 percent* of households (36.9 percent). Notably, the comprehensive income measure used here includes not just wages and capital gains and other sources of "market-based" income, but also includes in-kind benefits from employers and government, often thought to disproportionately supplement resources for those at the middle and bottom of the income scale.

The sharp rise in income inequality in the United States between 1979 and 2007 is apparent in every major data source and is universally recognized by researchers. **Figure 1H** shows the share of growth in total household incomes (holding the number of households constant) that accrued to the top 5 percent and top 1 percent using various income concepts ranging from exclusively market-based incomes (e.g., wages, capital gains) to more comprehensive measures of income

Figure 1G Share of total household income growth attributable to various income groups, 1979–2007

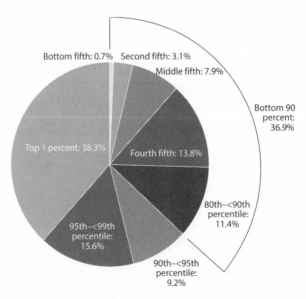

Note: Data are for comprehensive income.

Source: Authors' analysis of Congressional Budget Office (2010a)

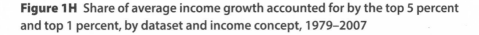

Figure 1H Share of average income growth accounted for by the top 5 percent and top 1 percent, by dataset and income concept, 1979–2007

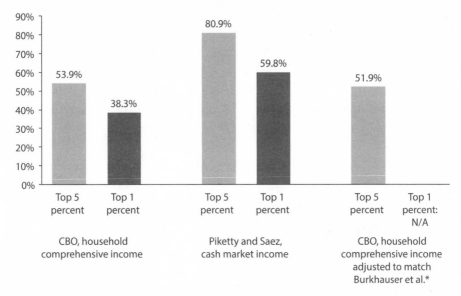

* As described in Chapter 2, this bar uses Burkhauser's income concepts for CBO income data because CBO income data are not top-coded.

Source: Authors' analysis of Piketty and Saez (2012, Table A-6); Congressional Budget Office (2010a); Burkhauser, Larrimore, and Simon (2011, Table 4)

(including employer benefits, government cash transfers, and in-kind support such as Medicare and Medicaid). The key lesson is that every source shows a dramatic increase in inequality; the source showing the *least* increase in inequality from 1979 to 2007 still shows the top 5 percent gained over half of the income growth over this period. (A more detailed discussion of the various sources is available in Chapter 2.)

Figure 1I shows the gap in income growth rates at different points in the distribution. Between 1979 and 2007 (the last year before the Great Recession), incomes of the top 1 percent of households in the income distribution rose by 240.5 percent. But incomes of the middle fifth of households grew only 19.2 percent over the 28-year period.

This huge divergence in household income growth, a divergence apparent in all data sources and across all income measures and across all units of observation (i.e., households, families, individuals), was overwhelmingly driven by divergence in pre–tax-and-transfer incomes ("market-based incomes"). Because the federal income tax remains progressive (though far less so than it used to be) and because many components of government transfers are thought to boost incomes at the low and middle segment of the income scale, incomes measured post–tax and

Figure 1I Change in real annual household income, by income group, 1979–2007

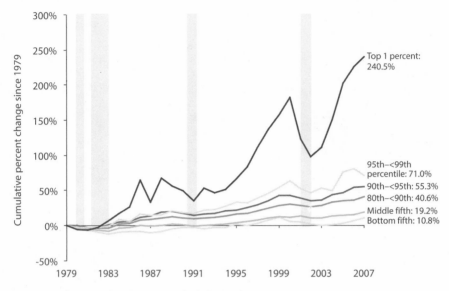

Note: Data are for comprehensive income. Shaded areas denote recessions.

Source: Authors' analysis of data from the Congressional Budget Office (2010a)

transfers are generally more equal across the distribution at any point in time. But between 1979 and 2007, the inequality-reducing effect of taxes and transfers actually *declined* across most measures of inequality. Nevertheless, the declining boost to income shares at the low and middle portions provided by tax-and-transfer policies pales in comparison to the degree to which market-based income generated increasing inequality.

We close this discussion of overall income inequality with two observations. First, it is not inevitable that market economies generate chronically rising inequality, as **Figure 1J** demonstrates. The American economy delivered extraordinarily equal, and much more rapid, growth in family incomes between 1947 and 1979 than between 1979 and 2007. For example, in the earlier period, incomes of the middle fifth grew 2.4 percent annually, compared with 1.9 percent annual growth in incomes of the top 5 percent. In the later period, annual income growth for the middle fifth had fallen to 0.6 percent, compared with 2.0 percent for the top 5 percent.

Second, the sheer amount of income transferred to the top in recent decades has been enormous, and had inequality not risen over this time, there would have been enough income to *significantly* increase family incomes at the bottom and middle. A straightforward demonstration of this is provided in **Figure 1K**, which

Figure 1J Average family income growth, by income group, 1947–2007

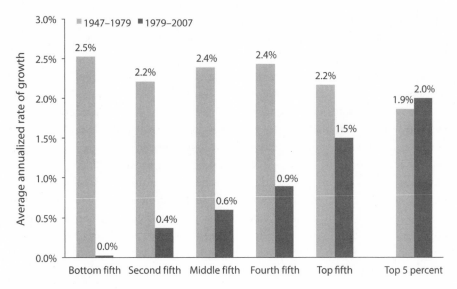

Note: Data are for money income.

Source: Authors' analysis of Current Population Survey Annual Social and Economic Supplement *Historical Income Tables* (Tables F-2, F-3, and F-5)

Figure 1K Income of middle-fifth households, actual and projected assuming growth equal to growth rate of overall average household income, 1979–2007

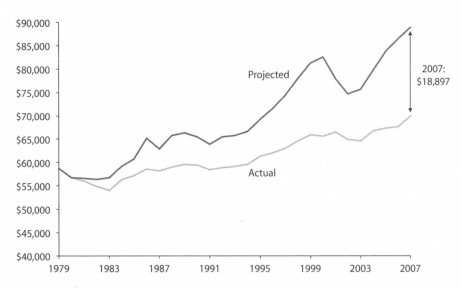

Note: Data are for comprehensive income.

Source: Authors' analysis of Congressional Budget Office (2010a)

compares actual middle-fifth household income growth with middle-fifth income growth had it grown at the same rate as overall average household income between 1979 and 2007. Had middle-fifth income grown at the same rate as overall average household income over this period, it would have been $18,897 higher in 2007—27.0 percent higher than it actually was.

Essentially, rising inequality imposed a tax of 27.0 percent on middle-fifth household incomes over this period. It is important to note that this drain on disposable household income is exponentially greater than the reductions posed by many policy matters that generate great heat among policymakers and economic commentators for allegedly overburdening households, such as the gross costs of regulations, the efficiency costs of progressive tax-and-transfer policy, the long-run costs of chronic budget deficits, or the burden that would stem from immediately fixing Social Security's 75-year financing shortfall with *only* an increase in the payroll tax. Policymakers who express rhetorical concern about American households' disposable incomes should pay much more attention to this 27 percent "inequality tax" on the households in the middle fifth of the income distribution. This inequality tax exceeds these households' effective federal income tax rate (3.3 percent) *by roughly eight times*. Even including the much larger (and less progressive) payroll tax (as well as the corporate income tax and excise tax), the federal tax bill for the middle fifth of households, 14.3 percent, is just over half the size of the inequality tax imposed on these households over recent decades.

Wage inequality and the break between wages and productivity

As is documented in Chapter 2, the divergence of market-based incomes that drove rising *overall* income inequality occurred because both labor incomes (wages) and capital-based incomes (profits, rents, and interest payments) became increasingly concentrated at the top, and because a growing share of overall incomes accrued to owners of capital rather than to workers (a trend expressed as the "shift from labor incomes to capital incomes").

Because wages are by far the dominant source of income for low- and middle-income households, it is important to examine trends in worker pay in the 1979–2007 era of rising inequality. **Table 1.2** provides data on some of these trends. The key finding is that between 1979 and 2007, growth in worker hourly wages at the 10th percentile and the median lagged overall productivity growth significantly. Worker hourly wages at the 10th percentile were essentially flat, while median wages grew about 0.3 percent each year in this 28-year period. In contrast, productivity, a measure of how much output is generated by the economy in each hour of work, grew by 1.7 percent annually.

The wedges between productivity growth and typical workers' pay are examined in great detail in Chapter 4. For example, Table 4.23 shows that roughly

Table 1.2 Key labor market indicators and living-standards benchmarks, 1979–2011 (2011 dollars)

	Payroll employment	Unemployment rate	Labor force participation rate	Working-age employment-to-population ratio	Median household income*	Working-age median family income*	Worker hourly wages			Total economy productivity
							10th percentile	Median	95th percentile	
1979	89,932	5.8%	63.7%	74.6%	$47,535	$58,659	$8.53	$15.21	$36.28	$36.03
1989	108,014	5.3 .	66.5	79.9	50,633	62,048	7.29	15.12	38.99	40.98
1995	117,298	5.6	66.6	79.8	49,944	61,621	7.42	14.84	41.09	44.21
2000	131,785	4.0	67.1	81.5	54,851	69,233	8.24	15.99	45.44	49.62
2007	137,598	4.6	66.0	79.9	54,499	68,893	8.45	16.40	49.39	57.22
2011	131,359	8.9	64.1	75.1	51,014**	63,967**	8.16	16.07	49.74	60.83
Change										
1979–1989	1.8%	-0.5 ppts.	2.8 ppts.	5.3 ppts.	0.6%	0.6%	-1.6%	-0.1%	0.7%	1.3%
1989–1995	1.4	0.3	0.1	-0.1	-0.2	-0.1	0.3	-0.3	0.9	1.3
1979–1995	1.7	-0.2	2.9	5.2	0.3	0.3	-0.9	-0.2	0.8	1.3
1995–2000	2.4	-1.6	0.5	1.7	1.9	2.4	2.1	1.5	2.0	2.3
2000–2007	0.6	0.6	-1.1	-1.6	-0.1	-0.1	0.4	0.4	1.2	2.1
1979–2007	1.5	-1.2	2.3	5.3	0.5	0.6	0.0	0.3	1.1	1.7
2000–2011	0.0	4.9	-3.0	-6.4	-0.7**	-0.8**	-0.1	0.0	0.8	1.9

*   Data are for money income.
**   Data are for 2010 (top panel) and 2000–2010 (bottom panel) due to data limitations.
***   Percent change numbers are annualized rates; percentage-point change numbers are cumulative change.

Source: Authors' analysis of Current Population Survey (CPS) public data series, CPS ASEC microdata and *Historical Income Tables* (Table H-5), CPS-ORG microdata, BLS Current Employment Statistics, and unpublished Total Economy Productivity data from BLS Labor Productivity and Costs program

half of the gap between productivity and median hourly pay (which includes nonwage compensation) from 1973 to 2011 can be explained by rising inequality *within* compensation (i.e., concentration within labor incomes, as mentioned previously), and roughly another fifth can be explained by the shift from labor incomes to capital incomes. In other words, rising economic inequality can explain about two-thirds of this failure of typical workers' pay to keep pace with overall economic growth, as measured by productivity.

Inequality within the wage distribution is shown in **Figure 1L**, which shows growth rates since 1979 at various points in the wage distribution. Between 1979 and 2007, real annual wages for the bottom 90 percent of wage earners grew 16.7 percent (which translates to a 0.6 percent annual growth rate), while wages for the top 1 percent grew 156.2 percent (or 3.4 percent annually). In short, the rise of inequality within wages has been extreme, and has put a very large wedge between typical workers' pay and productivity growth.

Because American households added so many more hours to the paid labor force between 1979 and 2007 and because the later 1990s provided a welcome period of strong across-the-board wage growth, the full extent of the wage disaster

Figure 1L Cumulative change in real annual wages, by wage group, 1979–2010

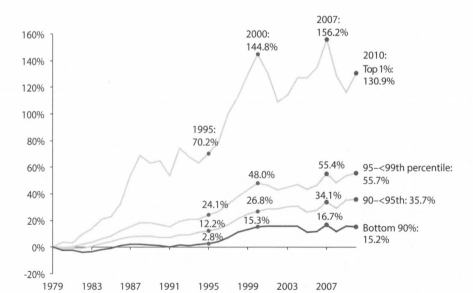

Note: Data are for individual wage earners. Trend lines show cumulative percent change since 1979.

Source: Authors' analysis of Kopczuk, Saez, and Song (2010) and Social Security Administration wage statistics

for the majority of American workers for *most* of the years between 1979 and 2007 has often been underappreciated. Between 1979 and 1995, for example, hourly wages at the 10th percentile and the median fell at average annual rates of 0.9 percent and 0.2 percent, respectively (shown in Table 1.2). (Undoubtedly, Americans started working more paid hours beginning in 1979 in part as a coping strategy to ensure some income growth despite poor wage performance.) And as noted later in this discussion, once the momentum of the late 1990s wage boom faded, both median and 10th-percentile wages fell for even most years during the economic expansion of the 2000s.

This long-term wage disaster should be a more pressing focus of policy. Rapid and stable growth in living standards for low- and middle-income Americans will only happen if wages and benefits grow in line with overall productivity. This did not happen for most years in the three decades before the Great Recession. And as we note in more detail in the conclusion of this chapter, the failure of wages to match productivity growth was a predictable consequence of many policy choices.

For a while, households compensated for wage stagnation with other ways to generate income and consumption growth, including, as noted earlier, by work-ing more paid hours and, especially in the 2000s, taking on debt. There are ob-vious limits and downsides to these coping strategies, and their use does not let policymakers off the hook. Though less immediately solvable than the current jobs crisis, the sluggish growth in hourly wages and their resulting diminishing capacity to drive income and consumption growth is an important challenge for policy going forward.

The atypical period of strong income and wage growth in the late 1990s offers some suggestions on ways to enable wage growth.

Strong income and wage growth in the atypical last half of the 1990s

The U.S. economy from the mid-1990s through the early 2000s delivered a brief respite from the wage (and consequently income) trends just described. Median hourly wages rose at an average annual rate of 1.5 percent between 1995 and 2000, after contracting 0.2 percent annually between 1979 and 1995 (Table 1.2). Hourly wage growth also accelerated at the 95th percentile (from 0.8 percent annually in 1979–1995 to 2.0 percent annually in 1995–2000) and at the 10th percentile (from falling 0.9 percent annually in 1979–1995 to rising 2.1 percent annually in 1995–2000).

In short, the late 1990s boom delivered both faster and more broad-based wage growth. And this faster wage growth, in turn, drove faster growth in incomes for typical American households. Median household incomes rose by 1.9 percent annually between 1995 and 2000, a rate more than six times as fast as the 0.3 per-cent average annual growth rate between 1979 and 1995 (as shown in Table 1.2).

Further, during the late 1990s it was hourly wage growth, and not just growth in hours worked, that provided the bulk of annual earnings gains (as we document in Chapter 2). The contrast between wage and income growth in late 1990s and in the broader periods of stagnation that preceded and followed it provides a useful preview of some of our findings on the role of economic policy in driving economic outcomes. In particular, this period affirms the importance of tight labor markets and increases in the minimum wage for producing acceptable wage and income growth.

Labor markets in the late 1990s were tighter than they had been for decades, in part because Alan Greenspan and the Federal Reserve broke with a key piece of economic orthodoxy in place since the inflation of the 1970s: that the "natural" or "non-accelerating inflation rate of unemployment" (the NAIRU) was well above 5 percent (or even 6 percent), and that a responsible Federal Reserve should set its policy interest rates at levels that would keep the economy from reaching unemployment rates below these, as too-low unemployment rates would spur inflation. In the late 1990s, Greenspan and the Federal Reserve admirably engaged in some pragmatic heterodoxy on the NAIRU—deciding to not raise rates until *actual* (rather than incipient) inflation appeared. They were encouraged in this stance by exogenous world events, such as currency and financial crises in Asia, Brazil, and Russia, that strongly demanded accommodative interest rates to keep world capital markets healthy.

This heterodoxy was well-rewarded. Unemployment fell far below officially sanctioned estimates of the NAIRU; in 2000, it actually fell below 4 percent for some months. These historically low unemployment rates assured jobs for millions of Americans who would not have had them had official NAIRU estimates strictly guided policy. And no jump in inflation occurred. In fact, what ended the late 1990s boom was not runaway inflation that demanded a monetary policy contraction, but the bursting of the stock market bubble in 2001. This is important to note, because many (including us) would argue that while the *sources* of the tight labor markets of the 1990s were unsustainable (very rapid growth in consumer spending and investment, both driven by a stock market bubble concentrated in information and communications technology), very low rates of unemployment and tight labor markets are not *in and of themselves* unsustainable. It is important to be clear that the late 1990s offered no evidence that there is a threshold unemployment rate (say, 5 percent) below which the economy cannot fall without suffering dire consequences. Instead, the lesson of this period is simply that tight labor markets are indeed sustainable, but they should be driven by stronger fundamentals than stock market bubbles.

A similarly useful break with economic orthodoxy occurred when Congress enacted federal minimum-wage increases. These increases, in 1996 and 1997, together raised the real value of the minimum wage by nearly 20 percent, though it remained substantially below its historic high. As shown in Table 1.2, these increases in a key labor standard boosted wages at the bottom end of the wage distribution (particularly wages of women, as covered in Chapter 4). And many measures of "bottom-tail" inequality (or how much low-wage earners' growth lagged that of other groups) stabilized or even declined slightly following the increase. Importantly, these salutary wage effects were not accompanied by any discernible downward pressure on employment growth—either at the aggregate level or within smaller labor markets more directly affected by minimum-wage increases.

Economic mobility has neither caused nor cured the damage done by rising inequality

The debate over the extent, causes, and implications of rising economic inequality has raged for decades. A recurring argument from those seeking to minimize the implications of rising inequality is that the American economy provides tremendous opportunities for economic mobility, i.e., to change one's economic position. So, even if there is large measured inequality of economic outcomes at any *single point in time*, inequality of economic outcomes throughout lifetimes and across generations is likely greatly reduced, they argue. Further, they say, although inequality in recent decades has grown much faster in the United States than in its advanced-country peers, this rise in American inequality is compensated for (or possibly even driven by) the much greater opportunities for crossing class lines in the American economy.

These claims about the importance of mobility in either generating or ameliorating the sharp increase in "point-in-time" inequality are simply incorrect. While an outlier in the extent of inequality growth (inequality has risen much faster in the United States than in peer countries in recent decades), the United States is *not* an outlier in the economic mobility it provides people over their lifetimes and across generations; it is, if anything, *below average* in this regard when compared with peer countries.

Figure 1M charts correlations between the earnings of fathers and sons—an "intergenerational elasticity" measure that increases as mobility declines—in 17 OECD countries. As the figure shows, the United States has the fifth-lowest economic mobility of the 17 countries examined, ahead only of Slovenia, Chile, Italy, and the United Kingdom.

Further, there has been no substantial increase in mobility to counteract the sharp rise in inequality since 1979 in the United States. **Figure 1N** displays data on the correlation between parental income and sons' earnings in selected years between 1950 and 2000. This measure also rises as mobility declines. This intergenerational correlation declined in the decades between 1950 and 1980 but increased steadily thereafter.

Figure 1M Intergenerational correlations between the earnings of fathers and sons in OECD countries

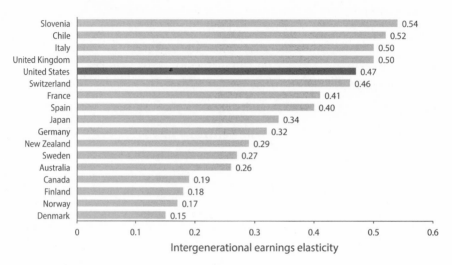

Note: The higher the intergenerational elasticity, the lower the extent of mobility.

Source: Adapted from Corak (2011, Figure 1)

Figure 1N Elasticities between parental income and sons' earnings, 1950–2000

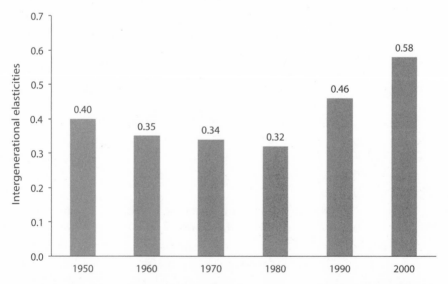

Note: The higher the intergenerational elasticity (IGE), the lower the extent of mobility. The IGEs shown are for 40- to 44-year-old sons.

Source: Authors' analysis of Aaronson and Mazumder (2007, Table 1)

While some other measures of economic mobility show a less clear-cut pattern, the preponderance of evidence suggests that mobility has likely declined in recent decades and clearly has not significantly increased, and it has certainly not increased enough to neutralize the steep rise in inequality over the last three decades.

Today's private economy: Not performing for middle-income Americans

Almost universally, researchers acknowledge growing economic inequality as a fact of American economic history in recent decades. Recently, however, a number of "revisionist" studies have claimed that middle-income families have managed to carve out acceptable rates of living-standards growth despite this large rise in inequality.

These studies tend to focus on family or household incomes, not just hourly wages, as incomes for households or families can be boosted simply by adding more hours to the paid labor force. Further, these revisionist studies argue that more "comprehensive" measures of income that include benefits from employers and government transfers show a much healthier rate of growth in middle-income households' living standards than would be surmised looking only at measures of "money income."

Middle-income growth lags average income growth and historical income growth rates

It is true that incomes of households in the middle of the income distribution have grown faster when measured by the data on "comprehensive" incomes than when measured by the strict "money" incomes available in more-conventional data sources. A core finding of the revisionist literature is that comprehensive income for the middle fifth of households rose by 19.1 percent between 1979 and 2007, as measured by data methods used by the CBO measures of household income. (Note that this rate of middle-fifth household income growth comes from unrounded CBO data, and thus differs from the 19.2 percent rate in Figure 1I, which comes from rounded, publicly available CBO data.)

But this cumulative growth rate does not mean that the private sector of the American economy is performing well for middle-income families. First, while this growth rate is sufficiently far from zero to qualify as "significant" or "rapid" for some observers, it is inadequate when measured against more meaningful benchmarks—such as what it would have been had it simply grown as fast as overall average incomes (which grew more than 50 percent over the same period, buoyed by the extraordinarily rapid growth at the top of the income scale, as was shown in Figure 1K). Second, this rate of middle-fifth income growth, which

translates to 0.6 percent annual growth, doesn't come close to our available measure of income growth from 1947 to 1979, when middle-fifth family income
grew 2.4 percent annually (shown in Figure 1J earlier).

Third, the sources of this 19.1 percent growth of comprehensive incomes are
not evidence that the private economy has delivered for American workers. They
instead reflect the strength of the American social insurance programs—Social
Security, Medicare, and Medicaid—as well as the impressive ability of American
households to steadily increase their work hours (as well as climb the educational
ladder over time). Fourth, the data on comprehensive incomes are technically
flawed because they count, as income, rapidly rising health expenditures made on
behalf of households by employers and the government without accounting for
the excessive health care inflation that has absorbed large portions of the increase
in this particular source of income.

Social insurance programs, not private sources, account for the majority of middle-fifth income growth

Government transfers (including unemployment insurance, food stamps, Temporary Assistance to Needy Families and, most relevant for middle-income households, Social Security, Medicare, and Medicaid) accounted for fully 53.6 percent
of comprehensive-income growth of middle-fifth households between 1979 and
2007. Labor earnings, conversely, accounted for just 6.1 percent of this growth.
A surprisingly large share of overall income growth for middle-income households—31.9 percent—was driven by rising pension incomes. This rise in pension
incomes for the middle fifth is clearly a bright spot in the otherwise disappointing
contribution of the private economy to middle-income living-standards growth
between 1979 and 2007. However, pension incomes are highly unlikely to continue to contribute so much to household income growth for the middle fifth,
given the steadily declining rates of pension coverage over the past three decades.

Growing shares of income are dedicated to holding families harmless against rising medical costs

Employer-sponsored health insurance benefits contributed roughly 12.5 percent to overall middle-fifth income growth between 1979 and 2007, and an
even greater share—22.9 percent—between 2000 and 2007. But we believe the
income growth stemming from these benefits is overstated because the overall
price deflator that the CBO uses to measure the value of these employer-provided
health benefits actually does not include employer-provided health insurance premiums in the "basket" of goods and services whose prices it tracks. Thus, it fails to
reflect how cost inflation of these medical goods and services has risen much more
rapidly than overall prices over the last three decades.

If these employer-sponsored health benefits are valued more appropriately with a medical cost deflator, then the value of these benefits to middle-income households actually *shrank* between 1979 and 2007, as rising health care inflation swamped the rise in nominal dollars spent by employers on health care benefits. This same logic applies to the value of health benefits provided through government transfers, predominantly Medicare and Medicaid. When deflated by a medical care price index, the value of these benefits rose less than a third as fast as indicated under an overall price index deflator. If all health benefits are deflated appropriately with the medical price deflator, then overall middle-fifth income growth between 1979 and 2007 was actually 6.3 percentage points lower than indicated by the raw CBO data—essentially knocking off a third of total income growth during that period.

Beyond the technical issue of price deflators, this discussion of health care benefits is important to keep in mind when evaluating how well the private American economy is working to generate living-standards growth for middle-income households. If a growing share of employee compensation and government transfers must be dedicated to holding these households harmless against health care inflation exceeding that in the United States' advanced-country peers, this cannot be counted as a success of the private American economy.

Households have to work more to achieve income gains

The small contribution (just 6.1 percent, as documented in Chapter 2) made by annual wages to overall income growth for the middle fifth of households in the income distribution should not be glossed over. Wages (and imputed taxes, which for the middle fifth are dominated by wage-linked payroll taxes) accounted for nearly two-thirds (65.8 percent) of overall income earned by households in this group in 2007, so the very small contribution to growth made by this income source over time is startling.

Part of this very small contribution is explained by the fact that elderly households (who have much lower annual wages) grew as a share of the middle fifth, rising from 15.2 percent in 1979 to 22.1 percent in 2007. Yet even looking strictly at the annual earnings growth of working-age households provides little reason to believe that this compositional change is hiding a happy story about the labor market and middle-income households. This is because changes in work hours have been substantial, and have been responsible for the large majority of overall increases in annual wage earnings. For example, working-age households worked an average of 222 more hours in 2007 than in 1979.

As documented in Table 2.17 in Chapter 2, between 1979 and 2007, average annual wages for working-age households in the middle fifth rose by just 12.0 percent over the entire 28 years. Of this 12.0 percent growth, 85.9 percent was accounted for by rising hours worked by these households. Further, more than 90 percent of the growth in average annual wages over this 28-year period was concentrated between 1995 and 2000. If one removed the influence of these five years, then annual wages for the middle fifth would have risen by only 1.1 percent over the entire 28 years, and this would have been the net result of hours rising by more than 8 percent while hourly pay fell.

Assessing what the private economy is really delivering to middle-income Americans

Table 1.3 summarizes the effects of the influences just described on the trajectory of middle-fifth household income growth. The first row shows growth in comprehensive income, as documented by the CBO. The next row shows this same growth, but with both employer-provided health benefits and Medicare/Medicaid benefits deflated with a health-specific deflator. This change alone reduces the income growth in 1979–2007 from 19.1 percent to 12.7 percent. The next row keeps employer-provided health benefits deflated by health-specific deflators, but strips out all growth in government cash transfers as well as Medicare and Medicaid. This change further reduces the growth of middle-fifth household income in 1979–2007 from 12.7 percent to just 5.9 percent. The next row subtracts the effect of growing hours of paid work in the middle fifth, which brings the cumulative growth figure down to 4.9 percent.

By stripping out those elements adding to measured income growth that cannot be attributed to the private U.S. economy generating decent outcomes, we

Table 1.3 Middle-fifth household income, minus selected key sources, 1979–2007

	1979	1989	1995	2000	2007	1979– 2007
Comprehensive household income	$58,751	$59,724	$61,334	$65,637	$69,949	19.1%
With health care deflated properly	58,751*	58,685	59,025	63,151	66,234	12.7
Without cumulative contributions of:						
Government transfers	$58,751*	$57,166	$56,071	$60,049	$62,209	5.9%
Hours worked	58,751*	60,678	60,050	61,783	61,623	4.9
Pensions	58,751*	59,233	57,654	58,363	58,050	-1.2

* Data are held at 1979 levels to compute change from 1979 to 2007.
Note: Data are for comprehensive income and include employer-sponsored health insurance.

Source: Authors' analysis of Congressional Budget Office (2010a and 2010b), Current Population Survey Annual Social and Economic Supplement microdata, and Bureau of Labor Statistics Consumer Price Indices database

provide a clearer assessment of how well the private economy is delivering for middle-income Americans. And a cumulative growth rate of 4.9 percent across 28 years offers little to brag about. Again, whether it is government transfers, rapidly rising health care prices, or the tenacity of American earners in working longer hours (even while becoming a more educated and experienced workforce), none of these influences seems to provide any obvious evidence that the private economy is working well for these middle-income families. The last row strips out the influence of rising pension income, which actually pushes overall comprehensive income growth for the middle fifth of households over the entire 1979 to 2007 period negative. While pension incomes are mostly privately generated income, trends in pension coverage (documented later in this introduction and in later chapters) suggest rising pension incomes will not boost middle-fifth incomes substantially in coming decades.

Today's economy: Different outcomes by race and gender

As this book, and our research in general, shows, there is actually no one economic "state of working America" but rather an America that is experienced differently, and often unequally—not only by class but by race and gender.

As with the differences by income group highlighted earlier, disparities by race are sometimes staggering.

Many more than just two Americas

Figure 10 illustrates an example that is particularly salient now. It compares the unemployment rates of whites, blacks, and Hispanics from 1979 to 2011. In this period, black and Hispanic unemployment always far exceeded white unemployment. It is telling to note that when the overall unemployment rate peaked at 10.0 percent in October 2009 and commentators rightly labeled it a national catastrophe demanding sustained attention from policymakers, it was still far below the *average* rate of African American unemployment across the entire post-1979 period: 12.2 percent. Likewise, when the annual white unemployment rate reached 8.0 percent in 2010, it was still below the 9.8 percent average rate of African American unemployment in the economic expansion and recovery preceding the Great Recession. These data support the claim that African Americans have essentially been living through a perpetual, slow-motion recession. As this book was nearing completion, in July 2012, the overall unemployment rate was 8.3 percent—roughly the same as the African American unemployment rate during all of 2007, the last full year of economic expansion before the Great Recession.

Again we note that adverse labor market trends cannot be blamed on workers' lack of skills. The ratio of the African American unemployment rate to the white

Figure 1O Unemployment rate, by race and ethnicity, 1979–2011

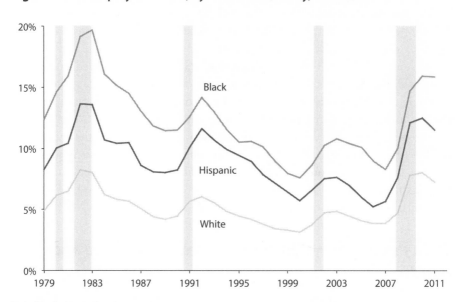

Note: Shaded areas denote recessions.

Source: Authors' analysis of basic monthly Current Population Survey microdata

unemployment rate is roughly the same for every educational category; for example, the unemployment rate of African American college graduates is roughly double that of white college graduates. Influences other than workers' own skills must be shaping labor market developments, and those influences deserve scrutiny.

Another staggering racial difference identified in *The State of Working America* is the ratio of median white household wealth to median black household wealth, displayed in **Figure 1P**. Even in 1992, the peak of black/white equality in wealth holdings, these differences were huge; median African American wealth was just 16.8 percent of median white wealth. By 2010—after the housing bubble had burst and destroyed $7 trillion in equity in residential real estate (the most widely held type of wealth)—median African American wealth was just 5.0 percent of median white wealth.

Racial economic disparities also appear in the provision of social insurance by private employers. The United States is unique among advanced nations in tying much of this social insurance, particularly health insurance and pensions for retirement income, to the employment relationship. While this part of the American social compact has frayed in recent decades, as employers withdrew an increasing share of these valuable worker benefits, these benefits were never

Figure 1P Median wealth by race, 1983–2010

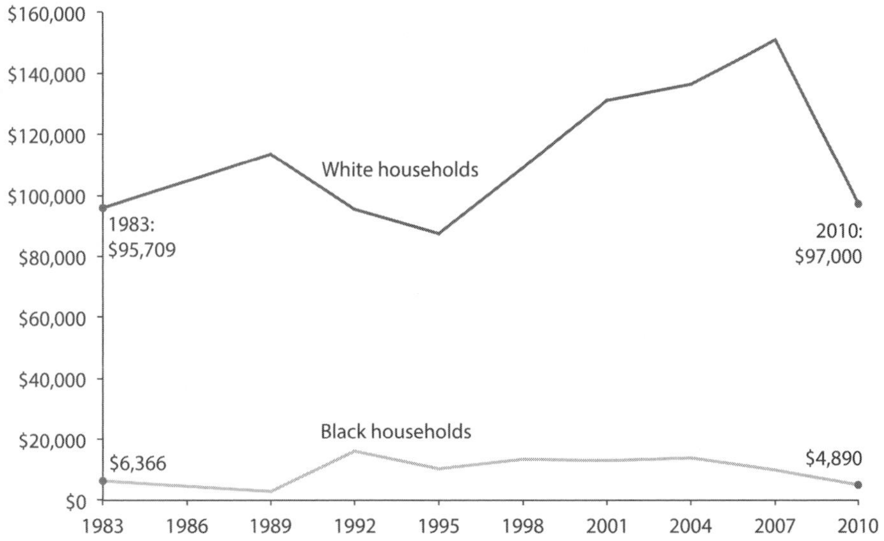

Source: Authors' analysis of Wolff (2012)

near-universal, and their unraveling is occurring at vastly different rates depending on population group.

Table 1.4 shows the incidence of employer-sponsored pension and health insurance coverage by race and ethnicity for business cycle peak years between 1979 and 2007, and for 2010. Health insurance and pension coverage rates of whites were higher than rates of blacks and Hispanics in each year shown. Coverage rates of Hispanics were lowest. In fact, in most of the years observed there was a roughly 2-to-1 difference in pension coverage rates of white workers relative to Hispanic workers, even in 2007. Further, there was no movement toward equality in employer-provided health or pension benefits from 1979 to 2010: Ratios of white-to-black and white-to-Hispanic pension and health coverage rates either held steady or actually increased over this period. Worst of all, while relative rates did not change much, absolute pension and health coverage rates declined steadily among all racial groups.

Male and female America

Disparities in employer-provided health and pension benefits also appear between genders. **Table 1.5** shows the change in employer-provided health and pension coverage for men and women. Encouragingly, perhaps, it shows that gender gaps in both pension and health coverage narrowed, quite rapidly in pensions, between

Table 1.4 Employer-provided health insurance and pension coverage, by race and ethnicity, 1979–2010

	1979	1989	1995	2000	2007	2010	Change 1979–2010
Pension coverage							
White	52.2%	46.1%	49.5%	53.7%	50.3%	48.2%	-3.9
Black	45.8	40.7	42.6	41.3	39.1	37.7	-8.1
Hispanic	38.2	26.3	24.7	27.5	24.8	23.9	-14.3
Health insurance coverage							
White	70.3%	64.0%	61.7%	62.7%	59.6%	57.8%	-12.5
Black	63.1	56.3	53.0	55.4	52.4	49.5	-13.6
Hispanic	60.4	46.0	42.1	41.8	37.3	36.3	-24.1

Note: Data are for private-sector wage and salary workers age 18–64 who worked at least 20 hours per week and 26 weeks per year.

Source: Authors' analysis of Current Population Survey Annual Social and Economic Supplement microdata

Table 1.5 Employer-provided health insurance and pension coverage, by gender, 1979–2010

	1979	1989	1995	2000	2007	2010	Change 1979–2010
Pension coverage							
Men	56.9%	46.9%	48.6%	50.3%	45.4%	43.6%	-13.3
Women	41.3	39.6	42.5	45.8	43.6	41.9	0.6
Health insurance coverage							
Men	75.4%	66.8%	62.6%	63.2%	58.4%	55.8%	-19.6
Women	59.4	54.9	53.3	53.6	51.8	49.9	-9.5

Note: Data are for private-sector wage and salary workers age 18–64 who worked at least 20 hours per week and 26 weeks per year.

Source: Authors' analysis of Current Population Survey Annual Social and Economic Supplement microdata

1979 and 2010. Less encouragingly, these gaps shrank predominantly because men *lost* coverage rather than because women gained coverage; women experienced large reductions in health coverage and very slight increases in pension coverage over the period examined, while men experienced even larger reductions in health coverage and substantial losses in pension coverage.

Similarly, the gap between the median hourly wage of men and that of women has been more than halved since 1973. In 2011, the median hourly wage of women was 84.0 percent of the median hourly wage of men, up from 63.1 percent in 1973. But this rapid narrowing of the gender wage gap occurred mostly due to a steady fall in the male median wage during the 1980s and early 1990s (but also because of steady modest growth of the female median wage). However, in 2011 a female college graduate earned $24.31 an hour, $7.50, or about 24 percent, less than a male college graduate that same year ($31.81)—and roughly $3.00, or 11 percent, less than a male college graduate earned in 1979 ($27.29), more than 30 years ago.

No one 'American economy'

These disparities in economic outcomes by race, ethnicity, and gender teach us a valuable lesson about the "American economy": There is no one "American economy." While headline numbers on economic performance—such as gross domestic product, average income, and productivity—provide information about many important issues, on the most salient question about the American economy—"How well is it working to provide most American households with acceptable growth in living standards?"—these top-line numbers are either insufficient or even misleading. While disparities by race, ethnicity, and gender are often easily recognized by even casual observers of economic developments, very large (and obviously interrelated) disparities also exist by economic class. For example, productivity growth, one of the most-followed economic statistics, was nearly identical in two periods: 1995–2000 and 2001–2006. Yet performance of key indicators of living standards growth for typical American households, such as hourly wage growth and household income, was much stronger during the earlier period. This insight, that one must dig deeply into data to answer what seem like basic questions about the performance of the American economy, is the driving motivation behind *The State of Working America*.

Conclusion: The struggling state of working America is policy-driven

As noted in past editions, *The State of Working America* is a work of data analysis, not a policy manifesto. Yet it is data analysis that we seriously hope helps to propel policy changes that improve the economic prospects of all Americans. Other publications by the authors identify a range of policy actions called for by the trends captured in the book. Here we briefly sketch out what the data suggest about the fingerprints of policy—both policy commission and omission—on the trajectory of economic outcomes in recent decades. Our criticism of policy failures does not constitute a rejection of public-sector intervention in the private economy. Instead we criticize the way in which the instruments of economic policy are often seized by corporate interests and already-wealthy individuals to direct more economic rewards their way.

The most fundamental lesson is that the generally dismal performance of wages and incomes of low- to middle-income workers and households cannot be chalked up to large, disembodied forces like "technological change." The implied claim of those who attribute rising inequality to such bloodless factors is twofold. First, it suggests that little can be done to change the status quo pattern of economic rewards flowing to the top. Second, it argues that the skewed distribution of income growth is simply a side effect of well-functioning markets, labor markets in particular, which leaves the task of addressing inequity solely to government tax-and-transfer policy changes.

This perspective is clearly wrong: Policy changes drive economic outcomes, and there's nothing to suggest that the U.S. private economy, particularly the U.S. labor market, functions so well and fairly that it should never be tampered with.

For example, the evidence in Chapter 4 argues strongly that labor-market institutions such as unions and the minimum wage increase the bargaining power of low- and middle-income workers, raising their pay and economic security without unduly impairing labor-market efficiency.

As explained in Chapter 4, unions reduce wage inequalities because they raise wages more at the bottom and in the middle of the wage scale than at the top. Unions also improve pay and working conditions for the broader workforce as union compensation norms and workplace practices become more generalized throughout the economy (indeed, many fringe benefits, such as pensions and health insurance, were first provided in the union sector). According to one study that captured both these direct and indirect effects, declining unionization accounted for about a third of the growth of male wage inequality and a fifth of the growth of female wage inequality between 1973 and 2007. Further, unions provide a political check on excessive managerial pay. These findings and many others suggest that anything that reduces the power and reach of unions in the U.S. economy will increase wage and income inequality. Given this, policy maneuvers aimed at checking or even rolling back the reach of unions (such as those employed by powerful political movements against state public employee unions in Wisconsin, Ohio, and other states in 2011 and 2012) could have powerful, negative effects on economic outcomes.

Chapter 4 also reviews what happened when the failure to increase the federally legislated minimum wage in the 1980s allowed rising inflation to shave 30 percent off its real value: a severe drop in wages of low-wage women, who are the chief beneficiaries of the legislated minimum. Increases in the minimum wage in the early and late 1990s largely halted this erosion. Yet despite further increases by

2009, the real minimum wage in 2011was about 20 percent lower than in 1968, meaning low-wage workers, despite being older and better-educated than in the late 1960s, had a lower wage floor.

Other examples of policy changes that have directed more resources toward the top end of the income and wage distributions include the combination of sharply lower maximum marginal tax rates and the deregulation of the financial sector in the decades preceding the Great Recession. Congress deregulated the activities allowed by the financial sector but did not withdraw the explicit and implicit government guarantees that support financial institutions, such as federal deposit insurance and the implicit guarantee of the debt of Fannie Mae and Freddie Mac. It seems to us that financial deregulation provided the *opportunity* for well-placed actors in finance to get paid large amounts of money to hide risks they should have been managing, while declining tax rates on high incomes provided a strong *motive* for them to do so. To put it bluntly, the returns to rule-rigging (or even outright rule-breaking) are made much larger when your marginal tax rate is halved. As noted in Chapter 4, a distinct aspect of rising inequality in the United States is the wage gap between wage earners in the top 1.0 percent (and top 0.1 percent) and other earners, and a key driver of wage growth of this top tier is the increased size and high pay of the financial sector.

Policies choose sides. Which economic agents should be shielded from the pressures of globalization, and which should be left exposed? Which interests should be prioritized in the policymaking targets of the Federal Reserve? Whose voice should be heeded in debates related to corporate governance? In these cases and many more, policy in the last three decades has tilted toward corporate interests and what is best for the already-affluent—the segments of society that have done well while most Americans' incomes and wages have lagged.

Behind this realization lies an important point: The chain of causality runs *from* such dysfunctional policy choices *to* disappointing outcomes experienced by most American individuals and households. This may seem obvious, especially in the aftermath of the Great Recession. But the prevailing orthodoxy in both economics and policymaking circles assigns responsibility for sluggish living standards growth and rising inequality to the workers and households experiencing them. According to this belief, it is not policy failure, but instead a failure of initiative, skills, or cultural values on the part of workers themselves that prevents them from sharing in the fruits of economic growth.

This orthodoxy should surely not survive the Great Recession. Between December 2007 and February 2010, the U.S. economy shed 8.7 million jobs. American workers didn't lose their skills or initiative or decide to take a mass vacation during this time. Instead, they were failed by policymakers acting on behalf of the interests of the wealthy and against the interests of average Americans. Policymakers who did not rein in the obvious-in-real-time housing bubble while it was inflating, largely because doing so would have meant imposing regulatory limits on the powerful financial sector. Policymakers who were complacent about (or even complicit in) stagnating hourly wages in the years leading up to the Great Recession, even as households and families boosted borrowing and increased their overall economic fragility in part to compensate for these stagnant wages. Then, when the bubble burst, policymakers who were willing to put as much money on the line as was needed to make incumbent actors in the financial sector whole, but were not willing to put as much money on the line as was needed to fully restore health to the labor market where the vast majority of Americans secure their livelihoods.

This relationship between policy and outcomes, so clear in the slide toward the Great Recession, is also behind much of the United States' post-1979 economic history. Many valuable economic policy institutions established before this period—the social insurance programs such as Social Security, Medicare, Medicaid, and unemployment insurance—have actually been a primary and rare source of strength in bolstering economic security for low- and middle-income households. Yet these same programs have often weathered political attack from those who do not prioritize living-standards growth at the low and middle segments of the income scale. At the same time, in decision after decision in the post-1979 period, policy changes were made that nearly all economic analysts agreed would predictably increase economic inequality—and this is exactly what happened. Yet these changes did not spur any boost in overall growth to compensate for the rise in inequality. While other publications by the authors of this book lay out these policies and better alternatives, we close our discussion here with a proven policy equal to the challenges we face and relevant to today's economic situation.

The policy good for everybody in the fractured U.S. economy: Ensuring rapid recovery to full employment

As noted, the trends identified in this book reveal many disparate "American economies," divided by economic status, gender, race, ethnicity, and other factors. It might seem impossible to find policies that can benefit them all. But it is not. A key finding that emerges again and again throughout our investigation of American living standards is that tight labor markets provide large benefits across-the-board to American households, while high rates of unemployment are nearly universally damaging. Tight labor markets lead to both faster growth and growth rates that are more uniform up and down the wage and income scale.

The power of tight labor markets to spur broadly shared growth can be seen in the period of low unemployment in the late 1990s. While American family incomes posted impressive gains across-the-board, incomes of African American families grew even more rapidly. In fact, median African American family-income growth was greater during the late 1990s than it was during the height of the Civil Rights revolution.

This relationship between labor markets and outcomes also applies to poverty rates. While rising inequality contributed greatly to a sad delinking of overall U.S. economic growth and poverty reduction beginning in the 1970s, poverty is not—contrary to much discussion—utterly unmoved by larger economic trends. For example, the tight labor markets of the late 1990s were associated with a rapid reduction in the overall poverty rate, while elevated rates of unemployment in the 1980s led to a large increase in poverty rates. Even at full employment, pockets of poverty that remain should receive sustained, targeted policy attention.

These admittedly basic observations about the destructiveness of chronically high unemployment and the potential of tight labor markets to equalize living-standards growth and reduce poverty are particularly important as the American economy remains deeply depressed following the economic shock of the Great Recession.

And, as we noted earlier, today's pressing crisis of joblessness is economically solvable. Even more encouraging, there is no obvious powerful economic interest that benefits from the current, extraordinarily high unemployment rates. When the economy approaches full employment and wages for low- and middle-income workers look poised to rise, then some corporate interests may seek to slow growth to keep their labor costs, and overall inflation, in check. But now, with the unemployment rate still far above rates that prevailed in the quarter century before the Great Recession began, no group would seriously worry about runaway wages, and all would welcome the boost to bottom lines from more-rapid economic growth.

In short, the crisis of jobs brought on by the Great Recession and still-unfinished recovery should be solvable from both economic and political perspectives. And yet it lingers. Given this, it should not shock anyone wrestling with the evidence in this book that few policy changes have helped, and in fact most have hindered, low- and middle-income households for decades. It is past time for this to change.

Table and figure notes

Tables

Table 1.1. Key labor market indicators and living-standards benchmarks, 2000–2011. Underlying data are from the Current Population Survey (CPS) public data series; the CPS Annual Social and Economic Supplement microdata and *Historical Income Tables* Table H-5, "Race and Hispanic Origin of Householder–Households by Median and Mean Income: 1967 to 2010"; CPS Outgoing Rotation Group microdata (see Appendix B for details on CPS-ORG microdata); the Bureau of Labor Statistics Current Employment Statistics; and unpublished Total Economy Productivity data from the Bureau of Labor Statistics Labor Productivity and Costs program.

Table 1.2. Key labor market indicators and living-standards benchmarks, 1979–2011. See note for Table 1.1.

Table 1.3. Middle-fifth household income, minus selected key sources, 1979–2007. Underlying data for income, transfers, and pensions are from the Congressional Budget Office Web resource, *Average Federal Taxes by Income Group*, "Sources of Income for All Households, by Household Income Category, 1979 to 2007" [Excel spreadsheet] and unpublished data related to the resource. Underlying data for health care deflation are from the Bureau of Labor Statistics *Consumer Price Indexes* database. Underlying data for hours worked are from Current Population Survey Annual Social and Economic Supplement microdata; see Appendix A for details on microdata. Income data are deflated using a health care deflator, and then the contributions of additional transfers, hours worked, and pensions since 1979 are taken out in sequence. Note that the unpublished CBO data are unrounded, and produce slightly different income dollar values and thus an income growth rate for the middle fifth (19.1 percent) that differs by .1 percentage point from the income growth rate from the rounded, publicly available CBO data underlying Figure 1I. Note that the "hours worked" increases in some periods because total earnings in the CBO data dropped *more* than hourly earnings in the CPS data (which is where the hourly earnings are measured from) over this period. This implies that hours dropped more than hourly earnings over this period in the CBO data. In other words, if you remove the effect of hours (i.e., leave only the effect of hourly earnings), total earnings will rise.

Table 1.4. Employer-provided health insurance and pension coverage, by race and ethnicity, 1979–2010. Underlying data are from Current Population Survey Annual Social and Economic Supplement microdata; see Appendix A for details.

Table 1.5. Employer-provided health insurance and pension coverage, by gender, 1979–2010. Underlying data are from Current Population Survey Annual Social and Economic Supplement microdata; see Appendix A for details.

Figures

Figure 1A. Payroll employment and the number of jobs needed to keep up with the growth in the potential labor force, Jan. 2000–Dec. 2011. Underlying data are from the Bureau of Labor Statistics Current Employment Statistics public data series and a 2012 Congressional Budget Office report, *The Budget and Economic Outlook*, Table 2-3, "Key Assumptions in the

CBO's Projection of Potential GDP." Since the CBO estimates of the size of the potential labor force are annual, the annual values are assigned to June of each year and extrapolated for the monthly figure.

Figure 1B. Home prices and their impact on residential investment and housing wealth, 1995–2011. Underlying data are from Case, Quigley, and Shiller (2005); Shiller (2012); Bureau of Economic Analysis National Income and Product Accounts, Table 1.1.5, "Gross Domestic Product"; and Federal Reserve Board, Flow of Funds Accounts of the United States. Home prices are indexed such that 1997=100, and residential investment and the wealth effect on consumption are relative to the 1997 average as a share of GDP.

Figure 1C. Employment-to-population ratio, age 25–54, 1995–2011. Underlying data are from the Current Population Survey public data series.

Figure 1D. Unemployment rate and real median-wage decline, 1991–2011. Underlying data for the unemployment rate are from the Current Population Survey public data series. The unemployment rate is lagged by one year in the figure. Underlying data for median wages are from CPS Outgoing Rotation Group microdata; see Appendix B for details.

Figure 1E. Change in real family income of the middle fifth, actual and predicted, 2000–2018. Underlying data are from the Current Population Survey public data series on unemployment and from CPS Annual Social and Economic Supplement *Historical Income Tables*, Table F-2, "Share of Aggregate Income Received by Each Fifth and Top 5 Percent of All Families, All Races: 1947– 2010"; Table F-3, "Mean Income Received by Each Fifth and Top 5 Percent of Families, All Races: 1966 to 2010"; and Table F-5, "Race and Hispanic Origin of Householder—Families by Median and Mean Income." Real family income is indexed such that 2000=100. The projections are based on a regression analysis, based roughly on Katz and Krueger (1999), that uses the annual change in inflation-adjusted income of families in the middle fifth of the money income distribution as the dependent variable and the level of unemployment as the independent variable. The projections then use the regression parameters to forecast annual changes in middle-fifth family income based on unemployment forecasts through 2018 that are made by the Congressional Budget Office and Moody's Economy.com, a division of Moody's Analytics.

Figure 1F. Cumulative change in total economy productivity and real hourly compensation of selected groups of workers, 1995–2011. Productivity data, which measure output per hour of the total economy, including private and public sectors, are from an unpublished series available from the Bureau of Labor Statistics Labor Productivity and Costs program on request. Wage measures are the annual data used to construct tables in Chapter 4: median hourly wages (at the 50th percentile) from Table 4.4 and hourly wages by education from Table 4.14. These are converted to hourly compensation by scaling by the real compensation/wage ratio from the Bureau of Economic Analysis National Income and Product Accounts (NIPA) data used in Table 4.2.

Figure 1G. Share of total household income growth attributable to various income groups, 1979–2007. Underlying data are from the Congressional Budget Office *Average Federal Taxes by Income Group*, "Sources of Income for All Households, by Household Income Category, 1979 to 2007" [Excel spreadsheet]. Each group's contribution to overall income growth is calculated by multiplying the change in its average income from 1979 to 2007 by its share of the distribution (where, for example, the share of the distribution for the top 1 percent is .01), and dividing the result by the change in overall average income growth over the same time period. For pretax income calculations of the 90th–<95th percentile and 95th–<99th percentile, see Figure 2M notes.

Figure 1H. Share of average income growth accounted for by the top 5 percent and top 1 percent, by dataset and income concept, 1979–2007. Underlying data are from Piketty and Saez (2012, Table A-6); Congressional Budget Office, *Average Federal Taxes by Income Group*, "Sources of Income for All Households, by Household Income Category, 1979 to 2007" [Excel spreadsheet]; and Burkhauser, Larrimore, and Simon (2011), Table 4, "Quintile Income Growth by Business Cycle Using Each Income Series." Each income concept's contribution to overall income growth is calculated by multiplying the change in its average income from 1979 to 2007 by its share of the distribution (where, for example, the share of the distribution for the top 1 percent is .01) and dividing the result by the change in overall average income growth over the same time period.

Figure 1I. Change in real annual household income, by income group, 1979–2007. Underlying data are from the Congressional Budget Office, *Average Federal Taxes by Income Group*, "Sources of Income for All Households, by Household Income Category, 1979 to 2007" [Excel spreadsheet]. Cumulative growth is calculated by dividing the average pretax income in the base year (1979) into average pretax income in each subsequent year (1980–2007). The data provide average pretax income for the bottom, second, middle, fourth, and top fifths, and for the top 10, 5, and 1 percent. For the 80th–<90th percentile, average pretax income is calculated by subtracting the aggregate income of the top 10 percent from aggregate income of the top fifth and dividing by the total number of households in the 80th–<90th percentile. Aggregate income is calculated by multiplying the number of households in each income group by average pretax income. The number of households is calculated by subtracting the number of households in the top 10 percent from the number of households in the top fifth. This same procedure is done between the top 10 percent and top 5 percent to calculate average pretax income for the 90th–<95th percentile and between the top 5 percent and top 1 percent to calculate the average pretax income for the 95th–<99th percentile. Data are inflated to 2011 dollars using the Consumer Price Index Research Series Using Current Methods (CPI-U-RS) and then indexed to 1979=0. Note that this publicly available CBO dataset is rounded, and produces slightly different income dollar values and thus an income growth rate for the middle fifth (19.2 percent) that differs by .1 percentage point from the income growth rate from the unpublished, unrounded CBO data underlying Table 1.3.

Figure 1J. Average family income growth, by income group, 1947–2007. Underlying data are from CPS Annual Social and Economic Supplement *Historical Income Tables*, Table F-2, "Share of Aggregate Income Received by Each Fifth and Top 5 Percent of All Families, 1947–2010"; Table F-3, "Mean Income Received by Each Fifth and Top 5 Percent of Families, All Races: 1966–2010"; and Table F-5, "Race and Hispanic Origin of Householder—Families by Median and Mean Income." Data are inflated to 2011 dollars using the CPI-U-RS.

Figure 1K. Income of middle-fifth households, actual and projected assuming growth equal to growth rate of overall average income, 1979–2007. Underlying data are from the Congressional Budget Office *Average Federal Taxes by Income Group*, "Sources of Income for All Households, by Household Income Category, 1979 to 2007" [Excel spreadsheet]. Data for the middle fifth are shown as is and when applying the cumulative growth rate of the average income for all households.

Figure 1L. Cumulative change in real annual wages, by wage group, 1979–2010. Data taken from Kopczuk, Saez, and Song (2010), Table A-3. Data for 2006 through 2010 are extrapolated from 2004 data using changes in wage shares computed from Social Security Administration wage statistics (data for 2010 are at http://www.ssa.gov/cgi-bin/netcomp.cgi). The final results of the paper by Kopczuk, Saez, and Song printed in a journal used a more restrictive definition of wages so we employ the original definition, as recommended in private correspondence with Kopczuk. SSA provides data on share of total wages and employment in annual wage brackets such as for those earning between $95,000.00 and $99,999.99. We employ the midpoint of the bracket to compute total wage income in each bracket and sum all brackets. Our estimate of total wage income using this method replicates the total wage income presented by SSA with a difference of less than 0.1 percent. We used interpolation to derive cutoffs building from the bottom up to obtain the 0–90th percentile bracket and then estimate the remaining categories. This allows us to estimate the wage shares for upper wage groups. We use these wage shares computed for 2004 and later years to extend the Kopczuk, Saez, and Song series by adding the changes in share between 2004 and the relevant year to their series. To obtain absolute wage trends we used the SSA data on the total wage pool and employment and computed the real wage per worker (based on their share of wages and employment) in the different groups in 2011 dollars.

Figure 1M. Intergenerational correlations between the earnings of fathers and sons in OECD countries. The figure is adapted from Corak (2011), Figure 1, "Comparable Estimates of the Intergenerational Elasticity between Father and Son Earnings for the United States and Twenty Four Other Countries." "Earnings" refers to wages.

Figure 1N. Elasticities between parental income and sons' earnings, 1950–2000. Data are from Aaronson and Mazumder (2007), Table 1, "Estimates of the IGE Using Census IPUMS Data." Data reflect annual family income for the parents and annual earnings for the sons.

Figure 1O. Unemployment rate, by race and ethnicity, 1979–2011. Underlying data are basic monthly Current Population Survey microdata. As with other CPS microdata analyses presented in the book, race/ethnicity categories are mutually exclusive (i.e., white non-Hispanic, black non-Hispanic, and Hispanic any race).

Figure 1P. Median wealth by race, 1983–2010. Underlying data are from the 2010 Survey of Consumer Finances (SCF) data prepared in 2012 by Edward Wolff for the Economic Policy Institute. The definition of wealth used in this analysis of the SCF is the same definition of wealth used in the analysis of the SCF conducted by Bricker et al. (2012), except that the Bricker et al. analysis includes vehicle wealth, while this analysis does not.

CHAPTER 2

Income
Already a 'lost decade'

Income is at the core of living standards for American families and households. Income received from work, returns on investments, and/or government benefits is what enables families and households to secure food and shelter, cover unexpected costs (such as for hospital stays or roof repairs), withstand periods of joblessness, save for children's education, and ensure a comfortable retirement.

Three key issues arise when analyzing the trajectory of American incomes in recent decades: the large cost inflicted by the Great Recession on American incomes and the long shadow it is likely to cast on income growth in the next decade, the steep and broadly recognized rise in income inequality since the late 1970s, and the contested question of just how well those in the middle of the income distribution (i.e., the middle class) have fared in the face of this rising inequality, and what their change in circumstances tells us about how to assess American economic performance over that time.

While it is generally recognized that the Great Recession dealt a harsh blow to American family and household incomes, our analysis reveals that the business cycle preceding the recession was already shaping up as a lost decade for American incomes. Between the business cycle peaks of 2000 and 2007, most measures of typical American incomes registered either negligible gains or outright losses. Median household income, for example, fell by 6 percent over the entire period. Similarly, median income of working-age families never recovered its 2000 peak in the years leading up to the Great Recession.

This poor performance during an economic recovery and expansion was then followed by the severe setback to incomes during the Great Recession. Median income of working-age families, for example, fell 7.1 percent between 2007 and 2010 (from $68,893 to $63,967). Further, the strong relationship between income growth (or lack thereof) and unemployment implies that if full labor-market recovery from the Great Recession takes as long as forecasters predict, nearly two decades likely will pass before American incomes regain lost ground and return to their 2000 levels. This is an underappreciated economic calamity.

The steep rise in inequality in recent decades is familiar to many readers and has been the subject of many previous editions of *The State of Working America*. It is widely acknowledged that American families and households with the highest incomes (the top 1 percent, for example) have been claiming an increasingly large share of overall income. Further, the amount of additional income they have received is economically significant and greatly constrains how much income growth is left over for others to enjoy. Take one example: Between 1979 and 2007 (the last year before the Great Recession) the top 1 percent of households claimed more of the total income growth generated in the U.S. economy (38.3 percent) than that claimed by the bottom 90 percent of households (36.9 percent), even when including the value of government transfers (such as Social Security) and employer-provided benefits. In that same period, income of the top 1 percent of households grew 240.5 percent, compared with 10.8 percent for the bottom fifth of households and 19.2 percent for the middle fifth of households.

This rising inequality has been primarily driven by developments in market incomes, particularly the rapid concentration of income derived from labor (labor earnings, also referred to as "wages" in this book) and income derived from capital ownership (such as interest, dividends, and capital gains) in the hands of households at the top of the income scale. Trends in taxes and transfers (together, "nonmarket incomes") have generally failed to counter this concentration of market incomes, and have actually heightened inequality of market incomes by some measures. For example, the net effect of taxes and transfers boosted overall income of the bottom fifth of households by 37.2 percent in 1979 but just 28.3 percent in 2007.

In addition to the growing concentration within both labor- and capital-derived incomes, there has been a large increase in the share of overall income coming from owning capital and a decrease in the share coming from other sources, notably from work (labor income). This shift from labor-derived to capital-derived income in recent decades has contributed significantly to the growing share of income claimed by households at the top of the income distribution. From 1979 to 2007, the share of overall income claimed by the top 1 percent of households rose from 9.6 percent to 20.0 percent, or 10.4 percentage points, compared with the 7.0 percentage-point gain that would have occurred without the shift towards capital-based incomes. This means that for the top 1 percent of households, nearly one-third of their income share increase was driven by this shift toward capital-based income.

The last section of this chapter addresses the controversial question, "How well did middle-income households and families do in the decades leading up to the Great Recession?" Recent revisionist literature has downplayed the economic significance of rising inequality by claiming that households and families in the middle of the income distribution have managed significant income gains despite rising inequality, when the value of in-kind benefits (such as medical care) and government transfers is included in income measures. But these analyses consider any income growth above zero to be "significant." We argue for more analytic discipline, asserting that income gains for specific groups of households should be measured against benchmarks of performance for the overall economy. Further, we argue that the economic value of these medical benefits are overstated due to a technical flaw in how they are deflated; adjusting for the flaw greatly reduces the contribution they make to income growth for the middle fifth of households. Lastly, we argue that the sources of these income gains must be examined to determine whether the private economy is performing efficiently or fairly.

On the first issue—proper benchmarks—we note that while comprehensive incomes of households in the middle fifth of the income distribution grew 19.1 percent between 1979 and 2007, incomes in 2007 would have been 27 percent greater had they kept pace with the overall average income growth over the period (see Chapter 1). Of course, this overall average growth rate was buoyed by the extraordinarily fast income growth at the very top of the income distribution. But in a real sense, rising inequality can be described as a 27-percent tax on middle-income growth over these years—an implicit tax that dwarfs the impact of any real-world tax these households face. (For this calculation we used unrounded data provided by the Congressional Budget Office, which shows middle-fifth incomes grew 19.1 percent, rather than the 19.2 percent growth rate, from publicly available data, cited earlier.)

On the second issue—the value of medical benefits—we note that more-optimistic portrayals of middle-income growth over this period rely heavily on flawed assumptions about how to value the nominal payments made to families to cover the costs of health care. When these health care payments are properly deflated to reflect the very rapid health care cost inflation from 1979 to 2007, income growth of middle-income households is much reduced. Roughly one-third of the overall 19.1-percent income growth in these years is erased if we use a correct medical-care-specific price deflator for these benefits.

On the third issue—the sources of these income gains—we argue they do not indicate efficiency or fairness in the overall economy, particularly in boosting growth for middle-income households over these decades. Although incomes of middle-income households grew between 1979 and 2007, this growth was driven to a large degree by government transfer payments, primarily Social Security, Medicare, and Medicaid. The growth of these social insurance programs is a clear policy victory in that they are doing what they are designed to be doing: boosting growth and economic security for American households. However, there is little reason to take the growth of these programs as evidence that the private economy is being managed well or fairly for middle-income households.

Further, to the degree that market-based incomes (which, for the middle fifth of households, overwhelmingly come from wages) have contributed to rising total incomes in recent decades, it is not due to increasing hourly wages (a claim documented more fully in Chapter 4). Rather, much of the rise in annual wages for middle-fifth households has been driven by increased hours of work. Working-age households in the middle fifth increased average annual hours worked by 327 between 1979 and 2007. Married couples with children in the middle of the income distribution increased their average annual hours worked by 577 hours between 1979 and 2007. These increased hours certainly purchased higher incomes, but it is incorrect to equate higher income with increased living standards without reckoning for the *cost* of working this much more.

The relatively stagnant hourly wage growth over these decades is particularly dismaying when we realize that households in the middle fifth made extraordinary efforts to increase their educational attainment and also gained more potential labor market experience. For example, the share of workers in middle-income households who had a four-year college degree or more education rose from 14.5 percent in 1979 to 22.3 percent in 2007, an increase of more than 50 percent.

All in all, once we account for this increased effort on the part of American households, it is hard to find much evidence that the private economy has been particularly friendly to the longstanding American aspiration for improving living standards.

There is one exception to this generally poor labor market performance for middle-income households: the economic boom in the late 1990s. More than 90 percent of the growth in average annual wages for working-age households between 1979 and 2007 occurred between 1995 and 2000. Growth in annual earnings during these years was driven *more* by rising hourly wages than by increased hours of work. Without this brief period of genuine labor market success, the labor market for middle-income households during the three decades before the Great Recession would have been uniformly disastrous.

In short, there have been some clear victories in the march to better living standards in the decades preceding the Great Recession—the rise of social insurance programs and the brief period of genuine labor market tightness that spurred broad-based wage growth in the late 1990s—but family and household incomes over the business cycle from 2000 to 2007 experienced the weakest growth on record. And, as this chapter will demonstrate, there is plenty of reason to worry about what is to come.

Table notes and figure notes at the end of this chapter provide documentation for the data, as well as information on methodology, used in the tables and figures that follow.

The basic contours of American incomes

Analyses of American incomes often examine family or household income. Following the official U.S. Census Bureau definitions, a family is a group of two or more people related by birth, marriage, or adoption who reside together, whereas a household consists of all the people who occupy a housing unit. All families are, by definition, also part of a household, but the reverse is not necessarily true (for example, single-person households are not considered to be a family). In this chapter we document trends in both the family and household income distributions, specifying in each case which data series is under discussion. When families are grouped by race and ethnicity, the household head's race or ethnicity is used to categorize the family.

Using families as the unit of analysis allows us to study data over a longer time period (family income data are available from 1947 to 2010). Using household data, however, takes advantage of the greater detail available in public datasets for the post-1979 period. In addition, household data capture more of the population, because every person included in the annual Census survey of income (the Current Population Survey Annual Social and Economic Supplement) is placed into a household, but not necessarily into a family.

It is important to recognize that the average size of families and households changes over time. Between 1979 and 2007—the period examined most thoroughly in this chapter—the average size of families and households declined in nearly every income group. This means that, all else equal, growth in family or household income per person was faster than growth in total family or household income over this period. Some analysts contend that growth in family or household income per person is the only relevant measure of living standards and that income data unadjusted for changing family and household size over long periods therefore underestimate income growth.

There is at least a grain of truth to this argument: Clearly a household income of $100,000 is consistent with a much higher living standard if the household consists of a single person rather than a family of six. However, it is not entirely clear that diminishing family and household size can be interpreted as a pure economic good. Take the case of families with children, which have experienced roughly the same reduction in size as most other family and household categories. Although it sounds odd to non-economists to think of it this way, it is true that part of a family's decision about the number of children to have rests on the family's concept of children as "consumption goods;" if the price of having and raising children rises sharply relative to other consumption goods, this can lead families to having fewer children and consuming more of other goods. Because size-adjusted household income is adjusted by the number of "children" but not by the number of "other consumption goods," this switch from one way that families spend resources (having children) to other ways (consuming other goods) automatically boosts some measured incomes. Similarly, if families decide to have fewer children because they don't expect income growth sufficient to ensure that their children are raised well, this could also mechanically raise size-adjusted income measures. For these reasons, we are unconvinced that the mechanical boost to size-adjusted household and family incomes should be banked as an unambiguous increase in living standards.

In addition, focusing simply on size-adjusted family or household income growth would entail making some very strong assumptions. The first assumption is that family or household resources are indeed evenly shared among all members, and that intra-household distribution has not changed over the decades. The second assumption is that nothing is changing in the wider economy to increase or decrease the economies of scale available from consumption goods that determine the potential costs and benefits of cohabitation. Imagine, for example, that the relative price of goods that cannot be shared among household members (medical care or education, for example) rises sharply over time while the relative price of goods that can be shared (rental costs, appliances) falls sharply. These relative price changes would diminish the cost of living in smaller households. Shrinking household size would be a rational response to changes in the economy, yet it reflects a genuine decline in utility (a rise in the price of something that cannot be shared among members of the household). Yet, to sterilize this change, to just mechanically adjust for household size, would fail to note this utility loss.

Because we are uncomfortable making the strong assumptions needed to focus solely on size-adjusted income levels, we report income levels for households and families unadjusted for changing family size. Although adjusting for family and household size changes would result in a higher income growth rate between 1979 and 2007, it would not generally affect trends in income distribution (as nearly all income groups experienced roughly similar changes in household size).

Family and household money income

Table 2.1 shows real average family "money income" by income fifth and of families in the top 5 percent of the income distribution. The data are presented for the business cycle peak years 1947, 1979, 1989, 2000, and 2007 as well as for 1995, the midpoint during the 1990s business cycle after which incomes grew rapidly across the board, and for 2010, the latest year for which we have data. "Money income" refers to earnings from work; government cash payments, such as Social Security and unemployment benefits; profits, interest payments, rents, and other cash income accruing to owners of businesses and capital assets; and other miscellaneous sources of cash income. Though capital gains are part of money income,

Table 2.1 Average family income, by income group, 1947–2010 (2011 dollars)

	Income fifth					Breakdown of top fifth	
	Bottom	Second	Middle	Fourth	Top	80th–<95th percentile	Top 5 percent
Real money income							
1947	$7,808	$18,584	$26,548	$36,075	$67,152	$53,097	$109,317
1979	17,318	37,442	56,466	77,740	133,340	111,995	197,373
1989	16,575	38,561	59,906	86,189	162,284	129,724	259,965
1995	16,508	38,035	59,550	87,129	175,047	133,327	300,208
2000	18,444	42,171	66,279	97,682	204,946	152,205	363,167
2007	17,430	41,550	66,651	99,667	202,335	155,298	343,448
2010	15,464	38,235	62,268	94,893	193,308	150,016	323,183
Average annual change							
1947–1979	2.5%	2.2%	2.4%	2.4%	2.2%	2.4%	1.9%
1979–1989	-0.4	0.3	0.6	1.0	2.0	1.5	2.8
1989–1995	-0.1	-0.2	-0.1	0.2	1.3	0.5	2.4
1995–2000	2.2	2.1	2.2	2.3	3.2	2.7	3.9
2000–2007	-0.8	-0.2	0.1	0.3	-0.2	0.3	-0.8
1979–2007	0.0	0.4	0.6	0.9	1.5	1.2	2.0
2007–2010	-3.9	-2.7	-2.2	-1.6	-1.5	-1.1	-2.0

Source: Authors' analysis of Current Population Survey Annual Social and Economic Supplement *Historical Income Tables* (Tables F-2, F-3, and F-5)

they are not included in Table 2.1 because they are not included in the annual Current Population Survey (CPS) supplement that collects the data. Also not in the table, because they are not considered to be money income, are in-kind benefits from government or private sources, such as food stamps, housing vouchers, Medicaid, and employer contributions for health insurance premiums. Much of this section of the chapter focuses on money income because it is the measure most reliably tracked by the CPS Annual Social and Economic Supplement and allows for detailed analysis over a long period, in some cases six and a half decades. Later sections in this chapter examine datasets that include more comprehensive sources of income.

To construct the table, families were ranked from lowest to highest by income levels and then broken into equal fifths, with the top fifth broken down into families between the 80th and 95th percentiles and families in the top 5 percent. The underlying data do not allow finer breakdowns within the top 5 percent (such as the top 1 percent), but data from other sources presented later in this chapter allow for detailed upper-percentile breakdowns.

The table highlights a key theme of this chapter: Between 1947 and 1979, family income growth was relatively uniform across the income distribution, but between 1979 and 1995, family income growth was greater further and further up the income distribution. In the late 1990s, growth was rapid and uniform among the bottom four-fifths and even more rapid at the very top. Then, between 2000 and 2007, income growth was weak across the board, even among families in the upper reaches of the income distribution, largely due to the decline in incomes associated with the burst of the stock market bubble in 2001. Later analysis will show that families at the very top of the distribution did well after the initial stock market decline hit its trough.

Average real income of the middle fifth of families grew from $56,466 in 1979 to $62,268 in 2010, an increase of 10.3 percent. Average real income of the top fifth rose from $133,340 to $193,308 (45.0 percent), and average real income of the top 5 percent increased from $197,373 to $323,183 (63.7 percent).

These disparate growth patterns hold for household incomes, though the data for households do not go back as far as for families. **Table 2.2** demonstrates that the average money incomes of households are lower than those of families. This makes sense, as single-person households, a group with lower-than-average incomes, are not included in family income data. The table also shows the same sharp rise in inequality after 1979 that was shown in family incomes. Income growth of households in the middle fifth lagged behind that of the top fifth in each period except 2000 to 2007, when middle-fifth incomes shrank just slightly less (0.1 percent less) than top-fifth incomes. Average real income of the middle fifth grew from $47,432 in 1979 to $50,865 in 2010, an increase of just 7.2 percent. Average real income of the top fifth rose from $124,917 to $174,985 (40.1 percent), and average real income of the top 5 percent increased from $190,513 to $296,763 (55.8 percent).

Table 2.3 shows the money income thresholds for income fifths and the top 5 percent of families and households. Whereas the previous table showed average income for these groups, this table shows their income ranges. These thresholds may help readers determine their own place in the income distribution. The thresholds also highlight the extent of income inequality in the upper end of the income distribution. For example, while Table 2.1 shows that the average income of the top 5 percent of families was $323,183 in 2010, Table 2.3 shows that the minimum income needed to be in the top 5 percent was much lower—$206,675. This means that even within the top 5 percent, families and households make much more at the upper end than at the lower end of the range.

Table 2.2 Average household income, by income group, 1967–2010
(2011 dollars)

	Income fifth					Breakdown of top fifth	
	Bottom	Second	Middle	Fourth	Top	80th–<95th percentile	Top 5 percent
Real money income							
1967	$9,420	$26,100	$41,668	$58,300	$104,920	$84,725	$165,505
1979	11,566	28,769	47,432	69,606	124,917	103,052	190,513
1989	12,249	30,475	50,658	76,626	149,790	119,051	242,009
1995	12,229	29,890	49,979	76,830	160,332	121,539	276,710
2000	13,266	33,123	55,159	85,747	185,812	137,866	329,650
2007	12,530	31,937	54,202	85,815	182,205	139,097	311,527
2010	11,382	29,540	50,865	81,534	174,985	134,393	296,763
Average annual change							
1967–1979	1.7%	0.8%	1.1%	1.5%	1.5%	1.6%	1.2%
1979–1989	0.6	0.6	0.7	1.0	1.8	1.5	2.4
1989–1995	0.0	-0.3	-0.2	0.0	1.1	0.3	2.3
1995–2000	1.6	2.1	2.0	2.2	3.0	2.6	3.6
2000–2007	-0.8	-0.5	-0.2	0.0	-0.3	0.1	-0.8
1979–2007	0.3	0.3	0.4	0.7	1.2	0.9	1.5
2007–2010	-3.2	-2.6	-2.1	-1.7	-1.3	-1.1	-1.6

Source: Authors' analysis of Current Population Survey Annual Social and Economic Supplement *Historical Income Tables* (Table H-3)

Table 2.4 introduces some elements of nonmoney income by displaying the sources of comprehensive income by income fifths and for the top 10 percent of households (separated into three mutually exclusive groups) in 2007. The table uses the household "comprehensive income" measure from the Congressional Budget Office, which includes several income sources (such as employer-sponsored health benefits and noncash government transfers in the "in-kind" column) that are not included in the CPS money income data.

As the table shows, money income (represented in this table by all the rows "Wages" through "Cash transfers") made up a large majority of total comprehensive income—86.1 percent. It also shows that the relative importance of income sources differed greatly among income fifths. For example, wages account for around 60 percent of total income for the middle three-fifths of the income distribution, yet

Table 2.3 Minimum income thresholds for family and household income, by income group, 1947–2010 (2011 dollars)

| | Real money income threshold, by fifth | | | | | |
	Bottom	Second	Middle	Fourth	Top	Top 5 percent
Family income						
1947	$0	$13,952	$22,513	$30,529	$43,318	$71,099
1979	0	28,471	46,817	66,326	91,330	146,517
1989	0	28,027	49,038	71,455	104,292	173,318
1995	0	27,945	48,336	71,783	105,890	181,206
2000	0	31,345	53,340	80,094	119,340	209,126
2007	0	30,225	53,705	81,355	122,183	213,928
2010	0	27,527	49,514	76,483	117,333	206,675
Household income						
1979	$0	$20,211	$37,534	$57,748	$83,731	$135,297
1989	0	21,184	40,281	61,910	94,064	160,685
1995	0	21,102	39,440	61,550	95,433	165,591
2000	0	23,405	43,100	68,142	106,791	189,666
2007	0	22,010	42,413	67,254	108,474	191,999
2010	0	20,631	39,243	63,683	103,222	186,515

Note: The bottom fifth begins at the first percentile, the second fifth at the 20th percentile, the middle fifth at the 40th percentile, the fourth fifth at the 60th percentile, and the top fifth at the 80th percentile of the income distribution.

Source: Authors' analysis of Current Population Survey Annual Social and Economic Supplement *Historical Income Tables* (Tables F-1 and H-1)

Table 2.4 Sources of pretax comprehensive income, by income group, 2007 (2011 dollars) *Part 1 of 2*

	Income fifth					Breakdown of top 10%			Average all households
	Bottom	Second	Middle	Fourth	Top	90th–<95th percentile	95th–<99th percentile	Top 1 percent	
Households (millions)	24.6	22.2	22.9	23.0	23.7	6.0	4.7	1.2	116.88 (Total)
Share of total pretax income									
Wages	50.5%	59.3%	60.5%	63.2%	48.4%	61.8%	55.6%	26.7%	54.3%
Proprietors' income	6.0	2.6	1.9	1.6	2.6	2.8	4.8	1.6	2.4
Other business income	0.1	0.6	0.9	1.1	8.2	3.3	7.3	15.5	4.6
Interest and dividends	1.0	1.2	1.9	2.6	7.6	5.0	7.1	12.1	5.2
Capital gains	0.3	0.4	0.6	1.1	13.8	3.8	6.3	31.3	8.1
Pensions	1.9	4.1	7.1	8.2	5.2	7.6	5.9	1.1	5.8
Cash transfers	20.3	12.2	9.6	6.6	2.3	3.3	2.3	0.4	5.7
In-kind income	15.4	13.1	11.1	8.7	3.6	5.2	3.5	0.6	6.9
Imputed taxes	4.4	5.1	5.3	5.7	7.3	6.5	6.0	9.5	6.5
Other income	0.2	1.4	1.2	1.2	1.2	1.2	1.0	1.3	0.6
Total	100.0	100.0	100.0	100.0	100.0	100.0	100.0	100.0	100.0
Average									
Wages	$10,082	$27,346	$42,341	$64,528	$139,009	$121,552	$174,477	$542,615	$56,561
Proprietors' income	1,198	1,199	1,330	1,634	7,467	5,511	15,008	32,516	2,500
Other business income	20	277	630	1,123	23,551	6,580	22,803	315,001	4,792
Interest and dividends	200	553	1,330	2,655	21,828	9,890	22,130	245,904	5,416
Capital gains	60	184	420	1,123	39,635	7,451	19,908	636,099	8,437
Pensions	379	1,891	4,969	8,372	14,935	15,047	18,435	22,355	6,041
Cash transfers	4,053	5,626	6,719	6,739	6,606	6,410	7,082	8,129	5,937

Table 2.4 Sources of pretax comprehensive income, by income group, 2007 (2011 dollars) *Part 2 of 2*

	Income fifth					Breakdown of top 10%			Average all households
	Bottom	Second	Middle	Fourth	Top	90th–<95th percentile	95th–<99th percentile	Top 1 percent	
In-kind income	$3,075	$6,041	$7,768	$8,883	$10,339	$10,138	$11,039	$12,194	$7,187
Imputed taxes	878	2,352	3,709	5,820	20,966	12,745	18,971	193,065	6,771
Other income	40	646	840	1,225	3,446	2,362	3,245	26,419	625
Total	19,965	46,114	69,985	102,102	287,208	196,838	313,616	2,032,265	104,163
Shares of total income categories claimed by each group									
Wages	3.8%	9.2%	14.7%	22.5%	49.9%	11.0%	12.4%	9.9%	100.0%
Proprietors' income	9.8	8.8	10.1	12.5	58.8	11.0	23.4	13.0	100.0
Other business income	0.1	1.0	2.4	4.3	92.3	6.5	17.7	62.5	100.0
Interest and dividends	0.8	2.0	4.9	9.8	82.6	9.5	16.6	47.1	100.0
Capital gains	0.2	0.4	1.0	2.6	95.8	4.6	9.5	77.9	100.0
Pensions	1.3	5.9	16.0	27.1	49.7	12.7	12.2	3.8	100.0
Cash transfers	14.4	18.1	22.3	22.5	22.7	5.6	4.8	1.4	100.0
In-kind income	9.0	16.0	21.3	24.4	29.3	7.3	6.2	1.7	100.0
Imputed taxes	2.7	6.6	10.8	17.0	62.9	9.7	11.3	29.3	100.0
Other income	0.7	9.9	13.3	19.5	56.6	9.8	10.6	22.0	100.0
Average	4.0	8.3	13.1	19.1	55.5	9.6	12.0	19.9	100.0

Source: Authors' analysis of Congressional Budget Office (2010a)

only 26.7 percent of total income for the top 1 percent of households. Conversely, capital incomes (interest and dividends, capital gains, and business income other than proprietors' income) were less than 5 percent of total income for each fifth in the bottom four-fifths but 58.9 percent for the top 1 percent. This disproportionate importance of capital income for the top 1 percent of households will become important in later sections as we explore the sources of growing inequality since 1979.

Because "proprietors' income" measures the earnings of businesses owned and operated by a single owner/employee, it is difficult to cleanly parse into either wage or capital income. In this chapter we tend to leave this income in its own category. Given that it is a small and shrinking share of overall comprehensive income (falling from 3.0 to 2.4 percent of overall income between 1979 and 2007), its inclusion in any particular income category would not significantly change trends or levels.

Median family income as a metric of economic performance

Changes over the full income distribution are examined later in the chapter; here, we focus on a commonly cited metric of economic performance—growth in median family money income. Median family income is simply the income of the family that is at the exact center of the income distribution, with half of families having higher incomes and half having lower incomes. **Figure 2A** charts real median family income from 1947 to 2010.

With a little squinting, we can see that median family income either grew much more slowly or fell during recessions (shaded grey on the graph) before generally beginning to grow shortly after the recessions ended. A key thing to notice about this figure is how long it took median family income to recover its

Figure 2A Real median family income, 1947–2010

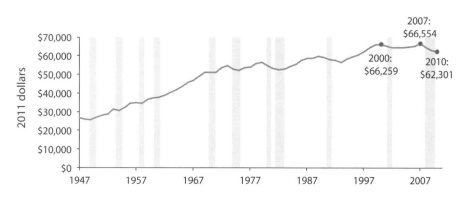

Note: Data are for money income. Shaded areas denote recessions.

Source: Authors' analysis of Current Population Survey Annual Social and Economic Supplement *Historical Income Tables* (Table F-5)

pre-recession level following the recessions of the early 1980s, the early 1990s, and the early 2000s—seven full years in each case. Further, even when median family income finally did surpass its previous 2000 peak in 2007, it was only 0.4 percent higher—$66,554 versus $66,259 (and by 2010 was back down to $62,301). In short, median family income growth has taken much longer to achieve real gains following recessions in recent decades than during pre-1980 business cycles. The next section of this chapter, which addresses the Great Recession and American incomes, will provide evidence that the sluggish growth of median family incomes following recessions is likely to continue in the coming years.

Median family income growth in the 2000s was even worse for working-age families, as shown in **Figure 2B**. Real median income of this group (which excludes families headed by persons more than 64 years old) never regained its 2000 peak of $69,233 following the 2001 recession. By 2007, it had only recovered to $68,893, 0.5 percent below the 2000 peak. By 2010, in the wake of the Great Recession and its aftermath, the median income of working-age families was $63,967, 7.6 percent below the 2000 peak. Even if the median income of working-age families began growing at the relatively rapid annual rate that characterized the 1989–2000 business cycle (1.0 percent average annual growth), the

Figure 2B Real median income of working-age families, 1975–2010

Note: Data are for money income. Shaded areas denote recessions.

Source: Authors' analysis of Current Population Survey Annual Social and Economic Supplement microdata

2000s peak would not be reached until 2018—constituting nearly two decades of lost income growth for this group.

A look at income by income fifths

Of course, median family income represents only one point in the U.S. income distribution. **Figure 2C** shows average annualized income growth for family income fifths (calculated by ranking incomes from lowest to highest and then dividing into fifths) as well as for the top 5 percent of families. Between 1947 and 1979, income growth was relatively uniform for all fifths and even the top 5 percent. Average annual growth rates ranged from 1.9 percent (for the top 5 percent) to 2.5 percent (for the bottom fifth).

The 1979–2007 period had a very different pattern, with faster growth among the higher-income fifths and the fastest growth for families in the top 5 percent. These data clearly reveal the contrast between the broadly shared growth seen from World War II through the 1970s and the concentrated-at-the-top growth seen since.

Figure 2C Average family income growth, by income group, 1947–2007

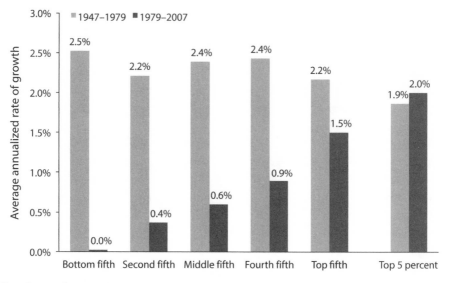

Note: Data are for money income.

Source: Authors' analysis of Current Population Survey Annual Social and Economic Supplement *Historical Income Tables* (Tables F-2, F-3, and F-5)

Median family income by race, ethnicity, and nativity

Family money income differs significantly by racial and ethnic group. **Table 2.5** shows real median family income by race and ethnicity for business cycle peaks, as well as for 1995, and 2010. It also shows income earned by black and Hispanic families as a share of white median family income. In 2010, for example, the median income was $39,715 for black families and $40,785 for Hispanic families; both were less than 63 percent of white median family income, which was $65,138.

While Table 2.5 shows that white families have consistently higher levels of income than African American or Hispanic families, it also highlights trends in median income growth. For example, both white and black families experienced

Table 2.5 Median family income, by race and ethnicity, 1947–2010 (2011 dollars)

	White	Black*	Hispanic**	As a share of white family income	
				Black	Hispanic
1947	$27,807	$14,216	n.a.	51.1%	n.a.
1969	53,120	32,537	n.a.	61.3	n.a.
1979	59,013	33,417	$40,910	56.6	69.3%
1989	63,004	35,393	41,062	56.2	65.2
1995	62,494	38,057	36,005	60.9	57.6
2000	69,259	43,983	44,983	63.5	64.9
2007	69,886	43,545	44,003	62.3	63.0
2010	65,138	39,715	40,785	61.0	62.6
Average annual change					
1947–1969	3.0%	3.8%	n.a.		
1969–1979	1.1	0.3	n.a.		
1979–1989	0.7	0.6	0.0%		
1989–2000	-0.1	1.2	0.8		
1995–2000	2.1	2.9	4.6		
2000–2007	0.1	-0.1	-0.3		
1979–2007	0.5	0.8	0.2		
2007–2010	-2.3	-3.0	-2.5		

* Prior to 1967, data for blacks include all nonwhites.
** Persons of Hispanic origin may be of any race.
Note: Data are for money income.

Source: Authors' analysis of Current Population Survey Annual Social and Economic Supplement *Historical Income Tables* (Table F-5)

their highest annual income growth rates between 1947 and 1967 (3.0 and 3.8 percent, respectively) while income growth for both racial groups dropped to essentially zero between 2000 and 2007 (white median family income grew an average of 0.1 percent annually and African American median family income shrank by 0.1 percent annually).

Another key finding of this table is shown visually in **Figure 2D**. Between 1947 and 1969, the relative incomes of African American families rose substantially—from 51.1 percent of white family incomes to 61.3 percent. In the 1970s and 1980s, this relative progress reversed and, by 1989, the median income of African American families was only 56.2 percent of median white family income. However, rapid growth in the 1990s pushed this relative income to a historic high of 63.5 percent by 2000, an increase of 7.3 percentage points over the 1989 level. But by 2007 this relative income had declined to 62.3 percent, and by 2010 it was down to 61.0 percent. In 2010, median income was $65,138 for white families, compared with $40,785 for Hispanic families and $39,715 for black families.

This fluctuation foreshadows a key finding of the next section: Typical American families and households need low rates of unemployment if they are to achieve fast gains in income (especially gains that are not just purchased by working longer hours), and the benefits of low unemployment disproportionately accrue to often-disadvantaged groups of workers. In fact, the tight labor markets of the late 1990s were actually a prime driver of relative income gains for African Americans, gains that were comparable to those experienced during the height of the Civil Rights revolution.

Figure 2D Black median family income, as a share of white median family income, 1947–2010

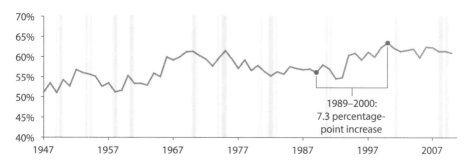

Note: Data are for money income. Shaded areas denote recessions.

Source: Authors' analysis of Current Population Survey Annual Social and Economic Supplement *Historical Income Tables* (Table F-5)

Lastly, it is also worth looking at the basic contours of American incomes by nativity status. Many economic observers have tried to excuse the poor growth in median incomes in recent decades by arguing that a rise in the share of poorer immigrants in the population is pulling down median incomes through composition effects. The idea is that if a substantial number of new immigrants enter the country and have below-median incomes, they would bring down the overall U.S. median income even if the income distribution of those already here did not change. **Figure 2E** shows median family income growth by nativity status since 1993 (the first year data on nativity status are available). This series shows that median income growth for native families very closely matched overall median income growth between 1993 and 2010, with cumulative growth of 12.2 percent for native families and 10.2 percent growth overall. The fact that growth trends for native-born families are very similar to the overall growth trends means that a rising share of immigrants over this period cannot explain poor median income growth.

Of course, this exercise simply tests the composition effect of nativity status on income growth. If competition from immigrants did push down wages of native-born workers, then simply removing immigrant families from these data would not remove this effect (since it is embedded in the native-born incomes).

Figure 2E Median family income growth, by nativity, 1993–2010

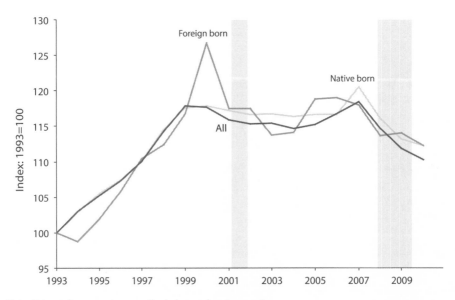

Note: Data are for money income. Shaded areas denote recessions.

Source: Authors' analysis of Current Population Survey Annual Social and Economic Supplement microdata

However, the clear responsiveness of both immigrant and native-born family incomes to overall economic conditions (incomes rose sharply during the tight labor markets of the late 1990s and had sluggish growth during the low-employment-growth 2000s) does suggest that overall economic trends seem to be a first-order determinant of income growth for both sets of families.

The Great Recession and American incomes

What is now known as the Great Recession officially began in December 2007 and ended in June 2009. Yet the economy did not begin registering reliable employment growth until the last quarter of 2010. By the end of 2010, this extended period of economic weakness had taken a heavy toll on American incomes. This section examines the actual and projected effects of the Great Recession on various income and demographic groups.

Impact by income group

Figure 2F shows declines in family money incomes between 2007 and 2010 by income fifth. Over the downturn that began with the Great Recession, family money incomes declined significantly for all income fifths, with the

Figure 2F Change in average family income, by income group, 2007–2010

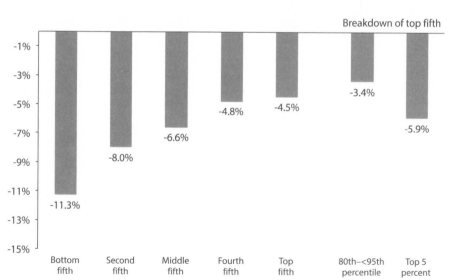

Note: Data are for money income.

Source: Authors' analysis of the Current Population Survey Annual Social and Economic Supplement *Historical Income Tables* (Table F-3)

lower fifths hit hardest: Incomes fell 11.3 percent for the bottom fifth (from $17,430 to $15,464 as shown in Table 2.1), 6.6 percent for the middle fifth (from $66,651 to $62,268), and 4.5 percent for the top fifth (from $202,335 to $193,308).

This pattern is familiar. **Figure 2G** shows the fall in real family incomes for the bottom and middle income fifths over the past three downturns, beginning with the business cycle peak year before the start of each recession. In each instance, the income decline caused by the recession is larger for the lowest income fifth than for the middle fifth, as workers at the lower end of the income distribution tend to be harder hit by job loss and hours reductions during downturns than are workers further up the income scale.

However, Figure 2F does display a perhaps-surprising feature of recent recessions: income losses experienced by families at the very top of the income distribution. Incomes of the top 5 percent of families fell 5.9 percent between 2007 and 2010—a loss greater than that suffered by families in the fourth and top fifths of the distribution. There is, however, a reasonable explanation for this pattern (documented in a longer timespan in Figure 2H ahead). A large share of income of families at the top of the income distribution is linked directly to asset

Figure 2G Change in real family income from business cycle peak years 1989, 2000, and 2007

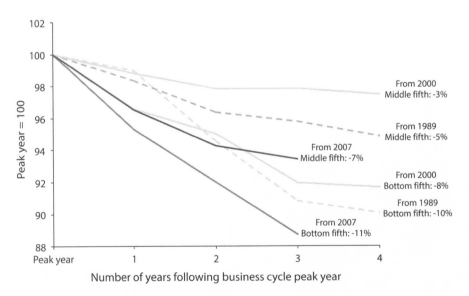

Note: Data are for money income.

Source: Authors' analysis of Current Population Survey Annual Social and Economic Supplement *Historical Income Tables* (Table F-3)

markets (through the exercise of stock options and bonuses tied to measures of corporate profitability, for example). These asset markets lost significant value when the stock market bubble of the early 2000s and the housing market bubble of the mid-to-late 2000s burst. Under such conditions, income declines at the very top of the income distribution often exceed those in the next lower groups and (though not the case in 2007–2010) are sometimes even larger than at the bottom of the distribution.

Some economic observers have argued that the income decline among families at the top implies that the Great Recession "solved" the problem of economic inequality. This is almost surely not the case.

Capital gains are an important source of income for the most affluent households, constituting 21.9 percent of total comprehensive income for the top 5 percent of households in 2007. Because it is tied to stock market valuations, capital gains income tends to fall sharply during recessions, and this is precisely what happened following the stock market crash at the end of 2008.

However, capital gains also tend to rise sharply once economic recovery begins, and capital gains incomes of the most affluent households tend to rise. **Figure 2H** plots the value of the Standard and Poor's index of 500 companies (a

Figure 2H Average capital gains of the top 5% of the income distribution and the S&P 500 composite price index, 1979–2011

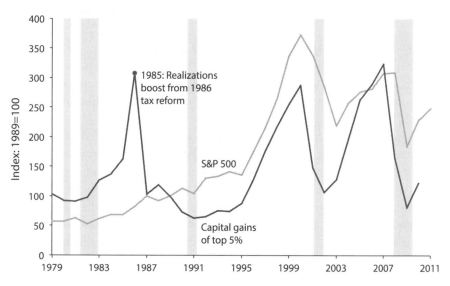

Note: Income distribution is for tax units. A tax unit consists of the people represented on a single tax return. Shaded areas denote recessions.

Source: Authors' analysis of Piketty and Saez (2012, Table A-6 and A-8) and Shiller (2012)

leading measure of stock market health) between 1979 and 2011 against capital gains income for the top 5 percent of tax units in the income distribution between 1979 and 2010. It shows that the capital gains incomes of these households closely follow asset values. This largely explains the big drops and rapid recoveries of high incomes during and after recessions. In short, there is a persistent upward trend in income growth for those at the top of the income distribution that is only temporarily halted during recessions accompanied by stark drops in stock values (as the last two recessions have been). Extrapolating from the recovery in the stock market in the last two years, it would be safe to bet that incomes at the top of the income distribution will register much stronger recovery than incomes below the top in 2011 and beyond. It should also be noted that wage and salary incomes of the highest-income households are also often tied to stock market performance, because these households tend to receive stock options and bonuses linked to firm performance. In short, the highest incomes do tend to fall further when recessions are associated with stock market declines, but tend also to quickly rise following the market's recovery.

Impact by race and ethnicity

Income declines caused by the Great Recession have also differed by race and ethnic group, with racial and ethnic minority households experiencing the largest declines. **Figure 2I** shows that between 2007 and 2010, real median household income declined 5.4 percent for the median white household, 7.2 percent for the median Hispanic household, 7.5 percent for the median Asian American household, and 10.1 percent for the median African American household.

Income losses projected for years to come

While the Great Recession officially ended in 2009, the damage to family income growth from elevated unemployment is likely not over. The unemployment rate averaged 8.9 percent in 2011, and is generally not expected to fall below 7 percent until 2016.

Figure 2J shows, from 2000 onward, the actual and projected family income growth for the middle fifth of the income distribution. The projected paths are modeled based on the relationship between income growth and the unemployment rate from 1948 to 2010. The projected unemployment rates for 2012 and later come from two prominent economic forecasts—one by the Congressional Budget Office (CBO) and one by Moody's Analytics. Our forecast overestimated income growth in the 2000s because the decade's unemployment rates, low by historical standards, did not translate into large income gains (as emphasized in the previous section). That is, incomes grew less than expected in the 2000s given relatively low unemployment rates.

Figure 2I Change in real median household income, by race and ethnicity, 2007–2010

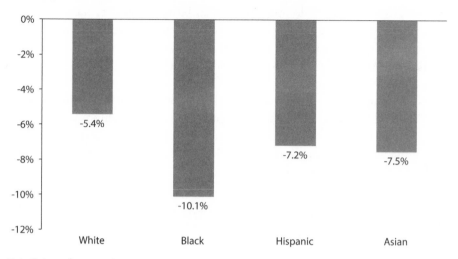

Note: Data are for money income.

Source: Authors' analysis of Current Population Survey Annual Social and Economic Supplement *Historical Income Tables* (Table H-5)

Figure 2J Change in real family income of the middle fifth, actual and predicted, 2000–2018

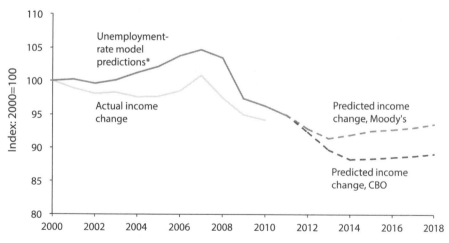

* Path of income growth projected by a model based on the relationship between income growth and the unemployment rate from 1948–2010.

Note: Data are for money income.

Source: Authors' analysis of Current Population Survey Annual Social and Economic Supplement *Historical Income Tables* (Tables F-2, F-3, and F-5) and analysis based on forecasted unemployment rates from Congressional Budget Office (2012) and Moody's Analytics (2012)

However, the statistical relationship captured in the prediction line does reflect the turning point in family income in 2007 and does a decent job of predicting the extent of income declines after 2007: Actual incomes of the middle fifth fell by 6.7 percent, compared with a projected 8.0 percent decline.

The outcome of this exercise for 2012 and later is grim. Using the CBO unemployment forecast, income of the middle fifth of families in 2018 will still be more than 10 percent below the 2000 level. Even under the more-optimistic Moody's Analytics unemployment forecast, middle fifth income will not reach its 2000 level by 2018. This analysis suggests again that roughly two decades are likely to pass before typical families regain the level of income they had in 2000, due to the weak income performance of the 2000s expansion combined with the very long reach of the Great Recession.

Rising inequality of American incomes

As shown earlier in Figure 2C, family income growth since 1979 has become vastly more unequal than growth between 1947 and 1979. This section explores income inequality, first tracking trends in family income and thereafter focusing on household income. Switching to analyses of household income has two advantages. First, as already mentioned, household data capture more people because virtually everyone in the population belongs, by definition, to a household, while not everyone belongs to a family. Second, crucial aspects of the debate about American income inequality in recent years have centered around some forms of income that are not captured in the publicly available annual CPS data on family money incomes. In particular, noncash transfers and compensation such as housing assistance, Medicare, Medicaid, and contributions to employer-sponsored health insurance (ESI) premiums are not available in the data commonly used to chart family incomes. However, the Congressional Budget Office has released a series of reports on the distribution of household incomes and taxation that use publicly unavailable data to apportion these noncash benefits across the distribution of households. Much of the following analyses will draw on this extraordinarily useful dataset.

Family income inequality
Figure 2K charts money income growth for families at the 20th percentile, the median, and the 95th percentile of the income distribution since 1947. The results are striking—income growth that was nearly uniform across income levels for decades diverges markedly after 1979. From 1947 to 1979, annual family incomes at the 20th and the 95th percentiles grew 2.3 percent on average while median family income grew 2.4 percent. But between 1979 and 2007, average annual income of families at the 20th percentile grew just 0.2 percent (from $28,471 in 1979 to $30,225 in 2007), compared with 0.6 percent for median families (from

Figure 2K Income growth for families at the 20th, 50th, and 95th percentiles, 1947–2010

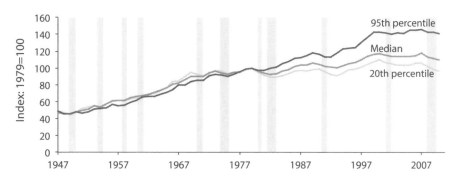

Note: Data are for money income. Shaded areas denote recessions.

Source: Authors' analysis of Current Population Survey Annual Social and Economic Supplement *Historical Income Tables* (Tables F-1 and F-5)

$56,553 in 1979 to $66,554 in 2007) and 1.4 percent for families at the 95th percentile (from $146,517 in 1979 to $213,928 in 2007).

This pattern is important for a couple of reasons. First, it demonstrates that rising inequality is not inevitable in advanced market economies—the United States and other rich countries have had extended periods of rapid overall economic growth with gains broadly shared across the income distribution. Second, it shows that the increasing inequality documented in the post-1979 household data that follow is not unique to this dataset but appears in analyses of all datasets of American incomes over time, regardless of whether they track family or household income.

Before turning to household data based on comprehensive incomes, we will use the family money income data to examine the influence of nativity status on rising inequality. As noted earlier in the chapter, many economic observers blame the sluggish growth of median family incomes on the "compositional effect" of a rising share of immigrant families in the United States at the bottom of the income distribution. That argument was shown to be false, since the median family income of native-born Americans scarcely differed from the median family income of all Americans between 1993 and 2010 (see Figure 2E).

Figure 2L illustrates the possible effect of nativity status on income inequality by displaying income growth of the 20th percentile, the median, and the 95th percentile of all families and of just native-born families. The trends for all families and native-born famililes track each other closely, meaning that the growing income inequality in recent decades is not simply due to a growing share of non-native families in the U.S. population.

Figure 2L Income growth for families at the 20th, 50th, and 95th percentiles, by nativity, 1993–2010

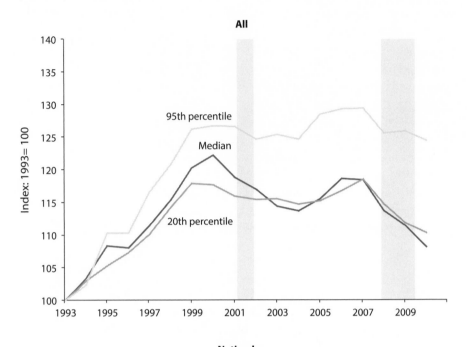

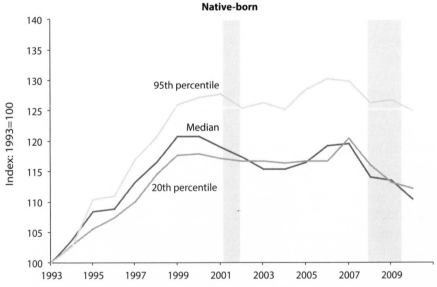

Note: Data are for money income. Shaded areas denote recessions.

Source: Authors' analysis of Current Population Survey Annual Social and Economic Supplement microdata

Unequal growth of comprehensive household incomes suggests diverging well-being

The CBO data used in the following analyses of household income are based on "comprehensive income." This income measure includes market incomes (earnings from labor, dividends, interest payments, realized capital gains, and rents and other business income that accrue to owners of capital), transfer payments from government (cash transfers, such as Social Security and unemployment insurance benefits, and noncash transfers, such as housing vouchers, food stamps, Medicare, and Medicaid), noncash employment income (the value of employer-sponsored insurance paid to employees by employers), and imputed taxes (taxes, such as the corporate income tax or the employer portion of payroll tax, that are nominally paid by non-households but that, as most economists agree, are actually borne by households in the form of lower wages and incomes).

Measuring comprehensive income allows us to assess trends in living standards across the distribution of household income (though perhaps not perfectly—instances where the CBO may overstate income gains are discussed later in this section). However, the measure can lead to faulty conclusions about the related question of how well the private U.S. economy is generating increasing living standards. As will be noted at the end of this chapter, the income gains of American households in recent decades are not clear evidence that the private U.S. economy is generating efficient and fair outcomes. Rather, these gains are often evidence of just how hard American households have worked, by supplying more hours of labor to the paid labor markets and ensuring that they constantly upgrade their educational levels and work experience.

Figure 2M illustrates a key finding on comprehensive income trends by showing a striking pattern in average income growth by income group: Income growth is strongly positively correlated with a household's rank in the income distribution, and the gap in income growth between the highest-income households and the rest is enormous. For example, the top 1 percent of households registered cumulative income growth of 240.5 percent between 1979 and 2007, while households in the bottom and middle fifths of the income distribution posted gains of 10.8 and 19.2 percent, respectively.

Importantly, although income growth for households between the 80th and 90th percentiles and 90th and 95th percentiles was substantial (40.6 and 55.3 percent, respectively), this growth still far lagged that at the top: Income growth of households between the 80th and 90th percentiles was just 16.9 percent of growth for the top 1 percent, while that of households between the 90th and 95th percentiles was just 23.0 percent of growth for the top 1 percent. While this chapter has a special focus on how households in the middle of the income distribution have been faring, it is important to note that in terms of income

Figure 2M Change in real annual household income, by income
group, 1979–2007

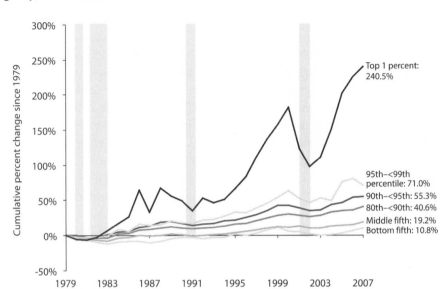

Note: Data are for comprehensive income. Shaded areas denote recessions.

Source: Authors' analysis of data from the Congressional Budget Office (2010a)

growth the top 1 percent has been pulling away, not just from the middle, but
from other households in the top income fifth.

Sharp rise in income inequality apparent
in every major data source

The sharp rise in income inequality in the United States between 1979 and 2007
is apparent in every major data source and is almost universally recognized by
researchers. **Table 2.6** shows the growth in average incomes accounted for by the
bottom 95 percent, top 5 percent, and top 1 percent of the population analyzed
by various income data sources and measures.

At first glance, these estimates are perhaps surprisingly bimodal. For example, CPS data show that the share of overall average household money income
growth attributable to the top 5 percent of households in the household money
income distribution was 37 percent (a contribution far in excess of their share
of the population). A study that supplements CPS data with estimates of taxes
paid and of in-kind incomes from employer-provided benefits and government
transfers (Burkhauser, Larrimore, and Simon 2011) found that the top 5 percent
of households accounted for 26.6 percent of overall average household income

Table 2.6 Share of average income growth accounted for by the bottom 95 percent, top 5 percent, and top 1 percent, by dataset and income concept, 1979–2007

	Bottom 95 percent	Top 5 percent	Top 1 percent
Top-coded			
Burkhauser et al.; CPS household money income, adjusted	73.4%	26.6%	—
CPS household money income	63.0	37.0	—
Not top-coded			
CBO, household comprehensive income	46.1	53.9	38.3%
Piketty and Saez, cash market income	19.1	80.9	59.8
CBO, household comprehensive income adjusted to match Burkhauser et al.*	48.1	51.9	—

* Capital gains are excluded, post–tax-and-transfer growth is shown, and in-kind benefits such as health care are allowed to boost bottom-fifth incomes to the same degree as allowed by Burkhauser, Larrimore, and Simon (2011).

Source: Burkhauser, Larrimore, and Simon (2011, Table 4), Current Population Survey Annual Social and Economic Supplement Historical Income Tables (Table H-3), Congressional Budget Office (2010a), authors' analysis of Piketty and Saez (2012, Table A-6)

growth, an estimate of broadly similar magnitude—differing by just slightly over 10 percentage points—to the estimate using the unadjusted CPS data.

On the other hand, datasets that use Internal Revenue Service sources for the highest-income households, such as those on household income from the CBO (2010a) and on tax units from Piketty and Saez (2012), show much higher shares of average income growth accounted for by the top 5 percent of the income distribution. The top 5 percent of households accounted for 53.9 percent of average household comprehensive income growth according to CBO data that, as mentioned earlier, uses IRS sources for top incomes and also includes the in-kind income tracked by Burkhauser, Larrimore, and Simon (2011) and capital gains. The widely referenced dataset from Piketty and Saez, published in 2003 and updated to 2010 (Piketty and Saez 2012), tracks only cash, market-based incomes; it indicates that the top 5 percent of tax units accounted for 80.9 percent of average growth from 1979 to 2007. (A tax unit consists of the people represented on a single tax return.)

The differences between these estimates seem to be largely due to whether the data used to construct the growth rates of the top 5 percent were "top-coded." Top-coding refers to when incomes above a given threshold are given a single uniform value; it is generally done in publicly available datasets to ensure confidentiality of the highest-income units in the sample. But because so much income growth in recent decades has occurred at the very top of the income distribution, datasets that include this top-code show much smaller increases in inequality than datasets that are not top-coded. The CPS data on household money income, and the Burkhauser, Larrimore, and Simon (2011) data based on the CPS data but that add in other types of income, are top-coded. The Piketty and Saez data and the CBO comprehensive income data are not top-coded, and this largely explains why they capture the greater increase in the gap between average growth of the top 5 percent, and everybody else.

The last row in the table provides calculations based on the CBO data but adjusted to exactly match the Burkhauser, Larrimore, and Simon (2011) concepts; it strips out capital gains, shows post-tax, post-transfer growth, and allows in-kind benefits such as health care to boost bottom-fifth incomes to the same degree estimated by Burkhauser and coauthors. Using the Burkhauser concepts, the CBO data, which are not top-coded, display much larger increases in inequality than do the CPS data, which are top-coded.

Piketty and Saez's widely referenced dataset confirms inequality trends shown in this chapter

One of the most referenced datasets showing the rise in American inequality in recent decades was published by Thomas Piketty and Emmanuel Saez in 2003 and is regularly updated. The Piketty and Saez data are incredibly valuable for several reasons. First, it is an extremely long data series, compiled from consistent, high-quality data from 1913 to 2010. In addition, the data are not "top-coded," meaning the highest incomes are included (including even the top 1.0 and 0.1 percent), enabling us to chart the full extent of rising inequality.

However, most of this chapter uses other income data sources, primarily because the Piketty and Saez data do not map perfectly to family or households incomes. Instead, Piketty and Saez use "tax units," the people represented on a single tax return. Further, the Piketty and Saez data show pretax and pretransfer market incomes, data which do not provide useful information for debates about how noncash income and transfers affect the bottom 99 percent of American incomes. Finally, the Piketty and Saez data do not provide breakdowns within the bottom 90 percent.

Nevertheless, the Piketty and Saez data are too important and useful to completely leave out of any discussion of American incomes. **Figure 2AA** compares their most iconic finding—the share of overall income claimed by the top 1 percent of American tax units—with the share of income claimed by the top 5 and top 1 percent of families or households from CBO and Current Population Survey datasets. All tell the same basic story about income inequality: Those with the highest incomes have claimed ever-greater shares of income in recent decades.

Figure 2AA Share of income held by high-income groups, 1913–2010

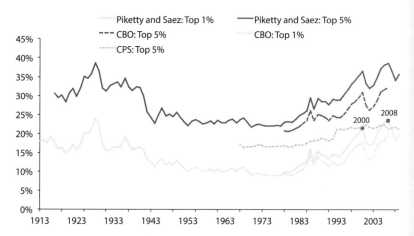

Note: Data show market income of tax units (Piketty and Saez), comprehensive household income (CBO), and household money income (CPS). All datasets except CPS include capital gains income. Sharp drops in income shares after 2000 and 2008 were due to the burst of the dot-com bubble in 2001 and the financial crisis of 2008.

Source: Authors' analysis of Piketty and Saez (2012, Table A-3), Congressional Budget Office (2010a), and Current Population Survey Annual Social and Economic Supplement *Historical Income Tables* (Table H-2)

The Piketty and Saez data also contribute to our discussion by showing that the rise in U.S. income inequality is unique in scale among all developed economies. Some other countries (mostly those that have pursued economic policies closer to those of the United States) have seen some increase in income inequality in recent decades, while others have seen very little increase. But no country in the developed world has experienced a rise in inequality as pronounced as that seen in the United States (**Figure 2AB**).

Figure 2AB Share of income held by top 1 percent in developed countries, 1913–2009

Note: Thin gray lines plot the share of market income held by the top 1 percent of tax units in Australia, Canada, Finland, Germany, Ireland, Netherlands, New Zealand, Norway, Spain, Sweden, and Switzerland.

Source: Authors' analysis of *The World Top Incomes* database (Alvaredo, Atkinson, Piketty, and Saez various years)

The limited impact of taxes and transfers relative to market income

Although tax and budget policies have dominated economic policy debates in recent years, it is useful to remember that the large increases in income inequality over recent decades have been overwhelmingly driven by market incomes, i.e., incomes households bring in before government taxes and transfers such as Social Security and unemployment benefits.

Figure 2N shows changes in the share of total income claimed by households in various income groups using two different measures of income shares. The lighter-shaded bar in each income category shows percentage-point changes in the market-income share (pretax, pre-transfer). For example, the market-income share of the middle fifth of households dropped by 3.1 percentage points between 1979 and 2007. The darker-shaded bar shows changes in the post-tax, post-transfer income share. For example, the post-tax, post-transfer income share of the middle fifth dropped by 2.4 percentage points over this period.

Figure 2N Change in the share of market income and post-tax, post-transfer income that households claim, by income group, 1979–2007

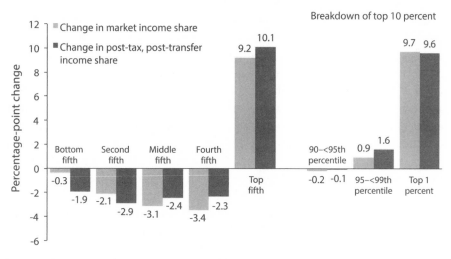

Source: Authors' analysis of Congressional Budget Office (2010a and 2010b)

The most striking aspect of this chart is that the bottom four-fifths of households (that is, 80 percent of Americans) lost income share, however defined, between 1979 and 2007. The big winners in terms of overall income shares (again, however defined) are the top 1 percent of households, which have seen their share of overall income rise by close to 10 percentage points (9.7 percentage points for market-income share and 9.6 percentage points for post-tax, post-transfer income share).

This chart also demonstrates that changes in post-tax, post-transfer income are largely determined by changes in market income. For example, gains in market incomes contributed a huge proportion (9.2 percentage points) of the entire 10.1 percentage-point increase in post-tax, post-transfer income shares of households in the top fifth. This means that any changes in government transfer policy (e.g., unemployment benefits and Social Security) or in tax policy have played relatively minor roles in changes of post-tax, post-transfer income; the key driver has been changes in market-based incomes, namely what households have received in wages, benefits, and capital incomes.

This does not negate the importance of tax and budget policies. Indeed, we could argue that lower tax rates on the very rich have given them extra incentive to secure policies that redistribute more market incomes to them. For example, they could choose to make it harder for low- and moderate-income workers to form unions or to fight increases in the minimum wage. However, the lesser role of tax and transfer policies in driving overall income growth does imply that efforts to improve the lot of low- and moderate-income families cannot rely solely on the tax-and-transfer system.

Still, it remains useful to examine what developments in tax-and-transfer payments have and have not done in affecting income inequality. By some measures, the changing effect of taxes and transfers on overall income inequality has exacerbated the trend towards growing inequality in market incomes. For example, the CBO (2011) shows that the change in taxes and transfers between 1979 and 2007 actually increased the Gini coefficient (a measure of inequality; a higher value indicates a less equal distribution of resources) of post-tax comprehensive income.

Indeed, taxes and transfers have been shown to be wholly ineffective in countering the large rise in market income inequality since 1979. **Figure 20**, which illustrates income groups' share of pretax and post-tax comprehensive income, highlights how ineffective tax policies have been in countering increasing inequality of market income. Each set of three bars corresponds to households in different segments of the income distribution. The first bar in each set shows the change in that group's income share—measured as the difference between pretax and post-tax

Figure 2O Effect of tax policies on each household income group's share of total income, 1979 and 2007, and the difference needed in 2007 to preserve 1979 post-tax shares

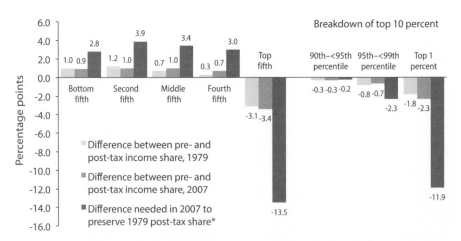

* This shows the degree to which the tax system would have needed to increase 2007 pretax income shares to keep each group's share of post-tax income stable from 1979 to 2007, given the increasing inequality of pretax income over this period.

Note: Data are for comprehensive income. The changes in the difference needed in 2007 to preserve 1979 post-tax shares do not sum to zero due to the presence of negative-income households in CBO data.

Source: Authors' analysis of Congressional Budget Office (2010a and 2010b)

share—due to tax policy in 1979. For example, in 1979, the tax system boosted the share of total income going to the bottom fifth of households by 1.0 percentage point and boosted the share of total income going to the second fifth by 1.2 percentage points. The second bar in each set shows the difference between pretax and post-tax share of total income in 2007. In 2007, the tax system boosted the share of total income going to the bottom fifth of households by 0.9 percentage points and increased the share of total income going to the second fifth by 1.0 percentage point, both slight declines relative to 1979. In other words, taxes boosted these groups' relative income shares less in 2007 than they did in 1979.

Given the deterioration in market income shares for the bottom four fifths of the income distribution shown in Figure 2N, the tax system actually would have had to do more to smooth out inequality just to keep their 1979 shares of post-tax income constant. The last bar in each set shows what boost the tax system would have needed to provide in order to keep each group's share of post-tax income stable from 1979 to 2007, given the increasing inequality in market income over this period. For the bottom fifth of households, the tax system would have needed to add 2.8 percentage points to pretax income share in 2007 to preserve their 1979 post-tax share; and the tax system would have needed to add 3.9 percentage points to income to restore the second fifth of households to their 1979 post-tax income share. Instead, the tax system boosted these groups' pretax share by 0.9 percentage points and 1.0 percentage point, respectively, in 2007. One way to interpret this is to say that the tax system, given underlying trends in market income, has not only boosted the bottom two fifths' pretax income share by less than it used to, it boosted it by less than one-third of what was needed to have kept the their post-tax income shares constant since 1979. Given this weak impact, it seems clear that changes in tax rates have, at best, been totally ineffective in combating large increases in inequality since 1979.

Actual data on tax rates demonstrate why this finding is unsurprising. Effective tax rates by income fifth have converged rapidly in recent years, and average federal tax rates for the top 1 percent of households fell from 37.0 percent in 1979 to 29.5 percent in 2007. While effective tax rates fell across the entire household income distribution, the overall effective rate for the entire income distribution only fell from 22.2 percent to 20.4 percent, a much smaller decline than that for the highest-income households. **Figure 2P** shows effective tax rates for households at various points in the income distribution.

The data in Figure 2P underlie most of the remaining examination of the tax-and-transfer system's impacts on inequality trends over recent decades. It is important to note that these data may well understate the decline in tax rates for the very richest households over time. First, the trend of declining rates on the highest incomes predates 1979, the starting point of the CBO data in the figure. Second, even as marginal rates have fallen, the rapid rise in incomes of the most well-off households actually increases their effective tax rates, all else equal,

Figure 2P Average effective federal tax rates, by household income group, 1979–2007

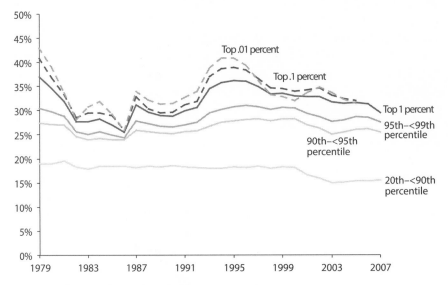

Note: Data are for comprehensive household income.

Source: Authors' analysis of Congressional Budget Office (2008 and 2010a)

by subjecting a greater share of their total income to the highest marginal rates. (Changes in effective tax rates are thus the net effect of legislated lowered rates and the higher rates that result from increased incomes.) The CBO data do not separate the changes in effective tax rates due to policy from those due to changes in the underlying income growth of rich households. Third, the CBO data do not include gift taxes and estate taxes. These taxes are paid disproportionately by the highest-income households and have fallen precipitously for decades.

Figure 2Q provides (at least partial) correction for the each of these three understatements. Based on the work of Piketty and Saez (2007), it provides effective tax rates that include gift taxes and estate taxes for finely grained income groupings over a longer period of time. The figure shows an extraordinary convergence of tax rates across the income distribution.

Table 2.7 details some of these tax changes using data from the CBO (2010a). The table clearly shows that the federal income tax remains progressive despite changes during the 2000s that eroded progressivity. In each year, average effective tax rates rose smoothly with income. Further, the large expansion of the Earned Income Tax Credit (EITC) during the Clinton administration greatly reduced low-income households' effective tax rate—which has actually been consistently

Figure 2Q Average effective federal tax rates, by income group, 1960–2004

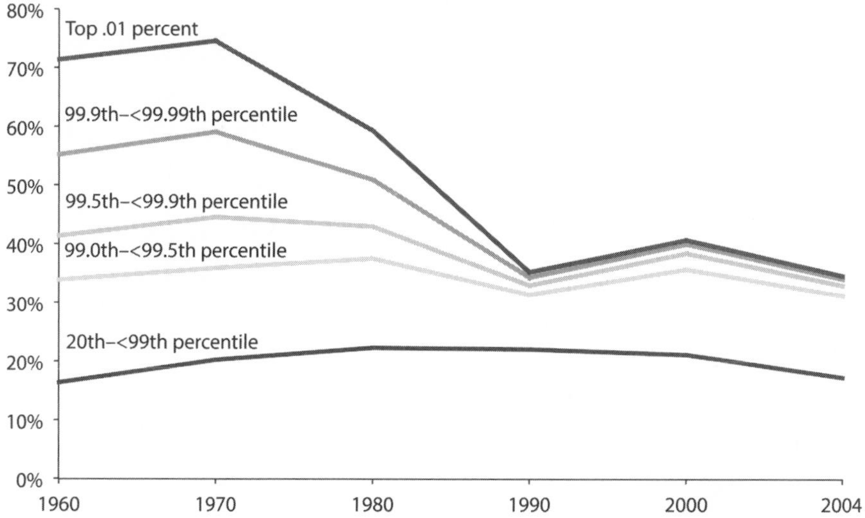

Note: Data are for tax units (people represented on a single tax return).

Source: Authors' analysis of Piketty and Saez (2007, Table 2)

negative in recent decades. While the federal income tax has remained progressive for any given year, policy has changed the level of its progressivity over time. Between 1989 and 2000, for example, the effective income tax rate on the top 1 percent of households rose from 19.9 percent to 24.2 percent, in large part because of tax increases on high-income households during the Clinton administration. Of course, as noted in the discussion of Figure 2P, the simple rates reported in this table do not fully reflect policy changes that reduced tax rates on high-income households. These households experienced fast income growth in the 1979-and-on period under discussion, which, all else equal, would have led to rising effective tax rates for them as more of their income was subject to the highest marginal rates. The fact that the effective income tax rate for the top 1 percent fell between 2000 and 2007 (from 24.2 percent to 19.0 percent) is testament to the impact of policies (the Bush administration tax cuts) that reduced tax rates at the high end.

The table also indicates the pronounced progressivity of the corporate income tax—a tax that in 2007 averaged less than 1 percent of income for the bottom 80 percent of households, but was 8.8 percent of income for the top 1 percent.

The table also shows that federal payroll taxes are much flatter (i.e., less progressive) than income taxes. Because the tax base for funding Social Security is capped (at just over $110,000 in 2012, for example), the payroll tax rate actually falls sharply at the high end of the income distribution, with the top 1 percent

Table 2.7 Effective tax rates for selected federal taxes, by income group, 1979–2007

Income group	Personal income tax				Payroll tax				Corporate income tax				Excise tax			
	1979	1989	2000	2007	1979	1989	2000	2007	1979	1989	2000	2007	1979	1989	2000	2007
Bottom fifth	0.0%	-1.6%	-4.6%	-6.8%	5.3%	7.1%	8.2%	8.8%	1.1%	0.6%	0.5%	0.4%	1.6%	1.8%	2.3%	1.6%
Second fifth	4.1	2.9	1.5	-0.4	7.7	8.9	9.4	9.5	1.2	0.8	0.6	0.5	1.3	1.2	1.4	1.0
Middle fifth	7.5	6.0	5.0	3.3	8.6	9.8	9.6	9.4	1.4	1.1	0.9	0.8	1.1	1.0	1.1	0.8
Fourth fifth	10.1	8.3	8.1	6.2	8.5	10.0	10.4	9.5	1.6	1.2	1.0	1.1	0.9	0.9	0.9	0.7
Top fifth	15.7	14.6	17.5	14.4	5.4	6.6	6.3	5.7	5.7	3.5	3.7	4.6	0.7	0.6	0.5	0.4
Top 10 percent	17.4	16.3	19.7	16.2	4.2	5.1	5.0	4.5	7.4	4.4	4.4	5.7	0.7	0.5	0.4	0.3
Top 5 percent	19.0	17.7	21.6	17.6	2.8	3.7	3.8	3.3	9.5	5.3	5.2	6.8	0.6	0.4	0.4	0.2
Top 1 percent	21.8	19.9	24.2	19.0	0.9	1.4	1.9	1.6	13.8	7.2	6.7	8.8	0.5	0.3	0.2	0.1
All	**11.0**	**10.2**	**11.8**	**9.3**	**6.9**	**8.1**	**7.9**	**7.4**	**3.4**	**2.3**	**2.4**	**3.0**	**1.0**	**0.8**	**0.9**	**0.6**

Note: Income groups reflect comprehensive household income.

Source: Authors' analysis of Congressional Budget Office (2010a)

paying only 1.6 percent of income in 2007, as opposed to the 9.4 percent paid by the middle fifth of households.

Figure 2R shows changes on the transfer side of tax-and-transfer policy. The bottom 40 percent of households saw outright declines in average annual cash transfer income (such as Social Security and unemployment benefit payments) between 1979 and 2007. For the bottom fifth this decline is large; they received $2,125 less in cash transfers in 2007 than they received in 1979. For the middle, fourth, and top income fifths, cash transfers have grown steadily over time, rising by $2,786, $3,562, and $3,409, respectively, between 1979 and 2007.

When one adds in the "fungible value" of government transfers for health care (i.e., the value of Medicare and Medicaid to recipients as calculated by the CBO), transfer income of the second fifth rises by $1,735 in 2007 as compared with 1979, still far less than the $6,019, $6,778, and $6,202 increase including these transfers for the middle, fourth, and top fifths, respectively.

These medical transfers have done little to boost the change in overall transfers received by the bottom fifth of households, changing the $2,125 cash loss into a $1,730 overall loss. However, part of the failure of medical transfers to boost incomes of the bottom fifth is a symptom of how the data are constructed.

Figure 2R Change in real cash and medical transfer income, by income group, 1979–2007

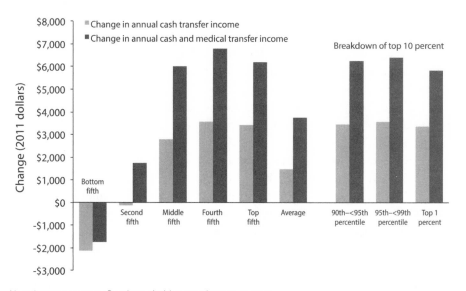

Note: Income groups reflect household comprehensive income.

Source: Authors' analysis of Congressional Budget Office (2010a and 2010b)

For each person who reports receiving these transfers, the CBO assigns an income value equal to the average per-beneficiary cost. But the CBO counts as a gain in comprehensive income only those parts of Medicaid and Medicare transfers that boost a household's potential for purchasing non-health-care-related goods. Because many poor households have incomes that are not much greater, and sometimes less, than the per-beneficiary cost of Medicaid and Medicare, this means that the boost to non-health-care-related consumption possibilities (i.e., the "fungible value" of these benefits) is quite small.

Lastly, we can combine data on taxes and transfers by income group to measure their net impact on household incomes. The basic data are provided in **Table 2.8**, which shows the effective tax rate as well as the transfer rate (the value of government transfer payments divided by comprehensive income). Lastly, the table calculates a net tax-and-transfer rate—the rate that shows how much the combination of taxes and transfers either boosts or reduces comprehensive incomes. Note that a negative "tax rate net of transfers" means that transfers are larger than taxes and therefore the tax-and-transfer system together provide an income boost to the household.

The findings for the bottom fifth of households are striking: The net effect of taxes and transfers boosted household incomes by 37.2 percent in 1979 but by only 28.3 percent in 2007. In other words, the tax rate net of transfers increased over this period by 8.8 percentage points for the bottom fifth, as shown in the last row of the table. For groups within the top 10 percent, particularly the top 1 percent of households, the tax rate net of transfers, while starting from a much higher level, moved in the other direction, dropping significantly between 1979 and 2007. However, the biggest "swing" in the tax rate net of transfers was actually for the middle fifth: In 1979 their tax rate net of transfers was 10.2 percent, but by 2007 it had dropped to -1.3 percent, meaning that in 2007 the incomes of the middle fifth were boosted 1.3 percent on average by the tax-and-transfer system.

The last row of the table summarizes the data by measuring how the change in the effect of the tax-and-transfer system between 1979 and 2007 affected household income.

The last three rows of Table 2.8 are displayed visually in **Figure 2S**. The lightest-shaded bar in each set shows that between 1979 and 2007 the tax rate declined across the entire income distribution, though the declines were greatest for the top 1 percent. But the transfer rate, depicted in the second bar in each set, increased for every group except the bottom fifth, for whom it dropped by 12.8 percentage points. Putting these two data points together, we find that the bottom fifth of the income distribution saw their tax rate net of transfers increase by 8.8 percent over this period, while rates for the top four fifths dropped, with particularly large declines for the middle fifth (11.5 percentage points), the fourth fifth (9.3 percentage points) and the top 1 percent (7.9 percentage points). Recall from

Table 2.8 Tax rate, transfer rate, and tax rate net of transfers, by income group, 1979–2007

	All households	Household income fifth					Breakdown of top 10 percent		
		Bottom	Second	Middle	Fourth	Top	90th–<95th percentile	95th–<99th percentile	Top 1 percent
1979									
Effective tax rate	22.2%	8.0%	14.3%	18.6%	21.2%	27.5%	28.7%	30.5%	37.0%
Transfer rate	8.3	45.2	19.2	8.4	4.9	2.6	0.4	0.4	0.2
Tax rate net of transfers	13.9	-37.2	-4.9	10.2	16.3	24.9	28.3	30.1	36.8
2007									
Effective tax rate	20.4%	4.0%	10.6%	14.3%	17.4%	25.1%	25.9%	27.5%	29.5%
Transfer rate	9.1	32.3	20.1	15.6	10.4	3.5	2.9	1.9	0.6
Tax rate net of transfers	11.3	-28.3	-9.5	-1.3	7.0	21.6	23.0	25.6	28.9
Percentage-point change, 1979–2007									
Effective tax rate	-1.8	-4.0	-3.7	-4.3	-3.8	-2.4	-2.8	-3.0	-7.5
Transfer rate	0.8	-12.8	0.9	7.2	5.5	1.0	2.5	1.5	0.4
Tax rate net of transfers	-2.6	8.8	-4.6	-11.5	-9.3	-3.4	-5.3	-4.5	-7.9

Note: Income groups reflect comprehensive income.

Source: Authors' analysis of Congressional Budget Office (2010a and 2010b)

Figure 2S Change in tax rate, transfer rate, and tax rate net of transfers, by income group, 1979–2007

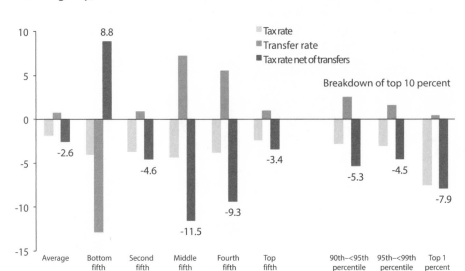

Note: Income groups reflect comprehensive income.

Source: Authors' analysis of Congressional Budget Office (2010a and 2010b)

Figure 2N, however, that favorable changes in the tax-and-transfer system for the middle portion of the income distribution did not even come close to offsetting their declining share of market income.

In conclusion, our review of market incomes vis-a-vis tax-and-transfer policy finds that most of the rise in inequality in recent decades has been driven by trends in market income. The equalizing effect of tax-and-transfer policy has been, at best, wholly ineffective in countering inequality and, at worst, has exacerbated the rise in market-driven inequality.

Factors behind the large rise in inequality of market incomes

There are basically three developments that caused the large increase in inequality of market incomes between 1979 and 2007: concentration of labor incomes, concentration of capital incomes, and a shift in the share of overall income from labor to capital incomes. Though not necessarily a significant contributor every year, each factor had a strong influence on rising inequality of market incomes during certain timespans within that period.

Market incomes of households can basically be classified as derived either from labor services or from ownership of capital assets. Labor services are work hours provided by household members to the paid labor force. Earnings from labor services depend on the amount worked and the pay per unit of work, usually hourly pay (wage and benefit) rates. Pay rates, in turn, depend on many factors, some of which likely reflect a given worker's underlying productivity (educational attainment and experience, for example), and some of which reflect historical and institutional influences on pay rates (such as industry, race and ethnicity, gender, and nativity status; Chapter 4 covers these influences in detail).

Capital incomes are the returns to owning physical and financial capital, i.e., claims to income generated by businesses or government plants and equipment. The income derived from owning this capital comes in the form of interest payments, dividends, realized capital gains, rent, and other business income. Essentially, capital incomes are the returns to holding wealth, whereas labor incomes are the returns to work.

On average, households in all income fifths generate some income from both sources. Obviously, a greater concentration of either labor or capital income in higher income brackets widens income inequality. But because capital incomes are much more concentrated at the top of the income distribution than labor incomes (Table 2.4 showed these shares for 2007), an overall shift in the share of all income from labor earnings to capital incomes will also tend to exacerbate income inequality. The next two figures and one table examine each of these factors in turn.

Figure 2T shows cumulative changes in real annual wages and salaries of households at various points on the income scale between 1979 and 2007. The data, which capture changes in how many household members work, how many hours they work, and how much they earn per hour, show the rapid relative growth of such labor income for the top 1 percent of households—183.4 percent, compared with only 1.7 percent for the middle fifth of households. Perhaps surprisingly, wages of the bottom fifth of households rose by a seemingly healthy 38.0 percent over this period. But given that average wages of this group were only $7,942 in 1979, this represents a per-household increase of only $3,017 over 28 years. Further, 87 percent of this increase occurred between 1994 and 1999, a period of rapid declines in unemployment that culminated in the lowest levels of unemployment in a generation. The lesson that very tight labor markets are needed to spur rapid wage growth for households at the bottom of the wage distribution is explored further in Chapter 4.

A commonly cited explanation for this divergence of labor earnings—rising educational disparities—does not seem particularly convincing as a key driver of the trend toward greater concentration of labor earnings. **Table 2.9** shows the changing educational composition of the workforce (as measured by work hours) by household income level. For households in each income distribution grouping, it shows the share of the total hours worked by workers with different education levels. The data suggest a large increase in educational attainment of the top 5 percent of working households: The share of work hours in this group accounted for by workers without a high school degree fell from 6.3 percent in 1979 to 1.2

Figure 2T Change in real annual household wages, by income
group, 1979–2007

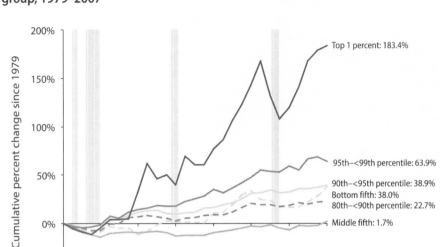

Note: Shaded areas denote recessions.

Source: Authors' analysis of Congressional Budget Office data (2010a)

---

percent in 2007, while the share of work hours by workers with an advanced degree rose from 24.3 to 36.9 percent.

However, the educational upgrading of other income groups is also dramatic.
For example, for households in the fourth income fifth, the share of all hours
accounted for by workers with a four-year college degree more than doubled between 1979 and 2007, rising from 11.4 percent to 23.8 percent. In the middle
fifth, the share with a college degree also saw a big jump, from 9.4 percent in
1979 to 16.7 percent in 2007, while the share with less than a high school degree
dropped by more than half, from 22.4 percent to 9.8 percent. The fact that increases in educational attainment at the top of the income distribution have not
dramatically outpaced increases in educational attainment lower down the distribution means that educational upgrading cannot explain the dramatic increases
in income inequality over this period.

Figure 2U is very similar to Figure 2T, charting cumulative growth in average annual capital income instead of labor income. This concentration of capital
income growth among high-income households is striking. Between 1979 and
2007, average capital incomes of the top 1 percent rose by 309.3 percent. Those

Table 2.9 Educational attainment, by income group, selected
years, 1979–2007 *(Part 1 of 2)*

	1979	1989	1995	2000	2007
Bottom fifth					
Less than high school	45.3%	35.5%	34.1%	32.6%	30.4%
High school only	33.4	40.1	36.9	38.7	37.8
Some college	15.2	18.0	23.0	21.9	23.7
College graduate	3.9	4.3	4.7	5.5	6.3
Advanced degree	2.3	2.1	1.3	1.2	1.8
Second fifth					
Less than high school	32.5%	23.1%	21.3%	20.6%	17.6%
High school only	39.4	44.3	41.7	39.6	39.2
Some college	19.1	22.5	26.5	28.9	30.1
College graduate	5.8	6.9	8.4	8.7	10.5
Advanced degree	3.3	3.3	2.3	2.2	2.6
Middle fifth					
Less than high school	22.4%	14.8%	12.2%	11.7%	9.8%
High school only	41.6	43.6	39.4	37.4	35.5
Some college	21.5	25.6	31.3	32.5	32.4
College graduate	9.4	10.6	13.5	14.2	16.7
Advanced degree	5.1	5.5	3.7	4.2	5.6
Fourth fifth					
Less than high school	17.4%	9.6%	7.3%	6.4%	4.9%
High school only	39.7	37.4	33.6	31.1	28.2
Some college	23.5	28.3	32.2	32.3	32.6
College graduate	11.4	15.7	19.2	21.8	23.8
Advanced degree	8.0	9.1	7.7	8.4	10.6
80th–<95th percentile					
Less than high school	11.3%	5.7%	3.4%	3.0%	2.4%
High school only	35.7	28.1	23.1	20.8	18.7
Some college	24.6	26.4	28.9	27.9	26.4
College graduate	15.5	22.5	28.7	30.5	32.5
Advanced degree	12.9	17.4	15.9	17.8	20.0

Table 2.9 Educational attainment, by income group, selected
years, 1979–2007 *(Part 2 of 2)*

	1979	1989	1995	2000	2007
Top 5 percent					
Less than high school	6.3%	2.2%	1.9%	1.5%	1.2%
High school only	24.5	16.0	13.5	9.8	8.3
Some college	23.0	20.7	19.3	18.3	16.9
College graduate	21.9	29.7	32.6	37.4	36.7
Advanced degree	24.3	31.4	32.7	33.1	36.9
All					
Less than high school	20.2%	13.2%	11.0%	10.7%	9.0%
High school only	37.4	36.1	32.3	30.6	28.6
Some college	22.1	25.0	28.7	29.0	29.0
College graduate	11.5	15.1	18.6	19.9	21.8
Advanced degree	8.8	10.6	9.4	9.8	11.7

Note: Educational attainment is measured by determining what share of a given income group's total hours
worked were worked by workers with a given education level.

Source: Authors' analysis of Current Population Survey Outgoing Rotation Group microdata

Figure 2U Change in real annual household capital income, by income
group, 1979–2007

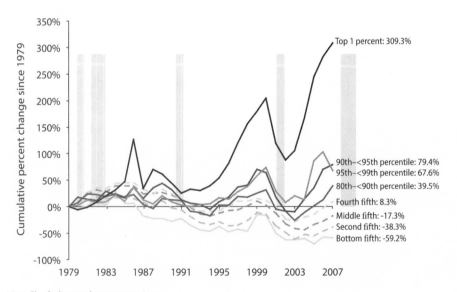

Note: Shaded areas denote recessions.

Source: Authors' analysis of Congressional Budget Office (2010a)

of the fourth fifth rose by only 8.3 percent, while average capital incomes of the bottom 60 percent of households actually fell.

Figure 2V shows the share of total capital income claimed by the top 1 percent, the 90th–<99th percentile, and the bottom 90 percent. In 1979, capital incomes were already substantially unequal—the top 1 percent of households claimed 39.4 percent of all capital income generated in the economy. However, by 2007 this share had ballooned to 65.0 percent. The share of capital income claimed by the remainder of the top 10 percent declined, from 28.3 percent to 20.3 percent over this period. However, the share of capital income claimed by the bottom 90 percent dropped the most. In 1979, the entire bottom 90 percent claimed less than a third (32.2 percent) of all capital income, and that fell to just 14.8 percent by 2007.

While the previous three figures have shown the generally recognized rising inequality of both labor earnings and capital income, **Table 2.10** documents the shift in aggregate income from labor to capital. As noted earlier, because the highest-income groups receive the bulk of capital income (increasingly so over the last 30 years), then a shift of total income toward more capital income and less labor income will exacerbate overall income inequality. This shift from labor to capital incomes between 1979 and 2007 is significant: The share of personal,

Figure 2V Share of total household capital income claimed, by income group, 1979–2007

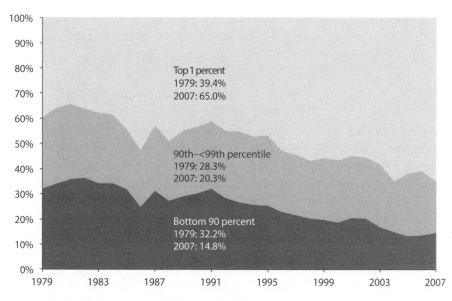

Source: Authors' analysis of Congressional Budget Office (2010a)

Table 2.10 Share of market-based personal income, by income type, selected years, 1959–2010

Income type	Share of income						
	1959	1973	1979	1989	2000	2007	2010
Total capital income	13.3%	13.8%	15.0%	20.8%	19.3%	19.7%	18.7%
Rent	4.2	2.2	1.1	1.0	2.6	1.3	3.2
Dividends	3.3	2.8	2.9	3.6	4.6	7.1	6.5
Interest	5.8	8.8	11.0	16.3	12.0	11.3	9.1
Total labor income	73.6%	75.6%	75.8%	71.2%	70.7%	70.5%	71.9%
Wages and salaries	68.0	66.0	63.4	58.7	59.0	57.6	57.8
Fringe benefits	5.5	9.5	12.4	12.5	11.7	12.9	14.1
Proprietors' income*	13.2%	10.6%	9.2%	8.0%	10.0%	9.8%	9.4%
Total market-based personal income**	100.0%	100.0%	100.0%	100.0%	100.0%	100.0%	100.0%
Realized capital gains**	1.64%	1.55%	1.4%	3.3%	7.7%	8.1%	2.4%

* Business and farmowners' income
** Total of listed income types
*** The fall in realized capital gains in 2010 is due to the economic impact of the 2007 recession.

Source: Authors' analysis of Bureau of Economic Analysis National Income and Product Accounts (Table 2.1), and Internal Revenue Service *SOI Tax Stats* (Table 1 and Historical Table 1)

market-based income accruing to capital owners rose from 15.0 to 19.7 percent during this time. This 4.7 percentage-point increase came mainly from a 5.3 percentage-point reduction in the share of overall income accounted for by wages and benefits of employees. Again, because capital income is much more concentrated than labor income (see Table 2.4) among high-income households, a shift from the latter to the former will, all else equal, tend to increase overall income inequality.

To highlight just how much this shift from labor to capital incomes between 1979 and 2007 affected trends in inequality, **Table 2.11** shows what would have happened had the share of total household income accounted for by capital (i.e., the "capital share") remained constant at the 1979 level over this time. First, note

Table 2.11 Effect of the shift from labor to capital income on the top 1 percent of households, selected years, 1979–2007 (2011 dollars)

Row		1979	1989	1995	2000	2007
1	Total capital income (billions)	$611,633	$965,322	$878,675	$1,593,798	$2,008,466
2	Top 1 percent capital income (billions)	$242,550	$433,743	$414,063	$902,701	$1,323,836
3	Top 1 percent's share of capital income	39.7%	44.9%	47.1%	56.6%	65.9%
4	Total household income (billions)	$5,139,775	$6,703,622	$7,446,395	$9,659,379	$11,220,480
5	Top 1 percent household income (billions)	$495,000	$857,200	$918,100	$1,706,430	$2,247,600
6	Top 1 percent's share of total household income	9.6%	12.8%	12.3%	17.7%	20.0%
7	Capital income as a share of total household income ("capital share")	11.9%	14.4%	11.8%	16.5%	17.9%
Counterfactual income, if 1979 capital share (11.9%) is held constant						
8	Counterfactual top 1 percent household income (billions)	$495,000	$794,265	$921,038	$1,499,045	$1,871,366
9	Counterfactual top 1 percent share of total household income	9.6%	11.8%	12.4%	15.5%	16.7%

Source: Authors' analysis of Congressional Budget Office (2010a)

that the overall income share of the top 1 percent of households rose from 9.6 percent to 20.0 percent—an increase of 10.4 percentage points—over this period (see row six in the table). Even allowing for the rise in the top 1 percent's share of capital income (row three), if the share of total household income accounted for by capital (row seven) had remained at its 1979 level instead of rising, the overall share of income claimed by the top 1 percent of households (row eight divided by row four) would have risen by only 7.0 percentage points—from about 9.6 percent to about 16.7 percent—rather than the actual 10.4 percentage-point increase (figures in the table are rounded to the nearest decimal place). Thus, the shift toward capital income accounted for roughly one-third (3.4 of 10.4 percentage points) of the increase in the total household income share claimed by the top 1 percent between 1979 and 2007.

The breakdown of income shares and the degree of tradeoff between capital and labor incomes shown in Table 2.11 is slightly complicated by categories such as proprietors' income, which can't be clearly defined as either labor or capital incomes. Thus, analysts often look at developments strictly within the corporate business sector to get a better sense of capital and labor income shares. All income in the corporate sector (which accounts for nearly 57 percent of the overall economy and 75 percent of the private economy) is classified strictly as either labor or capital incomes, so there is no ambiguity about which category is gaining or losing. **Table 2.12** documents the share of corporate-sector income accruing to capital owners versus to labor in recent decades. The table also conveys important information on not just capital's share of income but also profit rates and the capital-to-output ratio in the corporate sector.

An increase in the share of corporate income accruing to capital owners (the "capital share") can happen for one of two reasons—a rising capital-to-output ratio or a rising profit rate. The capital-to-output ratio is the value of the capital stock (physical capital used in production) in the corporate sector divided by total economic output in the sector. It is essentially a measure of how capital-intensive production is. If production becomes more capital-intensive over time (i.e., if the final cost of goods in the corporate sector reflects that proportionately more capital and less labor are used to produce the goods over time), then we should expect the share of capital incomes in the corporate sector to rise.

The profit rate is total capital income in the corporate sector divided by the value of the corporate capital stock. This is essentially the income generated per

Table 2.12 Corporate-sector income shares, profit rates, and capital-to-output ratio, selected years, 1959–2010

	Income share			Profit rate		Capital-to-output ratio
	Labor	Capital	Total	Pretax	Post-tax	
1959	77.5%	22.5%	100.0%	12.6%	6.9%	1.78
1969	79.1	20.9	100.0	13.0	7.8	1.61
1979	81.2	18.8	100.0	9.4	5.8	2.01
1989	80.0	20.0	100.0	10.8	7.8	1.85
1995	79.3	20.7	100.0	11.6	8.1	1.79
2000	81.2	18.8	100.0	11.0	7.8	1.71
2007	78.0	22.0	100.0	11.1	7.5	1.99
2010	73.8	26.2	100.0	13.3	9.6	1.97

Source: Authors' analysis of Bureau of Economic Analysis National Income and Product Accounts (Table 1.14) and Fixed Assets Accounts (Table 6.1)

unit of capital for capital owners. If the profit rate rises, then capital owners can enjoy a stable (or even rising) share of total income even if the output of the corporate sector is no more capital-intensive than before.

This relationship is somewhat analogous to hours worked and the hourly wage rate. There are basically two ways for workers to earn more money: work longer hours or earn a higher wage per hour worked. One can think of the capital-to-output ratio as the "effort" put forth by capital owners, while the profit rate is the return to this effort.

Table 2.12 shows that between 1979 and 2007, corporate-sector production did not become more capital intensive—the capital-to-output ratio remained essentially the same, at 2.01, in 1979, as in 2007, at 1.99. Yet the capital share of total corporate income rose from 18.8 percent to 22.0 percent, reflecting a large rise in the pretax profit rate from 9.4 percent to 11.1 percent. It is also worth noting that as effective corporate tax rates fell between 1979 and 2007, the post-tax profit rate rose even further—from 5.8 percent to 7.5 percent.

The pretax and post-tax profit rates are shown visually in **Figure 2W**. In addition to their sharp upward jumps in the mid-1990s and 2000s, their levels at the end of 2010 are also remarkable. By the end of 2010, the post-tax profit rate reached its highest level since the 10.7 percent rate in 1966.

Figure 2W Pretax and post-tax profit rates, 1959–2010

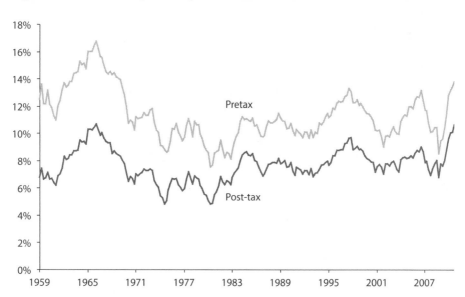

Source: Authors' analysis of data from Bureau of Economic Analysis National Income and Product Accounts, (Table 1.14) and Fixed Assets Accounts (Table 6.1)

Figure 2X demonstrates the influence of rising profit rates on the corporate income share accruing to capital owners. It shows the actual share of corporate income accounted for by capital and then shows what this share would have been had the 1979 profit rate held constant. In 2007, this difference was 3.4 percent of total corporate income (down from the peak difference of 6.5 percent in 2006, the year of peak profit rates). Corporate sector net value added was roughly $8.0 trillion in 2007; a 3.4 percent difference implies that roughly $270 billion went to capital owners rather than employees relative to a counterfactual with 1979 profit rates held constant. This is a substantial amount of money. If, for example, the corporate sector accounted for the same share of overall employment as it did for total economic output (57 percent in 2007), then this would imply that 78 million Americans were employed in the corporate sector in 2007. If this were the case, given that $270 billion could have gone to employee compensation had the profit rate in 2007 matched that of 1979, each of these employees could have had a roughly $3,400 raise that year (roughly 4.3 percent of average corporate-sector wages).

Finally, besides often being masked by a falling capital-to-output ratio, the shift between labor- and capital-derived shares of income is probably muffled by the fact that much of what is classified as labor income is actually tightly tied to movements in the price of capital assets. The most obvious example involves stock

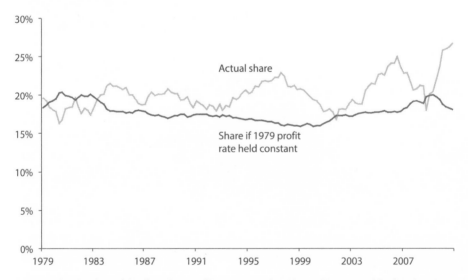

Figure 2X Capital share of total corporate-sector income, actual and counterfactual holding 1979 profit rate constant, 1979–2010

Source: Authors' analysis of data from Bureau of Economic Analysis National Income and Product Accounts (Table 1.14) and Fixed Assets Accounts (6.1)

options granted to CEOs and other highly paid wage and salary earners. When these options are exercised, the resulting income is classified as labor income, but the value of this income is directly dependent on valuation of the physical capital stock (through equity prices). These options tend to be granted to the highest-ranking managers of firms. All in all, they "look" much more like capital income than labor income—they rise and fall with the valuation of the physical capital stock, and they are even more concentrated among high-income households than the overall distribution of capital incomes. Freeman, Blasi, and Kruse (2009) estimate that in 2006 stock options accounted for about $65.1 billion in labor income that was probably better classified as capital income. Given that stock options were not nearly as large a component of managerial pay in the late 1970s, this increase almost surely means that any estimate of the shift from labor to capital incomes since then has been masked by the increasing, and quite likely inaccurate, classification of a large form of income payments (stock options) as labor income.

Figure 2Y provides a useful summary measure of the findings of this section on rising inequality, charting the shares of total income growth from 1979 to 2007 attributable to growth in the incomes of various subgroups. Between 1979 and

Figure 2Y Share of total household income growth attributable to various income groups, 1979–2007

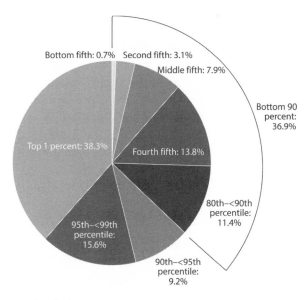

Note: Data are for comprehensive income.

Source: Authors' analysis of Congressional Budget Office (2010a)

2007, average pretax income rose by 51.4 percent, according the CBO data on comprehensive income. Figure 2Y shows that rising incomes of the top 1 percent accounted for fully 38.3 percent of this total growth. Further, the top 1 percent of households accounted for a larger share of overall average income growth between 1979 and 2007 than the bottom 90 percent of households combined (who accounted for 36.9 percent of overall average income growth). The top 10 percent accounted for 63.1 percent of total growth. What this means is that a very small slice of the population (the top 1 percent) is claiming large-enough shares of total income growth to significantly affect how much is left over from everybody else.

How much did middle-income living standards actually rise between 1979 and 2007?

It is clear that the Great Recession dealt a tough blow to living standards across the household income distribution. What is much more contested is how much living standards of middle-income households rose in the 28 years preceding the Great Recession. Also crucially important to the public debate is a related question that we examine in some detail: To what degree have the increases in living standards of middle-income families been gained not because the overall economy performed well for this group, but because these households contributed more work hours to the paid labor force and upgraded their educational attainment? Income increases obtained by contributing more hours to the labor force or raising educational attainment have implicit ceilings. There are only so many hours in a week and so many degrees that can be earned. In contrast, income increases earned by economy-wide growth in wages per hour (reflecting overall productivity growth) do not have any obvious ceiling. The durability of income growth will be much greater if it stems from ever-increasing wages per hour. Unfortunately, that is not how incomes at the middle generally have been raised in recent decades.

The relevance of controlling for hours worked by middle-income households is obvious: Income increases obtained by working more hours do not necessarily translate into increases in living standards. Leisure has value. More specifically, economists tend to think the value of leisure is best approximated by the income foregone when leisure is "consumed," and this foregone income is simply a worker's earnings per unit of work. The value of an hour of leisure for a worker who commands $20 an hour when doing paid work is $20; and the decision to work another hour to earn this $20 is also a decision to give up an hour's worth of leisure that is worth $20. Choosing to work may also require paying for services household members provided when they were not in the paid labor force, such as child care, transportation, preparation of meals, etc.

The relevance of controlling for educational upgrading is perhaps less clear. But it seems fair to account for education upgrades when comparing measures of middle-income households' economic performance to measures of overall economic growth (say, economy-wide productivity growth) to determine how much of the growth of middle-income households' living standards is purely exogenous to their own effort. In a well-functioning economy, when households invest time and money to increase their educational attainment, they should boost their own living standards as well as overall productivity growth.

In other words, when productivity is growing at all (which has indeed been true for the U.S. economy for more than a century), well-functioning capitalist economies ought to be able to generate growth in living standards even for a population that does not see substantial educational upgrading. But we know that the U.S. workforce has become substantially more educated in recent decades, which means that, all else equal (that is, even in a poorly performing economy), one should expect to see quite rapid increases in earnings and incomes of middle-income households.

This section provides a rough measure of how much of the increase in middle-income living standards derives from upgraded educational attainment rather than from share of overall productivity growth. We would argue that "credit" for the income increases obtained through rising educational attainment should be mostly given to the households themselves and not offered as evidence that the wider U.S. economy is doing a particularly good job in generating acceptable outcomes for middle-income households.

In our analysis of middle-income living standards we begin by defining how we measure living standards for middle-income households. Then we show the sources of income growth for middle-fifth families over selected years to determine how much income growth for this group is coming from market incomes versus other sources (government transfers, in particular) and to evaluate the future sustainability of these income gains given their sources. Next, we assess how much of the income gains resulting from market income growth were driven by increased effort on the part of households versus an increased return to that effort (i.e., inflation-adjusted hourly wage growth). In our discussion, "effort" pertains to both increased hours of work and to educational and experiential upgrading. Lastly, we use these trends to estimate the extent to which a well-functioning economy versus redistributive policies and increased household effort improved living standards for middle-income families.

Measuring living standards at the middle

The term "middle class" is difficult to define with precision. For the purposes of this section we examine the average income of the middle fifth of the household income distribution. In 2007, this middle class income was $69,985, according to a dataset compiled by the CBO that measures comprehensive incomes. The remainder of this section will draw largely on this CBO dataset, the chief advantage of which is that it measures many nonmoney components of income, the most important of which is health care benefits provided by public sources and employers, that are not tracked by the CPS annual survey's money income measures. Further, the CBO data track growth in realized capital gains, which have been a growing source of overall income, and one that is quite concentrated at the very top of the income distribution. The data go to 2007, which aligns with our examination of trends up to the Great Recession.

Figure 2Z demonstrates the differences in growth of average incomes using both the "money" or "comprehensive" definitions of income. The "money income" measure, which mirrors the "cash income" definition used by the Census Bureau in its annual Current Population Survey report on income, poverty, and health insurance coverage, likely is the most-cited measure of living standards at the middle of the income distribution. However, in recent years a number of "revisionist" studies have been released arguing that the economic trajectory of the American middle class has been much more positive than the CPS cash income series implies. We use the CBO comprehensive income data in much of the rest of this section in large part to assess the worth of this revisionist literature.

Figure 2Z Change in household income, as reported by CBO comprehensive income data and CPS money income data, by income group, 1979–2007

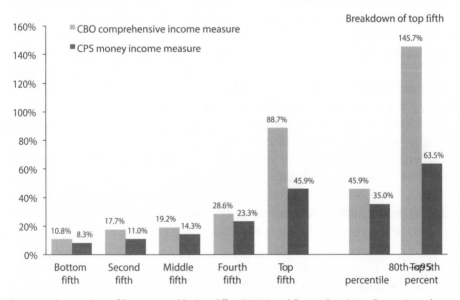

Source: Authors' analysis of Congressional Budget Office (2010a) and Current Population Survey Annual Social and Economic Supplement, *Historical Income Tables* (Table F-3)

It is true that the comprehensive-income data (which, as described previously in this chapter, include many sources of income excluded in the money income definition) show substantially faster growth than the money-income data across the entire income distribution. Average household money income for the middle fifth rose 14.3 percent between 1979 and 2007, while average household comprehensive income for this group rose 19.2 percent (from $58,700 to $69,985). For this fifth, this difference is largely explained by the rising share of noncash transfers and employee benefits in overall average incomes of the middle fifth. The much larger increase in comprehensive income for the top 5 percent of households (which rose from $269,956 to $663,172, or 145.7 percent compared with a 63.5 percent increase in money income) is largely driven by the CBO dataset's inclusion of the value of realized capital gains.

Sources of income for the middle fifth

Table 2.13 draws upon CBO comprehensive income data to show the sources of income for the middle fifth of the household income distribution for selected years. Unsurprisingly, wages (including imputed taxes, which for the middle fifth are dominated by payroll taxes, which are directly determined by underlying wages and assumed by the CBO to directly boost pretax income levels) make up the largest share of income for this group—accounting for $45,315 of its total $58,751 in income (in 2011 dollars) for 1979, or about 77 percent. However, the share of comprehensive income accounted for by wages has fallen over time— by 2007 wages accounted for $45,997 of $69,949 in comprehensive income, or about 66 percent. (The dollar values shown in the table are from unrounded CBO data, and thus differ slightly from those underlying Figure 2Z, which are from rounded CBO data.)

This table also charts the changes in various income sources over time. Over the entire 1979–2007 period, total average wages of the middle fifth rose only $682, or an average 0.1 percent growth each year over this period. (Recall that increases in household wages result from changes in three factors: the number of workers in the household; annual hours employed household members work, based on changes in weekly hours or weeks worked per year; and the inflation-adjusted hourly wage of employed workers.)

This growth in total household wages explains only 6.1 percent of the $11,198 increase in comprehensive income between 1979 and 2007. Capital-based incomes actually fell for the middle fifth over this period, dropping by a cumulative $455.

The bulk of the total increase in comprehensive income between 1979 and 2007 can be explained by growth in pension income, cash transfers, and in-kind income. Pension income refers to income currently received by retirees for past service (not employers' current payments into plans for incumbent workers, as they are sometimes classified in other data sources, such as the National Income

Table 2.13 Change in sources of comprehensive income, middle fifth of households, selected years, 1979–2007 (2011 dollars)

	Income	Wages and imputed taxes	Capital income	Pensions and other income	Cash transfers	In-kind income CPI-U-RS deflator* Employer-sponsored insurance	Medicare and Medicaid	Other in-kind	CPI-MC* Employer-sponsored insurance	Medicare and Medicaid
1979	$58,751	$45,315	$4,114	$2,247	$3,942	$2,163	$817	$154	$2,163	$817
1989	59,724	41,605	5,198	3,692	5,058	2,358	1,722	90	1,757	1,283
1995	61,334	40,936	3,785	4,642	5,992	2,976	2,843	160	1,795	1,715
2000	65,637	43,654	4,347	5,667	6,034	2,568	3,242	125	1,470	1,855
2007	69,949	45,997	3,658	5,820	6,739	3,558	4,050	126	1,821	2,073
Share of income										
1979	100.0%	77.1%	7.0%	3.8%	6.7%	3.7%	1.4%	0.3%	3.7%	1.4%
1989	100.0	69.7	8.7	6.2	8.5	3.9	2.9	0.2	3.0	2.2
1995	100.0	66.7	6.2	7.6	9.8	4.9	4.6	0.3	3.0	2.9
2000	100.0	66.5	6.6	8.6	9.2	3.9	4.9	0.2	2.3	2.9
2007	100.0	65.8	5.2	8.3	9.6	5.1	5.8	0.2	2.7	3.1
Average annual change										
1979–1989	0.2%	-0.9%	2.4%	5.1%	2.5%	0.9%	7.7%	-5.2%	-2.1%	4.6%
1989–1995	0.4	-0.3	-5.2	3.9	2.9	4.0	8.7	10.1	0.4	5.0
1995–2000	1.4	1.3	2.8	4.1	0.1	-2.9	2.7	-4.7	-3.9	1.6
2000–2007	0.9	0.7	-2.4	0.4	1.6	4.8	3.2	0.1	3.1	1.6
1979–2007	0.6	0.1	-0.4	3.5	1.9	1.8	5.9	-0.7	-0.6	3.4

	Income	Wages and imputed taxes	Capital income	Pensions and other income	Cash transfers	In-kind income CPI-U-RS deflator* Employer-sponsored insurance	Medicare and Medicaid	Other in-kind	CPI-MC* Employer-sponsored insurance	Medicare and Medicaid
Total change in 2011 dollars										
1979–1989	$972	-$3,709	$1,085	$1,446	$1,116	$195	$905	-$64	-$406	$466
1989–1995	1,610	-669	-1,414	950	934	618	1,122	70	37	432
1995–2000	4,303	2,718	562	1,024	42	-407	399	-35	-325	140
2000–2007	4,312	2,344	-688	153	705	989	808	1	351	218
1979–2007	11,198	682	-455	3,573	2,797	1,395	3,233	-28	-342	1,256
Share of total change										
1979–1989	100.0%	-381.5%	111.5%	148.6%	114.8%	20.0%	93.0%	-6.6%	-41.7%	47.9%
1989–1995	100.0	-41.6	-87.8	59.0	58.0	38.4	69.6	4.4	2.3	26.8
1995–2000	100.0	63.2	13.1	23.8	1.0	-9.5	9.3	-0.8	-7.6	3.3
2000–2007	100.0	54.4	-16.0	3.6	16.3	22.9	18.7	0.0	8.1	5.0
1979–2007	100.0	6.1	-4.1	31.9	25.0	12.5	28.9	-0.2	-3.1	11.2

* The last two columns deflate health care contributions by a medical care price deflator that accounts for faster growth in health care costs relative to other consumer goods.

Source: Authors' analysis of data from the Congressional Budget Office (2010a and 2010b)

and Product Accounts). As such, today's pension income accruing to the middle fifth largely reflects the past extent of pension coverage for this group. Cash transfers include items such as payments from unemployment insurance, veterans' benefits, and, as the largest category, Social Security payments. In-kind income is dominated by Medicaid, Medicare, and employer payments for ESI premiums.

Income growth for the middle fifth has been driven largely by elderly households' pension and transfer income

There is a common theme among these large sources of income growth for the middle fifth: They are payments heavily weighted towards older (and often retired) households. The share of elderly households in the middle fifth increased from 15.2 percent to 22.1 percent over this period, so it is not surprising that income flows directed disproportionately toward these households seemingly accounted for a large share of overall income growth in the middle.

But the share of total growth accounted for by these income categories (85.6 percent) is so large that it seems unlikely that the rising share of elderly households in the middle fifth is the only trend driving this dynamic. To get a sense of how much of overall income growth from 1979 to 2007 was driven by these income categories, note that growth in pension income ($3,573), cash transfers ($2,797), and in-kind income ($3,205) (in-kind income was mostly from government transfers such as Medicare and Medicaid, which totaled $3,233, and excluded employer payments for health insurance premiums for reasons discussed in the following section) all together account for $9,575, which is 85.5 percent of the total $11,198 increase in comprehensive income. Although some cash transfers are not directly targeted at older households, it seems safe to say that the growth in cash transfers over the 1979 to 2007 period was dominated by Social Security. Further, excluding employer contributions for health insurance premiums actually cuts out some income received by older households for retiree health insurance. All in all, these numbers point to a strong case that the large majority of the increase in middle fifth incomes was a function of pensions and government transfers directed toward elderly households.

Adjusting income for the truer contribution of health care transfers

With the exception of pension income, which is largely derived from past market activity, market incomes contributed comparatively little to income growth for the middle fifth of households. After pensions, the second-largest source of growth of market-based income (all data columns except cash transfers and in-kind income from government sources) for the middle fifth is the growth of employer contributions for health insurance premiums. Growth in this component of compensation lifted overall comprehensive income of the middle fifth by $1,395 between 1979 and 2007, 12.5 percent of the total increase.

Although these large increases in health-insurance-premium contributions cost employers real money, they are not clear evidence that the broader economy is working well for middle-income families because the contributions do not necessarily buy substantially higher living standards for these families. To gauge how much these premium contributions affect overall inflation-adjusted living standards, the CBO deflates the contributions (as well as other components of in-kind income that are related to health care) with the same overall price deflator applied to other income sources. Because the inflation measure behind the deflator—the consumer price index for urban consumers, research series (CPI-U-RS)—does not adequately reflect increases in health care costs, the CBO data likely overstates living standards growth. The CPI-U-RS (used by the authors in most sections of this book and by the CBO in their comprehensive income measures) does not even include employer contributions for health insurance premiums in the "basket" of goods that it tracks over time for price increases; only out-of-pocket health care costs are included in this basket. But because "income" via employer-sponsored health care premiums can only be used to purchase health care, it seems to us more appropriate to deflate it by a medical-care-specific price deflator.

This is especially important given that health care prices have grown far faster (by a factor of nearly 3-to-1) than prices of other consumer goods and services. The last two columns in Table 2.13 show the value of employer and government health benefits received by the middle fifth deflated using the medical care price deflator, the CPI-Medical Care (CPI-MC) from the Bureau of Labor Statistics rather than the overall CPI-U-RS used in the preceding columns. This adjusted method indicates that the value of health care benefits that the middle fifth received from employers actually declined from 1979 to 2007.

Although changing the deflator for employer-sponsored health care premiums seems like a relatively technical change to a small share of overall income, it actually results in a -$1,737 swing in comprehensive income growth between 1979 and 2007 (the difference between the $1,395 gain when deflated by the overall CPI-U-RS into a $342 decline when deflated with the CPI-MC). This adjustment effectively erases 15.5 percent of the entire rise in comprehensive income over that period.

Further, applying the same medical care deflator to the value of Medicaid and Medicare payments reduces growth of in-kind income going to the middle fifth by a further $1,977 (the difference between the $3,233 gain when using the CPI-U-RS deflator and the $1,256 gain using the CPI-MC). In all, deflating medical-related in-kind income by medical-specific price deflators erases $3,714 ($1,737 in ESI contributions plus $1,977 in Medicare and Medicaid payments) or about one-third of the $11,198 total gain in comprehensive income between 1979 and 2007.

Well-informed analysts have expressed doubt that the CPI-MC (and other medical care price deflators that show similar trends) fully captures underlying growth in the value of medical services provided in today's economy relative to decades past—in short, suggesting that the deflators show too large an increase in prices because they don't reflect that quality is improving. It is true that most medical-care deflators in essence show no inflation-adjusted increase in the value of medical care consumed in the United States between 1979 and 2007, even while a growing share of the overall economy is spent in this sector. But even if medical deflators cause too much of a "correction"—even if medical consumers are getting some increased value for their increased dollars spent (indeed it would be strange to think that today's workers would happily accept the medical care and technologies available only in 1979 as a perfect substitute for what they receive today), the value has clearly not kept pace with rapid health care price inflation.

To make the point polemically, health care wise, the U.S. economy is performing quite poorly, both for workers and employers. While U.S. workers might be unwilling to trade today's U.S. health care for 1979-vintage U.S. health care, they probably would happily accept 2010-vintage health care delivered in, say, France, as a perfect substitute (or even, if the World Health Organization's 2010 rankings are to be believed, a substantial improvement). And this French health care bundle was available at less than half the price of the U.S. health care bundle (OECD 2011).

In short, the CBO data, which show that government health care transfers (Medicare and Medicaid) and employer contributions to health care premiums contributed 41.4 percent to overall income growth of the middle fifth, likely significantly overstate these health care contributions. Adjusting government- and employer-sponsored health care benefits to account for higher inflation of health care prices relative to prices of other consumer goods shows that comprehensive income of the middle fifth of U.S. households grew 12.7 percent from 1979 to 2007, not 19.1 percent.

Disproportionate growth of transfers directed toward elderly households

The next two tables confirm the disproportionate growth of transfers directed toward elderly households suggested by Table 2.13. **Table 2.14** shows the sources of income for the middle fifth of "elderly households," households headed by persons age 65 and older. While average annual income of elderly households in the middle fifth rose by a cumulative $12,696 between 1979 and 2007 (from $45,839 to $58,535), average annual wages fell by $3,439, and capital incomes fell by $4,697. However, these declines were overwhelmingly offset by a $7,153 increase in pension income, a $5,413 increase in cash transfers (surely dominated by Social Security payments), and an $8,265 increase in in-kind income (dominated

Table 2.14 Change in sources of comprehensive income for elderly households in the middle fifth, selected years, 1979–2007 (2011 dollars)

	Income	Wages and imputed taxes	Capital income	Pensions and other income	Cash transfers	In-kind income
1979	$45,839	$12,517	$9,244	$6,192	$13,836	$4,049
1989	48,653	7,839	9,660	8,400	15,922	6,832
1995	50,616	8,400	5,902	10,467	16,679	9,168
2000	54,469	8,454	6,822	13,078	16,331	9,784
2007	58,535	9,079	4,548	13,345	19,250	12,314
Average annual change						
1979–1989	0.6%	-4.6%	0.4%	3.1%	1.4%	5.4%
1989–1995	0.7	1.2	-7.9	3.7	0.8	5.0
1995–2000	1.5	0.1	2.9	4.6	-0.4	1.3
2000–2007	1.0	1.0	-5.6	0.3	2.4	3.3
1979–2007	0.9	-1.1	-2.5	2.8	1.2	4.1
Total change						
1979–1989	$2,814	-$4,679	$415	$2,208	$2,086	$2,783
1989–1995	1,963	562	-3,758	2,067	757	2,336
1995–2000	3,853	54	921	2,611	-348	616
2000–2007	4,067	625	-2,274	267	2,919	2,531
1979–2007	12,696	-3,439	-4,697	7,153	5,413	8,265
Share of total change						
1979–1989	100.0%	-166.3%	14.8%	78.5%	74.1%	98.9%
1989–1995	100.0	28.6	-191.4	105.3	38.6	119.0
1995–2000	100.0	1.4	23.9	67.8	-9.0	16.0
2000–2007	100.0	15.4	-55.9	6.6	71.8	62.2
1979–2007	100.0	-27.1	-37.0	56.3	42.6	65.1

Note: Elderly households are age 65 and older.

Source: Authors' analysis of Congressional Budget Office (2010c)

by Medicaid and Medicare benefits). These findings support our conclusion that transfer payments and pension increases specifically accruing to elderly households played a major role in supporting middle-fifth incomes.

Table 2.15 undertakes the same analysis for non-elderly households. Even for this group, which should be much more dependent on labor earnings, wages accounted for less than half ($5,311) of the overall $12,133 increase in comprehensive income between 1979 ($61,062) and 2007 ($73,194). Somewhat surprisingly, the increase in pension income, $2,140, accounted for nearly a fifth of the total increase in income for non-elderly households in the middle fifth. If we assign the full value of employer contributions for health insurance premiums to this non-elderly group (which would, admittedly, be a small overstatement), then employer contributions for ESI added $2,019 to overall income between 1979 and 2007.

Table 2.16 combines the data from the previous three tables with data on the share of total households in the middle fifth that are elderly to show the shares of overall income growth of the middle fifth of the income distribution contributed by various household types and income sources. This allows us to examine how much of the growth of middle-fifth incomes was due to particular types of households (e.g., elderly versus non-elderly) and types of income (e.g., wages versus pensions versus cash transfers). To make the results fully comparable with others, we used the CPI-U-RS to deflate health benefits and transfers.

Reading down the first column in Table 2.16, we can see that average comprehensive income of the middle fifth in 1979 was $58,751. Of this, $6,958 was "contributed" by elderly households (computed by multiplying average elderly household income in 1979, $45,839, by the share of middle-fifth households that were elderly, 15.2 percent). The rest of the $58,751 was contributed by non-elderly households.

Reading down to the next block of rows, we can see that wages and imputed taxes overall contributed $45,315 to overall income of $58,751 in 1979. Of this contribution from wages, $1,900 came from elderly households while $43,415 came from non-elderly households.

In data columns 6 through 10, we track the change for each income type by household type for various time periods. In the last column, we show how much each household/income-type contributed to overall income growth for the middle fifth of households between 1979 and 2007. Probably the most striking finding is that annual wage earnings from non-elderly households contributed only $572, or 5.1 percent, of the $11,198 increase in overall middle-fifth incomes. Given that wages (including imputed taxes) constituted 65.8 percent of overall incomes of the middle fifth, this small share suggests that the lackluster performance of wages of non-elderly households bodes ill for future income growth.

As in Table 2.13, the last column in this table shows that pensions, cash transfers and in-kind income (minus employer-sponsored insurance) accounted

Table 2.15 Change in sources of comprehensive income for non-elderly households in the middle fifth, selected years, 1979–2007 (2011 dollars)

	Income	Wages and imputed taxes	Capital income	Pensions and other income	Cash transfers	Employer-sponsored insurance	In-kind income*
1979	$61,062	$51,184	$3,196	$1,541	$2,172	$2,550	$420
1989	62,785	50,941	3,965	2,391	2,055	3,010	424
1995	64,720	51,213	3,116	2,803	2,617	3,915	1,056
2000	69,495	55,813	3,491	3,106	2,477	3,456	1,151
2007	73,194	56,495	3,405	3,680	3,182	4,569	1,863
Average annual change							
1979–1989	0.3%	0.0%	2.2%	4.5%	-0.6%	1.7%	0.1%
1989–1995	0.5	0.1	-3.9	2.7	4.1	4.5	16.4
1995–2000	1.4	1.7	2.3	2.1	-1.1	-2.5	1.7
2000–2007	0.7	0.2	-0.4	2.5	3.6	4.1	7.1
1979–2007	0.6	0.4	0.2	3.2	1.4	2.1	5.5
Total change							
1979–1989	$1,723	-$243	$769	$850	-$117	$460	$4
1989–1995	1,935	271	-849	412	562	906	633
1995–2000	4,775	4,601	375	304	-140	-460	95
2000–2007	3,699	681	-86	574	705	1,114	711
1979–2007	12,133	5,311	210	2,140	1,010	2,019	1,443
Share of total change							
1979–1989	100.0%	-14.1%	44.6%	49.3%	-6.8%	26.7%	0.2%
1989–1995	100.0	14.0	-43.9	21.3	29.1	46.8	32.7
1995–2000	100.0	96.3	7.9	6.4	-2.9	-9.6	2.0
2000–2007	100.0	18.4	-2.3	15.5	19.1	30.1	19.2
1979–2007	100.0	43.8	1.7	17.6	8.3	16.6	11.9

* In-kind income does not include employer-sponsored insurance.

Source: Authors' analysis of Congressional Budget Office (2010c)

Table 2.16 Contributions to middle-fifth income growth, by income category and household type, selected years, 1979–2007 (2011 dollars)

								Change			
	1979	1989	1995	2000	2007	1979–1989	1989–1995	1995–2000	2000–2007	1979–2007	Share of 1979–2007 income change
Share of total households											
Elderly	15.2%	21.7%	24.0%	25.7%	22.1%	6.5	2.3	1.7	-3.5	7.0	
Non-elderly with kids	49.2	39.8	38.2	35.6	34.1	-9.4	-1.6	-2.6	-1.5	-15.1	
Non-elderly without kids	35.6	38.5	37.8	38.7	43.7	2.9	-0.8	0.9	5.0	8.1	
All non-elderly	84.8	78.3	76.0	74.3	77.9	-6.5	-2.3	-1.7	3.5	-7.0	
Average comprehensive income	$58,751	$59,724	$61,334	$65,637	$69,949	$972	$1,610	$4,303	$4,312	$11,198	100.0%
Elderly	6,958	10,538	12,150	13,985	12,959	3,580	1,612	1,835	-1,026	6,001	53.6
Non-elderly with kids	35,088	29,895	29,638	29,959	30,674	-5,193	-258	321	715	-4,414	-39.4
Non-elderly without kids	16,706	19,290	19,547	21,693	26,316	2,585	256	2,146	4,623	9,611	85.8
All non-elderly	51,794	49,186	49,184	51,652	56,990	-2,608	-1	2,468	5,338	5,196	46.4
Wages and imputed taxes	$45,315	$41,605	$40,936	$43,654	$45,997	-$3,709	-$669	$2,718	$2,344	$682	6.1%
Elderly	1,900	1,698	2,016	2,171	2,010	-202	319	154	-161	110	1.0
Non-elderly with kids	29,942	24,904	23,876	24,432	24,146	-5,038	-1,028	556	-286	-5,796	-51.8
Non-elderly without kids	13,473	15,004	15,044	17,051	19,842	1,531	40	2,007	2,791	6,369	56.9
All non-elderly	43,415	39,908	38,920	41,483	43,988	-3,507	-988	2,563	2,504	572	5.1
Capital incomes	$4,114	$5,198	$3,785	$4,347	$3,658	$1,085	-$1,414	$562	-$688	-$455	-4.1%
Elderly	1,403	2,092	1,417	1,752	1,007	689	-676	335	-745	-396	-3.5
Non-elderly with kids	1,711	1,702	1,363	1,481	1,561	-9	-339	118	80	-150	-1.3
Non-elderly without kids	1,000	1,404	1,005	1,114	1,090	404	-399	109	-23	90	0.8
All non-elderly	2,711	3,106	2,368	2,595	2,651	395	-738	227	56	-59	-0.5

	1979	1989	1995	2000	2007	Change					Share of 1979–2007 income change
						1979–1989	1989–1995	1995–2000	2000–2007	1979–2007	
Pensions and other income	$2,247	$3,692	$4,642	$5,667	$5,820	$1,446	$950	$1,024	$153	$3,573	31.9%
Elderly	940	1,819	2,513	3,358	2,954	880	693	845	-403	2,015	18.0
Non-elderly with kids	717	843	1,052	1,143	1,290	126	209	90	147	572	5.1
Non-elderly without kids	589	1,030	1,078	1,166	1,576	440	48	88	410	987	8.8
All non-elderly	1,307	1,873	2,130	2,309	2,866	566	257	179	557	1,559	13.9
Cash transfers	$3,942	$5,058	$5,992	$6,034	$6,739	$1,116	$934	$42	$705	$2,797	25.0%
Elderly	2,100	3,449	4,004	4,193	4,262	1,349	555	189	69	2,161	19.3
Non-elderly with kids	993	779	947	819	865	-214	168	-128	45	-128	-1.1
Non-elderly without kids	849	830	1,042	1,022	1,613	-19	211	-20	591	764	6.8
All non-elderly	1,842	1,610	1,989	1,841	2,478	-232	379	-148	636	636	5.7
Employer-sponsored insurance (ESI)	$2,163	$2,358	$2,976	$2,568	$3,558	$195	$618	-$407	$989	$1,395	12.5%
Elderly	—	—	—	—	—	—	—	—	—	—	—
Non-elderly with kids	—	—	—	—	—	—	—	—	—	—	—
Non-elderly without kids	—	—	—	—	—	—	—	—	—	—	—
All non-elderly	—	—	—	—	—	—	—	—	—	—	—
In-kind income minus ESI	$971	$1,812	$3,003	$3,368	$4,176	$841	$1,192	$364	$809	$3,206	28.6%
Elderly	615	1,480	2,201	2,512	2,726	865	721	311	214	2,112	18.9
Non-elderly with kids	1,725	1,667	2,400	2,084	2,813	-58	733	-316	729	1,088	9.7
Non-elderly without kids	794	1,022	1,378	1,340	2,195	228	356	-39	855	1,401	12.5
All non-elderly	2,519	2,690	3,778	3,424	5,008	170	1,088	-354	1,584	2,489	22.2

Source: Authors' analysis of Congressional Budget Office (2010c)

for 85.5 percent of overall income growth. Perhaps even more striking, however, is that pensions, cash transfers, and in-kind transfers minus ESI directed exclusively at elderly households accounted for 56.2 percent of overall income growth (18.0 percent from pensions, 19.3 percent from cash transfers, and 18.9 percent from in-kind transfers).

In short, this table suggests that labor-market-driven outcomes have not been an important contributor to the rise in incomes reported by CBO for the middle fifth of households in the income distribution from 1979 to 2007. The relative insignificance of wages on income growth is especially apparent when we account for inflation in medical care by deflating the gains from employer-provided health coverage and government-provided medical services. As discussed earlier, a correction for this reduces overall income growth for the middle fifth from 19.1 percent to 12.7 percent.

The role of hours worked and educational upgrading in wage growth

Although wages have made a relatively small contribution to wage growth for the middle fifth of households in the income distribution, wages still constitute by far the largest portion of middle-fifth household incomes. (Table 2.13 cites wages' 2007 share of comprehensive income as 65.8 percent, which includes 5.3 percent in "imputed taxes" that are largely employer-side payroll taxes based on their labor earnings). Further, annual labor earnings made such a small contribution to comprehensive income growth from 1979 to 2007 partially because non-elderly households shrank as a share of all households in the middle fifth over the period. Table 2.15 showed that annual wages of working-age households increased $5,311 from 1979 to 2007. Thus, determining how much of the gain in this crucial income category was a function of increased work effort rather than higher earnings per unit of work is key to assessing actual living-standards growth and projecting how well labor-market-derived incomes are likely to boost non-elderly middle-income households in coming years.

The next part of this section looks at how much of the overall increase in annual earnings of the middle fifth is driven by working more hours and upgrading education and experience. Such earnings gains attest to the ingenuity and tenacity of American households in striving for living-standards growth, and do not serve as strong evidence that the economy has been performing satisfactorily. In our view, gains achieved simply by working more are a gain in income, but a decline in leisure, which has at best an ambiguous effect on living standards.

To undertake this examination, we switch back to the CPS microdata, because the CBO data do not provide information on hours worked, educational attainment, or experience. **Table 2.17** shows, for groups across the money income (not comprehensive income) distribution, how much of the increase in annual wages of

Table 2.17 Contribution of hours versus hourly wages to annual wage growth for working-age households, by income group, selected years, 1979–2007 (2011 dollars) *Part 1 of 2*

	1979	1989	1995	2000	2007	Change				
						1979–1989	1989–1995	1995–2000	2000–2007	1979–2007
Real average annual wages										
All	$59,723	$65,858	$70,210	$78,883	$78,768	9.8%	6.4%	11.6%	-0.1%	27.7%
Bottom fifth	14,596	14,855	14,346	17,090	16,507	1.8	-3.5	17.5	-3.5	12.3
Second fifth	32,792	33,773	32,700	36,817	35,980	2.9	-3.2	11.9	-2.3	9.3
Middle fifth	49,260	51,729	50,561	56,335	55,560	4.9	-2.3	10.8	-1.4	12.0
Fourth fifth	66,410	71,972	72,651	80,791	81,220	8.0	0.9	10.6	0.5	20.1
80th–<95th percentile	91,395	103,913	107,185	120,541	123,076	12.8	3.1	11.7	2.1	29.8
Top 5 percent	128,656	159,249	219,365	264,547	254,701	21.3	32.0	18.7	-3.8	68.3
Annual hours worked										
All	3,092	3,286	3,317	3,378	3,314	6.1%	0.9%	1.8%	-1.9%	6.9%
Bottom fifth	1,716	1,884	1,837	1,977	1,880	9.4	-2.5	7.4	-5.0	9.2
Second fifth	2,543	2,797	2,811	2,908	2,787	9.5	0.5	3.4	-4.2	9.2
Middle fifth	3,007	3,273	3,323	3,395	3,335	8.5	1.5	2.2	-1.8	10.3
Fourth fifth	3,424	3,604	3,688	3,774	3,719	5.1	2.3	2.3	-1.5	8.3
80th–<95th percentile	3,816	3,976	4,005	4,035	3,997	4.1	0.7	0.7	-0.9	4.6
Top 5 percent	3,939	4,069	4,057	3,984	4,013	3.2	-0.3	-1.8	0.7	1.9
Real average hourly wages										
All	$19.32	$20.04	$21.17	$23.35	$23.77	3.7%	5.5%	9.8%	1.8%	20.8%
Bottom fifth	8.51	7.88	7.81	8.64	8.78	-7.6	-0.9	10.1	1.6	3.2
Second fifth	12.90	12.07	11.63	12.66	12.91	-6.6	-3.7	8.5	1.9	0.1

Table 2.17 Contribution of hours versus hourly wages to annual wage growth for working-age households, by income group, selected years, 1979–2007 (2011 dollars) *Part 2 of 2*

	1979	1989	1995	2000	2007	Change				
						1979–1989	1989–1995	1995–2000	2000–2007	1979–2007
Middle fifth	$16.38	$15.81	$15.22	$16.59	$16.66	-3.6%	-3.8%	8.7%	0.4%	1.7%
Fourth fifth	19.40	19.97	19.70	21.41	21.84	2.9	-1.4	8.3	2.0	11.8
80th–<95th percentile	23.95	26.14	26.76	29.87	30.79	8.7	2.4	11.0	3.0	25.1
Top 5 percent	32.66	39.14	54.07	66.40	63.47	18.1	32.3	20.5	-4.5	66.4
Contributions to annual wage growth										
Hours worked										
All						62.3%	14.5%	15.8%	1321.3%	25.0%
Bottom fifth						531.5	73.0	42.2	145.4	74.4
Second fifth						323.8	-15.4	28.6	184.7	99.0
Middle fifth						173.0	-66.2	20.0	130.1	85.9
Fourth fifth						63.9	245.3	21.7	-276.5	41.1
80th–<95th percentile						31.9	23.7	6.3	-45.0	15.6
Top 5 percent						15.2	-0.9	-9.7	-19.0	2.7
Hourly wages										
All						37.7%	85.5%	84.2%	-1221.3%	75.0%
Bottom fifth						-431.5	27.0	57.8	-45.4	25.6
Second fifth						-223.8	115.4	71.4	-84.7	1.0
Middle fifth						-73.0	166.2	80.0	-30.1	14.1
Fourth fifth						36.1	-145.3	78.3	376.5	58.9
80th–<95th percentile						68.1	76.3	93.7	145.0	84.4
Top 5 percent						84.8	100.9	109.7	119.0	97.3

Note: Income groups refer to working-age households in various sections of the income distribution as measured by money income. Percentage changes are approximated by taking the difference of natural logs of wages and hours.

Source: Authors' analysis of the Current Population Survey Annual Social and Economic Supplement microdata

working households is attributable to higher hourly pay versus how much is attributable to more hours worked throughout the year (which would include changes in the work status or work schedules of household members).

While there are many compelling findings in this table, we focus on trends for the middle fifth of households. Between 1979 and 2007, annual wages of the middle fifth increased 12.0 percent (from $49,260 to $55,560) (note that the increases and shares differ from Table 2.13 because these are different data sources and income concepts; see table notes). However, average annual hours worked rose by 10.3 percent (from 3,007 to 3,335), while average hourly wages rose by 1.7 percent (from $16.38 to $16.66); therefore, 85.9 percent of the rise in annual wages of the middle fifth was driven by increased work time.

Another striking finding of this table is that annual hours worked by the top 5 percent of households grew by only 1.9 percent over this period. Contrary to many claims that rising inequality is largely a function of workaholism among high-earners, all else equal, changes in work hours would have actually *reduced* inequality over the 1979 to 2007 period.

Another interesting finding from the table is further evidence that the labor market of the late 1990s was particularly favorable for workers across the board. Hourly earnings rose faster for more income groups between 1995 and 2000 than in any other subperiod within the 1979–2007 period. For the bottom four fifths, the vast majority of their earnings growth from 1979 to 2007 occurred in the late 1990s.

Table 2.18 takes a closer look at annual hours worked of a specific type of household: prime-age married couples (both spouses between age 25 and 54) with children. As with Table 2.17, we need to use CPS microdata to examine trends for this group, and we will focus the discussion here on households in the middle fifth of the money income distribution. From 1979 to 2007, there was little variance in the hours worked by men in this group, who tend to work more than full time, full year (they worked 2,200 hours in 2007, versus 52 weeks at 40 hours per week, or 2,080 hours), and thus there is little room for them to expand work hours. (This is known as a "ceiling effect," since annual hours are constrained by the available time in the day.) Women in this group, on the other hand, logged marked increases in annual hours worked, particularly over the 1980s. Between 1979 and 2007, women in the middle fifth increased their hours by 58.5 percent (from 891 hours to 1,413 hours), or 522 hours on average. This increase is the equivalent of over three months of full-time work. Of course, the increased time that married couples with children contribute as a unit to the paid labor market represents a challenge in terms of balancing work and family, challenges that are exacerbated by the lack of family-friendly workplace policies such as guaranteed paid leave, including family leave, sick leave, and vacations.

Table 2.18 Annual hours worked by married men and women age 25–54 with children, by income group, selected years, 1979–2010

	1979	1989	2000	2007	2010	Change 1979–2007	Change 2007–2010
Married women							
Bottom fifth	504	686	740	650	555	28.9%	-14.7%
Second fifth	733	1,006	1,186	1,160	1,101	58.2	-5.1
Middle fifth	891	1,228	1,401	1,413	1,382	58.5	-2.2
Fourth fifth	1,095	1,325	1,458	1,462	1,496	33.6	2.3
80th–<95th percentile	853	1,152	1,085	1,374	1,437	61.1	4.6
Top 5 percent	1,156	1,401	1,540	1,552	1,513	34.2	-2.5
Married men							
Bottom fifth	1,708	1,694	1,784	1,702	1,413	-0.4%	-17.0%
Second fifth	2,057	2,129	2,118	2,092	1,912	1.7	-8.6
Middle fifth	2,145	2,185	2,224	2,200	2,082	2.6	-5.4
Fourth fifth	2,190	2,247	2,300	2,258	2,212	3.1	-2.0
80th–<95th percentile	2,421	2,469	2,498	2,426	2,392	0.2	-1.4
Top 5 percent	2,260	2,337	2,359	2,325	2,279	2.8	-2.0
Combined							
Bottom fifth	2,213	2,380	2,525	2,352	1,967	6.3%	-16.4%
Second fifth	2,790	3,135	3,304	3,252	3,013	16.5	-7.3
Middle fifth	3,036	3,412	3,625	3,613	3,464	19.0	-4.1
Fourth fifth	3,284	3,571	3,758	3,720	3,708	13.3	-0.3
80th–<95th percentile	3,274	3,621	3,583	3,800	3,828	16.1	0.7
Top 5 percent	3,416	3,738	3,899	3,876	3,792	13.5	-2.2

Source: Authors' analysis of Current Population Survey Annual Social and Economic Supplement microdata

Table 2.19 examines how much of the increase in the middle fifth's annual wages is attributable to workers' increasing education and potential experience. Put simply, individuals in the middle fifth of the income distribution were better educated and somewhat older in 2007 than they were in 1979, and this should mechanically pull up their earnings. To undertake this calculation, we divided earners in the middle fifth of working-age households into 50 education/potential experience "cells," consisting of five educational categories (less than high school, high school degree only, some college attendance, college degree, and advanced degree) by 10 potential experience categories (0–5, 6–10, 11–15, 16–20, 21–25,

Table 2.19 Impact of increasing education and experience on hourly wages of individuals in the middle fifth of the income distribution, selected years, 1979–2007 (2011 dollars)

	1979	1989	1995	2000	2007	Change 1979–2007
Education						
Less than high school	22.4%	14.8%	12.2%	11.7%	9.8%	-12.6
High school only	41.6	43.6	39.4	37.4	35.5	-6.1
Some college	21.5	25.6	31.3	32.5	32.4	10.9
College degree	9.4	10.6	13.5	14.2	16.7	7.3
Advanced degree	5.1	5.5	3.7	4.2	5.6	0.5
Average potential experience (years)	17.8	17.3	18.2	19.1	20.0	2.2
Average hourly wages	$14.99	$15.14	$14.74	$16.11	$16.35	9.1%
Average hourly wages, 1979 weights*	$14.99	$14.60	$14.00	$15.36	$15.33	2.3%

* Hourly wage controlling for changes in education and experience.

Source: Authors' analysis of Current Population Survey Annual Social and Economic Supplement microdata

26–30, 31–35, 36–40, 41–45, and 46+ years an individual could have worked post-schooling, defined as age minus years of schooling minus 6).

For each year we calculate the share of earners in the middle fifth who fall into each of these 50 cells and each group's average hourly wage. We also calculate a "weight" for each cell, which is the share of total hours worked that are worked by individuals in that cell. Note that the overall hourly wage of the middle fifth is equal to the sum across cells of the weights multiplied by the hourly wage. Either higher cell wages or a movement of workers into higher-paid cells over time will increase the overall average wage. We look to see precisely how much wage growth is driven by movement into higher educational/experiential attainment cells and how much is due to higher wages given workers' levels of education and potential experience.

The first five rows of the table show the share of earners in the middle fifth with various levels of educational attainment in selected years between 1979 and 2007. The pattern toward educational upgrading is clear. For example, the share of earners in the middle fifth with a high school degree or less fell from 64.0 percent in 1979 to 45.3 percent in 2007. Conversely, the share with a four-year college degree or more rose from 14.5 percent to 22.3 percent.

The pattern toward increasing experience is evident in in the next row: Average potential experience among earners in the middle fifth increased from 17.8

years in 1979 to 20.0 years in 2007, a 2.2-year increase in potential work experience, on average.

The bottom two rows show the actual earnings per hour of the middle fifth and the hourly earnings that would result if the 1979 shares of educational attainment and potential experience were held constant over time. (It should be noted that the row "Average hourly wages" in Table 2.19 will not exactly match the hourly wages of the middle fifth in Table 2.17, due to the fact that Table 2.19 provides average hourly earnings of individuals, while Table 2.17 provides average hourly earnings of households.) The row "Average hourly wages, 1979 weights" is the result of a simple exercise that takes the educational and potential experience of 1979 as fixed (i.e., does not allow them to rise over time) and calculates a counterfactual growth in hourly earnings for earners in the middle fifth based on average hourly wages for these educational groups. In other words, this row shows what the growth in hourly wages would have been if the middle fifth had not increased their educational attainment and potential work experience.

Between 1979 and 2007, average hourly wages of the middle fifth increased by 9.1 percent. But if the effects of education and experience upgrades are removed, the increase is only 2.3 percent (as shown in the last row). Thus, over this period, three-quarters of the increase in earnings per hour was due to education and experience upgrading, not to the economy generating higher real wages for these workers independent of education and experience upgrades.

In short, educational and experiential upgrading, along with increased work hours, accounted for the vast majority of the growth of annual wages for those in the middle fifth of the income distribution between 1979 and 2007. Correspondingly, very little of the gains in annual wages were due to rising real wages independent of these factors.

Recall from Table 2.17 that 85.9 percent of the total increase in annual earnings of middle-fifth households between 1979 and 2007 was attributable to more hours being worked by these households, and only 14.1 percent was attributable to higher hourly wages. Furthermore, the calculations in Table 2.19 imply that 75 percent of that growth in hourly wages was attributable to the substantial educational and potential experience upgrading by the middle fifth, with only 25 percent attributable to higher real hourly wages for workers with a given amount of education or experience. Putting these together, less than 4 percent of the total increase in annual wages of households in the middle fifth of the income distribution is unaccounted for by more hours worked and education and experience upgrades.

Little of the growth of middle incomes can be attributed to a well-functioning economy

The comprehensive income data from the CBO provided in Table 2.13 suggested that average incomes of the middle fifth rose by 19.1 percent between 1979 and 2007. However, as Table 1.3 in Chapter 1 showed, about one-third of this growth is actually driven by the way health benefits are valued; valuing health benefits correctly (accounting for faster health care cost growth), reduces growth for the middle fifth to 12.7 percent. Furthermore, more than half of this growth was being driven by increased government transfers rather than developments in the market economy. Excluding the growth in cash transfers, Medicare and Medicaid, and other in-kind income apart from employer-sponsored health insurance, reduces growth for the middle fifth to 5.9 percent. Even further, about one-fifth of this growth was driven by the contribution to wages made by increased work hours. And even this ignores the fact that education and experience upgrading, documented earlier, generated nearly all growth in hourly wages over this time period.

When all of these factors are excluded, market-based incomes of households in the middle fifth of the income distribution rose just 4.8 percent from 1979 to 2007. This is the extent to which economic performance advanced the middle fifth of American households without the benefit of the large, public social insurance programs. Further, much of this 4.8 percent growth was concentrated in a single five-year burst in the late 1990s—a period of exceptionally tight labor markets and rapid growth in wage and salary incomes. In fact, nearly half of the 4.8 percent growth between 1979 to 2007 period was achieved between 1995 and 2000. It seems extraordinarily hard to argue that a U.S. economy that has generated 4.8 percent market-based income growth over 28 years (most of which was crammed into a five-year window) is performing satisfactorily and generating sustainable growth in middle-income living standards. Lastly, it is worth noting that most of these market-based income gains stem from rising pension incomes for the middle fifth. Given that today's pension incomes are a function of pension coverage rates that prevailed in the past, and given the trends in the rapid erosion of pension coverage rates in recent decades documented in Chapter 4, it is hard to believe that pension incomes will contribute this much to growth in middle-fifth incomes in decades to come.

Given all of this, it is hard to see how the period between 1979 and 2007 can be described as anything but disappointing for America's middle-income households. It is obvious from the gap between income growth of the middle fifth (19.1 percent) and overall income growth (51.4 percent) that sharply rising income inequality was a prime impediment to America's middle-income families reaching the full potential of income growth that the overall economy could have generated for them.

This does not mean that gains in middle-fifth incomes generated by pension income, Social Security, and health care for the elderly are insignificant. Improving retirement income security of elderly households is a positive outcome. After all, large social insurance programs such as Social Security, Medicare, Medicaid, and unemployment insurance were designed to lift living standards—or at least arrest their fall. They have succeeded in this goal. Further, the boost provided to today's middle-income households by employer-provided pension income earned from past work is another very positive economic outcome—substantial retirement income was once a luxury only available to a narrow segment of the workforce.

Yet we can celebrate these sources of living standards growth for the middle fifth while remaining concerned about their durability. The erosion of employer-provided pension coverage and quality in recent decades (surveyed in Chapter 4) suggests that employer-provided pensions will not continue to be a driver of income growth of elderly households. Further, the large social insurance programs (Social Security, Medicare, and Medicaid) that boosted income growth for the middle fifth over the nearly three decades preceding the Great Recession are under constant scrutiny, and the level of protection they will provide in the future is uncertain, hinging on political and policy decisions that will be debated continuously in the coming years.

Even if these social insurance programs are maintained and not reduced as some are advocating, they are unlikely to boost middle-fifth incomes by the same degree that they have in past decades, particularly if the health programs are deflated correctly. This is largely because a growing share of these social insurance expenditures will have to be dedicated just to covering rising health care costs. Additionally, the Social Security Administration is phasing in an increase of the normal retirement age to 67, which will lower annual benefits for workers who retire before they reach this new retirement age. In short, even if social insurance programs undergo no policy changes, the programs will contribute less to growth of middle-income living standards than provided during previous decades.

Conclusion

In recent decades, significant trends in American family and household incomes have broken sharply with the past. While incomes of families at the upper reaches of the income distribution have always far exceeded incomes at the middle and bottom segments of the distribution, the ratios between top and bottom (and top and middle) were actually quite stable for decades after World War II. In other words, overall income growth was shared proportionately across the American income distribution.

But since 1979, incomes at the top have soared while those at the middle and bottom have stagnated for long stretches, growing solidly only during the period of very tight labor markets in the late 1990s. Achieving economic growth that is both more rapid and more broadly shared—as was the case between 1947 and 1979—is perhaps the greatest economic challenge confronting the United States.

The years between 2007 and 2010 magnified this challenge. What we now know as the Great Recession has already taken a large toll on incomes of most Americans, with declines across the income distribution as well as across racial and ethnic groups. Worse, the continued slow labor market recovery indicated by projected slow declines in unemployment suggests that incomes will also likely be slow to recover. Recall Figure 2J, which suggests typical families are unlikely to regain the level of income they had in 2000 by 2020. The prospect of two decades of lost income growth is quite likely, and this is troubling indeed.

While no serious economic analyst denies the rise in inequality since 1979, experts do contest whether middle-income households can achieve living standards growth even in the face of this rising inequality. Some of those arguing that middle-income growth in the decades preceding the Great Recession was acceptable simply define the threshold of decent economic performance as growth exceeding zero. It is true that incomes of middle-income families grew between 1979 and 2007. However, this chapter has shown that a very large share of that income growth derived from pension incomes and transfer payments to elderly households and from government- and employer-provided medical benefits, the large boost from which declines if deflated by the medical care price deflator rather than the less appropriate deflator linked to the overall price index.

Only a small share of the income growth of middle-income families comes from rising labor earnings. Given that wages constitute the majority of overall income for families in the middle of the income distribution, the failure of wages to contribute significantly to income growth between 1979 and 2007 is also a cause for much concern. Worse, the large majority of annual wage growth during this period occurred because middle-income families worked more hours and became more educated and experienced over time. These influences boosting earnings growth—more hours worked, more education obtained, and more experience gained—speak very well of middle-income families' aspirations to carve out higher material standards of living. But they do not speak well of the overall economy's performance in helping families achieve these aspirations, nor do they bode well for similar middle-income growth in the coming decades.

Table and figure notes

Tables

Table 2.1. Average family income, by income group, 1947–2010. Underlying data are from Current Population Survey Annual Social and Economic Supplement *Historical Income Tables*, Table F-2, "Share of Aggregate Income Received by Each Fifth and Top 5 Percent of All Families, All Races: 1947– 2010," Table F-3, "Mean Income Received by Each Fifth and Top 5 Percent of Families, All Races: 1947 to 2010," and Table F-5, "Race and Hispanic Origin of Householder—Families by Median and Mean Income: 1947 to 2010." The years 1947, 1979, 1989, 2000, and 2007 are highlighted throughout the chapter because they are employment cycle peaks and are similar in nature to business cycle peaks. 1995 represents a midway point between cycles to show the growth or stagnation of the period. 2010 is highlighted because it is the most recent year for which data are available. Data are inflated to 2011 dollars using the CPI-U-RS (Consumer Price Index Research Series Using Current Methods).

Table 2.2. Average household income, by income group, 1967–2010. Underlying data are from Current Population Survey Annual Social and Economic Supplement *Historical Income Tables*, Table H-3, "Mean Income Received by Each Fifth and Top 5 Percent, All Races: 1967 to 2010." Data are inflated to 2011 dollars using the CPI-U-RS.

Table 2.3. Minimum income thresholds for family and household income, by income group, 1947–2010. Underlying data are from Current Population Survey Annual Social and Economic Supplement *Historical Income Tables*, Table F-1, "Income Limits for Each Fifth and Top 5 Percent of Families (All Races): 1947 to 2010," and Table H-1, "Income Limits for Each Fifth and Top 5 Percent of All Households: 1967 to 2010." Data are inflated to 2011 dollars using the CPI-U-RS.

Table 2.4. Sources of pretax comprehensive income, by income group, 2007. Underlying data are from the Congressional Budget Office, *Average Federal Taxes by Income Group*, "Sources of Income for All Households, by Household Income Category, 1979 to 2007" [Excel spreadsheet]. Shares of pretax income, by income source, are given by CBO for the bottom, second, middle, fourth, and top fifth, and the top 10, 5, and 1 percent. Average pretax income is defined as the sum of each income groups' wages, proprietors' income, other business income, interest and dividends, capital gains pensions, cash transfers, in-kind income, imputed taxes, and other income. For the purposes of this chapter, capital income is defined as the sum of capital gains, interest and dividends, and other business income categories. Sources of income for the groups are calculated by multiplying the shares of each income source by average pretax income. To calculate average pretax income by source for the 95th–< 99th percentile, the aggregate incomes of the top 5 percent were subtracted from the aggregate incomes of the top 10 percent and divided by the total number of households in the 95th–<99th percentile. Aggregate income is calculated by multiplying the number of households in each income group by average pretax income source. The number of households is calculated by subtracting the number of households in the top 5 percent from the number of households in the top 10 percent. The same calculation is done for the 95th–<99th percentile using the top 5 percent and the top 1 percent. The share of total income categories claimed by each group is calculated by dividing the aggregate income for each income source in each income group by the total aggregate income for all households, minus negative income. Data are inflated to 2011 dollars using the CPI-U-RS.

Table 2.5. Median family income by race and ethnicity, 1947–2010. Underlying data are from Current Population Survey Annual Social and Economic Supplement *Historical Income Tables*, Table F-5, "Race and Hispanic Origin of Householder—Families by Median and Mean Income: 1947–2010." Unlike with CPS microdata analyses presented in the book, race and ethnicity categories are not mutually exclusive (i.e., persons of Hispanic origin may be of any race, and white and black Hispanics are counted in the white and black columns as well as the Hispanic column). Data are inflated to 2011 dollars using the CPI-U-RS.

Table 2.6. Share of average income growth accounted for by the bottom 95 percent, top 5 percent, and top 1 percent, by dataset and income concept, 1979–2007
Underlying data are from Piketty and Saez (2012, Table A-6); Current Population Survey Annual Social and Economic Supplement *Historical Income Tables*, Table H-3, "Mean Household Income Received by Each Fifth and Top 5 percent;" Congressional Budget Office *Average Federal Taxes by Income Group,* "Sources of Income for All Households, by Household Income Category, 1979 to 2007" [Excel spreadsheet]; and Burkhauser, Larrimore, and Simon (2011), Table 4, "Quintile Income Growth by Business Cycle Using Each Income Series." Each income concept's contribution to overall income growth is calculated by multiplying the change in its average income from 1979 to 2007 by its share of the distribution (where, for example, the share of the distribution for the top 1 percent is .01), and dividing the result by the change in overall average income growth over the same time period.

Table 2.7. Effective tax rates for selected federal taxes, by income group, 1979–2007. Underlying data are from the Congressional Budget Office, *Average Federal Taxes by Income Group,* "Average Federal Tax Rates for All Households, by Comprehensive Household Income Quintile, 1979–2007" [Excel spreadsheet]. CBO defines individual income taxes as taxes attributed directly to households paying those taxes; social insurance (payroll) taxes are taxes attributed to households paying those taxes directly or paying them indirectly through their employers. Corporate income taxes are attributed to households according to a household's share of capital income, and federal excise taxes are attributed to households according to their consumption of the taxed good or service.

Table 2.8. Tax rate, transfer rate, and tax rate net of transfers, by income group, 1979–2007. Underlying data are from the Congressional Budget Office *Average Federal Taxes by Income Group,* "Average Federal Tax Rates for All Households, by Comprehensive Household Income Quintile, 1979–2007," "Sources of Income for All Households, by Household Income Category 1979 to 2007" [Excel spreadsheets] and unpublished data related to the same report on the composition of in-kind income, with a breakout for health spending (both government transfers and employer-sponsored insurance benefits). The tax rate is taken directly from the first Excel spreadsheet cited here, while the transfer rate is calculated as the share of cash transfers and Medicare and Medicaid spending in comprehensive income.

Table 2.9. Educational attainment, by income group, selected years, 1979–2007. Underlying data are from Current Population Survey Annual Social and Economic Supplement microdata; see Appendix A for details. The data are sorted by household income and placed into the income groupings. Then, an hours-weighted measure of the share of all hours worked by workers with the given educational attainment is constructed for each of the income groupings.

Table 2.10. Share of market-based personal income, by income type, selected years, 1959–2010. Underlying data for total capital income, rent, dividends, interest, total labor income, wages and salaries, fringe benefits, and proprietors' income are from Bureau of Economic Analysis National Income and Product Accounts, Table 2.1, "Personal Income and Its Disposition." Underlying data for realized capital gains come from the Internal Revenue Service, *SOI Tax Stat–Individual Time Series Statistical Tables*, Historical Table 1, "All Individual Income Tax Returns: Sources of Income and Tax Items, Tax Years 1913–2005," and Table 1, "Individual Income Tax Returns: Selected Income and Tax Items for Specified Tax Years, 1999–2009." Rent, dividends, interest, total labor income, wages and salaries, fringe benefits, proprietors' income, and net capital gains are divided by the total market income (the sum of total capital income, total labor income, and proprietors' income) for select years.

Table 2.11. Effect of the shift from labor to capital income on the top 1 percent of households, selected years, 1979–2007. Underlying data are from the Congressional Budget Office, *Average Federal Taxes by Income Group*, "Sources of Income for All Households, by Household Income Category, 1979 to 2007" [Excel spreadsheet]. The counterfactual holds the share of all income accounted for by capital income constant at its 1979 level. By implication, this means that all non-capital income sources rise over that time period (since overall income growth is assumed to remain the same). This extra non-capital income is distributed across income groupings in proportion to their actual income shares over time. Then the counterfactual income level of the top 1 percent is calculated and compared with actual trends. Data are inflated to 2011 dollars using the CPI-U-RS.

Table 2.12. Corporate sector income shares, profit rates, and capital-to-output ratio, selected years, 1959–2010. Underlying data are from the Bureau of Economic Analysis National Income and Product Accounts, Table 1.14, "Gross Value Added of Domestic Corporate Businesses in Current Dollars and Gross Value added of Nonfinancial Domestic Corporate Business in Current and Chained Dollars" and BEA Fixed Assets Accounts, Table 6.1, "Current-Cost Net Stock of Private Fixed Assets by Industry Group and Legal Form of Organization." Total income shares are the sum of labor and capital income, specifically the sum of line items Compensation and Net Operating Surplus to get net value added in NIPA Table 1.14. Labor share is the share of compensation in net value added and capital is net operating surplus over net value added. Pretax profit rate is the net operating surplus divided by private fixed corporate assets, line item 2 from Table 6.1. Post-tax profit rate is the net operating surplus, without taxes, divided by private fixed corporate assets. The capital-to-output ratio is private fixed corporate assets divided by the constructed net value added.

Table 2.13. Change in sources of comprehensive income, middle fifth of households, selected years, 1979–2007 (2011 dollars). Underlying data are from the Congressional Budget Office, *Average Federal Taxes by Income Group*, "Sources of Income for All Households, by Household Income Category, 1979 to 2007" [Excel spreadsheet], as well as unpublished data related to the same CBO Web resource on the composition of in-kind income, with a breakout for health spending (both government transfers and employer-sponsored insurance benefits). "Imputed taxes" are taxes that are not directly paid by households to government (such as the employer's share of the payroll tax), but which are "paid" in the form of lower wages and thus are added by the CBO to actual, observed wages to produce the measure of "pretax" income. "Other income" in the pensions category includes withdrawals from 401(k) plans and traditional pensions and a small category of "other income" that CBO links with pension income in its reports. Note that the unpublished CBO data are unrounded, and produce slightly different income dollar values than the publicly available CBO dataset underlying Figures 2M and 2Z. For deflation of health care benefits (both transfers and employer-provided) we use the Consumer Price Index for medical care (CPI-MC) instead of the Consumer Price Index for Urban Consumers, Research Series (CPI-U-RS) that is used throughout the book.

Table 2.14. Change in sources of comprehensive income for elderly households in the middle fifth, selected years, 1979–2007. Underlying data are unpublished data on income source by family type from the Congressional Budget Office related to its 2010 Web resource, *Average Federal Taxes by Income Group.* "Imputed taxes" are taxes that are not directly paid by households to government (such as the employer's share of the payroll tax), but which are "paid" in the form of lower wages and thus are added by the CBO to actual, observed wages to produce the measure of "pretax" income. "Other income" in the pensions category includes withdrawals from 401(k) plans and traditional pensions, and a small category of "other income" that CBO links with pension income in its reports. The income levels for "Wages and imputed taxes" column and the "Pensions and other income" columns are calculated by the sum of the product of the shares of wages and imputed taxes multiplied by average pre-tax income for each income group and the sum of the product of the share of pensions and other income multiplied by average pretax income. The contribution to shares from income sources is calculated by multiplying the change in the types of income sources by the changes in the total income for elderly households. Data are inflated to 2011 dollars using the CPI-U-RS.

Table 2.15. Change in sources of comprehensive income for non-elderly households in the middle fifth, selected years, 1979–2007. Underlying data are unpublished data on income source by family type from the Congressional Budget Office related to its 2010 Web resource, *Average Federal Taxes by Income Group.* "Imputed taxes" are taxes that are not directly paid by households to government (such as the employer's share of the payroll tax), but which are "paid" in the form of lower wages and thus are added by the CBO to actual, observed wages to produce the measure of "pretax" income. "Other income" in the pensions category includes withdrawals from 401(k) plans and traditional pensions, and a small category of "other income" that CBO links with pension income in its reports. The income levels for "Wages and imputed taxes" column and the "Pensions and other income" columns are calculated by the sum of the product of the shares of wages and imputed taxes multiplied by average pretax income for each income group and the sum of the product of the share of pensions and other income multiplied by average pretax income. The contribution to shares from income sources is calculated by multiplying the change in the types of income sources by the changes in the total income for non-elderly households. Data are inflated to 2011 dollars using the CPI-U-RS. Note that the unpublished CBO data are unrounded, and produce slightly different income dollar values than the publicly available CBO dataset underlying Figures 2M and 2Z.

Table 2.16. Contributions to middle-fifth income growth, by income category and household type, selected years, 1979–2007. Underlying data are unpublished data on income source by family type from the Congressional Budget Office related to its 2010 Web resource, *Average Federal Taxes by Income Group.* Data are inflated to 2011 dollars using the CPI-U-RS.

Table 2.17. Contribution of hours versus hourly wages to annual wage growth for working-age households, by income group, selected years, 1979–2007. Underlying data are from Current Population Survey Annual Social and Economic Supplement microdata; see

Appendix A for details. Households are ranked in the same way as in the Congressional Budget Office data—by household income divided by the square root of household size. Average annual wages and annual hours worked for each income group are then calculated, and a household average for hourly wages is calculated by dividing annual wages by annual hours. Data are inflated to 2011 dollars using the CPI-U-RS.

Table 2.18. Annual hours worked by married men and women age 25–54 with children, by income group, selected years, 1979–2010. Underlying data are from the Current Population Survey Annual Social and Economic Supplement microdata; see Appendix A for details.

Table 2.19. Impact of increasing education and experience on hourly wages of individuals in the middle fifth of the income distribution, selected years, 1979–2007. Underlying data are from Current Population Survey Annual Social and Economic Supplement microdata; see Appendix A for details. Households are ranked in the same way as in the Congressional Budget Office data—by household income divided by the square root of household size. Fifty age/experience "cells" are created (five educational categories by 10 potential experience categories). Average hourly earnings are calculated for each cell. To get the counterfactual wage growth that would have happened *without* education and experience upgrading, we hold the 1979 cell weights (i.e., the shares of total hours worked in each year by a given cell) constant, but allow the within-cell wage growth to occur. Data are inflated to 2011 dollars using the CPI-U-RS.

Figures

Figure 2A. Real median family income, 1947–2010. Underlying data are from Current Population Survey Annual Social and Economic Supplement *Historical Income Tables*, Table F-5, "Race and Hispanic Origin of Householder—Families by Median and Mean Income: 1947 to 2010." Data are inflated to 2011 dollars using the CPI-U-RS.

Figure 2B. Real median income of working-age families, 1975–2010. Underlying data are from Current Population Survey Annual Social and Economic Supplement microdata; see Appendix A for details. Data are inflated to 2011 dollars using the CPI-U-RS.

Figure 2C. Average family income growth, by income group, 1947–2007. Underlying data are from Current Population Survey Annual Social and Economic Supplement *Historical Income Tables*, Table F-3, "Mean Income Received by Each Fifth and Top 5 Percent of Families, All Races: 1966 to 2010." Data are inflated to 2011 dollars using the CPI-U-RS.

Figure 2D. Black median family income, as a share of white median family income, 1947–2010. Underlying data are from Current Population Survey Annual Social and Economic Supplement *Historical Income Tables*, Table F-5, "Race and Hispanic Origin of Householder—Families by Median and Mean Income: 1947 to 2010."

Figure 2E. Median family income growth, by nativity, 1993–2010. Underlying data are from Current Population Survey Annual Social and Economic Supplement microdata; see Appendix A for details. Data is inflated to 2011 dollars using the CPI-U-RS and then indexed to 1993=100.

Figure 2F. Change in average family income, by income group, 2007–2010. Underlying data are from Current Population Survey Annual Social and Economic Supplement *Historical*

Income Tables, Table F-3, "Mean Income Received by Each Fifth and Top 5 Percent of Families, All Races: 1966 to 2010." Data are inflated to 2011 dollars using the CPI-U-RS.

Figure 2G. Change in real family income from the business cycle peak years 1989, 2000, and 2007. Underlying data are from Current Population Survey Annual Social and Economic Supplement *Historical Income Tables*, Table F-3, "Mean Income Received by Each Fifth and Top 5 Percent of Families, All Races: 1966 to 2010." Data for each recession are indexed to the business cycle peak year preceding the recession=100.

Figure 2H. Average capital gains of the top 5% of the income distribution and the S&P 500 composite price index, 1979–2011. Underlying data are from Piketty and Saez (2012, Tables A-6 and A-8) and Shiller (2012). The inflation-adjusted S&P 500 data are taken directly from Shiller and converted into an index (1989=100). Income derived from realized capital gains is taken from Piketty and Saez (2012) and converted into an index as well. The Shiller data can be found at: http://www.econ.yale.edu/~shiller/data.htm, and the Piketty and Saez data can be found at: http://elsa.berkeley.edu/~saez/TabFig2010.xls.

Figure 2I. Change in real median household income, by race and ethnicity, 2007–2010. Underlying data are from Current Population Survey Annual Social and Economic Supplement *Historical Income Tables*, Table H-5, "Race and Hispanic Origin of Householder—Households by Median and Mean Income: 1967–2010."

Figure 2J. Change in real family income of the middle fifth, actual and predicted, 2000–2018. Underlying data are from the Current Population Survey Annual Social and Economic Supplement *Historical Income Tables*, Tables F-2, F-3, and F-5. Data are inflated to 2011 dollars using the CPI-U-RS. The projections are based on a regression analysis, based roughly on Katz and Krueger (1999), that uses the annual change in inflation-adjusted income of families in the middle fifth of the money income distribution as the dependent variable and the level of unemployment as the independent variable. The projections then use the regression parameters to forecast annual changes in middle-fifth family income based on unemployment forecasts through 2018 that are made by the Congressional Budget Office and Moody's Economy.com, a division of Moody's Analytics.

Figure 2K. Income growth for families at the 20th, 50th, and 95th percentiles, 1947–2010. Underlying data are from Current Population Survey Annual Social and Economic Supplement *Historical Income Tables*, Table F-1, "Income Limits for Each Fifth and Top 5 Percent of Families (All Races): 1947 to 2010," and Table F-5, "Race and Hispanic Origin of Householder—Families by Median and Mean Income: 1947 to 2010." Data are inflated to 2011 dollars using the CPI-U-RS and then indexed to 1979=100.

Figure 2L. Income growth for families at the 20th, 50th, and 95th percentiles, by nativity, 1993–2010. Underlying data are from Current Population Survey Annual Social and Economic Supplement microdata; see Appendix A for details. Data are inflated to 2011 dollars using the CPI-U-RS and then indexed to 1993=100.

Figure 2M. Change in real annual household income, by income group, 1979–2007. Underlying data are from the Congressional Budget Office, *Average Federal Taxes by Income Group*, "Sources of Income for All Households, by Household Income Category, 1979 to 2007"

[Excel spreadsheet]. Cumulative growth is calculated by dividing the average pretax income in the base year (1979) into average pretax income in each subsequent year (1980–2007). The data provide average pretax income for the bottom, second, middle, fourth, and top fifths, and for the top 10, 5, and 1 percents. For the 80th–<90th percentile, average pretax income is calculated by subtracting the aggregate income of the top 10 percent from aggregate income of the top fifth and dividing by the total number of households in the 80th–<90th percentile. Aggregate income is calculated by multiplying the number of households in each income group by average pretax income. The number of households is calculated by subtracting the number of households in the top 10 percent from the number of households in the top fifth. This same procedure is done between the top 10 percent and top 5 percent to calculate average pretax income for the 90th–<95th percentile and between the top 5 percent and top 1 percent to calculate the average pretax income for the 95th–<99th percentile. Note that this publicly available CBO dataset is rounded, and produces slightly different income dollar values than the unpublished, unrounded CBO data underlying tables 2.13 and 2.16. Data are inflated to 2011 dollars using the CPI-U-RS, and then indexed to 1979=0.

Text Box Figure 2AA. Share of income held by high-income groups, 1913–2010. Underlying data are from Piketty and Saez (2012, Table A-3), Current Population Survey Annual Social and Economic Supplement *Historical Income Tables*, Table H-2, "Share of Aggregate Income Received by Each Fifth and Top 5 Percent of Households," and the Congressional Budget Office *Average Federal Taxes by Income Group* report, "Average Pre-Tax Income for All Households, by Household Income Category, 1979–2007" [Excel spreadsheet]. The top 5 percent share is shown because the CPS data do not allow examination of the top 1 percent.

Text Box Figure 2AB. Share of income held by top 1 percent in developed countries, 1913–2009. Underlying data are from *The World Top Incomes* database.

Figure 2N. Change in the share of market income and post-tax, post-transfer income that households claim, by income group, 1979–2007. Underlying data are from the Congressional Budget Office, *Average Federal Taxes by Income Group*, "Pre-Tax Income Shares All Households, by Household Income Category, 1979–2007," "After-Tax Income Shares for All Households, by Household Income Category, 1979–2007," and "Sources of Income for All Households, by Household Income Category, 1979 to 2007" [Excel spreadsheets] and unpublished health benefit data pertaining to this report. The shares of pre- and post-tax income are taken directly from the first two datasets cited here. The change in market income is then expressed as a share of the overall change in pretax income (transfers are essentially the only nonmarket income type that changes the pretax income shares).

Figure 2O. Effect of tax policies on each household income group's share of total income, 1979 and 2007, and the difference needed in 2007 to preserve 1979 post-tax shares. Underlying data are from the Congressional Budget Office, *Average Federal Taxes by Income Group*, "Average Federal Tax Rates for All Households, by Comprehensive Household Income Quintile, 1979–2007"and "Sources of Income for All Households, by Household Income Category, 1979 to 2007" [Excel Spreadsheets].

Figure 2P. Average effective federal tax rates, by household income group, 1979–2007. Underlying data are from the Congressional Budget Office, *Average Federal Taxes by Income Group*, "Average Federal Tax Rates for All Households, by Comprehensive Household Income Quintile, 1979–2007" [Excel spreadsheet] and "Effective Federal Tax Rates for All Households, by Comprehensive Household Income Category, 1979 to 2005 (Percent)" [Excel spreadsheet supplement to *Historical Effective Federal Tax Rates: 1979 to 2005*]. The tax rates for the top .01, top 0.1 and top 1.0 percent are given by CBO. The tax rates for the 20th–<90th percentile, 90th–<95th percentile, and the 95th–<99th percentile are calculated by taking an average of each income groups' tax rate weighted by their share of total income.

Figure 2Q. Average effective federal tax rates, by income group, 1960–2004. Underlying data are from Piketty and Saez (2007), Table 2, "Federal Rates by Income Groups, 1960 to 2004." The top .01 percent, the 99.9th–<99.99th percentile, 99.5th–<99.9th percentile, and 99.0–<99.5th percentile data are provided. The 20th–<99th percentile tax rate was calculated as an average of each income groups' tax rate weighted by their share of total income.

Figure 2R. Change in real cash and medical transfer income, by income group, 1979–2007. Underlying data are from the Congressional Budget Office, *Average Federal Taxes by Income Group*, "Sources of Income for All Households, by Household Income Category, 1979 to 2007" [Excel spreadsheet] and unpublished data related to the same report on the composition of in-kind income, with a breakout for health spending (both government transfers as well as employer-sponsored insurance benefits).

Figure 2S. Change in tax rate, transfer rate, and tax rate net of transfers, by income group, 1979–2007. Data in Figure 2S are a subset of the data in Table 2.8.

Figure 2T. Change in real annual household wages, by income group, 1979–2007. Underlying data are from the Congressional Budget Office *Average Federal Taxes by Income Group*, "Sources of Income for All Households, by Household Income Category, 1979 to 2007" [Excel spreadsheet]. Cumulative growth is calculated by dividing the average wages in the base year (1979) into average wages in each subsequent year (1980–2007). Average wages by income group are calculated by multiplying the share of wages by the average pretax income in each income group. See Figure 2M notes for calculations of the 80th–<90th percentile, 90th–<95th percentile, and 95th–<99th percentile. Data are inflated to 2011 dollars using the CPI-U-RS, and then indexed to 1979=0.

Figure 2U. Change in real household capital income, by income group, 1979–2007. Underlying data are from the Congressional Budget Office, *Average Federal Taxes by Income Group*, "Sources of Income for All Households, by Household Income Category, 1979–2007" [Excel spreadsheet]. Cumulative growth is calculated by dividing the average capital income in the base year (1979) into average capital income in each subsequent year (1980–2007). Average capital income by income group is calculated by multiplying the share of capital income by the average pretax income in each income group. See Figure 2M notes for calculations of the 80th–<90th percentile, 90th–<95th percentile, and 95th–<99th percentile; see Table 2.4 notes for explanation of capital income. Data are inflated to 2011 dollars using the CPI-U-RS, and then indexed to 1979=0.

Figure 2V. Share of total household capital income claimed, by income group, 1979–2007. Underlying data are from the Congressional Budget Office, *Average Federal Taxes by Income Group*, "Sources of Income for All Households, by Household Income Category, 1979 to 2007" [Excel spreadsheet]. The share of capital income is each income group's capital income share of the total capital income for all income groups. See Table 2.4 notes for the calculations for income group breakdowns and definition of capital income.

Figure 2W. Pretax and post-tax profit rates, 1959–2010. Underlying data are from the Bureau of Economic Analysis National Income and Product Accounts tables, Table 1.14, "Gross Value Added of Domestic Corporate Businesses in Current Dollars and Gross Value added of Nonfinancial Domestic Corporate Business in Current and Chained Dollars" and Fixed Assets Accounts tables, Table 6.1, "Current-Cost Net Stock of Private Fixed Assets by Industry Group and Legal Form of Organization." For calculations of pretax and post-tax profit rate, see Table 2.12 notes.

Figure 2X. Capital share of total corporate-sector income, actual and counterfactual holding 1979 profit rate constant, 1979–2010. Underlying data are from the Bureau of Economic Analysis, National Income and Product Accounts tables, Table 1.14, "Gross Value Added of Domestic Corporate Businesses in Current Dollars and Gross Value added of Nonfinancial Domestic Corporate Business in Current and Chained Dollars" and Fixed Assets Accounts tables, Table 6.1, "Current-Cost Net Stock of Private Fixed Assets by Industry Group and Legal Form of Organization." For calculations of pretax and post-tax profit rate, see Table 2.12 notes.

Figure 2Y. Share of total household income growth attributable to various income groups, 1979–2007. Underlying data are from the Congressional Budget Office *Average Federal Taxes by Income Group*, "Sources of Income for All Households, by Household Income Category, 1979 to 2007" [Excel spreadsheet]. Each group's contribution to overall income growth is calculated by multiplying the change in its average income from 1979 to 2007 by its share of the distribution (where, for example, the share of the distribution for the top 1 percent is .01), and dividing the result by the change in overall average income growth over the same time period. For pretax income calculations of the 90th–<95th percentile and 95th–99th percentile, see Figure 2M notes.

Figure 2Z. Change in household income, as reported by CBO comprehensive income data and CPS money income data, by income group, 1979–2007. Underlying data are from Congressional Budget Office *Average Federal Taxes by Income Group* report, "Sources of Income for All Households, by Household Income Category, 1979 to 2007" [Excel spreadsheet], and Current Population Survey Annual Social and Economic Supplement *Historical Income Tables*, Table F-3, "Mean Income received by each fifth and top 5 percent of all families, 1966–2010." Percentage change of household income is calculated between the years 1979 and 2007. Note that this publicly available CBO dataset is rounded, and produces slightly different income dollar values than the unpublished, unrounded CBO data underlying tables 2.13 and 2.16. Data are inflated to 2011 dollars using the CPI-U-RS, and then indexed to 1979=0.

CHAPTER 3

Mobility
Not offsetting growing inequality

The State of Working America documents growing economic inequality in the United States over the last few decades. Due to this rise in inequality, increases in living standards for most American families have lagged overall economic growth.

For many, these highly troubling developments could arguably be somewhat mitigated by increased economic mobility. If American families were regularly climbing up and down the income ladder even as the ladder's rungs grow farther apart, the historically high level of economic inequality may be of less concern.

In fact, some observers argue that inequality is not such a serious problem, as everyone has an equal chance of winding up at the top. Their assertion is the essence of the American Dream: Regardless of where you begin, if you work hard, you have opportunities to succeed.

This chapter examines mobility, a critical measure of economic well-being. Specifically, mobility measures the likelihood of moving up or down the distribution of incomes, earnings (i.e., labor income/wages), and wealth, comparing people and families relative to one another across time. If the data showed, for example, that many families are likely to move from the bottom fifth on the income or wealth scale to the top over time, or that children of wealthy families switch places with middle-class children when they become adults, we could conclude that the benefits of economic growth were more broadly shared than the inequalities highlighted in the other chapters suggest.

But the research does not find that increasing mobility is offsetting the increasingly skewed distribution of growth. Rather, most families are stuck in place while economic growth passes them by. In this respect, then, reality does not match the dream. Mobility—movement among economic classes—is much more restricted than in the opportunity-rich ideal of the American Dream.

Of course, some families do move up and down the income scale, but most maintain their relative positions, meaning that relative to other families in their age cohort, they remain at or near the income or wealth position in which they started out. According to one study discussed later, 61.0 percent of families that start in the bottom fifth are still there a decade later, while 52.2 percent of families that start in the top fifth finish there at the end of the decade. In addition, 84.3 percent of families starting out in the bottom fifth end up in the bottom two-fifths a decade later.

Intergenerational mobility—mobility across generations—is also not great in the United States. Your economic position in childhood largely determines your position in adulthood. Specifically, research highlights a significant correlation between parents' economic position and that of their adult children, implying that class barriers are such that children's economic fate is largely determined by their family's position on the income, earnings, or wealth scale. For example, one study found that two-thirds (66.7 percent) of sons of low-earning fathers end up in the bottom two-fifths, while only 18.1 percent make it to the top two-fifths. This persistence in relative position across generations suggests, for instance, that a middle-class child's chances of becoming a rich adult are low. If where you start out has a strong influence on where you end up, then the rate of economic mobility is low. More practically, if researchers can look at a child's characteristics—such as her race, parental income, neighborhood, and so on—and predict with some accuracy what her adult income, earnings, or wealth will be, then this is also evidence of low mobility.

American lore often emphasizes the idea that anyone with the gumption and smarts to prevail can travel up the income scale in his lifetime. In fact, conventional wisdom holds that mobility is higher in the United States than in the advanced economies in Europe (particularly Scandinavia) in part because their more extensive public sectors, income transfers, and social protections dampen the entrepreneurial spark that generates rags-to-riches stories. The evidence suggests otherwise. A study found that in Denmark, Norway, and Finland, parents' economic positions tend to be *less* correlated with their children's incomes as adults, meaning these nations have more intergenerational mobility than the United States.

One particularly disturbing aspect of U.S. mobility is the lower mobility of African Americans compared with whites. One study discussed later shows that nearly two-thirds (62.9 percent) of black children who start out in the bottom fourth on the income scale remain there as adults, compared with about one-third (32.3 percent) of white children. Another study finds that more than a third (34.1percent) of African American children who start out in middle-income families are downwardly mobile, ending up in poor families (in the bottom fifth on the income scale) as adults, compared with 15.6 percent of whites.

Unequal educational opportunities explain some of the lack of mobility in the United States. Children from rich families have much greater access to higher education than children from low-income families, even when controlling for innate skills. This educational barrier places profound limits on income mobility. Only 16 percent of children who grew up in low-income families and earned a college degree ended up low-income (in the bottom fifth of the income distribution) as adults. In contrast, nearly half (45 percent) of low-income children who didn't graduate from college ended up in the bottom fifth as adults. In other words, among children who grew up in low-income families, those who failed to graduate college were almost three times more likely than their college-educated peers to still be in the bottom fifth as adults.

This unequal distribution of opportunities leads to one of the central conclusions of this chapter: Americans who do not object to unequal outcomes, only to unequal opportunities, must realize that unequal outcomes themselves may lead to unequal opportunities.

It is one thing to have a society where some people are much more economically successful than others because they work harder, make better choices, or are just plain smarter. But when success favors those who are not necessarily more meritorious but are instead born wealthier, more connected, more powerful, whiter, male, etc., then it violates the basic American value of equal opportunity. Trends in inequality suggest that economic growth flows mostly to those at the top of the scale, meaning their children may have not only greater, but *increasingly* greater, access to quality education relative to children from less well-placed families. When some neighborhoods get parks, libraries, and grocery stores while others do not, this too restricts opportunity. When quality health care is more accessible to haves than the have-nots, then the latter face a mobility barrier borne of inequality.

If income concentration leads to a level of political influence that tilts against the have-nots, this too will reduce opportunity and ultimately lower the rate of economic mobility. If, for example, opportunity-enhancing programs that aid disadvantaged children (e.g., subsidized health care and policies to create jobs for their parents) are cut in order to maintain high-end tax cuts, then the likelihood that economically disadvantaged children will experience significant mobility is diminished.

Debates over policies that impede or advance mobility are particularly crucial now, in the face of more than three decades of growing income inequality. Recent cross-country evidence suggests that higher inequality is associated with lower mobility. It seems to make sense that when the gaps are wider, people have a harder time traversing them, and, if this is true, the United States may be facing a future of diminished mobility as income inequality increases. Regardless of the accuracy of this prediction, there is no evidence to suggest that mobility has *increased* to offset rising inequality. Income classes are further apart now than in the past, and families are no more likely to traverse that greater distance.

Figure notes at the end of this chapter provide documentation for the data, as well as information on methodology, used in the figures that follow.

Intragenerational mobility

One way to examine mobility is to look at whether and how far individuals and families move up or down the income scale over their lives. If where you start on the income scale has a strong influence on where you end, then the degree of economic mobility is low. If, on the other hand, where you start is largely unrelated to where you end, then mobility is high.

Lifetime mobility against the backdrop of generational stagnation

An important element of this line of research is that people and families generally follow a pattern of growing income throughout their lives. **Figure 3A** shows U.S. median family income over the prime working years (age 25–64) of the family's adult head ("householder"), by his or her year of birth. This plot is best read starting from the bottom right with the earliest birth cohort, 1885–1894, and reading counterclockwise, ending nearly 100 years later, with those born from 1975 to 1984. Because data only range between 1949 and 2009, only later years of the life cycle are available for early cohorts (because they were not observed when they were young), and only earlier years are available for more recent cohorts (who generally are still in the middle of their work lives).

This plot tells a crucial story about income growth in the United States. First, it shows that over the life cycle of the householder, family incomes typically increase over the first 20 prime working years. (That does not mean that families are mobile over that time or that their mobility has increased—this determination requires analyzing longitudinal data, which will be discussed shortly.)

Second, it shows that each cohort from the first birth cohort up through the early baby boomers (those born from 1945 to 1954) saw substantial income gains compared with the cohort that preceded them—though the gains from cohort to cohort generally slowed over that time. Perhaps most importantly, it shows that after the early baby boomers (at the top of the figure), the progress stops—judged by where their median family income falls at the end of the available data, birth cohorts following the early baby boomers have seen no additional improvements. In other words, the families headed by early baby boomers were the last to achieve higher living standards than the cohort that preceded them.

Figure 3A Median family income over the householder's working life, by birth cohort

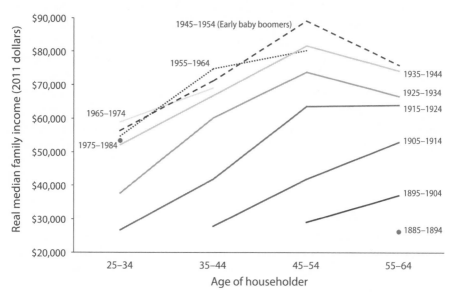

Note: Data range from 1949 to 2009.

Source: Authors' analysis of Current Population Survey Annual Social and Economic Supplement *Historical Income Tables* (Table F-11)

This loss of continually improving living standards for successive generations strikes at the heart of the American Dream. This figure suggests that today's middle-income families may not be doing as well as those of previous generations, and children may not achieve the economic success of their parents.

As troubling as the story underlying this figure is—a story told more fully in chapters 2 and 4 of this book—the message in this chapter is perhaps even more grim.

Mobility research, which goes beyond examining how families in a given age cohort compare with families in other cohorts, measures how well families do relative to one another over time. It finds that opportunities for families to move up are not as plentiful as the American Dream would suggest.

Family and individual mobility trends

The central question addressed in this section is: How far do families move up or down the income scale over their life spans? In other words, of those families that start at the bottom, middle, or top of the income distribution, what share are still there years later? Recall the analysis of Figure 3A: Identifying growth in a cohort's income from one decade to another can show whether families in the cohort are better or worse off in terms of absolute income, but is not sufficient to conclude that families in the cohort are upwardly mobile. Mobility requires changes in family income *relative* to incomes of other families in the cohort.

To make these relative comparisons, researchers assign each family (or person, in the case of individual mobility) to an income fifth at the beginning of the observation period, based on the income distribution at that time. At some later point (after some number of years, depending on data and the research question), new fifths are calculated so researchers can assess where families ended up. This approach allows a better comparison of families relative to their cohort as opposed to simply determining whether they are better or worse off in terms of their absolute incomes.

This type of analysis requires longitudinal data, survey data that follow individuals and families over time. One of the most frequently used data sources for mobility research is the Panel Study of Income Dynamics (PSID). Begun in 1968 with a sample of approximately 5,000 families, the PSID follows families and their descendants over time, tracking changes in incomes, behaviors, and living situations. The PSID was administered annually between 1968 and 1997, and every two years thereafter.

Acs and Zimmerman (2008a) use the PSID to track family income across income fifths over 10 years from 1994 to 2004. Using two-year averages to control for transitory income fluctuations, the lightly shaded bars in **Figure 3B** illustrate the share of families starting in the bottom fifth of the income distribution in 1994 that remained there or moved to higher income fifths by 2004. In a society with perfect mobility, all of the bars would equal 20 percent. As shown, 61.0 percent of those in the bottom fifth in 1994 remained in the bottom fifth in 2004, while about 16 percent reached at least the middle fifth of the income distribution (placing them in the top 60 percent of the income distribution). Using income levels from families in 2010 to translate these findings into more recent terms, these results suggest that only about 16 percent of families with incomes below $27,527 would reach at least $49,514 in income a decade later. Less than 1 percent of families with incomes below $27,527 would have incomes of $117,333 or more (placing them in the top fifth) a decade later. (See Table 2.3.)

The darkly shaded bars illustrate where those starting in the highest income fifth in 1994 were in 2004. More than half (52.2 percent) of those starting in the highest fifth were still there 10 years later, and more than a quarter (27.7 percent) had fallen to the next-highest fifth. Altogether, 92.4 percent were in or above the middle fifth.

While a family's position in the income distribution largely appears to persist from one decade to another, actual individual income may change from one year to the next. Dahl and Schwabish (2008) look specifically at wage income

Figure 3B Share of families in the bottom and top income fifths in 1994 ending up in various income fifths in 2004

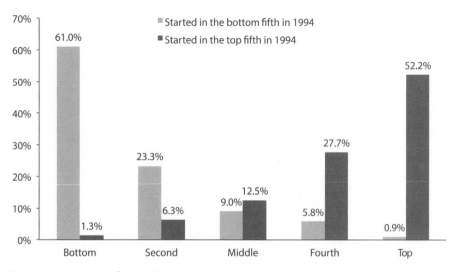

Source: Authors' analysis of Acs and Zimmerman (2008a, Table 2)

(earnings) and find that the extent of swings, or volatility, in workers' earnings from one year to the next depends on where one falls on the earnings scale. **Figure 3C** illustrates the share of workers at different earnings levels who experienced swings in annual real earnings of 25 percent or more from 2002 to 2003, and shows what portion of these shifts were increases or decreases. Workers in the bottom fifth of the earnings distribution were more than five times more likely to experience swings in earnings of 25 percent or more than those in the top fifth. Further, as a share of total fluctuations in earnings, those at the bottom were more likely to experience large drops than gains, while those at the top were more likely to experience large gains than drops. This higher earnings insecurity at the bottom may have contributed to the persistence in income position shown in the previous figure, as families may have experienced shocks to their financial well-being that kept them from moving ahead, or investing in their future.

Unlike data from the PSID, tax return data allow us to measure income and earnings mobility not just among fifths, but also within the top fifth. The U.S. Department of the Treasury (2007) examined income mobility in the United States from 1996 to 2005 using data from the tax returns of approximately 169,300 primary and secondary taxpayers (persons listed first and second on tax returns). The Treasury report breaks down the top 20 percent of taxpayers into the top 10, 5, and 1 percent of earners. Also unlike the earlier-cited PSID study, the Treasury study uses single-year estimates of income as opposed to two-year

Figure 3C Share of workers with large shifts in real annual earnings from 2002 to 2003, by earnings fifth

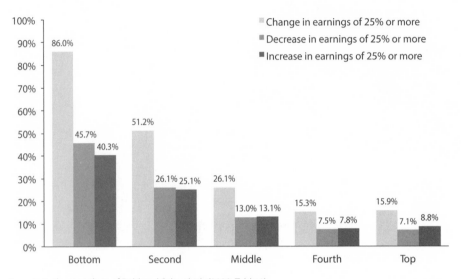

Source: Authors' analysis of Dahl and Schwabish (2008, Table 1)

averages, thereby increasing the likelihood of capturing transitory fluctuations, meaning that one specific year of data may not be particularly representative of how the tax filer was doing generally at that time (and therefore may overstate mobility at the top).

Using these data, **Figure 3D** illustrates the share of taxpayers in the top 1 percent, top 5 percent, and top 10 percent of the income distribution in 1996 who wound up in various income groups in 2005. This figure demonstrates considerable persistence in relative income at the high end of the income scale. Turning first to the darkly shaded bars, more than 40 percent of those who were in the top 1 percent of income in 1996 were still in the top 1 percent in 2005, and nearly 33 percent had fallen only to the next-highest level, where incomes were between the 95th and 99th percentiles. Taken together, nearly three-fourths (73.0 percent) of those who began in the top 1 percent were in the top 5 percent a decade later, and only about 14 percent fell into the bottom 80 percent. Nearly half (49.7 percent) of those who started in the top 5 percent of income were in the top 5 percent in 2005, which includes almost 15 percent in the top 1 percent. Nearly 73 percent of those in the top 10 percent of income in 1996 were in the top 20 percent in 2005.

In conclusion, Figures 3B and 3D illustrate the fact that many of those at the top and bottom of the income distribution tend to remain there over the span of a decade.

Figure 3D Share of taxpayers at the top of the income distribution in 1996 ending up in various income groups in 2005

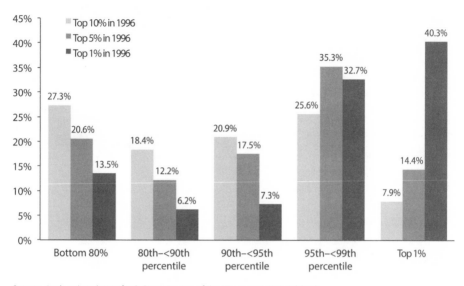

Source: Authors' analysis of U.S. Department of the Treasury (2007, Table 2)

Factors associated with intragenerational mobility

While many individuals and families maintain their place in the income distribution over 10 years, by no means does the United States have a totally stagnant, immobile society, where everyone is stuck in place decade after decade. But neither are Americans moving that far from where they start. Most who start at the bottom are there a decade later. The vast majority of those who start in the middle are still in or near the middle a decade later. Recent research has attempted to explore factors associated with these movements (or lack thereof), particularly movements to and from the bottom 20 percent of the income distribution.

In a regression framework, Acs and Zimmerman (2008b) use the PSID to examine which characteristics of individuals were related to either exiting or entering the bottom fifth of family income over two 10-year periods, 1984–1994 and 1994–2004 (**Figures 3E** and **3F**). As Figure 3E shows, being white and male are positively associated with upward mobility, while being disabled appears to impede upward mobility (the positive coefficient on disability in the latter period is not statistically significant).

The role of education is also pronounced: A household whose head has a high school education or more is far more likely than one whose head did not finish high school to leave the bottom fifth 10 years later. Although Acs and Zimmerman's analysis suggests that the interaction between marital status and work hours

Figure 3E Characteristics associated with leaving the bottom income fifth

Percent change in likelihood associated with characteristic

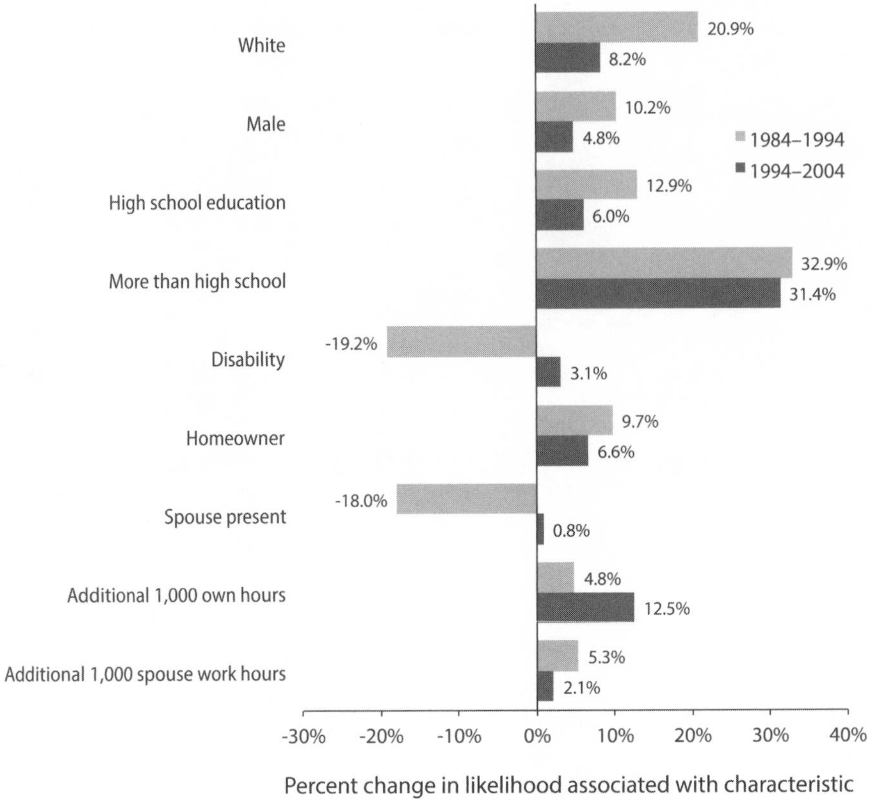

Note: Bars show how much the chance of leaving the bottom income fifth changes if the head of household has the identified characteristic relative to not having it (e.g., being white relative to being nonwhite or having a high school education relative to not having completed high school).

Source: Adapted from Acs and Zimmerman (2008b, Figure 5)

is complex and changing over time, it is clear that both the household head's and spouse's work hours are positively associated with leaving the bottom fifth.

Figure 3F illustrates factors associated with moving down into the bottom fifth of the income distribution. As already discussed, individuals and families tend not to move far over 10-year periods, so it is not surprising that households in the middle, fourth, and top fifths of income are increasingly less likely than those in the second lowest to enter the bottom fifth. Not being white or being disabled increases the likelihood of falling into the bottom fifth of income, while owning a home or having a spouse or other adult in the household decreases the likelihood of falling into the bottom fifth.

Figure 3F Characteristics associated with entering the bottom income fifth

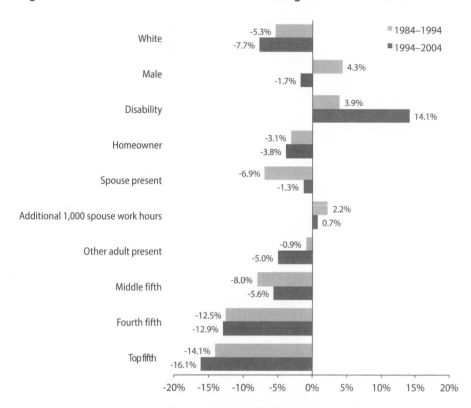

Percent change in likelihood associated with characteristic

Note: Bars show how much the chance of entering the bottom income fifth changes if the head of household has the identified characteristic relative to not having it (e.g., being white relative to being nonwhite). The change in likelihood associated with being in the middle, fourth, or top income fifth is relative to being in the second-lowest fifth.

Source: Adapted from Acs and Zimmerman (2008b, Figure 6)

It is clear that race, health, education, assets (in particular, owning a home), and other sources of family income are significant drivers of mobility in the United States. Some of these factors will be explored in greater depth later in this chapter.

Intergenerational mobility

While the prior section tracked family and individual mobility within generations as they age, this section examines mobility between generations. Intergenerational mobility is the relationship between the income of parents and that of their adult children. If one's position on the earnings, income, or wealth scale is largely a function of birth, then we are left with a more rigid society where even those with prodigious talents will be held back by entrenched class barriers. Conversely, if there is little correlation between parents' position and that of their children, we have a society with more fluidity among classes where one's economic fate can be directed through intelligence and hard work.

Economists measure the extent of intergenerational mobility by calculating the correlation between income or earnings of parents and that of their children once they grow up and earn their own income—this is known as intergenerational elasticity, or IGE. An IGE of zero would mean there is no relationship, and thus complete intergenerational mobility, with poor children just as likely as rich children to end up as rich adults. The higher the IGE, the greater the influence of one's birth circumstances on later life position.

Lee and Solon (2006) find an intergenerational elasticity of 0.49 between parents and sons and 0.46 between parents and daughters. An IGE of about one-half belies the notion of a totally fluid society with no class barriers. Yet, without various benchmarks against which to judge these correlations, it is difficult to know what to make of them. Using Solon's 1992 exercise relating IGEs to the likelihood of moving to different parts of the earnings distribution, **Figure 3G** attempts to put these intergenerational elasticities in perspective, and can assist in interpreting different IGE estimates across countries.

Taking different IGE estimates, the bars demonstrate the likelihood that sons of low-earning fathers (with earnings at or below the 10th percentile) would wind up at different points in the earnings distribution as adults. The lightly shaded bars show that while earnings mobility certainly exists at an IGE of 0.5—close to that of the United States—these children have a less than 60 percent chance of earning above the bottom fifth by adulthood. They have a 22.5 percent chance of surpassing the median and a very slight chance (4.5 percent) of ending up in the top fifth. Using wage levels from 2011, a son whose father earns about $8.52 an hour has about a 5 percent chance of earning more than $30.93 per hour as an adult. That son has only a 22.5 percent chance of exceeding wages of $17.72 an hour. (See Table 4.5.)

One way to judge the extent of mobility under these metrics is to determine how the probabilities in Figure 3G would change if the elasticity were 0.2 instead of 0.5. At the lower IGE (signifying a greater level of intergenerational mobility), the son has a 72.0 percent chance of moving out of the bottom fifth, a 39.5 percent chance of exceeding the median, and a 13.0 percent chance of reaching

Figure 3G Likelihood that sons of low-earning fathers end up above various earnings thresholds as adults, depending on estimated ease of mobility

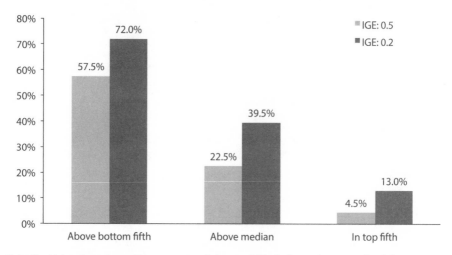

Note: The higher the estimated intergenerational elasticity (IGE), the lower the extent of mobility. Low-earning fathers are defined as those in the bottom 10th percentile.

Source: Authors' analysis of Solon (1989, Table 5)

the top fifth. In other words, his chances of becoming a middle or high earner are roughly double under the lower IGE scenario.

Cross-country comparisons

One of the most interesting areas of mobility research compares the extent of economic mobility across countries. Such comparisons shed light on the reality of the American Dream. The notion that low class barriers in America enable anyone who is willing and able to "pull themselves up by their bootstraps" and achieve significant upward mobility is deeply embedded in U.S. society. Conventional wisdom holds that class barriers in the United States are the lowest among the advanced economies, and that more Americans move up than Europeans.

Motivating this set of beliefs is the notion that there is a tradeoff between market regulation and mobility. The European economic model is characterized by higher taxes, greater regulation, more union coverage, universal health care, and a more comprehensive social contract. Because some see these policies and institutions as impediments to mobility, mobility is believed to be greater in the United States.

The belief that ambition and hard work are important in getting ahead is fairly pervasive in the United States, more so than among countries overall, according

Figure 3H Intergenerational correlations between the earnings of fathers and sons in OECD countries

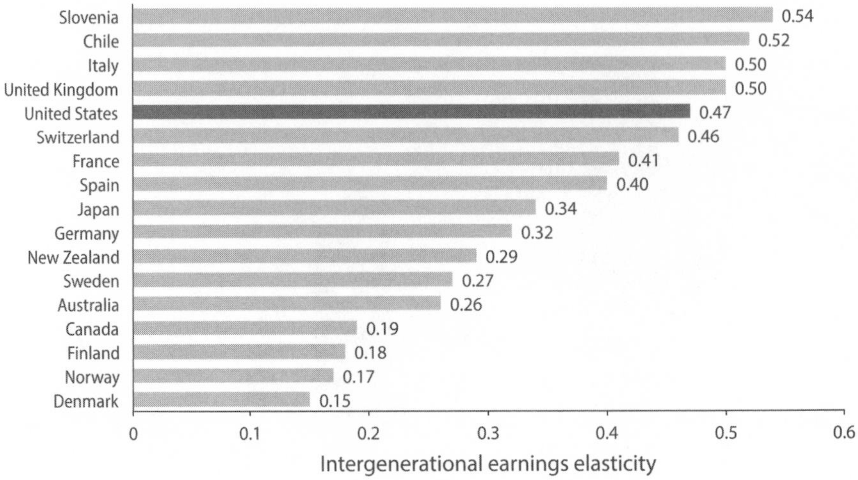

Note: The higher the intergenerational elasticity, the lower the extent of mobility.

Source: Adapted from Corak (2011, Figure 1)

to data from the International Social Survey Programme (ISSP), an annual re-search project covering various topics in social science research. In 2009, the ISSP surveyed people in 38 (mostly developed) countries on a series of questions about social inequality.

A full 91.4 percent of U.S. respondents said that ambition is "very impor-tant" or "essential" to getting ahead, compared with 71.7 percent of respondents from all the countries. An even higher share, 95.5 percent, of U.S. respondents said that hard work is very important or essential in getting ahead, compared with 76.2 percent of respondents from all the countries. Furthermore, a higher percentage of U.S. respondents (88.3 percent) said that working hard is a very important determinant of pay, compared with 77.7 percent of all respondents (International Social Survey Programme 2009).

While faith in the American Dream is deep, evidence suggests that the United States lacks policies to ensure the opportunities that the dream envisions. Ac-cording to the data, there is considerably more mobility in most other developed economies. **Figure 3H** uses intergenerational elasticities to illustrate correlations between earnings of fathers and sons in member countries of the Organisation for Economic Co-operation and Development (OECD) for which data are available. Except for the United Kingdom and Italy, the IGE of father-son earnings is higher in the United States than in the other OECD countries with similar incomes, meaning U.S. mobility is among the lowest of major industrialized economies. For example, the relatively low correlations between father-son earnings in Scandinavian countries provide a stark contradiction to the conventional wisdom. As Figure 3G showed, an IGE of 0.5, which is close to that of the United States (0.47), offers much less likelihood of moving up than an IGE of 0.2 or less, as characterizes Canada, Finland, Norway, and Denmark.

Further evidence of the lack of intergenerational mobility in the United States relative to peer countries is shown in **Figure 3I**. The figure presents the likelihood that sons of low-earning fathers (fathers in the bottom 20 percent of the wage distribution) end up in the bottom 40 percent or make it to the top 40 percent. Two-thirds (66.7 percent) of the sons of low-earning fathers in the United States end up in the bottom 40 percent, compared with about half in the other countries. Conversely, in the United States, only 18.1 percent of these sons of low-earning fathers make it to the top 40 percent, compared with 27.8 percent to 33.3 percent in the other countries.

The chance that a daughter who has a low-earning father remains in the bottom 40 percent is lower than that of sons, implying more mobility for girls than boys (**Figure 3J**). There is also more similarity across countries. Though research is only beginning to examine these gender differences, it is possible that mating patterns play a role: Higher-earning women, including those from humbler

Figure 3I Share of sons of fathers in the bottom earnings fifth ending up in the bottom or top two-fifths as adults, by country

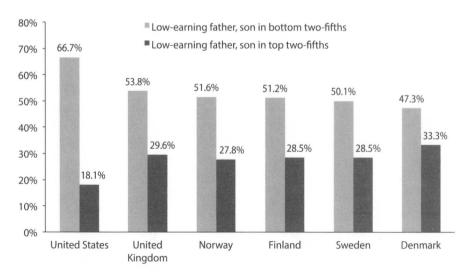

Source: Authors' analysis of Jäntti et al. (2006, Table 12)

Figure 3J Share of daughters of fathers in the bottom earnings fifth ending up in the bottom or top two-fifths as adults, by country

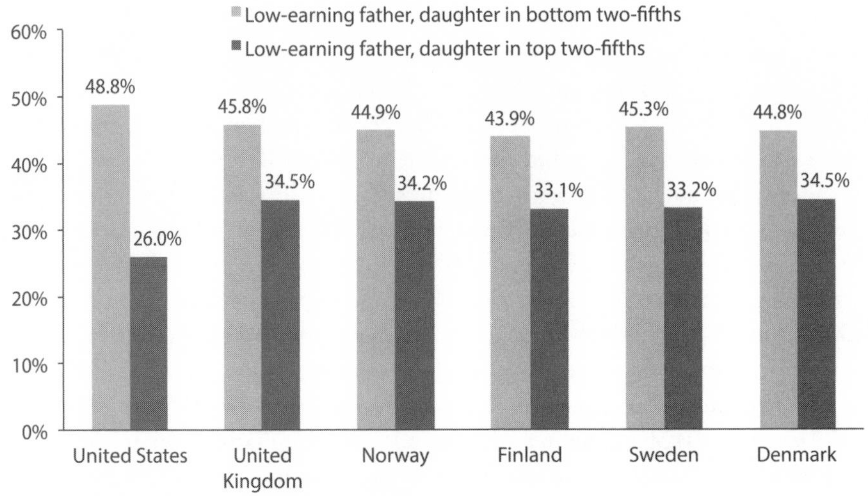

Source: Authors' analysis of Jäntti et al. (2006, Table 13)

backgrounds, tend to marry higher-earning men, and this weakens the association between their families' income while young and their incomes as adults. However, daughters of low-earning fathers in the United States are less likely to make it to the top 40 percent than daughters in the other countries pictured.

The impact of race, wealth, and education on mobility

According to polling data, more than 80 percent of Americans say they believe that hard work, ambition, staying healthy, and having a good education are essential or very important factors in upward economic mobility (Corak 2010). Only 28 percent reported that coming from a wealthy family is very important, and even fewer (15 percent) thought race was very important to economic mobility.

This section examines those beliefs by looking at the impact of race, wealth, and education. It dispels the myth that race is unimportant, and notes that since education is correlated with income, education is less of an equalizing influence than might seem the case: If children of highly educated parents have a better chance of achieving high levels of education themselves, this will lead to greater persistence of income positions (i.e., less mobility) across generations. Similarly, wealth is correlated across generations, as wealthy parents make bequests to their children. All these factors play a role in the income persistence, i.e., lack of mobility, documented thus far in this chapter.

Race

Figure 3K illustrates the extent of upward and downward mobility of children, by race. The figure focuses on children who started out in families in the bottom fourth of all families by income, and shows what share remained in the bottom fourth, and what share made it all the way to the top fourth as adults. Close to two-thirds (62.9 percent) of African American children who started out in the bottom fourth remained there as adults. The share of white children remaining in the lowest fourth was about half as large, at 32.3 percent.

Conversely, only 3.6 percent of African American children made it to the top fourth of the income scale as adults, compared with 14.2 percent of white children. Such results suggest that mobility barriers, while large for both groups, are steeper for blacks.

Figure 3L shows more significant backsliding by African American children compared with whites. The figure examines the share of children born in each earnings fifth who ended up in the bottom fifth of earnings as adults. About a quarter (26.3 percent) of white children and half (50.8 percent) of African American children ended up where they started, in the bottom earnings fifth. But even when they started out in middle-income families, more than one-third (34.1 percent) of African American children slid into the bottom fifth, compared with 15.6 percent of white children.

Figure 3K Share of children in the bottom income fourth ending up in either the bottom or top income fourth as adults, by race

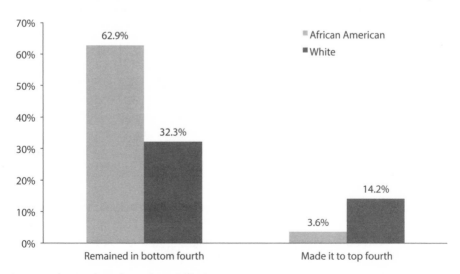

Source: Authors' analysis of Hertz (2006, Table 1)

Figure 3L Share of children from various earnings fifths ending up in the bottom fifth as adults, by race

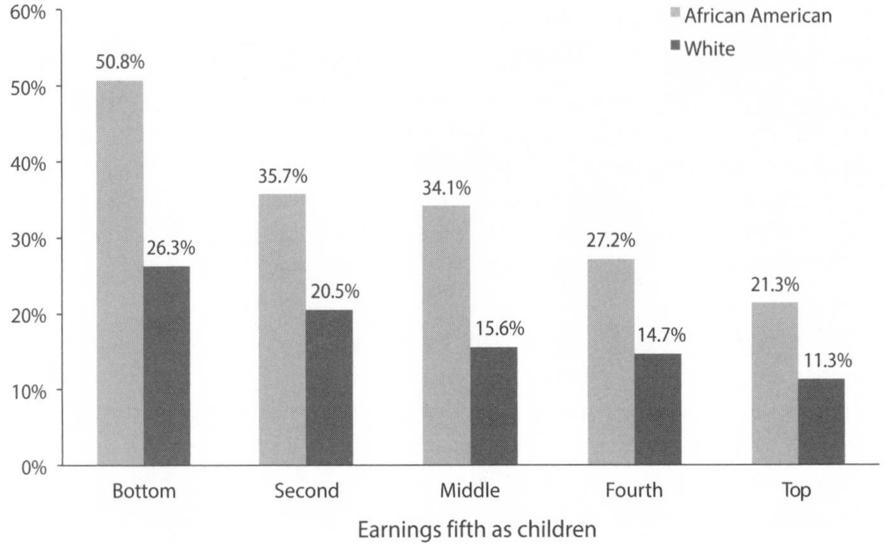

Source: Authors' analysis of Mazumder (2011, Table 7)

The finding that significant shares of children, especially African American children, are downwardly mobile warrants more careful study. One hypothesis is that middle-class African American children lack the social and societal supports—from informal networks to anti-discrimination rules—to keep them from losing ground. A related hypothesis, explored briefly below, is that higher returns to education in today's economy compared with a generation ago especially disadvantage children without access to higher education. Such access is often blocked for low-income children, even those with high cognitive skills. Since a greater share of minority children are in low-income families (see Chapter 7), they are more likely to lack access to higher education. But, as Figure 3L shows, even African American children from higher-earning families are nearly twice as likely to backslide to the lowest fifth as are white children from higher-earning families.

Wealth

Figure 3M shows the extent of wealth mobility of children given their parents' position. This figure shows the share of children who by their mid-30s reached a particular wealth fifth, given their parents' position on the wealth scale.

In a society with perfect mobility, all bars in the graph would equal 20 percent. However, more than a third (36 percent) of those with parents in the bottom

Figure 3M Share of children in the bottom and top wealth fifths ending up in various wealth fifths as adults

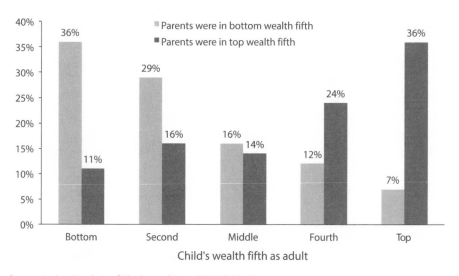

Source: Authors' analysis of Charles and Hurst (2002, Table 2)

wealth fifth ended up there as adults, while only 7 percent ended up in the top wealth fifth by their mid-30s. Adding the first two lightly shaded bars, 65 percent of children with parents in the bottom wealth fifth ended up in the bottom two-fifths (40 percent) of the wealth distribution. More than a third (36 percent) of the children of parents in the top wealth fifth also ended up in the top fifth, and 60 percent stayed in the top two-fifths.

To the extent that less wealth translates into a diminished ability to make educational investments that boost earning power, those at the bottom are even less likely to have the resources to move up themselves or create an environment enabling their children to move up. (For more detail on the distribution of wealth, see Chapter 6.)

Education

Education is a critical component of economic mobility. If children's educational attainment is closely correlated with that of their parents, a damaging class barrier inhibits merit-based mobility. As the findings presented in this section show, children from families with low incomes are much less likely to complete college, even after controlling for cognitive ability (as measured by test scores). This provides strong evidence of considerable barriers to opportunity.

One relevant issue is the quality of education accessible to children from families with different backgrounds. **Figure 3N** compares the family socioeconomic status—measured using a combination of family income and parents' educational attainment and occupation—of students in the entering classes at top-tier universities with the family socioeconomic status of students entering community colleges. In this study (Carnevale and Rose 2003), top-tier universities were defined as the nation's 146 most competitive four-year colleges, whose enrollments represent less than 10 percent of the nation's college freshman class (including four-year and two-year colleges). Nearly three-fourths (74 percent) of those entering top-tier universities came from families with the highest socioeconomic status, while 3 percent and 6 percent, respectively, came from the bottom and second-lowest socioeconomic groups—that is, the bottom half of families. In contrast, the family socioeconomic status of students entering community colleges was much more uniform.

Still, one might argue that those findings represent meritocracy at work—that students from socioeconomically advantaged families have, perhaps through their privileged positions, acquired the intellectual faculties required to gain admittance to and succeed at top schools. **Figure 3O** refutes this argument. The figure shows that even after controlling for academic ability, students of higher socioeconomic status are still more likely to complete college. Each set of bars

Figure 3N Share of entering classes at top universities and community colleges coming from families in various socioeconomic fourths

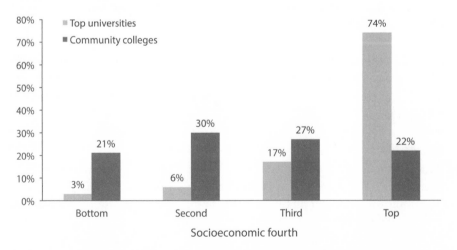

Note: Socioeconomic status is measured by a composite score that includes family income, parental education, and parental occupation.

Source: Authors' analysis of Carnevale and Rose (2003, Table 1.1)

Figure 30 Share of students completing college, by socioeconomic status and eighth-grade test scores

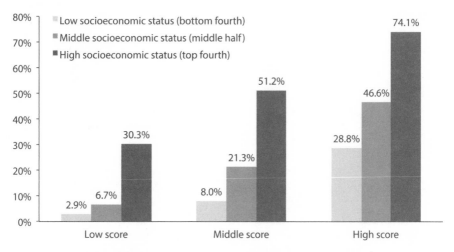

Note: Socioeconomic status is measured by a composite score that includes family income, parental education, and parental occupation.

Source: Authors' analysis of Fox, Connolly, and Snyder (2005, Table 21)

shows the share of students who completed college, based on family socioeconomic status and math test scores in eighth grade. For example, 2.9 percent of students with low scores and from families of low socioeconomic status completed college, compared with 30.3 percent of low-scoring students from high-socioeconomic-status families.

The fact that college completion was higher for each successive socioeconomic group among similarly scoring students is evidence that we do not have a completely meritocratic system. If opportunity were only a function of test scores, the bars within each score category would be equal. Instead, at every test-score level, higher socioeconomic status led to higher completion rates. Notably, 28.8 percent of high-scoring students from low-socioeconomic-status families completed college, just under the rate for low-scoring, high-socioeconomic-status students (30.3 percent). In other words, high-scoring students from families with low socioeconomic status are no more likely to complete college than low-scoring students from families with high socioeconomic status.

The barriers to higher education highlighted in these last two figures are costly in terms of reduced mobility, as shown in **Figure 3P**. By adding college completion to the intergenerational analysis, the figure reveals that educational achievement is an important mobility booster. The first set of bars shows that among children in the lowest-income families (in the bottom fifth of income),

Figure 3P Share of adults remaining in the same income fifth they were in as children, by college attainment

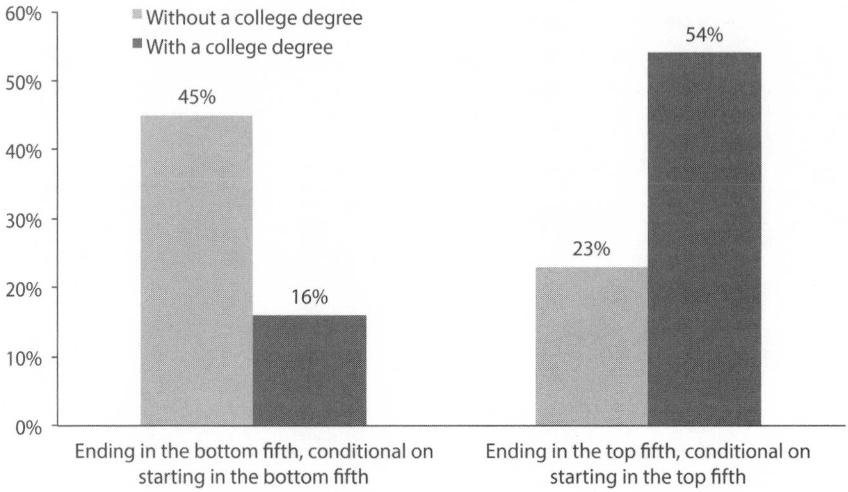

Source: Authors' analysis of Isaacs, Sawhill, and Haskins (2008, Figure 6)

college completion was strongly associated with leaving the bottom fifth in adulthood: Only 16 percent of those with a college degree remained low-income as adults, compared with 45 percent of those without a college degree. Similarly, 54 percent of high-income children who completed college were high-income (in the top fifth) as adults. While Figure 3O shows that high-socioeconomic-status children (defined as those in the top 25 percent) are much more likely to *complete* college, Figure 3P shows that 23 percent, or almost a fourth, of high-income children (defined here as those in the top 20 percent) who did *not* get a college degree still maintained their high-income status. Clearly, education *and* income/socioeconomic status matter for getting ahead and staying ahead.

An interesting corollary to the role of education in mobility is the financial return to education, that is, the wage advantage of more highly educated workers over those with less education. In the last few decades, the returns to education have increased. As Chapter 4 shows, increasing returns to education do not come close to explaining the dramatic increase in inequality over the last 30 years. Nevertheless, the increasing returns to education reinforce the immobility related to intergenerational educational attainment. That is, a child of a parent who went to college has a greater chance of attending college and thus a greater chance of benefitting from the higher relative wages earned by college-educated workers today compared with decades earlier.

These results do not imply that *everyone* should get a college degree. In fact, for the foreseeable future, the U.S. labor market will have a large number of jobs that do not require a college degree (see "Jobs of the future" in Chapter 4). While most college graduates come from the top of the income distribution, many people who are suited to go to college are not in the top of the income distribution. The policy objective is to make college accessible across the income distribution regardless of whether that is the appropriate goal for everyone.

Income inequality and mobility

The previous section explored how education, though providing no guarantee of rising from the lowest income levels, is key to getting ahead. This section examines whether income inequality itself could be driving lower mobility in the United States compared with other advanced economies. **Figure 3Q** examines the relationship between income inequality and intergenerational elasticities (IGEs) of earnings in a set of countries for which relatively comparable data can be found. In this figure, income inequality is measured by the Gini coefficient, a measure of dispersion wherein zero expresses perfect equality (everyone has exactly the same income) and one expresses maximal inequality (only one person has all the income). As explained earlier, an IGE number of zero would signify complete

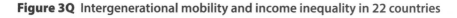

Figure 3Q Intergenerational mobility and income inequality in 22 countries

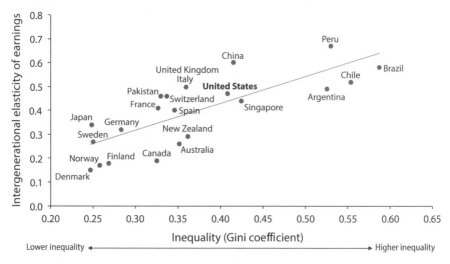

Note: The higher the Gini coefficient, the higher the inequality. The higher the intergenerational elasticity, the lower the extent of mobility. Equation for the trend line is y = 1.1253x − 0.0202 and the R² = 0.5934.

Source: Adapted from Corak (2012, Figure 2)

intergenerational mobility, with children in low-earning families just as likely to end up rich adults as children in high-earning families. The higher the IGE, the greater the influence of one's birth circumstances on later life position.

The line in the figure represents the simple regression of IGE on the inequality measure. While the IGEs across countries were calculated using different methodologies (for example uniform datasets are not available across countries), and the choice of when inequality should be measured is debatable (e.g., when the next generation is born, are teenagers, are adults, etc.), this figure illustrates a striking positive relationship between higher inequality and less mobility.

It is clear from Figure 3Q that the United States generally has higher inequality and lower mobility than many other developed countries—those shown to the lower left of the United States in the figure. If inequality does indeed lower mobility, the United States may face a future of diminished mobility as income inequality increases.

One explanation for why mobility may be lower in countries with more income inequality is suggested in **Figure 3R**. Since most advanced economies have less income inequality than the United States (see Chapter 2), the distance between income classes is smaller, so a family or an individual has less distance to cover to move from the bottom to the top. Figure 3R places the hypothetical European income distribution within that of the United States. Because income is far less dispersed (i.e., far less unequal) in the European Union, families that fall in the bottom fifth on the income scale are closer to those in the top fifth than is the case in the United States. All else equal, this would make it easier in Europe to move from one income fifth to another. Here, then, is another way in which the higher levels of inequality in the United States dampen the rates of mobility, in this case compared with other advanced, but more equal, economies.

Figure 3R Distance between income groups in the United States versus the European Union (hypothetical)

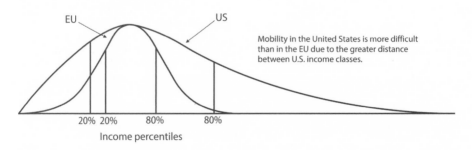

Source: Authors' illustration

It is important to remember that mobility refers to movements down the income distribution as well as up. Opportunities to move up hinge on some people moving down. Here, again, Figure 3R presents an important illustration of the income distribution in the United States versus that in Europe. Income at the 80th percentile in Europe is lower than in the United States, but income at the 20th percentile is higher. So, while Europeans can rise more quickly, if they fall, they will not fall quite as far. And, to the extent that the safety net is stronger in Europe than in the United States, the fall from higher income levels may be less of a concern. (For more on the international comparison of income distributions, particularly at the bottom, see Chapter 7.) The inadequate safety net and relative lack of opportunities for those at the bottom likely factor into the correlation between growing inequality and reduced mobility in the United States.

Has the American Dream become more or less attainable over time?

Though troubling, the high levels of income inequality reported in Chapter 2 could be somewhat less cause for alarm if successive generations of American families were able to ascend the income ladder even as the ladder's rungs grow farther apart. However, if the relationship between income inequality and mobility holds, as suggested by the previous section, then growing inequality in the United States suggests diminishing mobility.

This section examines how mobility has changed over time, exploring *trends* in intragenerational mobility, short-term income volatility, and intergenerational mobility. In short, research indicates that there has not been an acceleration in mobility that might offset the higher income inequality observed in Chapter 2.

To assess whether families are moving up or down the income distribution at an increasing or decreasing rate, we look at intragenerational income mobility— changes in families' positions in the income distribution over a relatively short time frame (generally 10 years). **Figure 3S** examines the share of people in the bottom and top family-income fifths who moved up or down, and moved far, over a 10-year period. For those who started in the top fifth at year one, moving far is defined as moving into the middle fifth or lower by year 10; similarly, for those who started in the bottom fifth, moving far entails moving to the middle fifth or higher.

Arguably, the data show increased persistence, as the richest fifth, for example, experienced a decline in those who moved down. The share of the top income fifth who moved down (the top line) between 1970 and 1980 was 48.8 percent, compared with 45.0 percent who moved down between 1995 and 2005. Those 3.8 percentage points may or may not be considered a significant increase in persistence; in other words, it may not be sufficient evidence to say that mobility has

Figure 3S Share of people in the bottom and top family income fifths moving along the income scale, 1970–1980 to 1995–2005

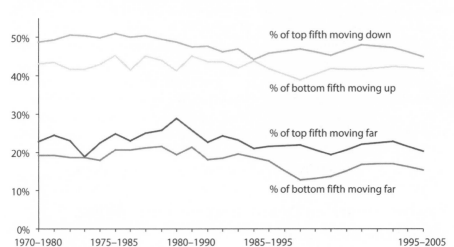

Note: Moving far means moving at least two income fifths (e.g., from the bottom to the middle fifth, or from the top to the middle fifth). Data are missing for 1986–1996, 1988–1998, 1990–2000, 1992–2002, and 1994–2004.

Source: Adapted from Bradbury (2011, Figure 2)

clearly decreased. However, it is clear that the share of top income earners who remained at the top did not shrink, evidence that mobility has clearly not increased. In fact, the share who remained in the top fifth fluctuated only 6.7 percentage points over the entire period.

Turning to the bottom line in the figure, the share of the bottom fifth who moved far (to the middle fifth or higher) fell 3.7 percentage points, while the range of estimates remained within 8.9 percentage points. Although many argue that greater income inequality in the United States is more acceptable if mobility is also greater, this figure clearly shows that mobility has not increased to offset the dramatic rise in inequality over the last 30 years.

Figure 3T focuses on another component of mobility: the probability of large income losses over two years. The figure reveals that the share of working-age individuals who experienced a large drop (50 percent or greater) in their family income climbed steadily—from about 4 percent or less in the early 1970s to nearly 10 percent in the early 2000s. While the likelihood of large income losses rises in recessions, a structural increase—an underlying increasing trend—is clear from the figure.

What conclusions can be drawn from the increase in short-term volatility? Analysts generally agree that an increase in income jumps and dips makes families

Figure 3T Share of working-age individuals experiencing a 50% or greater drop in family income over two years, 1971–2004

Note: Data after 1996 are every two years. Shaded areas denote recessions.

Source: Authors' analysis of Hacker and Jacobs (2008, Figure C)

more economically insecure; whereas a smooth, predictable income trajectory tends to benefit a family, increased "shocks," even if temporary, create the sense that a family's economic foundation may be shakier than previously thought. Thus, the trends shown here may help explain why many families report feeling less confidence in their own, and their children's, economic fate. (This is particularly true for lower earners, who experience more income volatility than higher earners, as shown earlier in Figure 3C.)

Survey data confirm this: Nearly half of young adults (18–34 years old) say that their generation will be worse off than their parents' generation (Demos and Young Invincibles 2011). But because recent polls may be highly influenced by young people's economic misfortunes in the Great Recession and its aftermath (see Chapter 5), it is valuable to examine the evidence on changes in intergenerational mobility over time.

The data certainly provide little evidence that mobility has increased in recent decades. **Figure 3U** examines the relationship between earnings of sons and income of their parents from 1950 to 2000 by graphing the implied intergenerational elasticity for 40- to 44-year-old sons in each decade. From 1950 through the 1970s, intergenerational mobility initially increased (as seen in declining elasticity). After 1980, mobility markedly declined (i.e., intergenerational elasticity increased), precisely at the same time that inequality increased (for example, see

Figure 3U Elasticities between parental income and sons' earnings, 1950–2000

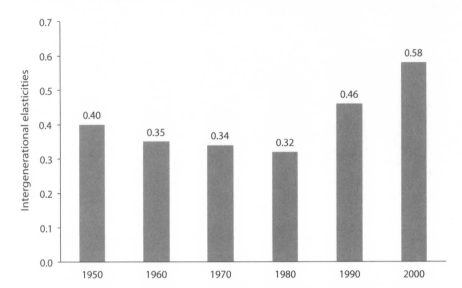

Note: The higher the intergenerational elasticity (IGE), the lower the extent of mobility. The IGEs shown are for 40- to 44-year-old sons.

Source: Authors' analysis of Aaronson and Mazumder (2007, Table 1)

Figure 2M in Chapter 2). Instead of increases in mobility that might have offset rising inequality, mobility decreased.

However, the evidence on decreasing mobility is by no means conclusive. Examining cohorts born between 1952 and 1975, Lee and Solon (2006) do not find major changes in intergenerational mobility. In many respects, it is too early to report definitive trends in mobility, particularly regarding the impact of increasing inequality. Nevertheless, it is clear that growing income inequality is expanding the distances between income classes; therefore, it would not be surprising if it were harder to jump income classes.

To more closely examine the role of opportunity in bridging the income gap over time, it again is important to review data on educational opportunities. Figures 3N, 3O, and 3P earlier in this chapter demonstrated unequal access to higher education and education's importance in moving up or remaining in the top of the income distribution. **Figure 3V** looks at how educational attainment as a function of parental income has changed over time.

The figure shows the share of 25-year-olds from each family income fourth who have not attained a college degree. The lightly shaded bars represent the share without a college degree from the earlier cohort (born 1961–1964), and the darkly shaded bars represent educational attainment of the cohort born nearly

Figure 3V Share of 25-year-olds from each family income fourth without a college degree, by birth cohort

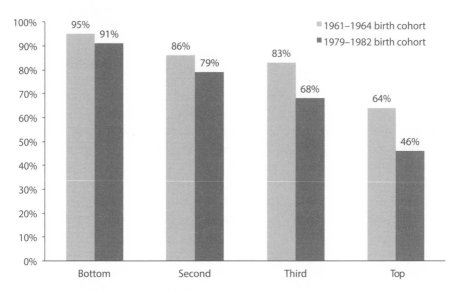

Note: Family income fourths are those of 25-year-olds when they were children.

Source: Authors' analysis of Bailey and Dynarski (2011, Figure 3)

20 years later (1979–1982). While the share of 25-year-olds without a college degree declined overall, the declines steadily increased from the bottom to the top income fourth. In other words, children from lower income groups were always more likely to lack a college degree than children from higher income groups, but those differences have become more pronounced.

Figure 3P, earlier, suggests that college education is an important mobility booster, while the lack of a college degree stunts upward mobility. Therefore, Figure 3V suggests that as those at the lower end of the income distribution continue to largely attain less than a college degree (the share without a college degree only declined from 95 percent to 91 percent), their position in the income distribution is likely to persist. Conversely, it appears that those whose family incomes fall in the top fourth are increasingly less likely to move downward over time (as the share of this group who did not obtain a college degree fell from 64 percent to 46 percent).

The findings on educational attainment hint that intergenerational mobility is likely to decline well into the future. It is too early to measure the full extent of mobility of cohorts born in periods of increasing inequality (such as the 1980s) because it is still too early in their work lives. However, the data presented in this chapter contradict the claim that increased mobility has offset rising inequality. Thus, policies that more actively encourage investment in human capital (such as those concerning health and education) could help slow these trends, making the American Dream more, instead of less, attainable.

Conclusion

Inequality means that some income earners claim a larger slice of the pie than others. Some might argue this is not such a significant problem if everyone has an equal chance of winding up at the top. Some even claim that this is the essence of the American Dream; that regardless of where you begin, if you work hard, you can have all the opportunities to succeed.

Unfortunately, income mobility—movement between income classes—is less common than broadly assumed. This suggests that the rising inequality of outcomes outlined in Chapter 2 is not counterbalanced by rising equality of opportunity.

As income and wealth become more concentrated in American society, so do access to higher education, to political power, to good neighborhoods with good schools, to decent health care, and ultimately to opportunity itself. This reality undermines a core American principle: fair opportunity for all. The indicators and trends investigated in this chapter warrant action. If market forces are failing to provide fair opportunities—and there is ample evidence to support this claim—then policy intervention is necessary.

Figure notes

Figure 3A. Median family income over the householder's working life, by birth cohort.
Data are from Current Population Survey Annual Social and Economic Supplement *Historical Income Tables*, Table F-11, "Age of Householder—Families, All Races by Median and Mean Income: 1947 to 2010." Data are inflated to 2011 dollars using the CPI-U-RS (Consumer Price Index Research Series Using Current Methods). Income measured is family money income, defined in Chapter 2.

Figure 3B. Share of families in the bottom and top income fifths in 1994 ending up in various income fifths in 2004. Data are from Acs and Zimmerman (2008a), Table 2, "Quintile Transitions, Two-Year Average Income (Relative Mobility)." Data for other years and relationships are available on *The State of Working America* website (http://stateofworkingamerica. org/).

Figure 3C. Share of workers with large shifts in real annual earnings from 2002 to 2003, by earnings fifth. Data are from Dahl and Schwabish (2008), Table 1, "Distribution of Changes in Workers' Annual Real Earnings from 2002–2003, by Sex, Age, and Earnings Quintile." The sample consists of workers age 25 to 55 who had earnings from employment covered by Social Security in 2002 or 2003. Earnings include wages and salaries, tips, and other forms of compensation; they exclude self-employment income and deferred compensation. Before the percentage change was calculated, earnings were adjusted for inflation using the CPI-U-RS.

Figure 3D. Share of taxpayers at the top of the income distribution in 1996 ending up in various income groups in 2005. Data are from U.S. Department of the Treasury (2007), Table 2, "The Degree of Mobility Remains Substantial after Restricting the Analysis to Taxpayers Included in the Panel of Tax Returns." The table uses the tax returns of primary and secondary nondependent taxpayers who were age 25 and older in 1996 and filed for both 1996 and 2005. Income cutoffs for the percentiles are based only on the tax returns of the panel population. Income is cash income in 2005 dollars.

Figure 3E. Characteristics associated with leaving the bottom income fifth. The figure is adapted from Acs and Zimmerman (2008b), Figure 5, "Characteristics Associated with Leaving the Bottom Quintile." Coefficients are based on a linear probability regression that includes these characteristics as well as dummy variables for age, the presence of children, and the presence of other adults in the household. *Own* and *spouse work hours* are measured in thousand-hour units. Acs and Zimmerman do not differentiate between spouses and permanent cohabiters, and interact the spouse hours variable with a dummy variable for the spouse's presence. Only characteristics with statistically significant coefficients in at least one time period are shown. In the 1984–1994 time period, the coefficients for *white, more than high school, disability*, and *spouse present* are statistically significant at the 99 percent confidence level; *high school education* is statistically significant at the 95 percent confidence level; and *male, homeowner, own hours*, and *spouse's hours* are statistically significant at the 90 percent confidence level. In the 1994–2004 time period, the coefficients for *more than high school* and *own hours* are statistically significant at the 99 percent confidence level.

Figure 3F. Characteristics associated with entering the bottom income fifth. The figure is adapted from Acs and Zimmerman (2008b), Figure 6, "Characteristics Associated with Entering the Bottom Quintile." Coefficients are based on a linear probability regression that includes these characteristics as well as dummy variables for age, education, the presence of children, and own work hours. *Own* and *spouse work hours* are measured in thousand-hour units. Acs and Zimmerman do not differentiate between spouses and permanent cohabiters, and interact the spouse hours variable with a dummy variable for the spouse's presence. Only characteristics with statistically significant coefficients in at least one time period are shown. In the 1984–1994 time period, the coefficients for *middle fifth*, *fourth fifth*, and *top fifth* are statistically significant at the 99 percent confidence level; *male* and *spouse present* are statistically significant at the 95 percent confidence level; and *spouse work hours* is statistically significant at the 90 percent confidence level. In the 1994–2004 time period, the coefficients for *disability*, *fourth fifth*, and *top fifth* are statistically significant at the 99 percent confidence level; *white* is statistically significant at the 95 percent confidence level; and *homeowner*, *other adult present*, and *middle fifth* are statistically significant at the 90 percent confidence interval.

Figure 3G. Likelihood that sons of low-earning fathers end up above various earnings thresholds as adults, depending on estimated ease of mobility. Data are from Solon (1989), Table 5, "Probability that Son's Long-Run Status Is in Specified Decile Given Percentile of Father's Status." Data are from the 1985 follow-up to the 1968 Panel Study of Income Dynamics. "Earnings" refers to wages.

Figure 3H. Intergenerational correlations between the earnings of fathers and sons in OECD countries. The figure is adapted from Corak (2011), Figure 1, "Comparable Estimates of the Intergenerational Elasticity between Father and Son Earnings for the United States and Twenty Four Other Countries." "Earnings" refers to wages.

Figure 3I. Share of sons of fathers in the bottom earnings fifth ending up in the bottom or top two-fifths as adults, by country. Data are from Jäntti et al. (2006), Table 12, "Intergenerational Mobility Tables—Earnings Quintile Group Transition Matrices Corrected for Age for Fathers and Sons." These results include only those father-son pairs that have non-zero earnings (wages).

Figure 3J. Share of daughters of fathers in the bottom earnings fifth ending up in the bottom or top two-fifths as adults, by country. Data are from Jäntti et al. (2006), Table 13, "Intergenerational Mobility Tables—Earnings Quintile Group Transition Matrices Corrected for Age for Fathers and Daughters." These results include only those father-daughter pairs that have non-zero earnings (wages).

Figure 3K. Share of children in the bottom income fourth ending up in either the bottom or top income fourth as adults, by race. Data are from Hertz (2006), Table 1, "Mobility Experience of Children Born in the Bottom Quartile, By Race." The quartile boundaries change over time, as real incomes grow. The black-white gap in the likelihood of upward mobility was statistically significant at the 1 percent level, and persists after controlling for one's starting position within the quartile, and for parental education.

Figure 3L. Share of children from various earnings fifths ending up in the bottom fifth as adults, by race. Data are from Mazumder (2011), Table 7, "Transition Matrices by Race Using SIPP-SSA Sample." Both panels use subsamples drawn from a sample of 16,782 men from the

Survey of Income and Program Participation and Social Security Administration data and use a multiyear average of sons' earnings over 2003–2007 and parents' earnings over 1978–1986.

Figure 3M. Share of children in the bottom and top wealth fifths ending up in various wealth fifths as adults. Data are from Charles and Hurst (2002), Table 2, "Intergenerational Transition Matrix of Age-Adjusted Log Wealth Position." The sample includes all PSID parent-child pairs in which the following conditions were met (1,491 pairs): Parents were in the survey in 1984–1989 and alive in 1989, the child was in the survey in 1999, the parent was not retired and was between age 25 and 65 in 1984, the child was between age 25 and 65 in 1999, and the child and parent both had positive wealth when measured.

Figure 3N. Share of entering classes at top universities and community colleges coming from families in various socioeconomic fourths. Data are from Carnevale and Rose (2003), Table 1.1, "Socioeconomic Status of Entering Classes." Socioeconomic status is measured by a composite score that includes family income, parental education, and parental occupation.

Figure 3O. Share of students completing college, by socioeconomic status and eighth-grade test scores. Data are from Fox, Connolly, and Snyder (2005), Table 21, "Percentage Distribution of 1988 Eighth-Graders' Educational Attainment by 2000, by Eighth-Grade Mathematics Achievement and Selected Student Characteristics: 2000." Socioeconomic status is measured by a composite score that includes family income, parental education, and parental occupation.

Figure 3P. Share of adults remaining in the same income fifth they were in as children, by college attainment. Data are from Isaacs, Sawhill, and Haskins (2008), Figure 6, "Chances of Getting Ahead for Children with and without a College Degree, from Families of Varying Income."

Figure 3Q. Intergenerational mobility and income inequality in 22 countries. The figure is adapted from Corak (2012), Figure 2, "More Inequality at a Point in Time Is Associated with Less Generational Earnings Mobility in Twenty Five Countries with Comparable Estimates of the Intergenerational Elasticity Between Father and Son Earnings." Note that data points for Italy and the United Kingdom overlap, and that the upward sloping line is the least squares fitted regression line.

Figure 3R. Distance between income groups in the United States versus the European Union (hypothetical). Authors' illustration.

Figure 3S. Share of people in the bottom and top family income fifths moving along the income scale, 1970–1980 to 1995–2005. The figure is adapted from Bradbury (2011), Figure 2, "Position-relative Origin-specific Mobility for Poorest and Richest Quintiles."

Figure 3T. Share of working-age individuals experiencing a 50% or greater drop in family income over two years, 1971–2004. Data are from Hacker and Jacobs (2008), Figure C, "Prevalence of a 50% or Greater Drop in Family Income." The line traces the share of individuals age 25 to 61 who experience a 50 percent or greater drop in before-tax total family income (adjusted for family size) from one year to two years later. Data after 1996 are only available every two years.

Figure 3U. Elasticities between parental income and sons' earnings, 1950–2000. Data are from Aaronson and Mazumder (2007), Table 1, "Estimates of the IGE Using Census IPUMS Data." Data reflect annual family income for the parents and annual earnings for the sons.

Figure 3V. Share of 25-year-olds from each family income fourth without a college degree, by birth cohort. Data are from Bailey and Dynarski (2011), Figure 3, "Fraction of Students Completing College, by Income Quartile and Year of Birth," which is based on data from the National Longitudinal Survey of Youth, 1979 and 1997. Family income fourths are those of 25-year-olds when they were children.

CHAPTER 4

Wages

The top, and very top, outpace the rest

Wage trends are the driving force behind trends in income growth and income inequality; wages and salaries constitute about three-fourths of total family income, and more than three-fourths of income of families in the broad middle class. Given the foundational nature of wages, it is discouraging that real hourly compensation (wages and benefits) of the median worker rose just 10.7 percent between 1973 and 2011. Most of this growth occurred in the late 1990s wage boom, and once the boom subsided by 2002 and 2003 real wages and compensation stagnated for most workers—college graduates and high school graduates alike. This makes the last decade a "lost decade" for wage growth. If high unemployment persists, as is likely, there will be another lost decade ahead. This chapter examines and explains the trends in wage growth and wage inequality in the last few decades that have generated this outcome.

A key feature of the labor market since 1973—one that was not present in prior decades—has been the stunning disconnect between the economy's potential for improved pay and the reality of stunted pay growth, especially since 2000. Productivity grew 80.4 percent between 1973 and 2011, when, as noted, median worker pay grew just 10.7 percent. Since 2000, productivity has grown 22.8 percent, but real compensation has stagnated across the board, generating the largest divergence between productivity and pay in the last four decades. Stagnant wage and benefit growth has not been due to poor overall economic performance; nor has it been inevitable. Rather, wage and benefit growth stagnated because the economy, as structured by the rules in place, no longer ensures that workers' pay rises in tandem with productivity.

The wedges between the growth of productivity and pay primarily are the increase in wage (and compensation) inequality and the declining share of overall income made up of wage (labor) income as it was displaced by income accruing to wealth—capital income such as profits, dividends, capital gains, and so on. The dynamic behind both of these wedges is worker disempowerment.

Wage inequality can best be understood when it is broken down into three widening wage gaps, each of which has had a differing historical trajectory. The gap within the "bottom," reflecting the difference between middle-wage (median-wage) earners and low-wage workers (10th-percentile wage earners), grew in the 1980s but has been stable or declining ever since. In contrast, the wage gap within the "top half," between high-wage (90th- or 95th-percentile wage earners) and middle-wage earners, has persistently grown since the late 1970s. The third wage gap is that between the very top wage earners, those in the top 1.0 percent and even the top 0.1 percent, relative to other high-wage earners. The very highest earners have enjoyed considerably better wage growth than all other workers for at least 30 years.

These shifts in wage inequality have derived from several key factors, which affect low-, middle-, and high-wage workers differently. High unemployment in the early and mid-1980s greatly increased wage inequality, especially at the bottom, and provided the context in which other forces—specifically, a weakening of labor market institutions and globalization—could drive up wage inequality. In contrast, the low unemployment of the late 1990s helped offset other factors driving up wage inequality. These other factors have included shifts in labor market policies and institutions, such as the severe drop in the minimum wage; deunionization; the increasing globalization of the economy (and accompanying trends in immigration, trade, and capital mobility); and the employment shift toward lower-paying service industries (such as retail trade) and away from manufacturing. High levels of unemployment in recent years have again weakened wage earners' prospects in the face of these other factors driving wage inequality.

The greatest increase in wage inequality at the bottom occurred among women and corresponded to the fall in the minimum wage over the 1980s, the high unemployment of the early and mid-1980s, and the expansion of low-wage retail jobs. High unemployment in the early and mid-1980s also knocked down wages of low-wage men and widened the wage gap at the bottom. The "90/50" and "95/50" gaps between high- and middle-wage earners have grown fairly steadily for 30 years, due to the continuing influence of globalization, deunionization, the shift to lower-paying service industries ("industry shifts"), high unemployment, and other factors that disempower workers.

Gaps at the very top grew greatly from 1979 to 2007 as the top 1.0 percent of earners more than doubled their share of total annual wages and the top 0.1 percent more than tripled their share of total wages. Wages at the top plummeted as stock prices fell in 2007–2009 but started a strong recovery in 2010. The disproportionate growth of wages at the top is closely linked to two factors: the huge growth in compensation of chief executive officers and managers, and the increasingly high wages in and expansion of the financial sector, the latter of which reflects the "financialization" of the economy. From 1978 to 2011, CEO compensation grew more than 725 percent, substantially more than the stock market and remarkably more than worker compensation, which grew by a meager 5.7 percent. Depending on the CEO compensation measure, U.S. CEOs in major companies earned 18.3 or 20.1 times more than a typical worker in 1965; this ratio grew to 29.0-to-1 or 26.5-to-1 in 1978 and to 58.5-to-1 or 53.3-to-1 by 1989. After peaking in 2000 and despite falling in the recent financial crisis, the CEO-to-worker compensation ratio was at 231.0-to-1 or 209.4-to-1 in 2011, substantially above the historic norm.

Rising inequality has been accompanied by deteriorating job quality for many workers, driven largely by a decline in the extent and quality of employer-provided benefits, most notably pensions and health insurance. Employer-provided health care coverage eroded from 1979 until 1993–1994, when it stabilized, and then began falling again after 2000; coverage dropped from 69.0 percent in 1979 to 58.9 percent in 2000 to 53.1 percent in 2010 (the latest year of data), a 5.8 percentage-point fall since 2000. Employer-provided pension coverage tended to rise in the 1990s but receded by 5.5 percentage points from 2000 to 2010 (the latest year of data) to just 42.8 percent. Pension plan quality also receded, as the share of workers in defined-benefit plans fell from 39 percent in 1980 to just 18 percent in 2004 (the latest year of data). Correspondingly, the share of workers with a defined-contribution plan (and no other plan) rose from 8 percent to 31 percent.

Young workers' prospects are a barometer of the strength of the labor market: When the labor market is strong for workers overall, the prospects for young workers are very strong, and when the labor market is weak, their prospects are very weak. Since 2000, wages have fallen among every key entry-level group—both high school and college graduates, and both men and women. For instance, in 2011 the entry-level hourly wages of young male and female high school graduates were roughly 9 percent lower than in 2000. Between 2000 and 2011, entry-level wages fell 7.6 percent for male college graduates and 6.0 percent for female college graduates.

A surprising feature of the post-2000 period is the dramatically disappointing wage trend for college graduates: From 2000 to 2011, the bottom 70 percent had stagnant or declining wages, and the bottom 90 percent had stagnant or declining wages from 2002 or 2003 to 2011. Poor wage growth occurred over roughly the last 10 years in nearly every occupation in which college graduates worked, including business and professional occupations. An increasing share of college graduates, especially younger college graduates, work in occupations that do not require a college education. These trends cast doubt on the oft-repeated story that wage inequality is increasing due to shortages of skilled and educated workers in a time of rapid technological change.

Wage inequality is, however, affected by the decline in unionization, which lowered wages in the middle. Unionized workers earn higher wages than comparable nonunion workers and also are 18.3 percent more likely to have health insurance, 22.5 percent more likely to have pension coverage, and 3.2 percent more likely to have paid leave. The erosion of unionization among blue-collar men (from 43.1 percent in 1978 to just 17.8 percent in 2011) accounted for about three-fourths of the 10.1 percentage-point growth of the white-collar/blue-collar wage gap among men from 1978 to 2011. Research incorporating the impact of unions on wage norms and standards as well as unionism's direct impact on unionized workers shows that weaker unions were a major factor in rising wage inequality, accounting for about a third of the growth of wage inequality among men and around a fifth of the growth of wage inequality among women from 1973 to 2007.

Low-wage workers, particularly women, have also been hard-hit by the decline in the real value of the minimum wage. In 2011, the real minimum wage was 12.1 percent lower than in 1967, meaning low-wage workers, despite being older and better-educated than in the late 1960s, had a lower wage floor. The weakness of the minimum wage is more apparent when noting that in 2011 it was just 37 percent of the typical worker's hourly wage, while in the late 1960s it averaged about half the typical worker's hourly wage. The lowering of the minimum wage in the 1980s caused a severe drop in wages of low-wage women, who are the chief beneficiaries of the legislated minimum.

Will the jobs of the future require far more skills and education and necessitate a wholesale upgrading of workforce educational attainment? The jobs of the future will, in fact, require greater education credentials, but not to any large extent. In 2010 the occupational composition of jobs required that 20.0 percent of the workforce have a college degree or more. This share will rise modestly to 20.5 percent in 2020 as a result of occupational change. Whether workers in the future enjoy higher wages will depend on whether wages rise for particular occupations rather than on whether there is any shift of workers into better-paid and more-skilled occupations.

The first half of this chapter documents changes in the various dimensions of the wage structure, that is, changes in average wages and compensation, and changes by occupation, gender, wage level (by decile and the top 1.0 percent), education level, age, and race and ethnicity. Shifts in the various dimensions of wage inequality are assessed and explained in the second half of the chapter, which focuses on particular factors such as unemployment, industry shifts, deunionization, the minimum wage, globalization, immigration, and technology/skills.

Table notes and figure notes at the end of this chapter provide documentation for the data, as well as information on methodology, used in the tables and figures that follow.

Describing wage trends

The initial part of this chapter presents the key trends in wages, benefits, and overall compensation that have driven the corresponding trends in wage income of families and households—particularly the trend of growing wage and income inequality. The focus is mainly on the hourly wages of individual workers because it is the dynamics of hourly wages that have dominated trends in annual wages. Data on all nonwage benefits and on particular benefits such as health insurance, pension benefits, and paid leave are also examined. The sections below review wage trends of workers differentiated by occupation, gender, wage level (by decile and the top 1.0 percent), education level, age, race, and ethnicity. The remainder of the chapter provides an explanation of the trends in wages and wage inequality.

The decade of lost wage growth

As highlighted in the analyses of incomes in Chapter 2, wage stagnation has been a key factor driving the stagnation (or decline) in incomes since 2000, a period including the entire business cycle from 2000 to 2007 as well as the recession and period of high unemployment from 2007 through 2011. This stagnation occurred as a consequence of the weak recovery of the 2002–2007 period and the recession-related income losses caused by the financial crisis and its aftermath.

The data presented in Chapter 2 showed that slower growth in hourly wages and a fall in annual work hours translated into poor growth in middle-class families' annual earnings (combining those of all earners in the family) during the last business cycle and the recession. This section further explores these trends by examining the hours and wages of individual workers. Specifically, this section highlights the wage trends underpinning the lost decade: Despite continued strong productivity growth, real hourly wages failed to improve for the vast majority of the workforce, including those with a college degree, during the 2002–2007 recovery period and the recession and its aftermath.

To understand the period starting in 2000, it is necessary to put it into the context of the extraordinary real wage growth of the late 1990s. Broad-based real wage growth took hold in 1996, due to falling and sustained low unemployment amid accelerated productivity growth (and a minimum-wage increase). This late 1990s wage boom stands out as the sole period of sustained real wage growth for low-wage and middle-wage workers since 1973, as will be explored below. The important point for our current discussion is that the momentum of wage growth in the late 1990s carried over into the decade of the 2000s, leading to real wage growth even during the downturn and continuing through 2003. This trend can

Figure 4A Cumulative change in total economy productivity and real hourly compensation of selected groups of workers, 1995–2011

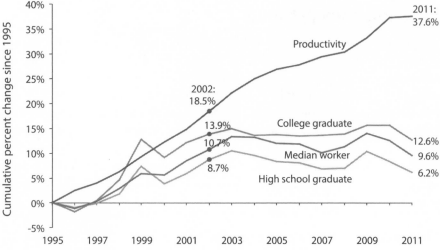

Source: Authors' analysis of unpublished Total Economy Productivity data from the Bureau of Labor Statistics Labor Productivity and Costs program, Bureau of Economic Analysis National Income and Product Accounts data, and Current Population Survey Outgoing Rotation Group microdata

be seen in **Figure 4A**, which shows the real hourly compensation growth (relative to 1995) of three groups of workers: high school graduates, college graduates, and the median worker, representing middle-wage workers. We start the analysis in 1995 since the productivity acceleration of the late 1990s happened soon thereafter. For all three groups, compensation grew strongly until 2003 and stagnated thereafter. (The strong bump in compensation in 2009 is the consequence of a decline in inflation that year so that even low nominal, i.e., not inflation-adjusted, compensation growth yielded a real compensation increase.) Figure 4A also includes the growth of economy-wide productivity, which grew strongly—37.6 percent—over the entire period of the late 1990s through 2011. In contrast, real hourly compensation grew a much more modest 12.6 percent for college graduates and just 9.6 percent for the median worker. The counterpoising of productivity and compensation trends highlights another key dimension of living standards and wage trends: the divergence between the economy's increased ability to provide rising living standards and its failure to do so. This will be explored in further detail later in this chapter.

With this framework in mind, we now turn to an exploration of various trends in the growth of wages, benefits, and compensation.

Contrasting work hours and hourly wage growth

To understand changes in wage trends, it is important to distinguish between trends in annual, weekly, and hourly wages. Trends in annual wages, for instance, are driven by changes in both hourly wages and the amount of time spent working (weeks worked per year and hours worked per week). Likewise, weekly wage trends reflect changes in hourly pay and weekly hours.

Table 4.1 illustrates the importance of distinguishing between annual, weekly, and hourly wage trends. For instance, from 2007 to 2010, the years of the recent downturn, average annual wages fell 0.3 percent annually. The reason for this drop was the large decline in average annual hours worked, which fell 1.2 percent annually, rather than any trend in hourly wages (which actually grew 0.9 percent annually). The point is that trends in both weekly wages and annual wages

Table 4.1 Average wages and work hours, 1967–2010 (2011 dollars)

	Productivity per hour (2005=100)	Real wage levels			Hours worked		
		Annual wages	Weekly wages	Hourly wages	Annual hours	Weeks/ year	Hours/ week
1967	52.3	$29,555	$678.58	$17.24	1,716	43.5	39.3
1973	60.2	34,378	791.40	20.50	1,679	43.4	38.6
1979	64.2	34,632	789.79	20.34	1,703	43.8	38.8
1989	73.1	37,685	830.34	21.13	1,783	45.4	39.3
1995	78.8	38,768	843.83	21.22	1,827	45.9	39.8
2000	88.5	43,616	929.04	23.24	1,876	46.9	40.0
2007	102.0	43,615	920.91	23.16	1,883	47.4	39.8
2010	108.2	43,194	928.18	23.79	1,815	46.5	39.0
Annual growth rate*							
1967–1973	2.4%	2.5%	2.6%	2.9%	-0.4%	0.0%	-0.3%
1973–1979	1.1	0.1	0.0	-0.1	0.2	0.2	0.1
1979–1989	1.3	0.8	0.5	0.4	0.5	0.3	0.1
1989–2000	1.7	1.3	1.0	0.9	0.5	0.3	0.2
1989–1995	1.3	0.5	0.3	0.1	0.4	0.2	0.2
1995–2000	2.3	2.4	1.9	1.8	0.5	0.4	0.1
2000–2007	2.0	0.0	-0.1	-0.1	0.1	0.1	-0.1
2007–2010	2.0	-0.3	0.3	0.9	-1.2	-0.6	-0.6

* Log growth rate

Source: Authors' analysis of unpublished Total Economy Productivity data from the Bureau of Labor Statistics Labor Productivity and Costs program, Current Population Survey Annual Social and Economic Supplement microdata, and Murphy and Welch (1989)

are affected by trends in work time, such as weekly hours or weeks worked yearly. In other periods the annual wage growth was boosted by increased annual hours worked. In fact, this was true in every business cycle in the 1970s, 1980s, 1990s, and 2000s, as can be seen by the increased growth in annual hours.

Table 4.1 shows the sharp acceleration in hourly wage growth (to 1.8 percent) from 1995 to 2000, which was a clear departure from the measly 0.1 percent growth of the earlier part of that business cycle (1989–1995) and the 0.4 percent growth of the prior business cycle (1979–1989). Despite strong productivity growth in the succeeding business cycle, 2000–2007 (nearly on par with the 2.3 percent growth of the late 1990s), real hourly wage growth was stagnant (-0.1 percent). The stronger real wage growth of the 2007–2010 period is an artifact of the fall in energy prices that led to negative inflation in 2009.

Not surprisingly, trends in family income correspond to the shift from strong annual wage growth in the late 1990s to the falloff in income among working-age families in the next business cycle (2000–2007). For instance, the strong pickup in overall wage growth in the late 1990s, along with an even stronger increase in wage growth at the bottom end of the wage scale (detailed below), is the main factor behind the widespread improvements in family income (discussed in Chapter 2) and reductions in poverty (discussed in Chapter 7) seen in the late 1990s.

This chapter focuses on the hourly pay levels of the workforce and its subgroups in order to distinguish changes in earnings resulting from more (or less) pay from those stemming from more (or less) work. Also, the hourly wage can be said to represent the "true" price of labor (exclusive of benefits, which we analyze separately). Moreover, changes in the distribution of annual earnings have been predominantly driven by changes in the distribution of hourly wages and not by changes in work time. Chapter 5 addresses employment, unemployment, underemployment, and other issues related to changes in work time and opportunities.

Contrasting compensation and wage growth

A worker's pay, or total compensation, is made up of both nonwage payments, referred to as fringe benefits, and wages. Much of the analysis in this chapter focuses on wages because there are no data on workers' hourly compensation, including benefits, that can be analyzed by wage level, race/ethnicity, gender, or education. But the available data do allow an examination of overall compensation trends and how they differ from overall wage trends.

Table 4.2 uses the two data series that are available to examine changes in compensation. We employ the wage and compensation data that are part of the National Income and Product Accounts (NIPA) to track the historical trends from 1948 to 1989. These NIPA data are the Commerce Department's measure of the size of the national economy, termed the gross domestic product. Compensation levels exceed wage levels because they include employer payments for

Table 4.2 Average hourly pay and pay inequality, 1948–2011 (2011 dollars)

	Wages and salaries	Benefits*	Total compensation	Benefit share of compensation
*Real hourly pay (NIPA)***				
1948	$9.69	$0.53	$10.21	5.1%
1989	20.14	4.61	24.75	18.6
Annual percent change				
1948–1973	2.6%	7.3%	3.0%	
1973–1979	0.2	5.2	1.0	
1979–1989	0.8	1.0	0.8	
*Real hourly pay (ECEC)***				
1987	$21.08	$5.30	$26.38	20.1%
1989	20.68	5.30	25.98	20.4
1995	20.23	5.18	25.41	20.4
2000	21.43	4.79	26.22	18.3
2007	22.74	5.60	28.34	19.8
2011	22.53	5.57	28.10	19.8
Annual percent change				
1989–2000	0.3%	-0.9%	0.1%	
1989–1995	-0.4	-0.4	-0.4	
1995–2000	1.2	-1.6	0.6	
2000–2007	0.9	2.3	1.1	
2007–2011	-0.2	-0.2	-0.2	

Measures of inequality	Wages		Compensation	
	Std. dev.	Gini	Std. dev.	Gini
1987	0.564	0.317	0.597	0.326
1997	0.578	0.329	0.620	0.346
2007	0.592	0.340	0.639	0.354
Change, 1987–2007	**0.028**	**0.023**	**0.042**	**0.028**

* Includes payroll taxes, health, pension, and other nonwage benefits
** Deflated by personal consumption expenditures (PCE) index for all items, except health, which is deflated by PCE medical index. NIPA data are for the entire economy; ECEC data are for the private sector.

Source: Authors' analysis of Bureau of Labor Statistics National Compensation Survey employment cost trends and benefits data, Bureau of Economic Analysis National Income and Product Accounts, and Pierce (2010)

health insurance, pensions, and payroll taxes (primarily payments toward Social Security and unemployment insurance). We track more recent trends with data on the private sector drawn from the Bureau of Labor Statistics Employer Costs for Employee Compensation (ECEC) survey, a more detailed source that provides the value of wages and employer-provided benefits for each year since 1987, the first survey year. These data vary from those in NIPA because they describe only the private sector (government employment is excluded) and because the definition of "hours worked" is different.

It is important to note that these compensation data are averages covering the entire economy or private sector, from low-paid hourly workers to high-paid executives. Since we know there has been a sizable rise in wage inequality, we also know that trends in wages or compensation of the "average" worker diverge sharply from (i.e., rise faster than) trends for typical or median workers. Therefore, compensation trends presented in Table 4.2 do not correspond to those experienced by middle-wage or typical workers.

Measured over the long term, benefits have become a more important part of the average worker's total compensation package. In 1948 payroll taxes and health and pension benefits made up only 5.1 percent of compensation. By 1989 the share had risen to 18.6 percent. But the benefit share of compensation has remained largely flat since 1987—according to ECEC data, it was 20.1 percent in 1987 and 19.8 percent in both 2007 and 2011. In other words, the growth of total compensation has largely paralleled that of wages over the last 20 or 30 years. It is still worthwhile to track each component measure of compensation separately when possible because they can, and have, diverged in particular periods (benefits even fell in the late 1990s but then regained ground in recent years). One implication of compensation and wages growing roughly in tandem is that analyses (such as the one below) that focus on wage trends are using an appropriate proxy for compensation, at least on average. However, analyses of wage growth sometimes overstate the corresponding growth of compensation, as in the latter 1990s, and sometimes understate compensation growth, as in 2000–2007.

Table 4.2 also presents inequality measures for compensation and wages in 1987, 1997, and 2007. Inequality of compensation is greater than inequality of wages in each year using either the standard deviation (a measure that shows the degree to which data vary from the average) or the Gini coefficient measure, a measure of dispersion wherein zero expresses perfect equality (everyone has exactly the same wage) and one expresses maximal inequality (only one person has all the wage income). Moreover, the growth of inequality between 1987 and 2007 was greater for total compensation than for wages, meaning that adding benefits to the overall picture does not negate findings using wage data but actually strengthens them. Again, these results may differ when considering particular time periods or when examining particular aspects of the pay structure, such as the difference between the top and the middle versus the difference between the middle and the bottom.

From 2000 to 2007, benefits grew much faster than average wages, 2.3 percent annually versus 0.9 percent, but since benefits made up less than 20 percent of compensation, the rise in total compensation (1.1 percent annually) was closer to the wage trend. A different trend prevailed in the late 1990s, when benefits declined by 1.6 percent annually while wages rose 1.2 percent. Hourly total compensation, in fact, grew faster from 2000 to 2007 than in the late 1990s; while wage growth slowed in the later period, compensation growth accelerated. This comparison is a bit skewed for reasons we have identified previously—the momentum of fast wage growth in the late 1990s carried over into the early part of the 2000s but then disappeared. The trends over the recovery from 2002 to 2007 (after the earlier wage momentum had subsided) affirm this, as annual wage and compensation growth in that period were just 0.4 percent and 0.7 percent, respectively (not shown in the table).

Over the four years since the recession began in 2007, compensation fell 0.2 percent a year, in line with the 0.2 percent annual declines in both benefits and wages.

Trends in specific benefits such as health insurance and pensions are examined later in this chapter.

Wages of production and nonsupervisory workers

The pattern of growth or decline in wages of the various segments of the workforce since 1973 in characterized by at least three distinct "wage regimes"—one from 1973 to 1995 that consisted of stagnant average wage growth and real wage reductions for the vast majority, one from 1995 into the early 2000s that was characterized by broad-based real wage growth, and one that encompasses the recovery starting in 2002 to 2003 and includes the recessionary period following 2007, a new period of stagnant real wages.

The data in **Table 4.3** and **Figure 4B** show wage trends for the 80 percent of employment consisting of either production workers in manufacturing or nonsupervisory workers in other parts of the private sector. This category includes factory workers, construction workers, and a wide variety of service-sector workers ranging from restaurant and clerical workers to nurses and doctors; it leaves out higher-paid managers and supervisors. These data allow us to start our analysis in 1947. (Note that Table 4.3 and Figure 4B refer to wages as "earnings," in keeping with how the Bureau of Labor Statistics describes the data.)

From 2007 to 2011 hourly wages of production/nonsupervisory workers grew 0.7 percent a year. In the business cycle from 2000 to 2007, hourly wages grew 0.5 percent per year, though growth was only 0.2 percent a year during the 2002–2007 recovery (not shown on Table 4.3). As discussed earlier, the momentum of the strong wage growth of the late 1990s carried over into the first few years of the 2000s. Annual wage growth over the entire 2000–2007 period was substantially less than the 1.4 percent annual growth of the 1995–2000 period.

The differences in trends between the early and latter parts of the 1989–2000 period are striking: Hourly wages fell 0.1 percent a year from 1989 to 1995 and then grew 1.4 percent a year from 1995 to 2000, a turnaround of 1.5 percentage points. The business cycles of the 1970s and 1980s were the most disappointing periods for wage growth, as real wages of production/nonsupervisory

Table 4.3 Hourly and weekly earnings of private production and nonsupervisory workers, 1947–2011 (2011 dollars)

	Real average earnings	
	Hourly	Weekly
1947	$10.67	$428.98
1967	16.79	636.48
1973	18.74	690.63
1979	18.31	651.82
1989	17.17	592.72
1995	17.08	586.44
2000	18.32	628.57
2007	18.91	640.23
2011	19.47	654.87
Annual percent change		
1947–1967	2.3%	2.0%
1967–1973	1.9	1.4
1973–1979	-0.4	-1.0
1979–1989	-0.6	-0.9
1989–2000	0.6	0.5
1989–1995	-0.1	-0.2
1995–2000	1.4	1.4
2000–2007	0.5	0.3
2007–2011	0.7	0.6
1979–2011	0.2	-0.1

Note: Private production and nonsupervisory workers account for more than 80 percent of wage and salary employment.

Source: Authors' analysis of Bureau of Labor Statistics Current Employment Statistics

workers fell 0.6 percent annually from 1979 to 1989 and 0.4 percent annually from 1973 to 1979.

Over the longer term, from 1979 to 2011, wages were up only slightly, from $18.31 in 1979 to $19.47 in 2011, growth of just 0.2 percent per year over 32 years—virtually stagnant—despite some rapid growth in the late 1990s. This is in stark contrast to the early postwar trends: Between 1947 and 1967 real hourly earnings grew by 2.3 percent annually, and from 1967 to 1973 the growth was still a strong 1.9 percent each year. Figure 4B tracks the change in hourly wages and compensation of production/nonsupervisory workers over the entire period.

Figure 4B Real hourly earnings and compensation of private production and nonsupervisory workers, 1947–2011

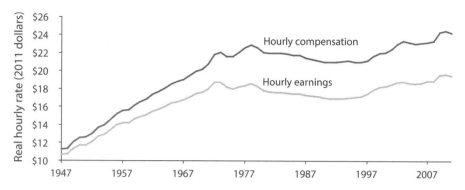

Note: Private production and nonsupervisory workers account for more than 80 percent of wage and salary employment.

Source: Authors' analysis of Bureau of Economic Analysis National Income and Product Accounts data and Bureau of Labor Statistics Current Employment Statistics

Wages and compensation both grew strongly from 1947 to 1973 and then stagnated for typical workers after 1973 (other than in the late 1990s).

Table 4.3 also shows that the trend in weekly earnings corresponds closely to that of hourly earnings. However, weekly earnings grew more slowly (or fell faster) in each of the subperiods between 1947 and 1989 because weekly work hours declined. The weekly earnings of production and nonsupervisory workers in 2011 were $654.87 (in 2011 dollars), roughly similar to weekly earnings in 1979 and more than $35 less than in 1973.

Wage trends by wage level

For any given trend in average wages, particular groups of workers will experience different outcomes if wage inequality grows, as it has throughout approximately the last three decades. The pattern of inequality has shifted over time: Inequality grew across the board in the 1980s, and grew between the top and the middle throughout the 1990s and 2000s. This is why it is important to peer beneath the "average" and examine wage trends of groups of workers differentiated by occupation, education level, and so on. However, any analysis comparing different groups necessarily overlooks possible changes in inequality *within* the groups. This section examines wage trends by wage level, or percentile (the 60th percentile, for instance, is the wage at which a worker earns more than 60 percent of all earners but less than 40 percent of all earners), an analysis that has the advantage of capturing all of the changes in the wage structure. Though all of the wage shifts can be noted by this analysis, the changes across groups (by education or age) and within groups (among those with particular education or ages) remain to be identified.

Table 4.4 provides data on wage trends for workers at each decile (every tenth percentile) in the wage distribution, thus allowing an examination of wage growth (or decline) of low-, middle-, and high-wage earners. Data are presented for the 95th percentile, the best measure of wages at the top of the wage structure that can be provided with these data (other data that can track wages in the top 1.0 percent and the top 0.1 percent are reviewed in a later section). The data are presented for the business cycle peak years of 1973, 1979, 1989, 2000, and 2007 as well as for 1995 (the point during the 1990s business cycle after which wages grew dramatically) and for 2011 (the last year for which data are available). The table also shows the percent change in wages over certain time periods. The

Table 4.4 Hourly wages of all workers, by wage percentile, 1973–2011 (2011 dollars)

	Wage by percentile*									
	10	20	30	40	50	60	70	80	90	95
Real hourly wage										
1973	$8.07	$9.75	$11.58	$13.47	$15.45	$17.72	$20.58	$23.53	$29.57	$37.10
1979	8.53	9.73	11.43	13.45	15.21	17.64	20.84	24.29	29.71	36.28
1989	7.29	9.08	10.89	13.01	15.12	17.66	21.01	25.12	31.72	38.99
1995	7.42	9.07	10.84	12.75	14.84	17.57	20.94	25.35	32.76	41.09
2000	8.24	10.15	11.85	13.71	15.99	18.92	22.43	27.25	35.62	45.44
2007	8.45	10.25	11.97	14.04	16.40	19.46	23.10	28.50	38.23	49.39
2011	8.16	9.86	11.74	13.88	16.07	19.03	23.00	28.80	38.49	49.74
Percent change										
1973–1979	5.7%	-0.1%	-1.3%	-0.2%	-1.6%	-0.5%	1.3%	3.2%	0.5%	-2.2%
1979–1989	-14.6	-6.7	-4.7	-3.3	-0.6	0.1	0.8	3.4	6.8	7.5
1989–2000	13.1	11.8	8.9	5.4	5.8	7.1	6.8	8.5	12.3	16.5
1989–1995	1.8	-0.1	-0.5	-2.0	-1.8	-0.5	-0.3	0.9	3.3	5.4
1995–2000	11.1	11.9	9.4	7.5	7.7	7.7	7.1	7.5	8.7	10.6
2000–2007	2.5	1.0	1.0	2.5	2.6	2.9	3.0	4.6	7.3	8.7
2007–2011	-3.4	-3.9	-1.9	-1.2	-2.0	-2.2	-0.5	1.0	0.7	0.7
1979–2011	-4.3	1.3	2.7	3.2	5.7	7.9	10.3	18.6	29.6	37.1

* The xth-percentile wage is the wage at which x% of the wage earners earn less and (100-x)% earn more.

Source: Authors' analysis of Current Population Survey Outgoing Rotation Group microdata

bottom row presents the percent change in wages over the entire 1979–2011 period as a metric for assessing the longer-term trend; it uses 1979 as the last year of low unemployment (the cyclical peak) before the period of steady growth in wage inequality took hold.

From 2007 to 2011 wages fell for the bottom 70 percent of the workforce and rose by 1 percent or less at the 80th, 90th, and 95th percentiles. Some of this erosion stems from higher inflation in 2011 driven by rising energy prices. However, the main cause of eroded real wages has been low nominal wage growth, the result of recessionary conditions. For instance, the median wage fell a total of 2.0 percent between 2007 and 2011, and no matter how low inflation would have been absent higher energy prices, there still would have been a decline in inflation-adjusted wages of the median worker between 2007 and 2011.

Wage growth was very modest in the prior business cycle from 2000 to 2007, with the median rising just 2.6 percent. As noted previously, all of the wage growth between 2000 and 2007 occurred in the first few years of that period and was due to the momentum from the fast wage growth of the late 1990s. Wage growth was significantly higher for wage earners at the 90th and 95th percentiles, who saw their wages grow 7.3 percent and 8.7 percent, respectively. On the other hand, low-wage workers at the 10th percentile had wage growth comparable to that of the median worker. Thus, from 2000 to 2007 wage inequality grew between the top and the middle but not between the middle and the bottom, as we will explore further.

Wages grew strongly across the board from 1995 to 2000, rising at least 7 percent at every wage level. Remarkably, the fastest growth—over 11 percent—occurred at the two bottom wage levels (the 10th and 20th percentiles). However, workers with the very highest wages, at the 95th percentile, saw almost comparable wage growth of 10.6 percent. Wages grew more slowly at every wage level from 2000 to 2007 compared with 1995–2000. Wage deceleration in the 2000s has been pervasive, especially since 2003.

The deterioration in real wages from 1979 to 1995 (looking at the 1979–1989 and 1989–1995 periods) was both broad and uneven. Wages were stagnant or fell for the bottom 60 percent of wage earners from 1979 to 1995 and grew modestly for higher-wage workers; the growth was just 3.4 percent at the 80th percentile from 1979 to 1989 and another 0.9 percent from 1989 to 1995. Wage growth at the 90th and 95th percentiles, however, was more than double that at the 80th percentile from 1979 to 1995. Starting in the early 1990s, low-wage workers experienced wage growth either more than or comparable to that of middle-wage workers, so that the wage gap between the middle and bottom lessened and then stabilized. Increases in the minimum wage in the early and late 1990s and the drop in unemployment in the late 1990s can explain this trend. For much of the last decade, the rates of wage growth for low- and middle-wage

Figure 4C Cumulative change in real hourly wages of men, by wage percentile, 1979–2011

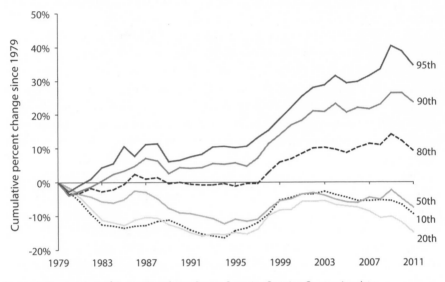

Source: Authors' analysis of Current Population Survey Outgoing Rotation Group microdata

workers were about equal. Thus, the pattern of wage inequality since 1989 has generally been one of continual expanding of the wage gap between the highest earners and middle-wage earners but more or less parallel wage growth for low- and middle-wage workers.

This overall picture, however, masks different outcomes for men and women. **Figure 4C** shows the cumulative change in real hourly wages (relative to 1979) of men at key wage levels. The long-term pattern is that wages of median male work-ers and of low-wage men have been and remain below their 1979 levels despite strong wage growth in the late 1990s. In contrast, wages have improved modestly for men at the 80th percentile, growing just 9.3 percent over 32 years. High-wage men at the 90th and 95th percentiles did substantially better, with wages growing 23.6 percent and 34.6 percent, respectively. Figure 4C thus shows that low- and middle-wage men have fared comparably, and not so well, and that the wage gap between those at the top and those in the middle and bottom has expanded con-tinuously over the last three decades, a theme explored throughout this chapter.

Table 4.5 provides the wage levels and changes in wages in relevant time periods for men at every wage decile in the same manner as Table 4.4 did for all workers. **Table 4.6** presents comparable wage data for women (women's wages are far lower than those of men at every decile; the gender wage gap is discussed in a later section). From 2007 to 2011, real hourly wages of most men declined,

Table 4.5 Hourly wages of men, by wage percentile, 1973–2011

					Wage by percentile*					
	10	20	30	40	50	60	70	80	90	95
Real hourly wage (2011 dollars)										
1973	$9.53	$12.23	$14.42	$16.53	$18.74	$21.24	$23.38	$26.90	$34.27	$41.30
1979	9.39	11.94	14.37	16.72	19.13	21.73	24.37	28.30	34.46	41.32
1989	8.35	10.45	12.83	15.19	17.68	20.81	24.07	28.20	35.33	43.87
1995	8.05	10.16	12.08	14.53	17.03	19.91	23.39	27.97	36.46	45.60
2000	8.97	10.99	13.14	15.57	18.21	21.18	24.93	30.25	40.30	50.46
2007	8.88	10.92	13.13	15.62	18.29	21.48	25.63	31.52	41.94	54.31
2011	8.52	10.16	12.45	14.95	17.72	20.76	25.00	30.93	42.58	55.61
Percent change										
1973–1979	-1.5%	-2.4%	-0.4%	1.1%	2.1%	2.3%	4.2%	5.2%	0.6%	0.1%
1979–1989	-11.1	-12.5	-10.7	-9.1	-7.6	-4.2	-1.2	-0.4	2.5	6.1
1989–2000	7.4	5.2	2.4	2.5	3.0	1.8	3.6	7.3	14.1	15.0
1989–1995	-3.6	-2.8	-5.8	-4.4	-3.7	-4.4	-2.8	-0.8	3.2	4.0
1995–2000	11.5	8.2	8.7	7.2	6.9	6.4	6.6	8.2	10.5	10.7
2000–2007	-1.0	-0.7	0.0	0.4	0.4	1.4	2.8	4.2	4.1	7.6
2007–2011	-4.1	-6.9	-5.2	-4.3	-3.1	-3.4	-2.4	-1.9	1.5	2.4
1979–2011	-9.3	-14.9	-13.3	-10.6	-7.4	-4.5	2.6	9.3	23.6	34.6

* The xth-percentile wage is the wage at which x% of the wage earners earn less and (100-x)% earn more.

Source: Authors' analysis of Current Population Survey Outgoing Rotation Group microdata

with the median wage falling 3.1 percent and low-wage men losing from 4.1 to 6.9 percent. The fall in wages in this period was less among women, who experienced essentially stagnant wages at the median (down 0.2 percent) and losses of 2.8 percent and 0.4 percent, respectively, at the 20th and 10th percentiles. Wages eroded or stagnated among the bottom 80 percent of both men and women and rose among those in the upper 10 percent.

Among men over the 2000–2007 period, wages declined slightly or were relatively stagnant for the bottom 50 percent, but grew at least 4.0 percent at the 80th and 90th percentiles and 7.6 percent at the 95th percentile. Thus, the wage gap between the top and the middle continued to grow strongly from 2000 to 2007. This trend contrasts with the strong broad-based wage growth of the latter 1990s, when low-wage workers fared better than middle-wage workers. What makes the late 1990s remarkable is that the strong wage growth not only was lost afterwards but was preceded by many years of substantial wage erosion for

Table 4.6 Hourly wages of women, by wage percentile, 1973–2011

	Wage by percentile*									
	10	20	30	40	50	60	70	80	90	95
Real hourly wage (2011 dollars)										
1973	$6.71	$8.34	$9.39	$10.50	$11.83	$13.31	$15.00	$17.29	$21.38	$25.27
1979	8.14	8.82	9.58	10.68	11.99	13.63	15.18	17.66	21.98	25.98
1989	6.79	8.36	9.68	11.12	12.92	14.77	17.39	20.84	26.16	31.54
1995	7.10	8.46	9.89	11.38	13.07	15.06	17.89	21.86	28.10	34.92
2000	7.83	9.32	10.74	12.44	14.20	16.41	19.44	23.62	31.04	38.13
2007	7.99	9.52	10.96	12.87	14.91	17.33	20.61	25.54	33.62	41.92
2011	7.95	9.25	10.81	12.70	14.89	17.37	20.64	25.29	34.20	43.33
Percent change										
1973–1979	21.3%	5.8%	2.1%	1.8%	1.3%	2.4%	1.2%	2.1%	2.8%	2.8%
1979–1989	-16.6	-5.2	1.0	4.1	7.8	8.4	14.6	18.0	19.0	21.4
1989–2000	15.4	11.5	11.0	11.9	9.9	11.2	11.8	13.4	18.7	20.9
1989–1995	4.6	1.2	2.3	2.4	1.1	2.0	2.9	4.9	7.4	10.7
1995–2000	10.4	10.2	8.5	9.3	8.6	9.0	8.7	8.0	10.5	9.2
2000–2007	2.0	2.1	2.1	3.5	5.0	5.6	6.0	8.1	8.3	9.9
2007–2011	-0.4	-2.8	-1.3	-1.3	-0.2	0.2	0.2	-1.0	1.7	3.4
1979–2011	-2.3	4.8	12.9	18.9	24.2	27.5	36.0	43.2	55.6	66.8

* The xth-percentile wage is the wage at which x% of the wage earners earn less and (100-x)% earn more.

Source: Authors' analysis of Current Population Survey Outgoing Rotation Group microdata

middle- and low-wage workers. For instance, between 1979 and 1989, the median male hourly wage fell 7.6 percent, and low-wage (10th percentile) men lost 11.1 percent. In the early 1990s, across-the-board wage declines of roughly 3–6 percent affected the bottom 70 percent of male earners. The pattern of male wage deterioration shifted between the 1980s and the early 1990s; in the 1980s, wages fell most at the lower levels, while in the early 1990s wages eroded comparably in the middle and at the bottom. It is also noteworthy that 1979–1995 was a disappointing period even for high-wage men: At the 90th percentile they earned $34.46 per hour in 1979 and only 5.8 percent more, $36.46, in 1995. Thus, though high-wage men did relatively better than other men from 1979 to 1995, their absolute wage growth was minimal.

Figure 4D shows the cumulative percent change in real hourly wages (relative to 1979) of women at key wage levels. Wage growth for women has been stronger than for men at every wage level. Low-wage women at the 10th percentile were the

Figure 4D Cumulative change in real hourly wages of women, by wage percentile, 1979–2011

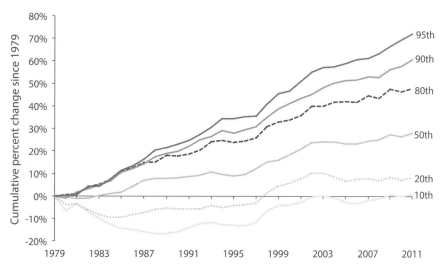

Source: Authors' analysis of Current Population Survey Outgoing Rotation Group microdata

only group to not experience any wage growth between 1979 and 2011, whereas the bottom 60 percent of men saw wage declines. As shown in Table 4.6, wages of the median woman grew by 24.2 percent from 1979 to 2011, with the gap between low- and middle-wage women's wages growing mostly in 1979–1995. Higher-wage women fared far better than middle-wage and lower-wage women for the entire period and had considerable improvement—66.8 percent and 55.6 percent, respectively—at the 95th and 90th percentiles.

Wages grew more among women than men over 2000–2007. They rose about 3–6 percent for the 40th to 70th percentiles and about 2 percent for the lowest-wage women at the 30th percentile and below (Table 4.6). The highest-wage women, those at the 95th percentile, enjoyed 9.9 percent wage growth in this period.

As with men, women's wages rose much more strongly across the board from 1995 to 2000 than in both the preceding and ensuing periods. It is notable that wage growth in this period was fairly even among all women, from 8.0 percent to 10.5 percent. In the earlier part of that same business cycle, from 1989 to 1995, wage growth was mediocre from the 20th to the 70th percentiles, ranging from about 1 percent to 3 percent. Wages grew more for the lowest-wage women, up 4.6 percent at the 10th percentile, reflecting the minimum-wage increases in those years. This was a sharp departure from the severe wage losses of low-wage women in the 1980s. Higher-wage women fared the best in 1989–1995, as they did in nearly all other periods examined.

There were tremendous disparities in wage growth among women in the 1980s. Low-wage women at the 10th percentile experienced a very large wage decline of 16.6 percent, while those at the 20th percentile had a 5.2 percent loss. Not surprisingly, the value of the minimum wage fell tremendously during this same period. In contrast to the wage losses at the bottom, the wage of the median woman grew 7.8 percent and that of the highest-wage women grew roughly 20 percent.

Shifts in low-wage jobs

Another useful dimension of the wage structure to analyze is the proportion of workers earning low, or poverty-level, wages. **Figures 4E** and **4F** present these trends by gender and race/ethnicity, respectively. The measure presented in these figures is the share of workers earning equal to or less than the "poverty-level wage," the hourly wage that a full-time, year-round worker must earn to sustain a family of four at the official poverty threshold. The poverty wage was $11.06 in 2011 (in 2011 dollars), based on the official poverty level for a family of four

Figure 4E Share of workers earning poverty-level wages, by gender, 1973–2011

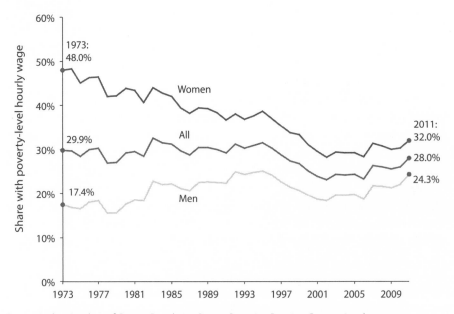

Source: Authors' analysis of Current Population Survey Outgoing Rotation Group microdata

Figure 4F Share of workers earning poverty-level wages, by race and ethnicity, 1973–2011

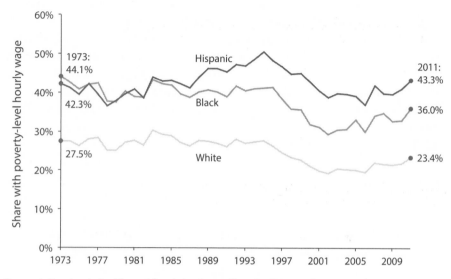

Source: Authors' analysis of Current Population Survey Outgoing Rotation Group microdata

in 2011 of $23,010. The poverty-level wage is roughly equal to two-thirds of the median hourly wage.

Women are much more likely to earn poverty-level wages than men. In 2011, 32.0 percent of women earned poverty-level wages or less, significantly more than the share of men (24.3 percent). Overall, 28.0 percent of workers, more than one in every four, earned poverty-level wages in 2011.

The trend in the share of workers earning poverty-level wages corresponds to the story outlined at the start of this chapter: Momentum in reducing poverty-wage jobs began in the late 1990s, then dissipated. The share of workers earning poverty-level wages has grown in the recessionary years among both men and women. The share of women earning poverty-level wages fell dramatically from 48.0 percent in 1973 to roughly 30 percent in 2000 and was relatively stable thereafter until the rise during the recent recessionary years. The story is different for men. They increasingly fell into low-wage work in the 1980s, a trend that was reversed in the late 1990s wage boom. But after the increase of the last few years, the share of men in low-wage work, at 24.3 percent in 2011, is substantially greater than in 1973, when just 17.4 percent of men earned low wages. The overall trends in the share of workers earning poverty-level wages are primarily driven by trends among women, since women are disproportionately the ones earning these low wages.

As seen in Figure 4F, the share of minority workers earning low wages is substantial—36.0 percent of black workers and 43.3 percent of Hispanic workers in 2011. Minority women are even more likely to be low earners—38.1 percent of black women and 47.3 percent of Hispanic women in 2011 (not shown in the figure). Figure 4F shows the decline from 1996 to 2002 in the share of white workers earning poverty-level wages and the bump up in the recent recessionary years. The decline in the shares earning poverty-level wages was steeper among both black and Hispanic workers in the late 1990s, reflecting the fact that persistent low unemployment disproportionately benefits disadvantaged and minority workers. That is also why the recent recession had a more adverse impact on black and Hispanic workers, sharply lifting the share earning low wages.

Trends year-by-year and by race/ethnicity and gender, plus trends in other wage groups (multiples of the poverty-level wage), are available on the State of Working America website at stateofworkingamerica.org/data/.

Trends among very high earners fuel growing wage inequality

Newly available data on the labor earnings of the very highest earners allow a look back to nearly the beginning of the last century, though the focus here is the period since 1947, and especially since 1979. The data cover annual earnings because they are drawn from the wage records in the Social Security system. Since these data are for annual wages and salaries, the trends reflect both changes in hourly wages, which we have been exploring, and changes in annual hours worked (based on changes in weekly hours and weeks worked per year).

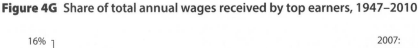

Figure 4G Share of total annual wages received by top earners, 1947–2010

Source: Authors' analysis of Kopczuk, Saez, and Song (2010) and Social Security Administration wage statistics

Figure 4G presents the share of total annual wages received by the top 1.0 percent and top 0.1 percent of earners from 1947 through 2010. Wages shares of these and lower-earning groups are presented in **Table 4.7**. The average annual wages (see **Table 4.8**) of the top 1.0 percent and top 0.1 percent of earners, respectively, were $590,633 and $2,153,347 in 2010 (in 2011 dollars). Figure 4G shows that the top 1.0 percent of earners' share of earnings was relatively stable from 1947 into the 1970s but then nearly doubled, from 7.3 percent in 1979 to 14.1 percent in 2007, before declining during the recession to 12.9 percent in 2010 (the latest year of available data). The growth of the earnings share of those in the top 0.1 percent, the upper 10th of the top 1.0 percent, was even sharper over this period, more than tripling from 1.6 percent in 1979 to 5.7 percent in 2007 before falling to 4.7 percent in 2010. The erosion of the top earners' share of all earnings in the recession reflects the scaling back of stock options income (which is counted as wages) as the stock market declined in the wake of the financial crisis. As the stock market revived in 2010 the top earners started to regain some of the prior erosion in their share of earnings: In 2010 the top 1.0 percent

Table 4.7 Change in wage groups' shares of total wages, 1979–2010

	Share of annual wages					Change in share			
	1979	2004	2007	2009	2010	1979–2004	1979–2007	2007–2010	1979–2010
Bottom 90%	69.8%	62.5%	61.1%	62.3%	61.5%	-7.3	-8.8	0.5	-8.3
Bottom fifth	3.8	3.3	—	—	—	-0.5	—	—	—
Second fifth	9.4	8.1	—	—	—	-1.3	—	—	—
Middle fifth	15.6	13.6	—	—	—	-2.0	—	—	—
Fourth fifth	24.1	21.4	—	—	—	-2.8	—	—	—
Next tenth	17.0	16.1	—	—	—	-0.9	—	—	—
Top 10%									
90th to 99th percentile	22.8%	24.6%	24.9%	25.5%	25.6%	1.8	2.0	0.7	2.7
90th–<95th	10.8	10.9	10.8	11.2	11.2	0.1	0.1	0.4	0.4
95th–<99th	12.1	13.8	14.1	14.3	14.4	1.7	2.0	0.3	2.3
Top 1.0%	7.3%	12.9%	14.1%	12.2%	12.9%	5.6	6.7	-1.1	5.6
99th–<99.5th	2.6	3.3	—	—	—	0.8	—	—	—
99.5th–<99.9th	3.1	4.7	—	—	—	1.5	—	—	—
99.9th–100th (Top 0.1%)	1.6	4.9	5.7	4.3	4.7	3.3	4.0	-0.9	3.1

Source: Authors' analysis of Kopczuk, Saez, and Song (2010) and Social Security Administration wage statistics

Table 4.8 Change in annual wages, by wage group, 1979–2010 (2011 dollars)

	Average annual wages (2011 dollars)					Change			
	1979	2004	2007	2009	2010	1979–2004	1979–2007	2007–2010	1979–2010
Bottom 90%	$26,276	$30,380	$30,653	$30,476	$30,278	16%	17%	-1%	15%
Bottom fifth	6,367	7,241	—	—	—	14	—	—	—
Second fifth	15,866	18,194	—	—	—	15	—	—	—
Middle fifth	27,239	30,791	—	—	—	13	—	—	—
Fourth fifth	42,178	48,240	—	—	—	14	—	—	—
Next tenth	59,300	72,732	—	—	—	23	—	—	—
Top 10%									
90th to 99th percentile	$88,681	$123,603	$128,873	$128,577	$129,752	39%	45%	1%	46%
90th–<95th	75,200	98,331	100,814	101,788	102,074	31	34	1	36
95th–<99th	105,531	155,194	163,947	162,063	164,350	47	55	0	56
Top 1.0%	255,792	581,047	655,251	553,069	590,633	127	156	-10	131
99th–<99.5th	179,613	299,779	—	—	—	67	—	—	—
99.5th–<99.9th	272,565	525,967	—	—	—	93	—	—	—
99.9th–100th (Top 0.1%)	569,590	2,207,706	2,634,121	1,946,058	2,153,347	288	362	-18	278

Source: Authors' analysis of Kopczuk, Saez, and Song (2010) and Social Security Administration wage statistics

regained 0.7 of the 1.9 percentage points lost from 2007 to 2009 (Table 4.7). Should the stock market continue to improve, it can be expected that the earnings share of the top 1.0 percent will return to near or above the share obtained in 2007. Even if top earnings do not return to the heights of 2007, the earnings share will clearly remain far above that of the mid-1990s and of the late 1970s. That is, we will certainly not see any major reversal of wage inequality between the top earners and the vast majority. This is the consequence of earnings growth of 131 percent for the top 1.0 percent compared with just 15 percent for the bottom 90 percent from 1979 to 2010 (Table 4.8).

Wages of the very highest earners have grown much faster than those of most workers. As **Figure 4H** shows, the growth of real annual wages of the bottom 90 percent from 1979 to 2007, before the recession began, was 16.7 percent. When the recent recessionary years are added, the bottom 90 percent's annual wages grew just 15.2 percent from 1979 to 2010. In contrast, wages grew 156.2 percent for the top 1.0 percent of earners between 1979 and 2007, nearly 10 times as fast as wage growth among the bottom 90 percent over the same period. Taking the recession into account, the top 1.0 percent had wage growth of 130.9 percent from 1979 to

Figure 4H Cumulative change in real annual wages, by wage group, 1979–2010

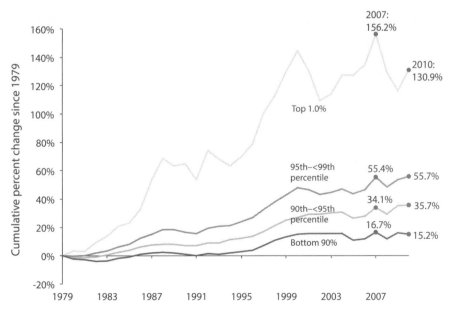

Source: Authors' analysis of Kopczuk, Saez, and Song (2010) and Social Security Administration wage statistics

2010. The top sliver (top 0.1 percent) of earners saw by far the fastest wage growth, enjoying a 278 percent increase from 1979 to 2010 (Table 4.8). In contrast, the group of earners from the 95th to the 99th percentile experienced wage growth of 55.7 percent from 1979 to 2010, less than half that of the top 1.0 percent though nearly four times that of the bottom 90 percent. These data thus illustrate a key characteristic of the wage inequality we have experienced over the last few decades: The gap between the vast middle of wage earners and the top earners has grown, but so has the gap between the top and the very top earners, with the upper one-thousandth (the top 0.1 percent) and the upper one-hundredth (the top 1.0 percent) faring far better than those just below them in the wage hierarchy. These growing wage gaps, between the top and the middle and between the very top and other top wage earners, represent two of the three key wage gaps that need to be explained in order to understand the growth of wage inequality.

One important cause of this fast growth of wages for the very highest wage earners is the rapid increase of corporate chief executive officers' pay, a subject explored in a later section.

Trends in benefit growth and inequality

The analysis in the preceding pages shows that real wages of a wide array of workers—high school graduates, college graduates, the median worker—have been flat since 2002 or 2003 depending upon the data series examined. In contrast, wages grew strongly between 1995 and 2002 or 2003, after declining or growing only minimally for the bottom 70 percent of wage earners after 1979. Also, total compensation (see the discussion of Table 4.2), the real value of both wages and fringe benefits, grew at the same pace as wages over the 1979–2011 period, though sometimes wages grew faster than compensation (as in the late 1990s) and sometimes more slowly (e.g., 2000–2007). Benefits grew faster than wages during much of the latter period, but since benefits make up a small share of compensation (18–20 percent), their growth was not associated with fast compensation growth overall. Fast growth in health care costs and pensions helped benefit growth exceed wage growth after 2000. In this section, we examine changes in health and pension coverage of different groups of workers and discuss another important benefit, paid leave.

Table 4.9 provides a breakdown of the growth in nonwage compensation, or benefits, using the Bureau of Labor Statistics Employer Costs for Employee Compensation data (the aggregate amounts appeared in Table 4.2). These data, based on a survey of employers, show that the value of total nonwage compensation, including health and pension/retirement plans and payroll taxes, remained over $5.00 per hour from 1987 to 1995. Following a 1.8 percent annual fall in the late 1990s, costs of health and pension/retirement plans ("voluntary benefits") grew rapidly (3.0 percent annually) in 2000–2007, with a net increase of $0.35 per

Table 4.9 Specific fringe benefits, 1987–2011 (2011 dollars)

	Voluntary benefits			Payroll taxes	Total nonwage compensation
	Pension	Health*	Subtotal		
Real hourly benefits					
1987	$0.91	$2.24	$3.15	$2.15	$5.30
1989	0.74	2.33	3.06	2.24	5.30
1995	0.76	2.10	2.86	2.32	5.18
2000	0.77	1.84	2.61	2.18	4.79
2007	0.95	2.26	3.21	2.40	5.60
2011	1.00	2.31	3.31	2.31	5.62
Annual dollar change					
1989–2000	$0.00	-$0.04	-$0.04	$0.00	-$0.05
1989–1995	0.00	-0.04	-0.03	0.01	-0.02
1995–2000	0.00	-0.05	-0.05	-0.03	-0.08
2000–2007	0.03	0.06	0.09	0.03	0.12
2007–2011	0.01	0.01	0.03	-0.02	0.00
Annual percent change					
1989–2000	0.4%	-2.1%	-1.5%	-0.2%	-0.9%
1989–1995	0.5	-1.7	-1.2	0.6	-0.4
1995–2000	0.3	-2.6	-1.8	-1.3	-1.6
2000–2007	3.0	3.0	3.0	1.3	2.3
2007–2011	1.4	0.5	0.8	-0.9	0.1

* Deflated by medical care price index
Note: Data are for March.

Source: Authors' analysis of Bureau of Labor Statistics National Compensation Survey–Employment Cost Trends

hour from 1995 to 2007. Note, however, that this 12.4 percent rise in voluntary benefit costs occurred at the same time that productivity grew 29.4 percent. Total nonwage compensation stagnated over the recessionary years from 2007 to 2011.

Table 4.9 also provides data on health and pension/retirement benefits per hour worked. It might be surprising to see that the real value of employer-provided health care benefits per hour worked has not grown appreciably since the late 1980s. It should be noted that health benefits in this table are adjusted for the inflation in medical care rather than for inflation in the average consumer basket of goods, because health care in the average consumer basket reflects

Table 4.10 Employer-provided health insurance coverage, by demographic and wage group, 1979–2010

| Group* | Health insurance coverage (%) | | | | | | Change | | | | |
	1979	1989	1995	2000	2007	2010	1979–1989	1989–2000	2000–2007	2007–2010	1979–2010
All workers	69.0%	61.5%	58.5%	58.9%	55.0%	53.1%	-7.4	-2.7	-3.9	-1.9	-15.9
Gender											
Men	75.4%	66.8%	62.6%	63.2%	58.4%	55.8%	-8.7	-3.6	-4.8	-2.6	-19.6
Women	59.4	54.9	53.3	53.6	51.8	49.9	-4.5	-1.3	-1.8	-1.9	-9.5
Race											
White	70.3%	64.0%	61.7%	62.7%	59.6%	57.8%	-6.3	-1.2	-3.2	-1.8	-12.5
Black	63.1	56.3	53.0	55.4	52.4	49.5	-6.8	-0.9	-3.0	-2.9	-13.6
Hispanic	60.4	46.0	42.1	41.8	37.3	36.3	-14.3	-4.3	-4.5	-1.0	-24.1
Education											
High school	69.6%	61.2%	56.3%	56.2%	51.1%	47.9%	-8.4	-5.0	-5.0	-3.2	-21.6
College	79.6	75.0	72.1	71.3	68.8	66.4	-4.6	-3.8	-2.5	-2.4	-13.3
Wage fifth											
Bottom	37.9%	26.4%	26.0%	27.4%	24.3%	20.5%	-11.5	1.0	-3.0	-3.8	-17.4
Second	60.5	51.7	49.5	50.9	45.9	43.6	-8.8	-0.8	-5.0	-2.3	-16.9
Middle	74.7	67.5	62.9	63.9	60.3	59.4	-7.2	-3.6	-3.6	-0.9	-15.3
Fourth	83.5	78.0	74.0	73.7	69.8	68.8	-5.5	-4.3	-3.9	-1.0	-14.6
Top	89.5	84.7	81.5	79.9	76.9	76.1	-4.7	-4.8	-3.0	-0.8	-13.4

* Private-sector wage and salary workers age 18–64 who worked at least 20 hours per week and 26 weeks per year

Source: Authors' analysis of Current Population Survey Annual Social and Economic Supplement microdata

out-of-pocket costs and not the costs to employers (therefore, the weight of health care in the overall basket is small). When examining changes in living standards, as we do in this table, it is important to be able to assess whether the amount of health care being purchased for a worker has grown, and that can only be achieved using a health-care-specific inflation measure. Pension benefits costs were stable in the 1990s, reflecting a shift to less-expensive, defined-contribution plans (discussed below)—but pension costs have grown steeply since 2000 and are responsible for most of the increase in benefit costs since 1989.

Table 4.11 Employer-provided pension coverage, by demographic and wage group, 1979–2010

Group*	Pension coverage (%)						Change				
	1979	1989	1995	2000	2007	2010	1979–1989	1989–2000	2000–2007	2007–2010	1979–2010
All workers	50.6%	43.7%	45.8%	48.3%	44.6%	42.8%	-7.0	4.6	-3.7	-1.8	-7.8
Gender											
Men	56.9%	46.9%	48.6%	50.3%	45.4%	43.6%	-10.1	3.4	-4.9	-1.8	-13.3
Women	41.3	39.6	42.5	45.8	43.6	41.9	-1.7	6.2	-2.2	-1.7	0.6
Race											
White	52.2%	46.1%	49.5%	53.7%	50.3%	48.2%	-6.1	7.6	-3.4	-2.1	-3.9
Black	45.8	40.7	42.6	41.3	39.1	37.7	-5.1	0.7	-2.2	-1.4	-8.1
Hispanic	38.2	26.3	24.7	27.5	24.8	23.9	-11.9	1.2	-2.6	-0.9	-14.3
Education											
High school	51.2%	42.9%	43.2%	43.8%	38.8%	36.3%	-8.3	0.9	-5.0	-2.5	-14.9
College	61.0	55.4	58.8	63.7	58.2	56.1	-5.6	8.3	-5.4	-2.2	-4.9
Wage fifth											
Bottom	18.4%	12.7%	13.7%	16.3%	14.1%	13.7%	-5.7	3.6	-2.2	-0.4	-4.7
Second	36.8	29.0	32.0	35.8	31.6	31.6	-7.7	6.8	-4.3	0.0	-5.2
Middle	52.3	44.5	47.0	50.9	47.6	46.2	-7.8	6.4	-3.3	-1.4	-6.2
Fourth	68.4	60.0	63.2	64.8	59.9	57.2	-8.3	4.8	-5.0	-2.6	-11.1
Top	78.5	72.8	74.8	74.8	69.9	67.9	-5.8	2.1	-4.9	-2.0	-10.7

* Private-sector wage and salary workers age 18–64 who worked at least 20 hours per week and 26 weeks per year

Source: Authors' analysis of Current Population Survey Annual Social and Economic Supplement microdata

As Table 4.2 showed, inequality of compensation grew faster than that of wages between 1987 and 2007, which means that benefits inequality also grew faster than wage inequality. **Tables 4.10** and **4.11** examine changes in employer-provided health insurance and pension coverage, respectively, of different demographic groups and by wage fifth between 1979 and 2010 (the last year of available data). The share of workers covered by employer-provided health care plans—meaning covered by their own employer and not a spouse's employer—dropped a steep 15.9 percentage points, from 69.0 percent in 1979 to 53.1 percent in 2010 (Table 4.10). As **Figure 4I** illustrates, health care coverage eroded

Figure 4I Share of private-sector workers with employer-provided health insurance, by race and ethnicity, 1979–2010

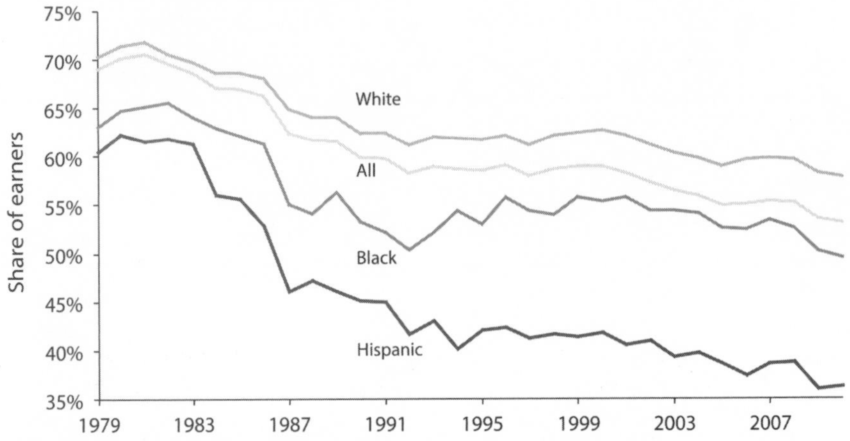

Note: Sample is of private-sector wage-and-salary earners age 18–64 who worked at least 20 hours per week and 26 weeks per year. Coverage is defined as being included in an employer-provided plan for which the employer paid for at least some of the coverage.

Source: Authors' analysis of Current Population Survey Annual Social and Economic Supplement microdata

from 1979 until 1992, when it stabilized through the late 1990s, but began falling again after 2000.

The 5.8 percentage-point erosion of employer-provided health care coverage from 2000 to 2010 was driven by eroded coverage in every racial/ethnic, education, gender, and wage group. The erosion of coverage was larger among men (down 7.4 percentage points) than women (down 3.7 percentage points) and declined roughly 5.0 percentage points among whites, blacks, and Hispanics. Coverage eroded for both high school graduates (8.2 percentage points) but also among college graduates (4.9 percentage points). Health coverage declined for every wage group, with those in the bottom 40 percent of the wage structure losing more ground even though they had less to lose.

Over the longer period from 1979 to 2010, health care coverage declined about twice as much among men (down 19.6 percentage points) as among women (down 9.5 percentage points) and comparably among whites and blacks; Hispanics, though, suffered by far the largest drop—24.1 percentage points. The pattern in the erosion of health insurance coverage by wage level shows growth in inequality in the 1980s, with greater erosion the lower the wage. The 1990s, however, saw modest extensions of coverage for the bottom 20 percent, while erosion continued for middle- and high-wage workers. Coverage eroded for all wage groups from 2000 to 2007 and 2007 to 2010, and over the longer period,

1979–2010, employer-provided health insurance coverage declined considerably for each wage fifth, though somewhat more the lower the wage. Along education lines there is also evidence of growing inequality: Employer-provided health insurance coverage fell 21.6 percentage points among high school graduates but fell a smaller but still sizable 13.3 percentage points among college graduates (high school graduates were 12.6 percent less likely to have coverage than college graduates in 1979 but 27.8 percent less likely in 2010).

The impact of rising health care costs on wage growth—i.e., the extent to which rising health care expenses for employers came at the expense of wage growth—is explored later in this chapter, along with the potential impact on wage inequality over the last two decades.

Employer-provided pension plan coverage (Table 4.11) eroded by 3.7 percentage points from 2000 to 2007 and another 1.8 percentage points between 2007 and 2010. This decline represents a sharp break from the 1990s, when pension coverage grew across the board (likely due to the increase in defined-contribution plans, as will be discussed shortly). In 2000 almost half the workforce (48.3 percent) had an employer-provided pension plan, a share nearly as large as in 1979. The recent erosion, however, lowered pension coverage to just 42.8 percent in 2010. The erosion since 2000 was widespread, occurring among both high school and college graduates and at every wage level. Among wage fifths, those with the highest wages and the highest coverage rates tended to lose the most ground since 2000 (they had more to lose). Much of the workforce now has very little pension coverage. Only 36.3 percent of high school graduates and just 31.6 percent of wage earners in the second fifth had coverage in 2010, and those in the bottom fifth had just 13.7 percent coverage. Less than a fourth of Hispanic workers and only 37.7 percent of black workers enjoyed employer-provided pension coverage in 2010. The coverage among men and women was comparably low in 2010, though men had much higher coverage than employed women back in 1979 or even in 1989. This is one area where we are seeing less inequality: Coverage among men has declined precipitously since 1979, while declines in recent years have returned women's coverage to its 1980s level.

From 1979 to 2010 pension coverage declined overall by 7.8 percentage points. The pattern by wage level shows coverage dropping relatively evenly across wage groups in the 1980s and rising across the board in the 1990s, with coverage expanding the most in the middle. Coverage declined across each wage fifth between 2000 and 2010 and over the entire 1979–2010 period. Lower-wage workers are now very unlikely to have jobs with employer-provided pension plans (as previously mentioned, only 13.7 percent were covered in 2010), and less than half of middle-wage workers have pension coverage. It should be noted that there was little coverage for low-wage workers to lose—just 18.4 percent for the bottom fifth and 36.8 percent for the second-lowest fifth in 1979. In 2010, the highest-wage workers were about 5.0 times as likely to have pension coverage as the lowest-wage workers (67.9 percent versus 13.7 percent). Changes in pension coverage by education show growing inequality: Over the 1979–2010 period, pension coverage fell 14.9 percentage points among high school graduates but 4.9 percentage points among college graduates.

The widening coverage of employer-provided pension plans in the 1990s was most likely due to the expansion of 401(k) and other defined-contribution pension plans. These plans differ from defined-benefit plans, which are generally considered the best plans from a worker's perspective because they guarantee a fixed payment in retirement based on preretirement wages and years of service, regardless of stock market performance. Unfortunately, the latest data to examine these trends are for 2004. **Figure 4J** shows that a much larger share of workers are now covered by defined-contribution plans, in which employers make contributions (to which employees often can add) each year. With this type of plan, a worker's retirement income depends on his or her success in investing these funds, and investment risks are borne by the employee rather than the employer. Therefore, the shift from traditional defined-benefit plans to defined-contribution plans represents an erosion of pension quality. Figure 4J shows a dramatic erosion in the share of workers covered by defined-benefit plans, a decline from 39 percent in 1980 to just 18 percent in 2004. Correspondingly, the share of workers with a defined-contribution plan (and no other plan) rose from

Figure 4J Share of pension participants in defined-contribution and defined-benefit plans, 1980–2004

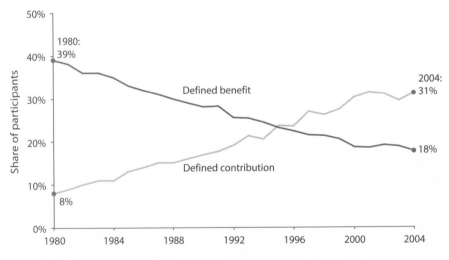

Note: Data are for private-sector workers.

Source: Authors' analysis of Center for Retirement Research (2006)

8 percent to 31 percent. Chapter 6 provides further discussion of pensions and retirement assets and income.

Table 4.12 broadens our discussion of benefits to focus on various types of paid leave such as sick leave, family leave, holidays, and vacation. Such leave is embedded in the wage data presented in this chapter, as workers surveyed report wages based on the days for which they were paid and not just for days worked. This table, therefore, surfaces the fact that access to such leave is very unequal and, for those who have such leave, there is great inequality in the leave that is provided. For instance, the top panel shows that only 67 percent of civilian workers (including all private-sector workers and state and local government workers but excluding

Table 4.12 Share of workers with paid leave, by wage group, 2011

| | Percent with access to: | | | |
	Paid sick days	Paid vacation	Paid family leave	Number of paid holidays*
All	67%	74%	12%	8
By wage				
Bottom 10 percent	23%	40%	4%	5
Lowest quarter	36	53	5	6
Second quarter	69	83	11	8
Third quarter	79	89	14	9
Top quarter	88	78	19	10
Top 10 percent	90	75	20	10
By union status				
Union	84%	74%	15%	10
Nonunion	64	74	11	8

	Number of paid sick days by length of service*				Number of vacation days by length of service*			
	1 yr	5 yrs	10 yrs	20 yrs	1 yr	5 yrs	10 yrs	20 yrs
All	9	9	10	10	10	14	17	19
Union	10	11	11	12	10	14	17	21
Nonunion	8	9	9	10	10	14	17	19

* For those with such paid leave
Note: Data are for civilian workers, defined as workers in the private sector and state and local government but not the federal government.

Source: Authors' analysis of Employee Benefits Survey tables (Bureau of Labor Statistics 2011)

federal workers) were provided any paid sick leave, and far fewer, just 12 percent, were provided any paid family leave. Paid vacations are more prevalent, with 74 percent of workers eligible. The great disparities in the provision of paid leave are revealed in the breakdowns of access by wage level. Only 23 percent of those in the bottom 10 percent of the wage scale were provided paid sick leave, compared with 90 percent among the top 10 percent of earners. In short, the higher the wage, the more likely a worker is to be provided paid sick leave. Paid family leave follows that same pattern, though the provision is far less than for paid sick leave at every wage level. Only 4 percent of workers in the bottom 10 percent of the wage structure had paid family leave, while 20 percent of those in the top 10 percent did.

The average worker is paid for eight holidays (Table 4.12), which is two fewer than the number of federal holidays each year. Those at the bottom of the wage structure enjoy five or six paid holidays on average, while those at the top have about twice as many paid holidays (10).

Table 4.12 also provides a breakdown of access to paid leave by union status. Unionized workers are more likely to have paid sick days (84 percent) than nonunion workers (64 percent), a bit more likely to have paid family leave, and equally likely to have paid vacation (74 percent). Union workers average 10 paid holidays, two more than the average nonunion worker.

Table 4.12 also has data on the number of paid sick and vacation days provided for workers at different lengths of service. (The data are only for those workers who are provided these types of paid leave.) Those provided paid sick leave have nine days provided early in their tenure, and starting at 10 years they receive an additional 10th paid sick day. Union workers have two more days of paid sick leave at each length of service when compared with nonunion workers. Vacation days rise more with service, starting at 10 days for those with just one year of service and reaching 19 days for those with 20 years of service. Union and nonunion workers who receive paid vacation have a comparable amount of leave except for very senior workers, among whom union workers enjoy a bit more (an additional two days) vacation time.

Dimensions of wage inequality

In this section we shift the discussion from describing wage and benefit trends to focusing on the many dimensions of one of the key wage trends: growing wage inequality. To explore the factors behind wage inequality, we first need to understand which particular groups are faring well or poorly compared with others, and how these wage gaps have changed over time.

The data presented up to this point have shown the stagnation of wages and overall compensation between 1979 and 1995 and the strong wage growth in the late 1990s that carried into the 2000s but waned after 2002 or 2003. **Table 4.13** and related figures present key wage differentials, by gender (excluding race and

Table 4.13 Dimensions of wage inequality, by gender, 1973–2011

		Wage gap*							Change				
		1973	1979	1989	1995	2000	2007	2011	1973–1979	1979–1989	1989–2000	2000–2007	2007–2011
A. Total wage inequality**													
90/10 (x/y)	Men	128.0%	130.0%	144.3%	151.1%	150.3%	155.3%	160.9%	2.0	14.3	6.0	5.0	5.7
	Women	115.9	103.2	134.9	137.6	137.7	143.7	145.9	-12.7	31.8	2.8	6.0	2.1
90/50	Men	60.3	58.8	69.2	76.1	79.5	83.0	87.7	-1.5	10.4	10.2	3.6	4.7
	Women	59.2	60.6	70.5	76.5	78.2	81.3	83.2	1.4	9.9	7.7	3.1	1.9
50/10	Men	67.6	71.1	75.1	75.0	70.8	72.3	73.3	3.5	3.9	-4.2	1.4	1.0
	Women	56.7	42.5	64.4	61.1	59.5	62.4	62.7	-14.2	21.9	-4.9	2.9	0.2
B. Between-group inequality**													
Education													
College/high school	Men	25.1%	20.2%	34.0%	37.1%	42.0%	44.1%	44.8%	-4.9	13.8	8.0	2.1	0.7
	Women	36.5	25.0	40.0	46.7	47.9	48.5	48.7	-11.5	15.0	7.9	0.6	0.2
High school/less than high school	Men	22.3	22.0	22.1	26.5	26.0	25.2	28.7	-0.3	0.1	3.9	-0.7	3.4
	Women	26.2	21.3	26.4	29.8	29.5	27.7	26.2	0.0	0.1	0.0	0.0	0.0
Experience****													
Middle/young (35 yrs/25)	Men	22.0%	21.5%	25.7%	26.9%	22.9%	24.3%	27.5%	-0.5	4.1	-2.8	1.4	3.2
	Women	8.0	9.5	17.8	21.7	18.4	20.9	22.4	1.5	8.3	0.6	2.5	1.5
Old/middle (50 yrs/35)	Men	3.4	8.2	12.4	12.7	8.8	9.4	11.8	4.7	4.3	-3.7	0.7	2.4
	Women	-2.0	0.4	2.1	5.3	4.7	8.3	8.6	2.4	1.7	2.5	3.7	0.3
C. Within-group inequality***													
	Men	42.3%	42.8%	46.7%	47.8%	48.1%	50.1%	50.7%	1.4%	9.0%	3.0%	4.2%	1.1%
	Women	41.8	40.2	44.7	46.7	45.8	48.4	48.5	-3.8	11.4	2.4	5.7	0.2

* Log wage differential
** Log wage ratio of x/y
*** Simple human capital regression of log wages; see table notes
**** Ratio x/y
***** Mean square error from same regressions as education and experience

Source: Authors' analysis of Current Population Survey Outgoing Rotation Group microdata

gender differentials), from 1973 to 2011. Any explanations of growing wage inequality (covered later) must be able to explain the movement of these wage differentials.

Gaps between higher- and lower-wage workers

The top section of Table 4.13 shows the trends in the 90/10 wage differential and its two components, the 90/50 and 50/10 wage differential. These differentials reflect the growth in overall wage inequality and follow the wage levels presented in Tables 4.5 and 4.6. The 90/10 wage gap, for instance, shows the degree to which high-wage workers—defined here as those who earn more than 90 percent but less than 10 percent of the workforce—fared better than low-wage workers, defined here as those who earn at the 10th percentile. The 90/50 wage gap shows how high earners fared relative to middle earners, and the 50/10 wage gap shows how middle earners fared relative to low earners. For example, men at the 90th percentile in 2011 earned wages 160.9 percent greater than those of men at the 10th percentile. (These differentials are presented in "logged" differentials to place them on the same scale as other differentials presented in the table, which are drawn from wage regressions using logged wages as the dependent variable.)

The values (not "logged") of the 90/50 and 50/10 wage gaps of men and women, respectively, are shown in **Figures 4K** and **4L** (in both figures as a ratio

Figure 4K Wage gaps among men, 1973–2011

* Ratio of workers' wages at the higher earnings percentile to workers' wages at the lower percentile

Source: Authors' analysis of Current Population Survey Outgoing Rotation Group microdata

of wages at the higher to lower percentiles). As the figures show, wage inequalities have grown since 1979, although the patterns differ across time periods. For
instance, among both men and women the pattern of growing inequality through
most of the 1980s (through about 1987–1988) differed from the pattern thereafter. From 1979 to 1989 (as we saw in the analysis of wage deciles in Tables 4.4
through 4.6), there was a dramatic across-the-board widening of the wage structure, with the top pulling away from the middle and the middle pulling away from
the bottom. In the late 1980s, however, the wage gap in the bottom half of the
wage structure, as reflected in the 50/10 ratio, began shrinking among men, stabilized in the early 1990s, then shrank until the mid-2000s, when it proceeded to
grow again. Among women the 50/10 wage gap grew sharply until the late 1980s
but has been relatively stable since then. On the other hand, the 90/50 wage gap
among both men and women continued to widen throughout the 1980s, 1990s,
and 2000s. This widening of the wage gap at the top is even more pronounced
between wage earners at the 95th and 50th percentiles, as shown in **Figure 4M**.
(The 95th percentile is the highest wage we can track in these data with technical precision. However, the Social Security data on annual earnings presented in
Table 4.8 show a widening inequality between the very top earners in the top 1.0
and top 0.1 percent, and wage earners in the rest of the top 10 percent.)

Figure 4L Wage gaps among women, 1973–2011

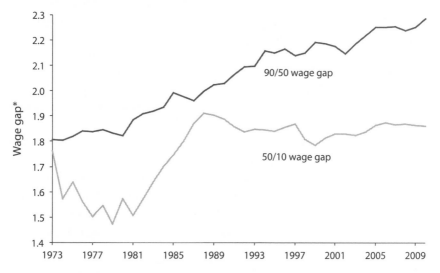

* Ratio of workers' wages at the higher earnings percentile to workers' wages at the lower percentile

Source: Authors' analysis of Current Population Survey Outgoing Rotation Group microdata

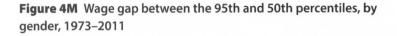

Figure 4M Wage gap between the 95th and 50th percentiles, by gender, 1973–2011

* Ratio of workers' wages at the 95th earnings percentile to wages at the 50th percentile

Source: Authors' analysis of Current Population Survey Outgoing Rotation Group microdata

These disparate trends between high- versus middle-wage growth and middle- versus low-wage growth should focus attention on how causal factors affect particular portions of the wage structure—very top, top, middle, or bottom—rather than on how causal factors affect inequality generally. This break in trend in the late 1980s (when inequality in the bottom half stopped expanding and started falling among men, and stopped expanding and began stagnating among women) raises the possibility of a differing mix of factors increasing overall inequality in the 1980s and thereafter, or a shift over time in the impact of a particular factor, such as technology or globalization (we will visit this issue when we examine the impact of both trade and technology).

The trends in recent years, 2000–2011, may signal a return to the 1980s pattern of an across-the-board widening of wage inequality (even if the overall wage gap at the bottom has grown modestly). At the top, the wage gap (95/50 or 90/50) has grown more sharply among men but has continued its growth among women as well (see Figure 4M for the 95/50 gap by gender). Overall wage inequality, measured by the 90/10 ratio, grew more rapidly among men and women from 2000 to 2011 than in the 1990s.

Gaps between workers with different education and experience levels

Analysts decompose, or break down, growing wage inequality into two types of inequality—"between group" and "within group." In addition to depicting total wage inequality, Table 4.13 presents trends in two types of "between group" inequalities: the growing wage differentials between groups of workers defined by their *education* levels and by their labor market *experience* (measured as x/y where the wage of x exceeds the wage of y). The most frequently discussed differential is the "college wage premium"—the wage gap between (four-year) college graduates and high school graduates. In this analysis the premiums discussed, such as the college premium, are "regression-adjusted," which means that the analysis controls for the impact of other factors such as experience, marital status, race, ethnicity, and region of residence. Thus, the education premium presented here will differ from one computed by simply dividing the college wage by the high school wage (because the calculation here takes account, for instance, of the differing age and racial distribution of each group).

The college wage premium (see **Figure 4N**) fell in the 1970s among both men and women but exploded in the 1980s, growing about 14 percentage points for

Figure 4N College wage premium, by gender, 1973–2011

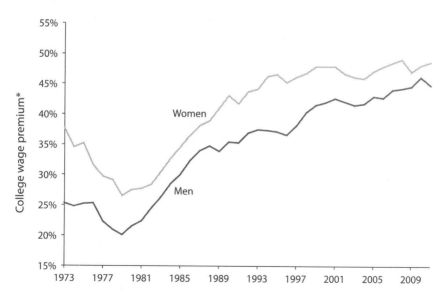

* Percent by which wages of college graduates exceed those of otherwise equivalent high school graduates, regression adjusted

Source: Authors' analysis of Current Population Survey Outgoing Rotation Group microdata

each. Growth then slowed after 1989. The pattern of growth of this key education differential in the 1990s and beyond, however, differed between men and women. Among men the college premium grew only modestly in the early 1990s—year-by-year trends (discussed later) show it to be relatively flat between 1988 and 1996—but it grew strongly thereafter until 2001 and modestly from 2001 until 2011. Thus, the 1990s growth in the college premium for men primarily occurred in the last few years of that period, with modest growth since 2001. Among women, however, the college wage premium grew steadily but modestly in the early 1990s and then was relatively stable after 1995 through 2011 (a modest growth of 2.0 percentage points over those 16 years).

Table 4.13 also presents the trends in another education differential—between those completing high school and those without high school degrees, the "high school premium." This differential would be expected to affect the wage distribution in the bottom half, as less than 10 percent of the workforce has less than a high school education, and high school graduates make up about a third of the workforce (as will be discussed later). The high school premium has been remarkably stable, especially relative to the trends in the college premium. Among men the high school premium ranged from 22.0 percent to 26.5 percent from 1973 through 2007. The bump up of the high school premium from 2007 to 2011 may reflect the hard times in construction, which provided decent wage opportunities for men lacking a high school degree. Among women the high school premium rose in the 1980s (after falling in the 1970s) and increased again in the 1990s. But it has fallen in value since 2000 and in 2011 was about the same as in 1989 (and 1973).

One reason for the relative stability of the high school premium is that, even as having a high school degree was becoming more economically valuable, the share of workers without a high school degree dramatically declined. It may also be the case that growth of the "high school wage" was diminished because a larger share of workers completing high school (which is our measure here) have an equivalency degree rather than a traditional diploma. Nevertheless, since this wage differential grew modestly among men over the last 30 years, one can conclude that this education differential has not been a driving force behind the changes in the 50/10 wage gap among men (which grew in the 1980s and declined thereafter). Among women, the wage gap between middle- and low-wage workers was far higher in 2011 than in 1979, yet the high school premium has only grown modestly. This suggests that changing wage differentials at the bottom among women are only weakly, at best, related to changing education differentials.

Experience, or age, is another way of categorizing "skill." Experience differentials reflect the wage gaps between older and middle-aged and younger workers. Among men, at least since 1979, there has not been any sizable increase in experience differentials, although young men's wages fell relative to those of middle-aged men in the recent recessionary years. Among women, however, experience differentials have grown between older and middle-aged women and between middle-aged and younger women. Most of the deterioration of younger women's wages relative to those of middle-aged women developed in the 1980s, consistent with the rapid decline in value of the minimum wage (which would affect younger women heavily). The wage gap between older and middle-aged women workers grew over 1973–1995 and then again in 2000–2007.

The gap between workers with comparable education and experience

Within-group wage inequality—wage dispersion among workers with comparable education and experience—has been a major dimension of growing wage inequality. Unfortunately, most discussions of wage inequality focus exclusively on the between-group dimensions discussed earlier, even though within-group wage inequality is by far the most important dimension of wage inequality's growth. The growth of within-group wage inequality is presented in the last section of Table 4.13, with changes measured in percent. These data show that within-group inequality grew slightly among men in the 1970s and 1990s but grew strongly in the 1980s (9.0 percent) and the 2000s (over 5.0 percent). Among women, within-group inequality fell in the 1970s, grew by 11.4 percent in the 1980s, grew by a modest 2.4 percent in the 1990s, and grew a bit more rapidly in recent years. Within-group inequality is explored further in Tables 4.19 and 4.20.

The measure of within-group wage inequality in Table 4.13 is a "summary measure" describing changes across the entire wage distribution. Within-group wage inequality reflects the changes in wages among workers with similar attributes such as education and experience, so it can be thought of as aggregating the inequalities among young college graduates and middle-aged high school graduates and so on. Unfortunately, such a measure does not help us understand changes in particular measures of wage inequality, such as the 90/50 and 50/10 differentials presented in the top portion of the table. This shortcoming is particularly troublesome for an analysis of the period after the late 1980s, in which inequalities were expanding at the top (i.e., the 90/50 differential) but shrinking or stable at the bottom (i.e., the 50/10 differential). A summary measure of inequality by definition reflects the net effect of the two disparate shifts in wage inequality since the late 1980s, and probably as a result the change in within-group wage inequality from 1989 to 2011 appears small. But it is clear that within-group wage inequality grew substantially in the 1980s.

Since changes in within-group wage inequality have been a significant factor in various periods, it is important to be able to explain and interpret these trends. In a later section, we show that over half of the growth of wage inequality since 1979 has been from growing within-group inequality. Unfortunately, the interpretation of growing wage inequality among workers with similar "human capital" has not been the subject of much research. Some analysts suggest it re-flects growing premiums for skills that are not captured by traditional human capital measures available in government surveys. Others suggest that changing "wage norms," employer practices, and institutions are responsible.

We now turn to a more detailed examination of between-group wage differ-entials such as education, experience, and race/ethnicity, as well as an examination of within-group wage inequality.

Rising education/wage differentials

Changes in the economic returns to education affect the structure of wages by changing the wage gaps between different educational groups. The growth in "ed-ucation/wage differentials," or premiums, has led to greater wage inequality since 1979 but to a different degree in each decade (see Table 4.13 and Figure 4N). The rise of the college premium helps to explain the relatively faster wage growth among high-wage workers. Changing education/wage differentials, it should be noted, are not causal in and of themselves. After all, a change in the minimum wage can affect the wage gap between high school graduates and those lacking a high school degree. In this light, examining education/wage differentials is an intermediate step in examining the factors that have generated wage inequality. This section examines wage trends among workers at different levels of education and begins the discussion, carried on through the remainder of the chapter, of the causes of rising education/wage differentials and of overall wage inequality.

Table 4.14 presents the wage trends and employment shares (percentage of the workforce) of workers at various education levels from 1973 to 2011. It is common to point out that the wages of "more-educated" workers have grown faster than the wages of "less-educated" workers since 1979, with the real wages of less-educated workers generally falling sharply (or rising more slowly from 1995 to 2000). This pattern of wage growth is frequently described in terms of a rising differential, or premium, between the wages of the college-educated and high school–educated workforces (as shown earlier in Table 4.13).

The frequent categorizing of workers as either "less educated" (and faring relatively poorly) or "more educated" (and faring relatively better) is potentially misleading. As we will show shortly, in some periods the better-educated workers do not fare so well. Moreover, the group labeled "less educated" actually compris-es about 70–75 percent of the workforce during most of this period and has skills and education levels that exceed those of most workers in the world. As the table shows, in 2011 the share of the U.S. workforce age 18–64 lacking a high school degree or an equivalent degree was just 8.4 percent. Last, it is notable that the college-educated group consists of two groups: one with just four years of college, and another more-educated group (advanced degree); the wage trends of these two groups have frequently diverged, so it makes sense—in fact, it is absolutely necessary—to examine them separately.

Wages have grown far more slowly for every education group since 2000 than in the late 1990s. The contrast is even starker when one looks at the wage growth during the 2002–2007 recovery after the wage momentum from the late 1990s had subsided (as seen in Figure 4A earlier) and the jobless recovery took hold, as well as during the recessionary years after 2007, when wages fell for every group except for those with advanced degrees (whose wages rose a scant 0.1 percent each year). These are disappointing outcomes for a period since 2000 when there was such fast productivity growth.

Table 4.14 Hourly wages by education, 1973–2011 (2011 dollars)

	Less than high school	High school	Some college	College degree	Advanced degree
Real hourly wage					
1973	$14.93	$17.11	$18.43	$24.96	$30.17
1979	14.85	16.67	17.82	23.36	28.53
1989	12.69	15.47	17.37	24.36	31.40
1995	11.46	15.15	16.93	25.16	33.10
2000	11.92	16.04	18.23	27.99	35.42
2007	12.34	16.24	18.31	28.65	36.31
2011	11.82	15.89	17.57	27.99	36.40
Annual percent change					
1973–1979	-0.1%	-0.4%	-0.6%	-1.1%	-0.9%
1979–1989	-1.6	-0.7	-0.3	0.4	1.0
1989–2000	-0.6	0.3	0.4	1.3	1.1
1989–1995	-1.7	-0.3	-0.4	0.5	0.9
1995–2000	0.8	1.1	1.5	2.2	1.4
2000–2007	0.5	0.2	0.1	0.3	0.4
2007–2011	-1.1	-0.5	-1.0	-0.6	0.1
Share of employment					
1973	28.5%	38.3%	18.5%	10.1%	4.5%
1979	20.1	38.5	22.8	12.7	6.0
1989	13.7	36.9	26.0	15.6	7.9
2000	10.8	31.9	29.8	18.8	8.7
2007	9.8	29.6	29.6	20.9	10.1
2011	8.4	28.0	30.4	21.9	11.3

Source: Authors' analysis of Current Population Survey Outgoing Rotation Group microdata

Over the 1979–2007 period, the simple story is that the greater the education level of the group, the more wages rose, although the extent of the differences varied across particular time periods. From 1979 to 1995 the wages of those with less than a college degree actually declined, while those of college-educated workers rose modestly (Table 4.14). It is notable that this group of workers with less than a four-year college degree who saw falling wages from 1979 to 1995 comprised more than three-fourths of the workforce in 1989. Between 1995 and 2000 (up until 2002 actually) real wages grew for all educational groups while, as just discussed, after 2002 wages failed to grow for those with a high school education or at most a college degree. One interesting pattern to note is that those with advanced degrees (master's degrees, professional degrees in law, medicine, and so on) sometimes saw their wages grow faster than those with just a college degree (1979–1989, 1989–1995) but sometimes saw slower wage growth (1995–2000) and sometimes comparable growth (2000–2007).

The increased wage differential between college-educated workers (referring to those with a college degree but no further degree) and those with less education is frequently ascribed to a relative increase in employer demand for workers with greater skills and education. This interpretation follows from the fact that the wages of college-educated workers increased relative to others' wages despite an increase in their relative supply, from 12.7 percent of the workforce in 1979 to 20.9 percent in 2007. That is, since, all else being equal, the increased relative supply of college-educated workers would be expected to reduce the college wage, the relative increase of the college wage implies strong growth in employer demand for more-educated workers, presumably reflecting technological and other workplace trends.

This interpretation correctly concludes that there has been a rising relative demand for college graduates in the last 30 years or so. However, demand also increased during the preceding 30 years, when wage inequality did not rise. As we will explore below, rising relative demand, driven by technology, can be the cause of rising education differentials and wage inequality if the growth of relative demand accelerated, i.e., was faster recently than in the past.

Yet an increased relative demand for educated workers is only a partial explanation, especially if it is credited to a benign process of technology or other factors that lead to a higher value for education and thus bid up the wages of more-educated workers. Note, for instance, that the primary reason for an increased wage gap between college-educated and other workers is the precipitous decline of wages among the non-college-educated workforce from 1979 to 1995 and not any strong growth in the college wage (it increased a modest 0.4 percent or 0.5 percent annually in this time period). Moreover, as discussed below, there are many important factors generating education differentials that may not reflect technology-driven changes in the relative demand for education and skill; these might include high unemployment, the shift to low-wage industries, declining unionization, a falling minimum wage, and import competition.

Tables 4.15 and **4.16** present trends in wage and employment shares of men and women in each education group. Among men, as with all workers, real wages declined in the recessionary years after 2007 in every education group, including college graduates, except for those with advanced degrees, whose wages were basically stagnant. Wage growth from 2000 to 2007 was modest, especially compared with the faster wage growth for each education group in the late 1990s. Wages of those with a college degree or less either stagnated or declined during the recovery years from 2002 to 2007 (not shown in the table). The exceptionally strong wage

Table 4.15 Hourly wages of men, by education, 1973–2011 (2011 dollars)

	Less than high school	High school	Some college	College degree	Advanced degree
Real hourly wage					
1973	$17.45	$20.69	$21.15	$28.54	$31.70
1979	17.13	20.08	20.88	27.29	31.06
1989	14.39	17.95	19.80	27.93	34.73
1995	12.61	17.08	19.03	28.30	36.65
2000	13.08	18.09	20.62	31.77	39.71
2007	13.37	18.03	20.45	32.78	41.17
2011	12.71	17.53	19.45	31.81	41.34
Annual percent change					
1973–1979	-0.3%	-0.5%	-0.2%	-0.7%	-0.3%
1979–1989	-1.7	-1.1	-0.5	0.2	1.1
1989–2000	-0.9	0.1	0.4	1.2	1.2
1989–1995	-2.2	-0.8	-0.7	0.2	0.9
1995–2000	0.7	1.2	1.6	2.3	1.6
2000–2007	0.3	0.0	-0.1	0.4	0.5
2007–2011	-1.3	-0.7	-1.3	-0.8	0.1
Share of employment					
1973	30.6%	34.4%	19.2%	10.3%	5.4%
1979	22.3	35.0	22.4	13.2	7.1
1989	15.9	35.2	24.4	15.7	8.8
2000	12.6	32.1	27.7	18.5	9.1
2007	12.0	31.1	27.3	19.9	9.8
2011	10.2	30.2	28.3	20.8	10.6

Source: Authors' analysis of Current Population Survey Outgoing Rotation Group microdata

Table 4.16 Hourly wages of women, by education, 1973–2011 (2011 dollars)

	Less than high school	High school	Some college	College degree	Advanced degree
Real hourly wage					
1973	$10.53	$13.03	$14.08	$19.50	$25.82
1979	11.00	13.04	14.00	17.73	22.71
1989	9.98	12.91	14.96	20.24	26.38
1995	9.63	13.04	14.92	21.72	28.56
2000	10.06	13.77	15.97	24.04	30.37
2007	10.52	14.08	16.34	24.59	31.34
2011	10.32	13.83	15.82	24.31	31.76
Annual percent change					
1973–1979	0.7%	0.0%	-0.1%	-1.6%	-2.1%
1979–1989	-1.0	-0.1	0.7	1.3	1.5
1989–2000	0.1	0.6	0.6	1.6	1.3
1989–1995	-0.6	0.2	0.0	1.2	1.3
1995–2000	0.9	1.1	1.4	2.1	1.2
2000–2007	0.6	0.3	0.3	0.3	0.5
2007–2011	-0.5	-0.5	-0.8	-0.3	0.3
Share of employment					
1973	25.6%	44.0%	17.5%	9.9%	3.1%
1979	17.2	43.0	23.4	12.0	4.4
1989	11.2	38.8	27.8	15.4	6.8
2000	8.8	31.6	32.0	19.1	8.4
2007	7.4	28.0	32.2	22.0	10.4
2011	6.5	25.7	32.6	23.1	12.1

Source: Authors' analysis of Current Population Survey Outgoing Rotation Group microdata

growth in the late 1990s stands apart from the long-term trend over the 16 years from 1979 to 1995, when wages fell sharply among non-college-educated men. The decline was sizable even among men with "some college"—8.9 percent from 1979 to 1995. The wage of the average high school–educated male fell more, 15.0 percent, from 1979 to 1995, while the wages of those without a high school degree fell 26.4 percent. By contrast, the wages of male college graduates rose, but more modestly than commonly thought—just 3.7 percent from 1979 to 1995. Year-by-year data show that male college wages in the 1979–1995 period peaked in 1988 (and fell thereafter).

Over the 1979–2011 period the pattern of growing wages for college-educated males (almost entirely due to the 1995–2000 period) and declining or stagnant wages for non-college-educated males meant a rise in the relative wage, or wage premium, for male college graduates. As shown in Table 4.13, the estimated college/high school wage premium (controlling for experience, race, and other characteristics) grew from 20.2 percent in 1979 to 34.0 percent in 1989 and to 44.8 percent by 2011. As previously mentioned, however, there was a flattening of the male college/high school wage premium from 1988 to 1996, particularly in the early 1990s (as shown in Figure 4N). Since there was not an acceleration of the supply of college-educated men, this slower growth in the premium implies, within a conventional demand-supply framework, that growth in the relative demand for college workers slowed in that period. From 1996 to 2000, however, this key education differential among men jumped again, followed by another period of flat college wage premiums for men and a bump up during the post-2007 recessionary years. Thus, the growth in the male college wage premium has been relatively modest since 1988, with the exception of the late 1990s.

As we have seen in our earlier examinations of the wage structure, women's wages have grown faster than men's in nearly every category (wage deciles, shrinkage of poverty-level wages, etc.). However, the same general pattern of relative wages—that is, who does better—prevails among women as among men (Table 4.16). From 2007 to 2011 wages fell for women with college degrees and those with less education, as happened for men, although the fall in wages was less among women. From 2000 to 2007, wages among women of all education groups rose modestly, with little variation among education groups. Wages rose 0.3 percent annually for those with a high school degree, some college, and a college degree, and a bit faster for those without a high school degree and those with an advanced degree. Year-by-year data (not shown in Table 4.16) show that wages during the 2000–2007 business cycle peaked in 2003 among women with college degrees or less education—a group comprising about 90 percent of women workers in 2007. Thus, there was pervasive wage stagnation or decline among women after 2003 in nearly every education group, parallel to the disappointing trends among men.

In the late 1990s wages grew much more strongly among women in every education group, with the familiar pattern of college graduates having the fastest growth (even greater than among those with advanced degrees). In the 1979–1989 and 1989–1995 periods, wages were stagnant among high school–educated women but fell significantly (12.4 percent) among those without a high school degree. Women with some college saw significant wage gains in the 1980s (unlike their male counterparts), but not in the early 1990s. College-educated women (those with college or advanced degrees) saw strong wage growth throughout the 1979–1995 period, faring by far the best among all gender-education categories. This pattern of wage growth resulted in growth of the college/high school wage differential comparable to that of men from 1979 to 1989 (Table 4.13), from 25.0 percent in 1979 to 40.0 percent in 1989. It further increased to 46.7 percent in 1995 (with this 1989–1995 increase being higher than among men). However, the college wage premium among women has barely budged since 1995, rising only 2 percentage points to 48.7 percent in 2011. Thus, the education wage gap grew more among women than among men from 1979 to 1995 and then stagnated thereafter, while it continued to rise somewhat among men after 1995. From 1979 to 1995 the relative losers among women—the non-college-educated—saw relatively stagnant wages, whereas among men the wages of those same groups fell.

Even though the wages of college-educated women have grown rapidly since 1979, a female college graduate in 2011 earned $24.31 an hour—$7.50, or about 24 percent, less than a male college graduate that same year and roughly $3.00, or about 11 percent, less than a male college graduate earned in 1979, more than 30 years ago. Thus, the gender wage gap among college graduates has shrunk but remains sizable.

Table 4.17 shows a breakdown of employment in 2011 by the highest degree attained and by gender and nativity status. Some 33.2 percent of those employed

Table 4.17 Educational attainment of the employed, by gender and nativity, 2011

	Percent of employment			Native born	Foreign born
	Men	Women	All		
Highest degree attained					
Less than high school	10.2%	6.5%	8.4%	5.1%	25.9%
High school/GED	30.2	25.6	28.0	28.4	25.7
Some college	19.0	20.5	19.7	21.3	11.3
Associate degree	9.3	12.2	10.7	11.4	6.9
College degree	20.8	23.1	21.9	22.7	17.9
Advanced degree*	10.6	12.1	11.3	11.1	12.3
Total	100.0	100.0	100.0	100.0	100.0
Cumulative education level					
High school or less	40.4%	32.1%	36.4%	33.5%	51.6%
Less than a college degree	68.6	64.8	66.8	66.2	69.8
College degree or more	31.4	35.2	33.2	33.8	30.2
Advanced degree*	10.6	12.1	11.3	11.1	12.3

* Includes law degrees, Ph.D.s, M.B.A.s, and similar degrees

Source: Authors' analysis of Current Population Survey Outgoing Rotation Group microdata

had at least a four-year college degree: 21.9 percent had a college degree only, and 11.3 percent also had a graduate or professional degree. Correspondingly, 66.8 percent of people employed had less than a college degree: 8.4 percent did not complete high school, 28.0 percent completed high school or obtained a GED, another 19.7 percent attended college but earned no degree beyond high school, and 10.7 percent held an associate degree. These data reinforce the earlier observation that the poor wage performance experienced by the "less educated" (frequently defined by economists as those without a college degree) between 1979 and 1995 and then in the 2002–2007 recovery affected a very large share of the workforce. This is important to note because the language used in public discussion frequently asserts that the "less educated" or "unskilled" have done poorly, leaving the impression that they are a small part of the population. But if "less educated" implicitly corresponds to those without a four-year college degree—who constitute about two-thirds of employed people—then it is rather misguided to consider this group as small. It was even more misguided during the 1980s, when this group comprised between about 75 percent and 80 percent of those employed.

Also worth noting is that workers with more than a high school degree but less than a four-year college degree now make up a group larger in size (30.4 percent of unemployment) than high school graduates (28.0 percent) and almost as large as those with at least a bachelor's degree (33.2 percent). Also noteworthy is that female workers have substantially more education than male workers; women have a larger share with associate degrees, college degrees, and advanced degrees.

The educational attainment of the workforce differs by immigration status. Native-born workers are more likely to have at least a college degree than foreign-born workers. Immigrants are more likely to have advanced degrees (12.3 percent versus 11.1 percent), but fewer have just college degrees (17.9 percent versus 22.7 percent). The starkest difference between foreign- and native-born workers is that immigrants are far more likely to lack a high school education (25.9 percent) than natives (5.1 percent). The data underlying Table 4.17 show that half of all workers who lack a high school credential are immigrants.

Figure 4O provides a further breakdown of the "less than high school" or "high school dropout" category by race and ethnicity. Only 4.1 percent of native-born whites and 6.7 percent of native-born blacks lack a high school degree, while 11.6 percent of native-born Hispanics do. Thus, there are very small proportions of native-born workers without a high school credential, and this is quite remarkable given that in 1973 (when the immigrant workforce was smaller) 28.5 percent of workers lacked a high school credential. Across racial and ethnic groups, a larger share of immigrants lacks a high school credential. Hispanic immigrants have by far the greatest concentration of workers without a high school credential, at 44.3 percent.

Figure 40 Share of the employed lacking a high school degree, by race/ethnicity and nativity status, 2011

Source: Authors' analysis of basic monthly Current Population Survey microdata

Young workers' wages

Young workers' prospects are an apt barometer of the strength of the labor market. When the labor market is strong for workers the prospects for young workers are very strong, and when the labor market is weak their prospects are very weak. This is because young workers tend to be more readily laid off in downturns and have the hardest time finding employment when jobs are scarce. In general, younger workers are "marginal workers." The recent decade affirms this general finding, as the wages of entry-level workers have fared extremely poorly during this period of general wage stagnation. This happened as well from 1973 to 1995, when the most dramatic erosion of wages was among young workers. Also consistent with this volatility of young workers' wages is that young workers experienced the fastest wage growth over the 1995–2000 period of booming wages.

Table 4.18 presents trends in wages of entry-level high school and college graduates by gender, where an entry-level worker is defined as one who has been in the workforce long enough to potentially have one to seven years of experience. It is interesting to note that in the recent period of disappointing wage growth, wages actually fell among every entry-level group, both high school and college graduates and both men and women. That is, real wages fell for entry-level men and women high school *and* college graduates in the years between 2000 and 2007, and there were steep wage declines for *each* group of entry-level workers

Table 4.18 Hourly wages of entry-level and experienced workers, by gender and education, 1973–2011 (2011 dollars)

	Real hourly wage							Change				
	1973	1979	1989	1995	2000	2007	2011	1979–1989	1989–2000	2000–2007	2007–2011	1979–2011
High school												
Men												
Entry*	$15.92	$15.64	$12.59	$11.67	$12.82	$12.70	$11.68	-19.5%	1.8%	-0.9%	-8.0%	-25.3%
Age 34–40	22.75	22.39	19.47	18.66	19.44	19.43	18.42	-13.0	-0.2	-0.1	-5.2	-17.7
Age 49–55	23.97	23.88	21.96	20.94	20.80	20.89	20.61	-8.0	-5.3	0.4	-1.3	-13.7
Women												
Entry*	$11.66	$11.56	$10.30	$9.96	$10.93	$10.23	$9.92	-10.8%	6.1%	-6.4%	-3.1%	-14.2%
Age 34–40	13.38	13.50	13.51	13.64	14.52	14.69	14.14	0.0	7.5	1.2	-3.7	4.7
Age 49–55	13.95	13.89	14.21	14.31	15.24	15.78	15.35	2.3	7.3	3.5	-2.7	10.5
College												
Men												
Entry**	$21.11	$20.61	$21.07	$19.51	$23.47	$22.88	$21.68	2.2%	11.4%	-2.5%	-5.2%	5.2%
Age 34–40	34.07	32.03	31.17	31.88	35.33	37.10	36.24	-2.7	13.4	5.0	-2.3	13.1
Age 49–55	35.11	35.50	35.05	35.20	36.41	36.39	36.40	-1.3	3.9	-0.1	0.0	2.5
Women												
Entry**	$17.69	$16.30	$18.34	$17.95	$20.00	$19.67	$18.80	12.5%	9.0%	-1.6%	-4.4%	15.4%
Age 34–40	21.11	18.68	21.18	23.86	25.99	27.15	27.39	13.4	22.7	4.4	0.9	46.6
Age 49–55	20.14	18.91	20.56	23.94	25.19	27.04	27.11	8.8	22.5	7.3	0.3	43.4

* Entry-level wage measured as wage of those from 19 to 25 years old
** Entry-level wage measured as wage of those from 23 to 29 years old

Source: Authors' analysis of Current Population Survey Outgoing Rotation Group microdata

in the recessionary years between 2007 and 2011. As a result, growth since 2000 has been far worse than pre-2000. For example, between 2000 and 2011, hourly wages of entry-level high school graduates fell 8.9 percent for men and 9.3 percent for women; for college-educated men and women at the entry level, wages over that period fell 7.6 percent and 6.0 percent, respectively. This contrasts with the extremely strong wage growth for each of these groups from 1995 to 2000, when wages rose roughly 10 percent for entry-level high school men and women, 20.3 percent for entry-level college men, and 11.4 percent for entry-level college women. This change illustrates the vast swing in wages of entry-level workers between a period of strong wage growth and one with stagnant wages.

The longer-term trends in the hourly wages of entry-level high school graduates are shown in **Figure 4P**. The wage boom of the late 1990s carried over into the first few years of the 2000s for most workers, but it ended in 2001 for these entry-level workers, and wages have fallen since (except in 2009 for women and 2007 for men). Figure 4P also shows the dramatic deterioration of wages for entry-level high school men over the 1979 to 1996 period, an indicator of the loss of earning power among non-college-educated men and the consequent even larger loss for younger workers. Entry-level wages of female high school graduates have remained significantly below those of their male peers, and their wages also fell substantially from 1979 to 1996.

Figure 4P Real entry-level wages of high school graduates, by gender, 1973–2011

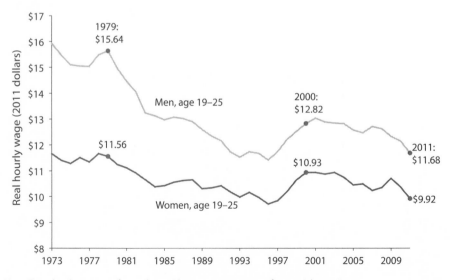

Note: Entry-level wages are for workers with one to seven years of potential experience.

Source: Authors' analysis of Current Population Survey Outgoing Rotation Group microdata

As a result, despite the strong wage increases in the late 1990s, the entry-level wages of men and women high school graduates in 2011 were far below their levels of 1979 or 1973. For instance, the entry-level hourly wage of a young male high school graduate in 2011 was 25.3 percent less than the wage of the equivalent worker in 1979, a drop of roughly $4.00 per hour (in 2011 dollars). Among women, the entry-level high school wage fell 14.2 percent in this period, a drop of $1.64. Note that wages in entry-level jobs held by high school–educated women are still roughly 15 percent less than those in jobs held by their male counterparts in 2011, though that gap has narrowed from about 26 percent in 1979.

Entry-level wages fell among both female and male college graduates from 2000 to 2007, 2.5 percent among men and 1.6 percent among women, and tumbled further in the recessionary years after 2007 (**Figure 4Q**). This means that young college graduates who finished their education in the last five years or so are earning significantly less than their older brothers and sisters who graduated in the late 1990s. The poor wage growth in this last decade contrasts markedly with the period of strongly rising wages for entry-level male college graduates from 1995 to 2000, when wages grew 20.3 percent. In the prior 16 years, from 1979 to 1995, the male entry-level college hourly wage fell more than a dollar. Thus, the period of falling wages since 2000 does not stand as the exception to the rule

Figure 4Q Real entry-level wages of college graduates, by gender, 1973–2011

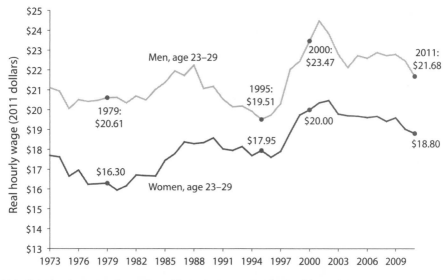

Note: Entry-level wages are for workers with one to seven years of potential experience.

Source: Authors' analysis of Current Population Survey Outgoing Rotation Group microdata

for young male college graduates; it is the wage boom of the late 1990s that seems exceptional. In 2011 the hourly wage of entry-level male college graduates was just a bit over $1.00 higher than in 1979, a rise of 5.2 percent over 32 years.

The wages of female college graduates (including those with advanced degrees) have grown more strongly than the wages among any other group of women, and this strength is reflected in the long-term trend among entry-level female college graduates; their wages grew 15.4 percent, or $2.50, from 1979 to 2011. In this light, the erosion of wages among entry-level female college graduates since 2000 stands out, with a fall of 1.6 percent from 2000 to 2007 and a 4.4 percent decline from 2007 to 2011. In the most recent decade, the most-educated workers (college graduates) with the newest skills (young college graduates) did not fare well at all, as their wages fell even as overall productivity in the economy continued to soar.

The wage trends for older workers, those 34–40 years old and 49–55 years old, were generally more positive than for the youngest workers among both education groups and for men as well as women (Table 4.18).

The erosion of job quality for young workers can also be seen in their lower likelihood of receiving employer-provided health insurance or pensions. In particular, we are focused on whether entry-level workers receive these benefits from

Figure 4R Share of recent high school graduates with employer health/pension coverage, 1979–2010

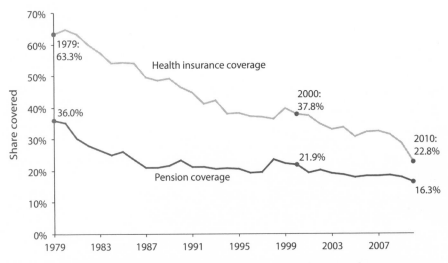

Note: Sample is of private wage-and-salary earners age 19–25 who worked at least 20 hours per week and 26 weeks per year. Coverage is defined as being included in an employer-provided plan where the employer paid for at least some of the coverage.

Source: Authors' analysis of Current Population Survey Annual Social and Economic Supplement microdata

Figure 4S Share of recent college graduates with employer health/pension coverage, 1979–2010

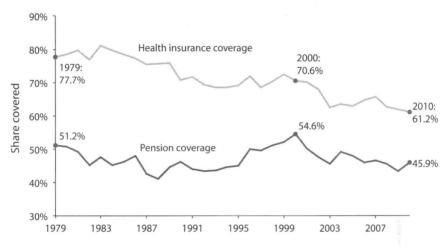

Note: Sample is of private wage-and-salary earners age 23–29 who worked at least 20 hours per week and 26 weeks per year. Coverage is defined as being included in an employer-provided plan where the employer paid for at least some of the coverage.

Source: Authors' analysis of Current Population Survey Annual Social and Economic Supplement microdata

their *own* employers (not from their parents' employers). **Figures 4R** and **4S** show the rate of employer-provided health insurance and pension coverage in entry-level jobs for high school and college graduates, respectively. Employer-provided health insurance among recent high school graduates fell by roughly half, from 63.3 percent to 32.5 percent, between 1979 and 2007—even before the substantial erosion to just 22.8 percent in 2010 (the latest available data). Employer-provided health insurance coverage is perhaps the single best indicator to workers as to whether they have a good-quality job. This dramatic erosion of health coverage among young high school–educated workers, then, is a telling indicator of their loss of good jobs over the last few decades. Pension coverage fell over this period as well, from an already low 36.0 percent in 1979 to an even lower 16.3 percent in 2010.

Health insurance coverage also fell among recent college graduates, but not as drastically as among recent high school graduates. The share covered was 77.7 percent in 1979, 70.6 percent in 2000, and 61.2 percent in 2010. The fall since 2000 therefore exceeded the fall over the entire 1979 to 2000 period. The fact that employer-provided coverage is much higher among entry-level college graduates than entry-level high school graduates tells us that there remain significant economic benefits for completing college. But the fact that employer-provided health insurance coverage is increasingly less likely to be provided to entry-level college graduates tells us that job quality among college graduates is deteriorating. Pension coverage among young college graduates follows the overall pattern discussed in an earlier section. It fell between 1979 and the late 1980s and then regained its earlier level by 1998, presumably because of increased participation in defined-contribution plans. However, this group's pension coverage fell from 2000 to 2010 by 8.7 percentage points, from 54.6 percent to 45.9 percent. This sharp reduction in both health and pension benefits for young college graduates over the last decade indicates a substantial job quality problem even for those with high educational attainment.

The growth of within-group wage inequality

The data presented so far illustrate the various dimensions of wage inequality. The between-group inequality of workers by both education and experience (or age) can be characterized as a growth in differentials in education and experience, which are sometimes labeled as an increase in the "returns to education and experience" or as a shift in the rewards or price of skill. We now examine in greater depth the growth of *within-group* wage inequality, the inequality among workers with similar education and experience.

This growth in within-group wage inequality was shown earlier in Table 4.13. The analysis in **Table 4.19** illustrates the growth of this type of inequality by presenting wage trends of low-, middle-, and high-wage high school and college-educated workers, by gender, where low, middle, and high earners refer, respectively, to those with wages at the 10th, 50th (median), and 90th percentiles. The data show a growing wage gap among college graduates and high school graduates.

Because of rising within-group inequality, the wage growth of the median or "typical" worker within each group has been less than that of the average worker within each group. For instance, the median wage of the male high school graduate fell 19.7 percent from 1979 to 2011, compared with a 12.7 percent drop in the group's average wage (Table 4.15). Similarly, the wage growth of male college graduates in the 1979–2011 period was 16.5 percent at the average (Table 4.15) but only 9.0 percent at the median (Table 4.19).

Table 4.19 shows that, while the high (90th percentile) wage among female college graduates grew 53.7 percent from 1979 to 2011, the low (10th percentile) wage in this group rose just 11.5 percent, a 42.2 percentage-point disparity. Similarly, wage trends at the top of the college male wage ladder (26.0 percent growth) and the bottom (a 6.0 percent decline) diverged dramatically from 1979 to 2011. Wage disparities among high school graduates grew over the last few decades but not as much as among college graduates.

Table 4.19 Hourly wages by wage percentile, gender, and education, 1973–2011 (2011 dollars)

	Real hourly wage							Change				
	1973	1979	1989	1995	2000	2007	2011	1979–1989	1989–2000	2000–2007	2007–2011	1979–2011
High school												
Men												
Low	$10.57	$9.79	$8.42	$8.18	$8.93	$8.70	$8.33	-14.0%	6.1%	-2.6%	-4.3%	-14.9%
Median	19.06	18.67	16.34	15.07	15.88	15.84	15.00	-12.5	-2.8	-0.3	-5.3	-19.7
High	31.13	30.47	28.81	27.71	29.07	29.61	29.80	-5.4	0.9	1.8	0.7	-2.2
Women												
Low	$7.16	$8.17	$6.68	$6.97	$7.64	$7.61	$7.64	-18.2%	14.3%	-0.4%	0.4%	-6.4%
Median	11.83	11.56	11.56	11.39	12.17	12.19	12.01	0.0	5.4	0.1	-1.5	3.9
High	19.57	19.73	20.82	21.05	21.87	21.94	22.09	5.5	5.0	0.4	0.6	12.0
College												
Men												
Low	$13.05	$12.63	$11.93	$11.41	$13.04	$12.54	$11.87	-5.5%	9.3%	-3.8%	-5.4%	-6.0%
Median	24.50	23.81	24.74	24.41	26.97	26.98	25.96	3.9	9.0	0.0	-3.8	9.0
High	45.69	43.74	44.85	47.70	52.20	56.33	55.10	2.5	16.4	7.9	-2.2	26.0
Women												
Low	$10.04	$9.07	$9.41	$9.59	$10.65	$10.79	$10.12	3.7%	13.2%	1.3%	-6.3%	11.5%
Median	17.34	15.75	18.18	19.34	20.92	20.87	20.25	15.4	15.0	-0.2	-3.0	28.5
High	27.39	26.77	31.67	35.84	40.12	41.69	41.15	18.3	26.7	3.9	-1.3	53.7

Note: Low, median, and high earners refer, respectively, to those earning the 10th, 50th, and 90th percentile wage.

Source: Authors' analysis of Current Population Survey Outgoing Rotation Group microdata

The question remains, however, as to how much the growth in overall wage inequality in particular time periods has been driven by changes in inequality among groups of workers with different education levels or other measures of skill (between-group wage inequality) versus changes in inequality among workers with comparable education or skill (within-group wage inequality). It would also be useful to know the role of the growth of between- and within-group inequality on growing wage inequality at the top (the 90/50 differential) versus the bottom (the 50/10 differential), but measurement techniques for answering this question are not readily available.

Table 4.20 presents the trends in overall wage inequality (as measured by the standard deviation of log hourly wages) and the trends in within-group and between-group wage inequality. These measures allow an examination of how much of the change in overall wage inequality in particular periods was due to changes in within-group wage inequality and between-group wage inequality (primarily changes in the differentials for education and experience).

The data in Table 4.20 indicate that almost 60 percent of the growth of wage inequality since 1979 (to either 2007 or 2011) was driven by the growth of within-group wage inequality. Among women, for instance, overall wage inequality, measured as a standard deviation (dispersion around the average) of log wages, grew 0.140 from 1979 to 2007, of which 0.082 was due to growth of within-group inequality. Similarly, 0.073, or 63.8 percent, of the 0.114 increase in overall male wage inequality from 1979 to 2007 was due to growing within-group inequality.

There were very different trends in particular subperiods. For this analysis Table 4.20 departs from the strictly business cycle periods examined in other tables (though they can be constructed from the data presented) and examines changes in inequality measures for the 1979–1995 period, the late 1990s period (1995–2000), and then the business cycle from 2000 to 2007 and the post-2007 trend. The growth of wage inequality in the earliest period, from 1979 to 1995, was driven by both within-group inequality and between-group inequality, with the within-group wage changes contributing about 55 to 56 percent of the growth of overall wage inequality. Most of the longer-term growth in wage inequality occurred in this early period. The late 1990s saw no change in wage inequality among men and a reduction in wage inequality among women. Wage inequality remained stable among men because growing within-group wage inequality was offset by falling between-group wage inequality. Among women it was falling within-group wage inequality that reduced overall wage inequality in the late 1990s.

The patterns of 1979–1995 returned in the 2000–2007 cycle, with wage inequality growing again, but this time it was primarily driven by within-group wage changes, which accounted for about 80 percent of the growth of wage inequality. This corresponds to our earlier finding that the college premium and other between-group differentials did not expand much in this period even though wage

Table 4.20 Contribution of within-group and between-group inequality to total wage inequality, 1973–2011

	Women				Men			
	Overall wage inequality*	Between-group inequality**	Within-group inequality***	Contribution of within-group inequality (3)/(1)	Overall wage inequality*	Between-group inequality**	Within-group inequality***	Contribution of within-group inequality (3)/(1)
	(1)	(2)	(3)		(1)	(2)	(3)	
1973	0.478	0.061	0.418	87.3%	0.506	0.083	0.423	83.6%
1979	0.446	0.044	0.402	90.1	0.506	0.078	0.428	84.7
1989	0.529	0.082	0.447	84.5	0.579	0.112	0.467	80.7
1995	0.562	0.095	0.467	83.1	0.595	0.118	0.478	80.2
2000	0.552	0.094	0.458	82.9	0.595	0.114	0.481	80.8
2007	0.586	0.102	0.484	82.7	0.620	0.119	0.501	80.8
2011	0.593	0.108	0.485	81.8	0.635	0.128	0.507	79.9
Change, subperiods								
1979–1995	0.116	0.051	0.065	56.1%	0.089	0.040	0.049	55.2%
1995–2000	-0.009	-0.001	-0.009	91.8	0.000	-0.003	0.003	****
2000–2007	0.033	0.007	0.026	78.0	0.025	0.005	0.020	80.9
2007–2011	0.008	0.006	0.001	14.8	0.014	0.009	0.005	37.7
Change, longer-term								
1979–2007	0.140	0.057	0.082	58.9	0.114	0.041	0.073	63.8
1979–2011	0.147	0.064	0.084	56.7	0.129	0.050	0.078	60.9

* Measured as standard deviation of log wages

** Reflects changes in education, experience, race/ethnicity, marital status, and regional differentials

*** Measured as mean square error from a standard (log) wage regression

**** Not applicable because denominator is zero

Source: Authors' analysis of Current Population Survey Outgoing Rotation Group microdata

inequality, mostly in the top half, grew strongly. The recessionary period after 2007 saw wage inequality continue to grow, but the character shifted again, relying more on the between-group changes. This is also what we saw in Table 4.13 as experience differentials and some education differentials expanded. These trends may reflect the more difficult experience of younger workers and those with less education in this very deep downturn; therefore, these trends may not persist as unemployment falls over the next few years—an interesting trend to watch.

Table 4.20 makes clear that any explanation of growing wage inequality must go beyond explaining changes in skill, education, experience, or other wage differentials and be able to explain growing inequalities within each of these categories, since they account for more than half of all the growth in overall wage inequality.

Wage inequality by race/ethnicity and gender

Race and ethnicity have long played an important role in shaping employment opportunities and labor market outcomes, and **Table 4.21** examines changes in those dimensions of the wage structure. Wage trends are presented by gender for two indicators of the middle of the wage structure (the median hourly wage and the average hourly wage of high school–educated workers) for four populations: white, black, Hispanic, and Asian. (A finer breakdown of groups—for example, subpopulations of Hispanics—is not possible because of sample size limitations; for the same reason, trends for the 1980s are unavailable. Also, note that our definitions of race/ethnicity categories exclude Hispanics from the white, black, and Asian groups.)

From 2000 to 2007 growth in the male median wage was relatively modest or stagnant for whites, Hispanics, and blacks. The 10.7 percent rise among Asian men is an exception, though most of that growth occurred by 2003. The wage trends among male high school graduates tell a similar story of largely stagnant wages for each racial/ethnic group from 2000 to 2007, including Asians (the Asian male high school wage is far below the median Asian wage so, unlike other racial/ethnic groups, it reflects a different part of the wage structure than the median). Wages deteriorated among middle-earning men over the 2007 to 2011 period regardless of race or ethnicity and regardless of measure—median or high school wages. Over the 1989–2000 period, the male high school wage fared poorly among each racial/ethnic group, except Asians, despite strong wage growth in the late 1990s. There have been large wage gaps between black and white men, and Hispanic and white men, since 1989. For example, examining wages averaged over the 2009–2011 period, the wage gap between black and white men, measured here as the ratio of black to white hourly wages, was about 79 percent among high school graduates and 72 percent among median-wage workers. Measured over the same period, the wage gap between Hispanic and white men, measured as the ratio of Hispanic to white hourly wages, was about 83 percent

Table 4.21 Hourly wage growth by gender and race/ethnicity, 1989–2011 (2011 dollars)

	Real hourly wage					Change				
	1989	1995	2000	2007	2011	1989–2000	1989–1995	1995–2000	2000–2007	2007–2011
Men										
Median wage										
White	$19.01	$18.29	$19.84	$20.33	$19.76	4.4%	-3.8%	8.5%	2.4%	-2.8%
Black	13.76	13.37	14.56	14.61	14.26	5.8	-2.8	8.9	0.3	-2.4
Hispanic	12.79	11.65	12.84	13.23	12.74	0.4	-8.9	10.2	3.0	-3.7
Asian	17.77	17.57	19.80	21.92	21.41	11.4	-1.1	12.7	10.7	-2.3
High school wage*										
White	$18.67	$17.86	$19.08	$19.16	$18.80	2.2%	-4.3%	6.8%	0.4%	-1.8%
Black	14.91	14.29	15.32	14.93	14.61	2.7	-4.2	7.2	-2.5	-2.1
Hispanic	15.47	14.68	15.48	15.97	15.31	0.1	-5.1	5.5	3.1	-4.1
Asian	16.33	15.93	16.99	17.20	16.22	4.1	-2.4	6.6	1.2	-5.7
Women										
Median wage										
White	$13.31	$13.63	$14.88	$15.95	$15.89	11.8%	2.4%	9.2%	7.2%	-0.4%
Black	11.86	11.73	13.04	13.27	13.13	9.9	-1.1	11.2	1.8	-1.1
Hispanic	10.58	10.37	11.04	11.65	11.77	4.3	-2.0	6.5	5.5	1.0
Asian	13.78	14.02	15.91	16.55	16.42	15.4	1.8	13.4	4.0	-0.8
High school wage*										
White	$13.11	$13.31	$14.09	$14.57	$14.42	7.5%	1.6%	5.8%	3.4%	-1.0%
Black	12.09	11.99	12.94	13.24	12.69	7.0	-0.9	8.0	2.3	-4.2
Hispanic	12.17	12.26	12.74	12.98	12.79	4.7	0.8	3.9	1.9	-1.5
Asian	12.48	12.62	13.57	13.22	13.02	8.8	1.1	7.6	-2.6	-1.5

* Average wage of high school–educated workers

Source: Authors' analysis of Current Population Survey Outgoing Rotation Group microdata

among high school graduates and 65 percent among median-wage workers. These wage gaps among men have neither expanded nor shrunk appreciably since 1989, indicating that the growth of male wage inequality has not been grounded in expanded racial/ethnic wage gaps.

Wage growth among women has generally been stronger than among men in recent decades, as discussed previously. However, wage growth for men exceeded that for women from 2000 to 2007 among Asians, and among Hispanics men did better by one measure (high school wages) but not by the other measure (median wages). In the recessionary years after 2007, wages fell for both men and women, but the fall was greater among men in nearly every race and ethnic group. Post-2007, Hispanic men seem to have suffered the largest wage declines among men, and black women had the greatest wage declines among women. From 1989 to 2000, Asians had the largest wage gains among men and women. Hispanics, on the other hand, saw the least wage growth among both men and women.

As with men, there have been large wage gaps between women of different races and ethnicities. Examining wages averaged over the 2009–2011 period, wages of black female high school graduates were about 89 percent of those of their white counterparts, while black median-wage workers earned about 84 percent as much as comparable white women. Ratios of Hispanic to white women's wages in 2009–2011 were 89 percent among high school graduates and 74 percent among median-wage workers. There has been some growth in these wage gaps among women, ranging from 3 to 6 percentage points. Thus, some of the increased wage inequality among women corresponds to greater racial/ethnic inequalities.

A common theme has been that women's wages have generally fared better than men's over the last few decades. **Table 4.22** presents the median wages of men and women and the ratio of women's to men's hourly wage as a way to describe the trend in the gender differential over time. In 1973 the ratio of the female median wage to the male median wage was 63.1 percent and, except for the 1970s, this ratio has increased in every time period; it stood at 84.0 percent in 2011. Thus, the wage gap between the genders was roughly halved over this time period. The rapid closing of the gender gap occurred primarily between 1979 and 1995, mostly as the result of a steady fall in the male median wage during the 1980s and the early 1990s but also because of a steady modest growth of the female median wage.

Another important dimension to examine is how the gender wage gap has changed for the various cohorts of workers over the postwar period and by age

Table 4.22 Gender wage gap, 1973–2011 (2011 dollars)

	1973	1979	1989	1995	2000	2007	2011
Real median hourly wage							
Women	$11.83	$11.99	$12.92	$13.07	$14.20	$14.91	$14.89
Men	18.74	19.13	17.68	17.03	18.21	18.29	17.72
Ratio women/men	63.1%	62.7%	73.1%	76.7%	78.0%	81.5%	84.0%

Source: Authors' analysis of Current Population Survey Outgoing Rotation Group microdata

Figure 4T Gender wage gap, by age cohort

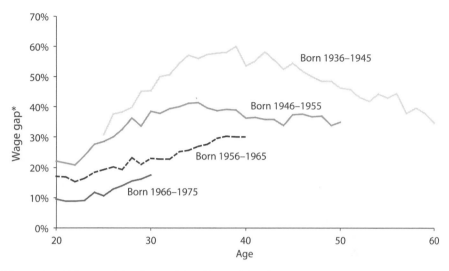

* Percent by which women's hourly wage is less than men's hourly wage

Source: Authors' analysis of Moore and Shierholz (2007)

within each cohort. **Figure 4T** shows the gender wage gap via the female *disadvantage* in wages at particular ages for several birth cohorts (such as those born between 1946 and 1955 or between 1956 and 1965). It is clear that in each cohort the wage gap rises from when workers enter the workforce in their 20s to the late 30s or age 40. For instance, for those born between 1956 and 1965 the gender wage gap was about 21 percent when they were in their late 20s but rose to 29 percent by their late 30s. Perhaps most important, the wage gap has lessened over time, as the gap is less for each succeeding cohort (since each successive cohort's line is lower than that of the preceding cohort). For example, women born between 1936 and 1945 were paid 58 percent less per hour worked than men when they were in their late 30s; for women born 20 years later, the gender wage gap was just half that large, 29 percent.

Research shows that shifts in skills, educational attainment, the gender composition of work, reductions in discrimination, changing social norms, and other factors have contributed to the closing of the gender gap.

Productivity and the compensation/productivity gap

Productivity growth, which is the growth of the output of goods and services per hour worked, provides the basis for the growth of living standards. However, the experience of the vast majority of workers in recent decades has been that productivity growth actually provides only the *potential* for rising living standards. Recent history, especially since 2000, has shown that wages and compensation of the typical worker and income growth of the typical family have lagged tremendously behind the nation's fast productivity growth. In contrast, the hourly compensation of a typical worker grew in tandem with productivity over the 1948 to 1973 period. This section examines the divergence between productivity growth and real hourly compensation growth for the typical (median) worker, focusing on the three "wedges," or factors, behind the divergence. These wedges explain the gap between the more than 80 percent growth in productivity from 1973 to 2011 and the correspondingly weak growth of real hourly compensation of the median worker, just 10.7 percent.

Figure 4U presents both the cumulative growth in productivity per hour worked of the total economy (inclusive of the private, government, and nonprofits sectors) since 1948 and the cumulative growth in inflation-adjusted average hourly compensation of private-sector production/nonsupervisory workers (who make up over 80 percent of payroll employment; their wages and compensation were presented in Table 4.3 and Figure 4B). Productivity and the typical worker's hourly compensation grew together from 1948 until 1973. After 1973, however, productivity grew strongly, especially after 1995, while the typical worker's compensation was relatively stagnant. This divergence of pay and productivity has

Figure 4U Cumulative change in total economy productivity and real hourly compensation of production/nonsupervisory workers, 1948–2011

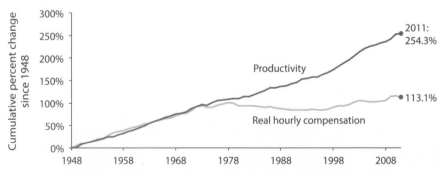

Note: Data are for compensation of production/nonsupervisory workers in the private sector and productivity of the total economy.

Source: Authors' analysis of unpublished Total Economy Productivity data from Bureau of Labor Statistics Labor Productivity and Costs program, wage data from BLS Current Employment Statistics program, and Bureau of Economic Analysis National Income and Product Accounts

Figure 4V Cumulative change in hourly productivity, real average hourly compensation, and median compensation, 1973–2011

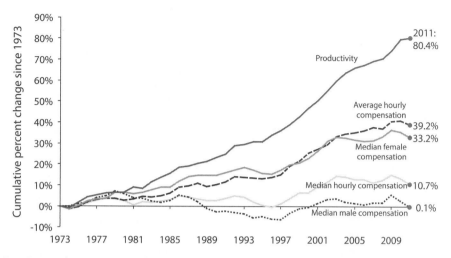

Note: Data are for compensation of production/nonsupervisory workers in the private sector and productivity of the total economy.

Source: Authors' analysis of unpublished Total Economy Productivity data from the Bureau of Labor Statistics Labor Productivity and Costs program, data from the Bureau of Economic Analysis National Income and Product Accounts, and Current Population Survey Outgoing Rotation Group microdata

meant that many workers were not benefiting from productivity growth—the economy could afford higher pay but was not providing it.

Figure 4V provides more detail on the productivity/pay disparity from 1973 to 2011 by charting the cumulative growth since 1973 in productivity, average hourly compensation, and median hourly compensation of all workers, men, and women. As Figure 4V illustrates, productivity grew 80.4 percent from 1973 to 2011, enough to generate large advances in living standards and wages if productivity gains were broadly shared. But average compensation—which includes the pay of CEOs and day laborers alike—lagged productivity growth, 39.2 percent versus 80.4 percent. This "wedge" between worker compensation and overall productivity growth—that of average worker pay not keeping up with productivity—partly reflects the *shift from wage income (labor income) to capital income* described in Chapter 2.

Hourly compensation of the median worker grew even less, just 10.7 percent. Most of the growth in median hourly compensation occurred in the late 1990s period of strong recovery; excluding the 1995 to 2000 period, median hourly compensation grew just 4.9 percent between 1973 and 2011. (As Figure 4A showed at the start of this chapter, productivity and median hourly compensation growth diverged markedly between 2000 and 2011.) This second "wedge," of the median worker (whether male or female) not enjoying growth in compensation as fast as that of higher-wage workers, especially the very highest paid, reflects growing *wage and benefit inequality*.

A third "wedge" not visible in Figure 4V but examined later has to do with the different measures of prices used to compute productivity growth versus compensation growth. The output measure used to compute productivity is converted to real, or constant (inflation-adjusted), dollars based on the components of national output (GDP). Average hourly compensation and the measures of median hourly compensation are converted to real, or constant, dollars based on measures of price change in what consumers purchase. Prices for national output have grown more slowly than prices for consumer purchases. Therefore, the same growth in nominal, or current dollar, wages and output yields faster growth in real (inflation-adjusted) output (which is adjusted for changes in the prices of investment goods, exports, and consumer purchases) than in real wages (which is adjusted for changes in consumer purchases only). That is, workers have suffered worsening "terms of trade," in which the prices of things they buy (i.e., consumer goods and services) have risen faster than prices of the items they produce (consumer goods but also capital goods). Thus, if workers consumed microprocessors and machine tools as well as groceries, their real wage growth would have been better and in line with productivity growth. In any case, it is important to examine this *terms-of-trade wedge between productivity and compensation growth*.

Table 4.23 depicts the basic trends in compensation and productivity and provides a breakdown (decomposition) that identifies the contribution of each factor to the productivity/median compensation gap in particular subperiods and overall from 1973 to 2011. The particular subperiods usually chosen in our analyses are business cycle peaks—years of low unemployment—with some exceptions. However, for this discussion the two business cycles, 1979–1989 and 1989–2000, are divided into the periods 1979–1995 and 1995–2000 to separate the period of low productivity growth from the period starting in 1995 when productivity growth accelerated.

Panel A shows the annual growth rates of median hourly wages and compensation, average hourly compensation, and hourly productivity. All measures are for the total economy, covering all sectors of the economy. The annual growth of the productivity/median hourly compensation gap is also presented for each period. That gap grew 1.3 percent a year from 1973 to 2011; it grew most quickly from 2000 to 2011 and from 1979 to 1995. Table 4.23 also shows that productivity accelerated in the late 1990s, growing 2.33 percent each year, far above the productivity growth of 1973–1995. Productivity growth since 2000 has remained much higher than during the "stagnation" of 1973–1995 but less than the productivity growth of the late 1990s.

Table 4.23 Factors contributing to the productivity/compensation gap, 1973–2011

	1973–1979	1979–1995	1995–2000	2000–2011	1973–2011
A. Basic trends (annual change)					
Median hourly wage	-0.26%	-0.15%	1.50%	0.05%	0.10%
Median hourly compensation	0.56	-0.17	1.13	0.35	0.27
Average hourly compensation	0.59	0.55	2.10	0.95	0.87
Productivity	1.08	1.29	2.33	1.88	1.56
Productivity/median compensation gap	0.52	1.46	1.21	1.53	1.30
B. Explanatory factors (percentage-point contribution to gap)					
Inequality of compensation	0.02	0.72	0.97	0.59	0.61
Shift in labor's share of income	0.03	0.23	-0.40	0.69	0.25
Divergence of consumer and output prices	0.46	0.51	0.64	0.24	0.44
Total	0.52	1.46	1.22	1.52	1.29
C. Explanatory factors (percent contribution to gap)					
Inequality of compensation	4.8%	49.6%	80.0%	38.9%	46.9%
Shift in labor's share of income	5.5	15.4	-32.5	45.3	19.0
Divergence of consumer and output prices	89.7	35.0	52.5	15.8	34.0
Total	100.0	100.0	100.0	100.0	100.0

Note: Rows in panels A and B show log annual change.

Source: Authors' analysis of Mishel and Gee (2012, Table 1)

Panels B and C show the percentage-point and percent contribution, respectively, of the explanatory factors behind the divergence of productivity and median hourly compensation. The first is the growing inequality of compensation, which is represented in this analysis by the changing ratio of average hourly to median hourly compensation. The second is the shift in labor's share of income, which is captured by changes in the nominal share of compensation in national output (GDP). The third factor is the divergence of consumer and output prices, the terms-of-trade wedge based on the change in consumer prices (with health benefits deflated by a medical index and the remaining portions of compensation deflated by consumer prices) relative to prices of national output.

The large productivity/median compensation gap from 2000 to 2011 was driven primarily by growing compensation inequality and the decline in labor's share of income; these two factors account for 38.9 percent and 45.3 percent, respectively, of the total gap. Terms of trade, or price divergences, were smaller in this period than in any other and accounted for only a small part, 15.8 percent, of the growing gap between productivity and median compensation.

Median hourly compensation accelerated in the late 1990s but not as much as productivity did, a divergence that generated a 1.21 percent gap on average each year from 1995 to 2000. This gap occurred despite labor's share of income *increasing*. In contrast, the earliest period, 1973–1979, saw no appreciable growth in compensation inequality or change in labor's share; the productivity/median compensation divergence primarily reflected price differences.

From 1973 to 2011 roughly half (46.9 percent) of the growth of the productivity/median compensation gap was due to increased compensation inequality, and about a fifth (19.0 percent) was due to a loss in labor's income share. About a third of the gap was driven by price differences.

Explaining the growing inequality of wages and compensation is the task of the rest of this chapter. It will follow a brief discussion of shifts in labor's share of income and the terms-of-trade effect.

The decline in the share of income accruing to workers has reduced workers' wage growth—meaning wages have grown less than they would have otherwise, as was examined directly in Chapter 2. There, we saw that the share of capital income in the corporate sector has grown significantly, driven by a comparably large increase in profitability, or the return to capital per dollar of plant and equipment. For instance, the share of income in the corporate sector going to capital income in the 2000s, especially in the recessionary years after 2007, was the highest in nearly 70 years. The share going to compensation was correspondingly at a low point. As explained in Chapter 2, the historically high returns to capital in 2007 relative to 1979 were equivalent to 3.4 percent, or $269 billion, of corporate-sector income. Had this amount of income not transferred from compensation to capital income, workers could have had a $3,400, or 4.3 percent, compensation increase. The transfer from compensation to capital income was even larger in 2010, as the capital income share of corporate income grew even larger. As a cause of the loss of wages for the typical worker, the income redistribution from labor to capital has been large when compared with factors such as the shift to services, globalization, the drop in union representation, or any of the other prominent explanations for growing wage inequality discussed in this chapter.

As for the terms-of-trade factor, there are two ways that the divergence in prices can be viewed. One way is to dismiss the divergence as a technical difference and to treat the associated productivity/pay gap as unimportant and uninteresting. The second way is to note that the widely articulated assumption that gains in labor productivity translate into improvements in living standards implies that these two price series—consumption and output—must converge in the long run. Given that this convergence has not occurred for several decades, the second view suggests that productivity is not translating fully into improved living standards, and that the divergence between consumption prices and output prices represents another mechanism by which workers are not benefiting from economic growth. Rather than being dismissed or set aside, the terms-of-trade disadvantage workers have faced—and its one-third share of the growth of the productivity/median compensation gap—deserves serious inquiry and a full explanation. Unfortunately, little research has been done in this area. In any case, the implication is that the "typical" worker is not benefiting fully from productivity growth.

The bottom line is that from 1973 to 2011 the 10.7 percent growth of real hourly compensation of the median worker greatly lagged the 80.4 percent productivity growth in the economy, a gap of 69.7 percentage points. Roughly two-thirds (65.9 percent) of that gap can be explained by rising inequality of compensation (meaning higher-wage workers garnered a hugely disproportionate share of the compensation gains) and a declining share of income accruing to labor compensation (and a corresponding increase accruing to capital income, or returns to wealth). Had this rise in compensation inequality and fall in labor's income share not occurred, the real hourly compensation of the median worker would have risen by 56.7 percent, 46 percentage points higher (65.9 percent of the 69.7 percentage-point gap between productivity and median compensation growth) than the actual 10.7 percent growth. That is a sizable loss for middle-wage and other workers. In short, over the last four decades the economy had the demonstrated potential to raise middle-wage workers' living standards far more than it actually did, and a redistribution of compensation to highly paid wage workers and a redistribution of income from workers to wealth holders prevented that from happening.

Factors driving wage inequality

Having described wage trends and the various dimensions of wage inequality, we turn to examining drivers of wage inequality. Rather than considering growing wage inequality as a whole, our approach is to examine the factors behind the growth of the three key wage gaps—those between the very top and top, the top and middle, and the middle and the bottom. These gaps have grown at different paces and in different periods and are not necessarily driven by the same factors. Therefore, the discussion of each factor driving wage inequality focuses on the magnitude of the impact, the timing of the impact, and the gap(s) affected. In some cases the discussion focuses on the impact of a factor on key education or occupation wage gaps, such as those between college-educated and high school–educated workers, or between white- and blue-collar workers. These other wage gaps have been frequently used in the literature and generally reflect the wage gap between the top and the middle.

Unemployment

Macroeconomic conditions greatly affect wage growth and wage inequality and are too often overlooked in explanations of rising wage and income inequality. Macroeconomic conditions reflect the overall health of the economy and determine whether it is producing below its capacity, as indicated by high unemployment and excess production capacity. Generally, slack in the economy is driven by monetary policy (e.g., the growth of the money supply and interest rates), fiscal policy (e.g., the size of the government surplus or deficit, with increasing deficits adding to demand and thereby lessening slack), and the U.S. international position (i.e., trade deficits and the flow of investment dollars abroad or from abroad to the United States). The recession that started in 2007 was the result of the burst of the housing bubble and the financial crisis that ensued (which suggests that financial regulation should also be listed as an additional macroeconomic policy). Macroeconomic factors that affect wage growth include not only those that limit or generate slack—reflected in unemployment and underemployment—but also those that shape productive potential or productivity, such as public and private investment, technological change, workforce skills, and work organization (how factors of production are combined).

Productivity growth and unemployment play key roles in driving wage trends. Productivity growth provides the potential for real wage gains and helps explain trends in wage growth. Unemployment, on the other hand, affects both average wage growth and wage inequality. The divergence of productivity and compensation growth was discussed in the last section; this section focuses on other macroeconomic factors influencing wage inequality, particularly the extent of unemployment and underemployment (trends in these factors are explored in detail in Chapter 5).

The burdens of an underperforming economy and high unemployment are not equally shared; lower- and middle-income families and racial and ethnic minorities are more likely to experience unemployment, underemployment, and slower wage growth because of a weak economy. For many years, until the last two decades, white-collar workers and high-wage workers were less affected by unemployment and recessions. Unsurprisingly, therefore, high unemployment is a factor that widens wage and income inequality.

There are a number of mechanisms through which high unemployment affects wages and, especially, affects wages differently for different groups of workers. The wages of groups that have lower wages; less education, experience, or skill; and less power in the labor market are generally more adversely affected by high unemployment and underemployment. In other words, those already disadvantaged in the labor market become even more disadvantaged in a recession or in a weak economy. Conversely, as unemployment falls in a recovery and stays low, the greatest benefit accrues to those with the least power in the labor market—non-college-educated, blue-collar, minority, young, and low-wage workers.

Why do these workers benefit disproportionately during a recovery? First, these groups experience the greatest employment decline in a downturn and the greatest employment growth in a recovery. This greater-than-average gain in employment reflects higher demand for these workers and consequently provides them with a greater increase in leverage with employers, a position that generates higher wages. Second, as unemployment drops, more opportunities for upward mobility arise for these workers, as they switch jobs either to a new employer or within the same firm. Third, unions are able to bargain higher wages when unemployment is low. Fourth, macroeconomic conditions and institutional and structural factors interact in important ways. For instance, the U.S. economy in the early 1980s experienced a surge of imports and a growing trade deficit, a decline in manufacturing, a weakening of unions, and a large erosion of the minimum wage that coincided with (and, as was the case with trade and manufacturing problems, partly caused) the rising unemployment at that time.

The impact of these trade and institutional factors on wage inequality was surely greater because they occurred at a time of high unemployment. For example, the impact of trade on wages (discussed in a later section) was greater because the recession had already induced a scarcity of good jobs. It should not be surprising that the most radical restructuring of wages (a tremendous growth in wage inequities) and the substantial real wage reductions for non-college-educated workers occurred during the period of very high unemployment from 1979 to 1985.

The persistently high unemployment of the last few years makes understanding the impact of unemployment on wage growth and on wage inequality critically important, especially because it appears that it will be many years before any "normal" rate of unemployment is attained.

The sensitivity (how much they would rise) of hourly wages of low-, middle-, and high-wage workers to a 1 percentage-point fall in unemployment, by gender, is presented in **Figure 4W**. This sensitivity is based on estimates of a well-known model that captures how much wages changed when the unemployment rate changed by 1 percentage point over 1979–2007. The relationship between unemployment and wage growth is assumed to be symmetrical, so these data also show the effect of a rise in unemployment if one simply changes the "sign" from positive to negative. As mentioned earlier, low-wage workers are more affected by changes in unemployment than are middle-wage workers, who, in turn, are more affected than are high-wage workers. The greater impact of unemployment

Figure 4W Increase in worker wages from a 1 percentage-point fall in
unemployment, by wage group

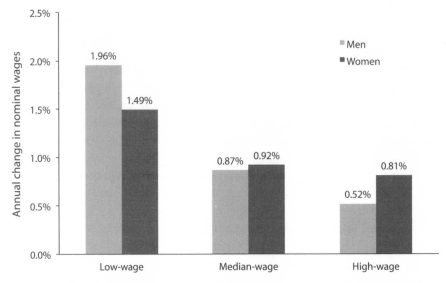

Note: Low-, median-, and high-wage refer, respectively, to wages at the 10th, 50th, and 90th percentiles.

Source: Authors' analysis of Current Population Survey Outgoing Rotation Group microdata

on low-wage men than on low-wage women may be due to women's wages being
lower and more substantially protected by the minimum wage.

Table 4.24 illustrates the impact of rising and falling unemployment on
wages and wage inequality over three periods: the high unemployment years of
1979–1985 and 2006–2011 and the years of persistent, decreasing unemployment from 1995 to 2000. Panel A shows the basic trends in unemployment and
wage inequality of each period. Unemployment is measured for all workers and
is illustrated in two ways: the change from the first to the last year of the period,
and the cumulative amount of unemployment in the period that was either over
or below the starting level, a measure designed to show the volume of unemployment over those years. For instance, in the six years from 1979 to 1985 the
unemployment rate (measured annually) was a total of 13.9 percentage points
over the starting rate of 5.8 percent. The volume of unemployment in the current downturn, 2006–2011, already exceeds that of the period encompassing the
early 1980s downturn, even though the current downturn is shorter by one year.
Unfortunately, there is more high unemployment ahead. To show wage inequality
trends, Panel A also provides the changes in the wage gaps at the bottom (between

Table 4.24 Impact of rising and falling unemployment on wage levels and gaps, 1979–2011

	1979–1985 (High unemployment)		1995–2000 (Low unemployment)		2006–2011 (High unemployment)	
	Men	Women	Men	Women	Men	Women
A. Basic trends (actual change)						
Unemployment rate change	1.4	1.4	-1.6	-1.6	4.3	4.3
Cumulative higher/lower unemployment rate*	13.9	13.9	-5.0	-5.0	15.2	15.2
50/10 wage gap (log)	9.6	17.2	-4.1	-1.8	2.7	-0.4
90/50 wage gap (log)	8.7	8.0	3.0	1.0	3.1	2.7
B. Estimated cumulative impact of unemployment on:						
1) Hourly wages**						
Low wage	-25.2%	-18.4%	11.1%	8.2%	-29.4%	-21.5%
Median wage	-11.1	-11.6	4.9	5.2	-13.0	-13.6
High wage	-6.6	-10.2	2.9	4.6	-7.7	-11.9
2) Wage ratios (log)						
50/10	14.1	6.8	-6.2	-2.9	16.4	7.9
90/50	4.5	1.5	-2.0	-0.6	5.3	1.7
C. Unemployment contribution to change in:						
50/10 wage gap (log)	146%	39%	150%	168%	617%	-2123%
90/50 wage gap (log)	52	18	-66	-61	169	64

* How much the unemployment rate exceeded or fell below the starting level across the span of the period, measured in percentage points
** Wages at the 10th, 50th, and 90th percentiles of the wage distribution

Source: Authors' analysis of Current Population Survey Outgoing Rotation Group microdata and Current Population Survey public data series using model from Katz and Krueger (1999)

workers at the 50th and 10th percentiles of the wage distribution) and at the top (between the 90th and 50th percentiles).

Estimates of the cumulative impact of unemployment on wage levels of low-, middle-, and high-wage workers and on the two wage gaps are presented in Panel B. These estimates reflect how sensitive the particular wage levels are to both unemployment changes and the volume of unemployment. The data show substantial downward pressure on wages from high unemployment, particularly at the bottom end. This downward pressure can be offset by factors that prevent wages from falling. One factor is "nominal wage rigidity," in which wage erosion primarily takes the form of reducing the growth of nominal (not inflation-adjusted) wages rather than reducing wages outright. A second factor is the minimum wage, which limits downward pressure from unemployment on wages at the bottom, especially among women (as noted earlier).

Higher unemployment, by putting more downward pressure on low than middle wages, and more pressure on middle than high wages, is a force for increasing the wage gap at the bottom (the 50/10 gap) and the top (the 90/50 gap), with the impact being greater at the bottom.

Panel C illustrates that the impact of unemployment on the wage gaps completely explains some of the observed changes in wage inequality during these particular periods. For instance, the 9.6 (log) percentage-point increase in men's 50/10 wage gap between 1979 and 1985 was less than the estimated unemployment impact of 14.1 percentage points, suggesting that without the volume of excess unemployment in that period we would not have observed any growth in the wage gap at the bottom for men, and in fact might have seen some narrowing. A substantial amount of the increased wage gap at the bottom among women in that same period, 6.8 percentage points of the 17.2 percentage-point change, was due to higher unemployment. Similarly, lower unemployment in the late 1990s pushed toward less wage inequality. The fact that wage inequality at the top continued to grow in the late 1990s is due to the presence of other factors driving up wage inequality there. Correspondingly, the wage gap at the bottom for both men and women fell in the late 1990s and would have fallen even further if not for other factors pushing inequality up while falling unemployment was pushing it down.

In the current downturn the large volume of high unemployment has exerted tremendous downward pressure on wages at the bottom (which, other factors aside, would have led to hourly wage decreases of 29.4 percent and 21.5 percent among men and women, respectively). Wages have not been able to fall as much as unemployment "demands" because of nominal wage rigidity and the minimum wage. The failure of wages to fall absolutely is very much a positive factor in maintaining wages and spending in the downturn and recovery. Note that the weight of unemployment on wages at the median or middle wage was about 13 percent for both men and women between 2006 and 2011, equivalent to more than 2 percent downward wage growth per year. This downward pressure on wages from high unemployment will continue to limit wage growth (and any concern about cost-inspired inflation) in the recovery for many years to come. And it is one reason that the lost decade of wage growth starting in 2002/2003 may be coupled with many more years of lost wage growth ahead.

The shift to low-paying industries

Another factor that contributes to growing inequality and lower pay, especially for non-college-educated workers, is a changing mix of industries in the economy. Such changes include the continued shift from goods-producing to service-producing industries and at times to lower-paying service industries. The shift in the industry mix of employment matters because some industries pay more than others for workers of comparable skill.

These industry employment shifts result from trade deficits and deindustrialization as well as from differential patterns of productivity growth across industries. (Industries facing the same growth in demand for their goods and services will generate more jobs the slower their productivity growth.) This section examines the significant erosion of wages and compensation of workers resulting from the employment shift to low-paying industries since the early 1980s.

Despite a common perception, the industry-shift effect is not the simple consequence of some natural evolution from an agricultural to a manufacturing to a service economy. For one thing, a significant part of the shrinkage of manufacturing is trade-related. More important, industry shifts would not provide downward pressure on wages if service-sector wages were more closely aligned with manufacturing wages, as is the case in other countries. Moreover, since health care coverage, vacations, and pensions in this country are related to the specific job or sector in which a worker is employed, the industry distribution of employment matters more in the United States than in other countries. An alternative institutional arrangement found in other advanced countries sets health, pension, vacation, and other benefits through legislation in a universal manner regardless

Table 4.25 Annual pay in expanding and contracting industries, 1979–2007

Annual pay	Industries		Difference		Annual impact
	Contracting	Expanding	Dollars	Percent	
Compensation (2011 dollars)					
2000–2007	$70,673	$60,048	-$10,625	-15.0%	-0.1%
1989–2000	57,809	45,130	-12,679	-21.9	-0.2
1979–1989	58,932	40,403	-18,528	-31.4	-0.3
Wages and salaries (2011 dollars)					
2000–2007	$58,449	$51,602	-$6,846	-11.7%	-0.1%
1989–2000	47,792	38,731	-9,061	-19.0	-0.1
1979–1989	48,077	36,999	-11,078	-23.0	-0.2

Source: Authors' analysis of Bureau of Economic Analysis National Income and Product Accounts and Bureau of Labor Statistics Current Employment Statistics

of sector or firm. Therefore, the downward pressure of industry shifts on wages and compensation can be said, in part, to be the consequence of the absence of institutional structures that lessen inter-industry pay differences.

The extent of the adverse effect of industry shifts on wages and compensation is examined in **Table 4.25**, which shows the annual wages and compensation of expanding and contracting industries in each business cycle since 1979. When industries with above (or below) average pay levels expand employment share, they raise (or lower) the average pay. The wages and compensation of "expanding" industries reflect the pay levels of each industry that experienced a rise in the share of total employment, weighted by the extent of the expansion in employment shares. These calculations show that expanding industries in 2000–2007 paid annual compensation of $60,048, or 15.0 percent less than contracting industries, which paid $70,673. The expansion of employment in lower-paid industries from 2000 to 2007 depressed compensation and wage growth by 0.1 percent each year. Thus, industry shifts in recent years have been *less* adverse than in the years 1979–1989, when the impact was to reduce compensation growth by 0.3 percent annually. This reduced impact is due to a lower pay gap between expanding and contracting industries in the 2000s than in the 1980s and to a diminished shift from one to the other in recent years. Nevertheless, this analysis shows that industry employment shifts have been consequential; they lowered average compensation by 5.3 percent between 1979 and 2007 (based on the annual impact times the number of years in each period).

Employer health care costs

Escalating health care costs and their effects on publicly provided health care programs and private insurance premiums remain a central concern of public policy, families, and employers. Controlling health care costs, for instance, was a key objective in the development of recent health care reform proposals. This section concerns the extent to which rising *employer* health care costs have squeezed wage growth and contributed to rising wage inequality. This discussion augments the analyses of the effect of health care and other benefits on household income and living standards growth (discussed in chapters 1 and 2) and on changes in real compensation and compensation inequality (examined earlier in this chapter).

Earlier in this chapter, we found that compensation inequality grew more than inequality of wages (Table 4.2) and that benefits grew faster than wages in some periods and not in others, such that the share of total compensation allocated to benefits had not grown since 1987. This indicates that the real value of benefits grew at the same rate as real wages over this period.

When we focus on growth in real compensation and real family incomes, and thus on living standards, we measure health care costs in inflation-adjusted terms to determine whether workers and families are enjoying greater health care services. This, in turn, means applying a specific medical services inflation measure to health care costs, since medical services inflation is consistently greater than overall inflation. (A health-specific deflator is needed because the measure of the inflation affecting consumers/families—used to adjust wages—has a limited health care component that only includes out-of-pocket costs and not the broader costs of increased spending by employers.)

In contrast, the potential health care squeeze on wages examined in this section must be analyzed in nominal (non-inflation-adjusted) terms. The issue is whether rising employer costs for health insurance premiums leave less of planned compensation available for wage growth. For this purpose, we simply measure the rise in employer health care spending regardless of the inflation in medical services.

In the analysis that follows it is assumed that higher health spending by employers offsets the possibility of higher wages dollar-for-dollar. This is the conventional way of proceeding. In reality, this is unlikely to be the case for all types of workers at all times; the actual outcome will depend upon the bargaining power of workers relative to employers. But assuming a one-to-one tradeoff allows an estimation of the *maximum* potential squeeze of health care costs on wages.

Table 4.26 uses data from the National Income and Product Accounts to show employer costs for employee group health insurance as a share of wages

Table 4.26 Employer health care costs as a share of wages, 1948–2010

	Health cost share
1948	0.5%
1973	2.9
1979	4.5
1989	6.4
1995	7.3
2000	7.2
2010	8.9
Annual percentage-point change	
1948–1973	0.10
1973–1979	0.26
1979–2010	0.14
1979–1989	0.19
1989–2000	0.07
2000–2010	0.17

Source: Authors' analysis of Bureau of Economic Analysis National Income and Product Accounts

back to 1948. In that year employer health care costs were the equivalent of just 0.5 percent of total wages; by 2010 (the latest year for these data) they were 8.9 percent of wages. The table also presents the annual percentage-point growth of the health care share of wages to examine how quickly health care costs grew, relative to wages, in various subperiods. The fastest growth, 0.26 percentage points per year, occurred during the 1973–1979 business cycle, so in these years wage growth was 0.26 percentage points per year slower because of rising health care costs. Between 1979 and 2010 the growth was 0.14 percentage points annually, just a bit faster than the annual growth of 0.10 percentage points in the postwar period from 1948 to 1973; the difference amounts to less than one-tenth of one percentage point per year. This pattern suggests that rising health care costs were not an important factor in explaining why wages were stagnant over the 1980s through 2000s relative to the early postwar period.

A closer look at patterns of health care cost acceleration and deceleration over subperiods allows us to examine the contention that accelerating health care costs led to wage stagnation in the 2000s. Health care costs rose slowly (by 0.07 percentage points annually) between 1989 and 2000, after growing 0.19 percentage points annually in the 1980s. The deceleration of health care costs in the 1990s could explain a small (0.12 percentage-point annual) acceleration of wage growth in the 1990s relative to the 1980s. Similarly, the reemergence of health care cost growth relative to wages in the 2000s (to 0.17 percentage points annually, comparable to growth in the 1980s) can potentially explain a small (0.1 percentage-point annual) deceleration of wage growth in the 2000s. According to these data, therefore, rising health care costs in the 2000s, as in earlier periods, were not a major determinant of the pattern of wage growth.

It is possible, however, that health care cost increases have a larger impact on wages of particular groups of workers. In particular, some analysts have claimed that employer health care cost increases in the 2000s are responsible for the middle-class wage stagnation of recent years. **Table 4.27**, which draws on an analysis of the Medical Expenditure Panel Survey, examines this possibility by looking at health care costs as a share of wages by wage fifth.

Employer health care costs are generally largest, relative to wages, for those in the second and middle fifths, lower for those in the first and fourth fifths, and lowest for the highest-wage workers, and they are above average for the bottom four-fifths. (Note that these shares are computed for *all* workers in each fifth, including those who have no employer-provided health insurance.) The net impact of several factors generates this pattern. One factor is that coverage by employer-provided health benefits rises with wage level, which up to a point leads health costs as a share of wages to rise with wages. A second factor is that premiums are fixed per month; thus, an employer pays the same amount regardless of wages paid or hours worked that month. Since health care costs are spread over fewer hours of work for low-wage workers (who work fewer annual hours), fixed premiums

Table 4.27 Employer health care costs as a share of wages, by wage fifth, 1996–2008

| | Wage fifth | | | | | |
	Bottom	Second	Middle	Fourth	Top	Average
A. Health share of annual wages						
1996	8.2%	9.2%	8.0%	6.9%	4.4%	6.1%
2001	9.5	11.0	10.3	7.9	4.9	7.1
2008	9.3	12.8	11.9	9.7	6.2	8.5
B. Total change in share						
1996–2001	1.3	1.8	2.3	1.0	0.5	1.0
2001–2008	-0.2	1.8	1.6	1.8	1.3	1.4
C. Annual change in share						
1996–2001	0.3	0.4	0.5	0.2	0.1	0.2
2001–2008	0.0	0.3	0.2	0.3	0.2	0.2
1996–2008	0.1	0.3	0.3	0.2	0.2	0.2

Source: Authors' analysis of Burtless and Milusheva (2012) based on Medical Expenditure Panel Survey

push up the health shares at the bottom. A third factor is that although health care benefits provided become increasingly expensive as one moves up the wage scale, the extent to which the quality of health benefits improves probably starts to diminish at some point, which would lead health care cost shares to diminish for higher-wage workers relative to low- and middle-wage workers.

Panel C in Table 4.27 shows the annual change in the health care cost share of annual wages during each period. Over the entire period, 1996–2008, health care costs relative to wages rose slightly more (0.1 percentage points faster per year) in the middle than the top, contributing modestly (1.2 percentage points) to the growth of the 90/50 wage ratio (which grew 12.1 percentage points, according to the annual data used for Table 4.4). This assumes that the wages and health care cost increases of workers at the 90th and 50th percentiles correspond to those of workers in the top and middle fifths, respectively. The difference between the growth of health care costs relative to wages in the middle and the bottom wage fifths was 0.2 percentage points a year over the 1996–2008 period and served to *narrow* wage differences between the middle and the bottom.

Panel C also provides information on the acceleration or deceleration of rising health care costs in the 2000s (2001–2008) relative to the late 1990s (1996–2001). Health care costs, relative to wages, grew faster in the 1990s than in the

Figure 4X Employer health care costs as a share of annual wages, by wage fifth, 1996–2008

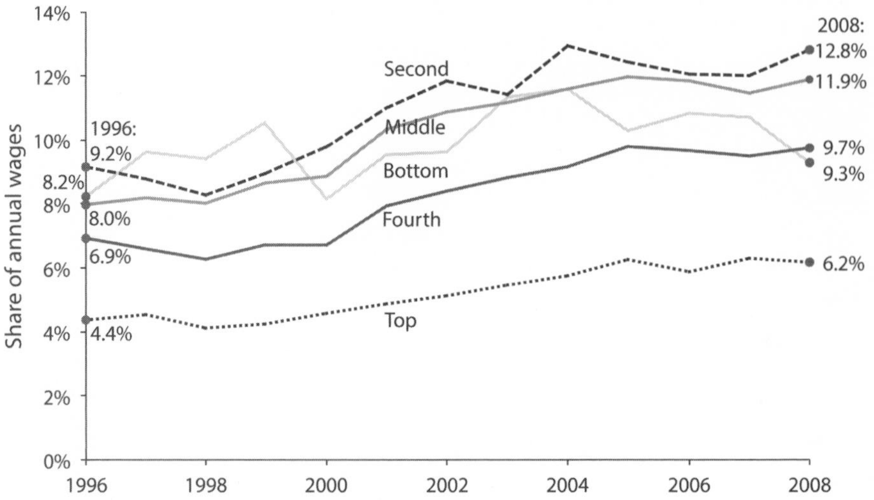

Source: Authors' analysis of Burtless and Milusheva (2012) based on Medical Expenditure Panel Survey

2000s for the bottom three-fifths of wage earners, a pattern that suggests rising health costs cannot explain the deceleration of wage growth for this group (which encompasses the median) in the 2000s.

Figure 4X, which shows the annual trends for each fifth, illustrates that employer health care costs as a share of wages were relatively stable from 1996 to 2000 and from 2004/2005 through 2008, but rose steeply from 2000 to 2004/2005. The rise in health care costs thus preceded the slowdown in wages, which began in 2002 or 2003, depending upon the wage data series used. Rising health care costs might have contributed to the wage slowdown if there were a lag in the impact, but the slowdown in the rise in health care costs as a share of wages in 2004/2005 was not followed by any wage acceleration. All in all, other than slightly contributing to the narrowed wage gap between the middle and the bottom and to a slight expansion of the wage gap between the middle and the top (as explained earlier in this discussion), it is hard to see a major health care squeeze on wages explaining the recent trends in either wage growth or wage inequality overall and for the middle class.

These findings should be put into a broader context. They do not suggest that rising health care costs have had no material effect on pay or (more importantly) living standards. The steady increase in the share of total compensation accounted for by health care costs indeed has the potential to squeeze cash wages, and the degree to which this increase is driven by excess health care inflation rather than more or better care is a drag on the growth of living standards. Over time, this accumulated slow and steady drag is not trivial, and if it continues for several more decades the accumulated damage to potential wage growth would be quite significant.

This analysis has examined only employer contributions to health care and their effect on wages. If workers and their families are devoting an ever-growing share of their own wages to insurance premiums or out-of-pocket costs for health care, then rising health costs will negatively affect living standards. An increase in taxes to cover the growing costs of health care paid for by government would have the same effect.

Trade and wages

The process of globalization since the 1980s has been an important factor in both slowing the growth rate of average wages and reducing the wage levels of workers with less than a college degree. In more recent years trade and globalization have begun to affect white-collar and college-educated workers to a great extent as well. The increase in international trade and investment flows affects wages through several channels. First, increases in imports of finished manufactured goods, especially from countries where workers earn only a fraction of what U.S. workers earn, reduce manufacturing employment in the United States. While increases in exports create employment opportunities for some domestic workers, imports mean job losses for many others. Large, chronic trade deficits over the last three decades suggest that the jobs lost to import competition have outnumbered the jobs gained from increasing exports. Given that export industries tend to be less labor intensive than import-competing industries, even growth in "balanced trade" (where exports and imports both increase by the same dollar amount) would lead to a decline in manufacturing jobs.

Second, imports of intermediate manufactured goods (used as inputs in the production of final goods) also help to lower domestic manufacturing employment, especially for production workers and others with less than a college education. The expansion of export platforms in low-wage countries has induced many U.S. manufacturing firms to purchase part of their production processes from low-wage countries. Since firms generally find it most profitable to purchase the most labor-intensive processes, the increase in intermediate inputs from abroad has hit non-college-educated production workers hardest.

Third, low-wage competition and greater world capacity for producing manufactured goods can lower the prices of many international goods. Since workers' pay is tied to the value of the goods they produce, lower prices from international competition, despite possible lower inflation, can lead to a reduction in the wages of U.S. workers, even if imports themselves do not increase.

Fourth, in many cases the mere threat of direct foreign competition or of the relocation of part or all of a production facility can lead workers to grant wage concessions to their employers. This is referred to as the "threat effect."

Fifth, the large increases in direct investment flows (i.e., investment in production plants and equipment) to other countries have meant reduced investment in the domestic manufacturing base and significant growth in foreign manufacturers' capacity to compete directly with U.S.-based manufacturers.

Sixth, the effects of globalization go beyond those workers exposed directly to foreign competition. As trade drives workers out of manufacturing and into lower-paying service jobs, not only do their own wages fall, but the new supply of workers to the service (or other) sectors (from displaced workers plus young workers not able to find manufacturing jobs) helps to lower the wages of similarly skilled workers already employed in service jobs. That is, globalization's impact is not just on those who are directly displaced by trade or face international competition but also on those workers with similar skills throughout the economy.

Last, trade in services has gained prominence in recent years as call center operations, computer programming, doctor support services (reading X-rays, for instance), research and development, and other white-collar services have been transferred (or purchased) abroad, sometimes to countries with far lower wages than those in the United States, most notably India and China. Less is known about this recent phenomenon, sometimes called "offshoring," but it seems to be a mechanism through which globalization now adversely affects white-collar jobs and wages (and will increasingly do so). Not only are jobs directly displaced, but the wage growth of still-employed white-collar workers threatened by offshoring is constrained.

This section briefly examines the role of international trade and investment in recent changes in the U.S. wage structure. Since the preceding list of channels through which globalization affects wages is not complete and not fully quantifiable, this analysis *understates* the impact of globalization on wages in the 1980s, 1990s, and 2000s.

Figure 4Y presents the trends in the imports and exports of goods as well as the size of the trade deficit in goods relative to GDP over the postwar period. Trade was balanced for the most part from 1947 through the end of the 1970s. A large deficit emerged in the mid-1980s as exports fell and imports continued to grow. Exports recovered after the fall-off in the dollar's value in the late 1980s and helped to close the deficit by the early 1990s. The goods trade imbalance spiked in the mid-1980s, rising to 2.6 percent of GDP (up 2.7 percentage points of GDP from 1980 to 1986). This escalation of the trade deficit and the rapid growth of imports are associated with a major restructuring of wages (and a fall in real wages for many workers) that occurred in the early 1980s. The trade deficit fell below 1.0 percent of GDP in the early 1990s before rising rapidly in the late 1990s to 4.0 percent of GDP in 2000. The pace quickened between 2000 and 2007,

Figure 4Y Imports, exports, and trade balance in goods as a share of U.S. GDP, 1947–2011

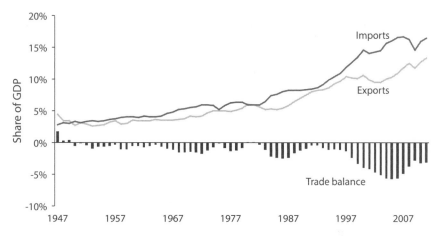

Source: Authors' analysis of Bureau of Economic Analysis National Income and Product Accounts

however, as the imbalance grew to 5.6 percent of GDP in 2004–2006. To the extent that the trade deficit is a proxy for trade's impact on wages of middle- and low-wage workers, the timing of growing trade deficits coincides with generally rising wage inequality during two recoveries, one in the late 1990s and the other in the early and mid-2000s.

An important characteristic of globalization has been the rising importance of trade with lower-wage, developing countries, especially since the end of the 1980s. This development is illustrated in **Figure 4Z** by the growth in the share of manufacturing imports originating in developing countries (measured as a share of GDP). In 1973, imports from low-wage countries equaled only 0.9 percent of GDP and, despite a rapid rise in imports in the 1980s, they reached only 2.6 percent of GDP in 1989. By 2000, however, imports from low-wage countries had nearly doubled in importance, registering 5.1 percent of GDP, and they grew even further to 6.1 percent of GDP by 2007, at which point they made up more than half of all manufacturing imports. By 2011 imports from low-wage countries had grown further to 6.3 percent of GDP even though manufacturing imports as a whole had declined. Industries subject to foreign competition have seen a growth of such competition over the last 30 years, and this competition increasingly comes from lower-wage countries. In fact, the rise in imports between 1979 and 2011 was primarily due to greater imports from low-wage nations: About three-fourths (4.7 percentage points) of the 6.0 percentage-point rise in manufacturing imports as a share of GDP was due to imports from low-wage countries.

Figure 4Z Manufacturing imports as a share of U.S. GDP, 1973–2011

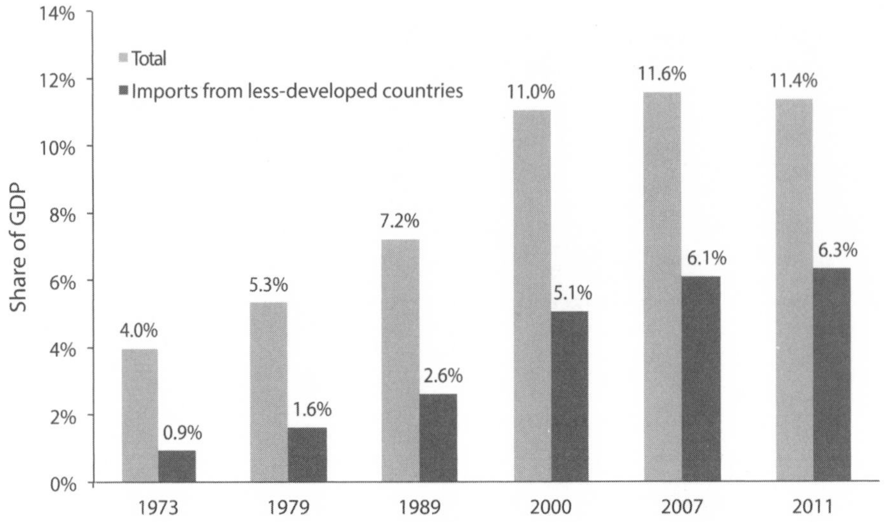

Source: Authors' analysis of USITC trade data and BEA National Income and Product Accounts

We further explore the changes in the composition of trade by examining the relative (to the United States) productivity levels of nations to which the United States exported and from which it received imports since the early 1970s. A nation's productivity level is an indicator of its wage level and its level of development; thus, a lower relative productivity level of our import partners indicates increased competition from developing, lower-wage countries. As **Figure 4AA** shows, U.S. export and import trading partners had equivalent productivity levels in 1973, at roughly 57 percent of U.S. productivity, and this parity prevailed through 1989. However, by 2000 the productivity levels of U.S. import trading partners had fallen. Between 2000 and 2011 our exports became increasingly focused on higher-productivity nations, and the productivity levels of the countries where our imports originate fell further. These trends imply that our trade imbalances with lower-wage nations grew in scale in the 2000s.

The growth in the trade deficit and increased global competition from lower-wage countries can, and would be expected to, adversely affect the wages of non-college-educated workers relative to others. This is because any potential gains from trade would be created through such a mechanism—a redeployment of workers and capital into more highly skilled or capital-intensive industries, a movement that lessens the need for non-college-educated workers.

We now turn to an examination of the types of jobs that were lost as trade competition and the trade deficit grew and as job losses in import-sensitive

Figure 4AA Relative productivity of U.S. trading partners, 1973–2011

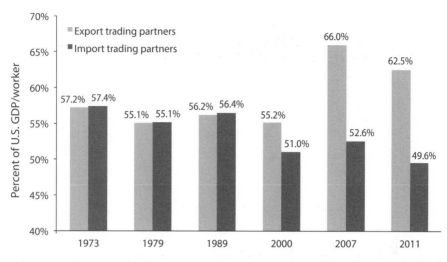

Note: Bars show trading partners' productivity as a share of U.S. productivity.

Source: Authors' analysis of United States International Trade Commission Tariff and Trade DataWeb and the Penn World Table (Heston, Summers, and Aten 2011)

industries exceeded job gains in export industries. In periods of low unemployment, it may be the case that a trade deficit does not cause actual job loss because workers displaced by rising imports can find employment in nontraded sectors such as services. Nevertheless, even with low unemployment, a trade deficit will affect the composition of jobs (to less manufacturing and more services), thereby affecting wage inequality. In this light, **Table 4.28** indicates how trade flows affect the composition of employment by education level by separately showing the impact on those with a four-year college degree or more and those without a four-year college degree. This analysis relies on information on the types of jobs in each industry and the changes in imports and exports by industry. By using an input-output model, the analysis can examine how jobs across the economy are affected, including jobs that feed into other industries (e.g., how steel workers are affected by fewer car sales).

To examine the shifts in globalization's effects over time, it is worthwhile to first examine the 1980s, a period when large trade imbalances and related job losses became important and very visible to the public. In 1979 imports and exports were comparable, as were the numbers of jobs created by exports (3.1 million) and lost to imports (3.4 million). Translating these numbers into jobs by education level, we can see that manufacturing trade in 1979 cost 335,000 "less than college" jobs while generating 66,000 "college or more"

Table 4.28 Impact of trade balance in manufacturing on employment and wages, by education, 1979–2005

	1979	1989	2000	2005	Change 1979–2005
Trade (millions of dollars)					
Imports (M)	$112,235	$379,426	$1,012,856	$1,288,223	$1,175,988
Exports (X)	116,585	272,167	625,892	685,077	568,492
Net trade (X–M)	4,350	-107,259	-386,964	-603,146	-607,496
Trade-related employment (thousands)					
Imports (M)	3,412	5,623	10,910	9,936	6,525
Exports (X)	3,142	3,615	6,564	4,597	1,455
Net trade (X-M)	-269	-2,008	-4,346	-5,339	-5,070
Education intensity of trade (share of jobs)					
Imports (M)					
Less than college	89.8%	85.6%	79.0%	77.8%	-12.0%
College or more	10.2	14.4	21.0	22.2	12.0
Exports (X)					
Less than college	86.8%	80.9%	76.6%	73.5%	-13.3%
College or more	13.2	19.1	23.4	26.5	13.3
Net trade (X-M) employment impact on:					
Employment level (thousands)					
Less than college	-335	-1,891	-3,590	-4,354	-4,019
College or more	66	-117	-757	-985	-1,051
Total	-269	-2,008	-4,346	-5,339	-5,070
Relative employment (change as share of group employment)					
Less than college	-0.5%	-2.3%	-3.8%	-4.6%	-4.2%
College or more	0.4	-0.5	-2.1	-2.5	-2.9
Relative change	-0.8	-1.8	-1.7	-2.1	-1.3

Source: Bivens (2008)

jobs. After imports grew faster than exports in the 1980s, trade cost about 2 million jobs in 1989, with most of the job erosion (about 1.9 million) among jobs not requiring a college degree. In 1989, this job loss for non-college-educated workers was equivalent to a 2.3 percent loss in their employment, or a 1.8 percent loss relative to the employment loss of college graduates (0.5 percent). Therefore, trade disproportionately affected the non-college-educated workforce. Consequently, non-college-educated and middle- and lower-wage workers disproportionately bore the costs and pressures of trade deficits and global competition in the 1980s.

Interestingly, trade-related job losses were more evenly spread across education levels in the 1990s. Trade flows in the 1990s led to a loss of noncollege jobs equivalent to 3.8 percent of their total by 2000, a 1.5 percentage-point increase over the 2.3 percent loss in 1989. In percentage-point terms, this increased loss is roughly the same as that among "college or more" jobs, which rose from a 0.5 percent loss in 1989 to a 2.1 percent decline in 2000. By 2005 the trade-imposed job losses among jobs not requiring a college degree totaled more than 4.3 million, or 4.6 percent of their total. Job loss among "college or more" jobs had grown to nearly a million in 2005, or 2.5 percent of their total. Nevertheless, the impact of trade on noncollege jobs was nearly double that on jobs requiring a college degree in 2005, so that employment of those without a college degree fell 2.1 percent relative to employment of those with a college degree. Thus, the pattern of job erosion due to trade depressed opportunities for non-college-educated workers relative to those with more education.

The last column in Table 4.28 shows the changes over the 1979–2005 period: a loss of about 4 million noncollege jobs and an erosion of their relative employment of 1.3 percent. This analysis probably overstates the adverse trade impact on the higher education group because of one of its underlying assumptions: that when an industry loses jobs, it does so proportionately across types of jobs (e.g., a 10 percent loss of jobs in an industry means 10 percent fewer jobs in each category within the industry). Since the response to lost export opportunities or displacements from greater imports has almost surely fallen disproportionately on the non-college-educated workforce of each industry (rather than on white-collar or technical workers), this analysis understates the degree to which trade and globalization affect non-college-educated workers relative to those with college degrees.

The data presented so far suggest that trade, particularly with low-wage developing countries, accelerated the long-term decline in manufacturing and related employment. The data also suggest that the fall in employment opportunities was especially severe for non-college-educated manufacturing production workers. Since millions of trade-displaced workers sought jobs in nonmanufacturing sectors, trade also worked to depress the wages of comparable workers employed outside manufacturing. The result has been to weaken the wages of middle- and low-wage workers relative to those of high-earning workers.

It is difficult to quantify the other channels, discussed at the beginning of this section, through which the increase in international trade and investment flows affects wages—channels such as the threat effect of imports and plant relocation on U.S. manufacturing wages and the reality of large-scale international direct investment flows. Nevertheless, these effects are likely to be as large as, or larger than, those that are more readily quantifiable.

To gauge the impact of globalization, particularly the rising competition from lower-wage nations, on wages and wage inequality, we examine the results of a "computable general equilibrium" model developed by economist Paul Krugman in the mid-1990s. What drives this model's estimates of the impact of trade on wage inequality is the share of trade coming from low-wage developing countries. The model answers two questions: How much would global prices (both of products and labor) have to change in order to make goods from less-developed countries unprofitable to send to the U.S. market, and how much would U.S. wages change in response? In other words, what would U.S. wages (and domestic product prices) be but for the opportunity to trade with less-developed countries? The larger the real-world share of trade with less-developed countries in any given year, the larger the hypothetical change in prices and wages needed to zero it out, and the larger the impact of trade on American wages. All imports in this analysis are manufacturing imports originating from less-developed countries (excluding services, oil, and other natural resource imports). The model assesses the impact of this trade on the hourly wage differential between those with a college degree or more and other workers (with this latter category combining those with "some college," high school, or "less than high school" educations); this differential is referred to as the college/noncollege wage gap.

In 1979, when such trade with less-developed countries made up just 1.8 percent of GDP, the model shows a modest 2.7 percent widening of the college/noncollege wage gap as a result of this trade (**Table 4.29**). In 1995, when trade with low-wage nations had risen to 3.6 percent of GDP, the relative impact on the wage gap was correspondingly higher, at 5.6 percent. However, between 1979 and 1995 developing-country trade's growing impact on the wage gap (a 2.9 percentage-point increase) was equivalent to 16.7 percent of the 17.2 percentage-point rise in the college/noncollege wage gap in this period. By 2011 the trade share from low-wage countries had risen to 6.4 percent of GDP, substantially greater than the 2.5 percent share in 1989. The wage impact of this increased trade from low-wage countries was 10.0 percent in 2011, 4.4 percentage points higher than in 1995. Because the college/noncollege wage gap rose only modestly in this period, from 46.1 percent in 1995 to 50.9 percent in 2011, the increased impact of trade on relative wages (a rise of 4.4 percentage points) accounted for 93.4 percent of the growth of the college/noncollege wage gap since the mid-1990s. Thus, increased competition from low-wage countries has been a strong factor pushing toward greater wage inequality since 1995, and without it the growth in the gap would have been trivial, from 46.1 percent to 46.5 percent. Over the entire 1979–2011 period, trade from low-wage nations caused a 7.3 percentage-point rise in

Table 4.29 Impact of trade with low-wage countries on college/noncollege wage gap

	1973	1979	1989	1995	2000	2007	2011	Change		
								1979–1995	1995–2011	1979–2011
Manufacturing trade penetration (as share of GDP)*										
Less-developed country (LDC) trade	1.0%	1.8%	2.5%	3.6%	4.6%	5.6%	6.4%	1.8	2.8	4.7
China trade	0.0	0.0	0.2	0.5	0.8	1.8	2.0	0.5	1.6	2.0
*College/noncollege wage gap***										
	36.9%	28.9%	41.5%	46.1%	48.2%	49.2%	50.9%	17.2	4.8	22.0
Estimated impact of trade on college/noncollege wage gap										
All LDC trade	1.6%	2.7%	4.0%	5.6%	7.3%	8.8%	10.0%	2.9	4.4	7.3
China trade***	0.0	0.0	0.3	0.7	1.2	2.8	3.2	0.7	2.5	3.2
Trade share of college/noncollege wage gap								*Percent of change*		
All LDC trade	4.3%	9.5%	9.5%	12.1%	15.0%	17.9%	19.7%	16.7%	93.4%	33.2%
China trade***	0.0	0.1	0.6	1.6	2.5	5.7	6.3	4.1	51.6	14.4

* "Penetration" is the average of the import share and the trade share to reflect current imbalance but also impact of balanced trade.
** Log hourly wage differential between those with a college or advanced degree and all other workers
*** Based on China share of LDC trade share, which assumes China trade impact equals other LDC trade impact

Source: Update of Bivens (2008) reanalysis of Krugman (1995) using 2011 USITC and NIPA data

the college/noncollege wage gap, accounting for a third of the entire growth in this education wage differential.

Much of the growth in U.S. trade with less-developed countries has originated from China, and Table 4.29 provides an estimate of the impact of the growth of U.S.-China trade on the college/noncollege wage gap. These estimates simply apportion to China an impact based on its share of less-developed country imports. Trade with China grew by 1.6 percentage points of GDP from 1995 to 2011, accounting for more than half of the total growth (2.8 percentage points of GDP) in less-developed country imports. Consequently, the trade with China served to expand the college/noncollege wage gap by 2.5 percentage points, or 51.6 percent of the total 4.8 percentage-point growth in the college/noncollege wage gap from 1995 to 2011.

In the early 2000s globalization's adverse impacts seemed to be moving up-scale, affecting so-called knowledge workers such as computer programmers, scientists, and doctors as work previously performed in the United States was relocated to other countries. This phenomenon of offshoring high-tech, white-collar work is noteworthy because the workers affected, especially computer-related professionals, are frequently discussed as the winners in the globalization process. If the jobs of such highly educated workers are now at risk in the global economy, it makes one wonder which jobs cannot be moved offshore.

Two factors seem to have made offshoring of white-collar work a potentially significant phenomenon. One is that technology, particularly fast Internet and other communications technology, makes coordination and transmission of work worldwide much easier. A second factor is what could be called a "supply shock" arising from the availability of millions of highly educated workers in places such as China, India, Eastern Europe, Russia, and elsewhere who are willing to do the work for a lower wage than U.S. workers.

Hard data that could inform us of the extent of offshoring and how much more to expect in the future are not available because our data systems are not well suited to measuring trade in services (including that which is transferred over the Internet) as opposed to goods. Even if the current level of offshoring is mod-est, the high public profile of this practice and the statements from firms of their intentions to intensify their offshoring are sufficient to depress wage expectations in the relevant labor markets.

Offshoring has also emerged as a concern for many workers at a time when the labor market for college-educated workers, especially new college graduates, has not been robust. As discussed earlier, wages of entry-level college graduates have declined since 2000, and employer benefits provided to new graduates have dimin-ished as well. The review of unemployment and employment trends in Chapter 5 describes a number of employment problems confronting college graduates.

Table 4.30 shows the results of two methods of assessing how vulnerable jobs are to offshoring. The first is presented in Panel A and relies on an analysis of which occupations are most offshorable. It then uses the occupational results to characterize the education and skill requirements of the particular jobs that are most offshorable. Each occupation was rated as either highly offshorable, offshorable, highly non-offshorable, or non-offshorable. Given these ratings and information about the total employment level and the education and skill require-ments of each occupation, it is possible to determine the amount of employment that falls into each category and the characteristics of jobs in each. Offshorable or highly offshorable in this context denotes, based on the nature of the job, whether the work is *potentially* offshorable. Only a fraction of such jobs will actually be offshored; nevertheless, just the potential of being offshored will likely suppress wage growth in these occupations.

Table 4.30 Characteristics of offshorable and non-offshorable jobs

A. Analysis of occupations	Highly offshorable	Offshorable	Non-offshorable	Highly non-offshorable	All
Total offshorable employment					
Level	9,517,000	22,116,667	9,525,167	104,976,167	146,135,001
Share	6.5%	15.1%	6.5%	71.8%	100.0%
Annual salary	$36,246	$42,775	$33,116	$33,020	$34,713
By education (percent)					
High school or less	28.5%	42.4%	41.4%	45.2%	43.5%
Some college	37.8	27.0	35.6	27.7	28.8
College or more	33.8	30.6	23.0	27.1	27.8
Total	100.0	100.0	100.0	100.0	100.0

B. Survey methods	Percent offshorable		
	Self-classified	Inferred	Externally coded
Less than high school	18.6%	14.3%	11.8%
High school or GED	17.3	19.8	19.3
Some college	22.4	22.1	23.8
Associate degree	22.9	22.8	17.1
College degree	34.6	42.8	26.4
Advanced or professional degree	37.0	38.5	16.9

Source: Authors' analysis of Bernstein, Lin, and Mishel (2007); Blinder (2007); Blinder and Krueger (2009, Table 4); and Bureau of Labor Statistics Occupational Employment Statistics

This occupational analysis shows that 6.5 percent of employment is highly offshorable and another 15.1 percent is offshorable, translating into about 31.6 million of today's jobs that are vulnerable to future offshoring. This group of vulnerable occupations is more than three times the employment of the manufacturing sector. More of the highly offshorable occupations require at least a college degree (33.8 percent of the jobs) than do the jobs that are in either of the non-offshorable categories (23.0 percent and 27.1 percent). Likewise, the jobs most vulnerable to being offshored are more likely to require some college, indicating that they are middle-wage jobs. Occupations in the offshorable category have somewhat more education requirements than the average in the economy (30.6 percent require a college degree or more versus 27.8 percent economy-wide).

It is interesting to note that occupations vulnerable to offshoring pay more than other occupations. For instance, the annual wages in the highly offshorable and offshorable occupations are, respectively, $36,246 and $42,775, far higher than the roughly $33,000 of pay in both of the non-offshorable categories. **Figure 4AB** shows the wage premium of offshorable jobs, i.e., the percent more that such jobs pay than comparably skilled jobs that are not offshorable. Overall, offshorable occupations pay 10.8 percent more; among jobs requiring at least a college degree the offshorable jobs pay 13.9 percent more. This analysis seems to confirm fears that offshoring threatens some of the best U.S. jobs, both in terms of their pay and the education required to obtain them.

The second method of assessing the potential for offshoring in particular occupations is presented in Panel B of Table 4.30. The researchers used three methods of analyzing survey data to determine whether a job was offshorable. The first, called "self-classified," asked survey respondents to assess whether their job is offshorable based on the difficulty someone in a remote location would have in performing the job. The second method, "inferred," used information on the nature of a respondent's job to assess whether it is offshorable. The third method, "externally coded," used professional coders to assess offshorability based on respondents' descriptions of their job tasks. For all three methods, the share of jobs that are offshorable was generally higher the more education the job required.

That offshorable jobs are highly paid and require above-average education credentials tells us that globalization will assert greater downward pressure on the wages of these vulnerable jobs and jobs like them throughout the economy.

Figure 4AB Wage premium of offshorable jobs, by gender and education

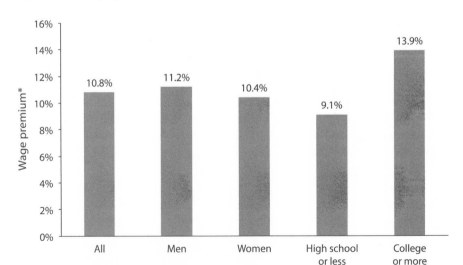

* The percent more that such jobs pay than comparably skilled jobs that are not offshorable

Source: Bernstein, Lin, and Mishel (2007)

It does not follow, however, that globalization will be more of a burden to the more highly educated and better-paid workforce; globalization will be increasingly evident in greater import flows and international competition in a wide variety of industries and occupations that have already experienced competition from producers in low-wage countries—an impact, as we have seen, that has disproportionately fallen on the non-college-educated workforce. Though white-collar workers have started to face more international competition, it may be a while before they face as much as do typical blue-collar workers.

Immigration

Another aspect of globalization is immigration. Immigrants' share of the U.S. labor force declined over the first half of the last century but began to grow in the 1970s. **Table 4.31** shows the immigrant share of the workforce from 1940 to 2011 for all immigrants and for those from Mexico, the largest single source

Table 4.31 Mexican and other immigrants' share of U.S. workforce, by gender, 1940–2011

	Share of workforce* (Decennial Census)							Share of workforce* (CPS)		Change		
	1940	1950	1960	1970	1980	1990	2000	2000	2011	1980–1990	1990–2000	2000–2011
Immigrants												
All	9.8%	7.3%	6.0%	5.2%	6.5%	8.8%	13.2%	13.4%	16.2%	2.3	4.4	2.8
Mexican	0.3	0.4	0.4	0.4	1.1	2.0	4.0	3.9	5.1	0.9	2.0	1.2
Other	9.5	6.9	5.6	4.8	5.4	6.8	9.2	9.6	11.1	1.4	2.4	1.5
Immigrant men												
All	10.9%	7.8%	6.1%	5.0%	6.4%	9.4%	14.5%	15.0%	17.9%	3.0	5.1	2.9
Mexican	0.4	0.4	0.4	0.5	1.3	2.5	5.1	5.0	6.4	1.2	2.6	1.4
Other	10.5	7.4	5.7	4.5	5.1	6.9	9.4	10.0	11.5	1.8	2.5	1.5
Immigrant women												
All	6.9%	6.0%	5.9%	5.4%	6.5%	8.2%	11.7%	11.6%	14.2%	1.7	3.5	2.6
Mexican	0.2	0.2	0.3	0.3	0.9	1.4	2.8	2.5	3.5	0.5	1.4	1.0
Other	6.7	5.8	5.6	5.1	5.6	6.8	8.9	9.1	10.7	1.2	2.1	1.6

* Population 18 to 64 years old

Source: Borjas and Katz (2005, Figure 1) and authors' analysis of Current Population Survey basic monthly microdata

country today. These data indicate that the growth in immigrant workers' share of the labor force nearly doubled in each decade starting in 1970 through 2000; the immigrant share grew 1.3 percentage points in the 1970s, 2.3 percentage points in the 1980s, and 4.4 percentage points in the 1990s. The immigrant share continued to grow between 2000 and 2007 but at a somewhat slower annual rate than in the 1990s, and there was minimal growth during the recessionary years from 2007 to 2011. By 2011 immigrants made up 16.2 percent of the workforce, more than triple the share in 1970. Immigration from Mexico contributed 42.4 percent of the growth in immigrants as a share of the workforce between 1970 and 2011, with a greater role among men.

A rise in immigration increases the available supply of labor in the United States and thus tends to reduce wages if all else is constant (which it rarely is). If one workforce group—say, those without a high school degree—experiences the largest growth in immigration, then that group will have wage growth inferior to (or real wage declines greater than) that of less-affected groups. Since the largest share of immigrants is found among those without a high school degree, native workers without a high school education would be most affected by immigration. (Recall from Table 4.17 that 5.1 percent of the native-born workforce had less than a high school education in 2011, compared with 25.9 percent of immigrant workers.) A particular concern is whether new immigrants adversely affect the relative employment and wages of other disadvantaged populations (e.g., the less-educated portion of the black workforce, native Hispanics, and Hispanics who immigrated some time ago) where a disproportionate share of workers lack a high school degree. The impact of immigrants on native-born workers' relative wages could also be felt by those with high school degrees or above to the extent these workers compete for jobs in the same occupations and industries.

One offsetting factor is that immigrants may be "complements" to, rather than "substitutes" for, native-born workers; in other words, immigrant workers can facilitate the employment of other workers (presumably more-skilled workers) or raise the effectiveness of capital investments (thereby raising productivity). This does not have to be a case of being perfect substitutes or complements, as there may be varying degrees of complementarity. (An illustration of complementarity is that native workers are more likely to concentrate in jobs that require strong English skills, and immigrants tend to concentrate in jobs that do not. For example, in restaurant jobs, natives might be waiters and waitresses and immigrants might be dishwashers.)

Also, the increased supply of immigrant workers could in some circumstances be offset by a rapid growth in demand for those particular types of workers. Unfortunately, economic analyses have been unable to clearly identify the impact of increased immigration on the absolute wages and employment of other workers. However, a consensus exists that immigration heavily weighted toward those lacking a high school degree or having just a high school degree will increase wage inequality at the bottom; it may not force wages of the "less educated" to fall, but it will lead these wages to rise less than wages of workers with more education.

A first step in understanding the impact of immigration is to examine the gender and education composition of immigrants so as to assess which demographic groups are affected. **Table 4.32** shows the composition of the immigrant workforce by education and gender and divides the immigrants into those from Mexico and those from other nations. In 2011, a majority of Mexican immigrants,

Table 4.32 Educational attainment of immigrants, by gender, 1940–2011

	Share of workers (Decennial Census)							Share (CPS)	
	1940	1950	1960	1970	1980	1990	2000	2000	2011
Mexican men									
High school (H.S.) dropouts	94.6%	91.2%	88.3%	82.6%	77.2%	70.4%	63.0%	64.6%	57.0%
H.S. graduates	3.0	6.7	6.7	11.7	14.3	19.0	25.1	22.2	28.3
Some college	1.0	1.5	2.7	3.6	5.7	7.8	8.5	9.3	9.7
College graduates	1.4	0.6	2.4	2.2	2.9	2.8	3.4	3.8	5.1
Non-Mexican men									
H.S. dropouts	84.4%	76.4%	64.5%	45.5%	30.2%	21.0%	17.0%	18.5%	14.6%
H.S. graduates	9.2	14.5	16.8	23.9	26.7	26.0	25.8	24.6	24.5
Some college	2.8	4.0	8.3	11.7	15.2	21.3	20.9	19.7	19.9
College graduates	3.7	5.1	10.4	18.9	27.9	31.7	36.3	37.3	41.0
Mexican women									
H.S. dropouts	84.5%	82.4%	83.9%	77.3%	72.9%	64.7%	57.0%	57.3%	48.5%
H.S. graduates	12.5	10.3	11.4	16.9	17.7	21.9	26.6	24.0	28.8
Some college	2.1	4.4	2.7	4.5	7.0	10.5	11.8	13.4	15.2
College graduates	0.9	2.9	2.0	1.4	2.4	3.0	4.5	5.2	7.6
Non-Mexican women									
H.S. dropouts	79.2%	68.5%	59.3%	43.9%	30.1%	20.0%	15.5%	16.6%	12.1%
H.S. graduates	15.8	22.3	25.5	33.7	35.2	31.1	27.6	27.1	24.7
Some college	2.8	5.0	9.6	12.6	16.8	24.0	24.4	22.6	23.2
College graduates	2.2	4.2	5.7	9.9	17.9	24.9	32.6	33.7	40.0

Source: Borjas and Katz (2005, Table 2) and authors' analysis of Current Population Survey basic monthly microdata

57.0 percent of men and 48.5 percent of women, did not have a high school education. Among non-Mexican immigrants the share without a high school degree (12.1 percent of women and 14.6 percent of men) was also larger than among native workers (5.1 percent, as seen in Table 4.17). Thus, immigration disproportionately adds to the supply of "less than high school" or "dropout" workers relative to other education levels: Half of the workforce in this group are immigrants while only 5.1 percent of native workers lack a high school credential.

At the other end of the education spectrum, Table 4.17 showed a slightly greater share of immigrants than native workers with advanced degrees, 12.3 percent versus 11.1 percent. However, more natives (22.7 percent) than immigrants (17.9 percent) have a college degree. Table 4.32 shows that non-Mexican immigrants are more likely to be college graduates (which includes those with advanced degrees) than native workers. For instance, roughly 40 percent of non-Mexican immigrants in 2011 had at least a college degree, a "college intensity" exceeding the roughly one-third of native workers with a college degree or higher (Table 4.17). The college intensity of non-Mexican immigrants has grown strongly in each decade among both men and women. Therefore, the impact of growing immigration has been broadly and increasingly felt, including among those with college or advanced degrees. To the extent that college-educated immigrants are substitutes for native college graduates, then immigration may have put downward pressure on the wages of those with a college degree or more and *lessened* wage inequality between high- and middle-wage earners.

As noted, the degree to which immigration adversely affects the wages of particular groups of workers, if at all, is a matter of some dispute among economists. Given the expected downward pressure on the wages of low-wage workers from increased immigration (assuming substitution between immigrants and natives), it is surprising that, while immigration grew faster in the 1990s, the wages at the bottom did better in the 1990s than in the 1980s and that, correspondingly, the 50/10 wage gap has been stable or declining since the late 1980s. However, two sets of increases in the minimum wage and many years of persistent low unemployment in the late 1990s may have offset the impact of immigration. There is not much evidence of an adverse impact of immigration on wages at the bottom in the 2000s. As Figures 4K and 4L showed, there was a fairly stable wage gap between the middle and the bottom in the 2000s. The 50/10 wage gap did grow among men during the current recessionary period, but during that time male immigration was stagnant and therefore unlikely to be associated with this trend.

Unionization

The percentage of the workforce represented by unions was stable in the 1970s but fell rapidly in the 1980s and continued to fall in the 1990s and the early

Figure 4AC Union coverage rate in the United States, 1973–2011

Source: Authors' analysis of Hirsch and Macpherson (2003) and updates from the *Union Membership and Coverage Database*

2000s, as shown in **Figure 4AC**. This falling rate of unionization has lowered wages, not only because some workers no longer receive the higher union wage but also because there is less pressure on nonunion employers to raise wages; the spillover or threat effect of unionism and the ability of unions to set labor standards have both declined. The possibility that union bargaining power has weakened adds a qualitative shift to the quantitative decline. This erosion of bargaining power is partially related to a harsher economic context for unions because of trade pressures, the shift to services, and ongoing technological change. However, analysts have also pointed to other factors, such as employers' militant stance against unions and changes in the application and administration of labor law, that have helped to weaken unions and their ability to raise wages.

Table 4.33 presents estimates of the union wage premium computed to reflect differences in hourly wages between union and nonunion workers who are otherwise comparable in experience, education, region, industry, occupation, and marital status. The union premium is presented as the extra dollars per hour and the percentage-higher wage earned by those covered by a collective bargaining contract. This methodology yields a union premium of 13.6 percent overall—17.3 percent for men and 9.1 percent for women.

Sizable differences exist in union wage premiums across demographic groups, with blacks and Hispanics having union premiums of 17.3 percent and 23.1 percent, respectively, far higher than the 10.9 percent union premium for whites.

Table 4.33 Union wage premium by demographic group, 2011

Demographic group	Percent union*	Union premium**	
		Dollars	Percent
Total	**13.0%**	**$1.24**	**13.6%**
Men	13.5	2.21	17.3
Women	12.5	0.67	9.1
White	**13.3%**	**$0.76**	**10.9%**
Men	14.1	1.79	14.9
Women	12.5	0.18	7.0
Black	**15.0%**	**$2.60**	**17.3%**
Men	15.8	3.05	20.3
Women	14.4	2.25	14.8
Hispanic	**10.8%**	**$3.44**	**23.1%**
Men	10.8	4.77	29.3
Women	10.7	2.06	15.7
Asian	**11.1%**	**$1.54**	**14.7%**
Men	9.9	1.53	16.6
Women	12.4	1.61	12.9
New immigrants (less than 10 years)			
Men	5.4%	$0.49	16.0%
Women	7.0	2.74	16.2
Other immigrants (more than 10 years)			
Men	10.4%	$2.13	16.7%
Women	12.7	0.57	8.8

* Union member or covered by a collective bargaining agreement
** Regression-adjusted hourly wage advantage of being in a union, controlling for experience, education, region, industry, occupation, race/ethnicity, and marital status

Source: Authors' analysis of Current Population Survey Outgoing Rotation Group microdata

Consequently, unions raise the wages of minorities more than of whites (the wage effect of unionism on a group is calculated as the unionism rate times the union premium), helping to close racial/ethnic wage gaps. Hispanic and black men tend to reap the greatest wage advantage from unionism, though minority women have substantially higher union premiums than their white counterparts. Unionized Asians have a wage premium somewhat higher than that of whites.

Unionized immigrant male workers obtain a premium comparable to that of male workers overall, whether they have immigrated relatively recently (within 10 years) or further back in time. Women who have immigrated recently have a higher union premium than women overall, 16.2 percent versus 9.1 percent. Immigrant women who have been in the United States more than 10 years have a union premium comparable to that of women overall.

Table 4.34 provides information on the union premium for three nonwage dimensions of compensation: health insurance, pensions, and paid time off. The first two columns present the characteristics of compensation in union and nonunion settings. The difference between the union and nonunion compensation packages is presented in two ways, unadjusted (simply the difference between the first two columns) and adjusted (for differences in characteristics other than union status, such as industry, occupation, and establishment size). The last

Table 4.34 Union premiums for health, retirement, and paid leave benefits

	Union	Nonunion	Difference		Union premium
			Unadjusted	Adjusted*	
Health insurance					
Percent covered	83.5%	62.0%	21.5	17.5	28.2%
Employee deductible	$200	$300	-$100	-$54	-18.0%
Employer share					
Single plan	88.3%	81.8%	6.5	9.1	11.1%
Family plan	76.3%	64.9%	11.4	10.1	15.6%
Retiree health coverage	76.6%	59.8%	16.7	14.6	24.4%
Pension					
Percent covered	71.9%	43.8%	28.1	23.6	53.9%
Employer costs (per hour)					
Defined benefit	—	—	—	$0.39	36.1%
Defined contribution	—	—	—	-0.11	-17.7%
Time off					
Vacation weeks	2.98	2.35	0.63	—	26.6%
Paid holiday/vacation (hours)	—	—	—	22.2	14.3%

* Adjusted for establishment size, occupation, industry, and other factors. Adjusted difference is used to calculate premium.

Source: Buchmueller, DiNardo, and Valletta (2001) and Mishel and Walters (2003, Table 4)

column presents the union premium, the percentage difference between union and nonunion compensation, calculated using the adjusted difference.

These data show that a union premium exists in every dimension of the compensation package. Unionized workers are 28.2 percent more likely to be covered by employer-provided health insurance, and their insurance is better: An 11.1 percent higher share of single-worker coverage is paid by the employer, and for family coverage the employer-paid share is 15.6 percent higher; deductibles are $54, or 18.0 percent, less for union workers; and union workers are 24.4 percent more likely to receive health insurance coverage in their retirement.

Similarly, 71.9 percent of union workers have employer-provided pensions, compared with only 43.8 percent of nonunion workers. When this difference is adjusted for characteristics other than union status, union workers are 53.9 percent more likely to have pension coverage. Union employers spend 36.1 percent more on defined-benefit plans but 17.7 percent less on defined-contribution plans. As defined-benefit plans are preferable, as discussed earlier, these data indicate that union workers are more likely to have the better form of pension plans.

Union workers also get more paid time off. Their nearly three weeks of vacation amount to about three days (0.63 weeks) more than nonunion workers receive. Including both vacations and holidays, union workers enjoy 14.3 percent more paid time off.

Table 4.35 provides a more refined analysis of the union wage premium by comparing the employer benefit costs in unionized settings with those in nonunion settings in comparable occupations and establishments, i.e., factories or offices. (Data are based on a survey of firms, whereas Table 4.34 used a survey of workers.) Specifically, the estimated union premium controls for the sector (public or private) in which the establishment is located, the establishment's size, the full-time or part-time status of its employees, and its detailed industry and region. Unionized workers are 18.3 percent more likely to have health insurance,

Table 4.35 Union impact on paid leave, pension, and health benefits

	Paid leave	Pension and retirement	Health insurance
Union impact on benefit incidence	3.2%	22.5%	18.3%
Union impact on benefit cost per hour			
Total impact	11.4%	56.0%	77.4%
Impact of greater incidence	3.4	28.4	24.7
Impact of better benefit	8.0	27.7	52.7

Source: Pierce (1999) and Mishel and Walters (2003, Table 3)

22.5 percent more likely to have pension coverage, and 3.2 percent more likely to have paid leave. Unionized employers pay more for these benefits because the benefits they provide are better than those offered by nonunion employers and because unionized employers are more likely to provide these benefits. For instance, unionized employers pay 77.4 percent more in health insurance costs per hour, 24.7 percent more because of the greater incidence and 52.7 percent because of the better benefit.

This analysis also shows that unionized employers pay 56.0 percent more per hour for pension plans, 28.4 percent from a greater incidence of providing pensions and 27.7 percent from providing better pensions. Similarly, unionized employers have 11.4 percent greater costs for paid leave, mostly because of the more extensive paid leave (the 8.0 percent "better benefit" effect).

The effect of the erosion of unionization on the wages of a segment of the workforce depends on the degree to which deunionization has taken place and the degree to which the union wage premium among that segment of the workforce has declined. **Table 4.36** shows the degree to which unionization and the union wage premium have declined by occupation and education level over the 1978–2011 period (1979 data were not available). These data, which are for men only, are used to calculate the effect of weakened unions (less representation and a weaker wage effect) over the period on the wages of particular groups and the effect of deunionization on occupation and education wage differentials. The focus, in particular, is on the role of deunionization on the widening wage differentials between blue-collar and white-collar occupations and between high school and college graduates.

Union representation fell dramatically among blue-collar and high school–educated male workers from 1978 to 2011. Among the high school–graduate workforce, unionization fell from 37.9 percent in 1978 to 14.9 percent in 2011, or by more than half. This decline obviously weakened the effect of unions on the wages of high school–educated workers. Because unionized high school graduates earned about 22 percent more than equivalent nonunion workers in 1978 (a premium estimated for this analysis, but not shown in the table, that declined to 17 percent in 2011), unionization raised the wage of the average male high school graduate (the "union wage effect") by 8.2 percent in 1978. Unions had a 0.9 percent impact on male college graduate wages in 1978, meaning that unions had the net effect of narrowing the college/high school wage gap by 7.3 percentage points in that year. The decline in union representation (and the lower union wage premium) from 1978 to 2011, however, reduced the union wage effect for male high school–educated workers to just 2.6 percent in 2011 while hardly affecting college graduates. Thus, unions closed the college/high school wage gap by only 2.0 percentage points in 2011. The lessened ability of unions to narrow this wage gap (represented by the drop from a 7.3 percent to a 2.0 percent narrowing effect)

Table 4.36 Effect of union decline on male wage differentials, 1978–2011

		1978	1989	2000	2011
Percent of workers in union ("union coverage")					
By occupation	White collar	14.7%	12.1%	11.2%	10.3%
	Blue collar	43.1%	28.9%	23.1%	17.8%
	Difference	-28.4	-16.7	-11.9	-7.5
By education	College	14.3%	11.9%	13.1%	12.1%
	High school	37.9%	25.5%	20.4%	14.9%
	Difference	-23.6	-13.6	-7.4	-2.9
*Union wage effect**					
By occupation	White collar	0.2%	0.0%	-0.2%	-0.2%
	Blue collar	11.5%	6.7%	4.3%	3.5%
	Difference (change in differential)	-11.3	-6.8	-4.5	-3.6
By education	College	0.9%	0.5%	0.9%	0.6%
	High school	8.2%	5.5%	3.1%	2.6%
	Difference (change in differential)	-7.3	-5.0	-2.3	-2.0

		1978–1989	1989–2000	2000–2011	1978–2011
Change in wage differential**	White-collar/blue-collar	5.0	4.2	0.9	10.1
	College/high school	13.0	8.0	2.8	23.9
Change in union wage effect	White-collar/blue-collar	-4.6	-2.3	-0.9	-7.7
	College/high school	-2.3	-2.5	-0.3	-5.1
Deunionization contribution to change in wage differential*	White-collar/blue-collar	-90.5%	-55.2%	-91.8%	-76.1%
	College/high school	-17.8	-30.7	-10.2	-21.2

* Union wage effect is "union wage premium" (estimated with simple human capital model plus industry and occupational controls) times union coverage; negative values in the difference row show how much unionization narrowed the wage gaps.
** Log wage gaps estimated with a simple human capital model
***Change in union wage effect on wage differential divided by overall change in differential

Source: Authors' update of Freeman (1991) using Current Population Survey Outgoing Rotation Group microdata

contributed 5.1 percentage points to the rise in the college/high school wage differential from 1978 to 2011 (shown in the "Change in union wage effect" portion of the table). This is equal to 21.2 percent of the total rise in this wage gap (shown in the "Deunionization contribution to change in wage differential" portion of the table). In other words, deunionization can explain about a fifth of the growth in the college/high school wage gap among men between 1978 and 2011.

The weakening of unionism had an even larger effect on blue-collar workers and on the wage gap between blue-collar and white-collar workers. The 43.1 percent unionization rate among blue-collar workers in 1978 and their 26.6 percent union wage premium (not shown in the table) boosted average blue-collar wages by 11.5 percent, thereby closing the white-collar/blue-collar wage gap by 11.3 percentage points in that year. The union impact on this differential declined as unionization and the union wage premium decreased, such that unionism reduced the white-collar/blue-collar differential by 3.6 rather than 11.3 percentage points in 2011, a 7.7 percentage-point weakening. This lessened effect of unionism can account for 76.1 percent of the 10.1 percentage-point growth of the white-collar/blue-collar wage gap between 1978 and 2011; the lessened effect was primarily driven by the enormous decline of unionism among blue-collar men, from 43.1 percent in 1978 to just 17.8 percent in 2011. In that 33-year period unionism among blue-collar workers lost much of its ability to set wage patterns and standards. The impact of this decline in unionization is underestimated here because it does not take account of the union impact on nonunion workers' wages.

Unions reduce wage inequalities because they raise wages more at the bottom and in the middle of the wage scale than at the top. Lower-wage, middle-wage, blue-collar, and high school–educated workers are also more likely than high-wage, white-collar, and college-educated workers to be represented by unions. These two factors—the greater union representation and the larger union wage impact for low- and mid-wage workers—are key to unionization's role in reducing wage inequalities.

The larger union wage premium for those with low wages, in lower-paid occupations, and with less education is shown in **Table 4.37**. For instance, the union wage premium for blue-collar workers in 1997, 23.3 percent, was far larger than the 2.2 percent union wage premium for white-collar workers. Likewise, the 1997 union wage premium for high school graduates, 20.8 percent, was much higher than the 5.1 percent premium for college graduates. The union wage premium for those with a high school degree or less, at 35.5 percent, was significantly greater than the 24.5 percent premium for all workers.

Table 4.37 presents a comprehensive picture of the impact of unions on wage inequality by drawing on the estimated union wage premiums for the different fifths of the wage distribution. The table presents the results of three different studies, and each demonstrates that the union premium is higher among lower-wage

Table 4.37 Union wage premium for subgroups

Subgroup	Percent union	Union wage premium*		
Occupation				
White collar (1997)	11.6%	2.2%		
Blue collar (1997)	20.8	23.3		
Education				
College (1997)	10.4%	5.1%		
High school (1997)	23.6	20.8		
All (1992, 1993, 1996)	n.a.	24.5		
High school or less	n.a.	35.5		

Wage distribution		*Estimated union wage premium*		
		Study 1	**Study 2**	**Study 3**
Bottom fifth	4.9%	17.2%	20.6%	24.2%
Second fifth	8.9	21.8	16.8	34.6
Middle fifth	14.0	20.6	13.7	30.8
Fourth fifth	20.3	15.5	10.7	24.5
Top fifth	19.1	12.4	6.1	6.1
Average effect		**19.0%**	**11.9%**	**n.a.**
Percent bottom 40% to top 40%	35%	140	223	193%

* Percent by which the wages of those covered by collective bargaining agreements exceed wages of comparable nonunion workers

Source: Mishel and Walters (2003, Table 2.3a); Gunderson (2003, Table 5.1 and Appendix C); and premium estimates by fifth from: 1) Gittleman and Pierce (2007), 2) Schmitt (2008), and 3) Card, Lemieux, and Riddell (2002). Union coverage by fifth from Schmitt (2008)

workers than among the highest-wage workers. This is illustrated in the last row, which shows the premium of the bottom two-fifths of earners as a percent of the premium of the top two-fifths; the results range from 140 percent to 223 percent. These numbers illustrate that unions generate a less unequal distribution of wages in the unionized sector by raising the wages of low- and middle-wage workers more than those of higher-wage workers. That is, lower-wage workers benefit more than higher-wage workers from coverage by a collective bargaining agreement. The countervailing factor, however, is that unionization rates are lower for low-wage workers than other workers.

There are several ways that unionization's impact on wages goes beyond the workers covered by collective bargaining agreements and extends to nonunion wages and labor practices. For example, in industries, occupations, and regions in which a strong core of workplaces are unionized, nonunion employers will frequently meet union standards or at least improve their compensation and labor practices beyond what they would have provided in the absence of a union presence. As noted earlier, this dynamic—the degree to which nonunion workers are paid more because their employers are trying to forestall unionization—is sometimes called the union threat effect.

A more general mechanism (without any specific "threat") through which unions affect nonunion pay and practices is the institution of norms and practices that have become more widespread throughout the economy, thereby improving pay and working conditions for the entire workforce. These norms and practices have particularly benefited the roughly 70 percent of workers who are not college educated. Many fringe benefits, such as pensions and health insurance, were first provided in the union sector and then became more commonplace. Union grievance procedures, which provide due process in the workplace, have been adapted to many nonunion workplaces. Union wage setting, which has gained exposure through media coverage, has frequently established standards for what workers expect from their employers. Until the mid-1980s, in fact, many sectors of the economy followed the patterns set in collective bargaining agreements. As unions have weakened, especially in the manufacturing sector, their ability to set broader patterns has diminished. However, unions remain a source of innovation in work practices (e.g., training and worker participation) and in benefits (e.g., child care, work-time flexibility, and sick leave).

A new study has focused attention on the impact on wages and wage inequality of declining unionization of industries in particular regions. **Table 4.38** presents the results of this study, which examined the direct impact of lower unionization, and also the impact of falling unionization, in industries within particular regions (using 18 industries and four regions) on the wages of similarly located nonunion workers. It assesses the impact of these factors on both between-group wage inequality (recall from earlier that this is the wage difference between workers with different characteristics, such as education levels and experience) and within-group wage inequality (inequality of wages among workers with similar education and experience, for instance). Among men, wage inequality (measured by the variance of log wages) grew 0.102 between 1973 and 2007, 0.055 from higher between-group wage inequality and 0.046 from higher within-group wage inequality. The biggest impact of direct deunionization was on within-group inequality because of the increasing inequality among nonunion workers (as unions declined, similar workers started having more dissimilar wages). The direct impact of declining unionization accounted for 20.2 percent of the growth of overall male wage inequality, and the impact of declining unionization within particular industry/region groups (i.e., the weakening union impact on nonunion wages and standards) explained another 13.7 percent of the

Table 4.38 Impact of deunionization on wage inequality, 1973–2007

	Change in wage inequality		
	Between-group	Within-group	Total growth
*A. Male wage inequality trends**			
Change in wage inequality	0.055	0.046	0.102
Direct deunionization effect	0.002	0.018	0.021
Union impact on nonunion wages and standards	-0.017	0.031	0.014
*Share of inequality growth explained***			
Direct deunionization effect	3.2%	40.3%	20.2%
Union impact on nonunion wages and standards	-30.1	66.0	13.7
Total union effect	-26.9	106.3	33.9
*B. Female wage inequality trends**			
Change in wage inequality	0.051	0.047	0.098
Direct deunionization effect	-0.003	0.004	0.001
Union impact on nonunion wages and standards	0.036	0.024	0.019
*Share of inequality growth explained***			
Direct deunionization effect	-5.2%	9.2%	1.7%
Union impact on nonunion wages and standards	-10.9	50.6	18.7
Total union effect	-16.1	59.8	20.4

* Percentage-point change in variance of log wages
** From original source, which used nonrounded data

Source: Authors' analysis of Western and Rosenfeld (2011, Table 2)

growth of overall male wage inequality. Overall, deunionization can explain about a third (33.9 percent) of the growth of male wage inequality from 1973 to 2007.

Among women the decline in unions had little direct impact on within-group inequality (9.2 percent), but the diminished ability of unions to set labor standards (as women experienced the decline in industry/region unionization) had a large impact, explaining more than half the rise of within-group wage inequality. Altogether, deunionization generated about a fifth (20.4 percent) of the growth of overall wage inequality among women.

The decline of union coverage and influence adversely affects men more than women and middle-wage men more than lower-wage men. Consequently, deunionization has its greatest impact among men on the growth of the wage gap between workers at the 90th percentile of wages and the 50th percentile—the 90/50 wage gap. In this light, it is not surprising that the period of rapid decline of union coverage from 1979 to 1984 (during a deep recession, and at a time when the manufacturing sector was battered by the trade deficit) was also one in which the male 90/50 wage gap grew the most. Recall from Table 4.36 that male blue-collar unionization fell from 43.1 percent in 1978 to just 28.9 percent in 1989, a drop that contributed to the rapid growth of male wage inequality in the 1980s. The decline of unionization in the 1990s and 2000s put continued downward pressure on middle-wage men and contributed to the continued growth of the 90/50 wage gap between high- and middle-wage men. The erosion of unions, however, has also affected nonunion wages, and the consequence has been a sizable increase in wage inequality among women as well as men.

The decline in the real value of the minimum wage

Table 4.39 and **Figure 4AD** track changes in the value of the minimum wage. Legislated increases in the federal minimum wage in both 2007 and 2008 boosted it from $5.15 in 2006 to $7.25 in 2009, its highest level in real terms since 1981. But even after this nearly 41 percent increase, the minimum wage in 2009 was still 7.8 percent less than its value in 1967 (in 2011 dollars). After two years of inflation the minimum wage in 2011 was 12.1 percent below the 1967 level. The minimum wage declined steeply and steadily between 1979 and 1989, when inflation whittled it down from $8.38 to $5.87 (in 2011 dollars), a fall of 29.9 percent. The legislated increases in the minimum wage in 1990 and 1991 and again in 1996 and 1997 raised the value of the minimum wage from 1989 to 2000 by 14.6 percent (in 2011 dollars). The value grew another 7.8 percent from 2000 to 2011.

A more appropriate way to assess the level of the current minimum wage in historical terms is to examine the minimum wage's share of the average worker's wage (as measured by the average hourly earnings of production/nonsupervisory workers), as shown in **Figure 4AE**. In 2011, the minimum wage was worth only about 37 percent of what an average worker earned per hour, not far above its lowest point, reached in 2006, in 47 years. In contrast, the minimum wage's share of the average wage was about 50 percent in the late 1960s, about 45 percent in the mid-1970s, and about 40 percent in the early 1990s. This analysis shows that the earnings of low-wage workers have fallen significantly behind those of other workers, and that the decline in the real value of the minimum wage is a causal factor in rising wage inequality.

Table 4.39 Value of the minimum wage, 1960–2011

	Minimum wage	
	Current dollars	2011 dollars
1960	$1.00	$6.65
1967	1.40	8.25
1973	1.60	7.24
1979	2.90	8.38
1989	3.35	5.87
1990	3.80	6.34
1991	4.25	6.85
1996	4.75	6.78
1997	5.15	7.20
2000	5.15	6.73
2007	5.85	6.35
2008	6.55	6.84
2009	7.25	7.60
2011	7.25	7.25
Period averages		
1960s	$1.29	$7.91
1970s	2.07	8.02
1980s	3.33	6.92
1990s	4.53	6.70
2000s	5.57	6.46
Percent change		
1979–1989		-29.9%
1989–2000		14.6
2000–2011		7.8
1967–2011		-12.1

Source: Authors' analysis of U.S. Department of Labor Wage and Hour Division (2009)

It has been argued that the minimum wage primarily affects teenagers and others with no family responsibilities. To address this claim, **Table 4.40** examines the demographic composition of the workforce that would benefit from an increase in the minimum wage in 2014 to $9.80, about 47 percent of the average wage. This analysis takes into account the many workers benefiting from a state minimum wage higher than the current federal level (discussed further below).

Figure 4AD Real value of the minimum wage, 1960–2011

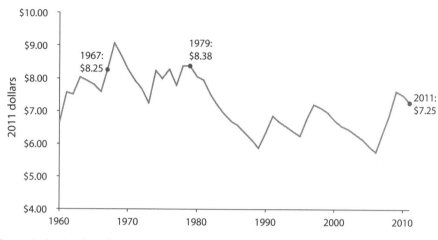

Source: Authors' analysis of U.S. Department of Labor Wage and Hour Division (2009)

Figure 4AE Minimum wage as a share of average hourly earnings, 1964–2011

Note: Earnings measured is average hourly earnings of production/nonsupervisory workers.

Source: Authors' analysis of U.S. Department of Labor Wage and Hour Division (2009) and Bureau of Labor Statistics Current Employment Statistics

Assessing who would benefit sheds light on who has been affected by the long-term drop in the real value of the minimum wage.

An analysis of only those earning between the current and the proposed new minimum wage would be too narrow, since a higher minimum wage would

Table 4.40 Characteristics of workers affected by proposed minimum-wage increase to $9.80 in 2014

	Directly	Indirectly*	Total	Total workforce
Total (millions)	19.5	8.9	28.4	127.4
Share of workforce	15.3%	7.0%	22.3%	100.0%
Gender				
Female	56.1%	51.1%	54.5%	48.3%
Male	43.9	48.9	45.5	51.7
Work hours				
Part time (<20 hrs/week)	17.1%	10.4%	15.0%	5.9%
Mid time (20–34 hrs/week)	33.9	24.4	30.9	14.5
Full time (35+ hrs/week)	49.1	65.2	54.1	79.6
Family status				
Married parent	15.9%	21.5%	17.6%	27.2%
Single parent	10.5	10.1	10.4	7.5
Age				
Age 20+	84.7%	95.0%	87.9%	96.6%
Under 20	15.3	5.0	12.1	3.4
Race/ethnicity				
White	56.2%	55.9%	56.1%	67.4%
African American	14.1	14.5	14.2	10.9
Hispanic	23.9	23.0	23.6	15.0
Asian	5.8	6.6	6.1	6.8
Industry				
Retail trade	24.5%	17.3%	22.2%	11.7%
Leisure and hospitality	23.4	14.3	20.6	9.4
Other	52.1	68.3	57.2	78.8
Occupation				
Sales	21.0%	12.5%	18.3%	10.5%
Service	37.7	31.3	35.7	18.0
Other	41.3	56.2	46.0	71.5

* Indirectly affected workers currently have a wage rate between $9.80 (the proposed minimum wage) and $12.35 (the proposed minimum wage plus the $2.55 increase from the current minimum wage of $7.25). They would receive a raise as employer pay scales adjust upward to reflect the new minimum wage.

Source: Cooper (2012) analysis of Current Population Survey Outgoing Rotation Group microdata

affect workers who earn more than but close to the proposed new minimum; they would receive increases if the minimum wage rises. For these reasons, Table 4.40 also includes other low-wage workers who would gain from the "spillover effect" of a higher minimum wage. The table presents information on these workers in the column labeled "Indirectly," a group totaling 8.9 million workers, or 7.0 percent of the workforce. The increase would affect 19.5 million workers directly, or 15.3 percent of the workforce. In total, the change in the minimum wage to $9.80 would affect a substantial group, 28.4 million workers, or 22.3 percent of the workforce. By this metric over a fifth of the workforce has been affected by the eroded value of the minimum wage.

A higher minimum wage would disproportionately affect women: They constitute a majority (54.5 percent) of those who would benefit, greater than their 48.3 percent share of the workforce. The vast majority (87.9 percent) of those who would be affected by the higher minimum wage are age 20 or over; thus, it is clear the increase would not mainly benefit teenagers. Similarly, single parents would disproportionately benefit from a higher minimum wage: 10.4 percent of those who would be affected are single parents, higher than their 7.5 percent share of the workforce. In addition, many beneficiaries (17.6 percent of the total) of the proposed minimum-wage increase are parents in a married-couple family; this share is less than their 27.2 percent share of the workforce. While minorities are disproportionately represented among the potential beneficiaries (23.6 and 14.2 percent are, respectively, Hispanic and African American), the majority, 56.1 percent, are white. A majority (54.1 percent) also work full time (at least 35 hours weekly), and another 30.9 percent work at least 20 hours but less than 35 hours each week.

Table 4.40 also shows that the beneficiaries of a potential minimum-wage increase are disproportionately concentrated in the retail and hospitality industries (42.8 percent are employed there, compared with just 21.1 percent of all workers), while other industries are underrepresented among this group. The demographic breakdown of those affected by the spillover effects of the proposed increase—those indirectly affected—is more inclusive of full-time and adult workers but has a similar racial/ethnic breakdown as the group directly affected.

The impact of the recent and proposed increases in the federal minimum wage is diminished somewhat compared with that of earlier increases because a substantial number of states have raised their own minimum-wage levels in recent years, reducing the number of workers affected by any proposed federal change. **Figure 4AF** contrasts the real value of the federal minimum wage with the share of the workforce covered by legislated state minimum wages that exceed the federal level. In 2007 31 states that were home to 70 percent of the nation's workforce had a minimum wage exceeding the federal level. By 2011 the number had declined to 17 states and about 41 percent of the workforce.

Another way to assess the importance of the minimum wage is to measure the share of total hours worked by workers earning at or below (some workers are not covered by minimum-wage laws) the legislated minimum (both federal and

Figure 4AF Real value of the federal minimum wage and share of workforce covered by higher state minimums, 1979–2011

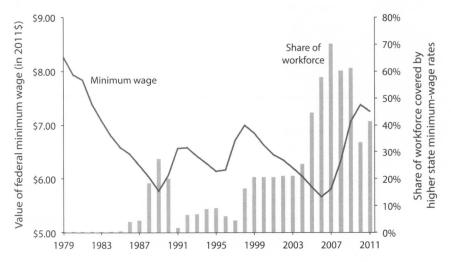

Source: Authors' analysis of U.S. Department of Labor (2009) and Cooper (2012) update of Shierholz (2009)

Figure 4AG Share of worker hours paid at or below the minimum wage, by gender, 1979–2009

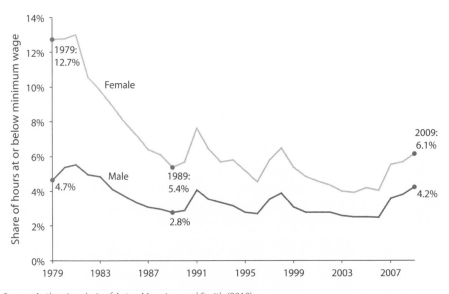

Source: Authors' analysis of Autor, Manning, and Smith (2010)

state). **Figure 4AG** illustrates that the minimum wage has been more important in setting a floor for women than for men and that there was a substantial erosion of the importance of the minimum wage for women in the 1980s. Since then the share of hours worked at or below the minimum wage has remained fairly low, except for a slight trend upward in the mid-2000s. It is notable that the 50/10 wage gap among women grew tremendously (as the 10th-percentile wage fell) in the 1980s, at the same time as the share of total hours worked by women workers earning at or below the legislated minimum fell.

Table 4.41 shows the impact of the minimum wage (including spillover impacts affecting workers just above the minimum) on the 50/10 wage gap among women, men, and overall in the years 1979–1991, when the value of the minimum wage eroded significantly, and over the longer period from 1979 to 2009. The results in Table 4.41 confirm that the deterioration in the minimum wage's value had a much larger impact on wages of women than of men. Between 1979 and 2009 the erosion of the minimum wage explained about two-thirds (65.5 percent) of the large 25.2 (log percentage point) expansion of the 50/10 wage gap among women but just over a tenth (11.3 percent) of the smaller 5.3 expansion of the 50/10 wage gap among men. For workers overall more than half (57.0 percent) of the increase in the 50/10 wage gap from 1979 to 2009 was accounted for by the erosion of the minimum wage. Curiously, the impact of the minimum wage on the 50/10 wage gap was less from 1979 to 1991 than from 1979 to 2009 even though the major decline of the value of the minimum wage occurred in the

Table 4.41 Minimum-wage impact on 50/10 wage gap, 1979–2009

	Change in 50/10 wage gap*		
	Actual change	Minimum-wage effect	Change explained by minimum wage
1979–1991			
Women	22.4	7.3	32.6%
Men	11.2	0.8	7.1
All	7.1	3.0	42.3
1979–2009			
Women	25.2	16.5	65.5%
Men	5.3	0.6	11.3
All	11.4	6.5	57.0

*Change in the (log) gap between wages of workers at the 50th percentile relative to wages of those at the 10th percentile

Source: Authors' analysis of Autor, Manning, and Smith (2010, Table 5)

1980s. Still, about a third of the 50/10 wage gap expansion among women from 1979 to 1991 can be explained by the falling value of the minimum wage.

The level of the minimum wage strongly affects the wage gains of low-wage workers, particularly low-wage women whose wages over the last few decades have essentially been set by the legislated minimum. Thus, the erosion of the minimum wage's value (along with high unemployment) led to a precipitous drop in the wages of low-wage women in the 1980s and to a large increase in the 50/10 wage gap. Wages among low-wage women (i.e., at the 10th percentile) stabilized in the late 1980s after these wages had descended close to their lowest possible level (i.e., near the minimum wage, where employers could still possibly hire) and as unemployment dropped. Thereafter, the 50/10 gap was flat or declined as unemployment fell to low levels in the late 1990s and as the federal government implemented two sets of increases in the minimum wage in the 1990s. Between 1999 and 2006, as the real value of the minimum wage eroded and unemployment rose, wage growth of low-wage women once again weakened, and the 50/10 wage gap grew. The legislated increases in the federal minimum wage that took effect in 2007, 2008, and 2009 kept the 50/10 wage gap among women from rising despite higher unemployment.

Executive and finance-sector pay

One distinct aspect of growing wage inequality is the gap between the very highest earners—those in the upper 1.0 percent or even upper 0.1 percent—and other high-wage earners, such as those at the 90th percentile (who earn more than 90 percent of all workers). These wage trends were reviewed in an earlier section. This section explores two key drivers of the wage increases in this top tier of wage earners: executive compensation and the increased size and high pay of the financial sector.

Our analysis first examines the role of executives and the financial sector in the growth of incomes of the top 1.0 and top 0.1 percent, and it then examines the growth of CEO compensation back to 1965, including the growth of the CEO-to-worker compensation ratio.

Table 4.42 draws on a study of tax returns to show the trend in the shares of total income (which includes wages and other types of income) of U.S. households accruing to the top 1.0 and top 0.1 percent of households. It further breaks down these two top income groups into households headed by either an "executive" (a group including managers and supervisors and hereafter referred to as executives) in a nonfinancial sector or by someone (executive or otherwise) working in the financial sector. (In Panel A, the household head is defined as the "primary taxpayer.")

Between 1979 and 2005 (the latest data available with these breakdowns) the share of total income held by the top 1.0 percent more than doubled, from 9.7 percent to 21.0 percent, with most of the increase occurring since 1993. The top

Table 4.42 Role of executives and financial sector in income growth of top 1.0% and top 0.1%, 1979–2005

	Share of total income*					1979–2005	
	1979	1993	1999	2001	2005	Change	Share
A. By rank and occupation of primary taxpayer							
Top 1.0%	9.7%	14.0%	19.3%	17.5%	21.0%	11.2	100%
Executives, managers, and supervisors (nonfinance)	3.8	5.6	7.8	6.5	7.9	4.0	36%
Finance workers, including executives	0.9	1.8	3.1	3.0	3.4	2.5	23%
Total, executives and finance workers	**4.8**	**7.4**	**10.9**	**9.4**	**11.3**	**6.5**	**58%**
Top 0.1%	3.3%	5.5%	9.3%	7.9%	10.3%	7.0	100%
Executives, managers, and supervisors (nonfinance)	1.6	2.8	4.5	3.5	4.7	3.1	44%
Finance workers, including executives	0.4	0.9	1.8	1.7	2.1	1.6	23%
Total, executives and finance workers	**2.0**	**3.7**	**6.3**	**5.2**	**6.7**	**4.7**	**67%**
B. Share of households with working spouse employed as executive or in finance							
Top 1.0%	10.0%	14.2%	16.1%	15.9%	15.7%	5.7	n/a
Top 0.1%	11.6	15.3	16.0	15.0	15.5	3.9	n/a

* Household income including capital gains

Source: Authors' analysis of Bakija, Cole, and Heim (2012, Tables 4, 5, 6a, and 7a)

0.1 percent led the way by more than tripling its income share, from 3.3 percent to 10.3 percent. This 7.0 percentage-point gain in income share of the top 0.1 percent accounted for more than 60 percent of the overall 11.2 percentage-point rise in the income share of the entire top 1.0 percent.

The table establishes that increases in income at the top were largely driven by households headed by someone who was either a nonfinance executive or in the financial sector as an executive or in some other capacity. Households headed by a nonfinance executive were associated with 44 percent of the growth of the top 0.1 percent's income share and 36 percent of the growth among the top 1.0 percent. Those in the financial sector were associated with nearly a fourth (23 percent) of the expansion of the income shares of both the top 1.0 and top 0.1 percent.

Together, finance workers and executives accounted for 58 percent of the expansion of income for the top 1.0 percent of households and two-thirds (67 percent) of the income growth of the top 0.1 percent of households.

This estimate of the impact of executives and finance on the growing incomes at the top does not include the role of earnings from spouses. These top-tier-income households frequently have employed spouses (though the data show the share of these households with an employed spouse did not grow between 1993 and 2005, the earliest and latest years for which data are available), and these spouses have increasingly been executives or employed in the financial sector. As the bottom section of Table 4.42 shows, the share of households with an employed spouse who was an executive or in finance, relative to all top 1.0 and top 0.1 percent households with or without spouses present, grew from 1979 to 1993 and held steady at roughly 15 percent thereafter. It is not possible to determine the role of these spouses in driving up top incomes without knowing whether the households' primary taxpayers were also executives or in finance, and these data are not available. However, the increased incomes earned by these spouses and their expanded role means that our analysis of the occupations of the "primary taxpayer" understates the total role of executives and the finance sector in driving up top incomes.

The 1980s, 1990s, and 2000s have been prosperous times for top U.S. executives, especially relative to other wage earners. The enormous pay increases received by chief executive officers of large firms have spillover effects (the pay of other executives and managers rises in tandem with CEO pay), but unfortunately no studies have established the scale of this impact.

Table 4.43 uses two measures of compensation to show trends in CEO pay since 1965. The measures differ only in their treatment of stock options: One incorporates stock options according to how much CEOs realized in that particular year (by exercising stock options available), and the other incorporates the value (the Black Scholes value) of stock options granted that year. Besides stock options, each measure includes the sum of salaries, bonuses, restricted stock grants, and long-term incentive payouts. It is possible to have broader measures of CEO compensation, but these would not be available for a historical series. The only historical CEO compensation data available (for 1965 to 1992) incorporate the value of stock options realized, and we use this series to extend the two measures back to 1965 (which explains why the growth from 1965 to 1978 is the same for both measures).

CEO compensation in Table 4.43 is the average of the annual compensation of the CEOs in the 350 publicly owned firms (i.e., they sell stock on the open market) with the largest revenue each year. For comparison, the table also presents the annual compensation of a private-sector production/nonsupervisory worker (a category that covers more than 80 percent of payroll employment), which allows us to compare CEO compensation to that of a "typical" private-sector worker.

Table 4.43 CEO compensation and CEO-to-worker compensation ratio, 1965–2011 (2011 dollars)

	CEO annual compensation (thousands)*		Worker annual compensation (thousands)		Stock market indices (infla- tion-adjusted)		CEO-to-worker compensation ratio***	
	Options realized	Options granted	Private- sector	Firms' industry**	S&P 500	Dow Jones	Options realized	Options granted
1965	$791	$750	$38	n/a	511	5,278	20.1	18.3
1973	1,033	980	45.8	n/a	451	3,881	22.1	20.1
1978	1,413	1,341	47.6	n/a	282	2,411	29.0	26.5
1989	2,631	2,496	44.0	n/a	525	4,081	58.5	53.3
1995	5,570	6,177	43.6	49.8	737	6,120	122.6	136.8
2000	19,482	19,977	45.9	52.0	1,730	13,006	383.4	411.3
2007	17,919	12,484	48.2	52.2	1,487	13,268	351.7	244.1
2008	17,491	11,648	48.4	53.0	1,183	10,902	314.9	225.7
2009	10,036	9,639	50.5	55.4	923	8,648	193.1	181.5
2010	12,042	11,003	50.9	56.0	1,092	10,215	228.0	205.9
2011	12,141	11,082	50.3	55.4	1,268	11,958	231.0	209.4
Percent change							**Change in ratio**	
1978–2011	759.3%	726.7%	5.7%	n/a	349.1%	395.9%	202.0	182.9
1965–1978	78.7	78.7	23.7	n/a	-44.7	-54.3	8.9	8.1
1978–2000	1,278.8	1,390.3	-3.6	n/a	513.0	439.3	354.4	384.9
2000–2011	-37.7	-44.5	9.7	6.6%	-26.7	-8.1	-152.4	-201.9

* "Options realized" compensation series includes salaries, bonuses, restricted stock grants, options exercised, and long-term incentive payouts for CEOs at the top 350 firms ranked by sales. "Options granted" compensation series includes salaries, bonuses, restricted stock grants, options granted, and long-term incentive payouts for CEOs at the top 350 firms ranked by sales.
** Annual compensation of production and nonsupervisory workers in the key industry of the firms in the sample
*** Based on averaging specific firm CEO-to-worker compensation ratios and not the ratio of averages of CEO and worker compensation

Source: Authors' analysis of data from Compustat ExecuComp database, Federal Reserve Economic Data (Stock Market Indexes), Bureau of Labor Statistics Current Employment Statistics, and Bureau of Economic Analysis National Income and Product Accounts

Last, from 1995 onward we can identify the average annual compensation of the production/nonsupervisory workers in the key industry of the firms included in the sample. We take this compensation as a more refined proxy for the pay of a "typical" worker in these particular firms. The pre-1995 historical benchmark years used in this analysis are the years for which data are available.

CEO compensation grew 78.7 percent between 1965 and 1978, about three times the growth of the compensation of private-sector workers. It is interesting that the stock market (as measured by the Dow Jones and S&P indices) fell by about half at the same time that CEO compensation grew by 78.7 percent. CEO compensation grew strongly over the 1980s but exploded in the 1990s; it peaked in 2000 at more than $19 million, a growth from 1978 to 2000 of about 1,279 or 1,390 percent, respectively, by the options-realized and the options-granted measures. This growth in CEO compensation far exceeded even the substantial rise in the stock markets, which grew in value by about 439 percent (Dow) and 513 percent (S&P) over the 1980s and 1990s. In stark contrast to both the stock market and CEO compensation growth was the 3.6 percent decline in the compensation of private-sector workers over the same period.

The fall in the stock market in the early 2000s led to a substantial paring back of CEO compensation, but by 2007 (when the stock market had mostly recovered) CEO compensation had returned close to its 2000 level, at least for the options-realized measure. The financial crisis in 2008 and the accompanying stock market tumble knocked CEO compensation down again. By 2011 the stock market had recouped much of the ground lost in the 2008 financial crisis, and CEO compensation had returned to either about $11.1 million measured by options granted or $12.1 million measured by options realized. Between 2010 and 2011 CEO compensation grew about 1 percent while the compensation of production and nonsupervisory workers fell by about 1 percent.

CEO compensation in 2011 is high by any metric, except when compared with its own peak in 2000, after the 1990s stock bubble. From 1978 to 2011, CEO compensation grew more than 725 percent, substantially more than the stock market and remarkably more than worker compensation, which grew by a meager 5.7 percent.

Table 4.43 also presents the trend in the ratio of CEO-to-worker compensation to illustrate the increased divergence between CEO pay and a typical worker's pay over time. This overall ratio is computed in two steps. The first step is to compute, for each of the largest 350 firms, the ratio of the CEO's compensation to the annual compensation of workers in the key industry of the firm (data on the pay of workers in any particular firm are not available). The second step is to average that ratio across all the firms. The data in the last two columns are the resulting ratios in specific years. The trends prior to 1992 are based on the changes in average CEO and private-sector worker compensation. The year-by-year trends are presented in **Figure 4AH**.

Depending on the CEO compensation measure, U.S. CEOs in major companies earned 18.3 or 20.1 times more than a typical worker in 1965; this ratio grew to 29.0-to-1 or 26.5-to-1 in 1978 and to 58.5-to-1 or 53.3-to-1 by 1989, and then it surged in the 1990s to hit 383.4-to-1 or 411.3-to-1 by 2000. The fall in the stock

Figure 4AH CEO-to-worker compensation ratio (options granted and options realized), 1965–2011

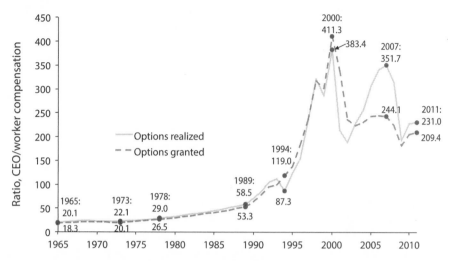

Note: "Options granted" compensation series data include salaries, bonuses, restricted stock grants, options granted, and long-term incentive payouts for CEOs at the top 350 U.S. firms ranked by sales. "Options realized" compensation series data include salaries, bonuses, restricted stock grants, options exercised, and long-term incentive payouts for CEOs at the top 350 firms ranked by sales.

Source: Authors' analysis of data from Compustat ExecuComp database, Bureau of Labor Statistics Current Employment Statistics, and Bureau of Economic Analysis National Income and Product Accounts

market after 2000 reduced CEO stock-related pay (e.g., options) and caused CEO compensation to tumble until 2002 and 2003. CEO compensation recovered to a level of 351.7 times typical-worker compensation by 2007, almost back to its 2000 level using the options-realized metric. Compensation based on options granted, however, returned only to 244.1-to-1 in 2007, still far below its heights in 2000.

The financial crisis in 2008 and accompanying stock market decline reduced CEO compensation after 2007–2008, as discussed previously, and the CEO-to-worker compensation ratio fell in tandem. By 2011 the stock market had recouped much of the value it lost following the financial crisis. Likewise, CEO compensation had grown from its 2009 low, and the CEO-to-worker compensation ratio had recovered to either 231.0-to-1 or 209.4-to-1, depending on the measure of options.

Though lower than in some other years in the last decade, the CEO-to-worker compensation ratio in 2011 (231.0-to-1 or 209.4-to-1) was far above the ratio in 1989 (58.5-to-1 or 53.3-to-1), 1978 (29.0-to-1 or 26.5-to-1), or 1965 (20.1-to-1 or 18.3-to-1). This illustrates that CEOs have fared far better than the typical worker, the stock market, or the U.S. economy over the last several decades.

Explaining wage inequality: Bringing the factors together

The approach to understanding growing wage inequality in this chapter has been to examine the factors behind the growth of the three key wage gaps (those between the very top and top, the top and middle, and the middle and the bottom) rather than to consider wage inequality as a unitary phenomenon. This is because the different parts of the wage structure have diverged at differing paces and at differing times as a result of various factors.

The wage gap at the bottom, the 50/10 gap, which captures the difference between wages of workers at the 50th percentile, or median, and those at the 10th percentile in the wage distribution, expanded from 1979 to the late 1980s (1986 for men, 1988 for women), grew much more for women than for men, and has been stable since then. It is not difficult to explain these trends. Rapid inflation and failure to raise the minimum wage lowered the real value of the minimum wage by roughly 30 percent from 1979 to 1989 (Table 4.39) and undercut the wages of low-wage women, as far fewer were protected by this wage floor (Figure 4AG). Roughly two-thirds of the growth of the 50/10 wage gap for women from 1979 to 2009 can be explained by minimum-wage trends (Table 4.41). The substantial unemployment of the early 1980s drove the 50/10 wage gap for men, which only stopped expanding after the unemployment rate reached 6.2 percent in 1987, down from a peak of 10.8 percent in late 1982. Unemployment also put significant downward pressure on the wages of low-wage women.

The growth of the wage gap at the very top, between those in the top 1.0 percent (or higher) and other high-wage earners, is primarily the result of two factors: the superlative growth of compensation of CEOs and other top managers (Table 4.43), and the increasingly high salaries in the financial sector and the expansion of finance (Table 4.42) the latter of which we could label "financialization." Together, these two factors accounted for at least 58 percent of the growth of the income share of the top 1.0 percent of households and 67 percent—two-thirds—of the increased income share of the top 0.1 percent of households from 1979 to 2005 (Table 4.42). It should be noted that the growth of the stock market greatly affects the wage trends at the very top because stock options that are exercised are counted as wage income.

The decades-long expansion of the wage gap within the top half of the wage structure, such as the growth of the 95/50 wage gap, also has identifiable causes. It is partly explained by the ongoing erosion of unionization and the declining bargaining power of unions along with the weakened ability of unions to set norms or labor standards that raise the wages of comparable nonunion workers. The decline of unions has affected middle-wage men more than any other group and explains about three-fourths of the expanded wage gap between white- and blue-collar men and over a fifth of the expanded wage gap between high school– and college-educated men from 1978 to 2011 (Table 4.36). An expanded analysis that includes the direct and norm-setting impact of unions shows that deunionization can explain about a third of the entire growth of wage inequality among men and around a fifth of the growth among women from 1973 to 2007 (Table 4.38).

International trade has been another factor suppressing wages in the middle of the wage structure, particularly since 1995. The college/noncollege wage gap grew modestly since 1995, rising 4.8 (log) percentage points, but this increase can almost totally be attributed to downward pressure exerted by trade on the wages of non-college-educated workers (Table 4.29). The emergence of high trade deficits and the import surge in the early 1980s also put substantial pressure on mid-level wages. This trade impact reinforced the pressure on low and mid-level wages exerted by the high unemployment of the early and mid-1980s. In addition, offshoring is now expanding the impact of globalization to higher-wage, white-collar workers. The shrinking share of employment in manufacturing and other high-paying sectors also reinforced the downward pressure on mid-level wages, an impact that was greatest in the 1980s, when it lowered hourly compensation 0.3 percent each year (Table 4.25).

Other factors not considered above have also put downward pressure on mid-level wages. Various industries were deregulated starting in the late 1970s, and in each of these industries—including airlines, trucking, interstate busing, telecommunications, utilities, and railroads—there was a strong adverse impact on the wages and compensation of blue-collar and other workers. Ongoing efforts to privatize public-sector functions have also put downward pressure on wages. Weakened labor standards (e.g., regarding overtime pay and independent contractor status) and generally weaker enforcement of labor standards also contribute to lower wages in the broad middle of the wage structure. At the same time, a weaker safety net, including the changes to what used to be called "welfare," empower employers because workers have fewer alternatives to less-than-desirable job conditions. Additionally, immigration policy in the form of temporary worker programs undercuts the wages of workers in such disparate fields as landscaping and hospitality, at the low end, to software engineering and computer programming, at the high end.

Rather than a disconnected list, these factors driving greater wage inequality are unified in a fundamental way: They are all the result of laissez-faire policies that strengthen the hands of employers and undercut the ability of low- and middle-wage workers to have good jobs and economic security. These laissez-faire policies (e.g., globalization, deregulation, weaker unions, and lower labor standards such as a weaker minimum wage) have all been portrayed to the public as providing goods and services at more competitive prices. Whatever the impact on prices, these policies have lowered the earning power of low- and middle-wage workers such that their real wages severely lag both productivity growth and wage growth of higher-wage workers. Further, monetary policies that aim to control inflation by tolerating (or causing) higher-than-necessary levels of unemployment have added to the forces disempowering the vast majority of workers and generating continuously greater wage gaps between those at the top and all other workers. These factors behind growing wage inequality can also be seen as the dynamics generating the erosion of labor's share of income.

Technology and skill mismatches

Some observers argue that wage inequality is the result of the failure of workforce skills to keep pace with the education and skills that workplace technologies demand. This is what is meant when increasing wage inequality and income inequality are attributed to a growing "education divide" fueled by an increasing mismatch between the education and skills of the workforce and the education and skills needed to fill available jobs. This education gap is sometimes described as a wage gap between "those with more and those with less education," and is sometimes referred to as "higher returns to education and skills." All of these labels are manifestations of a "technology story" of wage inequality. According to this story, technological change has raised the education and skill requirements of jobs while the workforce "supply" of those skills and education levels has lagged, forcing employers to bid up the wages of those with the requisite skills and education, thereby widening the education and skill wage gaps that fuel growing wage and income inequality.

A particularly prevalent storyline is that technology is generating a much greater need for college-educated workers, which leads to a much larger wage gap between workers with and without a college degree.

Technological change can affect the wage structure by displacing some types of workers and increasing demand for others. Unfortunately, because it is difficult to measure the extent and overall character of technological change (i.e., whether and how much change alters the worker skill levels needed), it is difficult to identify the role of technological change in recent wage trends. In fact, more than a few analysts have simply assumed that whatever portion of wage inequality is unexplained by more easily measured factors (such as trade, unionization, and so on) is the consequence of technological change. But this is the type of analysis said to simply "put a name to our ignorance."

This section examines whether technological change and growing skill mismatches (or skill shortages), including a growing unmet demand for college graduates, can explain the growth of the various dimensions of wage inequality described earlier in this chapter. Technological change has played a role in rising demand for education and skills in the last few decades, but not more so than in prior decades. Furthermore, the rapid expansion of workforce education and skill levels has been sufficient to satisfy the increased demand. The conclusion, then, is that technological change, skill mismatches, skill shortages, and the "education gap" have had very little to do with the growth of wage inequality. Rather, growing supply accompanied growing demand and, therefore, increasing wage gaps were the result of other factors. It is especially hard to attribute any of the growth of wage inequality since the mid-1990s to skill shortages or the education divide, as wage inequality rose rapidly but education-based wage gaps grew very modestly, and whatever growth in education wage gaps occurred was not necessarily due to technological change or skill shortages. Labor market trends among college graduates confirm this conclusion. Since 2002/2003, real wage growth among college graduates, including those in business and professional fields, has been disappointing, as has the erosion of employer-provided health and pension coverage. In addition, since 2000, more college graduates are working in jobs that do not require a college degree. Negative trends in wages, benefits, and job quality have been more extreme among younger college graduates, those considered best-equipped to fulfill demand for new technological skills.

What is the appeal of the technology story?

We are often told that the pace of change in the workplace is accelerating, and technological advances in communications, entertainment, Internet, and other technologies are widely visible. Thus it is not surprising that many people believe that technology is transforming the wage structure. But technological advances in consumer products do not in and of themselves change labor market outcomes. Rather, changes in the way goods and services are produced influence relative demand for different types of workers, and it is *this* that affects wage trends. Since many high-tech products are made with low-tech methods, there is no close correspondence between advanced consumer products and an increased need for skilled workers. Similarly, ordering a book online rather than at a bookstore may change the type of jobs in an industry—we might have fewer retail workers in bookselling and more truckers and warehouse workers—but it does not necessarily change the skill mix.

It is also easy to see why some economists would assume a large role for technology in growing wage inequality. First, growing wage inequality and the shift to more-educated workers have been caused more by shifts within industries than by shifts across industries (i.e., more service jobs, fewer manufacturing jobs). Second, according to research, technological change has traditionally been associated with increased demand for "more-educated" or "skilled" workers. As this chapter has documented, the wage premium for more-educated workers (i.e., college graduates) has risen over the last two decades, a pattern that to some analysts suggests an increase in what is called "skill-biased technological change" that is generating greater wage inequality.

Third, wages have risen the most for groups whose supply expanded the fastest (e.g., college graduates). Many economists reason that those fast-expanding groups would have seen their wages depressed relative to other groups unless there were other factors working strongly in their favor, such as rapid expansion in demand. Rapid technological change favoring more-educated groups seems a logical explanation for wages that increase at the same time as supply.

One complication in assessing any technology-related explanation is that technology's impact can vary in different periods, sometimes most adversely affecting the least-educated and sometimes hurting mid-level skilled workers. The challenge is to empirically trace how technology affects the demand for different types of skills in different periods.

Education gaps and wage inequality

Rising education wage gaps are the primary mechanism through which technology is said to increase wage inequality. The extent to which education wage gaps do not explain wage inequality is the extent to which the technology story of wage inequality is misdirected, at least in terms of the conventional story in the public discourse. Similarly, the extent to which technology does not explain education wage gaps is the extent to which the technology story falls short. According to our research, education wage gaps have had only a modest impact on overall wage inequality since 1995—and even when they have appeared to play a limited role, the greater education wage gaps have not been driven by technology.

Table 4.44 presents trends in wage gaps between key education and wage groups in order to assess how they correspond. The table shows change in the gaps from 1979 to 1995 and from 1995 to 2007, before the recession, and from 1995 to 2011, the most recent data. We use 1995 as the dividing year because it was about then that growth of education wage gaps flattened. The table shows that wage inequality in the top half of the distribution grew strongly from 1995 to 2011 and that this growth in inequality was largely not driven by education wage gaps. The table also shows that all of the education wage gaps grew far less between 1995 and 2011 than in 1979–1995. The wage gap between those with a high school education and those without a high school credential ("less than high school") rose modestly before 1995 and then stabilized. The wage gaps of those with a college degree or advanced degree relative to those with less education grew about a fourth as fast in the 1995–2011 period as in 1979–1995. For instance, the wage gap between those with at least a college degree relative to those without a college degree rose from 28.9 percent in 1979 to 46.1 percent in 1995, a rise of 1.08 percentage points a year. From 1995 to 2011, this wage gap grew 4.8 percentage points, or just 0.30 percentage points each year. Since these education wage gaps grew more slowly since 1995 and have made only a modest contribution to the various wage group wage gaps, it follows that the prima facie evidence for technology causing wage inequality is weak.

Table 4.44 Trends in education wage gaps, key wage group wage gaps, and relative supply of education, 1979–2011

	1979	1995	2007	2011	Average annual change		
					1979–1995	1995–2007	1995–2011
Education wage gaps*							
College/high school	23.5%	42.5%	46.4%	46.9%	1.19	0.33	0.28
Advanced degree/high school	32.4	62.3	66.6	69.6	1.87	0.35	0.46
College or more/noncollege	28.9	46.1	49.2	50.9	1.08	0.26	0.30
High school/less than high school	21.0	27.4	26.0	27.6	0.40	-0.11	0.01
Wage group wage gaps**							
50/10 (hourly)	57.8%	69.4%	66.3%	67.7%	0.72	-0.25	-0.10
95/50 (hourly)	86.9	101.8	110.2	113.0	0.93	0.70	0.70
Top 1.0/90th–95th (annual)	122.4	164.1	187.2	175.5	2.61	1.92	0.71
Relative supply (share of employment)							
College only (1)	12.7%	17.3%	20.9%	21.9%	0.29	0.30	0.29
Advanced degree (2)	6.0	8.1	10.1	11.3	0.13	0.17	0.20
College or more (1 + 2)	18.6	25.4	31.0	33.2	0.42	0.46	0.49

* Log point gaps based on regression-adjusted models with human capital controls
** Change in unadjusted log point wage gaps

Source: Authors' analysis of Current Population Survey Outgoing Rotation Group microdata and Tables 4.4 and 4.8 in this chapter

Additionally the table reveals how various education wage gap patterns correspond to the growth of the three key wage group wage gaps: between wages at the middle (50th percentile) and the bottom (10th percentile), known as the "50/10 gap"; between high and middle earners (the "95/50 gap"); and between the very top and other high earners (the gap between the top 1.0 percent and those making between the 90th and 95th percentile wage).

The 50/10 wage gap grew strongly in the early period but not at all in the latter period, which somewhat corresponds to the pattern of the high school/less-than-high-school differential. This would mean that technological change did not disadvantage low-wage workers relative to middle-wage workers since the late 1980s, as the wage gap did not grow at all (as discussed earlier, the 50/10 wage gap has been largely flat since the late 1980s). One reason the high school/

less-than-high-school differential didn't grow is that the share of workers without a high school credential declined enormously over these decades, falling from 20.1 percent in 1979 to just 8.4 percent in 2011 (Table 4.14). This is a clear case of supply shrinkage (in particular, of those without high school credentials) adjusting to increased relative demand (a reduced relative need for such workers). That is, there was a declining need for those without a high school degree as technology-related skill requirements grew, which would have, other things equal, generated growth in the high school/less-than-high-school differential as "less than high school" wages dropped. However, the shrinkage in the number of those without a high school degree compensated for the flagging demand for such workers.

In contrast, the wage gaps in the top half grew strongly pre- and post-1995, though growth was not as fast after 1995. The 95/50 wage gap grew 75 percent as fast from 1995 to 2011 as in the earlier period, and far faster than the growth of corresponding education wage gaps (e.g., growing 0.70 percentage points each year compared with the 0.30 percentage-point annual growth in the college or more/noncollege wage gap). The wage gap between the top 1.0 percent and other high earners grew strongly from 1995 to 2007, though education wage gaps grew very modestly. The reduction in this wage gap from 2007 to 2011 is due to the impact of the financial crisis on stock values and stock options (as discussed previously) and had nothing to do with trends in education wage gaps. In short, in 1995–2011, there was strong growth in the 95/50 wage gap and in the gap between the top 1.0 percent and other high earners, with the gap at the very top growing even faster from 1995 to 2007. This growth in wage inequality at the top occurred when education wage gaps grew modestly, suggesting that the connection between education wage gaps and overall wage inequality since 1995 has been very weak.

Even when the growth of education wage gaps corresponds to the growth of key wage group wage gaps, as in the 1980s, this does not necessarily indicate that technological change is the cause of the education gaps; many other factors affect education wage gaps. Earlier sections have demonstrated that changes in labor market institutions such as the minimum wage and unionization are responsible for some of the rise in education/wage differentials, and trade with low-wage nations has also had a substantial impact. These various factors have increased education wage gaps by lowering the wages of the noncollege workforce instead of bidding up college wages as they would do if the technology story were true. For instance, there was strong growth in the 50/10 wage gap in the 1980s and a corresponding (but much weaker) increase in the wage gap between high school graduates and those with no high school credential. Analyses presented earlier pointed to the declining value of the minimum wage and the persistent high unemployment of that period as the factors driving this wage inequality at the bottom, factors that lowered the wages of low-wage workers.

Similarly, the ongoing erosion of the union impact on wages has fueled the growth of the college/high school wage gap among both men and women. According to Table 4.36, deunionization can explain about one-fifth of the growth in the male college/high school wage premium from 1978 to 2011 and a quarter of the growth from 1989 to 2011 (not shown in the table), even without taking into account any effect of deunionization on nonunion workers (which would substantially raise this estimate of the impact of deunionization). Lastly, trade with low-wage nations has eroded the wages of noncollege workers, especially since 1995. This factor alone can explain almost the total rise in the college/noncollege wage gap from 1995 to 2011. If so, then technological change probably had no effect on that education wage gap after 1995 since trade and other factors can explain any post-1995 growth in education wage gaps.

To summarize, an alleged technology-driven growth in education wage gaps provides a very unsatisfactory explanation of rising wage inequality because the growth in education wage gaps only partially corresponds to that of key wage gaps, especially since 1995, and because other factors besides technology can explain much of the growth of education wage gaps.

The slowdown in the growth of demand for college graduates

The previous section examined the conventional assumption that education wage gaps are fueled by technology-driven changes in relative demand for more-educated or skilled workers, and showed that the role of technology is at best vastly overstated, given the proven influence of other factors on education wage gaps. This section looks specifically at the claim of technology-driven change itself. Technological change certainly has generated the need for a more educated workforce, and the workforce has indeed become far more educated. The share of the workforce without a high school degree has fallen sharply, and many more workers have college degrees (33.2 percent of the workforce had a four-year college or advanced degree in 2011, up from 18.7 percent in 1979, according to Table 4.14). Investment and technological change generally are associated with the need for more workforce skill and education—but this was true for the entire 20th century, and it therefore does not explain why wage inequality began to grow three decades ago. A convincing technology story must show that the impact of technology accelerated *relative to earlier periods* in order to explain why wage inequality started to grow in the 1980s, 1990s, and 2000s, and did not grow in prior decades.

To assess whether the role of technological change accelerated, we examine trends in the relative demand for more-educated and skilled workers (as a proxy). In fact, what we find is that the growth in the relative demand for college graduates has been historically slow in the 1990s and 2000s.

Figure 4AI presents estimates of the growth of the relative demand for college graduates (defined in this research as those with a four-year degree or more and some of those with an education beyond high school) for periods from 1940 to 2005. These estimates of relative demand are deduced from underlying trends in supply and wages.

What does the pattern tell us? First, the relative demand for college graduates grew in each period, albeit more in some periods than in others (except during the special circumstances of World War II, when wages grew faster for noncollege workers). And as we know from Table 4.14 and other data, there was a simultaneous shift toward more college graduates throughout this period. Therefore, we can safely say that skill-biased technological change has been ongoing for some time, leading to employers' increasingly greater needs for college graduates (or "skilled" workers). However, since 1980, the growth rate of relative demand for college graduates was not faster than the growth rate of relative demand over the prior 30 years. Thus, given that wage inequality grew faster in recent decades than in earlier decades when technologically driven demands for college graduates were at least as rapid, it is hard to conclude that a more rapid rise in technological change drove up wage inequality since 1980.

In particular, trends since 1990 do not support the argument that a technologically driven demand for college-educated workers has increased their wages and therefore expanded wage inequalities. Note that the relative demand for

Figure 4AI Growth in relative demand for college graduates, 1940–2005

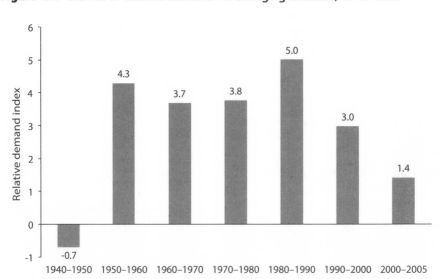

Source: Authors' analysis of Goldin and Katz (2008, Table 1)

college graduates grew more slowly in the 1990s than in any previous period since 1950 and that relative demand grew even more slowly from 2000 to 2005. This suggests that we are not in a time of historically rapid change in the need for education/skills in the workplace, at least if one equates a college degree with skilled labor. It also shows that the entire period since 1980 cannot be considered as one undifferentiated period of rapidly rising demand for college graduates.

The data comparing the 1979–1995 and 1995–2011 periods presented in Table 4.44 affirm the recent slowdown in relative demand for college graduates. The bottom panel shows the growth in relative supply of college graduates (college only, advanced degree, and both combined), which grew at roughly the same pace in each period (for college only) or a bit faster in the more recent period (for advanced degree and combined). As emphasized previously, the growth of the education wage gaps, most importantly the gap between those with at least a college degree and those with no college degree, slowed tremendously after 1995. The fact that the relative wage of college graduates grew more slowly while relative supply grew comparably across periods implies that the relative demand for college graduates slowed a great deal after 1995. This would be the case even with a slight uptick in supply growth (as in the combined group). Thus, these data affirm the findings of Figure 4AI.

The discussions in the last two sections show clear holes in the technology/education story. Only by ignoring factors such as institutional changes (the minimum wage, unionization, norms, etc.) and globalization (including immigration) that have also led to relatively higher wages for more-educated workers (primarily by depressing the wages of non-college-educated workers) can one accept the assumption that technology is the cause of all changes in education wage gaps. But if one accepts that assumption—and therefore accepts that increased relative demand for college graduates is a proxy for technological change—the slow relative demand for college graduates in recent years argues that technological change *decelerated*. It must have thus been a *weaker* force in generating wage inequality in recent years. Given that these other factors have been more important in the last few decades, it seems certain that technological change has played a smaller role in the last few decades, especially post-1995, than in the pre-1980 period.

Within-group wage inequality

As discussed previously, there are two dimensions of wage inequality—between-group wage differentials, such as those relating to different levels of education and experience, and within-group wage inequality that occurs among workers with similar education and experience. We have already seen that the key education wage gaps—an example of between-group wage differentials—do not readily support a technology story. The same is true for the growth of within-group inequality, which accounts for roughly 60 percent of the growth of overall wage inequality since 1979 (see Table 4.20). The growing wage gaps among workers with similar education and experience are not easily related to technological change unless they are interpreted as a reflection of growing economic returns to worker skills (such as motivation, aptitude for math, etc.) that are not easily measured (that is, the data and methods used to estimate education differentials cannot identify these kinds of differentials).

However, there are no signs that the growth of within-group wage inequality is associated with technological change. First, it has not grown faster in those industries where the use of technology grew the most (i.e., where computerization or capital investment were more rapid). Second, the economic returns to measurable skills (e.g., education) and unmeasurable skills (e.g., motivation) do not grow in tandem, which they would seem to do if they were both technologically driven. In fact, between-group and within-group inequality have not moved together in the various subperiods since 1973.

In addition, the timing of the growth of within-group wage inequality does not easily correspond to the technology story (see Table 4.20). For instance, consider what happened during the technology-led productivity boom of 1995–2000: Within-group wage inequality actually declined among women and was essentially flat among men. In contrast, within-group wage inequality grew rapidly in the low-productivity 1980s, faster even than after 2000 when productivity accelerated.

The labor market difficulties of college graduates

The veracity of the technology story rests heavily on the increasing relative wages of more-educated and skilled workers. However, while these workers have done better in *relative* terms, they have not fared well in *absolute* terms, especially in the last 10 years. As noted at the outset of the chapter there has been no net improvement in the real hourly wages and compensation of the average college graduate since 2003 (Figure 4A). Moreover, the wages of entry-level college graduates fell from 2000 to 2007 and from 2007 to 2011 (Table 4.18 and Figure 4Q). The failure of presumably the most technologically savvy college graduates, those of recent vintage, to see real wage gains runs counter to the technology story. The disappointing wage trends for college graduates are sometimes obscured in various analyses because of a focus on all college graduates (combining those with advanced degrees and those with terminal four-year degrees), and on relative, not absolute, wages. This section provides further evidence of the broad-scale wage and underemployment problems experienced by those with a college degree (but no further education) in the 2000s.

Real hourly wages have declined for roughly 70 percent of the college-educated workforce since 2000, as shown in **Figure 4AJ**, which presents the cumulative change in real wages of college graduates at the 20th, 50th, 70th, and 90th percentiles in wages. Perhaps more astonishing is that wages of college

Figure 4AJ Cumulative change in real hourly wages of college graduates, by decile, 2000–2011

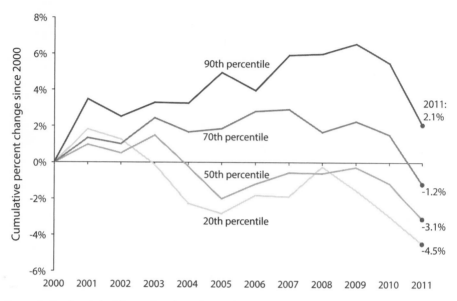

Source: Authors' analysis of Current Population Survey Outgoing Rotation Group microdata

graduates at the 90th percentile were lower in 2011 than in 2002. Since 2000, the vast majority of college graduates have not been winners from technological change, or in general.

The poor wage performance among college graduates is also apparent in nearly every key occupational category, as shown in **Table 4.45**, which presents wage trends for the nine most important occupations for college graduates. As discussed at the outset of the chapter, there was strong real wage growth in the first few years of the 2000s resulting from the momentum of the late-1990s wage boom, so the wage trends for 2000–2011 are generally better than those for 2002–2011 or 2003–2011. Because the wage data are volatile, providing data for both 2002–2011 and 2003–2011 checks for the robustness of the results. Real wages of college graduates fell for every key occupational group from 2003 to 2011, except for computer and mathematical science. From 2002 to 2011 there were four occupational categories with positive real wage growth for college graduates; however, even the occupation with the best real wage growth—computer and mathematical science—had growth of 3.2 percent over those nine years, an increase of about a third of 1 percent a year. It is fair to say that there was no occupation providing college graduates on average with good real wage growth after 2002 or 2003.

Table 4.45 Inflation-adjusted hourly wage trends of college graduates, by occupation, 2000–2011

Occupation	Share of all college graduates	Change 2000–2011	2002–2011	2003–2011
All college graduates	100.0%	0.2%	-2.2%	-1.9%
Management and business				
Management	17.6%	5.0%	-2.2%	-1.9%
Business and financial operations	9.2	0.3	0.7	-1.7
Professional and related				
Computer and mathematical science	5.4%	4.5%	3.2%	4.4%
Architecture and engineering	4.3	4.3	2.0	-0.6
Education, training, and library	10.6	1.7	-0.6	-2.2
Health care practitioner and technical	7.1	4.8	0.4	-1.1
Sales and office				
Sales and related	12.7%	-5.4%	-9.1%	-10.9%
Office and administrative support	9.9	-1.3	-4.6	-0.8
Production				
Transportation and material moving	4.5%	-10.0%	-12.1%	-6.8%
Subtotal of occupations shown	81.3%			

Source: Authors' analysis of Current Population Survey Outgoing Rotation Group microdata

Lastly, many college graduates have been forced to work in occupations that do not require a college education, a phenomenon labeled "underemployment." One advantage of having a college degree is the ability to "bump down" and displace others with less education. Nevertheless, this rise in underemployed college graduates signals that there has not been a growing unmet demand for college graduates in jobs that require such educations. **Figure 4AK** shows the change in college underemployment for young college graduates and for all college graduates from 2000 to 2010. Underemployment rose among young college graduates and all college graduates from 2000 to 2007, both years of low unemployment. This indicates that rising underemployment reflects shifts in the quality of jobs available to college graduates and not the lack of job availability overall, as would

Figure 4AK Underemployment of college graduates, by age, 2000–2010

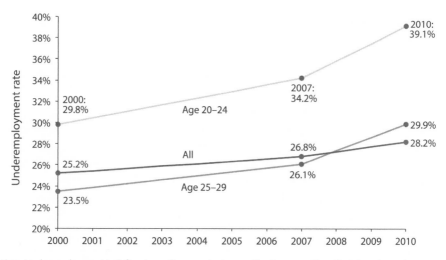

Note: Underemployment is defined as college graduates working in occupations that do not require a college degree to perform the work.

Source: Authors' analysis of Fogg and Harrington (2011, Table 1)

be the case in a recession. Unsurprisingly, the growth of underemployment among college graduates continued from 2007 to 2010.

It is difficult to see college graduates, at least those without any advanced degree, as winners in the labor market in the 2000s. College graduates do better than workers with less education, but their jobs have not provided real wage growth since 2002 or 2003. Furthermore, their jobs increasingly do not require a college degree and do not provide health or pension coverage (Tables 4.10 and 4.11). These patterns do not match the conventional technology story.

Jobs of the future

This section presents an analysis of the pay levels and education and skill requirements of the jobs projected by the Bureau of Labor Statistics to be created over the next 10 years. Some analysts examine which occupations are expected to grow at the fastest (and slowest) rates, while others examine which occupations will create the most (or least) absolute number of jobs. Our analysis assesses whether the types of jobs expected will significantly change wages earned or significantly raise the quality of work or the skill/education requirements needed to perform the work. This exercise requires an analysis of how the composition of jobs will change, that is, which occupations will expand or contract their *share* of overall employment.

Table 4.46 presents such an analysis for the 749 occupations for which the Bureau of Labor Statistics provides projections from 2010 to 2020. Through a shift-share analysis (weighting each occupation's characteristic, such as wage level, by its share of total employment) we can see what the characteristics of jobs were in 2010 and what they will be in 2020 if the projections are realized.

There are a few drawbacks to this analysis. First, it does not take into account how the job requirements of a particular occupation (one of the 749 we analyze) will change over the next 10 years. For example, will the education requirements of a loan officer or a parking lot attendant grow? In other words, the changing "content" of particular jobs is a dimension of future skill requirements not captured by our analysis. Second, we have no point of historical comparison (due to lack of data availability owing to changing occupational definitions) for judging whether what is expected in the future is fast or slow relative to the past. However, there is still much to learn from how occupational composition shifts will affect the job and wage structure.

Table 4.46 shows that employment will shift to occupations with very slightly higher median annual wages, raising annual wages by a minimal 0.07 percent over 10 years, which is essentially not at all. The analysis also shows the expected changes in the distribution of employment across wage levels—multiples of the poverty-level wage ($11.06 per hour). Occupational changes over the next 10 years are expected to modestly shrink the share of workers earning poverty-level wages and wages between 100 and 200 percent of the poverty wage. There is a corresponding shift to the two highest wage categories.

Drawing on the Bureau of Labor Statistics characterization of the education and training required to enter each occupation, the table shows that the jobs of the future will require greater education credentials, but not to any great extent. According to these data, the occupational composition of jobs in 2010 required that 15.5 percent of the workforce have a college degree, and 1.4 and 3.1 percent of jobs, respectively, required a master's degree or a doctoral or professional degree. By 2020 a slightly larger share of the workforce (a total of 0.5 percent across these three education credentials) will need these levels of education because of occupational upgrading. The jobs of 2020 will entail the need to expand the share of the workforce with an associate degree from 5.6 to 5.8 percent. In contrast, occupational requirements are such that 25.9 percent of the jobs could be filled by someone without a high school or equivalent degree in both 2010 and 2020.

The education levels of the current workforce, shown earlier in Table 4.17, far exceed the education levels required for entry into occupations in 2010 or even in 2020, as shown in **Figure 4AL**. For instance, the share of the employed with a college degree in 2011 (21.9 percent) exceeds those 15.8 percent of jobs

Table 4.46 Effect of changing occupational composition on wages and on education and training requirements, 2010–2020

Job characteristic	2010	2020	Change 2010–2020
Median annual wage (2010 dollars)	$39,250	$39,279	0.07%
*Share of workers by wage threshold**			**Percentage-point change**
0–100% of poverty	28.3%	28.0%	-0.3
>100–200% of poverty	41.5	41.2	-0.4
>200–300% of poverty	17.5	17.7	0.2
Over 300% of poverty	12.7	13.2	0.5
Education level needed for entry			
Less than high school	25.9%	25.9%	0.0
High school diploma or equivalent	43.4	42.6	-0.8
Some college, no degree	0.6	0.6	0.0
Post-secondary nondegree award	4.6	4.7	0.1
Associate degree	5.6	5.8	0.2
Bachelor's degree	15.5	15.8	0.3
Master's degree	1.4	1.5	0.1
Doctoral or professional degree	3.1	3.2	0.2
Training level needed for entry			
Short-term on-the-job training	40.7%	40.4%	-0.3
Moderate-term on-the-job training	17.5	17.3	-0.2
Long-term on-the-job training	4.9	4.8	-0.1
Apprenticeship	1.8	1.9	0.1
Internship/residency	3.8	3.8	0.1
None	31.4	31.8	0.4
Work experience needed for entry			
Less than one year	2.2%	2.2%	0.0
One to five years	12.0	11.7	-0.3
More than five years	3.2	3.0	-0.2
None	82.6	83.1	0.5

* The per-hour wage ranges are equivalent in 2011 dollars to (poverty levels for a four-person household): $11.06 and below (0–100%), $11.07–$22.12 (>100–200%), $22.13–$33.18 (>200–300%), and $33.19 and above (300%+).

Source: Thiess (2012, Tables 5 and 6) and Bureau of Labor Statistics Employment Projections (2012, Table 9)

Figure 4AL Education needed in 2020 workforce and education levels of the 2011 workforce

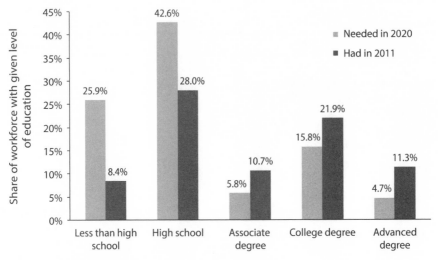

Note: Totals do not sum to 100% because some categories were omitted.

Source: Authors' analysis of Thiess (2012) and Current Population Survey Outgoing Rotation Group microdata

that will need a college degree for entry in the occupation structure of 2020. Similarly, as just mentioned, more than a fourth (25.9 percent) of the jobs in 2020 could be filled by those who lack a high school credential, a group ("less than high school") in 2011 that was far smaller, just 8.4 percent of those employed. This analysis suggests that the challenge ahead is to develop jobs with greater needs for more education rather than upgrading the workforce for jobs that are otherwise unlikely to exist.

Table 4.46 also provides an assessment of the training and experience needed to be employed in an occupation. The results suggest a slight shift to the occupations that require more training (such as apprenticeships) but also a shift toward occupations that require no prior training, meaning fewer occupations will require either "one to five" or "more than five" years' experience.

These projections show that occupational upgrading will continue, as the jobs created will be in occupations with somewhat higher educational requirements than today, but that the need can be readily met by the education already offered by today's workforce. Occupational change will not lead to the need for much more training or prior work experience before entering careers. If anything, the changes in education and training requirements in these projections are more modest than seen in earlier projections and do not appear extraordinary in any sense. Whether workers earn substantially more in the future than today will be determined primarily by how much wages in particular occupations rise rather than by any expected change in the occupational composition of jobs, including greater educational requirements.

Conclusion

The period since 2000 encompasses a few years in which the momentum from the late 1990s carried forward and brought real wage gains. However, real wages stopped growing when the 2001 recession took hold and unemployment and underemployment rose. Because of weak employment growth in the recovery, wage growth never picked up steam, and wages were flat through 2007. The Great Recession yielded persistent, high unemployment and disappointing wage growth. Consequently, the last decade has produced no improvement in real wages and a widening divergence between productivity and the wage or compensation of the typical worker. Wages of a broad range of workers, including those with either a high school or college degree, failed to improve. In addition, wage inequality has continued to grow between those at the very top and other very high earners, as well as between very high earners and those at either the 90th percentile or the median. The dip in wages at the top in the downturn and the associated stock market decline seems to have been a temporary setback for top-tier earners.

Structural factors such as the shift to lower-paying industries, increased trade competition, and deunionization have generated wage inequities and have eroded job quality. The erosion of the minimum wage (relative to past levels), sluggish job creation, continued competitive pressures from low-wage countries, and immigration have also taken their toll on the pay of low- and middle-wage earners. Young workers' wages and benefits have faltered the most, including the wages of young college graduates. In fact, the bottom 70 percent of college graduates had stagnant or falling wages over the last decade. The disappointing wage trends for blue-collar and non-college-educated workers from 1979 to 1995 have gone upscale in the 2000s; no major group of workers has escaped wage stagnation and eroded job quality.

Table and figure notes

Tables

Table 4.1. Average wages and work hours, 1967–2010. Productivity data, which measure output per hour of the total economy, including the private and public sectors, are from an unpublished series available from the Bureau of Labor Statistics Labor Productivity and Costs program on request. The wage-level data are based on the authors' tabulations of Current Population Survey Annual Social and Economic Supplement (CPS-ASEC, also known as the March CPS) microdata files using a series on annual, weekly, and hourly wages for wage and salary workers. See Appendix B for the sample definition and other information. The weekly and hourly wage data are "hour weighted," obtained by dividing annual wages by weeks worked and annual hours worked. The 1967 and 1973 values are derived from unpublished tabulations provided by Kevin Murphy from an update of Murphy and Welch (1989); they include self-employment as well as wage and salary workers. The values displayed in this table were bridged from CPS 1979 values using the growth rates in the Murphy and Welch series. Hours of work were derived from differences between annual, weekly, and hourly wage trends.

Table 4.2. Average hourly pay and pay inequality, 1948–2011. The data in the top panel are computed from the Bureau of Economic Analysis National Income and Product Accounts (NIPA) tables. "Wages and salaries" are calculated by dividing wage and salary accruals (NIPA Table 6.3) by hours worked by full-time and part-time employees (NIPA Table 6.9). "Total compensation" is the sum of wages and salaries and benefits (it includes payroll taxes and health, pension, and other nonwage benefits). Payroll taxes are calculated as total compensation (NIPA Table 6.2) minus the sum of volunteer benefits (sum of health and nonhealth benefits; see NIPA Table 6.11) and wages and salaries. "Benefits" is the difference between total compensation and wages and salaries. These data were deflated using the NIPA personal consumption expenditure (PCE, chain-weighted) index, with health insurance adjusted by the PCE medical care (chained) index. These data include both public- and private-sector workers.

The data in the Employer Costs for Employee Compensation (ECEC) panel come from the BLS National Compensation Survey's employment cost trends and benefits data and provide cost levels for March for private-sector workers, available starting in 1987. We categorize wages and salaries differently than BLS, putting all wage-related items (including paid leave and supplemental pay) into the hourly wage/salary column. This makes the definition of wages and salaries comparable to workers' W-2 earnings and to the definition of wages in the CPS Outgoing Rotation Group (ORG) data that are tabulated for other tables in this chapter. Benefits, in our definition, include only payroll taxes, pensions, insurance, and "other" benefits. The sum of wages and salaries and benefits makes up total compensation. It is important to use the ECEC (the current-weighted series) rather than the other series from the same National Compensation Survey (NCS) data, the ECI (the fixed-weighted series), because composition shifts (in the distribution of employment across occupations and industries) can have large effects over time. Employer costs for insurance are deflated by the medical-care component of the CPI-U-RS (Consumer Price Index Research Series Using Current Methods). All other pay is deflated by the CPI-U-RS for "all items." Inflation is measured for the first quarter of each year. Wage and compensation inequality measures are drawn from Pierce (2010). Pierce computes these from the NCS microdata, the data used to calculate the ECI and ECEC data.

Table 4.3. Hourly and weekly earnings of private production and nonsupervisory workers, 1947–2011. Underlying data are from the Bureau of Labor Statistics Current Employment Statistics program data from the *Employment, Hours, and Earnings–National* database, deflated using CPI-U-RS.

Table 4.4. Hourly wages of all workers, by wage percentile, 1973–2011. Table is based on analysis of CPS wage data described in Appendix B.

Table 4.5. Hourly wages of men, by wage percentile, 1973–2011. Table is based on analysis of CPS wage data described in Appendix B.

Table 4.6. Hourly wages of women, by wage percentile, 1973–2011. Table is based on analysis of CPS wage data described in Appendix B.

Table 4.7. Change in wage groups' shares of total wages, 1979–2010. Data are taken from Kopczuk, Saez, and Song (2010), Table A-3. Data for 2006 through 2010 are extrapolated from 2004 data using changes in wage shares computed from Social Security Administration wage statistics (data for 2010 at http://www.ssa.gov/cgi-bin/netcomp.cgi). The final results of the paper by Kopczuk, Saez, and Song printed in a journal used a more restrictive definition of wages so we employ the original definition, as recommended in private correspondence with Kopczuk. SSA provides data on share of total wages and employment in annual wage brackets such as for those earning between $95,000.00 and $99,999.99. We employ the midpoint of the bracket to compute total wage income in each bracket and sum all brackets. Our estimate of total wage income using this method replicates the total wage income presented by SSA with a difference of less than 0.1 percent. We use interpolation to derive cutoffs building from the bottom up to obtain the 0–90th percentile bracket and then estimate the remaining categories. This allows us to estimate the wage shares for upper wage groups. We use these wage shares computed for 2004 and later years to extend the Kopczuk, Saez, and Song series by adding the changes in share between 2004 and the relevant year to their series. To obtain absolute wage trends we use the SSA data on the total wage pool and employment and compute the real wage per worker (based on their share of wages and employment) in the different groups in 2011 dollars.

Table 4.8. Change in annual wages, by wage group, 1979–2010. See note to Table 4.7.

Table 4.9. Specific fringe benefits, 1987–2011. Table is based on ECEC data described in note to Table 4.2.

Table 4.10. Employer-provided health insurance coverage, by demographic and wage group, 1979–2010. Table is based on tabulations of CPS-ASEC data samples of private wage-and-salary earners ages 18–64 who worked at least 20 hours per week and 26 weeks per year. This sample is chosen to focus on those with regular employment. Coverage is defined as being included in an employer-provided plan for which the employer paid for at least some of the coverage. As with other CPS microdata analyses presented in the book, race/ethnicity categories are mutually exclusive (i.e., white non-Hispanic, black non-Hispanic, and Hispanic any race).

Table 4.11. Employer-provided pension coverage, by demographic and wage group, 1979–2010. Table is based on CPS-ASEC data on pension coverage, using the sample described in the note to Table 4.10. As with other CPS microdata analyses presented in the book, race/ethnicity categories are mutually exclusive (i.e., white non-Hispanic, black non-Hispanic, and Hispanic any race).

Table 4.12. Share of workers with paid leave, by wage group, 2011. Table is computed from the Employee Benefits Survey (Bureau of Labor Statistics 2011), *Holiday, Vacation, Sick, and Other Leave Benefits, March 2011,* data tables 34, 36, and 38; http://www.bls.gov/ncs/ebs/benefits/2011/benefits_leave.htm.

Table 4.13. Dimensions of wage inequality, by gender, 1973–2011. All of the data are based on analyses of the CPS-ORG data described in Appendix B and used in various tables. The measures of "total wage inequality" are natural logs of wage ratios (multiplied by 100) computed from Tables 4.5 and 4.6. The exception is 1979 data for women, which are 1978–1980 averages; we use these to smooth the volatility of the series, especially at the 10th percentile. The "between-group inequalities" are computed from regressions of the log of hourly wages on education categorical variables (advanced, college only, some college, less than high school with high school omitted), experience as a quartic, marital status, race, and region (4). The college/high school and high school/less-than-high-school premiums are simply the coefficient on "college" and "less than high school" (expressed as the advantage of "high school" over "less than high school" wages). The experience differentials are the differences in the value of age (calculated from the coefficients of the quartic specification) evaluated at 25, 35, and 50 years old. "Within-group wage inequality" is measured as the root mean square error from the same log wage regressions used to compute age and education differentials.

Table 4.14. Hourly wages by education, 1973–2011. Table is based on tabulations of CPS wage data described in Appendix B. See Appendix B for details on how a consistent measure of education was developed to bridge the change in coding in 1992.

Table 4.15. Hourly wages of men, by education, 1973–2011. See note to Table 4.14.

Table 4.16. Hourly wages of women, by education, 1973–2011. See note to Table 4.14.

Table 4.17. Educational attainment of the employed, by gender and nativity, 2011. Table is based on analysis of CPS wage earners. The data are described in Appendix B. The categories are as follows: "less than high school" is grade 1–12 or no diploma; "high school/GED" is high school graduate diploma or equivalent; "some college" is some college but no degree; "associate degree" is occupational or academic associate degree; "college degree" is a bachelor's degree; and "advanced degree" is a master's, professional, or doctoral degree.

Table 4.18. Hourly wages of entry-level and experienced workers, by gender and education, 1973–2011. Table is based on analysis of CPS wage data described in Appendix B. Entry-level wages are measured for a seven-year window starting a year after normal graduation, which translates to ages 19–25 for high school graduates and ages 23–29 for college graduates.

Table 4.19. Hourly wages by wage percentile, gender, and education, 1973–2011. Table is based on analysis of CPS wage data described in Appendix B.

Table 4.20. Contribution of within-group and between-group inequality to total wage inequality, 1973–2011. Data are from the CPS-ORG sample described in Appendix B. "Overall wage inequality" is measured as the standard deviation of log wages. "Within-group wage inequality" is the mean square error from log wage regressions (the same ones used for Table 4.13). "Between-group wage inequality" is the difference between the overall and within-group wage inequalities and reflects changes in all of the included variables: education, age, marital status, race, ethnicity, and region.

Table 4.21. Hourly wage growth by gender and race/ethnicity, 1989–2011. Table is based on analysis of CPS wage data described in Appendix B. As with other CPS microdata analyses presented in the book, race/ethnicity categories are mutually exclusive (i.e., white non-Hispanic, black non-Hispanic, and Hispanic any race).

Table 4.22. Gender wage gap, 1973–2011. Wages and ratios are based on 50th-percentile wages from Tables 4.5 and 4.6 (CPS-ORG data).

Table 4.23. Factors contributing to the productivity/compensation gap, 1973–2011. Table is based on analysis of Mishel and Gee (2012), Table 1. Mishel and Gee present a decomposition of the gap between productivity and median hourly compensation. This has been reconfigured to eliminate the gap between median hourly wages and compensation so the decomposition is between productivity and median hourly compensation.

Table 4.24. Impact of rising and falling unemployment on wage levels and gaps, 1979–2011. Table is based on analyses of yearly wage decile data from Tables 4.5 and 4.6 (see Appendix B), and of unemployment data using model from Katz and Krueger (1999). The unemployment rate is from the Current Population Survey. The simulated effect of change of unemployment presented in the table was calculated by regressing the log-change of nominal wages on the lagged log-change of the CPI-U-RS (but, following Katz and Krueger [1999], the coefficient is constrained to equal 1), the unemployment rate, lagged productivity growth, and dummies for various periods (1989–1995, 1996–2000, 2001–2007). Using these models, wages were predicted for the periods in the table given a simulated unemployment rate series in which unemployment remains fixed at its starting-year level. So in the 1979 to 1985 period, unemployment was fixed at its 1979 level and not allowed to rise (as actually happened) throughout the period. The "estimated cumulative impact of unemployment" shows the difference between actual wages and the wages when unemployment was held fixed in the starting year.

Table 4.25. Annual pay in expanding and contracting industries, 1979–2007. These data reflect the average (annual) wages, benefits, and compensation of the net new employment in each period based on changes in industry composition. The employment data are payroll counts from the BLS Current Employment Statistics, and the pay data are from 2008 Bureau of Economic Analysis NIPA tables (calculated per payroll employee). The pay of the net new employment is a weighted average of the pay by industry in which the weights are the changes in each industry's employment share over the period.

Table 4.26. Employer health care costs as a share of wages, 1948–2010. Table is based on analysis of National Income and Product Accounts data. Wage data are from NIPA Table 6.3, and group health insurance data are from NIPA Tables 6.11A-C, and 6.11D.

Table 4.27. Employer health care costs as a share of wages, by wage fifth, 1996–2008. Table is based on analysis of Burtless and Milusheva (2012) based on Medical Expenditure Panel Survey. The authors provide data by decile which we aggregated to fifths. The premiums include both those enrolled and not enrolled in employer plans. The premiums were estimated by Burtless and Milusheva using various imputation methods.

Table 4.28. Impact of trade balance in manufacturing on employment and wages, by education, 1979–2005. Table is based on analysis of Bivens (2008).

Table 4.29. Impact of trade with low-wage countries on college/noncollege wage gap, 1973–2011. Table is an update of Bivens's (2008) reanalysis of Krugman (1995) using 2011 data from the USITC Tariff and Trade DataWeb and Bureau of Economic Analysis National Income and Product Accounts.

Table 4.30. Characteristics of offshorable and non-offshorable jobs. Table reflects authors' analysis of the Bernstein, Lin, and Mishel (2007) analysis of data of Blinder (2007), matching Blinder's occupational codes to the BLS Occupational Employment Statistics (OES) survey (http://www.bls.gov/oes/) and Blinder and Krueger (2009) Table 4.

Table 4.31. Mexican and other immigrants' share of U.S. workforce, by gender, 1940–2011. Data are from Figure 1 in Borjas and Katz (2005) and authors' computations of Current Population Survey basic monthly microdata for 2000 and 2011.

Table 4.32. Educational attainment of immigrants, by gender, 1940–2011. Data are from Table 2 in Borjas and Katz (2005) and authors' computations of Current Population Survey basic monthly microdata for 2000 and 2011.

Table 4.33. Union wage premium by demographic group, 2011. "Percent union" is tabulated from CPS-ORG data (see Appendix B) and includes all those covered by unions. "Union premium" values are the coefficients on union in a model of log hourly wages with controls for education, experience as a quartic, marital status, region, industry (12) and occupation (9), race/ethnicity, and gender where appropriate. For this analysis we only use observations that do not have imputed wages because the imputation process does not take union status into account and therefore biases the union premium toward zero. See Mishel and Walters (2003). As with other CPS microdata analyses presented in the book, race/ethnicity categories are mutually exclusive (i.e., white non-Hispanic, black non-Hispanic, and Hispanic any race).

Table 4.34. Union premiums for health, retirement, and paid leave benefits. Table is based on Table 4 in Mishel and Walters (2003), which draws on Buchmueller, DiNardo, and Valletta (2001).

Table 4.35. Union impact on paid leave, pension, and health benefits. Table is based on Table 3 in Mishel and Walters (2003), which draws on Pierce (1999), Tables 4, 5, and 6.

Table 4.36. Effect of union decline on male wage differentials, 1978–2011. This analysis replicates, updates, and expands on Freeman (1991), Table 2, using the CPS-ORG sample used in other analyses (see Appendix B). The year 1978, rather than 1979, is the earliest year analyzed because we have no union membership data in our 1979 sample. "Percent union" is the share covered by collective bargaining. The "union wage premium" for a group is based on the coefficient on collective bargaining coverage in a regression of hourly wages on a simple human capital model (the same one used for estimating education differentials, as described in note to Table 4.13), with major industry (12) and occupation (9) controls in a sample for that group. The change in union premium across years, therefore, holds industry and occupation composition constant. Freeman's analysis assumed the union premium was unchanged over time. We allow the union premium to differ across years so changes in the "union effect" on wages (the union wage premium times union coverage) are driven by changes in the unionization rate and the union wage premium. The analysis divides the percentage-point change in the union effect on wage differentials by the actual percentage-point change in wage differentials (regression-adjusted with simple human capital controls plus controls for other education or occupation groups) to determine the deunionization contribution to the change in the wage gaps among men, which, as a negative percent, indicates contribution to the growth of the wage gaps.

Table 4.37. Union wage premium for subgroups. The analysis builds on Mishel and Walters (2003), Table 2.3A and Gundersen (2003), Table 5.1 and Appendix C. Premium estimates by fifth are from Schmitt (2008); Card, Lemieux, and Riddell (2002); and Gittleman and Pierce (2007). Union coverage by fifth is from Schmitt (2008).

Table 4.38. Impact of deunionization on wage inequality, 1973–2007. Table is based on analysis of Western and Rosenfeld (2011), Table 2.

Table 4.39. Value of the minimum wage, 1960–2011. Data, deflated using CPI-U-RS, are from the U.S. Department of Labor Wage and Hour Division (2009); http://www.dol.gov/whd/minwage/chart.htm.

Table 4.40. Characteristics of workers affected by proposed minimum-wage increase to $9.80 in 2014. Table is based on Cooper (2012) analysis of CPS Outgoing Rotation Group microdata. As with other CPS microdata analyses presented in the book, race/ethnicity categories are mutually exclusive (i.e., white non-Hispanic, black non-Hispanic, and Hispanic any race).

Table 4.41. Minimum-wage impact on 50/10 wage gap, 1979–2009. Analysis is of Autor, Manning, and Smith (2010), Table 5.

Table 4.42. Role of executives and financial sector in income growth of top 1.0% and top 0.1%, 1979–2005. Table is based on authors' analysis of Bakija, Cole, and Heim (2012) Tables 4, 5, 6a, and 7a, using tables that include capital-gains income. The Bakija, Cole, and Heim paper tabulates IRS tax returns and exploits the information on the primary and secondary taxpayer occupation data provided there.

Table 4.43. CEO compensation and CEO-to-worker compensation ratio, 1965–2011. Complete details on the data used to compute CEO compensation trends and the CEO-to-worker compensation ratio can be found in Mishel and Sabadish (2012), *Methodology for Measuring CEO Compensation and the Ratio of CEO-to-Worker Compensation* at http://www.epi.org/publication/wp293-ceo-to-worker-pay-methodology. We use executive compensation data from the ExecuComp database of Compustat, a division of Standard & Poor's. The ExecuComp database contains data on many forms of compensation for the top five executives at publicly traded U.S. companies in the S&P 1500 Index for 1992–2010. We employ two definitions of annual CEO compensation based on different ways of measuring option awards. "Realized direct compensation," referred to as "Options realized" in the table, is the sum of salary, bonus, restricted stock grants, options exercised, and long-term incentive payouts. It follows the definition of compensation used in previous editions of *The State of Working America*, which in turn adapted this definition from the *Wall Street Journal* (*WSJ*) annual report on CEO compensation (compensation reported by the *WSJ* has been compiled by various companies over the years, including Pearl Meyer, the Mercer Group, and the Hay Group and is the longest CEO pay series available to us). "Total direct compensation" (also a definition used in the *WSJ* series and labeled "Options granted" in the table) is the sum of salary, bonus, restricted stock grants, options granted (Compustat Black Scholes value), and long-term incentive payouts.

We define a CEO as an executive labeled a CEO by the variable CEOANN. Note that the executive flagged as the CEO may not necessarily be the highest-paid executive at the company. The CEOs included in our series are CEOs at the top 350 firms based on sales each year for 1992–2010.

Because no data for the compensation of an average worker in a firm exist, we create a proxy: the hourly compensation of a "typical" worker in a firm's key industry. The wage measure is the production/nonsupervisory worker hourly earnings in that industry, the same series used in Table 4.3 for the entire private sector. We obtain compensation by multiplying the compensation wage ratio computed from NIPA Tables 6.3C and 6.3D. The hourly wages of production and nonsupervisory employees in 2011 were $19.47, 21 percent higher than the median hourly wage, so our proxy severely overstates the compensation of a typical worker and understates the CEO-to-worker pay ratio.

We use the growth in CEO compensation in the *WSJ* series to extend the CEO compensation series and the CEO-to-worker compensation ratio series backward. The *WSJ* series conducted by Pearl Meyer covered the years 1965, 1968, 1973, 1978, 1989, and 1992. We convert the compensation series to constant dollars using the CPI-U-RS and calculate the ratio of CEO compensation in each year as a fraction of the 1992 CEO compensation level. We then apply these ratios to the CEO compensation for 1992 calculated from the ExecuComp data. This moves the series backward in time so that the growth of CEO pay is the same as in the Pearl Meyer/*WSJ* series but is benchmarked to the levels in the ExecuComp series.

We make a similar set of computations to obtain a historical series for the CEO-to-worker compensation ratio. We start with the Pearl Meyer/*WSJ* series in constant dollars and divide it by an estimate of private-sector annual compensation of production/nonsupervisory workers in the same year. The compensation series is the real hourly compensation series presented in Figure 4B multiplied by 2,080 hours.

Table 4.44. Trends in education wage gaps, key wage group wage gaps, and relative supply of education, 1979–2011. The gross wage gap data are computed from underlying yearly data with selected years presented in Tables 4.4 and 4.8. The education wage gaps are computed from the same regressions for which results on college/high school and high school/less-than-high-school wage premiums are reported in Table 4.13, regressions of the log of hourly wages on education categorical variables (advanced degree, college only, some college, less than high school with high school omitted), experience as a quartic, marital status, race, and region (4). The college or more/noncollege differential is drawn from a similar regression except there is only one education dummy variable for those with a college degree or advanced degree. This estimate was also used in the analysis of trade's impact on the college wage gap presented in Table 4.29.

Table 4.45. Inflation-adjusted hourly wage trends of college graduates, by occupation, 2000–2011. Table is based on tabulations of CPS-ORG data with a sample of those with a college degree (but no advanced degree). See Appendix B for information on the wage data.

Table 4.46. Effect of changing occupational composition on wages and on education and training requirements, 2010–2020. Table is based on analysis of Thiess (2012), Tables 5 and 6, and BLS Employment Projections Program (2012), Table 9.

Figures

Figure 4A. Cumulative change in total economy productivity and real hourly compensation of selected groups of workers, 1995–2011. Productivity data, which measure output per hour of the total economy, including private and public sectors, are from an unpublished series available from the Bureau of Labor Statistics Labor Productivity and Costs program on request. Wage measures are the annual data used to construct tables in this chapter: median hourly wages (at the 50th percentile) from Table 4.4 and hourly wages by education from Table 4.14. These are converted to hourly compensation by scaling by the real compensation/wage ratio from the Bureau of Economic Analysis National Income and Product Accounts (NIPA) data used in Table 4.2.

Figure 4B. Real hourly earnings and compensation of private production and nonsupervisory workers, 1947–2011. Wage data are from series used in Table 4.3. Wages are converted to hourly compensation by scaling by the real compensation/wage ratio from the NIPA data used in Table 4.2.

Figure 4C. Cumulative change in real hourly wages of men, by wage percentile, 1979–2011. See note to Table 4.5.

Figure 4D. Cumulative change in real hourly wages of women, by wage percentile, 1979–2011. See note to Table 4.6.

Figure 4E. Share of workers earning poverty-level wages, by gender, 1973–2011. Figure is based on analysis of Current Population Survey (CPS) wage data described in Appendix B. The poverty-level wage is calculated using an estimate of the four-person weighted average poverty threshold in 2011 of $23,010 (based on the 2010 threshold updated for inflation). This is divided by 2,080 hours to obtain a poverty-level wage of $11.06 in 2011. The poverty-level wage is roughly equal to two-thirds of the median hourly wage. This figure is deflated by CPI-U-RS (Consumer Price Index Research Series Using Current Methods) to obtain the poverty-level wage levels for other years. The threshold is available at the U.S. Census Bureau website.

Figure 4F. Share of workers earning poverty-level wages, by race and ethnicity, 1973–2011. See note to Figure 4E. As with other CPS microdata analyses presented in the book, race/ethnicity categories are mutually exclusive (i.e., white non-Hispanic, black non-Hispanic, and Hispanic any race).

Figure 4G. Share of total annual wages received by top earners, 1947–2010. See note to Table 4.7.

Figure 4H. Cumulative change in real annual wages, by wage group, 1979–2010. See note to Table 4.7.

Figure 4I. Share of private-sector workers with employer-provided health insurance, by race and ethnicity, 1979–2010. See note to Table 4.10.

Figure 4J. Share of pension participants in defined-contribution and defined-benefit plans, 1980–2004. Figure is based on Center for Retirement Research (2006), which used data from the Current Population Survey and the Department of Labor's Annual Return/Report Form 5500 Series.

Figure 4K. Wage gaps among men, 1973–2011. Figure is based on ratios of yearly hourly wage by decile data presented in Table 4.5.

Figure 4L. Wage gaps among women, 1973–2011. Figure is based on ratios of yearly hourly wage by decile data presented in Table 4.6.

Figure 4M. Wage gap between the 95th and 50th percentiles, by gender, 1973–2011. Figure is based on ratios of yearly hourly wage by percentile data presented in Tables 4.5 and 4.6.

Figure 4N. College wage premium, by gender, 1973–2011. Differentials are estimated with controls for experience (as a quartic), region (4), marital status, race/ethnicity, and education, which are specified as dummy variables for less than high school, some college, college, and advanced degree. Log of hourly wage is the dependent variable. Estimates were made on the CPS-ORG data as described in Appendix B, and presented in Table 4.13.

Figure 4O. Share of the employed lacking a high school degree, by race/ethnicity and nativity status, 2011. Figure is based on tabulations of the full monthly CPS. See Appendix B for details on data.

Figure 4P. Real entry-level wages of high school graduates, by gender, 1973–2011. See note to Table 4.18.

Figure 4Q. Real entry-level wages of college graduates, by gender, 1973–2011. See note to Table 4.18.

Figure 4R. Share of recent high school graduates with employer health/pension coverage, 1979–2010. Data are computed from annual data series developed for Tables 4.10 and 4.11. The definition of recent high school graduates is the same as used in Table 4.18 for entry-level workers who are high school graduates; ages 19–25.

Figure 4S. Share of recent college graduates with employer health/pension coverage, 1979–2010. Data are computed from annual data series developed for Tables 4.10 and 4.11. The definition of recent college graduates is the same as used in Table 4.18 for entry-level workers who are college graduates; ages 23–29.

Figure 4T. Gender wage gap, by age cohort. See Moore and Shierholz (2007).

Figure 4U. Cumulative change in total economy productivity and real hourly compensation of production/nonsupervisory workers, 1948–2011. Productivity is based on unpublished Total Economy Productivity data from the Bureau of Labor Statistics Labor Productivity and Costs program. Hourly compensation for production/nonsupervisory workers is based on the wage data series used in Table 4.3. Wages are converted to hourly compensation by scaling by the real compensation/wage ratio from the NIPA data used in Table 4.2.

Figure 4V. Cumulative change in hourly productivity, real average hourly compensation, and median compensation, 1973–2011. Productivity and average hourly compensation are based on unpublished Total Economy Productivity data from the Bureau of Labor Statistics Labor Productivity and Costs program. Average hourly compensation includes those who are self-employed as well as wage and salary workers. See Mishel and Gee (2012) for more details. Median wages for all, men, and women are based on the data presented in Tables 4.4, 4.5, and 4.6, respectively. Wages are converted to hourly compensation by scaling by the real compensation/wage ratio from the NIPA data used in Table 4.2.

Figure 4W. Increase in worker wages from a 1 percentage-point fall in unemployment, by wage group. Estimates are based on a model employed by Katz and Krueger (1999). Annual changes in log wages are regressed on unemployment, lagged log-changes in the CPI-U-RS (but, following Katz and Krueger the coefficient on this is constrained to equal 1), lagged productivity growth, and dummies for 1989–1995, 1996–2000, and 2001–2007 (excluded period is 1979–1988). The sample covers the years 1979–2007.

Figure 4X. Employer health care costs as a share of annual wages, by wage fifth, 1996–2008. Figure is based on analysis of Burtless and Milusheva (2012), based on Medical Expenditure Panel Survey. See note to Table 4.27.

Figure 4Y. Imports, exports, and trade balance in goods as a share of U.S. GDP, 1947–2011. Figure is based on authors' analysis of Bureau of Economic Analysis National Income and Product Accounts, Table 1.1.6.

Figure 4Z. Manufacturing imports as a share of U.S. GDP, 1973–2011. Figure is based on analysis of U.S. International Trade Commission Tariff and Trade data (series on manufacturing trade) and Bureau of Economic Analysis National Income and Product Accounts data on gross domestic product.

Figure 4AA. Relative productivity of U.S. trading partners, 1973–2011. Figure is based on analysis of United States International Trade Commission Tariff and Trade data and the Penn World Table (Heston, Summers, and Aten 2011). For each trading partner, their share of total imports was multiplied by their levels of GDP per worker relative to the United States (using data from the Penn World Tables). The resulting products were then summed to get the average productivity level of import trading partners. The same exercise was done for exports.

Figure 4AB. Wage premium of offshorable jobs, by gender and education. Figure is based on analysis of Bernstein, Lin, and Mishel (2007).

Figure 4AC. Union coverage rate in the United States, 1973–2011. Data are from Hirsch and Macpherson (2003), http://unionstats.gsu.edu/Hirsch-Macpherson_ILRR_CPS-Union-Database.pdf; updated at unionstats.com. The data on union coverage begin in 1977 and are extended back to 1973, based on percentage-point changes in union membership shares in Hirsh and Macpherson (2003).

Figure 4AD. Real value of the minimum wage, 1960–2011. Underlying data are from U.S. Department of Labor Wage and Hour Division (2009), deflated using CPI-U-RS; see note to Table 4.39.

Figure 4AE. Minimum wage as a share of average hourly earnings, 1964–2011. The data are the minimum wage divided by the average hourly earnings of production and nonsupervisory workers. Minimum-wage levels are from Table 4.39, and average hourly earnings are from the series used in Table 4.3.

Figure 4AF. Real value of the federal minimum wage and share of workforce covered by higher state minimums, 1979–2011. The figure is based on analysis of U.S. Department of Labor (2009) and Cooper (2012) update of Shierholz (2009).

Figure 4AG. Share of worker hours paid at or below the minimum wage, by gender, 1979–2009. Figure is based on analysis of Autor, Manning, and Smith (2010), Figure 1. Estimates are of the share of hours worked for reported wages equal to or less than the applicable state or federal minimum wage.

Figure 4AH. CEO-to-worker compensation ratio (options granted and options realized), 1965–2011. Figure is based on data developed for Table 4.43.

Figure 4AI. Growth in relative demand for college graduates, 1940–2005. Figure is based on authors' analysis of Goldin and Katz (2008), Table 1.

Figure 4AJ. Cumulative change in real hourly wages of college graduates, by decile, 2000–2011. Figure is based on authors' analysis of CPS-ORG data using a sample of college graduates (but no advanced degree). See Appendix B for data details.

Figure 4AK. Underemployment of college graduates, by age, 2000–2010. Figure is based on authors' analysis of Fogg and Harrington (2011), Table 1. "Underemployment" occurs when a college graduate works in an occupation that does not require a college education.

Figure 4AL. Education needed in 2020 workforce and education levels of the 2011 workforce. Figure is based on authors' analysis of Thiess (2012) for Table 4.46 and education attainment data from Table 4.17.

CHAPTER 5

Jobs

A function of demand

Employment is the foundation of family income and economic well-being for the vast majority of households that are not of retirement age. Even retired households need a strong past work history to enjoy economic security. It is through work that families have income to meet their material needs. Thus, whether the labor market is able to provide employment for willing workers is a key determinant of living standards.

Healthy job growth is growth that provides employment for all willing workers in a timely fashion. As we show, employment trends are driven by trends in aggregate demand (the total demand for goods and services in the economy). Simply put, jobs are created when demand for U.S. goods and services grows. The basic logic is straightforward—since workers provide goods and services, increasing demand for goods and services translates into job growth.

In periods of full employment, a healthy employment growth rate would be one that simply matches the growth rate of the labor force. But, contrary to assumptions often made by economists and policymakers, full employment is the exception rather than the rule in the U.S. labor market. An implicit message of this chapter is that ensuring healthy job growth requires an active macroeconomic policy that targets growth in aggregate demand sufficient to meet the growing supply of potential workers.

The business cycle from 2000 to 2007 failed dramatically in providing healthy job growth. After the strong job growth of the late 1990s (accompanied by an unemployment rate averaging 4.1 percent in 1999 and 2000) came the recession of 2001, which was followed by nearly two years of continued job loss. Job growth from 2000 to 2007 was the worst on record for a full business cycle, and this historically weak job creation was costly for families. The resulting lower rates of employment and consequent lack of upward pressure on wages translated into forgone increases in living standards. Then, at the end of 2007, the Great Recession began, causing the most severe and sustained job loss this country had seen in seven decades, with the loss of 8.7 million jobs over a period of more than two years, dismantling the already-weakened foundation of economic security for countless American families.

Although job growth in the *recovery* from the Great Recession has thus far been similar in strength to job growth in the weak early stages of the recoveries that followed the recessions of the early 1990s and early 2000s, the length and severity of the Great Recession created a much larger jobs deficit. By the end of 2011, the labor market was still more than 10 million jobs below what was needed to return to the pre-recession unemployment rate. Specifically, the labor market was down 5.8 million jobs from December 2007 and short the roughly 4.5 million jobs that should have been *added* between the end of 2007 and the end of 2011 simply to keep up with normal growth in the working-age population (see Figure 1A in Chapter 1).

Since the unemployment rate of racial and ethnic minorities tends to be much higher than the overall unemployment rate in good times and bad, the substantial increase in unemployment in the Great Recession and its aftermath meant the unemployment rate of racial and ethnic minorities spiked even more dramatically. The annual unemployment rate peaked at 9.6 percent in 2010. However, the unemployment rate of blacks in 2010 was 15.9 percent, and that of Hispanics was 12.5 percent. By 2011, the overall annual unemployment rate had dropped to 8.9 percent, but 15.9 percent of black workers and 11.5 percent of Hispanic workers were still unemployed.

A contentious issue in the aftermath of the Great Recession is whether the persistent high unemployment is in large part *structural*—unemployment that occurs when the skills of job seekers do not match the requirements of available jobs. We find that today's unemployment is broad-based—i.e., not limited to particular sectors or occupations, or to workers with or without certain skills or educational credentials. In other words, the high unemployment in the aftermath of the Great Recession is not predominantly structural, but instead driven by low aggregate demand, i.e., a general lack of demand for goods and services, which translates into a general lack of demand for workers.

Our discussion concludes with a look at the costs of job loss and unemployment. The negative impact of job loss on income is severe and long-lasting, and does not just affect laid-off workers, but also their children and families. In addition, young workers who enter the labor market for the first time during a downturn suffer long-lasting damage to their career trajectories and incomes.

Table notes and figure notes at the end of this chapter provide documentation for the data, as well as information on methodology, used in the tables and figures that follow.

Job creation is a macroeconomic outcome

Jobs are created when demand for U.S. goods and services—and therefore demand for workers who provide them—grows. The most comprehensive measure of economic activity is gross domestic product, which is the total value of goods and services produced in an economy. As is widely acknowledged, changes in GDP over relatively short periods are largely a function of shifts in aggregate demand. Thus, GDP growth can serve as a proxy measure of demand growth. GDP growth translates into employment growth except when employers meet demand by increasing hours worked per employee, or increasing productivity (the average amount produced per hour worked). As explained in the text box that follows, employment growth is equal to GDP growth minus the growth of average hours minus the growth of productivity.

The relationship between economic activity and job growth

The most comprehensive measure of economic activity is gross domestic product, which is the total value of goods and services produced in an economy and is often simply called output. To see the relationship between changes in economic activity and jobs, note that

(1) Output = (Output/Total hours worked) · (Total hours worked/ Employment) · Employment

Further noting that Output/ Total hours worked = Productivity, and Total hours worked/ Employment = Average hours, we find that

(2) Output = Productivity · Average hours · Employment

The terms in equation (2) can be rearranged to express employment as a function of output, average hours, and productivity in the following way:

(3) Employment = Output/(Average hours · Productivity),

and using a standard approximation, equation (3) can be expressed as growth rates, in particular by

(4) Employment growth = Output growth – Average hours growth – Productivity growth.

Table 5.1 examines growth in average annual employment (the total number of jobs in the economy), GDP, average hours worked, and productivity in the United States over the last nearly six-and-a-half decades. For the roughly 30 years following World War II, employment grew 1.7 percent per year on average. This employment growth was the result of strong annual GDP growth (3.8 percent) and a slight decline in average hours (-0.3 percent annually). GDP growth was strong enough over this period that plenty of new jobs were needed to meet the

Table 5.1 Average annual change in employment, GDP, hours, and productivity, 1948–2011

	Employment	GDP	Average hours	Productivity
1948–1979	1.7%	3.8%	-0.3%	2.4%
1979–1989	1.7	3.0	0.0	1.3
1989–2000	1.5	3.3	0.0	1.8
1989–1995	1.2	2.4	-0.1	1.3
1995–2000	1.9	4.3	0.0	2.3
2000–2007	0.5	2.4	-0.2	2.1
2007–2011	-1.3	0.2	-0.1	1.5
2007–2008	-0.7	-0.3	-0.3	0.8
2008–2009	-4.2	-3.5	-1.3	2.1
2009–2010	-0.9	3.0	0.9	3.1
2010–2011	0.9	1.6	0.5	0.2

Note: Employment growth = GDP growth – average hours growth – productivity growth.

Source: Authors' analysis of unpublished Total Economy Productivity data from the Bureau of Labor Statistics Labor Productivity and Costs program

growing demand for goods and services despite strong annual productivity growth (2.4 percent).

In the 1980s, employment growth remained strong, but both GDP growth and productivity growth were substantially weaker. Comparing these two periods (1948–1979 and 1979–1989) highlights that a given level of job growth can be achieved through different combinations of GDP growth, hours growth, and productivity growth. While the rate of job creation was the same in these two periods, GDP growth and productivity growth were much greater from 1948 to 1979. For a given level of job growth, faster GDP and productivity growth is much preferred because productivity growth provides the *potential* for wages and living standards to grow over time: For a given level of job growth, the faster productivity grows— i.e., the more workers produce on average in an hour—the higher the potential for rising wages. This is discussed further in chapters 1 and 4.

The 1990s maintained strong job growth with high GDP and productivity growth, particularly in the latter half of the decade. Strong job growth combined with strong productivity growth led to broad wage and income growth, as discussed in chapters 2 and 4.

The 2000–2007 business cycle was a reversal of the strength of the late 1990s. Annual job growth dropped to just 0.5 percent, the worst performance for a full business cycle on record. The slow job growth from 2000 to 2007 was caused by relatively weak GDP growth, most of which was absorbed by productivity growth. The historically weak job growth in turn translated into historically slow wage and income growth for most workers, discussed further in chapters 2 and 4.

And then the Great Recession began. When the housing bubble burst it caused a massive drop in demand for goods and services (and thus workers) as households losing wealth through declining home values pulled back on spending, home builders radically downsized after overbuilding during the bubble, and businesses facing shrinking demand for goods and services cut back on investments in plants and equipment. GDP dropped 3.8 percent between 2007 and 2009, and the economy shed jobs for more than two years. From December 2007 to February 2010, the economy lost 8.7 million jobs, with the bulk of those losses occurring between fall 2008 and mid-summer 2009.

Job growth from 2010 (the first full year of the recovery) to 2011 was a weak 0.9 percent, due to weak GDP growth and reinstatement of work hours that had been cut during the recession. Note that this weak job growth was *not* due to strong productivity growth, or "businesses doing more with less." While productivity growth was high from early 2009 to early 2010, it grew only 0.2 percent between 2010 and 2011. (In fact, productivity growth was comparatively weak before and after 2009–2010, so that over the full period from 2007 to 2011 productivity growth was a subdued 1.5 percent.)

What these trends in GDP, productivity, hours, and employment growth suggest is a simple truth that is far too often overlooked in labor market analyses: Rapid job growth will only occur when growth in aggregate demand is strong. Further, what are often called "jobless recoveries" (the weak job growth following the last three recessions) should actually be called "growthless and jobless recoveries" to emphasize that there is no mystery behind why employment rebounded so slowly; the economy simply did not grow fast enough to spur rapid job growth.

Zero is not the baseline for job growth

We know that overall economic growth is the main driver of job creation, but how do we judge whether economic growth is strong enough to provide enough jobs for our potential workforce? Later we delve much deeper into measures of slack in the labor market. Here we simply make the important point that at a minimum, the economy must add enough jobs every month to keep up with normal growth in the working-age population. In 2007, for example, there were 137.6 million jobs, and there were 231.9 million people of working age (typically defined as age 16 and older). This means there was one job for every 1.7 people of working age (this ratio is never 1-to-1 since not everyone of working age works or wants to work). Between 2007 and 2011, the working-age population grew a little less than 1 percent per year, which meant that there were nearly 8 million more people of working age in 2011 than in 2007. To provide one job for every

1.7 of these new workers, the economy should have added about 4.5 million jobs during this period—around 100,000 per month. In other words, the labor market would have needed roughly 100,000 jobs per month simply to "hold steady," i.e., to sustain the same share of working-age people with a job.

Figure 5A shows the number of jobs needed each month just to hold steady, along with the number of jobs actually created per month in each year from 1969 to 2011. The hold-steady number increases as the working-age population grows and decreases as the labor market weakens (the latter is perhaps counterintuitive, but recall that this is the hold-steady number, and if the share of the population with a job declines, the economy needs to create fewer jobs simply to hold steady at that lower level). As previously noted, the labor market currently needs around 100,000 jobs per month to hold steady (as has been true for most of the last four decades). The hold-steady line is the job market baseline; it is what monthly job growth should generally be judged against. If job growth is higher than the hold-steady level, the labor market is getting stronger and the unemployment rate generally would be decreasing. Alternatively, if job growth is lower than the hold-steady level, the labor market is weakening, and the unemployment rate generally would be increasing. Of course, when the unemployment rate is high,

Figure 5A Jobs needed each month to hold steady and actual monthly job growth, 1969–2011

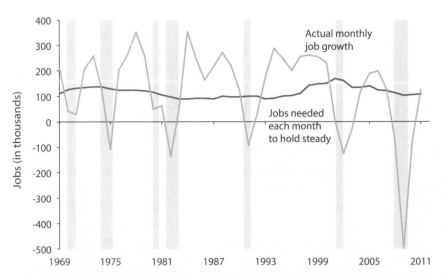

Note: To "hold steady" means to sustain the same share of working-age people with a job. See figure notes in the table and figure notes section for calculation of the hold steady line. Shaded areas denote recessions.

Source: Authors' analysis of Bureau of Labor Statistics Current Employment Statistics and Current Population Survey public data series

the economy needs job growth to be much, much faster than the hold-steady rate (in the aftermath of the severe job loss of the Great Recession, *three or four times* faster) to get back to full employment in a reasonable time frame.

What are today's jobs like?

This section provides a picture of what kind of jobs make up the U.S. labor market, and how the composition has changed over time. We present basic breakdowns by industry and firm size, and by occupation (many of which cut across industries—for example, an accountant might be employed in a construction firm or government agency or hospital). Finally, we offer a very broad measure of a "good job" and examine how the share of workers in good jobs has changed over time.

Industries

The economy can be roughly divided into goods-producing industries (manufacturing, construction, and mining) and service-producing industries (wholesale and retail trade, transportation and warehousing, utilities, information, financial activities, professional and business services, education and health services, leisure and hospitality, other services, and government). Over time, the U.S. economy has become more and more concentrated in producing services. In 1947, 61 percent of all jobs were in service-producing industries; six decades later, in 2007, it was 84 percent.

The ongoing shift can be seen in **Figure 5B**, which shows the distribution of jobs by industry (i.e., each industry's share of overall employment) at the last four business cycle peaks, and in 2011. It also shows the projected distribution in 2020. One salient point from this figure is that, with the exceptions of the decrease in manufacturing, the increase in health care and, to a lesser extent, the increase in professional and business services, the industry mix does not change very much or very quickly over time: All categories aside from manufacturing, health, and professional and business services changed by less than 3 percentage points—and most by *much* less—between 1979 and 2011. In other words, with some notable exceptions, the mix of industries employing workers has not changed dramatically over the last three decades. And looking at the projected distribution for 2020, it is not expected to change much over this decade, either, again with the notable exceptions of health care and manufacturing.

The sector that has seen the largest increase is health care. Note that in 1979 and 1989 data on health care and educational services are not available separately, and are thus not shown in the figure for those years, but *combined* they comprised 7.6 percent of employment in 1979 and 9.9 percent in 1989. Thus, health care alone grew from less than 7.6 percent in 1979 (not shown) to 11.2 percent in 2007 to 12.7 percent in 2011. Health care is also expected to see the

Figure 5B Distribution of employment, by industry, selected years, 1979–2011 (and 2020 projections)

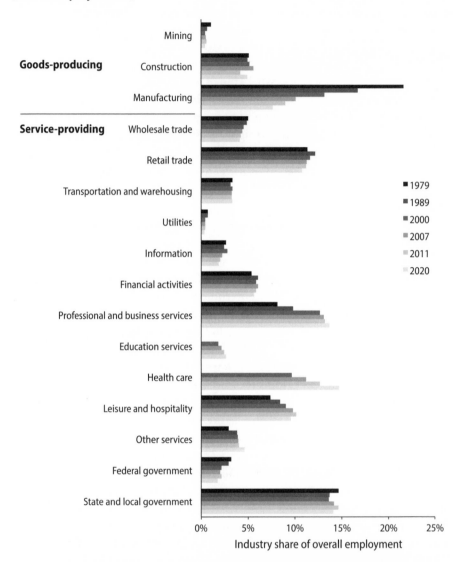

Note: Data for health care (which includes social assistance services, which is a very small share of the category) and education services are excluded from the figure in 1979 and 1989 because disaggregated data were not available for these industries.

Source: Authors' analysis of Bureau of Labor Statistics Current Employment Statistics, and BLS Employment Projections program (Table 2.1)

biggest increase this decade and is projected to make up 14.7 percent of employment by 2020.

The sector that has declined the most is manufacturing, dropping from 21.6 percent of all workers in 1979 to 10.1 percent in 2007 to 8.9 percent in 2011. Since manufacturing jobs traditionally have provided high wages and good benefits, especially for workers without a college degree, the decline of manufacturing has meant a decline in a crucial source of good jobs. Chapter 4 further investigates the impact of industry shifts on wages and compensation.

While manufacturing employment naturally tends to decline as a share of total employment as an economy advances, since around 1997, overvaluation of the dollar relative to the currencies of U.S. trading partners has significantly contributed to the loss of manufacturing jobs. Note that if the dollar is overvalued (i.e., too "strong" relative to other currencies), that makes U.S. goods more expensive to consumers around the world, which decreases our exports. At the same time, an overvalued dollar makes goods from around the world cheaper to U.S. consumers, which increases our imports. Because manufactured goods make up the bulk of our international trade, both of these things reduce the overall demand for U.S. manufactured goods, and cost jobs in manufacturing. In other words, an overvalued dollar hurts manufacturing job growth. For example, had the United States had balanced non-oil trade with the rest of the world in 2007 instead of running large trade deficits, there would have been about four million more U.S. manufacturing jobs (Scott 2008). As a point of comparison, in 2007 the United States had 13.9 million manufacturing jobs.

Firm size

Most private-sector workers in the United States are employed by relatively large firms. As shown in **Figure 5C**, more than 60 percent of workers work in firms with 100 or more workers, and close to 40 percent work in firms of 1,000 or more workers. Less than 20 percent work in firms of fewer than 20 workers. Figure 5C provides breakdowns for the first quarter of 2011 only, but it should be noted that these shares have remained relatively stable since 2000. Despite the fact that most workers are employed in large firms, there is a prominent public discourse focusing on the importance of small firms for job *creation*. Do small firms create a disproportionate number of jobs?

Figure 5D shows gross job gains (the number of jobs added in either opening or expanding private-sector establishments) and gross job losses (the number of jobs lost in either closing or contracting private-sector establishments), along with net job growth (the difference between gross job gains and gross job losses), by firm size. From 2000 to 2007, for example, firms with fewer than 20 workers, while constituting less than 20 percent of employment, accounted for nearly 40 percent of all gross job gains. But while small businesses do create a lot of jobs,

Figure 5C Distribution of employment, by firm size, 2011Q1

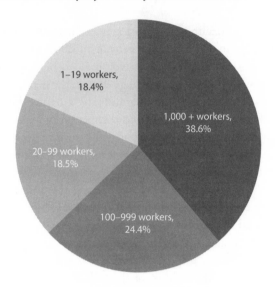

Note: Data are for private-sector workers. Shares do not total to 100 percent due to rounding.

Source: Authors' analysis of Bureau of Labor Statistics Business Employment Dynamics program (Table F)

they also *lose* a lot of jobs. From 2000 to 2007, firms with fewer than 20 workers also accounted for nearly 40 percent of all gross job losses. Considering both job gains and job losses, we find that firms with fewer than 20 people accounted for just around a third of all *net* gains over this period. This is still disproportionately high, but research shows that that is driven by startup firms, which tend to be small. In other words, small firms do not create a disproportionate share of net new jobs once the age of the firm is taken into account (see Haltiwanger, Jarmin, and Miranda 2010). Larger firms, perhaps unsurprisingly, tend to be less volatile. Firms with 1,000 or more employees employ nearly 40 percent of workers, but constituted less than 20 percent of all gross job gains and less than 20 percent of all gross job losses over this period. They did, however, make up nearly a quarter of all *net* gains over this period.

Occupations

Occupations can be broadly grouped into three categories—white collar (management, professional, sales, and office occupations), blue collar (farming and forestry, construction, maintenance, production, and transportation and material moving occupations), and service occupations (health care support, protective service, food preparation and serving, building and grounds cleaning and maintenance, and

Figure 5D Job gains, losses, and net employment change, by firm size, 2000–2011

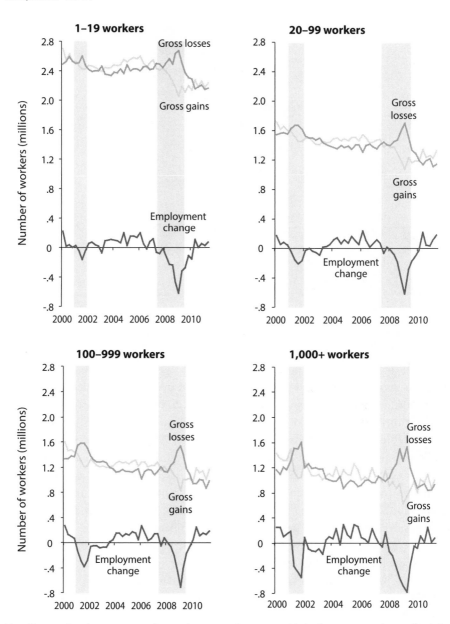

Note: Data are for private-sector workers and are quarterly, starting with the first quarter each year. Shaded areas denote recessions.

Source: Authors' analysis of Bureau of Labor Statistics Business Employment Dynamics program (Table 1)

Figure 5E Distribution of employment, by occupation, selected years, 1989–2011

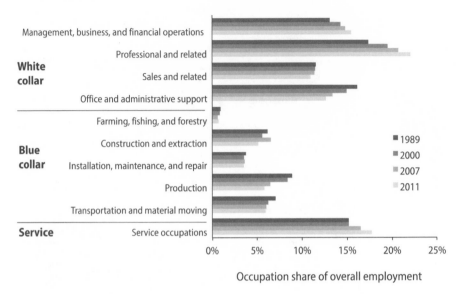

Occupation share of overall employment

Source: Authors' analysis of Current Population Survey public data series (Historical Table A-13)

personal care and service occupations). **Figure 5E** shows the distribution of jobs by major occupation (i.e., each occupation's share of overall employment) at the last three business cycle peaks, and in 2011. In the U.S. economy, the bulk of workers are in white-collar occupations (61 percent in 2011). That share has increased very modestly since the late 1980s (it was 58 percent in 1989). However, within white-collar occupations, there has been a shift—in particular, professional occupations' share has grown (from 17 percent in 1989 to 22 percent in 2011), as has management, business, and financial operations' share (from 13 percent in 1989 to 15 percent in 2011), while the share of jobs held by office and administrative support staff has declined (from 16 percent in 1989 to 13 percent in 2011).

Consistent with the shift from goods-producing to service-producing industries, there has been a shift from blue-collar to service occupations. In 1989, 27 percent of workers were in blue-collar jobs, but that had dropped to 21 percent by 2011. Around half of that drop was among production workers, whose share declined from 9 percent to 6 percent over this period. Service occupations' share, on the other hand, grew, from 15 percent in 1989 to 18 percent in 2011.

Job quality

Defining job quality is not straightforward. For example, a job would almost certainly be considered high quality if it paid well; offered good health and pension benefits; provided paid vacation, sick days, and family leave; and offered good working conditions, a good work schedule, and job security. A job with some but not all of those characteristics falls into a gray area. John Schmitt and Janelle Jones (2012) of the Center for Economic and Policy Research have defined a "good" job modestly as a job that meets three criteria—it must pay at least $18.50 per hour (the median male hourly wage in 1979 adjusted to 2010 dollars), offer health insurance, and offer a retirement plan of some kind. They have tracked the prevalence of good jobs over time.

Figure 5F presents good jobs (as defined above) as a share of total employment for recent business cycle peaks and for 2010. It also presents output per worker—the average value of goods and services produced by a worker in a year—as a benchmark for the economy's *potential* for generating better jobs for more workers over time. Output per worker increased 48.3 percent—from $69,903 to $103,659—from 1979 to 2010, underscoring that workers were getting more productive and the country as a whole was getting richer over this period. If those

Figure 5F Good jobs as a share of total employment, all workers and by gender, and output per worker, selected years,1979–2010

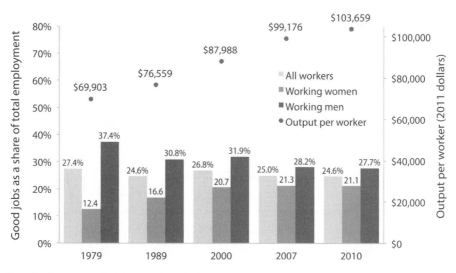

Note: See figure notes for definition of good jobs.

Source: Authors' analysis of Schmitt and Jones (2012) and unpublished Total Economy Productivity data from the Bureau of Labor Statistics Labor Productivity and Costs program

gains were broadly distributed across the workforce, one would expect to see the share of good jobs increase accordingly. Instead, the share of good jobs declined. From 1979 to 2007, the share of good jobs in the economy dropped 2.4 percentage points. By 2007, only 25.0 percent of jobs paid at least $18.50 per hour and offered health insurance and a retirement plan. From 2007 to 2010, while the number of people with jobs dropped dramatically due to the recession, output per worker continued to rise, from $99,176 in 2007 to $103,659 in 2010. However, the share of workers in good jobs remained essentially unchanged, dropping 0.4 percentage points. Altogether, while the value of the output workers produced rose dramatically from 1979 to 2010, the share of workers in good jobs shrank by 2.8 percentage points.

The decline in the share of good jobs is all the more troubling because it occurred when the workforce on average was becoming both older and more educated (a phenomenon that will be further discussed later in this chapter). All else equal, these factors would have *increased* the share of good jobs, as older and better-educated workers tend to be better able to secure quality employment because productivity tends to rise with both education and experience.

The figure also identifies important differences in the share of good jobs by gender. From 1979 to 2000, employed women made enormous progress by the good-jobs measure—the share in good jobs jumped from 12.4 percent to 20.7 percent. But over the 2000s the share of employed women with good jobs was essentially flat (a 0.3-percentage-point increase from 2000 to 2010). For men, the situation was much grimmer. From 1979 to 2000, the share of employed men with good jobs dropped 5.6 percentage points, and from 2000 to 2010, the share dropped an additional 4.2 percentage points. Altogether, the share of working men in good jobs dropped nearly 10 percentage points from 1979 to 2010.

Unemployment

The official definition of an unemployed person is someone who is jobless but available to work and actively seeking work (where "actively seeking" is defined as having looked for work in the last four weeks). The unemployment rate is the share of labor force participants (employed and unemployed people) who are unemployed. It is important to note that the unemployment rate is never expected to be zero. Even in a strong labor market, one characterized by "full employment," there are always some people without jobs who are seeking work—workers who have newly entered or re-entered the labor market in search of work, or who quit or were laid off from a previous job and are searching for a new one.

A key question is how much unemployment is the "right" level, one where job seekers can find a suitable job and employers can find suitable workers in a reasonable time frame. Another way to think of the "right" level of unemployment is the level where the demand for workers is roughly equal to the supply. If the demand is greater than the supply (i.e., if the unemployment rate is too low), then employers will have trouble finding the workers they need.

The primary concern with this situation is that it will cause wages to rise too fast (that is, faster than underlying productivity) as employers try to attract needed workers, and that this will fuel inflation. There is a debate about what is the lowest rate of unemployment that will *not* lead to increasing inflation (a theoretical rate that is often called the Non-Accelerating Inflation Rate of Unemployment, or the NAIRU). As a point of reference, however, it is useful to look to recent history: In the strong labor market of the late 1990s, the unemployment rate dropped dramatically—to a 4.1 percent average in 1999 and 2000—*and inflation did not accelerate.*

When demand for workers is *lower* than the supply (i.e., when the unemployment rate is elevated), problems occur at both the individual and economy-wide levels. When workers face job loss and unemployment, they and their families lose wages and benefits, and the adverse effects may last a very long time as career trajectories are interrupted. (Later in this chapter we further discuss the consequences of job loss and unemployment for individuals and their families.) The economy as a whole also loses the goods or services that would have been produced had they been working. In addition, because the purchasing power of unemployed workers is diminished, consumer demand declines, which leads to job loss for additional workers.

Figure 5G shows the unemployment rate from 1948 to 2011. Unsurprisingly, unemployment spikes sharply during recessions. What happens *after* recessions is also noteworthy. Up through the double-dip recession of the early 1980s, growth tended to be very strong once a recession ended, bringing the unemployment rate

Figure 5G Unemployment rate, 1948–2011

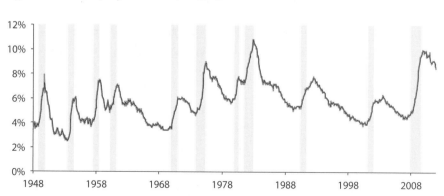

Note: Data are monthly and span Jan. 1948–Dec. 2011. Shaded areas denote recessions.

Source: Authors' analysis of Current Population Survey public data series

down quickly after it reached its peak. That is largely because recessions were essentially caused by the Federal Reserve, which raised interest rates to curb (either actual or incipient) inflation. This often meant that when it became clear that the economy had entered recession and the Federal Reserve lowered interest rates, a surge resulting from pent-up demand for interest-rate-sensitive goods (housing and durable goods, in particular) led to strong job growth, and the unemployment rate would drop.

But starting with the recession of the early 1990s, a different pattern has emerged, one characterized by slow growth following a recession, where the unemployment rate remains high for a very long time. This is largely because the last three recessions have *not* been caused by the Federal Reserve raising interest rates; there has been no need because inflation has been under control. Instead, these recessions were due to high levels of private-sector debt and the bursting of asset-market bubbles. (The early 1990s recession actually is a bit of a hybrid, with Federal Reserve tightening playing a role in the downturn, but asset-market deflation also clearly hampering recovery.) During this kind of recession and its aftermath, the Federal Reserve is in the situation of trying to stimulate the economy by cutting interest rates from levels that are not very high—or in the case of the Great Recession, basically zero. Further, since lowering interest rates stimulates the economy mainly by boosting the housing market, lowering interest rates may be ineffective anyway if housing is already overbuilt. So if fiscal policy—increasing net government spending to stimulate the economy—is not sufficiently expansionary, the recovery can take a long time to really take hold and raise employment growth to levels sufficient to absorb willing workers.

One thing to note in Figure 5G is that the unemployment rate in the 2000–2007 business cycle never returned to pre-recession levels before the Great Recession began. In 2000, the peak at the end of the 1989–2000 business cycle, the unemployment rate averaged 4.0 percent. But in 2007, the peak of the 2000–2007 business cycle, the unemployment rate averaged 4.6 percent, never regaining the strength of the late 1990s. The rise in the unemployment rate from 2000 to 2007 is unsurprising when we recall that the 2000–2007 business cycle is the weakest full business cycle on record in terms of job growth (see the discussion of Table 5.1).

Unemployment and age

A final thing to note in Figure 5G is that the unemployment rate in the Great Recession never got as high as it did during the downturn of the early 1980s, when it peaked at 10.8 percent at the end of 1982. In the Great Recession the unemployment rate peaked in October 2009 at 10.0 percent. Importantly, a key factor underlying that difference has nothing to do with better labor market conditions in the Great Recession, but simply with changes in the age composition of the labor force. The top panel of **Table 5.2** documents the aging of the labor

Table 5.2 Labor force share and unemployment rate, by age, 1979–2011

	1979	1989	2000	2007	2011	Change	
						1979–2007	2007–2011
Share of labor force							
Age 16–19	9.2%	6.4%	5.8%	4.6%	3.7%	-4.6	-0.9
20–24	15.0	11.4	10.0	9.9	9.9	-5.1	0.0
25–34	26.6	29.0	23.0	21.6	22.0	-5.0	0.3
35–44	18.8	24.7	26.3	23.2	21.3	4.4	-1.9
45–54	16.1	16.1	21.8	23.3	23.0	7.2	-0.3
55 and older	14.3	12.4	13.1	17.3	20.1	3.0	2.8
All	100.0	100.0	100.0	100.0	100.0		
Unemployment rate							
Age 16–19	16.1%	15.0%	13.1%	15.7%	24.4%	-0.4	8.7
20–24	9.2	6.9	7.2	8.2	14.6	-1.0	6.4
25–34	4.4	5.2	3.7	4.7	9.5	0.3	4.8
35–44	3.6	3.8	3.0	3.5	7.3	-0.1	3.9
45–54	3.2	3.2	2.5	3.2	7.1	0.0	3.9
55 and older	3.0	3.1	2.6	3.1	6.6	0.1	3.5
All	5.9	5.3	4.0	4.6	9.0	-1.2	4.3

Note: Percentage-point change shown in last two columns may not sum correctly due to rounding.

Source: Authors' analysis of Current Population Survey public data series

force by presenting the share of the labor force in different age categories at business cycle peak years between 1979 and 2007 and in 2011. In 1979 slightly less than half (49.2 percent) of the labor force was age 35 and older, but by 2007, almost two-thirds (63.8 percent) of the labor force was 35 and older, and 40.6 percent was 45 and older. The bottom panel of Table 5.2 shows that, for any given year, unemployment rates drop dramatically with age. For example, since 1979, the unemployment rate among teenagers has been at least 10 percentage points higher than among workers age 55 and older. Thus, the aging of the labor force would cause a decrease in overall unemployment rates *even if no individual age category experienced a decline in its unemployment rate.* From 1979 to 2007, the overall unemployment rate decreased by 1.2 percentage points, but *no* age categories experienced a decline that big—the largest change was a 1 percentage-point decline among workers age 20–24. All other categories experienced either much smaller declines or increases in their unemployment rates over this period. Thus, the fact that the unemployment rate was lower in 2007 than in 1979 was due in large part to the composition of the workforce shifting toward lower-unemployment age groups.

Figure 5H shows the unemployment rate, along with what the unemployment rate would have been if the age distribution of the labor force had not changed from 1979 (but with the unemployment rates within each age category changing as they actually did). In other words, the simulated unemployment rate demonstrates what the unemployment rate would have been if the age distribution were held constant over time. The simulation shows that without the aging of the labor force since 1979, the unemployment rate would have peaked at 11.6 percent in October 2009 (well above the highest rate in the downturn of the early 1980s) instead of its actual peak of 10.0 percent. This is one example of why it is problematic to compare the unemployment rate of today with that of earlier periods. A later section of this chapter offers further examples of how the unemployment rate of today is not entirely comparable with that of earlier periods because of changing labor force participation trends among different groups of potential workers.

Figure 5H Unemployment rate (actual and holding age distribution constant), 1979–2011

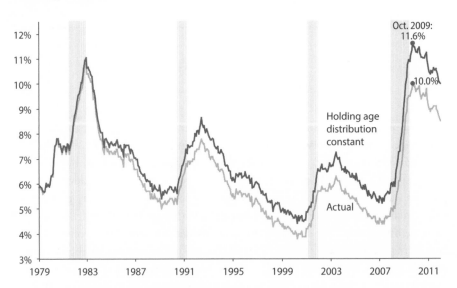

Note: Data are monthly and span Jan. 1979–Dec. 2011. Shaded areas denote recessions.

Source: Authors' analysis of Current Population Survey public data series

Unemployment and race/ethnicity, gender, and education

In addition to varying by age, unemployment rates differ enormously by other demographic characteristics, including by race and ethnicity, gender, and educational attainment. **Figure 5I** looks at unemployment rates by race and ethnicity. The figure shows that at nearly any given time over the last three decades, the unemployment rate of black workers was *more than twice as high* as that of white workers, and the unemployment rate of Hispanic workers was somewhere in between. During recessions the black-white gap in unemployment rates increases, as the unemployment rate of blacks increases more than that of whites. The same is true for the unemployment gap between Hispanic and white workers, though to a lesser extent. Between 2007 and 2010, the unemployment rate of whites increased by 4.2 percentage points (from 3.9 percent to 8.0 percent), while that of blacks increased by 7.7 percentage points (from 8.3 percent to 15.9 percent) and that of Hispanics increased by 6.8 percentage points (from 5.6 percent to 12.5 percent). (The actual percentage-point changes specified here do not match the difference between the shares because the shares are rounded.)

The highest annual unemployment rate of white workers since the onset of the Great Recession was 8.0 percent (in 2010), still less than the 8.3 percent 2007 (pre-recession) unemployment rate of blacks.

Figure 5I Unemployment rate, by race and ethnicity, 1979–2011

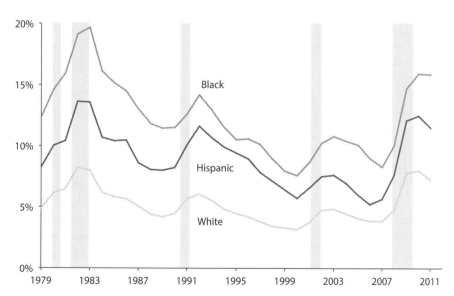

Note: Shaded areas denote recessions.

Source: Authors' analysis of basic monthly Current Population Survey microdata

Table 5.3 presents unemployment rates by educational attainment, with cross-tabulations by race and ethnicity. It first shows that in any time period, overall unemployment rates fall as educational attainment rises. For example, workers without a high school diploma have an unemployment rate that is typically more than five times as high as that of workers with an advanced degree. During economic downturns people with lower levels of education face greater increases in unemployment than those with higher levels of education—for example, between 2007 and 2010, unemployment among all workers without a high school diploma increased 8.5 percentage points, while unemployment among all workers with an advanced degree increased 1.8 percentage points. Note, however, that unemployment rates at all education levels more or less *doubled* between 2007 and 2010. The deterioration of demand for workers across the educational spectrum in the Great Recession and its aftermath is further examined in this chapter's discussion of structural and cyclical unemployment.

One of the most important points Table 5.3 makes is that large racial and ethnic disparities in unemployment exist across the educational spectrum. For example, white workers with a high school diploma but no more schooling saw their unemployment rate increase from 4.6 percent to 10.3 percent between 2007 and 2010, whereas similarly educated black workers saw their unemployment rate increase from 9.6 percent to 18.5 percent over the same period. Likewise, white workers with a college degree but no advanced degree saw their unemployment rate increase from 2.2 percent to 4.9 percent between 2007 and 2010, whereas black college graduates saw their unemployment rate increase from 3.5 percent to 9.8 percent. Note also that in any given year, the unemployment rate of black college graduates generally lies somewhere between the unemployment rate of white high school graduates and white workers with some college training but no college degree.

Table 5.4 presents unemployment rates by gender and education. During periods of relative strength in the labor market (such as in 2000 and 2007), men and women tend to have fairly similar unemployment rates (with the primary exception being that the unemployment rate of women without a high school degree is noticeably higher than that of men without a high school degree). During downturns, however, unemployment rates among men tend to increase much more than among women. Between 2007 and 2010, the overall male unemployment rate rose from 4.7 percent to 10.5 percent, while the overall female unemployment rate rose from 4.5 percent to 8.6 percent. This is largely due to the fact that men are overrepresented in many highly cyclical industries, such as manufacturing and construction, and are underrepresented in industries that tend not to see much job loss in recessions, such as education services and health services. In this chapter's section on job loss and gender in the Great Recession and its aftermath, we discuss this further.

Table 5.3 Unemployment rate, by education and race and ethnicity, 2000–2011

Education	Race and ethnicity	2000	2007	2010	2011	Change 2007–2010
Less than high school	All	9.4%	10.3%	18.8%	17.8%	8.5
High school	All	4.3	5.4	12.0	11.1	6.5
Some college	All	3.1	4.0	9.1	8.6	5.1
College degree	All	2.0	2.4	5.7	5.2	3.2
Advanced degree	All	1.4	1.7	3.5	3.3	1.8
Less than high school	White	8.4%	10.9%	19.2%	18.1%	8.3
	Black	16.8	18.7	30.6	31.7	11.9
	Hispanic	8.2	7.6	15.5	14.1	7.9
	Asian	8.2	5.7	13.6	12.2	7.9
High school	White	3.4%	4.6%	10.3%	9.2%	5.7
	Black	8.6	9.6	18.5	18.3	8.8
	Hispanic	5.1	5.5	13.5	12.3	8.0
	Asian	4.0	3.7	9.5	9.0	5.8
Some college	White	2.7%	3.5%	7.9%	7.2%	4.4
	Black	4.9	6.4	13.7	14.3	7.3
	Hispanic	3.8	4.6	10.8	10.2	6.2
	Asian	4.1	4.0	9.0	8.4	5.0
College degree	White	1.8%	2.2%	4.9%	4.5%	2.7
	Black	2.8	3.5	9.8	8.2	6.3
	Hispanic	2.5	2.9	7.1	6.9	4.2
	Asian	2.3	2.8	6.8	6.6	3.9
Advanced degree	White	1.3%	1.6%	3.2%	3.0%	1.6
	Black	2.2	2.5	5.7	5.8	3.1
	Hispanic	1.8	1.6	4.3	3.8	2.7
	Asian	1.6	1.9	3.8	3.6	1.9

Source: Authors' analysis of basic monthly Current Population Survey microdata

Table 5.4 Unemployment rate, by gender and education, 2000–2011

Gender	Education	2000	2007	2010	2011	Change 2007–2010
All		**4.0%**	**4.6%**	**9.6%**	**8.9%**	**5.0**
Men	**Total**	**3.9%**	**4.7%**	**10.5%**	**9.4%**	**5.8**
	Less than high school	8.6	9.7	18.8	17.1	9.1
	High school	4.3	5.6	13.2	11.8	7.5
	Some college	3.0	4.0	9.9	8.8	5.9
	College degree	1.8	2.4	5.9	5.2	3.5
	Advanced degree	1.4	1.6	3.3	3.2	1.7
Women	**Total**	**4.1%**	**4.5%**	**8.6%**	**8.5%**	**4.1**
	Less than high school	10.6	11.2	18.6	19.0	7.4
	High school	4.4	5.2	10.4	10.1	5.2
	Some college	3.2	4.0	8.3	8.5	4.3
	College degree	2.2	2.5	5.4	5.1	2.9
	Advanced degree	1.5	1.8	3.8	3.4	2.0

Source: Authors' analysis of basic monthly Current Population Survey microdata

Unemployment rates of foreign- and native-born workers

It is also instructive to dissect unemployment rates by whether workers were born inside or outside the United States. **Figure 5J** compares the unemployment rates of foreign- and native-born workers since 1994 (the earliest available year for these data). The figure shows that the unemployment rates of immigrants are buffeted by business-cycle dynamics to a greater degree than those of native-born workers. In other words, during expansions, immigrant unemployment rates drop more dramatically, and during contractions they increase more dramatically. During the expansion of the mid-2000s, the immigrant unemployment rate fell below that of native-born workers for the first time in this data series, but it crossed back above that of natives as the Great Recession took hold in 2008 and 2009. By 2011, the unemployment rates of native- and foreign-born workers were again similar, at 8.9 percent for native-born workers and 9.0 percent for foreign-born workers.

Figure 5J Unemployment rates of foreign-born and native-born workers, 1994–2011

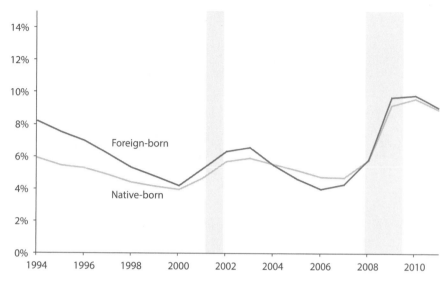

Note: Shaded areas denote recessions.

Source: Authors' analysis of basic monthly Current Population Survey microdata

Unemployment insurance benefits

Finally, it is important to note that the definition of unemployment has *nothing* to do with whether an unemployed person receives unemployment insurance (UI) benefits. To receive UI benefits, a worker must be unemployed (i.e., jobless but available to work and actively seeking work), but an unemployed worker may well not collect unemployment insurance benefits, or in fact may not even be eligible for them. Unemployed workers generally are eligible for UI benefits only if they are temporarily out of work through no fault of their own. For example, an employee who voluntarily quits or is fired for misconduct generally is not eligible for UI benefits. Further, new entrants to the labor market (e.g., new graduates) or re-entrants after a long absence (e.g., formerly stay-at-home parents) are not eligible.

Only employees who have recently worked can collect UI benefits, and even then the worker must have worked a minimum amount of time (generally longer than one year) and have received a minimum amount of earnings from his or her previous employer. In many states, workers are only eligible for UI benefits if they are looking for a full-time job. In addition, some states disqualify seasonal workers—and workers who were forced to leave their jobs because of, for example, medical reasons, also typically do not qualify for benefits.

Figure 5K Share of unemployed people with unemployment insurance benefits, 1989–2011

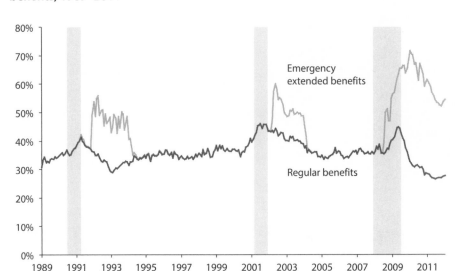

Note: Monthly data span Jan. 1989–Dec. 2011. Extended benefits are not seasonally adjusted. Shaded areas denote recessions.

Source: Authors' analysis of U.S. Department of Labor Unemployment Insurance program statistics and the Current Population Survey public data series

Figure 5K shows the share of unemployed people receiving unemployment insurance benefits, both regular state benefits and temporary emergency extensions of benefits passed by Congress during downturns in the labor market. With the exception of periods during and directly following recessions, generally only around 35 percent of the unemployed are eligible for and receive benefits. The share increases during downturns due both to temporary emergency extensions of benefits and to the fact that during recessions, a higher share of unemployed workers are unemployed because they were involuntarily laid off.

Due to the dramatic job loss in the Great Recession, the share of unemployed workers receiving benefits increased substantially; however, it still never exceeded 75 percent. Importantly, because so many unemployed workers faced such long spells of unemployment in the aftermath of the Great Recession, only about half of all workers receiving UI benefits received regular benefits—the rest had exhausted these and received emergency extended benefits. Long-term unemployment is discussed in greater depth later in this chapter.

Labor force participation:
Structural and cyclical changes

The labor force participation rate is the share of working-age people who are either employed or unemployed (jobless but actively seeking work). When there is a change in the labor force participation rate, the question that arises is whether the change is *structural* or *cyclical*. *Structural* changes are due to longer-run changes in the labor force attachment of a particular group, changes that have nothing to do with the strength or weakness of the broader economy. *Cyclical* changes are due to a change in demand for workers, as more people either are drawn into the labor market because of strong job prospects or, conversely, leave or never enter the labor market because of weak job prospects.

Perhaps the most dramatic structural change in the last century was the increased labor force participation of women. Their labor force participation rate nearly doubled from 1948 to 2000, increasing from 32.7 percent to 59.9 percent. Structural changes have also occurred in the labor force participation of different age groups. **Figure 5L** shows changes in the labor force participation rate of men and women in different age groups. Note that to try to isolate and examine structural changes over time, it is useful to look just through the year 2000; because the labor market has been so weak since that point, a significant portion of the post-2000 changes have likely been caused by weak demand for workers.

The share of young working-age men (age 16–24) in the labor force held roughly steady from 1959 to 1979, while young women's labor force participation grew steadily, substantially closing the gender gap in labor force participation among young workers. From 1979 to 2000, labor force participation of young men declined, while labor force participation of young women plateaued. Some, but certainly not all, of this trend can be explained by increasing college enrollment of young people.

Gender differences in trends among "prime-age" workers, those age 25–54, are dramatic. Labor force participation among prime-age women increased through 2000, with particularly dramatic increases in the 1970s. Prime-age men, on the other hand, experienced gradual decline in labor force participation from 1959 to 2000.

Male workers age 55 and older saw substantial declines in labor force participation until the early 1990s, as retirement became more available to a broader swath of workers. For older women, labor force participation stayed relatively flat over this period. Starting in the early 1990s, however, the labor force participation of both women and men age 55 and older began to rise, likely due in part to both health insurance and pensions. First, most people get some portion of their health insurance coverage through their employer, and since health care costs have risen significantly, workers are working longer to retain health insurance. Second, because pensions are becoming less and less likely to provide

Figure 5L Labor force participation rate, by age and gender, 1959–2011

Note: Shaded areas denote recessions. Darker shading denotes years past 2000.

Source: Authors' analysis of Current Population Survey public data series

adequate retirement income, people are working longer to improve their economic security in retirement.

Aside from *structural* changes just discussed, there are also *cyclical* changes in
the labor force participation rate. Because of the weak labor market since 2000,
and particularly since 2007, it is likely that labor force participation rates would
now be significantly higher if job prospects were better. The bottom row of **Table
5.5** shows that the labor force participation rate dropped from 66.0 percent in
2007 to 64.1 percent in 2011, a decline of 1.9 percentage points.

If the labor force participation rate *hadn't* dropped due to the weak labor
market—and instead the people who made up the decline in the labor force participation rate (those who dropped out or didn't enter) were in the labor force
and counted as unemployed—the unemployment rate would now be significantly
higher. Table 5.5 explores the possible impact of the cyclical decline in the labor
force participation rate since the start of the Great Recession on the unemployment rate. The table shows the labor force participation rate in 1989 and 2007
(two business cycle peaks) and in 2011 of men and women in different age groups.
It also shows what the labor force participation rate would have been in 2011 if,
from 2007 to 2011, it had followed its long-term trend. (Note that this exercise
ignores the fact that the weak labor market from 2000 to 2007 also probably
caused a cyclical decline in the labor force participation rate, and instead simply
uses the 1989–2007 trend in the labor force participation rate as the long-term

Table 5.5 Decline in the labor force participation rate from 1989 to 2011 and
its possible effect on the unemployment rate in 2011, by gender and age

Gender	Age	Labor force participation rate				Unemployment rate	
		1989	2007	2011	Counterfactual 2011 rate*	2011	Counterfactual 2011 rate**
Men	16–24	73.1%	61.5%	56.6%	59.8%	18.7%	23.1%
	25–54	93.7	90.9	88.7	90.3	8.2	9.8
	55+	39.6	45.2	46.3	45.9	7.0	6.1
Women	16–24	64.5%	57.2%	53.3%	56.5%	15.7%	20.5%
	25–54	73.7	75.4	74.7	75.6	7.6	8.8
	55+	23.0	33.2	35.1	35.8	6.2	8.1
All		**66.5%**	**66.0%**	**64.1%**	**65.4%**	**8.9%**	**10.7%**

* The column shows the labor force participation rate had it followed its long-term trend.
** The column shows the unemployment rate had the workers making up the difference between the 2011
   labor force participation rate and its long-term trend instead been in the labor force and unemployed.

Source: Authors' analysis of basic monthly Current Population Survey microdata

structural trend. This exercise thus likely *understates* the cyclical decline in labor force participation.)

For each group except men age 55 and older, the labor force participation rate in 2011 would have been higher if it had followed its long-term trend. For prime-age (25–54) male workers, it would have been 1.6 percentage points higher; for prime-age female workers, it would have been about 1.0 percentage point higher. Overall, the labor force participation rate would have been 1.3 percentage points higher. In other words, this exercise suggests that around one-third of the decline in the overall labor force participation rate between 2007 and 2011 was part of a long-term structural trend, and about two-thirds—1.3 percentage points out of the 1.9 percentage-point decrease—was due to a cyclical drop in the demand for workers.

The last two columns of the table give the unemployment rate in 2011, and what the unemployment rate would have been if the workers who made up the difference between the 2011 labor force participation rate and its long-term trend—i.e., the workers who dropped out of, or never entered, the labor force because of weak job prospects—had instead been in the labor force and counted as unemployed. For all groups except men age 55 and older, the unemployment rate in 2011 would have been higher. For prime-age men, it would have been nearly 10 percent in 2011 instead of 8.2 percent, and for prime-age women it would have been nearly 9 percent instead of 7.6 percent. Overall, the unemployment rate would have been 10.7 percent instead of 8.9 percent.

This shows how cyclical declines in the labor force mean that the unemployment rate may severely understate weakness in the labor market. It also illuminates the possibility that when job openings and hiring pick up significantly and sidelined workers seeing better job prospects begin searching for work, the unemployment rate may not fall (or will fall less than it otherwise would have) even though job opportunities have actually improved. A key message here is that changes in the unemployment rate are difficult to interpret during periods when there are also cyclical changes in labor force participation.

Beyond the unemployment rate: Other measures of labor market slack

As just discussed, the unemployment rate is an imperfect measure of changes in the strength or weakness of the labor market during times when the size of the labor force is affected by the state of the economy. However, there are a host of other available measures that are commonly used to help round out the picture of the strength of employment prospects.

Employment-to-population ratio

One of the most useful measures for assessing changes in the strength or weakness of job prospects during periods when the labor force is not growing normally is the employment-to-population ratio. This broad measure avoids issues related to changes in the labor force because it is simply the share of the relevant population with a job. **Figure 5M** shows changes in the employment-to-population ratio of 25–54 year olds. Looking at these "prime-age" workers is useful because their employment trends in recent years are generally not driven by other trends—such as increased college enrollment of young people or retiring baby boomers—but simply by aggregate demand for workers. The trends in the Great Recession and its aftermath are grim—the employment-to-population ratio of prime-age workers dropped from 80.2 percent in the first quarter of 2007 to 74.9 percent in the fourth quarter of 2009—an unprecedented fall. But perhaps even more startling is the lack of progress the following two years: From the fourth quarter of 2009 to the fourth quarter of 2011, the employment-to-population ratio stayed essentially flat. This suggests that the fall in the unemployment rate from the end of 2009 to the end of 2011 (see Figure 5G) was primarily because people dropped out of or didn't enter the labor market due to the lack of job prospects—not because an increasing share of potential workers found employment.

Figure 5M Employment-to-population ratio, age 25–54, by gender, 1989–2011

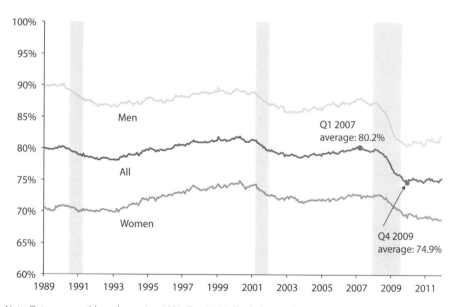

Note: Data are monthly and span Jan. 1989–Dec. 2011. Shaded areas denote recessions.

Source: Authors' analysis of Current Population Survey public data series

Underemployment

The definition of unemployment, by including only jobless workers who report that they are actively seeking work, overlooks jobless workers who want a job but have given up looking and those who have a job but can't get the hours they want or need. **Table 5.6** presents data on "underemployment," a more comprehensive measure of slack in the labor market than unemployment. Underemployment includes workers who meet the official definition of unemployment as well as: 1) those who are working part time but want and are available to work full time ("involuntary" part timers), and 2) those who want and are available to work and have looked for work in the last year but have given up actively seeking work ("marginally attached" workers). While this is the most comprehensive measure of labor underutilization available from the Bureau of Labor Statistics, it does not include workers who are underemployed in a "skills or experience" sense (as in, say, a mechanical engineer working as a barista). Unfortunately, there is no widely cited national measure of underemployment that includes people who are under-employed in this sense of the word (unless they are also working part time but want a full-time job). Nevertheless, the underemployment rate gets much closer than the regular unemployment rate to measuring the share of the labor force that is un- or underutilized.

According to Table 5.6, unemployed workers constitute just slightly more than half of the total underemployed population. Involuntary part-time workers make up about one-third, with the remaining roughly 10 percent accounted for by people who want a job but have given up actively seeking work and thus are not counted as unemployed (i.e., marginally attached workers). In the weak labor market of 2000–2007, the number of underemployed workers grew from 10.1 million to 12.9 million. In the Great Recession and its immediate aftermath, the

Table 5.6 Underemployment, 2000–2011 (in millions)

	2000	2007	2010	2011
Unemployed	5.7	7.1	14.8	13.7
Involuntary part time*	3.2	4.4	8.9	8.6
Marginally attached**	1.2	1.4	2.5	2.6
Total underemployed	10.1	12.9	26.2	24.9
Underemployment rate***	7.0%	8.3%	16.7%	15.9%

*   Want and are available for full-time work
** Not looking for work but want and would take a job and have looked for work sometime in the last year
***Total underemployed workers as a percent of the sum of the civilian labor force and marginally attached workers

Source: Authors' analysis of Current Population Survey public data series

Figure 5N Underemployment rate, by race and ethnicity, 2000–2011

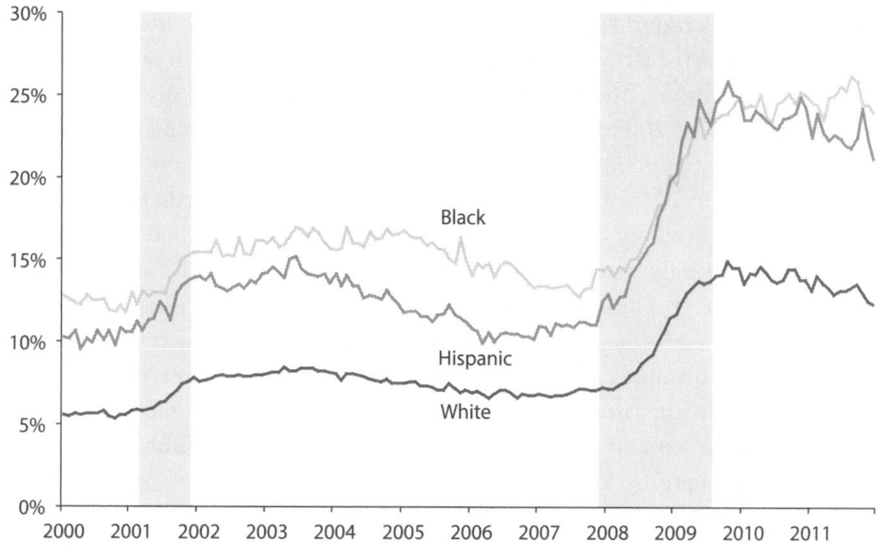

Note: Data are monthly and extend to December 2011. Shaded areas denote recessions.

Source: Authors' analysis of basic monthly Current Population Survey microdata

total number of underemployed workers climbed from 12.9 million in 2007 to 26.2 million in 2010, or 16.7 percent of the total workforce—more than one out of every six workers.

Figure 5N shows the underemployment rate by race and ethnicity. As with unemployment (Figure 5I), racial and ethnic minorities have much higher *underemployment* rates than white workers; the underemployment rate of blacks is typically about twice as high as that of whites. One substantive difference between Figure 5N (underemployment by race/ethnicity) and Figure 5I (unemployment by race/ethnicity) is that Hispanic underemployment is about as high as black underemployment in periods of high overall underemployment. In comparison, the *un*employment rate of Hispanics always falls firmly between the black and white unemployment rates. This difference arises because Hispanic workers are more likely to fall into the "involuntarily part time" category.

Long-term unemployment

Another important measure for understanding the job-finding prospects of unemployed workers is duration of unemployment. Perhaps the most frequently used unemployment duration measure is the share of unemployed workers who have been unemployed for more than six months. (Six months is the maximum length of regular unemployment insurance benefits in most states.) Being unemployed for more than six months is commonly referred to as "long-term" unemployment. **Figure 5O** shows the share of unemployed workers who have been out of work for more than six months. The increase in long-term unemployment over the business cycle from 2000 to 2007 is clear. In 2000, 11.4 percent of the unemployed were unemployed long term on average, but this increased to 17.5 percent in 2007. The length and severity of the Great Recession then caused an unprecedented rise in the share of unemployed out of work long term—to a peak of 45.5 percent in March 2011. Unsurprisingly, research (such as Valletta and Kuang 2012 and Rothstein 2012) shows that this dramatic and sustained increase is mainly due to severe and persistent weakness in the demand for labor and not such other factors as extended unemployment insurance benefits or a mismatch between worker skills and employer skill needs (the latter of which is discussed later in this chapter).

Who are the workers stuck in long-term unemployment? **Table 5.7** presents the long-term share by demographic group, education, and occupation. With the primary exception of age, the differences in long-term unemployment shares across different groups are generally small. This means that the characteristics of the long-term unemployed largely reflect those of the unemployed in general. Again, this is not surprising given the broad lack of demand for workers in the Great Recession and its aftermath. In 2011, 43.7 percent of the unemployed were unemployed long term. That was roughly the case among both men and women. Among different education categories there was also little variation: Workers with

Figure 5O Long-term unemployment, 1948–2011

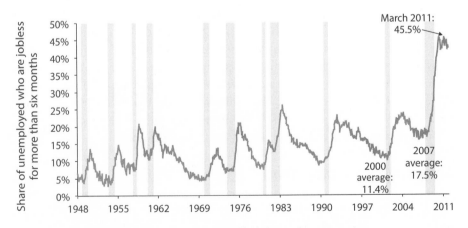

Note: Data are monthly and span Jan. 1948–Dec. 2011. Shaded areas denote recessions.

Source: Authors' analysis of Current Population Survey public data series

Table 5.7 Long-term unemployment, by demographic group, education, and occupation, 2000–2011

		2000	2007	2011
	All	**11.4%**	**17.6%**	**43.7%**
Gender	Men	12.2%	18.2%	44.0%
	Women	10.6	16.8	43.3
Education	Less than high school	10.6%	15.8%	39.0%
	High school	11.8	18.2	44.9
	Some college	10.8	17.2	45.1
	College degree	13.2	18.9	44.3
	Advanced degree	14.1	22.2	45.9
Race and ethnicity	White	9.6%	16.2%	42.4%
	Black	15.0	23.8	49.9
	Hispanic	12.2	14.3	39.8
Occupation	Management, business, and financial operations	14.7%	19.0%	49.7%
	Professional	10.6	19.0	42.4
	Service	11.3	16.5	39.8
	Sales	8.8	17.0	46.1
	Office and administrative support	11.9	17.8	48.6
	Farming, fishing, and forestry	8.0	14.8	22.9
	Construction and extraction	9.1	14.3	43.2
	Installation, maintenance, and repair	14.8	17.6	49.8
	Production, transportation, and material moving	13.0	19.5	46.3
Age	16–24	7.3%	11.9%	30.0%
	25–34	10.5	17.1	42.6
	35–44	13.5	19.8	47.6
	45–54	15.8	23.6	52.0
	55+	19.6	22.7	55.1

Note: Long-term unemployment measures the share of unemployed workers who have been unemployed for more than six months.

Source: Authors' analysis of basic monthly Current Population Survey microdata

higher levels of education generally had slightly higher long-term unemployment shares, but not consistently—long-term unemployment as a share of the unemployed was slightly lower among workers with a four-year college degree only than among workers with a high school degree or some college but no college degree. Among race there was slightly more but still limited variation: In 2011, the share of unemployed workers out of work long term was 49.9 percent for black workers, compared with 42.4 percent for white workers and 39.8 percent for Hispanic workers. There was also surprisingly little variation among different occupations. With the exception of farming, fishing, and forestry occupations, which have a very low long-term unemployment share of 22.9 percent, the share out of work long term only ranged from 39.8 percent in service occupations to 49.8 percent in installation, maintenance, and repair occupations.

The biggest differences are in age; in every year examined, older workers tended to get stuck in unemployment longer than younger workers. In 2011, the long-term unemployment share of workers under age 25 was 30.0 percent, compared with 55.1 percent for workers age 55 and older. This is an interesting contrast to Table 5.2, which showed that older workers tend to have much lower unemployment rates. While older workers have more job stability and are less likely to face unemployment, if they *do* become unemployed, they tend to get stuck in unemployment for longer periods. This makes sense—an older worker is much more likely to have developed a specific set of knowledge and skills during his or her career, so if an older worker is unemployed, finding a job that *matches* those specific skills can take much longer than it does for a younger worker. This difference is particularly pronounced when job openings in general are very scarce, such as during the Great Recession and its aftermath.

Over-the-year unemployment

The official unemployment rate measures the share of the labor force unemployed *in a given month*. But this understates the number of people who are unemployed at some point over a longer period, since someone who is employed in one month may become unemployed the next, and vice versa. **Figure 5P** shows both the average monthly unemployment rate and the "over-the-year" unemployment rate—the share of workers who experienced unemployment at some point during the year. In 2009, when job loss during the Great Recession was most severe, 9.3 percent of the labor force was unemployed per month on average. However, 16.4 percent of the labor force—nearly one out of every six workers—was unemployed *at some point* in 2009.

Figure 5P Unemployment rate, average monthly and
over-the-year, 2000–2010

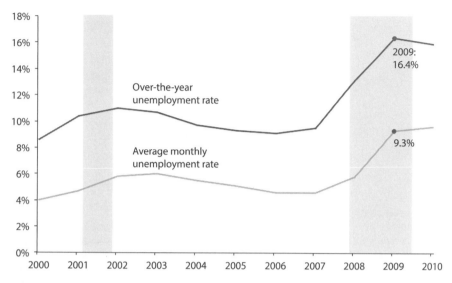

Note: Shaded areas denote recessions.

Source: Authors' analysis of Current Population Survey public data series and the Bureau of Labor Statistics
Work Experience of the Population

Job-seekers ratio

An intuitive measure of job seekers' prospects for finding work is the "job-seekers ratio," the ratio of unemployed workers to job openings. **Figure 5Q** shows this ratio since December 2000 (when job openings data first became available). It is important to note that this ratio does *not* measure the number of *applicants* per job opening (reliable national data do not exist on the number of job applications filed each month). Rather, this measure is literally the number of unemployed workers divided by the number of job openings each month. It thus reveals how many unemployed workers there are for each available job, regardless of how many applications are filed. In December 2000, the ratio of job seekers to job openings was 1.1-to-1. In other words, there was roughly one job seeker per job opening at the end of the expansion of the 1990s, when the unemployment rate was below 4 percent. Over the weak labor market of the 2000–2007 business cycle, this ratio never again fell to the December 2000 low, but it did fall to 1.4-to-1 in the spring of 2007, when the unemployment rate was 4.4 percent. In the Great Recession, the job-seekers ratio spiked dramatically, to 6.7-to-1 in summer 2009, when the unemployment rate was 9.5 percent. The job-seekers ratio was above 4-to-1 for all of 2009 and 2010 and for most of 2011; a job-seekers

Figure 5Q Job-seekers ratio, Dec. 2000–Dec. 2011

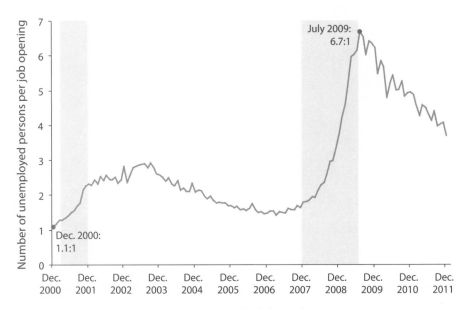

Note: Data are monthly and span Dec. 2000–Dec. 2011. Shaded areas denote recessions.

Source: Authors' analysis of Bureau of Labor Statistics Job Openings and Labor Turnover Survey and the Current Population Survey public data series

ratio above 4-to-1 means that there is simply no work for more than three out of four unemployed workers.

Voluntary quits

A final measure of the overall health of the labor market is, perhaps surprisingly, the number of *voluntary quits* in the labor market each month. All else equal, a larger number of voluntary quits represents a more dynamic labor market where job opportunities are plentiful. When job opportunities are plentiful, workers have the chance to change to jobs that better match their skills, experience, and interests and in which they are more productive and can command higher wages and better working conditions. During downturns, not only does hiring decrease, so does the number of voluntary quits, as outside job opportunities become scarce. **Figure 5R** shows the number of voluntary quits since December 2000. Between 2006 and 2009, the average number of voluntary quits each month dropped by more than 40 percent, from 3.0 million to 1.8 million, and by 2011 had only increased to 2.0 million. This represents an enormous drop in opportunities for the workforce, and demonstrates how persistent high unemployment hurts wage growth for workers with jobs; the lack of outside options reduces an important

Figure 5R Voluntary quits, Dec. 2000–Dec. 2011

Note: Data are monthly and span Dec. 2000–Dec. 2011. Shaded areas denote recessions.

Source: Authors' analysis of data from the Bureau of Labor Statistics Job Openings and Labor Turnover Survey

avenue for individuals to see wage growth (changing jobs). Furthermore, with limited outside options for their workers, employers do not have to pay substantial wage increases to keep the workers they need. The effect of recessions on wage growth is further discussed in Chapter 4.

Recovering from the Great Recession

Evidence showing the devastating impact of the Great Recession on employment, unemployment, labor force participation, and other measures of job opportunities has been woven throughout this chapter. This section directly compares the Great Recession with earlier recessions, and the current recovery with earlier recoveries. It also examines two special topics—gender and job loss in the Great Recession and its aftermath, and whether *structural* unemployment comprises a meaningful portion of the increase in unemployment in the Great Recession and its aftermath.

Comparing the Great Recession and its aftermath with earlier recessions and recoveries

Figure 5S directly compares job loss in percentage terms since the start of each of the last four recessions. It shows just how large job losses were in the Great Recession relative to the losses of earlier downturns. In December 2011, four years after the start of the Great Recession in December 2007, the number of jobs as a share of pre-recession employment was far lower than at any point during even the very deep recession of the early 1980s. By historical standards, job loss in the Great Recession and its aftermath was nothing the United States had seen in more than seven decades since the Great Depression.

In the discussion of Figure 5G, we pointed out that starting with the early 1990s recession, a pattern emerged of slow growth and stubbornly high unemployment following the end of recessions. To examine this more directly, in **Figure 5T** we reorient Figure 5S to compare job growth starting in *recoveries* instead of at the beginning of recessions. The top section of the figure shows that the number of jobs fell much further and faster during the Great Recession than in the previous three recessions. But looking to the right of the dotted line, it becomes clear

---

Figure 5S Job change since the start of each of the last four recessions

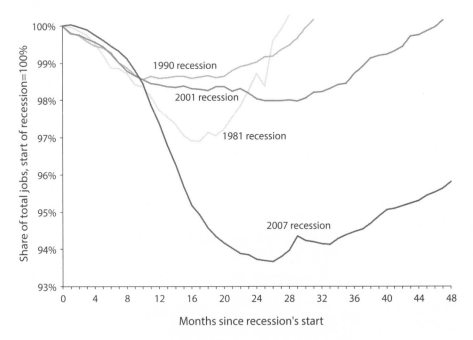

Source: Authors' analysis of Bureau of Labor Statistics Current Employment Statistics

Figure 5T Job change since the start of each of the last four recoveries

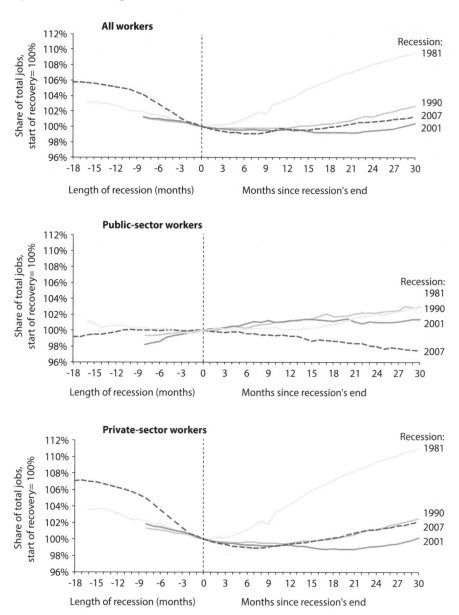

Note: The line for each recession begins at the official start of the recession, so the length of the line to the left of zero indicates the length of each recession. Data for public-sector workers exclude temporary Census workers.

Source: Authors' analysis of Bureau of Labor Statistics Current Employment Statistics

that job growth is not significantly weaker in the current recovery compared with the last two; it just slightly lags the job growth following the recession of 1990 and is actually faster than that of the recovery following the recession of 2001. The top section of Figure 5T underscores that the key difference between this recovery and the last two is the length and severity of the recessions that preceded them.

The bottom two sections of Figure 5T reveal an additional difference between this recovery and other recent recoveries—unprecedented public-sector job loss in the aftermath of the Great Recession. Private-sector job growth in the current recovery nearly matches that of the recovery following the early 1990s recession and is substantially stronger than that of the recovery following the early 2000s recession. But public-sector job losses in the current recovery—largely due to budget cuts at the state and local level—represent a large drag that was not weighing on earlier recoveries.

Job loss and gender in the Great Recession

Figure 5U looks at job loss during and after the Great Recession by gender. As the figure shows, men lost far more jobs than women did in the Great Recession (and, as shown in Table 5.4, the male unemployment rate rose much higher). In the

Figure 5U Job change, by gender, in the Great Recession and its aftermath (Dec. 2007–Dec. 2011)

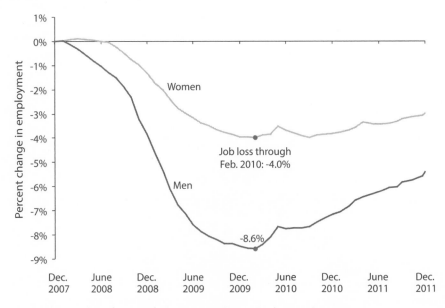

Source: Authors' analysis of Bureau of Labor Statistics Current Employment Statistics

period of overall job loss between the start of the recession in December 2007 and February 2010, men lost 6.0 million jobs, or 8.6 percent of their total December 2007 employment. By comparison, women lost 2.7 million jobs, or 4.0 percent. In December 2007, women held 48.8 percent of payroll jobs, but by August 2009, men's greater job loss had increased women's share of payroll jobs to 50.0 percent for the first time ever. Since the economy started regaining jobs, however, the gender dynamic in job growth has reversed—between February 2010 and the end of 2011, women gained 663,000 jobs while men gained 2.2 million, and the share of payroll jobs held by women dropped to 49.3 percent. However, Figure 5U also demonstrates that despite making up more ground, by the end of 2011 men were still in a far deeper hole than women relative to pre-recession employment levels (-5.4 percent for men compared with -3.0 percent for women).

It is important to note that greater net job loss for men from 2007 to 2011 can be more than explained by the fact that *before the recession started*, men were more concentrated in industries that would sustain the most dramatic job losses, while women were more concentrated in industries that would incur the least dramatic job losses, or even job gains. **Table 5.8** shows the distribution of workers across industries overall and by gender in 2007, and net job gains or losses within each industry overall and by gender from December 2007 to December 2011. The industries with the largest overall job losses, manufacturing (down 14.1 percent) and construction (down 25.9 percent), also employed a very large share of men; 14.0 percent of male workers were in manufacturing in 2007 (compared with 6.0 percent of female workers), and 9.4 percent of male workers were in construction (compared with 1.4 percent of female workers). The industries that employed the greatest shares of women in 2007, health care (18.5 percent) and state and local government (17.2 percent), were not as hard-hit. Between 2007 and 2011, health care *grew* by 7.8 percent, and state and local government fell by "only" 2.4 percent. In short, before the recession started, the gender-industry mix was such that men were positioned in industries that would bear much greater job loss, meaning that, all else equal, men would see greater job loss.

However, as the last column of Table 5.8 demonstrates, within industries, men often fared *better*. Women experienced a larger percentage net drop in jobs (or smaller percentage net gain in jobs) between 2007 and 2011 in 10 out of 16 major industries: manufacturing, wholesale trade, retail trade, transportation and warehousing, utilities, information, financial activities, professional and business services, health care, and leisure and hospitality. Women fared better only in mining, construction, educational services, other services, and government.

Figure 5V shows how employment of men and women would have evolved if, in December 2007, *men and women had had the same industry distribution* but if job changes by gender within each industry had evolved as they actually did between December 2007 and December 2011. Essentially, this exercise looks at job

Table 5.8 Industry distribution and job loss, by gender, 2007–2011

	Share of workers in various industries, 2007			Difference (women – men)	Net employment change, Dec. 2007–Dec. 2011			Difference (women – men)
	All	Women	Men		All	Women	Men	
Total nonfarm	100%	100%	100%		-4.2%	-3.0%	-5.4%	2.4
Mining	0.5%	0.1%	0.8%	-0.7	13.5%	16.4%	13.1%	3.3
Construction	5.5	1.4	9.4	-8.0	-25.9	-24.2	-26.1	1.9
Manufacturing	10.1	6.0	14.0	-8.0	-14.1	-18.6	-12.2	-6.4
Wholesale trade	4.4	2.7	5.9	-3.2	-7.8	-8.9	-7.3	-1.7
Retail trade	11.3	11.6	11.0	0.7	-5.4	-7.8	-3.0	-4.8
Transportation and warehousing	3.3	1.7	4.8	-3.2	-4.9	-10.1	-3.3	-6.8
Utilities	0.4	0.2	0.6	-0.3	0.4	-11.3	4.9	-16.2
Information	2.2	1.9	2.5	-0.5	-12.5	-16.8	-9.4	-7.3
Financial activities	6.0	7.4	4.7	2.7	-6.4	-8.2	-3.8	-4.4
Professional and business services	13.0	12.0	14.0	-2.0	-2.6	-3.2	-2.1	-1.0
Educational services	2.1	2.7	1.6	1.0	10.3	11.1	8.9	2.2
Health care and social assistance	11.2	18.5	4.2	14.3	7.8	6.8	11.8	-5.0
Leisure and hospitality	9.8	10.6	9.0	1.6	-0.7	-1.3	0.0	-1.3
Other services	4.0	4.3	3.7	0.5	-2.9	-1.7	-4.1	2.4
Federal government	2.0	1.8	2.2	-0.4	2.9	4.0	2.0	2.0
State and local government	14.2	17.2	11.5	5.7	-2.4	-2.0	-3.0	1.0

Note: Industry distribution shares may not total to 100 percent due to rounding.

Source: Authors' analysis of Bureau of Labor Statistics Current Employment Statistics

changes by gender in the Great Recession and its aftermath "controlling for industry." It shows that, all else equal, if men and women had had the same industry distribution going into the recession, job loss through the end of 2009 would have been very similar for men and women, but since then, men's job *gains* would have strongly outpaced women's. This simple exercise confirms that men's worse job losses in the Great Recession can be entirely explained by the industries in which men were concentrated before the recession started (i.e., controlling for industry, men and women saw very similar job loss from December 2007 to December

Figure 5V Simulated job change by gender in the Great Recession and its aftermath (Dec. 2007–Dec. 2011), controlling for industry

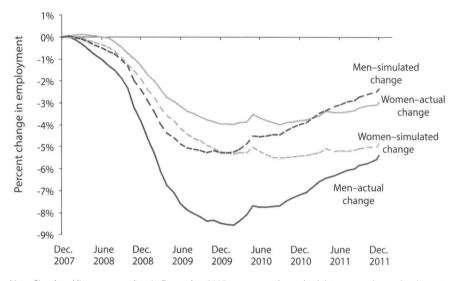

Note: Simulated lines assume that, in December 2007, women and men had the same industry distribution, but that male and female employment within each industry evolved as it actually did after 2007.

Source: Authors' analysis of Bureau of Labor Statistics Current Employment Statistics

2009). In the recovery, however, industry concentration does *not* fully explain the fact that men have seen stronger job growth. It does explain some of the gender difference in job growth in the recovery—in particular, women's disproportionate concentration in the public sector and the public sector's unprecedented job loss in the recovery (see the middle panel of Figure 5T) help explain why men have seen better employment growth in the recovery. However, industry concentration does not explain all of it—as Figure 5V shows, men are seeing stronger job gains in the recovery even after controlling for industry.

Unemployment in the aftermath of the Great Recession: Structural or cyclical?

Persistently high unemployment in the aftermath of the Great Recession has fueled a public debate about whether this unemployment is predominantly *cyclical* (caused by a lack of aggregate demand for workers—i.e., unemployment is high because employers don't need to hire) or *structural* (because the skills of job seekers do not match the requirements of available jobs—i.e., unemployment is high because employers want to hire but can't find the workers they need).

It is important to note that there are always labor market adjustments that create some degree of mismatch between the workers employers need and the workers who are available. The relevant question in a period of persistent high unemployment is whether that mismatch is an unusually large part of the unemployment story. The answer to this question has meaningful policy implications. If unemployment in the aftermath of the Great Recession is predominantly cyclical, then monetary and fiscal policy measures should be undertaken to bolster aggregate demand, which in that case would reduce unemployment without harmful side effects (in particular with little or no risk of accelerating inflation). But if unemployment is predominantly structural, attempts to bolster demand wouldn't help reduce unemployment, and might make things worse by accelerating inflation.

Perhaps the most important piece of information informing this discussion is the job-seekers ratio presented in Figure 5Q. This ratio shows that for all of 2009, 2010, and most of 2011, there have been more than *four times* as many unemployed workers as job openings. It cannot be the case that unemployment is being primarily driven by employers having job openings they can't fill (structural unemployment), because even if all job openings were filled immediately, more than three-fourths of unemployed workers would remain jobless.

Nevertheless, there is a great deal of further evidence that an increase in structural unemployment is not driving currently high unemployment. For example, if employers in certain sectors couldn't find suitable workers, we would expect to find industries with more job openings than unemployed workers—i.e., labor shortages. But there are no major sectors where this is happening. **Figure 5W** shows that the number of unemployed workers dramatically outnumbered job openings in every major sector in 2011. The sector with the lowest ratio of job seekers to job openings is mining, and even there it is nearly 2-to-1.

If structural unemployment were occurring in an *occupation* that exists in many industries, we might not find evidence of it in the industry breakdowns of Figure 5W. Job openings data do not exist by occupation, but unemployment data do, and, as shown in **Figure 5X**, they are revealing. If employers in particular occupations couldn't find enough workers, those occupations would not show a big increase in unemployment. However, Figure 5X shows a large increase in unemployment across all major occupation categories. The category with the smallest percent increase in unemployment is food preparation and serving, and even in that category there were nearly 70 percent more unemployed workers in 2011 than in 2007. In most occupations, the number of unemployed workers roughly doubled between 2007 and 2011.

An important thing to note in Figure 5X is that construction occupations do *not* stand out as an unusually large contributor to unemployment in the aftermath of the Great Recession. It is true that there was a big run-up in construction employment as the housing bubble inflated, and a dramatic drop in construction

Figure 5W Unemployed workers and job openings, by industry, 2011 (in millions)

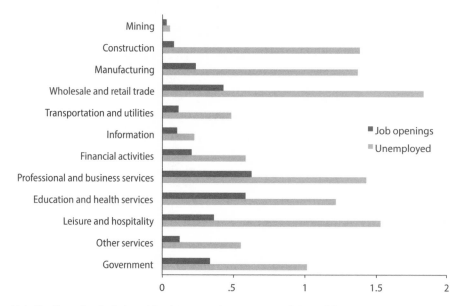

Note: Health services include social assistance service as a very small share of the category.

Source: Authors' analysis of Bureau of Labor Statistics Job Openings and Labor Turnover Survey and the Current Population Survey public data series

employment as the bubble burst and the recession took hold (see Table 5.8). But in proportional terms, the increase in unemployment among construction workers is very much in line with the increase in unemployment among workers in other occupations, which suggests that the skills of laid-off construction workers are at least as well-matched to the available jobs as those of laid-off workers in other occupations. In other words, unemployed construction workers are not driving today's unemployment (see also Schmitt and Warner 2011). Nor are they driving today's *long-term* unemployment, as shown in Table 5.7; in 2011, 43.2 percent of unemployed workers in construction and extraction occupations had been unemployed for more than six months, slightly *lower* than the overall share, 43.7 percent.

A final important place to investigate for evidence of structural unemployment is across education categories. As mentioned earlier (see Table 5.3), unemployment rates are much lower for workers with higher levels of education. Could this signal a shortage of workers with high levels of education? **Figure 5Y,** which shows the unemployment rate by education in 2007 and in 2011, reveals that while unemployment is substantially lower among workers with higher levels of education, they too have seen a large *percentage* increase in unemployment since

Figure 5X Unemployed workers, by occupation, 2007 and 2011 (in millions)

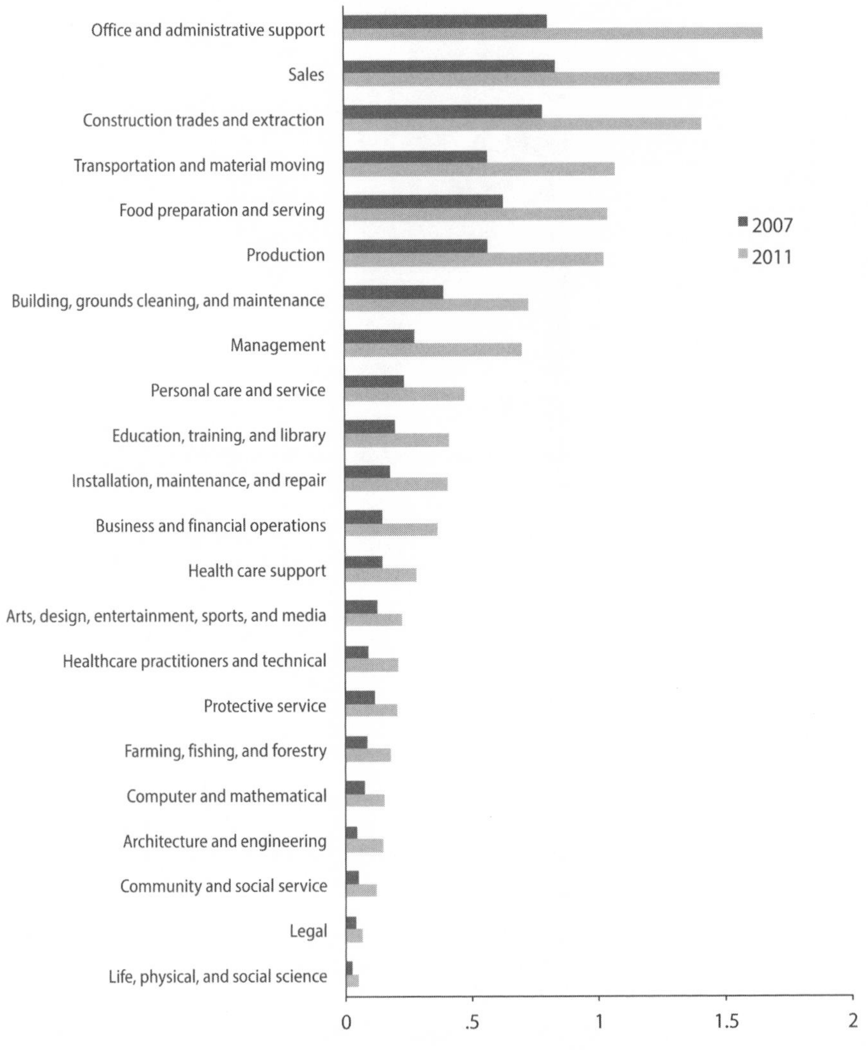

Source: Authors' analysis of basic monthly Current Population Survey microdata

before the recession started. Over the four years from 2007 to 2011, unemployment rates have roughly doubled in all categories. In other words, there has been a dramatic drop in demand for workers with even the highest levels of education.

In sum, data by industry, occupation, and education level all show a broad-based drop in demand for workers compared with before the recession started. This shows that the unemployment crisis in the aftermath of the Great Recession is primarily cyclical (caused by a drop in aggregate demand), not structural (in

Figure 5Y Unemployment rate, by education, 2007 and 2011

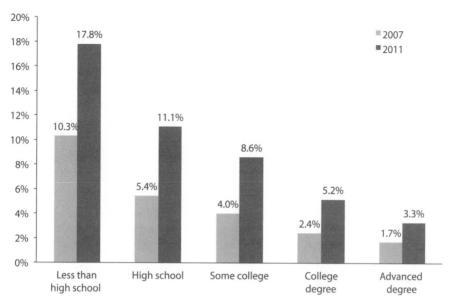

Source: Authors' analysis of basic monthly Current Population Survey microdata

other words, it is not caused by employers having difficulty finding the workers they need).

The consequences of job loss and unemployment for workers and their families

As mentioned in the earlier discussion of voluntary quits, workers who leave their jobs on their own accord but stay in the labor force generally move on to better circumstances in a new job with higher pay and improved working conditions. However, when workers lose their jobs involuntarily, they typically pay a large economic price. One cost is difficulty in finding a new job.

Figure 5Z shows the labor force status of workers who lost a job "not for cause" (i.e., due to a plant closing, a layoff, or the elimination of a job) at some point in the prior three years. The likelihood of reemployment for these workers is, unsurprisingly, cyclical—increasing in expansions and dropping in recessions. Less than half (47.4 percent) of workers who were laid off at some point from January 2007 to December 2009 were reemployed in January 2010—the lowest rate on record. The other 52.6 percent were unemployed or had dropped out of the labor force altogether.

Figure 5Z Labor force status of involuntarily displaced workers, 1984–2010

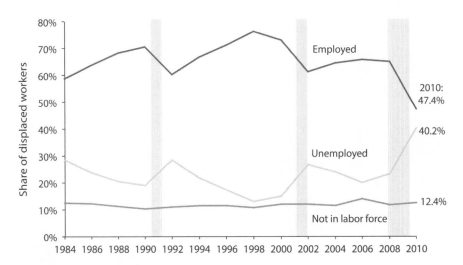

Note: Data are for workers who lost a job "not for cause" at some point in the prior three years. Shaded areas denote recessions.

Source: Authors' analysis of Farber (2011, Table 6)

Displaced workers able to find another job tend to earn wages that are substantially lower than those paid in their previous job. The wage impact is also cyclical; during recessions, displaced workers who find new jobs face very large wage losses. Those losses are lower in expansions, though generally still sizeable.

Figure 5AA shows the average weekly earnings loss of workers who were involuntarily displaced from a full-time job in the prior three years, both overall and separately for those who found a new full-time job. Overall, workers who lost a full-time job in 2007–2009 but were reemployed in either full- or part-time jobs in 2010 faced record weekly wage cuts of 21.8 percent on average. Some of this drop is certainly due to the large increase in people working part-time who want full-time jobs (see the earlier section on underemployment, particularly Table 5.6). But even restricting the analysis to displaced workers with the best outcomes—those who were able to find another full-time job—the drop is still a staggering 10.5 percent.

The one exception to the phenomenon of large wage cuts following displacement was in the very strong labor market of the late 1990s. Workers who involuntarily lost a full-time job in 1997–1999 but found new full-time employment by 2000 saw almost no drop (-0.2 percent) in wages at their new job.

Figure 5AA Average decline in weekly earnings for involuntarily displaced full-time workers who found new work, 1984–2010

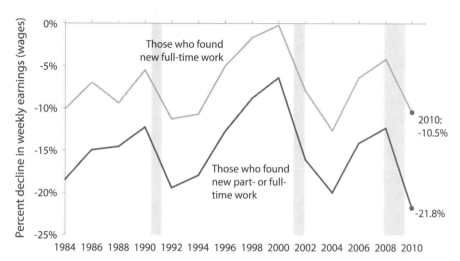

Note: Data are for workers who lost a full-time job at some point in the prior three years. Shaded areas denote recessions.

Source: Authors' analysis of Farber (2011, Table 16)

Judging from experiences in past recessions, the consequences of layoffs for displaced workers are not just severe, they are also long-lasting. The following discussion of the "scarring" effects of persistent high unemployment draws from a large body of research on these effects (Jacobson, LaLonde, and Sullivan 1993; von Wachter, Song, and Manchester 2009; Stevens 1997; Burgard, Brand, and House 2007; Sullivan and von Wachter 2009; Stevens and Schaller 2009; Oreopoulos, Page, and Stevens 2008; Oreopoulos, von Wachter, and Heisz 2008; and Kahn 2010).

This research shows that the average adult worker losing a stable job will see severe earnings reductions that last more than 15 to 20 years compared with what earnings would have been had the job not been lost. One of the reasons for this extended spell of depressed earnings is that the loss of a job is also often followed by a lengthy period of employment instability. Furthermore, in addition to financial hardship, displaced workers often experience declines in health during this period, which can lead to significant reductions in life expectancy (12 to 18 months).

Job losses also affect workers' children. Parental job loss is associated with reduced academic performance and higher rates of grade repetition. Even grimmer: The children of parents who lose work have substantially lower earning as *adults* than children from otherwise-similar families that didn't face job loss. Finally, the evidence from past recessions shows severe and long-lasting effects on young workers who are positioned to enter the labor market in a downturn. In particular, entering the labor market in a severe recession can lead to reduced earnings for up to 10 to 15 years. Young workers at all levels of educational attainment who enter the labor market during a downturn face higher rates of unemployment. And because of the scarcity of available jobs, these young workers are less likely to land a stable entry-level job that will lead to advancement, and are more likely to experience a lengthy period of instability in employment and earnings. All of these findings underscore the fact that economic recessions, which are often portrayed as short-term events, can and do cause long-lasting damage.

Conclusion

It is mainly through the job market that the country's economic growth reaches the vast majority of families not of retirement age. The great American jobs machine faltered from 2000 to 2007, producing the worst business cycle on record for job creation, and on its heels came the Great Recession and the most severe and sustained job loss this country had seen in seven decades. Although the recovery has been similar in strength to the recoveries that followed the recessions of the early 1990s and early 2000s, the length and severity of the Great Recession created a much deeper jobs deficit and a much higher unemployment rate this time around. When jobs are not plentiful, workers who do find employment are less likely to find a job that matches their skills and experience, and are less able to secure raises. And for workers who face job loss, the negative consequences for them and their families are severe and long-lasting.

Trends in job growth in recent decades—and especially during and after the Great Recession—offer a critical lesson: A healthy labor market is primarily a function of healthy growth in aggregate demand, while a sick labor market is a function of weak demand. This simple point is far too often ignored in debates about how to make labor markets more dynamic. Until the labor market regains is strength, strategies to boost demand and generate jobs must be a top national priority.

Table and figure notes

Tables

Table 5.1. Average annual change in employment, GDP, hours, and productivity, 1948–2011. Underlying data for total economy productivity are unpublished data provided to the authors by the Bureau of Labor Statistics Labor Productivity and Costs program.

Table 5.2. Labor force share and unemployment rate, by age, 1979–2011. Underlying data are from the Current Population Survey public data series.

Table 5.3. Unemployment rate, by education and race and ethnicity, 2000–2011. Underlying data are basic monthly Current Population Survey microdata.

Table 5.4. Unemployment rate, by gender and education, 2000–2011. Underlying data are basic monthly Current Population Survey microdata.

Table 5.5. Decline in the labor force participation rate from 1989 to 2011 and its possible effect on the unemployment rate in 2011, by gender and age. Underlying data are basic monthly Current Population Survey microdata. The counterfactual 2011 labor force participation rate is what the labor force participation rate would have been in 2011 if the labor force participation rate of each of 30 gender/age/education cells had continued on the same linear trend from 2007 to 2011 that they followed from 1989 to 2007, but if the relative sizes of those cells evolved as they actually did. (Note, there are three age groups: 16–24, 25–54, and 55+; and five education groups: less than high school, high school, some college, college degree, and advanced degree. The table presents aggregated results by gender and age.) The counterfactual 2011 unemployment rate is what the unemployment rate in 2011 would have been if the workers making up the difference between the actual and the counterfactual 2011 labor force participation rate were in the labor force and unemployed instead of out of the labor force.

Table 5.6. Underemployment, 2000–2011. Underlying data are from the Current Population Survey public data series. *Involuntary part time* refers to those who work part time for economic reasons, i.e., those who want and are available for full-time work, but who have had to settle for a part-time schedule. *Marginally attached* refers to those who are currently neither working nor looking for work but indicate that they want and are available for a job and have looked for work sometime in the past year.

Table 5.7. Long-term unemployment, by demographic group, education, and occupation, 2000–2011. Underlying data are from the Bureau of Labor Statistics Current Employment Statistics public data series.

Table 5.8. Industry distribution and job loss, by gender, 2007–2011. Underlying data are from the Bureau of Labor Statistics Current Employment Statistics public data series.

Figures

Figure 5A. Jobs needed each month to hold steady and actual monthly job growth, 1969–2011. *Actual monthly job growth,* the number of jobs added per month on average, comes from the Bureau of Labor Statistics Current Employment Statistics (CES) public data series. *Jobs needed each month to hold steady* is the number of jobs needed per month on average in a given year to maintain the same ratio of payroll jobs to the working-age population that prevailed at the end of the prior year (payroll jobs data come from the CES, and the size of the working-age population age 16 and older comes from the Current Population Survey public data series). A three-year rolling average of the working-age population in December is used because of large year-to-year variability in the population growth rate as measured by the CPS.

Figure 5B. Distribution of employment, by industry, selected years, 1979–2011 (and 2020 projections). Underlying data for 1979–2011 are from the Bureau of Labor Statistics Current Employment Statistics public data series. Underlying data for 2020 are from the Employment Projections program, Table 2.1, "Employment by Major Industry Sector."

Figure 5C. Distribution of employment, by firm size, 2011Q1. Underlying data are from the Bureau of Labor Statistics Business Employment Dynamics program, *National Firm Size Data—Supplemental Firm Size Class Tables*, Table F, "Distribution of Private Sector Employment by Firm Size Class, Not Seasonally Adjusted."

Figure 5D. Job gains, losses, and net employment change, by firm size, 2000–2011. Underlying data are from the Bureau of Labor Statistics Business Employment Dynamics program, *National Firm Size Data—Size Class 1 Tables*, Table 1, "Private Sector Firm-level Gross Job Gains and Job Losses: Seasonally Adjusted, Dynamic Method."

Figure 5E. Distribution of employment, by occupation, selected years, 1989–2011. Underlying data are from the Current Population Survey public data series, Historical Table A-13, "Employed and Unemployed Persons by Occupation, Not Seasonally Adjusted." Service occupations include health care support, protective service, food preparation and serving, building and grounds cleaning and maintenance, and personal care and service occupations.

Figure 5F. Good jobs as a share of total employment, all workers and by gender, and output per worker, selected years, 1979–2010. Good jobs shares are from Schmitt and Jones (2012), and output per worker is from the Bureau of Labor Statistics Labor Productivity and Costs program (unpublished Total Economy Productivity data provided to the authors upon request). Good jobs are defined as those that pay at least $18.50 per hour (the median male hourly wage in 1979 adjusted to 2010 dollars), have employer-provided health insurance where the employer pays at least some of the premium, and an employer-sponsored pension plan, including 401(k) and similar defined-contribution plans.

Figure 5G. Unemployment rate, 1948–2011. Underlying unemployment data are from the Current Population Survey public data series.

Figure 5H. Unemployment rate (actual and holding age distribution constant), 1979–2011. Underlying data are from the Current Population Survey public data series. The unemployment rate holding the age distribution constant since 1979 is the result of a simple exercise showing what the unemployment rate would be if the distribution of the labor force across age categories (ages 16–24, 25–34, 35–44, 45–54, and 55 and older) had not changed since January 1979, but the unemployment rates within each age category evolved as they actually did from January 1979 to December 2011.

Figure 5I. Unemployment rate, by race and ethnicity, 1979–2011. Underlying data are basic monthly Current Population Survey microdata. As with other CPS microdata analyses presented in the book, race/ethnicity categories are mutually exclusive (i.e., white non-Hispanic, black non-Hispanic, and Hispanic any race).

Figure 5J. Unemployment rates of foreign-born and native-born workers, 1994–2011. Underlying data are basic monthly Current Population Survey microdata.

Figure 5K. Share of unemployed people with unemployment insurance benefits, 1989–2011. Underlying data are from the Current Population Survey public data series and the U.S. Department of Labor's Unemployment Insurance Program Statistics, "Persons Claiming UI Benefits in Federal Programs (Expanded)" [Excel spreadsheet]. Extended benefits refer to those extended by Congress during downturns beyond the regular state-financed benefits. Shares are calculated by dividing the number of persons claiming regular benefits by the total number of unemployed persons, and by dividing the total number of persons claiming extended benefits or regular benefits by the total number of unemployed persons. Weekly unemployment insurance claims data are converted into monthly data from January 1989 to December 2011.

Figure 5L. Labor force participation rate, by age and gender, 1959–2011. Underlying data are from the Current Population Survey public data series.

Figure 5M. Employment-to-population ratio, age 25–54, by gender, 1989–2011. Underlying data are from the Current Population Survey public data series.

Figure 5N. Underemployment rate, by race and ethnicity, 2000–2011. Underlying data are basic monthly Current Population Survey microdata. As with other CPS microdata analyses presented in the book, race/ethnicity categories are mutually exclusive (i.e., white non-Hispanic, black non-Hispanic, and Hispanic any race).

Figure 5O. Long-term unemployment, 1948–2011. Underlying data are from the Current Population Survey public data series.

Figure 5P. Unemployment rate, average monthly and over-the-year, 2000–2010. Average monthly unemployment rate underlying data are from the Current Population Survey public data series, and over-the-year unemployment underlying data are from the U.S. Bureau of Labor Statistics *Work Experience of the Population* (annual economic news release).

Figure 5Q. Job-seekers ratio, Dec. 2000–Dec. 2011. Job openings data are from the U.S. Bureau of Labor Statistics Job Openings and Labor Turnover Survey, and unemployment data are from the Current Population Survey public data series.

Figure 5R. Voluntary quits, Dec. 2000–Dec. 2011. Underlying data are from the Bureau of Labor Statistics Job Openings and Labor Turnover Survey.

Figure 5S. Job change since the start of each of the last four recessions. Underlying data are from the Bureau of Labor Statistics Current Employment Statistics public data series. Data for each recession are indexed by the number of jobs in the first month of the recession. Monthly data span July 1989–December 2011.

Figure 5T. Job change since the start of each of the last four recoveries (all, private sector, and public sector). Underlying data are from the Bureau of Labor Statistics Current Employment Statistics public data series. Data for each recession are indexed by the number of jobs in the first month of the recession's recovery. Monthly data span July 1989–December 2011.

Figure 5U. Job change, by gender, in the Great Recession and its aftermath (Dec. 2007– Dec. 2011). Underlying data are from the Bureau of Labor Statistics Current Employment Statistics public data series. Data for each gender are indexed by the number of jobs held by workers of that gender in the first month of the recession.

Figure 5V. Simulated job change by gender in the Great Recession and its aftermath (Dec. 2007–Dec. 2011), controlling for industry. Underlying data are from the Bureau of Labor Statistics Current Employment Statistics public data series. The graph presents the results of an exercise showing how employment of men and women would have changed over the four-year period if, in December 2007, men and women had had the same industry distribution but if job changes by gender within each industry had evolved as they actually did between December 2007 and December 2011.

Figure 5W. Unemployed workers and job openings, by industry, 2011. Underlying data are from the Bureau of Labor Statistics Job Openings and Labor Turnover Survey and the Current Population Survey public data series.

Figure 5X. Unemployed workers, by occupation, 2007 and 2011. Underlying data are from basic monthly Current Population Survey microdata.

Figure 5Y. Unemployment rate, by education, 2007 and 2011. Underlying data are basic monthly Current Population Survey microdata.

Figure 5Z. Labor force status of involuntarily displaced workers, 1984–2010. Underlying data are from Farber (2011), Table 6, "Post-displacement Labor Force Status, 1984–2010."

Figure 5AA. Average decline in weekly earnings for involuntarily displaced full-time workers who found new work, 1984–2010. Underlying data are from Farber (2011), Table 16, "Proportional Change in Real Weekly Earnings, Full-Time Job Losers."

CHAPTER 6

Wealth
Unrelenting disparities

Preceding chapters have focused on what individuals and families bring in over a given time period, whether wages earned hourly or income received in a year. This chapter analyzes wealth. A family's (or individual's) wealth, or net worth, is the sum of assets, such as a home, bank account balances, stock holdings, and retirement funds (such as 401(k) plans and individual retirement accounts), minus liabilities, such as mortgages, credit card balances, outstanding medical bills, student loans, and other debts, at a point in time. As with wages and other income, wealth is a key determinant of a family's standard of living. Wealth makes it easier for families to invest in education and training, start a small business, or fund retirement. In addition, wealth—particularly liquid assets such as checking account balances, stocks, and bonds—can help families cope with financial emergencies related to unemployment or illness. More tangible forms of wealth, such as cars, computers, and homes, can directly affect a family's ability to participate fully in work, school, and community life.

Chapter 3 highlighted the class barriers evident in the strong correlation between family wealth in one generation and family wealth in subsequent generations in the United States. In the United States, children of poor parents are much more likely than other children to be poor as adults, and children of wealthy parents are much more likely than other children to be wealthy as adults. This lack of mobility violates a core American principal of equal opportunity for all. This chapter further investigates wealth in the United States, uncovering some important, if disturbing, findings.

The distribution of wealth in the United States is profoundly unequal—even more unequal than the highly skewed distributions of wages and income described in earlier chapters. In 2010, the wealthiest 1 percent of all households controlled a much larger share of national wealth (35.4 percent) than did the entire bottom 90 percent of households (which controlled just 23.3 percent of national wealth). The distribution of wealth has also become much more unequal over time. Between 1983 and 2010, nearly three-fourths (74.2 percent) of the total growth in household wealth accrued to the top 5 percent of households in the wealth distribution. For the bottom 60 percent of households, wealth *declined* from 1983 to 2010. The median household had 22.0 percent less wealth in 2010 than it did in 1983, with median household wealth dropping from $73,000 to $57,000 over those 27 years. In 2010, more than 1 in 5 households (22.5 percent) had either zero or negative wealth.

Racial and ethnic disparities in wealth are profound. The median net worth of black households was $4,900 in 2010, compared with $1,300 for Hispanic households and $97,000 for white households. Furthermore, about a third of black and Hispanic households (33.9 percent and 35.8 percent, respectively) had zero or negative wealth, compared with 18.6 percent of white households.

For all the talk of the "democratization of the stock market" since the 1980s, a surprisingly small share of households hold any stocks, including stocks held indirectly through retirement accounts and pension funds. In 2010, less than half (46.9 percent) of households owned any stock, and less than one-third (31.1 percent) of households owned more than $10,000 in stocks. The median black household and the median Hispanic household owned no stocks at all.

While stock market ups and downs garner much attention in the news media, housing equity is a far more important source of wealth for most households. In 2010, households in the middle fifth of the wealth distribution had an average net worth of $61,000, $39,300 of which was in home equity. This means that home equity made up nearly two-thirds (64.5 percent) of the wealth of "typical" households (those in the middle of the wealth distribution).

Therefore, though the destruction of home equity and other forms of wealth by the bursting of the housing bubble and resulting Great Recession affected households across the entire distribution, the wealth of middle-class households and those below was hit particularly hard. From 2007 to 2010 the average wealth of the top 1 percent of households dropped 15.6 percent, but median wealth dropped an astounding 47.1 percent. The middle fifth of households saw their housing equity drop 44.6 percent between 2007 and 2010, and in 2010 households in the bottom 40 percent of the wealth distribution had *negative* housing equity on average for the first time on record.

Table notes and figure notes at the end of this chapter provide documentation for the data, as well as information on methodology, used in the tables and figures that follow.

Net worth

Wealth, or net worth, is the sum of all assets minus the sum of all liabilities. Assets include resources such as homes, bank account balances, stock holdings, and funds in 401(k) plans and individual retirement accounts. Liabilities include mortgages, credit card debt, outstanding medical bills, student loan debt, and other debts. Calculations of net worth exclude assets held in defined-benefit pension plans because workers do not legally own these assets and thus do not benefit or suffer when these assets gain or lose value. For similar reasons, Social Security and Medicare are also excluded from net worth. (However, we later review the contributions of Social Security and defined-benefit pension plans to retirement security. Given the low levels of wealth held by most households, living standards in retirement greatly rely on implicit wealth from defined-benefit pension plans and Social Security.)

Net worth can be further subdivided into net nonfinancial (tangible) assets, and net financial assets. Net tangible assets are assets such as real estate and durable goods, minus mortgage debt. Net financial assets are assets such as stocks, bonds, mutual funds, and bank account balances, minus nonmortgage debt. **Figure 6A** shows average net worth per household, along with net tangible assets and net financial assets, from 1965 to 2012.

Figure 6A Average household net worth, net financial assets, and net tangible assets, 1965–2012 (2011 dollars)

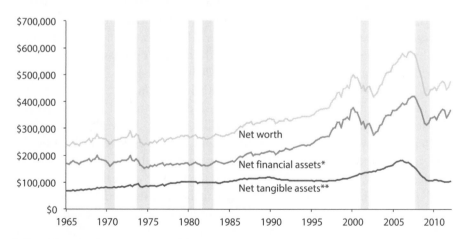

* Financial assets minus nonmortgage debt
** Housing and consumer durables minus home mortgages
Note: Data are quarterly and extend from the first quarter of 1965 to the first quarter of 2012. Shaded areas denote recessions.

Source: Authors' analysis of Federal Reserve Board Flow of Funds Accounts and Current Population Survey/ Housing Vacancy Survey, *Historical Tables* (Table 7)

For decades, the real average net worth of U.S. households grew at a relatively steady and modest pace—about 1.2 percent per year from 1965 to 1994. In the mid-1990s, net worth began to grow at a faster pace on average but also became increasingly volatile, as illustrated by two peaks (1999 and 2006) that were each followed by precipitous declines. During the first steep run-up in wealth, from 1994 to 1999, net worth, fueled by the dot-com bubble, grew 42.1 percent; as that bubble deflated, net worth declined 12.9 percent from 1999 to 2002. Net worth rebounded at a rapid pace from 2002 to 2006, but much of the increase was due to a growing housing bubble, which began inflating around 1997. After the housing bubble burst in 2006, net worth plummeted, dropping over 25 percent between 2006 and early 2009. Since 2009 it has rebounded slightly, growing over 12 percent between early 2009 and early 2012.

Net financial assets make up the majority of average net worth (though, as discussed later in the chapter, average net worth figures are skewed by the net worth of the very wealthy; most households have greater tangible assets, in particular housing value, than financial assets). Figure 6A shows that the trajectory of net financial assets closely mirrors that of overall net worth. However, between 1997 and 2005, growth in net worth was also bolstered by growth in tangible assets as the housing bubble inflated. Between 1997 and 2005 net tangible assets grew about 70 percent; after the housing bubble burst, they fell, dropping back to their pre-bubble levels by 2011.

The data underlying Figure 6A are from the Federal Reserve Board's Flow of Funds Accounts of the United States. These data are timely, but they do not allow for an analysis of how wealth is distributed across the population. We turn to the Survey of Consumer Finances (SCF) to conduct a distributional analysis, presented in the next set of tables and figures. This dataset, collected every three years by the Federal Reserve Board, is one of the country's primary sources of data on wealth. The latest data available are from 2010.

As mentioned, the distribution of wealth in the United States is dramatically more unequal than even the extremely unequal distributions of wages and income. **Table 6.1** shows the income distribution and the wealth distribution for 2010. It provides shares of total household income and wealth held by the top 1 percent, the next 9 percent (those between the 90th and 99th percentiles), and the bottom 90 percent of households in the income or wealth distributions. The 1 percent of households with the highest incomes received 17.2 percent of all income. At the same time, the 1 percent of households with the most wealth held 35.4 percent of all net worth. The entire bottom 90 percent of the income distribution received just 55.5 percent of all income, but that astoundingly small share dwarfs the share of wealth held by the bottom 90 percent of the wealth distribution, which was only 23.3 percent.

Table 6.1 Distribution of income compared with distribution of wealth, 2010

	Distribution of:	
	Household income	Household wealth (net worth)
Bottom 90%	55.5%	23.3%
90th–<99th percentile	27.3	41.3
Top 1%	17.2	35.4
All	100.0	100.0

Source: Wolff (2012)

The distribution of wealth has become more unequal over time, with the top 10 percent, and especially the top 5 percent, of the wealth distribution holding an increasing share of the country's total wealth. **Table 6.2** shows the share of wealth held by households in various segments of the wealth distribution. The top 5 percent of wealth holders have consistently held over half of all wealth, with their share increasing from 56.1 percent in 1983 to 63.1 percent in 2010. The bottom four-fifths of wealth holders have consistently held less than 20 percent of all wealth; their share decreased from 18.7 percent in 1983 to 11.1 percent in 2010, with *all* of that lost share migrating upward to the top 10 percent. The middle fifth of households held 2.6 percent of total wealth in 2010, its lowest recorded share. In 1983, middle-fifth households had 5.2 percent of wealth, which means their share of all wealth was cut in half between 1983 and 2010.

Table 6.3 shows overall average and median wealth, as well as average wealth by wealth group. As seen in Figure 6A, over the long run, *average* wealth grows along with an expanding economy, but also experiences short-run fluctuations due to business cycle dynamics, i.e., economic booms and busts. In 1983, average household wealth was $284,400; by 2007, it had roughly doubled to $563,800, its peak before the onset of the Great Recession. By 2010, average household wealth had dropped to $463,800, 17.7 percent below its 2007 level, but still 63.1 percent above its 1983 level and, as we saw in Figure 6A, it was again on an upward trajectory as the economy began to recover from the recession.

However, since all of the gains in wealth have gone to the top portion of the wealth distribution, *median* wealth, or the wealth of the typical household, has fared very poorly over the last three decades. Median wealth grew just 47.5 percent between 1983 and 2007, from $73,000 to $107,800, but with the housing bust and resulting Great Recession, all those gains and more were lost. Median wealth fell to $57,000 in 2010, meaning there was a 22.0 percent *decline* in the wealth of the typical household over the 27 years between 1983 and 2010. Over

Table 6.2 Change in wealth groups' shares of total wealth, 1962–2010

Wealth group*	1962	1983	1989	1998	2001	2007	2010	Change 1962–1983	Change 1983–2010
Bottom four-fifths	19.1%	18.7%	16.5%	16.6%	15.6%	15.0%	11.1%	-0.4	-7.6
Bottom	-0.7	-0.3	-1.5	-0.6	-0.4	-0.5	-1.2	0.4	-0.9
Second	1.0	1.2	0.8	0.8	0.7	0.7	0.2	0.2	-0.9
Middle	5.4	5.2	4.8	4.5	3.9	4.0	2.6	-0.2	-2.6
Fourth	13.4	12.6	12.3	11.9	11.3	10.9	9.4	-0.8	-3.2
Top fifth	81.0%	81.3%	83.5%	83.4%	84.4%	85.0%	88.9%	0.4	7.6
80th–<90th percentile	14.0	13.1	13.0	12.5	12.9	12.0	12.2	-0.9	-0.9
90th–<95th percentile	12.4	12.1	11.6	11.5	12.3	11.2	13.6	-0.2	1.5
Top 5%	54.6	56.1	58.9	59.4	59.2	61.8	63.1	-0.7	7.0
95th–<99th percentile	21.2	22.3	21.6	21.3	25.8	27.3	27.7	1.2	5.3
Top 1%	33.4	33.8	37.4	38.1	33.4	34.6	35.4	0.3	1.7
Total	100.0%	100.0%	100.0%	100.0%	100.0%	100.0%	100.0%		

* Wealth defined as net worth (household assets minus debts)
Source: Wolff (2012)

the same period, average wealth of the top 5 percent of households grew 83.1 percent, from nearly $3.2 million in 1983 to over $5.8 million in 2010.

Declines in average wealth due to the housing bust and resulting Great Recession were bigger in percentage terms for the bottom four-fifths of households than for groups in the top fifth of the wealth distribution. For example, between 2007 and 2010, middle-fifth household wealth dropped 45.3 percent while wealth of the top fifth dropped 14.0 percent. This is unsurprising given that households with less wealth tend to have a much larger share of their wealth in their homes. This feature of the wealth distribution, which will be discussed later in this chapter, underscores how the expansion and collapse of the housing bubble caused enormous damage to the balance sheets of middle-class households.

Table 6.3 shows that average household wealth grew $179,400 between 1983 and 2010, from $284,400 to $463,800. **Figure 6B** spotlights the increase in wealth inequality over this period by showing which groups in the wealth

Table 6.3 Change in average wealth, by wealth group, 1962–2010 (thousands of 2010 dollars)

Wealth group*	1962	1983	1989	1998	2001	2007	2010	Change			
								1962–1983	1983–2007	2007–2010	1983–2010
Average	$194.2	$284.4	$325.8	$361.5	$468.1	$563.8	$463.8	46.5%	98.2%	-17.7%	63.1%
Median	51.9	73.0	78.2	81.2	90.5	107.8	57.0	40.7	47.5	-47.1	-22.0
Bottom four-fifths	$46.2	$66.4	$67.1	$75.1	$91.1	$105.5	$64.2	43.6%	59.0%	-39.1%	-3.2%
Bottom	-7.1	-4.3	-24.6	-11.8	-10.1	-14.1	-27.5	—	—	—	—
Second	9.2	16.8	13.7	14.9	17.2	18.7	5.5	81.9	11.5	-70.7	-67.3
Middle	52.7	74.2	78.7	81.6	92.3	111.5	61.0	40.8	50.1	-45.3	-17.9
Fourth	130.1	178.7	200.7	215.8	265.1	306.0	216.9	37.4	71.2	-29.1	21.4
Top fifth	$785.8	$1,156.5	$1,360.6	$1,507.3	$1,975.8	$2,396.7	$2,061.6	47.2%	107.2%	-14.0%	78.3%
80th–<90th percentile	271.4	372.9	422.6	461.3	603.7	675.1	567.0	37.4	81.1	-16.0	52.1
90th–<95th percentile	480.3	690.5	756.6	834.0	1,154.2	1,263.4	1,263.4	43.8	83.0	0.0	83.0
Top 5%	2,120.2	3,189.9	3,840.8	4,272.5	5,541.7	6,973.2	5,841.9	50.5	118.6	-16.2	83.1
95th–<99th percentile	1,027.6	1,587.7	1,757.0	1,928.0	3,020.3	3,845.0	3,192.5	54.5	142.2	-17.0	101.1
Top 1%	6,490.6	9,598.6	12,176.0	13,650.2	15,627.3	19,486.1	16,439.4	47.9	103.0	-15.6	71.3

* Wealth defined as net worth (household assets minus debts)

Source: Wolff (2012)

Figure 6B Share of total household wealth growth accruing to various wealth groups, 1983–2010

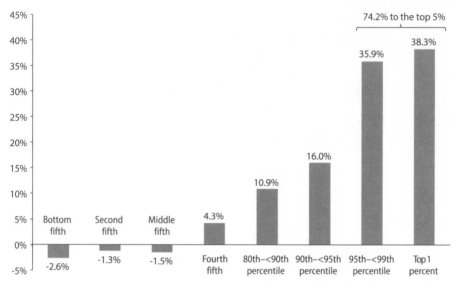

Source: Wolff (2012)

distribution actually claimed that increase in average household wealth. Nearly 40 percent (38.3 percent) of the increase in average household wealth between 1983 and 2010 accrued to the top 1 percent of the wealth distribution, and nearly three-fourths (74.2 percent) accrued to the top 5 percent of the distribution. For the bottom 60 percent of households, wealth *declined* from 1983 to 2010.

Figure 6C presents increasing wealth inequality in another way. The figure shows the ratio of the average wealth of the top 1 percent of households in the wealth distribution to the wealth of the median household. In 1962, the ratio was 125-to-1. In other words, the wealth of the wealthiest 1 percent of households averaged 125 times the wealth of the median household. However, that large disparity is dwarfed by today's wealth gap; in 2010, the wealthiest 1 percent of households had on average 288 times more wealth than the median household.

With **Figure 6D** we extend our analysis beyond the top 1 percent to the net worth of the "ultra wealthy," the 400 wealthiest people in the United States as captured in the "Forbes 400." The average annual net worth of the top 400 rises as asset bubbles inflate, drops when asset bubbles burst, and quickly bounces back. The rise of the dot-com bubble at the end of the 1990s and its fall, and then the rise of the housing bubble in the mid-2000s and its fall, are apparent in the figure. While the net worth of the ultra-wealthy dropped from 2007 to 2009, it began

Figure 6C Ratio of average top 1% household wealth to median wealth, 1962–2010

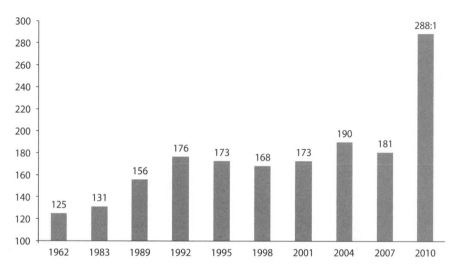

Source: Wolff (2012)

Figure 6D Average annual net worth of "Forbes 400" wealthiest individuals, 1982–2011 (billions of 2011 dollars)

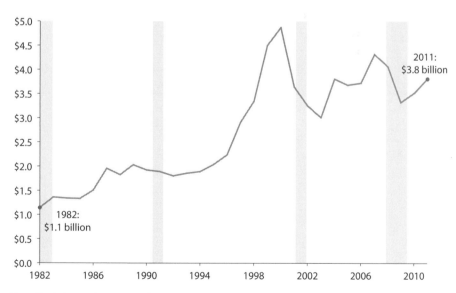

Note: Shaded areas denote recessions.

Source: Authors' analysis of Broom and Shay (2000) and *Forbes* (various years)

to rise again in 2010 and continued to rise in 2011. Overall, from 1982 to 2011, average wealth of the top 400 increased by 234 percent, from $1.1 billion to $3.8 billion. In 2011, the collective net worth of these 400 individuals was $1.5 trillion.

The price of admission to the top 400 has also increased substantially; in 2011, the minimum for being in the top 400 was $1.1 billion, nearly three times the $368.8 million threshold in 1982. And, perhaps unsurprisingly given the rising wealth inequality already documented in this chapter, gains were even greater for the wealthiest of the ultra-wealthy; in 1982, the net worth of the wealthiest person in the top 400 was $9.9 billion, but by 2011 it was six times higher, at $59.0 billion.

At the extreme other end of the wealth spectrum are a significant share of households with low, zero, or negative net worth. **Table 6.4** reports the share of all households with zero or negative net worth, and net worth of less than $10,000, from 1962 to 2010. In 2010, more than 1 in 5 households (22.5 percent) had zero or negative net worth, while another 12.6 percent had net worth of more than zero but less than $10,000. Thus, more than one-third (35.1 percent) of U.S. households had wealth holdings so low that they were extremely vulnerable to financial distress and insecurity. The share of households in this precarious position had held fairly steady for two-and-a-half decades, increasing 0.5 percentage points, from 27.7 percent to 28.2 percent, between 1983 and 2007. However, it

Table 6.4 Share of households with low net worth, 1962–2010 (2010 dollars)

	Zero or negative net worth	Positive but less than $10,000 net worth	Total net worth less than $10,000
1962	23.6%	8.4%	32.0%
1983	15.5	12.2	27.7
1989	17.9	11.3	29.2
1998	18.0	10.5	28.5
2001	17.6	10.5	28.0
2007	18.6	9.6	28.2
2010	22.5	12.6	35.1
Change			
1962–1983	-8.1	3.8	-4.3
1983–2007	3.1	-2.6	0.5
2007–2010	3.9	3.0	6.9

Source: Wolff (2012)

increased dramatically—by 6.9 percentage points—from 2007 to 2010, during the Great Recession and its aftermath.

The racial divide in net worth

The legacy of economic disadvantage for racial and ethnic minorities is apparent in persistent and profound racial and ethnic disparities in wealth, disparities that are far greater than racial and ethnic disparities in wages and incomes. Here we examine disparities in net worth by race and ethnicity; later in this chapter we examine disparities in assets and liabilities.

Table 6.5 shows that in 2010 the median net worth of black households was $4,900, just 5.0 percent of the median net worth of white households, $97,000. In 2010, the median net worth of Hispanic households was an even lower $1,300, just 1.4 percent of median white household net worth.

Persistent, large disparities also appear in shares of households with low net worth. In 2010, black and Hispanic households were nearly twice as likely as white households to have zero or negative net worth; 33.9 percent of black

Table 6.5 Median household wealth, and share of households with zero or negative wealth, by race and ethnicity, 1983–2010

	1983	1989	1998	2001	2007	2010	Change 1983–2007	Change 2007–2010
Median wealth* (thousands of 2010 dollars)								
Black	$6.4	$2.9	$13.4	$13.1	$9.7	$4.9	52.8%	-49.7%
Hispanic	—	—	4.0	3.6	9.6	1.3	—	-86.3
White	95.7	113.6	109.3	131.0	151.1	97.0	57.8	-35.8
Median wealth ratios (expressed as a percent)								
Black to white	6.7%	2.6%	12.2%	10.0%	6.4%	5.0%	—	—
Hispanic to white	—	—	3.7	2.8	6.3	1.4	—	—
Share of households with zero or negative net wealth								
Black	34.1%	40.7%	27.4%	30.9%	33.4%	33.9%	-0.7	0.5
Hispanic	—	—	36.2	35.3	33.5	35.8	—	2.3
White	11.3	12.1	14.8	13.1	14.5	18.6	3.2	4.0

* Wealth defined as net worth (household assets minus debts)

Source: Wolff (2012)

Figure 6E Median household wealth, by race and ethnicity, 1983–2010 (2010 dollars)

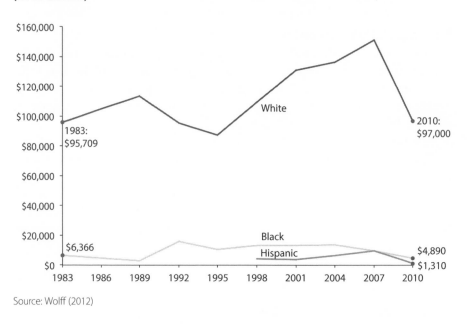

Source: Wolff (2012)

households and 35.8 percent of Hispanic households had zero or negative net worth, compared with 18.6 percent of white households.

These persistent wealth disparities are apparent in **Figure 6E**, which presents median wealth by race and ethnicity between 1983 and 2010. The figure also shows the damage to all groups' wealth during the Great Recession and its aftermath. Between 2007 and 2010, median white household wealth dropped $54,100. This was more in absolute terms than the $8,300 decline in median Hispanic household wealth and the $4,800 decline in median black household wealth. However, black and Hispanic households started from much lower levels of wealth and experienced considerably larger percentage declines in wealth. Median white household wealth declined 35.8 percent between 2007 and 2010, while median black household wealth dropped 49.7 percent and median Hispanic household wealth was all but wiped out over this period, dropping 86.3 percent.

Assets

As mentioned previously, net worth or wealth is determined by two components—assets and liabilities. This section further investigates assets, while the following section will further investigate liabilities. There are myriad assets households may possess, including houses, stocks, bonds, and bank account balances.

The distribution of assets varies significantly by the type of asset. Some assets, such as stocks and bonds, are highly concentrated among a relatively small share of households. Other assets, such as houses, are more widely held. The distributional differences of these assets are strongly related to overall wealth holdings. Wealthy households, for example, tend to hold a much higher percentage of their wealth in financial assets such as stocks and bonds, whereas less-affluent households, particularly those in the middle of the wealth distribution, typically hold most of their wealth in housing equity. This difference is one reason middle-class households were disproportionately affected when the housing bubble burst.

Table 6.6 shows that while the distribution across wealth groups of different types of household assets varies, it always strongly favors those at the top. In 2010 the wealthiest 5 percent of households owned about two-thirds (67.1 percent) of all stock, and an even larger share (79.9 percent) of stock not held in retirement accounts. Households in the bottom 80 percent of the wealth distribution held just 8.3 percent of all stock, and even less, 3.5 percent, of stock not held in retirement accounts. In comparison, housing equity is less skewed. However, the top 5 percent of households still held a highly disproportionate share (34.3 percent) of housing equity, a bigger share than the 29.9 percent held by the entire bottom 80 percent of households.

Table 6.6 Wealth groups' shares of household assets, by asset type, 2010

Wealth group	Stocks*	Stocks not held in retirement accounts**	Housing equity	Total assets
Bottom 95%	32.9%	20.1%	65.7%	44.8%
Bottom 80%	8.3	3.5	29.9	19.5
80th–<90th percentile	10.9	6.4	19.8	12.4
90th–<95th percentile	13.7	10.1	16.0	12.9
Top 5%	67.1	79.9	34.3	55.2
95th–<99th percentile	32.1	32.5	21.7	24.9
Top 1%	35.0	47.4	12.6	30.4
99th–<99.5th percentile	11.3	13.2	5.0	7.9
99.5th–100th percentile	23.7	34.3	7.7	22.4
Total	**100.0**	**100.0**	**100.0**	**100.0**

* Includes direct ownership of stock shares and indirect ownership through mutual funds, trusts, and IRAs, Keogh plans, 401(k) plans, and other retirement accounts
** Includes direct ownership of stock shares and indirect ownership through mutual funds and trusts

Source: Wolff (2012)

Table 6.7 shows how the various wealth groups' holdings of different types of assets have changed over time. In 2010, the wealthiest 1 percent of households owned an average of $3.5 million in total stocks (including stocks held in retirement accounts). The next 9 percent (those between the 90th and 99th percentiles) owned an average of $509,200 in total stocks. In comparison, the middle fifth of households held just $8,900 in stocks on average, and the bottom two-fifths of households held $1,700. These data confirm that stock ownership is not at all pervasive in or below the middle class, even taking into account stocks held indirectly in retirement plans. *Excluding* stocks held in retirement accounts, the typical wealth holder—represented by households in the middle fifth—owns next to nothing in stock, just $1,700. Stock holdings are further investigated later in the chapter.

In 2010, the wealthiest 1 percent of households held an average of $1.3 million in housing equity (housing assets minus mortgages). This was 24.7 percent less than their $1.7 million in housing equity in 2007, but still well above the $1.1 million in housing equity they held in 2001. Households lower in the wealth distribution fared much worse when the housing bubble burst. The middle fifth held just $39,300 in housing equity on average in 2010, 44.6 percent less than in 2007 and 15.5 percent less than the $46,500 average home equity they had 27 years earlier, in 1983. In 2010, households in the bottom two-fifths of the wealth distribution had *negative* housing equity. This means that on average, homeowners in the bottom two-fifths were "underwater" on their home loans in 2010, i.e., they owed more on their homes than their homes were worth. Housing is further investigated later in the chapter.

Table 6.8 shows average and median household assets (stocks, housing equity, and total assets) by race and ethnicity from 1983 to 2010. As shown in Table 6.7, households in the bottom 80 percent of the wealth distribution generally hold little in stocks, even including stocks held in retirement accounts. Table 6.8 shows that in 2010, the median black and median Hispanic households held *no* stocks, even including stocks held in retirement accounts, while the median white household held just $1,200 in stocks. Table 6.9, discussed later, provides a more direct look at the startlingly low share of households with any significant stock holdings, showing that the strong public narrative of the "democratization" of the stock market since the 1980s is at odds with the facts.

Although housing equity, as already mentioned, is more widely held than other forms of wealth such as stocks, the median black household and the median Hispanic household had zero housing equity over the entire period, while the median white household had $45,000 of housing equity in 2010 (a drop of more than one-third—37.1 percent—from their $71,500 in housing equity in 2007).

The median is a better indication of the "typical" household in a given category than the average, since the median is the value at which half of households

Table 6.7 Average household assets, by wealth group and asset type, 1962–2010 (thousands of 2010 dollars)

Asset type	Wealth fifth			Breakdown of top fifth		
	Bottom two	Middle	Fourth	80th–<90th percentile	90th–<99th percentile	Top 1%
Stocks						
1962	$0.4	$1.5	$5.9	$18.4	$164.8	$3,222.7
1983	0.5	2.1	6.1	16.1	135.0	2,092.5
1989	0.8	5.0	11.9	34.0	173.6	1,579.5
1998	2.2	12.3	36.9	106.3	389.9	3,378.2
2001	2.3	14.7	50.8	162.3	630.7	4,393.6
2007	1.8	10.4	35.8	111.1	534.9	4,281.0
2010	1.7	8.9	29.5	108.8	509.2	3,499.8
Stocks not held in retirement accounts						
1989	$0.3	$1.8	$4.2	$17.1	$87.7	$932.4
1998	0.5	3.5	13.7	50.3	256.6	3,245.8
2001	0.6	4.9	19.4	79.6	387.7	3,907.5
2007	0.4	3.0	14.3	49.5	346.4	3,701.3
2010	0.2	1.7	8.3	38.6	283.2	2,839.4
Housing equity						
1962	$3.5	$29.9	$59.7	$84.0	$102.5	$276.0
1983	5.4	46.5	93.6	141.2	233.1	683.6
1989	4.3	48.5	110.5	174.7	267.6	734.5
1998	5.4	48.0	98.0	149.7	262.0	737.4
2001	6.2	54.1	119.3	199.6	357.3	1,120.5
2007	8.0	71.0	159.7	273.1	535.6	1,731.4
2010	-0.1	39.3	114.6	204.1	431.9	1,303.5
Total assets						
1962	$20.9	$88.1	$165.8	$306.0	$770.1	$6,728.6
1983	23.0	109.1	223.5	438.7	1,180.3	10,145.9
1989	26.7	124.2	260.0	488.2	1,322.7	12,772.7
1998	34.1	142.9	279.2	549.6	1,495.2	14,028.3
2001	35.0	154.5	339.6	702.2	2,134.2	16,028.4
2007	50.2	210.3	422.6	801.3	2,652.3	19,990.2
2010	46.8	149.1	303.0	697.0	2,357.6	17,017.7

Source: Wolff (2012)

Table 6.8 Average and median household assets, by race/ethnicity and asset type, 1983–2010 (thousands of 2010 dollars)

	Median			Average		
	White	Black	Hispanic	White	Black	Hispanic
Stock						
1983	$0.0	$0.0	$0.0	$33.2	$0.4	$0.1
1989	0.0	0.0	0.0	35.4	2.7	1.7
1998	0.0	0.0	0.0	95.3	10.3	10.8
2001	3.1	0.0	0.0	164.3	18.0	14.6
2007	1.1	0.0	0.0	144.7	10.1	13.9
2010	1.2	0.0	0.0	129.9	12.3	10.8
1983–2007	—	—	—	335.5%	2,225.4%	12,132.4%
2007–2010	14.1%	—	—	-10.3%	21.9%	-22.3%
Housing equity						
1983	$50.7	$0.0	$0.0	$80.9	$28.7	$35.2
1989	51.0	0.0	0.0	95.9	33.7	33.1
1998	43.7	0.0	0.0	88.2	27.7	38.5
2001	57.9	0.0	0.0	118.4	28.4	35.2
2007	71.5	0.0	0.0	164.9	54.7	77.9
2010	45.0	0.0	0.0	124.6	39.4	39.7
1983–2007	41.2%	—	—	103.8%	90.4%	121.0%
2007–2010	-37.1%	—	—	-24.4%	-27.8%	-49.1%
Total assets						
1983	$125.3	$14.2	$10.5	$351.9	$73.0	$71.5
1989	164.2	8.4	3.8	458.3	87.1	99.1
1998	173.6	28.7	18.9	525.0	115.2	144.8
2001	200.0	42.1	10.2	647.9	120.9	138.4
2007	253.2	44.7	42.1	791.6	200.4	270.8
2010	205.0	28.1	20.0	702.5	136.1	153.9
1983–2007	102.2%	215.1%	301.1%	124.9%	174.5%	279.0%
2007–2010	-19.0%	-37.2%	-52.5%	-11.3%	-32.1%	-43.2%

Source: Wolff (2012)

have more and half have less. However, because median housing equity for black and Hispanic households is zero over the entire period, we turn to averages to provide some sense of how housing wealth has changed over time for these groups.

The average black household had $39,400 in housing equity in 2010, very close to the housing equity of the average Hispanic household ($39,700), and slightly less than a third of the housing equity of the average white household ($124,600). Between 2007 and 2010, the average black household lost 27.8 percent in housing equity, compared with a loss of 24.4 percent for the average white household. The average Hispanic household saw its home equity cut almost in half (falling 49.1 percent) between 2007 and 2010.

In 2010, the median black household held $28,100 in total assets, more than the $20,000 in total assets of the median Hispanic household but significantly less than the $205,000 in total assets of the median white household.

Stocks

This subsection and the next will look in more depth at two major asset categories, stocks and housing, respectively. While the stock market has experienced ups and downs throughout the last 50 years, stocks have been extremely volatile in the last two decades, as evident in **Figure 6F**, in which the two recent bubbles are unmistakable. The inflation-adjusted value of the Standard & Poor's composite index of the 500 largest U.S. firms (the S&P 500) increased 230 percent between 1989 and 2000, then lost over a third of its value between 2000 and 2003, after the dot-com bubble burst. The market regained more than 60 percent of those losses

Figure 6F U.S. stock market, 1955–2011

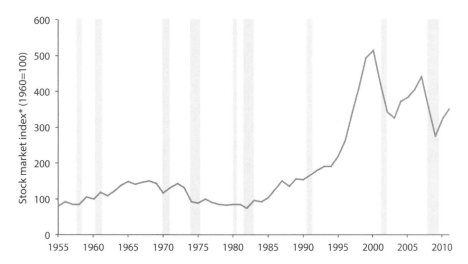

* Standard and Poor's 500 stock price index adjusted for inflation using CPI-U-RS and indexed to 1960=100.
Note: Shaded areas denote recessions.

Source: Authors' analysis of the *Economic Report of the President* (Council of Economic Advisers 2012)

by 2007, only to lose those gains and more during the steep decline from 2007 to 2009. The market began to climb again in 2009 and by 2011 had regained nearly half of what it lost between 2007 and 2009.

The strong rebound in stocks since 2009 amidst persistently high unemployment (see Chapter 5) highlights the disconnect between Wall Street's financial markets and Main Street's employers and workers. Despite minute-by-minute dissection of the stock market in the news media, the share of the population owning stock is surprisingly low, even when including shares purchased indirectly through retirement accounts. This means that the stock market has little or no direct financial importance to the majority of U.S. households—which is perhaps particularly surprising given the public discourse on how the stock market has "democratized" (the term implying stock holdings are no longer dominated by a tiny elite) since the 1980s.

As **Table 6.9** shows, even with the profound run-up in stocks in the latter half of the 1990s, in 2001 just over half (51.9 percent) of U.S. households held any stock, *including* stocks held in retirement plans, and just over a third (37.8 percent) had total stock holdings of $10,000 or more. In 2010, under half (46.9 percent) of all households had any stock holdings, and less than a third (31.1 percent) had stock holdings of $10,000 or more.

Stocks held outside of retirement accounts are a liquid asset; they can quickly be turned into cash without incurring significant losses. Just 14.3 percent of households owned $10,000 or more of this type of asset in 2010. Conversely, retirement stock holdings are largely nonliquid; premature withdrawals from IRAs and 401(k) accounts carry stiff tax penalties. Only around one-fourth (25.3 percent) of households had $10,000 or more in retirement stock holdings in 2010.

Table 6.9 Share of households owning stock, 1989–2010*

	1989	1998	2001	2007	2010
Any stock holdings (total)	31.7%	48.2%	51.9%	49.1%	46.9%
Stocks not held in retirement accounts	20.1	28.3	31.5	26.0	21.7
Stocks held in retirement accounts	19.5	26.0	41.4	40.2	40.0
Stock holdings of $10,000 or more (2010 dollars)	26.3%	30.1%	37.8%	32.4%	31.1%
Stocks not held in retirement accounts	16.1	20.3	22.0	17.6	14.3
Stocks held in retirement accounts	15.9	15.0	28.4	24.2	25.3

* Percentages in this table are shares of all U.S. households.

Source: Wolff (2012)

Figure 6G Wealth groups' shares of total household stock wealth, 1983–2010

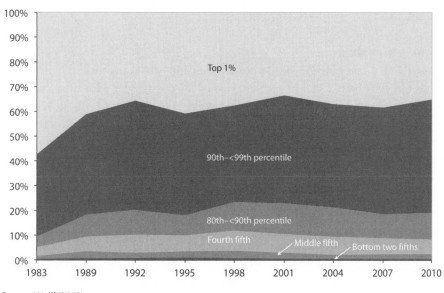

Source: Wolff (2012)

The imbalanced distribution of stock assets has persisted over time, as seen in **Figure 6G**. From 1989 to 2007, the wealthiest 1 percent of households never held less than one-third of all stock wealth. The top fifth of households consistently held about 90 percent of stock wealth, leaving approximately 10 percent for the bottom four-fifths of households. Because these data include stocks held in pension plans and retirement accounts, the shares capture the effect of the broad shift from defined-benefit pension plans to defined-contribution pension plans (a shift discussed both in Chapter 4 and later in this chapter). This figure shows that the vast "democratization of the stock market" since the 1980s—wherein the masses gained significant shares of the market through investment vehicles such as mutual funds, IRAs, and 401(k)s—*never actually happened.*

Housing

While stock market fluctuations garner much attention, housing equity is a far more important form of wealth for most households. In 2010, households in the middle fifth of the wealth distribution had an average net worth of $61,000 (Table 6.3), and $39,300 of that was in home equity (Table 6.7). In other words, home equity constituted nearly two-thirds (64.5 percent) of the wealth of households with "typical" wealth levels (i.e., those in the middle of the wealth distribution). Homeownership has long been associated with solid footing on the economic ladder. However, the housing boom and bust made that association more tenuous. This section examines homeownership and the effect of the housing meltdown on household wealth.

Homeownership

Figure 6H shows changes in the homeownership rate between 1965 and 2011. In 1965, 63 percent of homes were owned by the people who lived in them. The homeownership rate fluctuated somewhat in the following 30 years, including sharp increases in the late 1970s and declines in the early 1980s, but never exceeded 65.6 percent. But in the mid-1990s, homeownership rates began to rise dramatically, increasing from 64.0 percent in 1994 to 69.0 percent in 2004. Then, after the housing bust in 2006, the homeownership rate registered an unprecedented decline, falling to 66.1 percent in 2011.

As with other measures related to wealth, homeownership rates vary dramatically by income and demographics. **Figure 6I** shows, unsurprisingly, that higher-income households are more likely to own their homes. In 2009 (the most recent data available for this measure), 88.8 percent of households in the top fourth of the income distribution were homeowners, compared with just 47.0 percent in the bottom fourth. **Figure 6J** shows homeownership rates by race and ethnicity

Figure 6H Annual homeownership rate, 1965–2011

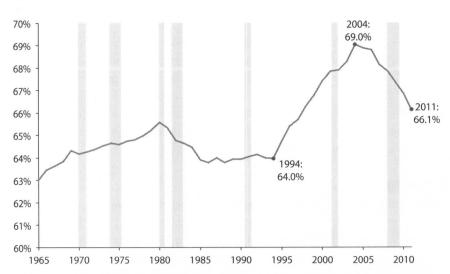

Note: The homeownership rate is the share of occupied housing units owned by their occupants. Shaded areas denote recessions.

Source: Current Population Survey/Housing Vacancy Survey, *Historical Tables* (Table 7)

Figure 6I Homeownership rate, by household income group, 2009

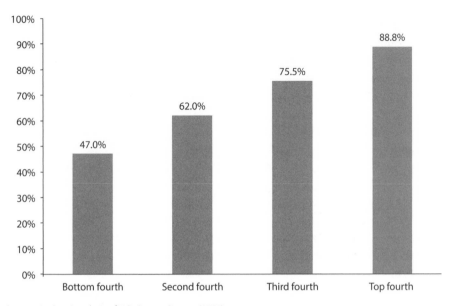

Source: Authors' analysis of U.S. Census Bureau (2009)

Figure 6J Homeownership rate, by race and ethnicity, 1975–2011

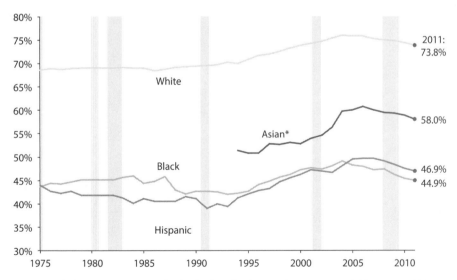

* Asian includes Native Hawaiian/Pacific Islander. Data for this population are unavailable prior to 1994.
Note: Data are unavailable from 1979 to 1982, and are substituted for by the 1978/1983 average. Shaded areas denote recessions.

Source: Current Population Survey (CPS) Annual Social and Economic Supplement and CPS/Housing Vacancy Survey *Annual Statistics: 2011* (Table 22)

from 1975 to 2011. In 2011, nearly three-fourths (73.8 percent) of white households, more than half (58.0 percent) of Asian households, less than half (44.9 percent) of black households, and less than half (46.9 percent) of Hispanic households owned their homes. Minority homeownership rates rose more than the white homeownership rate as the housing bubble inflated and fell further when it collapsed, with black households hit particularly hard; the black homeownership rate fell from 49.1 percent in 2004 to 44.9 percent in 2011.

The housing meltdown

As Table 6.7 showed, the collapse of the housing bubble had an enormous impact on the home equity of homeowners. **Figure 6K** shows the change in home prices from 1953 through the first quarter of 2012. The dramatic run-up in home prices from the mid-1990s to 2006 is striking, with annual increases from mid-2003 through mid-2005 in the double- or near-double-digits. However, this was ignored by central bankers and others responsible for the economic health of the country, who did nothing to halt the bubble's expansion. Home prices peaked in early 2006. Then the bubble burst and home prices began falling sharply, losing 35.7 percent between the first quarter of 2006 and the first quarter of 2009 and another 11.1 percent between the first quarter of 2009 and the first quarter of 2012. By early 2012, with home prices back at their 1998 values, it was likely

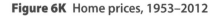

Figure 6K Home prices, 1953–2012

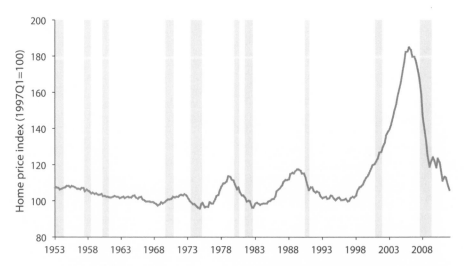

Note: Data are quarterly and extend from the first quarter of 1953 through the first quarter of 2012. Shaded areas denote recessions.

Source: Shiller (2012)

that the housing bubble had fully deflated and home prices were back on their long-run trajectory.

As mentioned earlier, home equity is the current market value of a home minus the outstanding balances of mortgages (including home equity loans). **Figure 6L** shows the ratio of homeowners' equity to the value of their homes, i.e., the share of home value that homeowners own outright. This share was fairly stable through the 1970s and 1980s, averaging 68.2 percent from 1969 through 1989, though it did decline somewhat throughout the 1980s. Around 1989, the share began a substantial decline, and had fallen to just under 58 percent by the middle of 1997. Homeowners' share of overall home value then fluctuated around 60 percent until early 2006, the peak of the housing bubble. This means that as home prices escalated dramatically between 1997 and 2006, the share of home value that homeowners owned did not. This is largely because homeowners increasingly took out home equity loans (as will be shown later in Figure 6O) and because homebuyers were increasingly likely to provide a relatively small down payment.

Underlying this activity was the belief—fueled by the news media and unchallenged by central bankers or others in charge of the country's economic health—that home prices would continue to rise or, at worst, level off after rising so spectacularly. Through home equity loans, homeowners used their accumulated equity to finance

Figure 6L Total homeowner equity as a share of total home values, 1969–2011

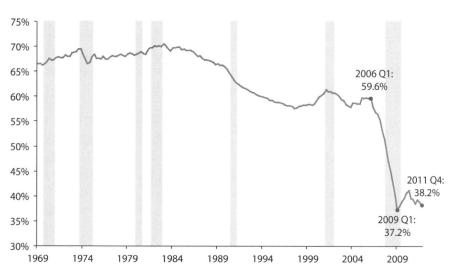

Note: Data are quarterly and extend from the first quarter of 1969 through the fourth quarter of 2011. Shaded areas denote recessions.

Source: Authors' analysis of Federal Reserve Board Flow of Funds Accounts

spending during a time of stagnating incomes and wages (as discussed in chapters 2 and 4). Families scrambled to get into the housing market because they thought buying a home would be a smart investment and that they would be priced out of the market if they waited. At the same time, barriers to homeownership were lowered for many homebuyers previously excluded from the market due to credit risk factors such as low income, a small down payment, or a troubled credit history. These and other buyers were targeted with new mortgage products, such as subprime mortgages with higher interest rates, and adjustable-rate mortgages with rates that escalated after initial terms.

Borrowers took out large home loans under the widespread belief that home prices would continue to rise and they could use their accumulating equity to refinance down the road. This false sense of security was never corrected by prominent policymakers, who should have used their regulatory powers to keep the housing bubble from inflating in the first place and, barring that, alerted Americans to the risks associated with the obvious financial market bubble.

Housing values began to fall in 2006, but home equity loans and mortgages did not, propelling a sharp decline in home equity as a share of home value, from 59.6 percent in the first quarter of 2006 to 37.2 percent in the first quarter of 2009. The ratio of home equity to value has since made up very little of that lost ground, and was at 38.2 percent in the fourth quarter of 2011. This means that creditors, including banks, own far more of the nation's housing stock than people do. As discussed earlier in this chapter, home equity is the primary source of wealth for a large majority of households, and therefore this decline in home equity has severely weakened the economic security of many, if not most, homeowners.

When housing prices began to drop in 2006, refinancing became more difficult as home equity fell, and mortgage delinquencies began to climb. **Figure 6M** shows the number of foreclosures per 1,000 owner-occupied dwellings from 2000 through 2011. From 2000 to 2005, there were an average of 2.4 foreclosures per 1,000 owner-occupied dwellings each quarter. Foreclosures rose steeply as home prices fell, reaching a peak of 7.5 foreclosures per 1,000 owner-occupied dwellings in the second quarter of 2009—more than triple the rate before the housing bubble burst. Overall, there were more than a million foreclosures in the first half of 2009. By the fourth quarter of 2011, the rate of foreclosures had dropped to 3.8 per 1,000 owner-occupied households, still far higher than before the housing bust. Therefore, while housing prices are no longer dropping, foreclosures remain elevated, underscoring that the fallout from the rise and fall of the housing bubble is far from over.

Retirement insecurity

Most Americans working today will enjoy less retirement security than their parents, a historic reversal that predates the Great Recession. According to the Center

Figure 6M Foreclosures per 1,000 owner-occupied dwellings, 2000–2011

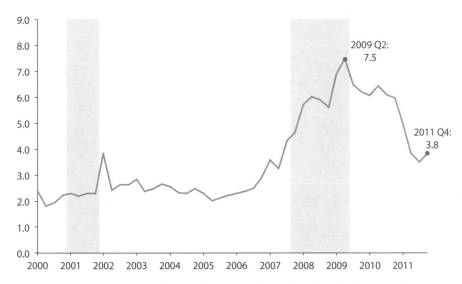

Note: Data are quarterly and extend from the first quarter of 2000 through the fourth quarter of 2011. Shaded areas denote recessions.

Source: Authors' analysis of Federal Reserve Bank of New York (2012) and Current Population Survey/ Housing Vacancy Survey, *Historical Tables* (Table 8)

for Retirement Research at Boston College, 41 percent of early baby boomers now entering retirement are at risk of a significant drop in living standards in retirement, even if they draw down all their savings, including home equity. The outlook is even worse for late baby boomers (48 percent of whom are at risk) and Gen Xers (56 percent of whom are at risk) (Munnell, Webb, and Golub-Sass 2009). This increase in retirement insecurity is driven in large part by the gradual increase in the official Social Security full retirement age (from age 65 for those born in 1937 or earlier to age 67 for those born in 1960 or later), which is equivalent to an across-the-board benefit cut for workers who retire at any given age, and the shift in the private sector from traditional defined-benefit pensions to 401(k)-style defined-contribution plans.

Though participation in employer-sponsored plans has stagnated at or below 50 percent for decades, when defined-benefit pensions were the norm many workers were still able to accrue substantial benefits over their working lives. However, the share of workers in employer-sponsored plans who were enrolled in defined-benefit pensions dropped from 88 percent in 1983 to 32 percent by 2010, while the share enrolled in defined-contribution plans rose from 38 percent to 81 percent in the same period (**Figure 6N**). Of households approaching or entering into

Figure 6N Enrollment in defined-benefit versus defined-contribution pension plans among workers with pension coverage, 1983 and 2010

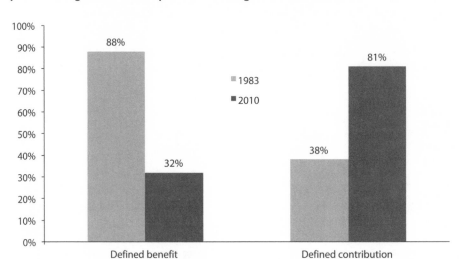

Note: Shares in a given year add up to more than 100 percent because some workers are enrolled in both types of plans. Of workers with pension coverage, 26 percent were enrolled in both types of plans in 1983, compared with 13 percent in 2010.

Source: Authors' analysis of Munnell (2012)

retirement (i.e., headed by someone age 55–64) who had one or more retirement accounts in 2010, the median value of all retirement accounts was $100,000, less than twice the median income for this age group, and a fraction of savings needed to maintain living standards in retirement, absent substantial other savings or pension benefits besides Social Security (Bricker et al. 2012).

Liabilities

Assets are one side of the ledger that tallies net worth; liabilities, or debts, are the other. Debt is not necessarily a problem; access to debt allows households to buy houses and cars, invest in education, and purchase other high-cost items that may provide services over many years. Debt may also be used to cope with short-term economic setbacks such as unemployment or illness. Debt becomes a burden only when required debt payments crowd out other economic obligations or opportunities or when it is accumulated for purposes that don't provide a worthwhile return (economic or otherwise).

Table 6.10 shows total debt, assets, and net worth across the wealth distribution from 1962 to 2010. For the middle fifth (i.e., households with "typical" levels

Table 6.10 Average household debt, assets, and net worth, by wealth group, 1962–2010 (thousands of 2010 dollars)

	Wealth fifth			Breakdown of top fifth		
	Bottom two	Middle	Fourth	80th–<90th percentile	90th–<99th percentile	Top 1%
Total debt						
1962	$19.8	$35.3	$35.7	$34.5	$46.6	$238.0
1983	16.8	34.9	44.8	65.8	91.1	547.3
1989	32.1	45.5	59.3	65.6	121.5	596.8
1998	32.6	61.2	63.4	88.2	140.4	378.1
2001	31.4	62.2	74.5	98.4	150.6	401.2
2007	47.8	98.9	116.4	127.0	241.4	545.8
2010	57.4	88.1	86.1	130.0	233.6	578.3
Total assets						
1962	$20.9	$88.1	$165.8	$306.0	$770.1	$6,728.6
1983	23.0	109.1	223.5	438.7	1,180.3	10,145.9
1989	26.7	124.2	260.0	488.2	1,322.7	12,772.7
1998	34.1	142.9	279.2	549.6	1,495.2	14,028.3
2001	35.0	154.5	339.6	702.2	2,134.2	16,028.4
2007	50.2	210.3	422.6	801.3	2,652.3	19,990.2
2010	46.8	149.1	303.0	697.0	2,357.6	17,017.7
Net worth						
1962	$1.1	$52.7	$130.1	$271.4	$723.6	$6,490.6
1983	6.3	74.2	178.7	372.9	1,089.3	9,598.6
1989	-5.5	78.7	200.7	422.6	1,201.2	12,176.0
1998	1.5	81.6	215.8	461.3	1,354.8	13,650.2
2001	3.5	92.3	265.1	603.7	1,983.6	15,627.3
2007	2.3	111.5	306.2	674.3	2,411.0	19,444.4
2010	-10.6	61.0	216.9	567.0	2,124.1	16,439.4

Source: Wolff (2012)

of wealth), average debt increased by 183.3 percent between 1983 and 2007, from $34,900 to $98,900. After the housing bust and the Great Recession, households began to pay down debt; between 2007 and 2010, average debt of middle-fifth households dropped by 10.8 percent, from $98,900 to $88,100. However, debt of the middle fifth was still 152.6 percent higher in 2010 than in 1983. Because assets of middle-fifth households grew only 36.6 percent between 1983 and 2010, middle-fifth net worth dropped between 1983 and 2010, from $74,200 in 1983 to $61,000 in 2010.

Table 6.11 shows median household debt by race and ethnicity between 1983 and 2010. Median debt of black households was $8,300 in 2010, down from $12,100 in 2007 but $6,700 greater than in 1983. Median debt of Hispanic households was $10,000 in 2010, also down from 2007 but $4,800 greater than in 1998 (the earliest data available). Median white household debt increased from $7,900 in 1983 to $37,000 in 2010. Racial and ethnic minority households typically have much less debt than white households. Median black household debt was 22.4 percent of median white household debt in 2010, while median Hispanic household debt was 27.0 percent of median white household debt. However, as shown in Table 6.8, racial and ethnic minority households also typically have fewer assets than white households, which is why racial and ethnic minority households tend to have much lower net worth than white households (as shown in Table 6.5).

Table 6.11 Median household debt, by race and ethnicity, 1983–2010 (thousands of 2010 dollars)

	White	Black	Hispanic	Median black debt as a share of white	Median Hispanic debt as a share of white
1983	$7.9	$1.6	—	20.2%	—
1989	13.7	1.4	—	10.3	—
1998	21.4	3.7	$5.2	17.5	24.4%
2001	23.8	7.4	4.9	31.1	20.7
2007	34.7	12.1	14.7	35.0	42.4
2010	37.0	8.3	10.0	22.4	27.0
Change					
1983–2007	337.8%	659.0%	—	—	—
2007–2010	6.6	-31.6	-32.1%	—	—

Source: Wolff (2012)

Table 6.12 Distribution of family debt by its purpose, 1989–2010

	1989	1995	1998	2001	2007	2010
Primary residence	66.5%	72.3%	70.0%	72.9%	71.8%	71.4%
Other residential property	8.8	8.2	7.8	6.5	10.8	10.5
Investments excluding real estate	3.9	1.0	3.3	2.8	1.6	2.0
Vehicles	10.6	7.6	7.6	7.8	5.5	4.7
Goods and services (including credit card debt)	6.1	5.7	6.3	5.8	6.2	5.7
Education	2.4	2.7	3.5	3.1	3.6	5.2
Other	1.7	2.4	1.5	1.1	0.5	0.4
Total	100.0	100.0	100.0	100.0	100.0	100.0

Source: Authors' analysis of Federal Reserve Board (2012a) and Bricker et al. (2012)

Table 6.12 presents a breakdown of total debt by the purpose of the debt from 1989 to 2010. One minor caveat about these data is that even though funds technically are borrowed for a particular purpose, they may in fact be used for something else. For example, a family may have the means to buy a house out-right but nevertheless takes out a mortgage and uses the freed-up funds for other purposes. Even so, the data provide a useful picture of how debt is used. With the notable exceptions of student loan debt and debt related to vehicle purchases, the distribution of debt by purpose has not changed substantially over this period, despite the considerable growth in debt levels, as shown in Table 6.10.

The large majority of family debt—71.4 percent in 2010—is tied to the purchase or improvement of a primary residence. This share grew from 66.5 percent in 1989 to 72.3 percent in 1995, but has since held relatively steady. Debt from the purchase of goods and services, which includes credit card debt, accounted for 5.7 percent of all debt in 2010, a moderate decrease from 6.2 percent in 2007. The 2007 share was little changed from 6.1 percent in 1989. One category that has significantly declined is the share of debt accounted for by vehicle purchases, which fell from 10.6 percent in 1989 to 4.7 percent in 2010.

Student loan debt

Debt incurred for education has substantially increased in the last two decades, as Table 6.12 shows. In 2010, education debt's share of overall debt was 5.2 percent, more than double its 1989 share, 2.4 percent. Though not shown in the table, the share of families with education debt also increased, from 15.2 percent to 19.2 percent between 2007 and 2010 alone. The *level* of student loan debt has also risen substantially. Among families with education debt, the average amount of that debt increased 14.0 percent—from $22,500 to $25,600—between 2007 and

2010. The median level of education debt of these families rose 3.4 percent over the same period, from $12,600 to $13,000 (Bricker et al. 2012).

Students assuming education loans are taking an implicit gamble that their extra human capital will be rewarded in the job market upon graduation. For this gamble to pay off, the job opportunities must be there. For many students graduating into the weak labor markets of the Great Recession and its aftermath, this gamble has led to great economic distress, through no fault of their own. And although most student loans have a six-month grace period before payments must begin, recent graduates without stable income may miss payments or default on their loans. According to researchers at the Federal Reserve Bank of New York, 27 percent of student loan debt holders had at least one past-due balance in the third quarter of 2011 (Brown et al. 2012).

Debt relative to disposable personal income

Figure 6O shows debt as a share of disposable income, for all debt and for various types of debt, from 1946 to 2011. Debt as a share of disposable personal income (personal income minus personal current taxes) was the highest on record in 2007, at 137.6 percent. That share dropped to 118.7 percent in 2011, as households reduced consumption and paid down debt relative to the housing bubble years.

As suggested by the data in Table 6.12, mortgage debt is the largest debt category. Mortgage debt as a share of disposable income declined from a 101.2 percent high in 2007 to 84.8 percent in 2011, the steepest drop on record. Consumer credit debt (consisting mostly of credit card debt and auto loans) also fell as a share of disposable income, from 24.5 percent in 2007 to 21.7 percent in 2011.

As homeownership rates and home values increased in the bubble years, so did home equity loans, as shown in Figure 6O. The steep growth rate in home equity loans during the bubble years indicates that households were increasingly spending their accumulated equity rather than saving it. While in retrospect this was a mistake, it was arguably a rational choice at the time, given the conventional wisdom that the housing boom would not bust—a belief that central bankers and others responsible for the economic health of the country did not debunk. Home equity loans as a share of disposable income dropped dramatically when the housing boom ended, from a peak of 10.9 percent in 2007 to 7.5 percent in 2011.

Debt service

As mentioned previously, debt is not necessarily a problem; access to credit can allow for great economic opportunities. Problems arise when debt payments begin to crowd out other economic obligations. A useful measure for assessing debt burden is the financial obligations ratio: the ratio of debt payments (including minimum required payments on mortgages, consumer debt, automobile leases,

Figure 60 Household debt as a share of disposable personal income, all and by type of debt, 1946–2011

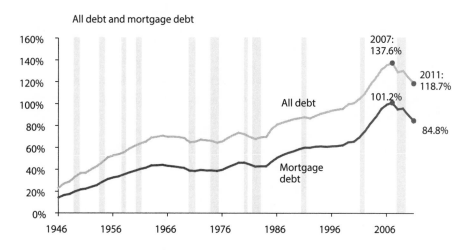

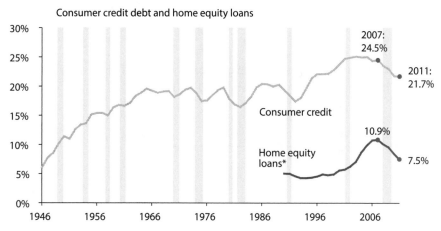

* Data for home equity loans are unavailable prior to 1990.
Note: Shaded areas denote recessions.

Source: Authors' analysis of Federal Reserve Board Flow of Funds Accounts

homeowners' insurance, property tax payments, and rent) to disposable personal income, expressed as a percent. **Table 6.13** provides the financial obligations ratio for renters and homeowners.

In 2011, renters spent an average of 24.1 percent of their disposable income on minimum debt payments, while homeowners spent an average of 14.4 percent (9.5 percent on mortgages and 4.9 percent on consumer debt). For renters, this was a moderate decline from 25.2 percent in 2007, due to households reducing consumption and paying down debt relative to the bubble years and to the downward pressure on the cost of rent as vacancy rates increased. From 1980 to 2007, the financial obligations ratio for renters changed little, increasing by 0.9 percentage points, from 24.3 percent to 25.2 percent.

Homeowners, on the other hand, substantially increased their share of disposable income devoted to minimum debt payments in the decades prior to the Great Recession: The share increased from 13.8 percent in 1980 to 17.5 percent in 2007, largely driven by an increase in mortgage payments. The financial obligations ratio for homeowners dropped significantly in the Great Recession and its aftermath, falling to 14.4 percent in 2011, also due to households reducing consumption and

Table 6.13 Household financial obligations as a share of disposable personal income, for renters and homeowners, 1980–2011

	Renters	Homeowners		
	Total	Total	Mortgage	Consumer
1980	24.3%	13.8%	8.3%	5.4%
1989	25.1	15.4	9.9	5.5
2000	29.6	14.9	8.7	6.2
2007	25.2	17.5	11.2	6.2
2011	24.1	14.4	9.5	4.9
Change				
1980–1989	0.8	1.7	1.6	0.1
1989–2000	4.5	-0.5	-1.2	0.7
2000–2007	-4.5	2.6	2.5	0.1
2007–2011	-1.0	-3.1	-1.7	-1.4
1980–2011	-0.2	0.6	1.2	-0.6

Note: The financial obligations ratio is the ratio of debt payments (including minimum required payments on mortgages, consumer debt, automobile leases, homeowners' insurance, property tax payments, and rent) to disposable personal income.

Source: Federal Reserve Board (2012b)

paying down debt relative to the bubble years, and to the fact that those who were able to hold on to their homes were better able to afford them.

Another measure of household debt service—the debt service ratio—is reported by income percentile in **Table 6.14**. As with the financial obligations ratio, the debt service ratio is a ratio of minimum debt payments to income, expressed as a percent. The debt service ratio, however, is a narrower measure than the financial obligations ratio because it does not include payments such as rent; it includes only payments on mortgage and consumer debt. Because these data include renters but do not count rental payments as debt, the values are pushed down, and disproportionately so at the lower end of the income scale. Nevertheless, Table 6.14 shows that households in the top 10 percent of the income distribution spend much less of their income on debt service than the bottom 90 percent of households. In 2010, households in the top 10 percent spent 9.4 percent of their income on servicing debt, less than half of the average of the bottom 90 percent, which was 19.6 percent.

Table 6.14 also shows the particularly large increase (from 17.7 percent to 23.5 percent) in household debt service as a share of income for households in the bottom fifth between 2007 and 2010. This was due predominantly to a decline in income during the Great Recession and its aftermath rather than an increase in debt service.

Table 6.14 Debt service as a share of family income, by income group, 1989–2010

	Bottom 90%						Top 10%
	Bottom fifth	Second fifth	Middle fifth	Fourth fifth	80th–<90th percentile	Total bottom 90%	
1989	14.1%	13.0%	16.3%	16.9%	15.7%	15.1%	8.7%
1998	18.7	16.5	18.6	19.1	16.8	18.1	10.3
2001	16.1	15.8	17.1	16.8	17.0	16.5	8.1
2007	17.7	17.2	19.8	21.8	19.8	19.2	8.4
2010	23.5	16.9	19.5	19.3	18.0	19.6	9.4
Change							
1989–2007	3.6	4.2	3.5	4.9	4.1	4.1	-0.3
2007–2010	5.8	-0.3	-0.3	-2.5	-1.8	0.4	1.0

Note: Household debt service is the ratio of payments on mortgage and consumer debt to family income.

Source: Bricker et al. (2012) and Federal Reserve Board (2012a)

It is important to note that neither the financial obligations ratio nor the debt service ratio captures the additional costs incurred by low-income families who must turn to nontraditional lending services and rapid-cash providers, such as pawn shops, nonbank check-cashing services, and payday lenders. The extraordinary fees often charged by these entities constitute a significant source of debt service expense for many low-income families.

Hardship

Debt service payments equal to more than 40 percent of household income are generally considered to represent economic hardship. **Table 6.15** looks at such hardship by income group. In all years, high debt burdens were, unsurprisingly, negatively associated with income. In 2010, 2.9 percent of households in the top 10 percent had high debt burdens, compared with 15.4 percent of middle-fifth households. In other words, close to 1 in 6 middle-income families spent more than 40 percent of their income on debt service. For households in the bottom fifth, it was more than 1 in 4 (26.1 percent). Furthermore, as with the data in Table 6.14, the data in Table 6.15 (and Table 6.16, following) include renters but not rental payments, so the share of low-income households struggling to meet debt and housing obligations is likely higher than the figures here indicate.

Table 6.15 Share of households with high debt burdens, by income group, 1989–2010

	Income fifth				Breakdown of top fifth	
	Bottom	Second	Middle	Fourth	80th–<90th percentile	Top 10%
1989	24.6%	14.5%	11.0%	5.8%	3.4%	1.9%
1998	29.9	18.3	15.8	9.8	3.5	2.8
2001	29.3	16.6	12.3	6.5	3.5	2.0
2007	26.9	19.5	14.5	12.9	8.2	3.8
2010	26.1	18.6	15.4	11.0	5.3	2.9
Change						
1989–2007	2.3	5.0	3.5	7.1	4.8	1.9
2007–2010	-0.8	-0.9	0.9	-1.9	-2.9	-0.9

Note: A high debt burden is a ratio of debt service payments to income greater than 40 percent.

Source: Bricker et al. (2012)

Table 6.16 Share of households late paying bills, by income group, 1989–2010

| | Income fifth | | | | Breakdown of top fifth | |
	Bottom	Second	Middle	Fourth	80th– <90th percentile	Top 10%
1989	18.2%	12.2%	5.0%	5.9%	1.1%	2.4%
1998	12.9	12.3	10.0	5.9	3.9	1.6
2001	13.4	11.7	7.9	4.0	2.6	1.3
2007	15.1	11.5	8.3	4.1	2.1	0.2
2010	21.2	15.2	10.2	8.8	5.4	2.1
Change						
1989–2007	-3.1	-0.7	3.3	-1.8	1.0	-2.2
2007–2010	6.1	3.7	1.9	4.7	3.3	1.9

Note: The table shows households with any payment past due 60 days or more.

Source: Bricker et al. (2012)

Another measure of the impact of debt on economic hardship is the share of households, by income level, that were late paying bills. In 2007, 7.1 percent of all households were at least 60 days late in paying at least one bill. **Table 6.16** shows the share of households late paying bills by income group. Not surprisingly, the share of households behind on their bills is strongly related to income. In 2007, very few (0.2 percent) of the top 10 percent of households were late in paying at least one bill, compared with 8.3 percent of middle-fifth households and 15.1 percent of bottom-fifth households. However, the share of households late in paying bills increased for all income groups in the Great Recession and its aftermath. By 2010, 2.1 percent of households in the top 10 percent of the income distribution were late paying at least one bill, compared with one out of every ten middle-fifth households (10.2 percent) and more than one out of every five bottom-fifth households (21.2 percent).

Bankruptcy

The opportunity to start anew through fair and reasonable bankruptcy is important for those who face insurmountable debt. The importance of this option is supported by research showing that misfortune—including job losses, medical emergencies, and divorce—precedes the vast majority of personal bankruptcies (Sullivan, Warren, and Westbrook 2000). Declaring bankruptcy allows an individual to obtain debt relief through either discharging or restructuring *nonmortgage* debt (in bankruptcy proceedings, only nonmortgage debts may be discharged; a bankruptcy court does not have the authority to modify mortgage loans on a primary residence).

Figure 6P tracks the rate of personal bankruptcies from 1989 through 2011. The rate of bankruptcies generally increased from 1989 through 2005, along with stagnating incomes and an increasing debt burden. At the 2005 peak, 9.6 out of 1,000 adults declared personal bankruptcy. The large jump in 2005 was partly due to people seeking to file bankruptcy prior to the October 2005 implementation of a new bankruptcy law that made personal bankruptcy more complicated and dramatically more expensive. As a result, the number of bankruptcy filings plummeted 70 percent from 2005 to 2006. However, as the Great Recession took hold and millions of people lost jobs and incomes, bankruptcies again began to rise. In 2010, despite the new law making bankruptcy more difficult and expensive, seven out of every 1,000 adults declared personal bankruptcy. That declined somewhat to 6.1 in 2011.

Figure 6P Consumer bankruptcies per 1,000 adults, 1989–2011

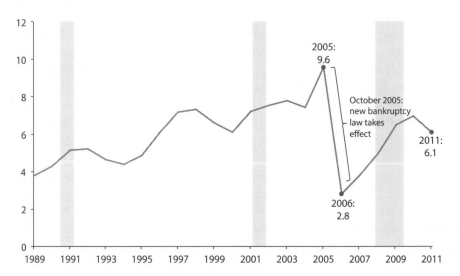

Note: Shaded areas denote recessions.

Source: Authors' analysis of bankruptcy statistics from the American Bankruptcy Institute (various years) and labor force statistics from the Current Population Survey

Wealth of U.S. citizens compared with citizens' wealth in peer countries

This chapter has demonstrated the low wealth holdings of the majority of Americans. But how does the wealth of people in the United States compare with that of people in peer countries? **Figure 6Q** shows the median wealth per adult in the United States and in 19 other advanced, industrialized nations. At $52,752, U.S. median wealth is the fourth-lowest among these 20 countries. Median wealth in Australia, Italy, Belgium, Japan, the United Kingdom, Switzerland, Ireland, France, Canada, Austria, Norway, and Finland is at least 60 percent higher than the median wealth in the United States.

Table 6.17 provides the data on median wealth per adult presented in Figure 6Q along with the mean (or average) wealth per adult. In each country, mean wealth is substantially greater than median wealth. The median is a better indication than the mean of the wealth of the "typical" adult, since the median is the value at which half of adults have less wealth and half have more wealth. However, the table also shows the ratio of mean-to-median wealth, which is a useful measure of wealth inequality. The higher the ratio (i.e., the higher the mean is above the median), the more wealth is held by a minority of people, and the greater the wealth inequality.

Figure 6Q Median wealth per adult in 20 advanced countries, 2011 (2011 U.S. dollars)

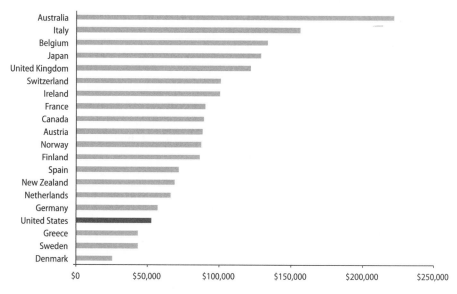

Source: Authors' analysis of Credit Suisse Research Institute (2011)

Table 6.17 Median and mean wealth per adult in 20 advanced countries, 2011
(2011 U.S. dollars)

	Median	Mean	Mean-to-median
Australia	$221,704	$396,745	1.8
Austria	88,112	194,207	2.2
Belgium	133,572	275,524	2.1
Canada	89,014	245,455	2.8
Denmark	25,692	239,057	9.3
Finland	86,286	174,895	2.0
France	90,271	293,685	3.3
Germany	57,283	199,783	3.5
Greece	43,571	105,843	2.4
Ireland	100,351	181,434	1.8
Italy	155,953	259,826	1.7
Japan	128,688	248,770	1.9
Netherlands	66,056	186,449	2.8
New Zealand	68,726	167,957	2.4
Norway	87,377	355,925	4.1
Spain	71,797	130,179	1.8
Sweden	43,297	284,146	6.6
Switzerland	100,901	540,010	5.4
United Kingdom	121,852	257,881	2.1
United States	52,752	248,395	4.7

Source: Authors' analysis of Credit Suisse Research Institute (2011)

The mean wealth in the United States, $248,395, places the United States firmly in the middle of its peers, 10th out of the 20 countries. However, since U.S. median wealth is so low, the ratio of mean-to-median wealth in the United States is very high. At 4.7, the United States has the fourth-highest ratio of mean-to-median wealth, meaning the United States has a very high level of wealth inequality relative to most of its peer countries.

Conclusion

The data presented here have highlighted the highly unequal distribution of wealth in the United States—with wealth inequality exceeding even the profoundly unequal distributions of income and wages described in earlier chapters. This discussion also exposed the fallacy that all or even most American households are invested in the stock market. Fewer than half of U.S. households have any stock holdings (including in retirement accounts and pension funds), and less than a third have stock holdings worth $10,000 or more. Most families depend on labor income alone to meet their financial obligations, and have very little in the way of a financial cushion that can be cashed in during times of economic hardship.

The loss of wealth due to the housing bust and the Great Recession further increased an already vast wealth divide. The richest 1 percent of American households saw 15.6 percent of their wealth eliminated between 2007 and 2010, but the middle fifth saw nearly half (45.3 percent) of their wealth eliminated. Many families that thought they had solid footing in the middle class have faced foreclosure and/or lengthy spells of unemployment. Moreover, the recovery (officially underway since June 2009) has been tepid—especially in the labor market—and has yet to bring substantial relief to those suffering from this economic shock. The rebound in stocks is of little help, given that most households have little to no stock holdings. To begin building wealth for the majority of U.S. households—wealth that is not inflated by an asset bubble—we must restore our economy to one in which wages and incomes across the distribution grow as the overall economy grows.

Table and figure notes

Tables

Table 6.1. Distribution of income compared with distribution of wealth, 2010. The table is based on unpublished analysis of 2010 Survey of Consumer Finances (SCF) data prepared in 2012 by Edward Wolff for the Economic Policy Institute. The definition of wealth used in this analysis of the SCF is the same definition of wealth used in the analysis of the SCF conducted by Bricker et al. (2012), except that the Bricker et al. analysis includes vehicle wealth, while this analysis does not.

Table 6.2. Change in wealth groups' shares of total wealth, 1962–2010. See note to Table 6.1.

Table 6.3. Change in average wealth, by wealth group, 1962–2010. See note to Table 6.1.

Table 6.4. Share of households with low net worth, 1962–2010. See note to Table 6.1.

Table 6.5. Median household wealth, and share of households with zero or negative wealth, by race and ethnicity, 1983–2010. See note to Table 6.1.

Table 6.6. Wealth groups' shares of household assets, by asset type, 2010. See note to Table 6.1.

Table 6.7. Average household assets, by wealth group and asset type, 1962–2010. See note to Table 6.1.

Table 6.8. Average and median household assets, by race/ethnicity and asset type, 1983–2010. See note to Table 6.1.

Table 6.9. Share of households owning stock, 1989–2010. See note to Table 6.1.

Table 6.10. Average household debt, assets, and net worth, by wealth group, 1962–2010. See note to Table 6.1.

Table 6.11. Median household debt, by race and ethnicity, 1983–2010. See note to Table 6.1.

Table 6.12. Distribution of family debt by its purpose, 1989–2010. Data for years 2001–2010 are from Bricker et al. (2012). Data for prior years are from the Federal Reserve Board's Survey of Consumer Finances, *Tables Based on the Internal Data.*

Table 6.13. Household financial obligations as a share of disposable personal income, for renters and homeowners, 1980–2011. Data refer to annual averages from the Federal Reserve Board (FRB), *Household Debt Service and Financial Obligations Ratios.* Per the FRB, the *financial obligations ratio (FOR)* adds automobile lease payments, rental payments on tenant-occupied property, homeowners' insurance, and property tax payments to the debt service ratio (an estimate of the ratio of debt payments on outstanding mortgage and consumer debt, to disposable personal income). The *homeowner mortgage FOR* includes payments on mortgage debt, homeowners' insurance, and property taxes, while the *homeowner consumer FOR* includes payments on consumer debt and automobile leases.

Table 6.14. Debt service as a share of family income, by income group, 1989–2010. Data are from Bricker et al. (2012), Table 17.

Table 6.15. Share of households with high debt burdens, by income group, 1989–2010. Data are from Bricker et al. (2012), Table 17.

Table 6.16. Share of households late paying bills, by income group, 1989–2010. Data are from Bricker et al. (2012), Table 17.

Table 6.17. Median and mean wealth per adult in 20 advanced countries, 2011. Data are from the Credit Suisse Research Institute's *Global Wealth Databook 2011.* Note that in international comparisons of income it is standard practice (including at EPI) to convert currencies using "purchasing power parity" (PPP) exchange rates instead of market exchange rates. PPPs are based on the price of buying a given "basket" of goods and services in each country, thereby equalizing the purchasing power of currencies. It should be noted that for these data, market exchange rates, not PPP exchange rates, are used to convert currencies to U.S. dollars. The authors of the report argue that there is a case to be made for using market exchange rates for international comparisons of wealth because in every country a large share of personal wealth is owned by households in the top few percentiles of the distribution, and these households tend to move their assets across borders with relative frequency. Results are not available using PPP exchange rates. It also should be noted that the ratio of mean to median is the same regardless of what exchange rates are used.

Figures

Figure 6A. Average household net worth, net financial assets, and net tangible assets, 1965–2012. Data for net worth and assets are from the Federal Reserve Board's Flow of Funds Accounts, Table B.100, "Balance Sheet of Households and Nonprofit Organizations." The data were adjusted for inflation using the CPI-U-RS (Consumer Price Index Research Series Using Current Methods), and divided by the number of U.S. households based on Census Bureau data. The household data are from the Current Population Survey/Housing Vacancy Survey *Historical Tables,* Table 7, "Annual Estimates of the Housing Inventory: 1965 to Present" (http://www.census.gov/hhes/www/housing/hvs/historic/index.html). The number of "owner occupied" homes was taken as a percentage of "total occupied" homes to calculate a percentage of homeownership.

Figure 6B. Share of total household wealth growth accruing to various wealth groups, 1983–2010. Data are derived from Table 6.3.

Figure 6C. Ratio of average top 1% household wealth to median wealth, 1962–2010. Data are derived from Table 6.3.

Figure 6D. Average annual net worth of "Forbes 400" wealthiest individuals, 1982–2011. Data for 1982 to 1999 are adapted from Broom and Shay (2000) Table 2, "'Forbes 400' Individual Fortunes." Data from 2000 to 2011 are from Forbes annual lists of the richest 400 Americans. All data are adjusted to 2011 dollars using the CPI-U-RS.

Figure 6E. Median household wealth, by race and ethnicity, 1983–2010. See note to Table 6.5.

Figure 6F. U.S. stock market, 1955–2011. Data on the Standard & Poor's composite index of the 500 largest U.S. firms (the S&P 500) are from the *Economic Report of the President* (Council of Economic Advisers 2012), tables B-95, "Historical Stock Prices and Yields, 1949–2003," and B-96, "Common Stock Prices and Yields, 2000–2011," deflated by the CPI-U-RS in 2011 dollars and indexed to 1960=100.

Figure 6G. Wealth groups' shares of total household stock wealth, 1983–2010. Data are derived from Table 6.6; see table note to Table 6.6.

Figure 6H. Annual homeownership rate, 1965–2011. Annual data are from the Current Population Survey/Housing Vacancy Survey, *Historical Tables*, Table 7, "Annual Estimates of the Housing Inventory: 1965 to Present," http://www.census.gov/hhes/www/housing/hvs/historic/index.html. To calculate the rate of homeownership, the number of owner-occupied homes was taken as a percentage of total occupied homes.

Figure 6I. Homeownership rate, by household income group, 2009. Data are from the U.S. Census Bureau's American Housing Survey, *National Data*, Table 3-12, "Owner Occupied Units," http://www.census.gov/housing/ahs/data/ahs2009.html, most recently published in 2009. Due to budget constraints, the two-year schedule for this survey was delayed in 2012, and 2011 data were not available in time for this publication.

Figure 6J. Homeownership rate, by race and ethnicity, 1975–2011. Data prior to 1994 are taken from the Current Population Survey (CPS) Annual Social and Economic Supplement, provided by the Census Bureau upon request. Data from 1994 onward are taken from the CPS/Housing Vacancy Survey, *Annual Statistics: 2011*, Table 22, "Homeownership Rates by Race and Ethnicity of Householder" (http://www.census.gov/hhes/www/housing/hvs/annual11/ann11ind.html). As with other CPS microdata analyses presented in this book, race/ethnicity categories are mutually exclusive (i.e., white non-Hispanic, black non-Hispanic, and Hispanic any race).

Figure 6K. Home prices, 1953–2012. Home price data are from Robert Shiller, of Yale University, who publishes a quarterly series of home price data, which was featured in his book *Irrational Exuberance* (http://www.econ.yale.edu/~shiller/data.htm). The home price index is set to 1997Q1=100.

Figure 6L. Total homeowner equity as a share of total home values, 1969–2011. Data are from the Federal Reserve Board's Flow of Funds Accounts, Table B.100, "Balance Sheet of Households and Nonprofit Organizations."

Figure 6M. Foreclosures per 1,000 owner-occupied dwellings, 2000–2011. Data on foreclosures are from the Federal Reserve Bank of New York's *Quarterly Report on Household Debt and Credit*; data series "Number of Consumers with New Foreclosures" (http://www.newyorkfed.org/newsevents/news/research/2012/an120227.html). The number of owner-occupied dwellings was taken from the Current Population Survey/Housing Vacancy Survey, *Historical Tables*, Table 8, "Quarterly Estimates of the Housing Inventory: 1965 to Present" (http://www.census.gov/hhes/www/housing/hvs/historic/index.html).

Figure 6N. Enrollment in defined-benefit versus defined-contribution pension plans among workers with pension coverage, 1983 and 2010. Figure produced from data in Munnell (2012), Figure 4.

Figure 6O. Household debt as a share of disposable personal income, all and by type of debt, 1946–2011. Data on disposable personal income, consumer credit liability, total liabilities, and mortgage liabilities are from the Federal Reserve Board's Flow of Funds data, Table B.100, "Balance Sheet of Households and Nonprofit Organizations." Data on home equity loans are from Flow of Funds data, Table L.218, "Home Mortgages," and are unavailable prior to 1990. The various liabilities are taken as shares of disposable personal income for display in the graphs.

Figure 6P. Consumer bankruptcies per 1,000 adults, 1989–2011. Data on bankruptcies are American Bankruptcy Institute Annual and Quarterly U.S. Bankruptcy Statistics, "Annual Business and Non-business Filings by Year" (http://www.abiworld.org/Content/NavigationMenu/NewsRoom/BankruptcyStatistics/Bankruptcy_Filings_1.htm). Data on the adult population are calculated with Current Population Survey labor force statistics, "Civilian Noninstitutional Population Series, Ages 18 and Over."

Figure 6Q. Median wealth per adult in 20 advanced countries, 2011. See note to Table 6.17.

Poverty
The Great Recession adds injury to insult

This book offers a detailed discussion of rising economic inequality as evident in growing inequality of wages, incomes, and wealth in America. This growing inequality, which helps explain stagnant income growth for most households for more than three decades, has also been a critical factor at the bottom of the income distribution. As income inequality increases, poverty becomes less responsive to overall growth because too little of that growth reaches individuals and families at the lower end of the income scale.

Before the mid-1970s, U.S. economic growth was associated with falling poverty rates (measured as the share of the population below the official poverty line). If that relationship had continued to hold, poverty would have been eradicated during the 1980s. It did not; the economy continued to grow, but poverty stopped falling.

Given the general wage stagnation and slow income growth everywhere but at the top, it is not surprising that little improved for those at the bottom over the last 30 years. Prosperity has not been broadly shared, and least of all for those at the very bottom.

Many Americans work in jobs that barely keep them above water. About one-fourth of workers earn poverty-level wages, wages at or below the wage a full-time, full-year worker would need to earn to reach the poverty threshold for family of four, which was $22,314 in 2010.

Furthermore, lower-wage workers are more susceptible to the ebbs and flows of the economy. Periods of high productivity and low unemployment tend to be associated with strong wage growth and reductions in poverty, as occurred in the strong economy of the 1990s. A decline in the unemployment rate has a larger effect on wages at the bottom: Wage gains from lower unemployment are roughly twice as high for the lowest-wage male workers as they are for middle- and high-wage workers.

As the unemployment rate rises, wages at the bottom of the wage distribution fall the most. It is no surprise that falling poverty reversed course in the weak economy of the 2000s, with across-the-board increases in poverty that were particularly large for families with children. Between 2000 and 2007, the workforce was highly productive but poverty increased, largely due to rising income inequality (and not, as some have wrongly claimed, from changes in the composition of American families).

With the Great Recession came steep increases in the poverty rate, from 12.5 percent in 2007 to 15.1 percent in 2010. Just over 46 million people in the United States were in poverty in 2010.

Poverty is even higher among certain demographic groups. In 2010, the poverty rates of Hispanics (26.6 percent) and of African Americans (27.4 percent) were more than two and half times the poverty rate of whites (9.9 percent). Minority children fared even worse: In 2010, close to half (45.8 percent) of young black children (under age 6) were in poverty, compared with 14.5 percent of white children.

The social safety net, namely Social Security, unemployment insurance, the Earned Income Tax Credit (EITC), and the Supplemental Nutritional Assistance Program (SNAP), among other programs, have prevented more-devastating outcomes. Unfortunately, the safety net in the United States has become weaker over time, and workers at the bottom end rely more heavily on wages and a strong economy to make ends meet. Unemployment insurance is particularly vital to countering increases in poverty in bad economic times. In 2010, unemployment insurance kept 900,000 children and 2.3 million non-elderly adults out of poverty even though one or more workers in these vulnerable households were laid off (Renwick 2011).

When we compare the United States to its international peers, it is clear how woefully inadequate the U.S. safety net is. While the top 1 percent in the United States claims a larger share of overall income than their counterparts in peer countries (see Chapter 2, Figure 2AB), it does not mean that U.S. families at the bottom of the income scale enjoy a similar relative economic advantage vis a vis their international peers. In fact, in the United States, earnings (wages) at the bottom, measured at the 10th percentile of the earnings distribution, are lower than in many U.S. peer countries. Therefore, when people fall out of the middle in the United States, they are more likely to fall further (in dollar terms) than their downwardly mobile peers in other countries. And, as shown in Chapter 3, those at the bottom in the United States are more likely to be stuck there generation after generation than low-income people in U.S. peer countries.

All of these factors play a role in the higher poverty rate in the United States compared with other developed countries, a comparison made possible by examining the "relative poverty" measure—the share of the population living in households with incomes below half of the household median income. This measure tracks economic distance between the poor and the middle.

In the late 2000s, the United States had the highest relative poverty rate among 23 Organisation for Economic Co-operation and Development (OECD) countries—17.3 percent compared with 9.6 percent on average among the other countries studied. The extent of child poverty in the United States is even more severe: More than one in five children in the United States lived in poverty in 2009—a share more than twice as high as in peer countries on average.

U.S. efforts to allocate resources to the bottom end of the income scale also lag peer countries: The United States spends 16.2 percent of gross domestic product on social programs, well below the vast majority of peer countries, which average 21.3 percent. Unsurprisingly, then, the U.S. safety net (the system of taxes, transfers, and social welfare benefits) is the least effective in terms of reducing poverty: The U.S. tax-and-transfer system reduced poverty by 9.7 percentage points in the late 2000s, compared with the average 17.4 percentage-point reduction by the tax-and-transfer systems in other peer countries. In short, peer countries are much more likely than the United States to step in where markets and labor policy fail in order to lift their most disadvantaged citizens out of poverty.

Table notes and figure notes at the end of this chapter provide documentation for the data, as well as information on methodology, used in the tables and figures that follow.

Poverty measurement

Dividing lines between income groups are somewhat arbitrary, and there are many ways to define "low income." In this section, we explore three different measures: the official poverty line, the Supplemental Poverty Measure recently designed by the U.S. Census Bureau, and a measure of relative poverty defined as the share who live below half of median income. In later sections, we explore low-income individuals and families by looking at those with poverty-level wages and those in the bottom of the wage or income distribution.

Official poverty line

The official poverty line was set in the 1960s at approximately three times a basic food budget, adjusted by family size and composition, and is updated annually by overall inflation. In 2010, the poverty line was $22,314 for a family of four, $22,113 for a family of four with two children, and $11,344 for a single individual under age 65.

The poverty rate is the share of people below the official poverty line. In 2010, the rate was 15.1 percent, or just over 46 million people. As shown in **Figure 7A**, the poverty rate fell fairly significantly from 1959, when it stood at 22.4 percent, to its historical low of 11.1 percent in 1973. Since then it has generally tracked business cycles, rising in recessions and falling in economic expansions. However, the poverty rate actually *increased* during the recovery that followed the 2001 recession, and when the Great Recession hit at the end of 2007, the poverty rate increased sharply—by 2.6 percentage points from 2007 to 2010.

Figure 7A also displays the "twice-poverty rate," officially the share of the population below twice the poverty line. This is an important measure to poverty researchers and many government programs because it recognizes that many people between 100 and 200 percent of the poverty line can find it hard to make ends meet. The share of the population below twice the poverty line, or below 200 percent of poverty, varies dramatically with business cycles. The latest data indicate that the twice-poverty rate rose 3.4 percentage points since the start of the Great Recession, from 30.5 in 2007 to 33.9 percent in 2010. In 2010, over one-third of Americans were living below twice the poverty line.

Figure 7A Poverty and twice-poverty rates, 1959–2010

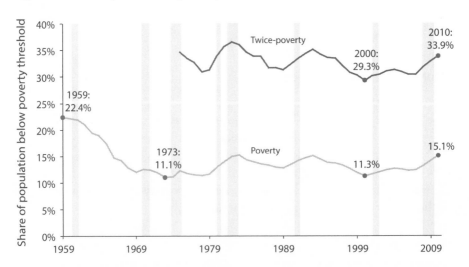

Note: The poverty rate is the share of the U.S. population with income below the official poverty line (where income is measured in terms of family income for persons in families and individual income otherwise) and the twice-poverty rate is the share with income below twice the official poverty line. Shaded areas denote recessions.

Source: Authors' analysis of Current Population Survey Annual Social and Economic Supplement *Historical Poverty Tables* (Tables 2 and 5)

In 2010, elderly individuals (people age 65 and older) had the lowest rates of poverty, followed by non-elderly adults, and then children (**Figure 7B**). Children under age 6 are nearly twice as likely to live in poverty as are adults age 18 to 64. This is explained partly by the fact that adults are usually at relatively early stages of their working lives when they have young children, and therefore are more likely to earn less than adults in later stages of their working lives. Figure 7B also demonstrates the dramatic decline in poverty rates from 1959 through the early 1970s, particularly for those age 65 and older. This large decline in overall poverty was due to a combination of economic factors discussed later in this section as well as the significant expansion of Social Security benefits, which especially reduced poverty among the elderly.

The dramatic changes in poverty rates over business cycles are clearer when examining subgroups of the U.S. population by race and ethnicity, and by age. **Figure 7C** highlights the stark disparities in poverty rates by race and ethnicity: The poverty rate of African Americans and Hispanics is nearly three times that of whites. While whites have lower poverty rates, their relatively flat poverty trend line conceals the fact that their poverty rates also rise and fall with business

Figure 7B Poverty rate, by age, 1959–2010

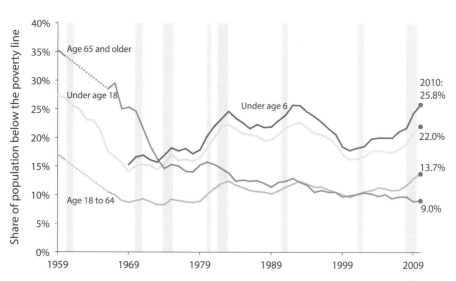

Note: For the age 18–64 and age 65 and older groups, no formal data exist for 1960–1965. The dotted lines denote a linear extrapolation between 1959 and 1966. Data for the under age 6 group begin in 1969. Shaded areas denote recessions.

Source: Authors' analysis of Current Population Survey Annual Social and Economic Supplement (CPS-ASEC) *Historical Poverty Tables* (Table 3) and CPS-ASEC microdata

Figure 7C Poverty rate, by race and ethnicity, nativity, and citizenship status, 1973–2010

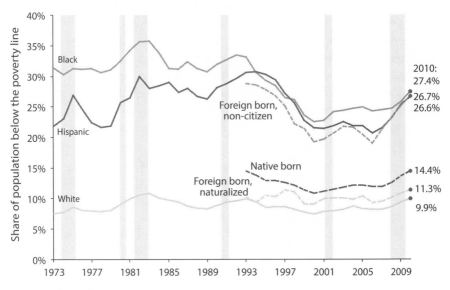

Note: Shaded areas denote recessions.

Source: Authors' analysis of Current Population Survey Annual Social and Economic Supplement *Historical Poverty Tables* (Tables 2 and 23)

cycles. What is most striking about the nonwhite population is the steep fall in poverty rates over the 1990s economic expansion. The declines in poverty among blacks and Hispanics in the mid- to late 1990s were due to a combination of macroeconomic factors, including high productivity and low unemployment, which increased wages across the entire income distribution and lifted many out of poverty.

Though immigrants on average have higher poverty rates than the native born, poverty differs between immigrant groups. As Figure 7C shows, foreign-born noncitizens have poverty rates over twice as high as foreign-born naturalized citizens. The poverty rates of noncitizens closely track those of Hispanics. While naturalized citizens likely differ in measurable ways from noncitizens (e.g., by country of origin, education/skills level, etc.), they also likely face certain economic advantages, such as broader job opportunities, that give them a leg up over noncitizens.

Figure 7D combines data on race and ethnicity, and age, to highlight the stark disparities between whites and minorities and the extent of poverty among African Americans and Hispanics. More than 1 in 3 African American and Hispanic children were poor in 2010, compared with about 1 in 8 white children.

Figure 7D Poverty rate, by race and ethnicity, and age, 2010

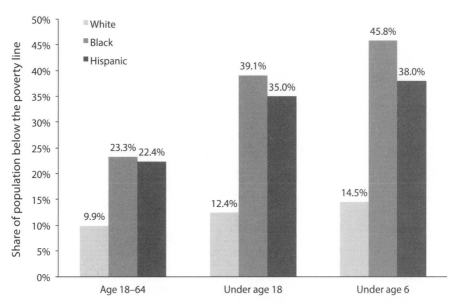

Source: Authors' analysis of Current Population Survey Annual Social and Economic Supplement (CPS-ASEC) *Historical Poverty Tables* (Table 3) and CPS-ASEC microdata

Nearly 46 percent of young black children (under age 6) lived in poverty in 2010, more than three times the rate of young white children.

Child poverty rates are a function of a family's income. In **Figure 7E,** the unit of observation shifts from persons to families, defined by the U.S. Census Bureau as households with two or more persons related through blood, marriage, or adoption. The poverty rate for all families was 11.7 percent in 2010, lower than the 15.1 percent poverty rate for persons, reflecting both the relatively high number of poor children and the inclusion of unrelated individuals in the person counts but not in the family counts. For families with children, the poverty rate was 18.3 percent in 2010.

The three remaining lines in Figure 7E refer to the poverty rates of three common family types: families with children that are female-headed, male-headed, and headed by married couples. Poverty rates of married couples with children are much lower—8.8 percent in 2010—in part because families can tap two earners when both spouses work in the paid labor market. In 2010, the poverty rate of female-headed families with children was 40.7 percent, more than four and a half times that of married-couple families with children and nearly 70 percent higher than that of male-headed families with children (24.2 percent). The poverty rate of female-headed families with children fell significantly through most of the

Figure 7E Poverty rates of various types of families, 1959–2010

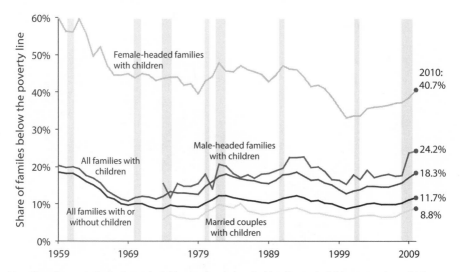

Note: Data for married couples with children and male-headed families with children are only available beginning in 1974. Shaded areas denote recessions.

Source: Authors' analysis of Current Population Survey Annual Social and Economic Supplement *Historical Poverty Tables* (Table 4)

1970s before increasing through the early 1980s, declined through the rest of that business cycle, fell sharply in the 1990s, and then climbed through the last entire business cycle (2000–2007), even when the economy was theoretically expanding. Male-headed families with children experienced similar fluctuations starting in the early 1980s, albeit with a particularly sharp jump in poverty in the Great Recession; 6.1 percentage points from 2008 to 2009. This increase was driven by the fact that men were harder hit by job loss in the recession (see Chapter 5 for additional gender-based labor market analyses).

The general decline of family poverty in the strong economy of the 1990s reversed course in the weakening economy of the 2000s, with across-the-board increases that were particularly large for single-mother and single-father families. This reversal highlights the cyclical effects of policy and the economy on lowering poverty, wherein those policies that tend to help reduce poverty in a strong economy or job market (e.g., the minimum wage) fail to help as much in a weaker one. (Both the characteristics of the economy of the late 1990s and antipoverty policy will be discussed in greater detail later in the chapter.)

As a measure of poverty, the poverty rate captures a snapshot in time, which misses the fact that different people cycle in and out of poverty over time. For instance, although the poverty rate averaged 13.8 percent across 2008 and 2009, far

Figure 7F Length of time in poverty over a two-year period, 2008–2009

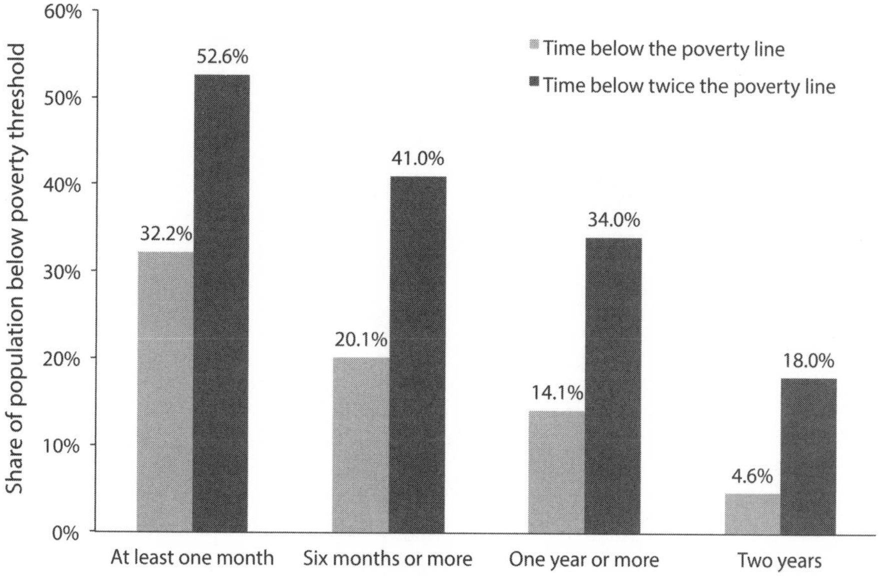

Source: Authors' analysis of U.S. Census Bureau Survey of Income and Program Participation microdata, 2008 panel

greater shares of people fell into poverty at some point in those years; as **Figure 7F** demonstrates, about one-third of the population fell below the poverty line for at least one month over that two-year period. In addition, about one-fifth of people were below the poverty line for at least six months in 2008–2009, and only 4.6 percent were in poverty the entire two years.

Figure 7F also illustrates "churning" below twice the poverty line. On average, 32.5 percent of people were below twice the poverty line during 2008 and 2009 (Figure 7A). However, when monthly income changes are taken into account, over half of the population fell below twice the poverty line for at least one month during those two years.

In short, many more people fall into poverty than suggested by the official rate, and an even greater number are at risk at any given time. Policies to reduce poverty need to recognize that poverty engulfs a much larger share of the U.S. population than annual averages suggest by providing a seamless and accessible safety net for those families threatened with falling into poverty even for short periods.

The need for such policies becomes more apparent when considering that, along with the poverty rate, the depth of poverty has increased. The poor are getting poorer. As shown in **Figure 7G**, a growing share of persons below the poverty line

Figure 7G Share of the poor in "deep poverty," 1975–2010

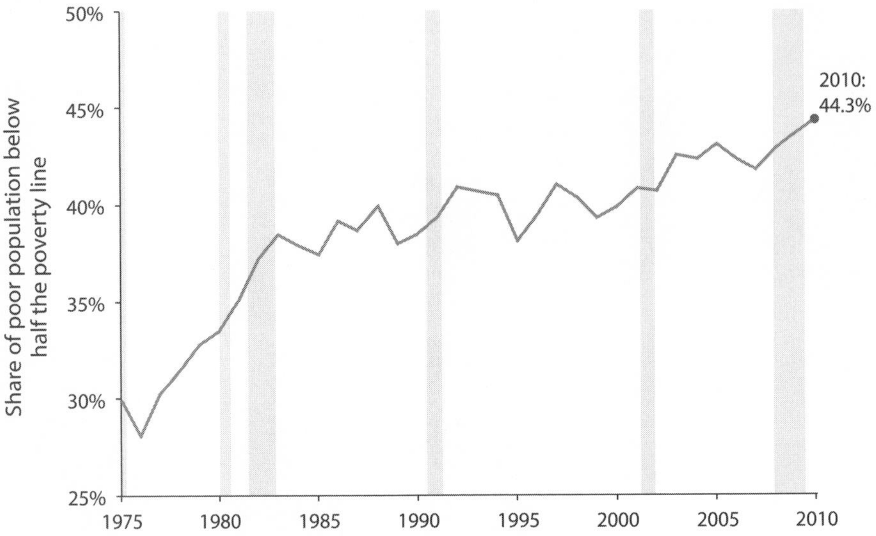

Note: Shaded areas denote recessions.

Source: Authors' analysis of Current Population Survey Annual Social and Economic Supplement *Historical Poverty Tables* (Tables 2 and 22)

have incomes below half of the poverty line. This is equivalent to $5,672 per year for one person under 65 years old or $11,057 for a family of four with two children.

In 2010, the share of the poor below half the poverty line reached a high of 44.3 percent. While many poor individuals have incomes close to the poverty threshold, a growing percentage are falling further behind. (A slight deepening occurred even through the later 1990s, when the overall poverty rate fell.) The tight labor market and income supports such as the Earned Income Tax Credit lifted those close to the poverty line above it but those left in poverty were probably the least able to take advantage of either a strong economy or such work-based supports.

Supplemental Poverty Measure

The current official U.S. poverty measure has been used since the 1960s, when it was devised as part of the "War on Poverty." This measure was primarily based on food consumption requirements and not on a full set of goods and services. The poverty line has been updated since the 1960s to reflect overall inflation, using the Consumer Price Index (CPI), but it has not changed to reflect cost increases of other essential consumption items such as housing or medical care, which consume an increasing share of families' budgets. To correct these and other short-comings, a government-appointed panel convened by the National Academy of Sciences in the mid-1990s was asked to update the way poverty is measured. Based on the panel's recommendations, an interagency technical working group for the U.S. Census Bureau was formed in conjunction with the Bureau of Labor Statistics to develop the Supplemental Poverty Measure, released by the Obama administration in 2011.

The Supplemental Poverty Measure seeks to better reflect both the resources families can access and the true cost of living. While the official poverty measure only counts pretax cash income, the supplemental measure redefines family resources to account for tax provisions such as the EITC and the value of government transfers such as food stamps and housing subsidies. Income is also adjusted

Table 7.1 Comparison of poverty measures

	Official poverty measure	Supplemental Poverty Measure
Threshold	Equal to three times the cost of "Economy Food Plan"	Equal to the 33rd percentile of expenditures on food, clothing, shelter, and utilities of consumer units with exactly two children, multiplied by 1.2
	Adjusted annually by change in the Consumer Price Index	Adjusted annually by the five-year moving average of expenditures on food, clothing, shelter, and utilities
	No geographic adjustment	Geographic adjustments for differences in housing costs
Resources included as income	Total family pretax cash income	Total family after-tax income (including credits such as the Earned Income Tax Credit)
		Includes value of near-cash benefits, such as SNAP, National School Lunch Program, WIC, housing subsidies, and LIHEAP
		Subtracts work-related expenses, such as child care and transportation costs
		Subtracts medical out-of-pocket expenses and child support paid

Note: SNAP is the Supplemental Nutrition Assistance Program; WIC is the Special Supplemental Nutrition Program for Women, Infants, and Children; and LIHEAP is the Low Income Home Energy Assistance Program.

Source: Authors' analysis of Short (2011)

for costs of child care, work-related transportation, and medical care. On the threshold side, the new measure seeks to better calculate the money it takes to live, i.e., pay for food, clothing, shelter, and utilities, by adjusting for average expenditures on these items (accounting for geographic differences in housing costs) as opposed to simply overall inflation. **Table 7.1** provides a detailed summary of how the official and supplemental measures are constructed.

Figure 7H compares poverty rates of people in different age groups under the official and supplemental poverty measures. For the entire population (the first set of bars), the poverty rate is higher under the more comprehensive supplemental measure because that measure is more realistic about what is required to achieve a minimum standard of living. But different groups fare differently. Under the supplemental measure, child poverty (the second set of bars) is lower because families with children are more likely to be beneficiaries of government transfers, while poverty of non-elderly adults is higher because the supplemental measure subtracts work-related expenses such as child care and transportation costs from income. The poverty rate of the elderly increases the most under the supplemental measure due to the higher medical expenses of the elderly. Components of the Supplemental Poverty Measure are discussed in further depth later in the chapter (see "Resources for low-income Americans").

Figure 7H Poverty rates, official and under the Supplemental Poverty Measure, by age group, 2010

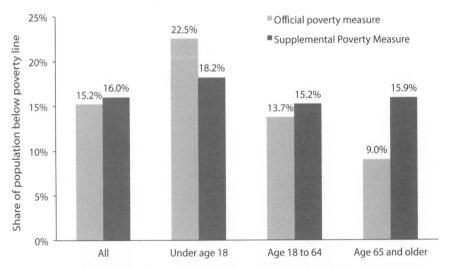

Note: Data in this figure differ from figures 7A and 7B because data in this figure include unrelated individuals under age 15.

Source: Authors' analysis of Short (2011, Table 1)

Relative poverty

Another way to measure poverty tracks the poor while accounting for changes in prevailing income levels among the non-poor. Such measures are called "relative" because they usually set the poverty threshold as a share of median income, which moves each year and typically rises in nominal terms.

The utility of this measure, besides being the norm in international comparisons, is that it tells how the poor fare relative to middle-income families (using median income as a proxy for middle-income families). Since the official poverty line is adjusted only for inflation, any time median income grows in real terms—faster than inflation—the poor lose relative ground. **Figure 7I** plots official poverty and relative poverty—the share of persons with one-half of median income—from 1979 to 2010. To be consistent with international comparisons later in this chapter, income in this context includes noncash transfers such as food stamps and housing subsidies. Income is measured in terms of family income for persons in families and individual income otherwise. As the figure shows, the official rate is considerably more cyclical: It fell over the expansion of the 1980s, and fell again, more so, in the 1990s, from a peak of 15.1 percent in 1993 to 11.3 percent in 2000. At the same time, the relative poverty rate fell less than a percentage point, from 18.5 percent in 1993 to 17.7 percent in 2000.

Figure 7I Official and relative poverty rate, 1979–2010

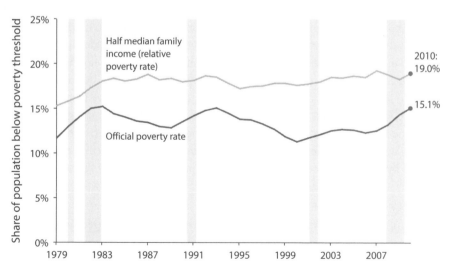

Note: Shaded areas denote recessions.

Source: Authors' analysis of Current Population Survey Annual Social and Economic Supplement (CPS-ASEC) *Historical Poverty Tables* (Table 2) and CPS-ASEC microdata

Relative poverty fell less because real median income rose in the 1990s (see Chapter 2), so the relative threshold of half the median was rising as well in real terms. Since, in relative terms, half median income grew at about the same rate as the median income, the poor remained about the same distance from the middle as before, while those poor by the official measure gained a great deal of ground in terms of reducing poverty.

Because the relative measure tracks economic distance between the poor and the middle class (in a way that absolute measures do not), it reveals the impact of changes in income inequality within the bottom half of the income distribution on poverty. The share of the population that is poor in relative terms hovered around 18 percent from the mid-1980s on, and was 19.0 percent in 2010. Thus, many more persons are poor in relative terms—their income is less than half the median—than in absolute terms. That such a significant share of the population remains relatively distant from the mainstream is an important dimension of the poverty problem.

The working poor

A large and growing share of income of poor households comes from wages earned from work. In 2007, about half of household income of those in the bottom fifth of the household income distribution came from wages. The discussion of Figure 7T later will explore more on this segment of the population, which, while not an exact fit with persons under the poverty line, represents another similar measure of relative deprivation.

Because wages are an important component of income for those at the bottom of the income distribution (other components are discussed later), it is important to examine the working poor. Who are they and what types of jobs do they have? For most of this section, the working poor are identified as those who earn "poverty-level wages," defined here as wages at or below the hourly wage that would give a family of four enough income to reach but not exceed the poverty threshold, given full-time, full-year work. In 2011, that wage was $11.06 per hour. Figures 4E and 4F in the wages chapter detail important trends in the share of workers earning poverty-level wages by gender and race and ethnicity; here we further explore these workers by examining their characteristics at a point in time (2011).

Poverty-level wages

This section compares the characteristics of workers earning poverty-level wages with the characteristics of those earning above poverty-level wages. In 2011, 28.0 percent of workers earned poverty-level wages (or $11.06 or less an hour), up from 23.1 percent in 2002 (from Figure 4E). The average wage among these poverty-wage workers was $8.66 an hour versus $25.85 for all other workers.

Figure 7J Demographic characteristics of poverty-level-wage workers vs. non-poverty-level-wage workers, 2011

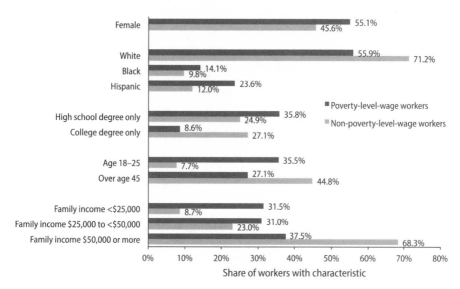

Note: Poverty-level-wage workers are defined as those earning at or below the wage a full-time, full-year worker would have to earn to give a family of four enough income to reach but not exceed the poverty threshold ($11.06 per hour in 2011).

Source: Authors' analysis of Current Population Survey Outgoing Rotation Group microdata

Figure 7J compares the demographic characteristics of poverty-wage and non-poverty-wage workers. Comparing each set of bars reveals categories in which poverty-wage workers are overrepresented (or underrepresented). Poverty-wage workers are more likely to be female, black, Hispanic, and young. They are also more likely to have only a high school degree. In fact, non-poverty-wage workers are more than three times as likely to have a college degree than poverty-wage workers.

The last set of bars in Figure 7J illustrate in what types of families poverty-wage workers reside, defined here as lower-income families (with incomes less than $25,000), middle-income families (with incomes of $25,000–<$50,000), and higher-income families (with incomes of $50,000 or more). Some have argued that many poverty-wage workers live in higher-income families, for example as children living at home. But the truth is that while some poverty-wage workers—about 37.5 percent—live in higher income families, most live in low- and middle-income families. About one-third of poverty-wage workers live in lower-income families, compared with 8.7 percent of non-poverty-wage workers.

Figure 7K Industry, occupation, and union status of poverty-level-wage workers vs. non-poverty-level-wage workers, 2011

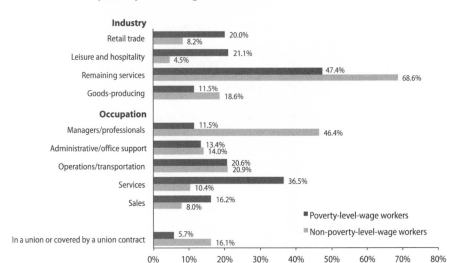

Note: Poverty-level-wage workers are defined as those earning at or below the hourly wage a full-time, full-year worker would have to earn to give a family of four enough income to reach but not exceed the poverty threshold ($11.06 per hour in 2011).

Source: Authors' analysis of Current Population Survey Outgoing Rotation Group microdata

Figure 7K displays several work-related characteristics of poverty-wage workers in 2011. Poverty-wage workers are disproportionately found in retail and leisure/hospitality, and are less likely to work in goods-producing industries and other services (such as finance or professional services). Turning to occupations, poverty-wage workers are far more likely to work in services or sales and far less likely to be managers or professionals. They are also considerably less likely to be in a union or covered by a union contract.

Job quality

Poverty-wage workers' much lower rate of unionization is significant not only because nonunion wages are likely to be lower but also because nonunion workers are less likely to have the benefits that tend to come with higher paying or unionized jobs. **Figure 7L** compares two such benefits: health insurance and pension coverage. Non-poverty-wage workers are about three times more likely to have employer-sponsored health insurance and nearly four times more likely to have employer-sponsored pension coverage as poverty-wage workers. Furthermore, poverty-wage workers generally are also far less likely to have paid-leave benefits.

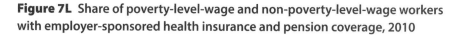

Figure 7L Share of poverty-level-wage and non-poverty-level-wage workers with employer-sponsored health insurance and pension coverage, 2010

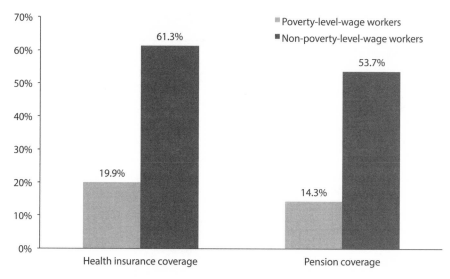

Note: Poverty-level-wage workers are defined as those earning at or below the hourly wage a full-time, full-year worker would have to earn to give a family of four enough income to reach but not exceed the poverty threshold ($10.73 per hour in 2010).

Source: Authors' analysis of Current Population Survey Annual Social and Economic Supplement microdata

As shown in Table 4.12, those in the bottom 10 percent of the wage distribution are only about one-third as likely to have paid sick days or paid family leave as workers overall.

Work hours

In this section, we switch gears to low-wage households (versus workers), which we define as households in the bottom fifth of the annual household earnings distribution (summing working members' wages). **Table 7.2**, which replicates a subset of information found in Table 2.17, separates annual earnings into hourly wages and annual hours, enabling us to determine how much of low-wage households' annual earnings growth between business cycle peak years 1979 and 2007 was driven by working more versus earning more per hour.

Annual earnings of the bottom fifth of working-age households rose by 12.3 percent between 1979 and 2007, as average overall earnings grew more than twice as fast at 27.7 percent. This represents a $1,911 growth in the bottom fifth's real annual earnings, about one-tenth the size of the average annual earnings growth of all working-age households ($19,045). Similarly, real hourly wages rose much

Table 7.2 Contribution of hours versus hourly wages to annual wage growth for working-age households, selected years, 1979–2007 (2011 dollars)

	1979	1989	1995	2000	2007	1995–2000	1979–2007
Real average annual wages							
All	$59,723	$65,858	$70,210	$78,883	$78,768	11.6%	27.7%
Bottom fifth	14,596	14,855	14,346	17,090	16,507	17.5	12.3
Annual hours worked							
All	3,092	3,286	3,317	3,378	3,314	1.8%	6.9%
Bottom fifth	1,716	1,884	1,837	1,977	1,880	7.4	9.2
Real average hourly wages							
All	$19.32	$20.04	$21.17	$23.35	$23.77	9.8%	20.8%
Bottom fifth	8.51	7.88	7.81	8.64	8.78	10.1	3.2
Contribution to annual wage growth							
Hours							
All	—	—	—	—	—	15.8%	25.0%
Bottom fifth	—	—	—	—	—	42.2	74.4
Hourly wages							
All	—	—	—	—	—	84.2%	75.0%
Bottom fifth	—	—	—	—	—	57.8	25.6

Note: The "bottom fifth" refers to the working-age households in the bottom fifth of the income distribution, as measured by money income. Percentage changes are approximated by taking the difference of natural logs of wages and hours.

Source: Authors' analysis of Current Population Survey Annual Social and Economic Supplement microdata

faster overall than for the bottom fifth between 1979 and 2007; 20.8 percent for all working-age households compared with 3.2 percent for the bottom fifth of working-age households. This translates into an increase in average hourly pay of $4.45 for all working-age households compared with $0.27 for those at the bottom.

Over the same period, annual hours of the bottom fifth rose by 9.2 percent, which means that about three-fourths—74.4 percent—of the rise in annual earnings of low-wage households was driven by increased work time. In stark contrast, only one-fourth (25.0 percent) of the growth in average working-age household earnings is derived from increased work hours; average annual earnings growth was driven primarily by increases in hourly wages, whereas annual earnings growth at the bottom was driven primarily by increases in annual hours worked.

One notable exception to this pattern is in the data for 1995 to 2000, which, as discussed earlier in the Wages chapter (Chapter 4), show how favorable the tight labor market of the late 1990s was to households at the bottom of the wage scale; hourly wages at the bottom grew 10.1 percent. Both annual earnings and hourly wages grew faster for the bottom fifth than overall. If the growth of the late 1990s had not happened, overall average hourly wage growth from 1979 to 2007 still would have been positive, but real wages of the bottom fifth of working-age households would have fallen. The following section explores factors that affect low-wage growth and subsequent changes to U.S. poverty rates.

Determinants of low incomes

Addressing the problem of U.S. poverty, however defined, requires exploring its many causes. To help explain why the poverty rate rises and falls, this section examines poverty alongside macroeconomic factors such as economic growth, unemployment, inequality, and wages; and then examines others factors such as education, family structure, and race.

The macro economy and poverty

Our examination of the relationship between macroeconomic growth and poverty begins with **Figure 7M**, which compares the actual poverty rate with a simulated poverty rate based on a model of the statistical relationship between

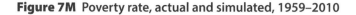

Figure 7M Poverty rate, actual and simulated, 1959–2010

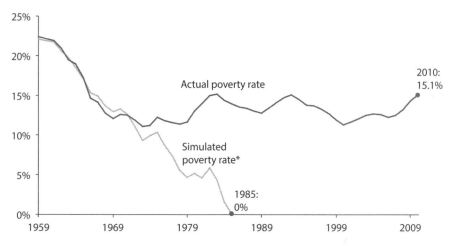

* Poverty rate simulated by a model based on the relationship between per capita GDP growth and the official poverty rate between 1959 and 1973.

Source: Authors' analysis of Current Population Survey Annual Social and Economic Supplement *Historical Poverty Tables* (Tables 2 and 4) and Bureau of Economic Analysis National Income and Product Accounts (Table 7.1). Analysis using Danziger and Gottschalk (1995)

growth in per capita gross domestic product (GDP) and poverty between 1959 and 1973. The model forecasts poverty quite accurately through the mid-1970s, when economic growth was broadly shared. Since then, the actual poverty rate has fluctuated cyclically within 4 percentage points above its trough in 1973. If the relationship between per capita GDP growth and poverty that prevailed from 1959 to 1973 (wherein as the country, *on average*, got richer, poverty dropped) had held, the poverty rate would have fallen to zero in the mid-1980s. The model's general results hold true, even under various alternative specifications. For instance, if we remove the elderly from the equation (not shown), non-elderly poverty still falls to zero in the 1980s, which tells us that the results shown were not driven by the increase in Social Security benefits over that period. And, when we rerun the model to control for the share of households headed by single mothers (not shown), we can demonstrate that family type did not drive these results.

Economic growth and poverty reduction clearly became decoupled in the mid-1970s, just as income inequality was taking off. As income inequality grows, poverty rates become less responsive to overall growth, because too little of that growth reaches the lower end of the income scale. Therefore, economic growth is a necessary factor in, but not *sufficient* for, broadly shared prosperity.

Faster productivity growth, which creates more income per hour worked, provides the potential for significant poverty reduction, but only if that income reaches the lower end of the income scale. An underappreciated way to ensure that income reaches those at the bottom is to sustain genuinely full employment by targeting the absolutely lowest unemployment rate consistent with non-accelerating inflation. **Figure 7N** compares the relationship between changes in productivity, unemployment, low-end wages, and poverty over the last three full business cycles and from 2007 to 2010.

The 1990s were characterized by strong productivity growth and falling unemployment. Productivity grew at a 2.1 percent annual rate during this period while the unemployment rate fell 1.3 percentage points from 1989 to 2000. This tightening labor market, particularly in the latter half of the decade, led to growth in wages at the low end (wages at the 20th percentile of the wage distribution grew 1.0 percent annually) and a decrease in the poverty rate (by 1.5 percentage points between 1989 and 2000). Full employment is critical for at least three reasons. First, the demand for labor in an economy at full-employment provides people with the jobs and work hours they need to make ends meet. Second, tight labor markets mean employers often must bid up wages and other measures of job quality to get and keep the workers they need. Third, full employment helps generate a more equitable distribution of growth because tighter labor markets help workers at the bottom of the wage scale more than other workers (as covered later in our discussion of Figure 7O).

Figure 7N Change in productivity, 20th-percentile wages, unemployment, and poverty, selected periods, 1979–2010

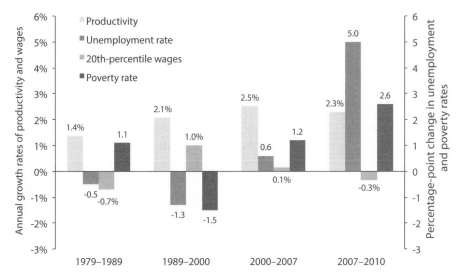

Source: Authors' analysis of Bureau of Labor Statistics Major Sector Productivity and Costs Index, Current Population Survey Outgoing Rotations Group microdata, CPS public data series, and CPS Annual Social and Economic Supplement *Historical Poverty Tables* (Table 2)

Unlike the 1990s expansion, the business cycles of the 1980s and 2000s did not translate into reductions in poverty. In the 1980s, annual productivity growth was lower than in other periods and unemployment fell only slightly. Wages at the 20th percentile fell and correspondingly poverty increased. In the 2000–2007 period, productivity grew more than in the prior two periods (by 2.5 percent annually) but unemployment also increased (up 0.6 percentage points across the period), and poverty grew (up 1.2 percentage points). During the 2007–2010 period, annual productivity growth remained relatively strong, but the unemployment rate skyrocketed, increasing by 5 percentage points (4.4 percentage points higher than the increase of the prior period). While this period does not represent a full business cycle, peak to peak, it still illustrates that failing labor markets are associated with falling wages at the bottom and sharply increasing poverty rates.

Falling unemployment, combined with increasing economic growth or rising productivity, is key to increasing wages at the bottom and reducing poverty. The critical role of full employment is particularly germane in the low-wage labor market. Unsurprisingly, there is a close relationship between low-end wage growth and poverty because wages are the largest component of incomes at the low end. However, wages of this group are also the most sensitive to a strong (or weak) labor market. **Figure 7O** makes this point by showing the impact on

Figure 7O Increase in wages from a 1 percentage-point decline in the unemployment rate, by gender

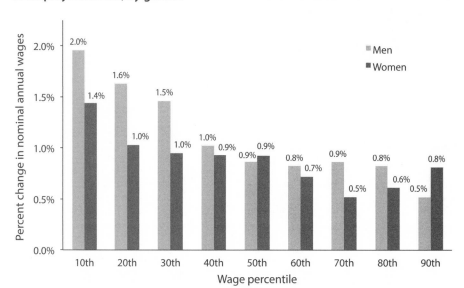

Source: Authors' analysis of Current Population Survey Outgoing Rotation Group microdata for 1979 to 2007. Analysis based on Katz and Krueger (1999)

nominal annual wage growth of a 1 percentage-point decline in the unemployment rate (based on data for 1979 to 2007). Note the steep downward "staircase," as the percent change in wages falls for nearly every consecutive wage percentile up the scale, particularly for men; clearly men at the lower end get the biggest wage boost from tighter job markets. For instance, for men at the 20th percentile, a 1-percentage-point decline in the unemployment rate is associated with a 1.6 percent increase in wages. According to these results, wage gains from lower unemployment are roughly twice as high for the lowest-wage male workers as they are for middle- and high-wage workers.

The impact of economic, demographic, and education changes on poverty rates

The previous analyses explored several important macroeconomic factors that play an important role in poverty reduction by boosting wages, and therefore incomes, at the bottom. **Table 7.3** extends our analyses to a different, larger set of factors commonly associated with changes in poverty over the past three decades: changes in the U.S. population's racial composition, education levels, and family structure (demographic factors), and overall income growth and income

Table 7.3 Impact of changes in U.S. economic and demographic composition on the poverty rate, selected periods, 1979–2010

	1979–1989	1989–2000	2000–2007	1979–2007	2007–2010
Actual change in poverty rate	1.2	-1.5	1.2	0.8	2.6
Change due to demographic shifts	-0.2	-0.6	-0.1	-0.8	0.3
Racial composition	0.4	0.4	0.1	0.9	0.0
Educational composition	-1.2	-1.1	-0.4	-2.7	0.2
Family structure	0.7	0.4	0.3	1.4	0.2
Change due to economic shifts	1.4	-0.9	1.2	1.7	2.3
Income change	-1.8	-2.1	0.1	-3.8	0.4
Income inequality	3.2	1.2	1.1	5.5	1.9

Note: Data may not sum due to rounding and the effect of the interactions between demographic characteristics, explained in the table note.

Source: Authors' analysis of Current Population Survey Annual Social and Economic Supplement microdata. Analysis based on Danziger and Gottschalk (1995)

---

inequality (economic factors). The first row shows the percentage-point change in the poverty rate across each subperiod shown, and the subsequent rows show how much (in percentage points) each factor contributed to that change. For example, the "education" row shows the percentage-point impact on the poverty rate made by changes in the educational composition of the U.S. population (in this case, an increasing share of individuals with higher levels of education translates into lower poverty). The "family structure" row shows how changes in the composition of U.S. families (e.g., more single-mother households) affected the poverty rate. (Table note 7.3 at the end of this chapter explains these calculations in detail.)

During the most recent full business cycle, 2000–2007, rising inequality of U.S. incomes (family income for people in families and individual income otherwise) contributed more than any other factor shown to the 1.2 percentage-point increase in the U.S. poverty rate. The minimal impact of the other factors generally canceled one another out. In other words, controlling for changes in racial, educational, and family structure composition, had income growth been more broadly shared over this period, poverty would have hardly increased from its most recent low in 2000. From 2007 to 2010, inequality continued to play the most significant role, though falling incomes also increased the poverty rate.

In the roughly three decades (1979–2007) leading up to the most recent recession, educational upgrading and overall income growth were the two biggest poverty-reducing factors, while income inequality was the largest poverty-increasing factor. Relative to these other factors, the racial composition of the U.S. population over this period (the growth of nonwhite populations with higher likelihoods of poverty) and changes in family structure (the growth of single mother households) have contributed much less to poverty, particularly in the last full business cycle, when racial composition contributed 0.1 percentage points and family structure 0.3 percentage points.

Up until the 2000s, when overall income growth was weak (or negative), rising incomes reduced poverty by about 2 percentage points (1.8 in the 1979–1989 cycle and 2.1 across 1989–2000). This finding aligns with Figure 7M, which established that, simply based on growth of real per capita GDP, poverty would have ended in the 1980s. That is, without inequality siphoning growth toward the top, a growing economy—with growth broadly shared—would have put a serious dent in poverty.

Figure 7P gives closer attention to the family structure component, which is often cited by those who discount economic explanations for poverty. Rather than inequality or the absence of full employment preventing growth from lowering poverty, they argue that changes in family structure, such as the increase in families headed by single mothers, are driving the higher poverty rates. According to this line of thinking, more jobs, stronger income growth, and less income inequality are secondary to marriage in decreasing poverty.

Figure 7P Impact of changes in family structure on the poverty rate, selected periods, 1979–2010

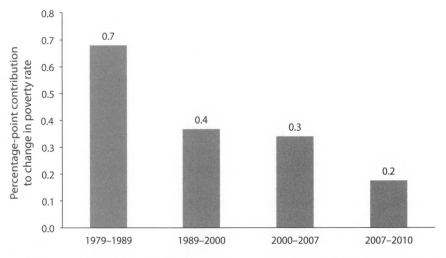

Source: Authors' analysis of Current Population Survey Annual Social and Economic Supplement microdata. Analysis based on Danziger and Gottschalk (1995)

The rationale for these arguments is that female-headed households with children have much higher poverty rates (as shown in Figure 7E) and that their formation contributed 1.4 percentage points to the increase in poverty from 1979 to 2007 (Table 7.3). However, Figure 7P shows a sharp fall in the impact of this factor. In each succeeding business cycle (including during the Great Recession), changes in the composition of U.S. families (changes dominated by increases in single-mother households) explained less of the increase in the poverty rate, with the effect largely fading out in the Great Recession and its aftermath, when the shift to more economically vulnerable families contributed only 0.2 percentage points to the growth in poverty rates.

Figure 7Q plots the impact of the economic and demographic factors shown in Table 7.3 for the roughly three-decade period prior to the Great Recession (three full business cycles). The impacts of income inequality and income growth were quantitatively large, but in opposite directions. Had income growth been equally distributed, which in this analysis means that all families' incomes would have grown at the pace of the average, the poverty rate would have been 5.5 points lower, essentially, 44 percent lower than what it was.

Figure 7Q Impact of changes in U.S. economic and demographic composition on the poverty rate, 1979–2007

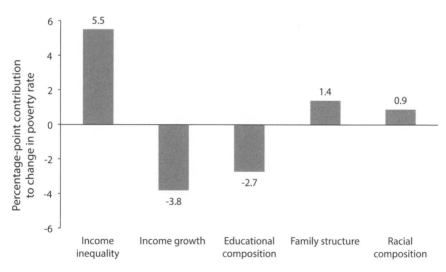

Note: The bars show by how much the poverty rate increased or decreased due to rising income inequality, income growth across the income distribution, and changes in the education levels, family structures, and racial composition of the U.S. population.

Source: Authors' analysis of Current Population Survey Annual Social and Economic Supplement microdata. Analysis based on Danziger and Gottschalk (1995)

Educational upgrading is often overlooked in these analyses. The low-income population in the United States has become considerably more highly educated over time, even with the influx of less-educated immigrants. More education tends to raise families' incomes; the third bar in the figure reveals that increased educational attainment (a dominant part of the change in the educational composition of the population) has been a potent force in lowering poverty rates.

In sum, our diagnosis of poverty's determinants reveals that the unequal distribution of income has, to a substantial degree, prevented poverty rates from falling in periods of strong economic growth. In the 2000s in particular, the workforce was highly productive, yet poverty increased. This rise had little to do with family formation. It had a great deal to do with rising inequality.

Resources for low-income Americans

While one of the most effective antipoverty programs is a U.S. economy that generates good jobs in a very tight labor market, government transfer programs can provide a valuable safety net. This section explores some of these antipoverty programs.

Figure 7R Per capita Social Security expenditures and the elderly poverty rate, 1959–2010

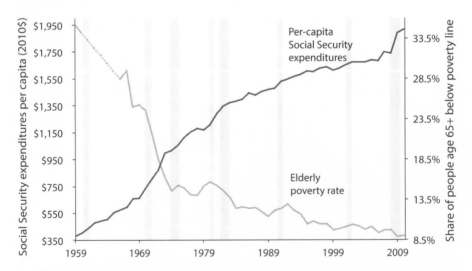

Note: The dotted line denotes a linear extrapolation between 1959 and 1966 (no formal data exist for 1960 to 1965). Shaded areas denote recessions.

Source: Authors' analysis of Current Population Survey Annual Social and Economic Supplement *Historical Poverty Tables* (Tables 2 and 3) and Social Security Administration trust fund data

As Figure 7B showed, poverty declined significantly among all age groups from 1959 through the early 1970s, and the largest and most continuous declines occurred among the elderly. **Figure 7R** shows that declines in elderly poverty are directly associated with sharp increases in per capita Social Security expenditures—evidence that direct government transfers keep many people from falling below the poverty line. Further evidence: The Census reported that 13.8 million elderly people would have been in poverty in 2010 had Social Security been unavailable in 2010 (Renwick 2011). That would have meant an elderly poverty rate of about 44 percent, compared with the actual poverty rate of 9.0 percent. But, Social Security lifts not only the elderly out of poverty. Without Social Security benefits to surviving family members or disabled individuals, the non-elderly poverty rate would have been 18.4 percent instead of 16.0 percent in 2010.

Other safety net programs help working families make ends meet and rise above poverty. Both the federal and state EITCs increase families' resources, while food stamps, public health insurance, child care subsidies, and housing vouchers reduce their annual expenses. **Figure 7S** illustrates how a set of targeted government programs affected overall poverty in 2010 by showing what the poverty

Figure 7S Poverty rate absent targeted government programs, by age group, 2010

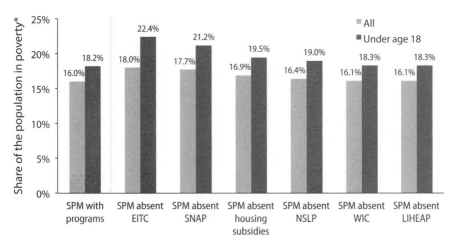

* As measured by the Supplemental Poverty Measure (SPM).
Note: The difference in the poverty rates between the first set of bars and each of the remaining sets is the extent to which each program reduced poverty. EITC is the Earned Income Tax Credit; SNAP is the Supplemental Nutrition Assistance Program; NSLP is the National School Lunch Program; WIC is the Special Supplemental Nutrition Program for Women, Infants, and Children; and LIHEAP is the Low Income Home Energy Assistance Program.

Source: Authors' analysis of Short (2011, Table 3a)

rate would have been absent each program, for the entire population and for children. The difference between the first set of bars, which show the shares of the overall and under-age-18 populations in poverty under the Supplemental Poverty Measure, and each subsequent set of bars is the extent to which each program reduced poverty. It is clear that many programs targeted to the poor disproportionately help children. The EITC was the largest poverty reducer for those under age 18, followed by the Supplemental Nutrition Assistance Program (SNAP, commonly referred to as food stamps).

While some components of this social safety net are available regardless of work status (e.g., SNAP), others are dependent on wage income (e.g., the EITC). In a strong labor market with low unemployment, work-dependent government supports lift many working poor out of poverty; however, a weak job market greatly curtails the effectiveness of these supports. The strength of other safety net programs, such as public health insurance, is also at risk when the economy is weak, as these programs depend on state financing at the same time as state budgets are stretched by the poor economy. Thus, unemployment insurance is vital to countering increases in poverty in bad economic times.

Using the methodology used to calculate the poverty prevention capacity of Social Security, we estimate that, absent unemployment insurance, the official poverty rate in 2010 would have been 23.2 percent for children (instead of 22.0 percent) and 14.9 percent for non-elderly adults (instead of 13.7 percent). Thus, unemployment insurance kept 900,000 children and 2.3 million non-elderly adults out of poverty in 2010 even though one or more workers in these vulnerable households were laid off.

In short, poverty can be greatly reduced by providing vulnerable households with direct subsidies such as Social Security, unemployment insurance, and the EITC and in-kind transfers such as food stamps and public health insurance, as well as by enacting policies that increase the minimum wage and workers' bargaining power (e.g., macroeconomic policies that target full employment, thereby lowering unemployment and securing wage gains across the income distribution). Used in combination, these policy levers can lower poverty rates as the United States pulls out of the downturn from the Great Recession.

Unfortunately, the safety net in the United States has weakened over time, and workers at the bottom rely more heavily on wages and a strong economy to make ends meet. **Figure 7T** displays the major sources of income for households in the bottom fifth of the income distribution from 1979 to 2007. The figure uses the household "comprehensive income" measure from the Congressional Budget Office, which includes "in-kind income" (i.e., employer-paid health insurance premiums, food stamps, school meals, housing assistance, energy assistance, and the fungible value (estimated fair value) of Medicare and Medicaid), and "cash transfers" (e.g., Social Security, unemployment insurance, and welfare programs such as Temporary Assistance for Needy Families (TANF)).

Figure 7T Share of bottom-fifth household income accounted for by wages, cash transfers, and in-kind income, 1979–2007

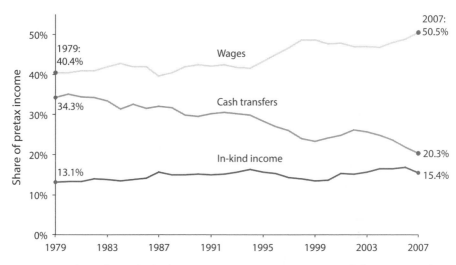

Note: Wages, cash transfers, and in-kind income comprise, on average, 88 percent of all pretax income for the bottom fifth. The other 12 percent is made up of capital gains, proprietors' income, other business income, interest and dividends, pensions, imputed taxes, and other income.

Source: Authors' analysis of Congressional Budget Office (2010a)

The share of comprehensive pretax income accounted for by wages rose from 40.4 percent in 1979 to 50.5 percent in 2007, an increase of 10.1 percentage points. Recall that for the bottom fifth of working-age households, increases in household annual wages stemmed primarily from increased annual hours worked rather than from increased hourly wages (Table 7.2). At the same time that wages became a more important source of household income for the bottom fifth, safety net programs' contributions to income held level or fell. From 1979 to 2007, the share of the bottom fifth's income accounted for by cash transfers fell 14.0 percentage points (from 34.3 percent to 20.3 percent), while the share accounted for by in-kind income rose a modest 2.3 percentage points, from 13.1 percent to 15.4 percent. Together, cash transfers and in-kind income dropped from 47.4 percent to 35.7 percent of income from 1979 to 2007.

International comparisons

In considering what can be done to alleviate poverty in the United States, it is useful to look at the experience of other developed countries. The first part of this section provides a general comparison of poverty and the earnings distribution in the United States and "peer" countries, largely countries within the OECD that have roughly similar GDP per hour worked as the United States. After comparing the bottom of the earnings distribution and poverty levels, we examine the extent to which resources go to the bottom, focusing specifically on the tax-and-transfer system that redistributes market income and provides a safety net to keep people out of poverty, or helps those who fall into poverty due to unexpected job losses or other events get back on their feet.

Poverty and the earnings distribution

One particular point of interest in international comparisons, shown in **Figure 7U,** is the ratio of earnings (wages) at the 10th percentile of the earnings distribution to earnings of the median worker. This measures how workers at the bottom fare in relation to the typical worker. A lower number implies more inequality. As the figure shows, earnings at the 10th percentile in the United States are less than half (47.4 percent) of those of the typical worker. This is the lowest share in the figure and is far below the (unweighted) peer average of 62.0 percent.

Figure 7U showed that earners at the 10th percentile in the United States are further from the U.S. median than 10th percentile earners in peer countries are

Figure 7U Earnings at the 10th percentile as a share of median worker earnings in selected OECD countries, late 2000s

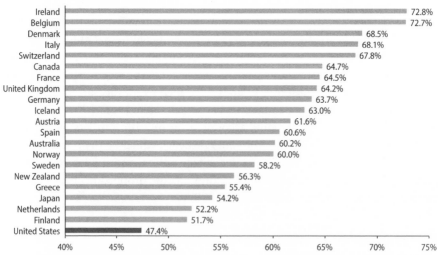

Note: Earnings is generally defined as gross earnings (wages prior to tax deductions or adjustments) for full-time, full-year workers.

Source: Authors' analysis of Organisation for Economic Co-operation and Development's *Distribution of Gross Earnings* metadata (data group labelled "late 2000s")

Figure 7V Earnings at the 10th percentile in selected OECD countries relative to the United States, late 2000s

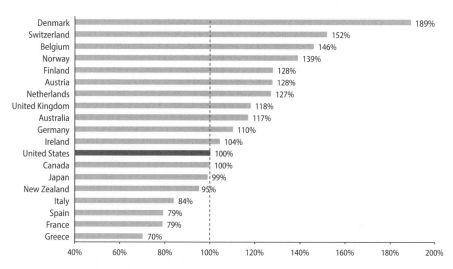

Note: Earnings is generally defined as gross earnings (wages prior to tax deductions or adjustments) for full-time, full-year workers.

Source: Authors' analysis of Organisation for Economic Co-operation and Development's *Distribution of Gross Earnings* metadata (data group labelled "late 2000s")

from their own countries' respective medians. However, median earnings vary across countries. Thus, the data in Figure 7U do not directly tell us how well-off (in terms of earnings) workers at the 10th percentile in other countries are compared with U.S. workers at the 10th percentile.

Figure 7V directly compares the level of earnings (a measure of livings standards) of low-earning workers in the United States with the living standards of low-earning workers in peer countries. The figure is scaled such that earnings at the 10th percentile in the United States equal 100 percent, making it easy to identify countries with higher relative earnings by their longer bars.

Despite the relatively high earnings at the top of the U.S. income scale (as illustrated in Chapter 2), inequality in the United States is so severe that low-earning U.S. workers are actually worse off than low-earning workers in all but seven peer countries. As shown in the figure, the United States ranks 12th out of the 19 peer countries shown.

Turning to an international comparison of poverty rates, we examine the share of the population living below half the median household income (similar to the relative measure of poverty from Figure 7I) in the United States and select OECD countries (**Figure 7W**). As with the previous two figures, this analysis draws on the OECD database.

Figure 7W Relative poverty rate in the United States and selected OECD countries, late 2000s

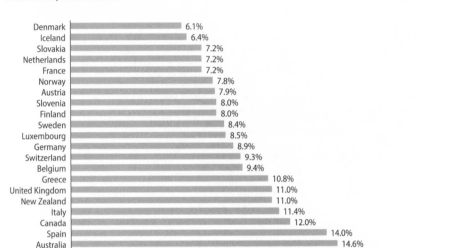

Note: The relative poverty rate is defined here as the share of individuals living in households with income below half of household-size-adjusted median income. Poverty rates are based on income after taxes and transfers.

Source: Authors' analysis of Organisation for Economic Co-operation and Development *Stat Extracts* (data group labelled "late 2000s")

According to the figure, in the late 2000s, 17.3 percent of the U.S. population lived in poverty—the highest relative poverty rate among OECD peers. The U.S. relative poverty rate was nearly three times higher than that of Denmark, which had the lowest rate (6.1 percent), and about 1.8 times higher than the (unweighted) peer country average of 9.6 percent.

While the overall relative poverty rate in the United States is higher than that of peer countries, the extent of child poverty is even more severe, as shown in **Figure 7X**. In 2009, the United States had the highest rate of child poverty, at 23.1 percent, meaning that more than one in five children in the United States lived in poverty (as measured by the share of children living in households with household income below half of median household income). This rate was almost five times higher than that of Iceland, which had the lowest rate, at 4.7 percent, and over two times higher than the (unweighted) peer-country average rate of 9.8 percent.

Another useful way to look at the extent of child poverty in the United States relative to other countries is to examine the child poverty gap, the distance between the poverty line (defined here as half of median household income) and

Figure 7X Child poverty rate in selected developed countries, 2009

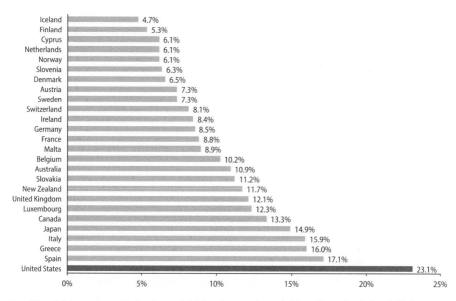

Note: The child poverty rate is the share of children living in households with income below half of household-size-adjusted median income.

Source: Adamson (2012, Figure 1b)

Figure 7Y Child poverty gap in selected developed countries, 2009

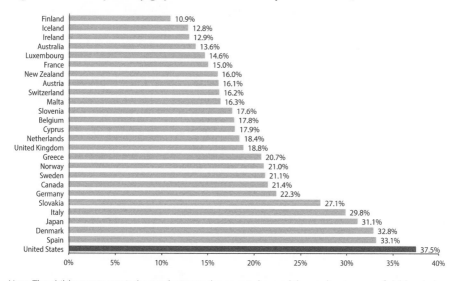

Note: The child poverty gap is the gap between the poverty line and the median income of children below the poverty line, taken as a share of the poverty line. The poverty line is defined as half of household-size-adjusted median income.

Source: Adamson (2012, Figure 7)

the median household income of children below the poverty line, expressed as a percentage of the poverty line. A smaller value means that the median household income of children below the poverty line is relatively close to the poverty line, while a larger number means the median household income of these children is further below the poverty line, i.e., that they are relatively more poor. **Figure 7Y** shows that the child poverty gap in the United States is 37.5 percent, the highest among peer countries. Therefore, not only is child poverty greater in the United States (Figure 7X), but children living in poverty in the United States also face higher relative deprivation than impoverished children in other developed countries. To some extent, this mimics the high rate of deep poverty in the United States shown in Figure 7G.

Resource allocation

To show how much taxes and transfer income affect poverty rates, we can compare poverty rates based on income calculations that include taxes and government transfers (Figure 7W) with rates based on income calculations that exclude them ("pretax and pre-transfer" poverty rates). While differences in the latter can be attributed to differences in market outcomes (such as the domestic economy but also a country's minimum wage, level of unionization, and other labor market institutions), the former reflects both market outcomes and variations in the extent of tax-and-transfer programs for low-income households. Differences between the two poverty rates are solely due to the government safety net.

Figure 7Z plots the differences between pre– and post–tax-and-transfer poverty rates in the United States and peer countries. (As with Figures 7I and 7W, the measure here is the relative poverty rate, the share of the population below half of median household income). For example, the pretax, pretransfer poverty rate in the United States in the late 2000s was 27.0 percent while the post-tax, post-transfer rate was 17.3 percent. The difference, 9.7 percentage points, is how much the U.S. tax-and-transfer system reduced the poverty rate. Among peer countries, the United States' tax-and-transfer system does the least to reduce the poverty rate. In contrast, tax-and-transfer programs reduced the poverty rate in France by 25.4 percentage points (from 32.6 percent to 7.2 percent after taxes and transfers). France's redistributive programs lower poverty by about 2.5 times as much as those of the United States. The (unweighted) average effect of peer countries' tax-and-transfer programs is a poverty-rate reduction of 17.4 percentage points—an effect nearly two times greater than that produced by tax-and-transfer programs in the United States.

Figure 7Z shows the effect of taxes and transfers on poverty rates, but does not show levels of social spending (for example, government expenditures on Medicare and Social Security in the United States). **Figure 7AA** shows total social expenditures as a share of GDP for the United States and select OECD countries

Figure 7Z Extent to which taxes and transfer programs reduce the relative poverty rate, selected OECD countries, late 2000s

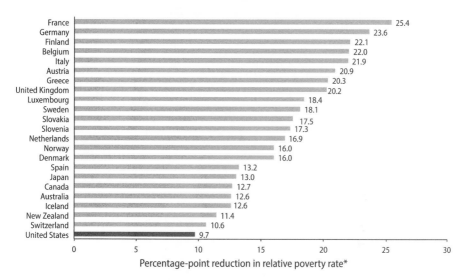

Note: This figure plots the differences between each country's pre– and post–tax-and-transfer relative poverty rate, where relative poverty is the share of individuals with income below half of household-size-adjusted median income.

Source: Authors' analysis of Organisation for Economic Co-operation and Development *Stat Extracts* (data group labelled "late 2000s")

plotted against their post-tax, post-transfer poverty rates (from Figure 7W), providing a clear picture of the relationship between social spending and poverty. The United States stands out as the country with the highest poverty rate and one of the lowest levels of social expenditures—16.2 percent of GDP, well below the vast majority of peer countries, which average 21.3 percent (unweighted). The figure suggests that relatively low social expenditures are at least partially implicated in the high U.S. poverty rate.

Together, Figures 7Z and 7AA demonstrate that peer countries are much more likely than the United States to step in where markets and labor policy fail in order to lift their most disadvantaged citizens out of poverty.

Figure 7AA Social expenditure and relative poverty rates in selected OECD countries, late 2000s

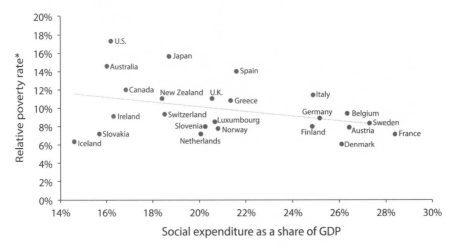

* The relative poverty rate is the share of individuals with income below half of household-size-adjusted median income. Poverty rates are based on income after taxes and transfers.
Note: Social expenditure is government expenditure on social programs, such as Social Security and Medicare in the United States. The equation for the trend line is $y = -0.2559x + 0.1528$ and the $R^2 = 0.1266$.

Source: Authors' analysis of Organisation for Economic Co-operation and Development *Stat Extracts* (data group labelled "late 2000s")

Conclusion

High and rising rates of poverty in the United States are yet another consequence of growing income inequality over the last three-and-a-half decades. Strong economic growth is no longer sufficient to reduce poverty. In periods of prosperity, economic gains have not been broadly shared, and least of all among those at the very bottom. In hard times, as in the Great Recession and its aftermath, an increasing number of families are falling into poverty, and, in many cases, deep poverty.

Historically, poverty has been greatly reduced by providing vulnerable households with direct subsidies such as Social Security and the EITC and in-kind transfers such as food stamps and public health insurance. Unfortunately, the safety net in the United States has weakened, and workers at the bottom rely more heavily on wages and a strong economy to make ends meet. A robust economy—with low unemployment—coupled with strong labor market institutions (e.g. a higher minimum wage, increased unionization) can help secure wage gains across the income distribution. Used in combination, a strong safety net and full employment policies can lower poverty rates.

Table and figure notes

Tables

Table 7.1. Comparison of poverty measures. Table is adapted from Short (2011), "Resource Estimates" table.

Table 7.2. Contribution of hours versus hourly wages to annual wage growth for working-age households, selected years, 1979–2007. See note to Table 2.17.

Table 7.3. Impact of changes in U.S. economic and demographic composition on the poverty rate, selected periods, 1979–2010. Underlying data are from Current Population Survey Annual Social and Economic Supplement microdata; see Appendix A for details. The methodology for this decomposition is taken from Danziger and Gottschalk (1995, Chapter 5), which explores the role of changes in socioeconomic characteristics (e.g., changes in average income, changes in income inequality, and demographic changes such as the change in racial groups' shares of the overall population) on the poverty rate (using the official poverty rate) between any two years. We focus specifically on the 1979–1989, 1989–2000, 2000–2007, 2007–2010, and 1979–2007 periods. To examine the impact of average income of the U.S. population on the poverty rate, we assign the average real income growth across the period to be the growth for all individuals between years t0 and t1 and simulate a new poverty rate. This procedure holds the shape of the distribution (inequality) constant in t0 while allowing incomes to grow equally for all individuals. This simulated poverty rate for t1 is then compared to the actual poverty rate in year t0, and the percentage-point difference is the change in the mean, i.e. the impact of income growth. The change due to income inequality is the percentage-point difference between the simulated poverty distribution in t1 and the actual poverty rate in t1.

We repeat this exercise using the demographic composition of each variable of interest to see the effect of these demographic changes on the overall poverty rate. First we calculate the weight of each demographic factor (such as individuals with college degrees) by its population share and simulate the poverty rate in t1 for all persons between t0 and t1, allowing for income to grow equally among all families and holding the demographic composition of the population in t0 constant. Then, we calculate a second simulated rate that incorporates both the mean income growth and the demographic changes across the period. The difference between these two simulated rates in t1 is the percentage point-change in the poverty rate due to demographic changes.

The interaction, or error, term states to what degree the demographic variables are conflated, which could lead to bias in measurement of a factor's impact. Since our error term is negative and relatively small (-.4 from 1979–2007), the reported relationship might slightly overstate the degree to which the simulated income decreases the poverty rate for each demographic group, but it is not enough to change the story.

Figures

Figure 7A. Poverty and twice-poverty rates, 1959–2010. Underlying data are from Current Population Survey Annual Social and Economic Supplement *Historical Poverty Tables*, Table 2, "Poverty Status, by Family Relationship, Race, and Hispanic Origin," and Table 5, "Percent of People by Ratio of Income to Poverty Level."

Figure 7B. Poverty rate, by age, 1959–2010. Underlying data are from Current Population Survey Annual Social and Economic Supplement *Historical Poverty Tables*, Table 3, "Poverty

Status, by Age, Race, and Hispanic Origin" and Current Population Survey Annual Social and Economic Supplement microdata (see Appendix A for details).

Figure 7C. Poverty rate, by race and ethnicity, nativity, and citizenship status, 1973–2010. Underlying data are from Current Population Survey Annual Social and Economic Supplement *Historical Poverty Tables*, Table 2, "Poverty Status, by Family Relationship, Race, and Hispanic Origin" and Table 23, "People in Poverty by Nativity." As with most other CPS data analyses presented in the book, race/ethnicity categories are mutually exclusive (i.e., white non-Hispanic, black non-Hispanic, and Hispanic any race).

Figure 7D. Poverty rate, by race and ethnicity, and age, 2010. Underlying data are from Current Population Survey Annual Social and Economic Supplement (CPS-ASEC) *Historical Poverty Tables*, Table 3, "Poverty Status, by Age, Race, and Hispanic Origin" and from CPS-ASEC microdata; see Appendix A for details. As with most other CPS data analyses presented in the book, race/ethnicity categories are mutually exclusive (i.e. white non-Hispanic, black non-Hispanic, and Hispanic any race).

Figure 7E. Poverty rates of various types of families, 1959–2010. Underlying data are from Current Population Survey Annual Social and Economic Supplement *Historical Poverty Tables*, Table 4, "Poverty Status, by Type of Family, Presence of Related Children, Race and Hispanic Origin."

Figure 7F. Length of time in poverty over a two-year period, 2008–2009. Underlying data are from Survey of Income and Program Participation microdata (2008 panel).

Figure 7G. Share of the poor in "deep poverty," 1975–2010. Underlying data are from Current Population Survey Annual Social and Economic Supplement *Historical Poverty Tables*, Table 2, "Poverty Status, by Family Relationship, Race, and Hispanic Origin," and Table 22, "Number of People Below 50 Percent of Poverty Level."

Figure 7H. Poverty rate, official and under the Supplemental Poverty Measure, by age group, 2010. Underlying data are from the U.S. Census Bureau's *Current Population Reports* (Short 2011), Table 1, "Number and Percent of People in Poverty by Different Poverty Measures: 2010."

Figure 7I. Official and relative poverty rate, 1979–2010. Underlying data are from Current Population Survey Annual Social and Economic Supplement *Historical Poverty Tables*, Table 2, "Poverty Status, by Family Relationship, Race, and Hispanic Origin," and Current Population Survey Annual Social and Economic Supplement microdata; see Appendix A for details. To be consistent with international comparisons, median income includes noncash transfers such as food stamps and housing subsidies.

Figure 7J. Demographic characteristics of poverty-level-wage workers vs. non-poverty-level-wage workers, 2011. Underlying data are from Current Population Survey Outgoing Rotation Groups microdata; see Appendix B for details. As with most other CPS microdata analyses presented in the book, race/ethnicity categories are mutually exclusive (i.e. white non-Hispanic, black non-Hispanic, and Hispanic any race).

Figure 7K. Industry, occupation, and union status of poverty-level-wage workers vs. non-poverty-level-wage workers, 2011. Underlying data are from Current Population Survey Outgoing Rotation Groups microdata; see Appendix B for details. Occupations do not sum to 100 percent because the figure excludes the "Other Occupations" category, which constitutes less than 2 percent of the workforce.

Figure 7L. Share of poverty-level-wage and non-poverty-level-wage workers with employer-sponsored health insurance and pension coverage, 2010. Underlying data are from Current Population Survey Annual Social and Economic Supplement microdata; see Appendix A for details. The analysis includes workers in both the private and public sectors and does not have age limits or work requirements. Coverage is defined as being included in an employer-sponsored plan for which the employer paid for at least some of the coverage.

Figure 7M. Poverty rate, actual and simulated, 1959–2010. Underlying data are from Current Population Survey Annual Social and Economic Supplement *Historical Poverty Tables*, Table 2, "Poverty Status, by Family Relationship, Race, and Hispanic Origin," and Table 4, "Poverty Status, by Type of Family, Presence of Related Children, Race and Hispanic Origin," and from Bureau of Economic Analysis National Income Product Accounts, Table 7.1, "Selected Per Capita Product and Income Series in Current and Chained Dollars." The analysis is an adaptation of analysis by Danziger and Gottschalk (1995), whose method was to regress the poverty rate of the growth of real per capita gross domestic product from 1959–1973 and then simulate poverty rates based on that simple model. The link between GDP and poverty in the earlier period (1959–1973) and the potential for GDP to eradicate poverty by the 1980s holds true for alternative specifications including using only the under-age-65 poverty rate (to remove elderly, the main recipients of Social Security, also growing over this period) and controlling for one target demographic: female headed families.

Figure 7N. Change in productivity, 20th-percentile wages, unemployment, and poverty, selected periods, 1979–2010. Productivity data, which measure output per hour, are from the Bureau of Labor Statistics Major Sector Productivity and Costs data; the figure shows the average annual growth rate of productivity over the periods covered. The figure also shows the average annual growth rate of wages at the 20th percentile of the wage distribution for the given periods, using data from Current Population Survey Outgoing Rotations Group microdata; see Appendix B for details. The percentage-point changes in the unemployment rate across the periods shown come from the monthly Current Population Survey public data series, while percentage-point changes in the poverty rate come from Current Population Survey Annual Social and Economic Supplement *Historical Poverty Tables*, Table 2, "Poverty Status, by Family Relationship, Race, and Hispanic Origin."

Figure 7O. Increase in wages from a 1-percentage-point decline in the unemployment rate, by gender. Estimates use Current Population Survey Outgoing Rotation Group microdata (see Appendix B), and are computed based on a model employed by Katz and Krueger (1999). Annual changes in log wages are regressed on unemployment, lagged log-changes in the CPI-U-RS (but, following Katz and Krueger the coefficient on this is constrained to equal 1), lagged productivity growth, and dummies for 1989–1995, 1996–2000, and 2001–2007 (excluded period is 1979–1988). The sample covers the years 1979–2007.

Figure 7P. Impact of changes in family structure on the poverty rate, selected periods, 1979–2010. The figure looks at the overall composition of family structure in the United States (e.g., the share of families headed by a single mother) and measures how much the change in the composition has affected the poverty rate in given periods. For more information on the methodology underlying the figure, see the note to Table 7.3.

Figure 7Q. Impact of changes in U.S. economic and demographic composition on the poverty rate, 1979–2007. See note to Table 7.3.

Figure 7R. Per capita Social Security expenditures and the elderly poverty rate, 1959–2010. Underlying data are from Current Population Survey Annual Social and Economic Supplement *Historical Poverty Tables*, Table 2, "Poverty Status, by Family Relationship, Race, and Hispanic Origin," and Table 3, "Poverty Status, by Age, Race, and Hispanic Origin." Data are also from Social Security Administration trust fund data, Table 4a1, "Old-Age and Survivors Insurance Trust Fund Expenditures."

Figure 7S. Poverty rate absent targeted government programs, by age group, 2010. Underlying data are from Short (2011), Table 3a, "Effect of Excluding Individual Elements on SPM Rates: 2010."

Figure 7T. Share of bottom-fifth household income accounted for by wages, cash transfers, and in-kind income, 1979–2007. Underlying data are from the Congressional Budget Office, *Average Federal Taxes by Income Group*, "Sources of Income for all Households, by Household Income Category, 1979 to 2007" [Excel spreadsheet]. The Congressional Budget Office definition of in-kind income includes employer-paid health insurance premiums, food stamps, school lunches and breakfasts, housing assistance, energy assistance, and the fungible value of Medicare and Medicaid, as estimated by the Current Population Survey. CBO's definition of cash transfers includes payments from Social Security, unemployment insurance, Supplemental Security Income, Aid to Families with Dependent Children, Temporary Assistance for Needy Families, veterans' benefits, and workers' compensation.

Figure 7U. Earnings at the 10th percentile as a share of median worker earnings in selected OECD countries, late 2000s. Underlying data are metadata from the Organisation for Economic Co-operation and Development's *Distribution of Gross Earnings of Full-time Employees and Gender Wage Gap* database. Earnings for all countries are defined as gross earnings for full-time, full-year workers, with the exception of Denmark, which is for all workers, the Netherlands, which is for full time, full-year equivalent workers, and Switzerland, which is net earnings for full-time workers. The shares are earnings at the 10th percentile as a share of the median earnings in each country's respective currency.

Figure 7V. Earnings at the 10th percentile in selected OECD countries relative to the United States, late 2000s. Underlying data are metadata from the Organisation of Economic Co-operation and Development's *Distribution of Gross Earnings of Full-time Employees and Gender Wage Gap* database. See note for Figure 7U on definition of earnings. Data for earnings at the 10th percentile are converted into weekly earnings and are then converted into equivalent U.S. dollars using a purchasing power parity index from the International Monetary Fund *World Economic Outlook Database*. The figure shows the share of each country's 10th percentile earnings relative to the 10th percentile earnings in the United States.

Figure 7W. Relative poverty rate in the United States and selected OECD countries, late 2000s. Underlying data are from the Organisation for Economic Co-operation and Development's *Stat Extracts* public data series. Household-size-adjusted income, or equivalent income, is household income divided by the square root of the household size. Countries were chosen based on their productivity per worker hour using the "PPP Converted GDP Laspeyres Per Hour Worked by Employees at 2005 Constant Prices" series from *Penn World Table Version 7.0* (Heston, Summers, and Aten 2011). We chose to exclude countries whose productivity is less than half that of the United States. The OECD data base uses slightly different methods than that found in 7I (e.g., its handling of taxes and transfers are different), therefore, the relative rates for the United States are not exactly the same.

Figure 7X. Child poverty rate in selected developed countries, 2009. Underlying data are from UNICEF Innocenti Research Centre Report Card 10 (Adamson 2012), Figure 1b, "Child Poverty Rate." The poverty rate is the percentage of children (age 0–17) living in households with equivalent income lower than 50 percent of the national median, where equivalent income is disposable income, adjusted for family size and composition. UNICEF uses a modified equivalence scale to adjust for household size by weighting the first adult in the household by 1, the subsequent adults by .5, and children under age 14 by .3, then summing the weights up and dividing total household income by the total weight. We chose countries based on their productivity per worker hour using the "PPP Converted GDP Laspeyres Per Hour Worked by Employees at 2005 Constant Prices" series from *Penn World Table Version 7.0* (Heston, Summers, and Aten 2011) and excluded countries whose productivity is less than half that of the United States.

Figure 7Y. Child poverty gap in selected developed countries, 2009. Underlying data are from UNICEF Innocenti Research Centre Report Card 10 (Adamson 2012), Figure 7, "The Poverty Gap." The child poverty gap is the distance between the poverty line and the median family income of children below the poverty line, expressed as a percentage of the poverty line. This is calculated by lining up all individuals in households by household-size-adjusted income (with children taking their family income value) and then locating the poverty line, which is 50 percent of national median income. UNICEF uses a modified equivalence scale to adjust for household size by weighting the first adult in the household by 1, the subsequent adults by .5, and children under age 14 by .3, then summing the weights up and dividing total household income by the total weight. The median income of children below the poverty line is then calculated. Then the gap between the poverty line and the median income of children is then taken as a share of the poverty line. For example, for a country with a median income of $50,000, the poverty line is $25,000. If the median income for children living below $25,000 is $15,000, the difference is $25,000-$15,000 = $10,000. This difference, taken as a share of the poverty line, yields a child poverty gap of $10,000/$25,000 (40 percent). We chose countries from the UNICEF list based on their productivity per worker hour using the "PPP Converted GDP Laspeyres Per Hour Worked by Employees at 2005 Constant Prices" series from *Penn World Table Version 7.0* (Heston, Summers, and Aten 2011), and excluded countries whose productivity is less than half that of the United States.

Figure 7Z. Extent to which taxes and transfer programs reduce the relative poverty rate, selected developed OECD countries, late 2000s. Underlying data are from the Organisation for Economic Co-operation and Development's *Stat Extracts* public data series. Household-size-adjusted income, or equivalent income, is household income divided by the square root of the household size. We chose countries based on their productivity per worker hour using the "PPP Converted GDP Laspeyres Per Hour Worked by Employees at 2005 Constant Prices" series from *Penn World Table Version 7.0* (Heston, Summers, and Aten 2011), and excluded countries whose productivity is less than half that of the United States.

Figure 7AA. Social expenditure and relative poverty rates selected in OECD countries, late 2000s. Underlying data are from the Organisation for Economic Co-operation and Development's *Stat Extracts* public data series. The relative poverty rate is the share of individuals living in households with income below half of household-size-adjusted median income, which is household income divided by the square root of the household size. We chose countries based on their productivity per worker hour using the "PPP Converted GDP Laspeyres Per Hour Worked by Employees at 2005 Constant Prices" series from the *Penn World Table Version 7.0* (Heston, Summers, and Aten 2011), and excluded countries whose productivity is less than half that of the United States.

Appendix A
CPS income measurement

This appendix explains the various adjustments made to microdata from the U.S. Census Bureau's Current Population Survey Annual Social and Economic Supplement (CPS-ASEC, commonly referred to as the March Supplement or March CPS) and the methodology used to prepare the data. The CPS is a monthly survey of unemployment and labor force participation prepared by the U.S. Census Bureau for the Bureau of Labor Statistics, and the CPS-ASEC is a special annual questionnaire that gathers income and earnings data. The microdata are raw untabulated survey responses. This microdata set is one of the data sources used for our analyses of family and household incomes as well as poverty. Each March, approximately 60,000 households are asked questions about their incomes from a wide variety of sources in the prior year (for example, the income data in the 2011 March CPS refer to 2010).

In order to preserve the confidentiality of respondents, the income variables in the public-use files of the CPS are top-coded, that is, values above a certain level are capped at a single common value. The reasoning is that since so few individuals, if any, have incomes above this "top-code," reporting the *exact* income number could allow somebody to use that information (along with other information from the March CPS, such as state of residence, age, ethnicity, etc.) to actually identify a specific survey respondent. Since income inequality measures are sensitive to changes in the upper reaches of the income distribution, this top-coding poses a challenge to analysts interested in both the extent of inequality in a given period and the change in inequality over time. We use an imputation technique, described below, that is commonly used in such cases to estimate the value of top-coded data. Over the course of the 1990s, Census top-coding procedures underwent significant changes, which also must be dealt with to preserve consistency. These methods are discussed below.

For most of the years of data in our study, a relatively small share of the distribution of any one variable is top-coded. For example, in 1989, 0.67 percent (i.e., two-thirds) of the top 1 percent of weighted cases are top-coded on the variable "earnings from longest job," meaning actual reported values are given for more than 99 percent of those with positive earnings. Nevertheless, the disproportionate influence of the small group of top-coded cases means their earnings levels cannot be ignored.

Our approach has been to impute the average value above the top-code for the key components of income using the assumption that the tails of these distributions follow a Pareto distribution. (The Pareto distribution is defined as $c/(x^{(a+1)})$, where c and a are positive constants that we estimate using the top 20 percent of the empirical distribution. More precisely, c is a scale parameter assumed known; a is the key parameter for estimation.) We apply this technique to three key variables: income from wage and salary (1968–1987), earnings from longest job (1988–2000), and income from interest (1968–1992). Since the upper tail of empirical income distributions closely follows the general shape of the Pareto distribution, this imputation method is commonly used for dealing with top-coded data. The estimate uses the shape of the upper part of the distribution (in our case, the top 20 percent) to extrapolate to the part that is unobservable due to the top-codes. Intuitively, if the shape of the observable part of the distribution suggests that the tail above the top-code is particularly long, implying a few cases with very high income values, the imputation will return a high mean relative to the case in which the tail above the top-code appears rather short.

Polivka and Miller (1998), using an uncensored dataset (i.e., without top-codes), show that the Pareto procedure effectively replicates the mean above the top-code. For example, Polivka and Miller's analysis of the use of the technique to estimate usual weekly earnings from the earnings files of the CPS yields estimates that are generally within less than 1 percent of the true mean.

As noted, the U.S. Census Bureau has lifted the top-codes over time in order to accommodate the fact that nominal and real wage growth eventually renders the old top-codes too low. For example, the top-coded value for "earnings from longest job" was increased from $50,000 in 1979 to $99,999 in 1989. Given the growth of earnings over this period, we did not judge this change (or any others in the income-component variables) to create inconsistencies in the trend comparisons between these two years.

However, changes made in the mid- to late 1990s data did require consistency adjustments. For these years, the Census Bureau adjusted the top-codes: Some were raised, some were lowered, and the new top-codes were determined by using the higher value of either the top 3 percent of all reported amounts for the variable or the top 0.5 percent of all persons. The bureau also used "plug-in" averages above the top-codes for certain variables. "Plug-ins" are group-specific average values taken above the top-code, with the groups defined on the basis of gender, race, and worker status. We found that the Pareto procedure was not feasible with unearned income, given the empirical distributions of these variables, so for March data from (survey year) 1996 forward, we use the "plug-in" values. Our tabulations show that, in tandem with the procedure described next regarding earnings, this approach avoids trend inconsistencies.

The most important variable that we adjust (i.e., the adjustment with the largest impact on family income) is "earnings from longest job." The top-code on this variable was raised sharply in survey year 1994, and this change leads to an upward bias in comparing estimates at or around that year to earlier years. (Note that this bias is attenuated over time as nominal income growth "catches up" to the new top-code, and relatively smaller shares of respondents again fall into that category.) Our procedure for dealing with this was to impose a lower top-code on the earnings data, to grow that top-code over time by the rate of inflation, and to calculate Pareto estimates based on these artificial top-codes. We found that this procedure led to a relatively smooth series across the changes in Census Bureau methodology.

For example, we find that, while our imputed series generates lower incomes among, say, the top 5 percent of families (because we are imposing a lower top-code) in the mid-1990s, by the end of the 1990s our estimates were only slightly lower than those from the unadjusted Census data. For 2001 forward we do not have any top-code adjustments.

Appendix B
Wage measurement

This appendix provides background information on the analysis of wage data from the Current Population Survey (CPS), which is best known for providing the monthly estimates of unemployment. The CPS is prepared by the U.S. Census Bureau for the Bureau of Labor Statistics (BLS). Specifically, for 1979 and beyond, we analyze microdata files that contain a full year's data on the outgoing rotation groups (ORG) in the CPS. (For years prior to 1979, we use the CPS May files; our use of these files is discussed later in this appendix.) We believe that the CPS-ORG files allow for timely and accurate analyses of wage trends that are in keeping with the familiar labor force definitions and concepts employed by BLS.

The sampling framework of the monthly CPS is a "rolling panel," in which households are in the survey for four consecutive months, out for eight, and then back in for four months. The ORG files provide data on those CPS respondents in either the fourth or eighth month of the CPS (i.e., in groups four or eight, out of a total of eight groups). Therefore, in any given month, the ORG file represents a quarter of the CPS sample. For a given year, the ORG file is equivalent to three months of CPS files (one-fourth of 12 months). For our analyses, we use a sample drawn from the full-year ORG sample, the size of which ranges from 160,000 to 180,000 observations during the 1979 to 1995 period. Due to a decrease in the overall sample size of the CPS, the ORG shrank to 145,000 cases from 1996 to 1998, and our most recent sample contains about 170,000 cases.

Changes in annual or weekly earnings can result from changes in hourly earnings or changes in time worked (hours worked per week or weeks worked per year). Our analyses focus on the hourly wage, which represents the pure price of labor (exclusive of benefits), because we are interested in changing pay levels for the workforce and its subgroups. This enables us to clearly distinguish changes in earnings resulting from more (or less) work from changes resulting from more (or less) pay. Most of our wage analyses, therefore, do not account for weekly or annual earnings changes due to reduced or increased work hours or opportunities for employment. An exception is Table 4.1, which presents annual hours, earnings, and hourly wages from the March CPS and shows that the overwhelming driver of annual wage trends between business cycle peaks has been trends in hourly wages.

In our view, the ORG files provide a better source of data for wage analyses than the traditionally used March CPS files. In order to calculate hourly wages from the March CPS, analysts must make calculations using three retrospective variables: the annual earnings, weeks worked, and usual weekly hours worked in the year prior to the survey. In contrast, respondents in the ORG are asked a set of questions about hours worked, weekly wages, and, for workers paid by the hour, hourly wages in the week prior to the survey. In this regard, the data from the ORG are likely to be more reliable than data from the March CPS. See Bernstein and Mishel (1997) for a detailed discussion of these differences.

Our subsample includes all wage and salary workers with valid wage and hour data, whether paid weekly or by the hour. Specifically, in order to be included in our subsample, respondents had to meet the following criteria:

- age 18–64

- employed in the public or private sector (unincorporated self-employed were excluded)

- hours worked within the valid range in the survey (1–99 per week, or hours vary—see discussion below)

- either hourly or weekly wages within the valid survey range (top-coding discussed below)

For those who met these criteria, an hourly wage was calculated in the following manner: If a valid hourly wage was reported, that wage was used throughout our analysis. For salaried workers (those who report only a weekly wage), the hourly wage was their weekly wage divided by their hours worked. Outliers, i.e., persons with hourly wages below 50 cents or above $100 in 1989 dollars (adjusted by the CPI-U-X1 consumer price index), were removed from the analysis. Starting from year 2002, we use dollars adjusted by the Consumer Price Index Research Series Using Current Methods (CPI-U-RS). These yearly upper and lower bounds are presented in **Table B.1**. CPS demographic weights were applied to make the sample nationally representative.

The hourly wage reported by hourly workers in the CPS excludes overtime, tips, or commissions (OTTC), thus introducing a potential undercount in the

Table B.1 Wage earner sample, hourly wage lower and upper limits, 1973–2011

	Lower	Upper		Lower	Upper
1973	$0.19	$38.06	1993	$0.58	$116.53
1974	0.21	41.85	1994	0.60	119.52
1975	0.23	45.32	1995	0.61	122.90
1976	0.24	47.90	1996	0.63	126.53
1977	0.25	50.97	1997	0.65	129.54
1978	0.27	54.44	1998	0.66	131.45
1979	0.30	59.68	1999	0.67	134.35
1980	0.33	66.37	2000	0.69	138.87
1981	0.36	72.66	2001	0.71	142.82
1982	0.39	77.10	2002*	0.70	140.05
1983	0.40	80.32	2003*	0.72	143.26
1984	0.42	83.79	2004*	0.74	147.06
1985	0.43	86.77	2005*	0.76	152.10
1986	0.44	88.39	2006*	0.78	156.90
1987	0.46	91.61	2007*	0.81	161.45
1988	0.48	95.40	2008*	0.84	167.66
1989	0.50	100.00	2009*	0.84	167.04
1990	0.53	105.40	2010*	0.85	169.78
1991	0.55	109.84	2011*	0.88	175.14
1992	0.57	113.15			

* Upper limit adjusted by CPI-U-RS

Source: Authors' analysis of Current Population Survey Outgoing Rotation Group microdata

hourly wage for workers who regularly receive tips or premium pay. OTTC is included in the usual weekly earnings of hourly workers, which raises the possibility of assigning an imputed hourly wage to hourly workers based on the reported weekly wage and hours worked per week. Conceptually, using this imputed wage is preferable to using the reported hourly wage because it is more inclusive. We have chosen, however, not to use this broader wage measure, because the extra information on OTTC seems unreliable. We compared the imputed hourly wage (reported weekly earnings divided by weekly hours) to the reported hourly wage; the difference presumably reflects OTTC. This comparison showed that significant percentages of the hourly workforce appeared to receive negative OTTC. These error rates range from a low of 0 percent of the hourly workforce in 1989–1993 to a high of 16–17 percent in 1973–1988, and persist across the survey change from 1993 to 1994. Since negative OTTC is clearly implausible, we rejected this imputed hourly wage series and rely strictly on the hourly rate of pay as reported directly by hourly workers, subject to the sample criteria discussed above.

For tables that show wage percentiles, we "smooth" hourly wages to compensate for "wage clumps" in the wage distributions. The technique involves creating a categorical hourly wage distribution, where the categories are 50-cent intervals, starting at 25 cents. We then find the categories on either side of each decile and perform a weighted, linear interpolation to locate the wage precisely on the particular decile. The weights for the interpolation are derived from differences in the cumulative percentages on either side of the decile. For example, suppose that 48 percent of the wage distribution of workers by wage level are in the $9.26–$9.75 wage "bin," and 51 percent are in the next higher bin, $9.76–$10.25. The weight for the interpolation (in this case, the median, or 50th percentile) is (50–48)/(51–48), or two-thirds. The interpolated median equals this weight, times the width of the bin ($.50), plus the upper bound of the previous bin ($9.75); $10.08 in this example.

In order to preserve the confidentiality of respondents, the income variables in the public-use files of the CPS are top-coded, that is, values above a certain level are capped at a single common value. The reasoning is that since so few individuals, if any, have incomes above this "top-code," reporting the exact income number could allow somebody to use that information (along with other information from the CPS, such as state of residence, age, ethnicity, etc.) to actually identify a specific survey respondent. For the survey years 1973–1985, the weekly wage is top-coded at $999.00; an extended top-code value of $1,923 is available in 1986–1997; the top-code value changes to $2,884.61 in 1998 and remains at that level. Particularly for the later years, this truncation of the wage distribution creates a downward bias in the mean wage. We dealt with the top-coding issue by imputing a new weekly wage for top-coded individuals. The imputed value is the Pareto-imputed mean for the upper tail of the weekly earnings distribution, based on the distribution of weekly earnings up to the 80th percentile (see Appendix A for a discussion of the Pareto distribution). This procedure was done for men and women separately. The imputed values for men and women appear in **Table B.2**. A new hourly wage, equal to the new estimated value for weekly earnings, divided by that person's usual hours per week, was calculated.

In January 1994, a new survey instrument was introduced into the CPS; many labor force items were added and improved. This presents a significant challenge to researchers who wish to make comparisons over time. The most careful research on the impact of the survey change has been conducted by BLS researcher Anne Polivka (1996). Interestingly, Polivka did not find that the survey changes had a major impact on broad measures of unemployment or wage

Table B.2 Pareto-imputed mean values for top-coded weekly earnings, and share top coded, 1973–2011 *Part 1 of 2*

	Share (percent hours)			Value	
	All	Men	Women	Men	Women
1973	0.11%	0.17%	0.02%	$1,365	$1,340
1974	0.16	0.26	0.01	1,385	1,297
1975	0.21	0.35	0.02	1,410	1,323
1976	0.30	0.51	0.01	1,392	1,314
1977	0.36	0.59	0.04	1,384	1,309
1978	0.38	0.65	0.02	1,377	1,297
1979	0.57	0.98	0.05	1,388	1,301
1980	0.72	1.23	0.07	1,380	1,287
1981	1.05	1.82	0.10	1,408	1,281
1982	1.45	2.50	0.18	1,430	1,306
1983	1.89	3.27	0.25	1,458	1,307
1984	2.32	3.92	0.42	1,471	1,336
1985	2.78	4.63	0.60	1,490	1,343
1986	0.80	1.37	0.15	2,435	2,466
1987	1.06	1.80	0.20	2,413	2,472
1988	1.30	2.19	0.29	2,410	2,461
1989	0.48	0.84	0.08	2,710	2,506
1990	0.60	1.04	0.11	2,724	2,522
1991	0.71	1.21	0.17	2,744	2,553
1992	0.77	1.28	0.22	2,727	2,581
1993	0.86	1.43	0.24	2,754	2,580
1994	1.25	1.98	0.43	2,882	2,689
1995	1.34	2.16	0.43	2,851	2,660
1996	1.41	2.27	0.46	2,863	2,678
1997	1.71	2.67	0.65	2,908	2,751
1998	0.63	0.98	0.25	4,437	4,155
1999	0.71	1.12	0.21	4,464	4,099
2000	0.83	1.38	0.24	4,502	4,179
2001	0.92	1.46	0.34	4,477	4,227
2002	0.91	1.44	0.33	4,555	4,252
2003	1.07	1.69	0.40	4,546	4,219
2004	1.19	1.90	0.42	4,611	4,195
2005	1.30	2.02	0.51	4,623	4,264
2006	1.49	2.26	0.65	4,636	4,328
2007	1.69	2.55	0.76	4,658	4,325

Table B.2 Pareto-imputed mean values for top-coded weekly earnings, and share top coded, 1973–2011 *Part 2 of 2*

	Share (percent hours)			Value	
	All	Men	Women	Men	Women
2008	1.95%	2.95%	0.87%	$4,723	$4,383
2009	2.09	3.20	0.92	4,872	4,403
2010	2.25	3.33	1.11	4,888	4,458
2011	2.26	3.30	1.14	4,792	4,477

Source: Authors' analysis of Current Population Survey Outgoing Rotation Group microdata

levels, though significant differences did surface for some subgroups (e.g., weekly earnings for those with less than a high school diploma and those with advanced degrees, and the unemployment rate of older workers). However, a change in the reporting of weekly hours did call for the alteration of our methodology. In 1994 the CPS began allowing people to report that their usual hours worked per week vary. In order to include nonhourly workers who report varying hours in our wage analyses, we estimated their usual hours using a regression-based imputation procedure, in which we predicted the usual hours of work for "hours vary" cases based on the usual hours worked of persons with similar characteristics. An hourly wage was calculated by dividing weekly earnings by the estimate of hours for these workers. The share of our sample that received such a wage in the 1994–2005 period is presented in **Table B.3**. The reported hourly wage of hourly workers was preserved.

BLS analysts Ilg and Haugen (2000), following Polivka (2000), did adjust the 10th-percentile wage because "changes to the survey in 1994 led to lower reported earnings for relatively low-paid workers, compared with pre-1994 estimates." We make no such adjustments for both practical and empirical reasons. Practically, the BLS has provided no adjustment factors for hourly wage trends that we can use—Polivka's work is for weekly wages. More important, the trends in 10th-percentile hourly wages differ from those reported by Ilg and Haugen for 10th-percentile weekly earnings. This is perhaps not surprising, since the composition of earners at the "bottom" will differ when measured by weekly rather than hourly wages, with low-weekly earners being almost exclusively part-timers. Empirically, Ilg and Haugen show the unadjusted 50/10 wage gap increasing between 1993 and 1994, when the new survey begins. In contrast, our 50/10 wage gap for hourly wages decreases between 1993 and 1994. Thus, the pattern of wage change in their data differs greatly from that in our data. In fact, our review of the 1993–1994 trends across all of the deciles shows no discontinuities whatsoever. Consequently, we make no adjustments to account for any effect of

Table B.3 Share of wage earners assigned an hourly wage from imputed weekly hours, 1994–2011

	Percent hours vary
1994	2.0%
1995	2.1
1996	2.4
1997	2.4
1998	2.5
1999	2.4
2000	2.4
2001	2.5
2002	2.5
2003	2.5
2004	2.7
2005	2.7
2006	2.5
2007	2.4
2008	2.4
2009	2.3
2010	2.1
2011	2.0

Source: Authors' analysis of Current Population Survey Outgoing Rotation Group microdata

the 1994 survey change. Had we made the sort of adjustments suggested by Polivka, our measured fall in the 50/10 wage gap in the 1990s would be even larger, and the overall pattern—wage gaps shrinking at 50/10, widening at 90/50, and, especially, at 95/50—would remain the same.

When a response is not obtained for weekly earnings, or an inconsistency is detected, an "imputed" response is performed by CPS using a "hot deck" method, whereby a response from another sample person with similar demographic and economic characteristics is used for the nonresponse. This procedure for imputing missing wage data appears to bias comparisons between union and nonunion members. We restrict our sample to the observations with non-imputed wages only for analysis of the union wage premium (Table 4.33).

Racial/ethnic demographic variables are also used in tables and in results reporting wage regression analyses. Starting in January of 2003, individuals are asked directly if they belong to Spanish, Hispanic, or Latino categories. Persons who report they are Hispanic also may select more than one race. For consistency, our race variable includes four mutually exclusive categories across years:

- white, non-Hispanic

- black, non-Hispanic

- Hispanic, any race

- all others

In January 2003, the CPS used the 2002 Census Bureau occupational and industry classification systems, which are derived from the 2000 Standard Occupational Classification (SOC) system and the 2002 North American Industry Classification System (NAICS). The new classification systems create breaks in existing data series at all levels of aggregation. Since we have built in "old" and "new" industry and occupation systems in our underlying 2000–2002 data, we use year 2000 as a break point to create consistent analyses with the "old" code for pre-2000 analysis and the "new" code for post-2000 analysis.

Beginning in 1992, the CPS employed a new coding scheme for education, providing data on respondents' highest degree attained. In earlier years, the CPS provided data on years of schooling completed. The challenge of making a consistent wage series by education level is to either make the new data consistent with the past or to make the old "years of schooling" data consistent with the new educational attainment measures. In prior editions of *The State of Working America*, we achieved a consistent series by imputing years of schooling for 1992 and later years, i.e., making the "new" consistent with the "old." In this version, however, we have converted the old data to the new coding following Jaeger (1997). However, Jaeger does not separately identify four-year college and "more than college" categories. Since the wages of these subgroups of the "college or more" group have divergent trends, we construct pre-1992 wages and employment separately for "four-year college" and "advanced." To do so, we compute wages, wage premiums, and employment separately for those with 16, 17, and 18-plus years of schooling completed. The challenge is to distribute the "17s" to the 16 years (presumably a four-year degree) and 18-plus years (presumably advanced) groups. We do this by using the share of the 17s that have a terminal four-year college degree, as computed in the February 1990 CPS supplement that provides both education codings: 61.4 percent. We then assume that 61.4 percent of all of the 17s are "college only" and compute a weighted average of the 16s and 61.4 percent of the 17s to construct "college only" wages and wage premiums. Correspondingly, we compute a weighted average of 38.6 percent (or 1 less 61.4 percent) of the 17s and the 18s to construct advanced "wages and wage premiums." Distributing the 17s affects each year differently depending on the actual change in the wages and premiums for 17s and the changing relative size of the 17s (which varies only slightly from 2.5 percent of men and women from 1979 to 1991).

We employ these education categories in various tables in Chapter 4, where we present wage trends by education over time. For the data for 1992 and later, we compute the "some college" trends by aggregating those "with some college but no degree beyond high school" and those with an associate or other degree that is not a four-year college degree.

Bibliography

Aaronson, Daniel, and Bhashkar Mazumder. 2007. *Intergenerational Economic Mobility in the U.S., 1940 to 2000*. Federal Reserve Bank of Chicago Working Paper 2005-12. http://www.chicagofed.org/webpages/publications/working_papers/2005/wp_12.cfm

Acs, Gregory, and Seth Zimmerman. 2008a. *Like Watching Grass Grow? Assessing Changes in U.S. Intragenerational Economic Mobility over the Past Two Decades*. A report of The Urban Institute and the Economic Mobility Project of The Pew Charitable Trusts.

Acs, Gregory, and Seth Zimmerman. 2008b. *U.S. Intragenerational Economic Mobility from 1984 to 2004*. A report of Economic Mobility Project of The Pew Charitable Trusts. http://www.urban.org/publications/1001226.html

Adamson, Peter. 2012. *Measuring Child Poverty: New League Tables of Child Poverty in the World's Rich Countries*. UNICEF Innocenti Research Centre Report Card 10. http://www.unicef.org.uk/Documents/Publications/RC10-measuring-child-poverty.pdf.

Alvaredo, Facundo, Tony Atkinson, Thomas Piketty, and Emmanuel Saez. Various years. *The World Top Incomes* [database]. http://g-mond.parisschoolofeconomics.eu/topincomes/

American Bankruptcy Institute. *Annual and Quarterly U.S. Bankruptcy Statistics* [data set]. Various years. http://www.abiworld.org/Content/NavigationMenu/NewsRoom/BankruptcyStatistics/Bankruptcy_Filings_1.htm

Autor, David, Alan Manning, and Christopher Smith. 2010. *The Contribution of the Minimum Wage to U.S. Wage Inequality Over Three Decades: A Reassessment*. Massachusetts Institute of Technology Working Paper. http://economics.mit.edu/files/3279\

Bailey, Martha J., and Susan M. Dynarski. 2011. *Gains and Gaps: Changing Inequality in U.S. College Entry and Completion*. National Bureau of Economic Research Working Paper No. 17633. www.nber.org/papers/w17633

Bakija, Jon, Adam Cole, and Bradley Heim. 2012. *Job and Income Growth of Top Earners and the Causes of Changing Income Inequality: Evidence from U.S. Tax Return Data.* http://web.williams. edu/Economics/wp/BakijaColeHeimJobsIncomeGrowthTopEarners.pdf

Bernstein, Jared, and Lawrence Mishel. 1997. "Has Wage Inequality Stopped Growing?" *Monthly Labor Review* (Bureau of Labor Statistics), vol. 120, no. 12, pp. 3–16. http://www.bls. gov/mlr/1997/12/art1abs.htm

Bernstein, Jared, James Lin, and Lawrence Mishel. 2007. "The Characteristics of Offshorable Jobs." Economic Policy Institute commentary, November 14. http://www.epi.org/publication/ webfeatures_viewpoints_characteristics_of_offshorable_jobs/

Bivens, Josh. 2008. *Everybody Wins, Except for Most of Us: What Economics Teaches About Globalization.* Washington, D.C.: Economic Policy Institute.

Blinder, Alan S. 2007. *How Many U.S. Jobs Might Be Offshorable?* Center for Economic Policy Studies Working Paper No. 60. http://www.princeton.edu/~ceps/workingpapers/142blinder. pdf

Blinder, Alan S., and Alan B. Krueger. 2009. *Alternative Measures of Offshorability: A Survey Approach.* Center for Economic Policy Studies Working Paper No. 190. http://www.princeton. edu/~ceps/workingpapers/190blinder.pdf

Borjas, George J., and Lawrence F. Katz. 2005. *The Evolution of the Mexican-Born Workforce in the United States.* National Bureau of Economic Research Working Paper No. 11281. http:// www.nber.org/papers/w11281

Bradbury, Katharine. 2011. *Trends in U.S. Family Income Mobility, 1969–2006.* Federal Reserve Bank of Boston Working Paper No. 11-10. http://www.bos.frb.org/economic/wp/ wp2011/wp1110.htm

Bricker, Jesse, Arthur B. Kennickell, Kevin B. Moore, and John Sabelhaus. 2012. "Changes in U.S. Family Finances from 2007 to 2010: Evidence from the Survey of Consumer Finances." *Federal Reserve Bulletin*, vol. 98, no. 2. http://www.federalreserve.gov/Pubs/Bulletin/2012/ PDF/scf12.pdf

Broom, Leonard, and William Shay. 2000. *Discontinuities in the Distribution of Great Wealth: Sectoral Forces Old and New.* Levy Economics Institute College Working Paper No. 308, prepared for "Saving, Intergenerational Transfers, and the Distribution of Wealth" conference, Bard College, June 2000.

Brown, Meta, Andrew Haughwout, Donghoon Lee, Maricar Mabutas, and Wilbert van der Klaauw. 2012. "Grading Student Loans," *Liberty Street Economics* (a blog of the Federal Reserve Bank of New York), March 5. http://libertystreeteconomics.newyorkfed.org/2012/03/ grading-student-loans.html

Buchmueller, Thomas C., John DiNardo, and Robert G. Valletta. 2001. *Union Effects on Health Insurance Provision and Coverage in the United States.* National Bureau of Economic Research Working Paper No. 8238. http://www.nber.org/papers/w8238

Bureau of Economic Analysis (U.S. Department of Commerce) Fixed Assets Accounts. Various years. *Fixed Assets Accounts Tables* [data tables]. http://bea.gov/iTable/iTable.cfm?ReqID=10&step=1

Bureau of Economic Analysis (U.S. Department of Commerce) National Income and Product Accounts. Various years. *National Income and Product Accounts Tables* [data tables]. http://bea.gov/iTable/iTable.cfm?ReqID=9&step=1

Bureau of Labor Statistics (U.S. Department of Labor) Business Employment Dynamics program. Various years. *National Business Employment Dynamics Data by Firm Size Class* [data charts and tables]. http://bls.gov/bdm/bdmfirmsize.htm

Bureau of Labor Statistics (U.S. Department of Labor) Consumer Price Indexes program. Various years. *All Urban Consumers: Chained Consumer Price Index (CPI)* [database]. http://bls.gov/cpi/

Bureau of Labor Statistics (U.S. Department of Labor) Current Employment Statistics program. Various years. *Employment, Hours and Earnings—National* [database]. http://www.bls.gov/ces/#data

Bureau of Labor Statistics (U.S. Department of Labor) Employment Projections program. Various years. *Employment Projections—Tables* [data tables]. http://www.bls.gov/emp/#tables

Bureau of Labor Statistics (U.S. Department of Labor) Job Openings and Labor Turnover Survey program. Various years. *Job Openings and Labor Turnover Survey* [database]. http://www.bls.gov/jlt/#data

Bureau of Labor Statistics (U.S. Department of Labor) Labor Productivity and Costs program. Various years. *Major Sector Productivity and Costs* and *Industry Productivity and Costs* [databases]. http://www.bls.gov/lpc/#data. (Unpublished data provided by program staff at EPI's request.)

Bureau of Labor Statistics (U.S. Department of Labor) National Compensation Survey—Employment Costs Trends. Various years. *Employer Costs for Employee Compensation* [economic news release]. http://www.bls.gov/ect/home.htm

Bureau of Labor Statistics (U.S. Department of Labor) Occupational Employment Statistics program. Various years. *Current Occupational Employment and Wages* [economic news release]. http://www.bls.gov/oes/

Bureau of Labor Statistics (U.S. Department of Labor) Work Experience of the Population (Annual) [economic news release]. Various years. http://www.bls.gov/news.release/work.toc.htm

Bureau of Labor Statistics (U.S. Department of Labor). 2008. "Updated CPI-U-RS, All Items and All items Less Food and Energy, 1978–2007." http://www.bls.gov/cpi/cpiurs1978_2007.pdf

Bureau of Labor Statistics (U.S. Department of Labor). 2011. *National Compensation Survey: Employee Benefits in the United States, March 2011*, Bulletin 2771. Data tables accessed through "Browse by Benefits" tab at http://bls.gov/ncs/ebs

Bureau of Labor Statistics (U.S. Department of Labor). Employment Projections program. 2012. "Employment Projections—2010–20" [news release]. www.bls.gov/news.release/pdf/ecopro.pdf

Burgard, Sarah A., Jennie E. Brand, and James S. House. 2007. "Toward a Better Estimation of the Effect of Job Loss on Health." *Journal of Health and Social Behavior*, vol. 48, no. 4, pp. 369–384.

Burkhauser, Richard V., Jeff Larrimore, and Kosali I. Simon. 2011. *A 'Second Opinion' on the Economic Health of the American Middle Class*. National Bureau of Economic Research Working Paper No. 17164. http://www.nber.org/papers/w17164

Burtless, Gary, and Sveta Milusheva. 2012. *Effects of Employer Health Costs on the Trend and Distribution of Social Security-Taxable Wages*. Center for Retirement Research at Boston College working paper.

Card, David, Thomas Lemieux, and W. Craig Riddell. 2002. *Unions and the Wage Structure*. http://faculty.arts.ubc.ca/tlemieux/papers/unions%20structure.pdf

Carnevale, Anthony, and Stephen Rose. 2003. *Socioeconomic Status, Race/Ethnicity, and Selective College Admissions*. A Century Foundation Paper. http://tcf.org/publications/2003/3/pb252

Case, Karl E., John M. Quigley, and Robert J. Shiller. 2005. "Comparing Wealth Effects: The Stock Market vs. the Housing Market." *Advances in Macroeconomics*, vol. 5, no. 1, pp. 1–34.

Center for Retirement Research. 2006. "Private Workers With Pension Coverage, by Pension Type, 1980, 1992, and 2004" [online chart]. Center for Retirement Research at Boston College.

Charles, Kerwin Kofi, and Erik Hurst. 2002. *The Correlation of Wealth Across Generations*. National Bureau of Economic Research Working Paper No. 9314. http://www.nber.org/papers/w9314

Compustat. Various years. ExecuComp database [commercial database product accessible by purchase]. http://www.compustat.com/products.aspx?id=2147492873&terms=Execucomp

Congressional Budget Office. 2008. *Historical Effective Tax Rates, 1979 to 2005: Supplement with Additional Data on Sources of Income and High-Income Households* (Supplement to *Historical Effective Federal Tax Rates: 1979 to 2005*), "Effective Federal Tax Rates for All Households, by Comprehensive Household Income Category, 1979 to 2005 (Percent)" http://cbo.gov/sites/default/files/cbofiles/ftpdocs/98xx/doc9884/12-23-effectivetaxrates_letter.pdf

Congressional Budget Office. 2010a. Average Federal Taxes by Income Group Web page portal. Excel data files accessible through the "Additional Data," "Supplemental Material," and "Additional Analyses" tabs. http://www.cbo.gov/publication/42870. (The web page provides supplemental material to the CBO report, Average Federal Tax Rates in 2007; http://cbo.gov/sites/default/files/cbofiles/attachments/AverageFedTaxRates2007.pdf)

Congressional Budget Office. 2010b. Unpublished health care data related to *Average Federal Tax Rates by Income Group* (see Congressional Budget Office 2010a).

Congressional Budget Office. 2010c. Unpublished income data by source and by family type related to *Average Federal Tax Rates by Income Group* (see Congressional Budget Office 2010a).

Congressional Budget Office. 2011. *Trends in the Distribution of Household Income Between 1979 and 2007.* Publication No. 4031. http://cbo.gov/sites/default/files/cbofiles/attachments/10-25-HouseholdIncome.pdf

Congressional Budget Office. 2012. *The Budget and Economic Outlook: Fiscal Years 2012 to 2022,* "Data Underlying Figures" [downloadable Excel file]. http://www.cbo.gov/publication/42905

Cooper, David. 2012. "A Rising Tide for Increasing Minimum Wage Rates." *Working Economics* (Economic Policy Institute blog), April 13. http://www.epi.org/blog/proposals-increasing-minimum-wage/

Corak, Miles. 2010. *Chasing the Same Dream, Climbing Different Ladders: Economic Mobility in the United States and Canada.* A report of The Economic Mobility Project of The Pew Charitable Trusts. http://www.pewstates.org/uploadedFiles/PCS_Assets/2010/PEW_EMP_US-CANADA.pdf

Corak, Miles. 2011. *Inequality from Generation to Generation: The United States in Comparison.* University of Ottawa.

Corak, Miles. 2012. Unpublished data provided to EPI upon request.

Council of Economic Advisers. 2012. *Economic Report of the President* together with *The Annual Report of the Council of Economic Advisers.* http://www.whitehouse.gov/administration/eop/cea/economic-report-of-the-President

Credit Suisse Research Institute. 2011. *Global Wealth Databook 2011.* https://infocus.credit-suisse.com/data/_product_documents/_shop/324292/2011_global_wealth_report_databook.pdf

Current Population Survey Annual Social and Economic Supplement. *Historical Income Tables* [data tables]. Various years. www.census.gov/hhes/www/income/data/historical/index.html

Current Population Survey Annual Social and Economic Supplement. *Historical Poverty Tables* [data tables]. Various years. http://www.census.gov/hhes/www/poverty/data/historical/people.html

Current Population Survey Annual Social and Economic Supplement microdata. Various years. Survey conducted by the Bureau of the Census for the Bureau of Labor Statistics [machine-readable microdata file]. Washington, D.C.: U.S. Census Bureau. http://www.bls.census.gov/ftp/cps_ftp.html#cpsmarch

Current Population Survey basic monthly microdata. Various years. Survey conducted by the Bureau of the Census for the Bureau of Labor Statistics [machine-readable microdata file]. Washington, D.C.: U.S. Census Bureau. http://www.bls.census.gov/ftp/cps_ftp.html#cpsbasic

Current Population Survey/Housing Vacancy Survey. Various years. *Annual Statistics: 2011* [data tables] http://www.census.gov/hhes/www/housing/hvs/annual11/ann11ind.html)

Current Population Survey/Housing Vacancy Survey. Various years. *Historical Tables* [data tables]. http://www.census.gov/hhes/www/housing/hvs/historic/index.html

Current Population Survey labor force statistics. Various years. *Labor Force Statistics Including the National Unemployment Rate* [database accessed through "one-screen data search tab"]. http://www.bls.gov/cps/#data

Current Population Survey Outgoing Rotation Group microdata. Various years. Survey conducted by the Bureau of the Census for the Bureau of Labor Statistics [machine-readable microdata file]. Washington, D.C.: U.S. Census Bureau. http://www.bls.census.gov/ftp/cps_ftp.html#cpsbasic

Current Population Survey public data series. Various years. Aggregate data from basic monthly CPS microdata are available from the Bureau of Labor Statistics through three primary channels: as *Historical 'A' Tables* released with the BLS Employment Situation Summary (http://www.bls.gov/data/#historical-tables), through the *Labor Force Statistics Including the National Unemployment Rate* database (http://www.bls.gov/cps/#data), and through series reports (http://data.bls.gov/cgi-bin/srgate).

Dahl, Molly, and Jonathan Schwabish. 2008. *Recent Trends in the Variability of Individual Earnings and Household Income.* Congressional Budget Office Publication No. 2996. http://www.cbo.gov/publication/41714

Danziger, Sheldon, and Peter Gottschalk. 1995. *America Unequal.* New York: Russell Sage Foundation; Cambridge, Mass.: Harvard University Press.

Demos and Young Invincibles. 2011. *The State of Young America: Economic Barriers to the American Dream, Poll Results.* http://www.demos.org/publication/state-young-america-poll

Farber, Henry S. 2011. *Job Loss in the Great Recession: Historical Perspective from the Displaced Workers Survey, 1984–2010.* National Bureau of Economic Research Working Paper No. 17040. http://www.nber.org/papers/w17040

Federal Reserve Bank of New York. 2012. *Quarterly Report on Household Debt and Credit— Underlying Data* [downloadable Excel files]. February. http://www.newyorkfed.org/newsevents/news/research/2012/an120227.html

Federal Reserve Board. 2012a. *2010 Survey of Consumer Finances—Tables Based on the Internal Data*. "Estimates in Nominal Dollars" [Excel file], updated July 19. http://www.federalreserve. gov/econresdata/scf/scf_2010.htm

Federal Reserve Board. 2012b. *Household Debt Service and Financial Obligations Ratios* [data release]. Last update June 22. http://www.federalreserve.gov/releases/housedebt/

Federal Reserve Board, Flow of Funds Accounts of the United States. Various years. Data download program. http://www.federalreserve.gov/datadownload/Choose.aspx?rel=Z.1

Federal Reserve Economic Data (FRED). Various years. Database maintained by the Federal Reserve Bank of St. Louis. http://research.stlouisfed.org/fred2/

Fogg, Neeta P., and Paul E. Harrington. 2011. "Rising Mal-Employment and the Great Recession: The Growing Disconnection between Recent College Graduates and the College Labor Market." *Continuing Higher Education Review*, vol. 75. http://www.drexel.edu/provost/ clmp/docs/CLMP_RisingMal-EmploymentandtheGreatRecession.pdf

Forbes. Various years. "The Forbes 400: The Richest People in America." http://www.forbes. com/forbes-400/list/#p_1_s_arank_All%20industries_All%20states_All%20categories_

Fox, Mary Ann, Brooke A. Connolly, and Thomas D. Snyder. 2005. *Youth Indicators 2005: Trends in the Well-Being of American Youth*. National Center for Education Statistics. http:// nces.ed.gov/pubs2005/2005050.pdf

Freeman, Richard B. 1991. *How Much Has De-unionization Contributed to the Rise in Male Earnings Inequality?* National Bureau of Economic Research Working Paper No. 3826. http:// www.nber.org/papers/w3826

Freeman, Richard B., Joseph R. Blasi, and Douglas L. Kruse. 2011. *Inclusive Capitalism for the American Workforce: Reaping the Rewards of Economic Growth through Broad-based Employee Ownership and Profit Sharing*. Center for American Progress. http://www.americanprogress. org/issues/2011/03/worker_productivity.html

Gittleman, Maury, and Brooks Pierce. 2007. "New Estimates of Union Wage Effects in the U.S." *Economics Letters*. Elsevier, vol. 95, no. 2, pp. 198–202.

Goldin, Claudia, and Lawrence F. Katz. 2008. *The Race between Education and Technology: The Evolution of U.S. Educational Wage Differentials, 1890 to 2005*. Harvard University and the National Bureau of Economic Research. http://www.nber.org/papers/w12984

Gundersen, Bethney. 2003. "Unions and the Well-being of Low-skill Workers." PhD diss., George Warren Brown School of Social Work at Washington University in St. Louis.

Hacker, Jacob S., and Elisabeth Jacobs. 2008. *The Rising Instability of American Family Incomes, 1969–2004: Evidence from the Panel Study of Income Dynamics*. Economic Policy Institute Briefing Paper No. 213. http://www.epi.org/publication/bp213/

Haltiwanger, John C., Ron S. Jarmin, and Javier Miranda. 2010. *Who Creates Jobs? Small vs. Large vs. Young.* National Bureau of Economic Research Working Paper No. 16300. http://www.nber.org/papers/w16300

Hertz, Tom. 2006. *Understanding Mobility in America.* The Center for American Progress. http://www.americanprogress.org/kf/hertz_mobility_analysis.pdf

Heston, Alan, Robert Summers, and Bettina Aten. 2011. *Penn World Table Version 7.0* [database]. Center for International Comparisons of Production, Income and Prices at the University of Pennsylvania. http://pwt.econ.upenn.edu/php_site/pwt_index.php

Hirsch, Barry, and David Macpherson. 2003. "Union Membership and Coverage Database from the Current Population Survey: Note." *Industrial and Labor Relations Review,* vol. 56, no. 2, pp. 349–54. http://unionstats.gsu.edu/Hirsch-Macpherson_ILRR_CPS-Union-Database.pdf

Ilg, Randy E., and Steven E. Haugen. 2000. "Earnings and Employment Trends in the 1990s." *Bureau of Labor Statistics Monthly Labor Review,* vol. 123, no. 3, pp. 21–33. http://www.bls.gov/opub/mlr/2000/03/art2full.pdf

Internal Revenue Service SOI Tax Stats. *Various years. Individual Time Series Statistical Tables [data tables].* http://www.irs.gov/uac/SOI-Tax-Stats---Individual-Time-Series-Statistical-Tables

International Monetary Fund. 2011. *World Economic Outlook Database: September 2011 Edition.* http://www.imf.org/external/pubs/ft/weo/2011/02/weodata/index.aspx

International Social Survey Programme. 2009. *2009 Social Inequality IV* [data tables accessed through "Archive and Data" tab]. http://www.issp.org/index.php

Isaacs, Julia B., Isabel V. Sawhill, and Ron Haskins. 2008. *Getting Ahead or Losing Ground: Economic Mobility in America.* A report of The Brookings Institution and the Economic Mobility Project of The Pew Charitable Trusts. http://www.brookings.edu/research/reports/2008/02/economic-mobility-sawhill

Jacobson, Louis, Robert LaLonde, and Daniel Sullivan. 1993. "Earnings Losses of Displaced Workers." *American Economic Review,* vol. 83, no. 4, pp. 685–709.

Jaeger, David A. 1997. "Reconciling the Old and New Census Bureau Education Questions: Recommendations for Researchers." *Journal of Economics and Business Statistics,* vol. 15, no. 3, pp. 300–309. http://www.djaeger.org/research/pubs/jbesv15n3.pdf

Jäntti, Markus, Knut Røed, Robin Naylor, Anders Björklund, Bernt Bratsberg, Oddbjørn Raaum, Eva Österbacka, and Tor Eriksson. 2006. *American Exceptionalism in a New Light: A Comparison of Intergenerational Earnings Mobility in the Nordic Countries, the United Kingdom and the United States.* Institute for the Study of Labor (IZA) Discussion Paper Series No. 1938. http://ftp.iza.org/dp1938.pdf

Kahn, Lisa B. 2010. "The Long-Term Labor Market Consequences of Graduating from College in a Bad Economy." *Labour Economics*, vol.17, no. 2, pp. 303–316.

Katz, Lawrence F., and Alan B. Krueger. 1999. *The High-Pressure U.S. Labor Market of the 1990s*. Princeton University Industrial Relations Section Working Paper No. 416. http://dataspace.princeton.edu/jspui/bitstream/88435/dsp01dr26xx37d/1/416.pdf

Kopczuk, Wojciech, Emmanuel Saez, and Jae Song. 2010. "Earnings Inequality and Mobility in the United States: Evidence from Social Security Data Since 1937." *The Quarterly Journal of Economics*, February. http://elsa.berkeley.edu/~saez/kopczuk-saez-songQJE10mobility.pdf

Krugman, Paul. 1995. "Growing World Trade: Causes and Consequences." *Brookings Papers on Economic Activity*, vol. 26, no. 1, pp. 327–377.

Lee, Chul-In, and Gary Solon. 2006. *Trends in Intergenerational Income Mobility*. National Bureau of Economic Research Working Paper No. 12007. http://www.nber.org/papers/w12007

Mazumder, Bhashkar. 2011. *Black-White Differences in Intergenerational Economic Mobility in the US*. Federal Reserve Bank of Chicago Working Paper 2011-10. http://www.chicagofed.org/webpages/publications/working_papers/2011/wp_10.cfm

Mishel, Lawrence, and Kar-Fai Gee. 2012. "Why Aren't Workers Benefiting From Labour Productivity Growth in the United States?" *International Productivity Monitor*, no. 23. http://www.csls.ca/ipm/ipm23.asp

Mishel, Lawrence, and Natalie Sabadish. 2012. *Methodology for Measuring CEO Compensation and the Ratio of CEO-to-Worker Compensation*. Economic Policy Institute Working Paper No. 293. http://www.epi.org/publication/wp293-ceo-to-worker-pay-methodology/

Mishel, Lawrence, and Matthew Walters. 2003. *How Unions Help All Workers*. Economic Policy Institute Briefing Paper No. 143. http://www.epi.org/publication/briefingpapers_bp143/

Moody's Analytics. 2012. Moody's Economy.com, *MyEconomy.com* [subscription only database].

Moore, Quinn, and Heidi Shierholz. 2007. "A Cohort Analysis of the Gender Wage Gap." Unpublished manuscript.

Munnell, Alicia H. 2012. *401(k) Plans in 2010: An Update from the SCF*. Center for Retirement Research at Boston College Issue in Brief, no. 12-13. http://crr.bc.edu/wp-content/uploads/2012/07/IB_12-13.pdf

Munnell, Alicia H., Anthony Webb, and Francesca Golub-Sass. 2009. *The National Retirement Risk Index: After the Crash*. Center for Retirement Research at Boston College Issue in Brief no. 9-22. http://crr.bc.edu/wp-content/uploads/2009/10/IB_9-22.pdf

Murphy, Kevin, and Finis Welch. 1989. *Recent Trends in Real Wages: Evidence From Household Data*. Paper prepared for the Health Care Financing Administration of the U.S. Department of Health and Human Services. University of Chicago.

National Bureau of Economic Research. 2010. "U.S. Business Cycle Expansions and Contractions." http://nber.org/cycles/cyclesmain.html

Oreopoulos, Philip, Marianne Page, and Ann Huff Stevens. 2008. "The Intergenerational Effects of Worker Displacement." *Journal of Labor Economics*, vol. 26, no. 3, pp. 455–483.

Oreopoulos, Philip, Till von Wachter, and Andrew Heisz. 2008. *The Short- and Long-Term Career Effects of Graduating in a Recession: Hysteresis and Heterogeneity in the Market for College Graduates*. IZA (Institute for the Study of Labor) Discussion Paper No. 3578. http://www.columbia.edu/~vw2112/papers/iza_dp3578.pdf

Organisation for Economic Co-operation and Development (OECD). Various years. *Distribution of Gross Earnings of Full-time Employees and Gender Wage Gap* [Metadata Excel file]. http://www.oecd.org/document/34/0,3746,en_2649_33927_40917154_1_1_1_1,00.html#deciles

Organisation for Economic Co-operation and Development (OECD). Various years. *OECD. Stat Extracts* [databases]. http://stats.oecd.org/

Organisation for Economic Co-operation and Development (OECD). 2011. OECD *StatExtracts*, "Health Status" data. http://stats.oecd.org/Index.aspx?DatasetCode=HEALTH_STAT

Pierce, Brooks. 1999. *Compensation Inequality*. U.S. Department of Labor, Bureau of Labor Statistics Working Paper No. 323. http://www.bls.gov/ore/pdf/ec990040.pdf

Pierce, Brooks. 2010. "Recent Trends in Compensation Inequality." In Katharine Abraham, James Spletzer, and Michael Harper, eds., *Labor in the New Economy*. Cambridge, Mass.: National Bureau of Economic Research. http://www.nber.org/books/abra08-1

Piketty, Thomas, and Emmanuel Saez. 2007. "How Progressive is the U.S. Federal Tax System? A Historical and International Perspective." *Journal of Economic Perspectives*, vol. 21, no. 1, pp. 3–24.

Piketty, Thomas, and Emmanuel Saez. 2012. Downloadable Excel files with 2010 data update to tables and figures in Piketty, Thomas, and Emmanuel Saez. 2007. "Income and Wage Inequality in the United States 1913–2002," in A.B. Atkinson and Thomas Piketty, eds., *Top Incomes over the Twentieth Century. A Contrast Between Continental European and English-Speaking Countries*. Oxford University Press (a series update to "Income Inequality in the United States, 1913–1998," published in the *Quarterly Journal of Economics* in 2003, vol. 118, no. 1). Excel files accessed at http://elsa.berkeley.edu/~saez/

Polivka, Anne. 1996. "Data Watch: The Redesigned Current Population Survey." *Journal of Economic Perspectives*, vol. 10, no. 3, pp. 169–180. www.jstor.org/discover/10.2307/213852 7?uid=3739704&uid=2129&uid=2&uid=70&uid=4&uid=3739256&sid=47699137007457

Polivka, Anne. 2000. "Using Earnings Data from the Current Population Survey." Bureau of Labor Statistics working paper. http://papers.ssrn.com/sol3/papers.cfm?abstract_id=261190

Polivka, Anne E., and Stephen M. Miller. 1998. "The CPS after the Redesign: Refocusing the Economic Lens." In *Labor Statistics Measurement Issues*, eds. John Haltiwanger, Marilyn E. Manser, and Robert Topel, pp. 249–289. Chicago: University of Chicago Press.

Renwick, Trudi. 2011. "Income, Poverty, and Health Insurance Coverage: 2010—Poverty" [PowerPoint presentation]. U.S. Census Bureau, September. http://www.census.gov/newsroom/releases/pdf/2010_Report.pdf

Rothstein, Jesse. 2012. *The Labor Market Four Years into the Crisis: Assessing Structural Explanations*. National Bureau of Economic Research Working Paper No. 17966. http://www.nber.org/papers/w17966

Schettkat, Ronald, and Rongrong Sun. 2008. *Monetary Policy and European Unemployment*. Schumpter Discussion Papers, Schumpter School of Business and Economics, University of Wuppertal, Germany. http://d-nb.info/993773516/34

Schmitt, John. 2008. *The Union Wage Advantage for Low-wage Workers*. Center for Economic Policy and Research. http://www.cepr.net/index.php/publications/reports/the-union-wage-advantage-for-low-wage-workers/

Schmitt, John, and Janelle Jones. 2012. *Where Have All the Good Jobs Gone?* Center for Economic and Policy Research. http://www.cepr.net/index.php/publications/reports/where-have-all-the-good-jobs-gone

Schmitt, John, and Kris Warner. 2011. *Deconstructing Structural Unemployment*. Center for Economic and Policy Research. http://www.cepr.net/index.php/publications/reports/deconstructing-structural-unemployment

Scott, Robert E. 2008. *The Burden of Outsourcing*. Economic Policy Institute Briefing Paper No. 222. http://www.epi.org/publication/bp222/

Shierholz, Heidi. 2009. *Fix It and Forget It: Index the Minimum Wage to Growth in Average Wages*. Economic Policy Institute Briefing Paper No. 251. http://www.epi.org/page/-/pdf/bp251.pdf

Shiller, Robert. 2012. *Online Data Robert Shiller*. Historical housing market data and stock market data [Excel files] used in *Irrational Exuberance* (Princeton University Press 2000). Accessed August, 2012. http://www.econ.yale.edu/~shiller/data.htm

Short, Kathleen. 2011. "The Research Supplemental Poverty Measure: 2010," *Current Population Reports* (U.S. Census Bureau), November. http://www.census.gov/prod/2011pubs/p60-241.pdf

Social Security Administration. Trust Fund Data. Various years. "Old-Age and Survivors Insurance Trust Fund Expenditures" [data table]. http://www.ssa.gov/OACT/STATS/table4a1.html

Social Security Administration. Wage Statistics. Various years. *Wage Statistics [database]*. http:// www.ssa.gov/cgi-bin/netcomp.cgi

Solon, Gary. 1989. *Intergenerational Income Mobility in the United States*. IRP Discussion Paper No. 894–889. Institute for Research on Poverty at the University of Wisconsin-Madison.

Stevens, Ann Huff. 1997. "Persistent Effects of Job Displacement: The Importance of Multiple Job Losses." *Journal of Labor Economics*, vol. 15, no. 1, part 1, pp. 165–188.

Stevens, Ann Huff, and Jessamyn Schaller. 2009. *Short-run Effects of Parental Job Loss on Children's Academic Achievement*. National Bureau of Economic Research Working Paper No. 15480. http://www.nber.org/papers/w15480

Sullivan, Daniel, and Till von Wachter. 2009. "Job Displacement and Mortality: An Analysis Using Administrative Data." *The Quarterly Journal of Economics,* vol.124, no. 3, pp. 1265–1306.

Sullivan, Teresa A., Elizabeth Warren, and Jay Lawrence Westbrook. 2000. *The Fragile Middle Class: Americans in Debt*. New Haven, Conn.: Yale University Press.

Thiess, Rebecca. 2012. *The Future of Work: Trends and Challenges for Low-wage Workers*. Economic Policy Institute Briefing Paper No. 341. http://www.epi.org/publication/bp341-future-of-work/

Union Membership and Coverage Database. Various years. http://unionstats.com/

United States International Trade Commission (USITC). Various years. *USITC Interactive Tariff and Trade DataWeb*. http://dataweb.usitc.gov/

U.S. Census Bureau. 2009. *American Housing Survey, National Data* [data tables]. http://www. census.gov/housing/ahs/data/national.html

U.S. Census Bureau. Survey of Income and Program Participation microdata. 2008 panel. [machine-readable microdata file]. Washington, D.C.: U.S. Census Bureau. http://www.census.gov/sipp/

U.S. Department of Labor. Unemployment Insurance program. Various years. *Program Statistics* [database]. http://workforcesecurity.doleta.gov/unemploy/finance.asp

U.S. Department of Labor, Wage and Hour Division. 2009. "Federal Minimum Wage Rates Under the Fair Labor Standards Act." http://www.dol.gov/whd/minwage/chart.pdf

U.S. Department of the Treasury. 2007. *Income Mobility in the U.S. from 1996 to 2005*. http:// www.treasury.gov/resource-center/tax-policy/Documents/incomemobilitystudy03-08revise. pdf

Valletta, Rob, and Katherine Kuang. 2012. *Why is Unemployment Duration So Long?* Federal Reserve Bank of San Francisco Economic Letter No. 2012-03. http://www.frbsf.org/publications/economics/letter/2012/el2012-03.html

von Wachter, Till, Jae Song, and Joyce Manchester. 2009. *Long-Term Earnings Losses due to Mass-Layoffs During the 1982 Recession: An Analysis Using U.S. Administrative Data from 1974 to 2004.* Columbia University. http://www.columbia.edu/~vw2112/papers/mass_layoffs_1982.pdf

Wall Street Journal. CEO compensation survey. Various years. Compensation reported by the WSJ has been compiled by various companies over the years, including Pearl Meyer, the Mercer Group, and the Hay Group. *The Wall Street Journal/Hay Group Survey of CEO Compensation,* published May 8, 2011, is available at http://graphicsweb.wsj.com/php/CEOPAY11.html

Western, Bruce, and Jake Rosenfeld. 2011. *Unions, Norms, and the Rise in American Wage Inequality.* Harvard University Department of Sociology paper. http://www.wjh.harvard.edu/soc/faculty/western/pdfs/Unions_Norms_and_Wage_Inequality.pdf

Wolff, Edward. 2012. Unpublished analysis of the Federal Reserve Survey of Consumer Finances prepared in 2012 for the Economic Policy Institute.

Index

Note: References to tables and figures are in italics.

About EPI

The Economic Policy Institute (EPI), a nonprofit, nonpartisan think tank, was founded in 1986 to improve the lives of America's low- and moderate-income families by producing reliable economic research, insightful analysis, and visionary policy solutions.

EPI was the first, and remains the premier, think tank focusing on the economic condition of low- and middle-income Americans and their families. EPI believes every worker deserves a good job with fair pay, affordable health care, and retirement security.

EPI's research is original, reliable, and objective, and it spans a broad range of economic issues. EPI analyses are a trusted resource for policymakers, the media, and state research organizations. *The State of Working America*, published 12 times since 1988 and now available at stateofworkingamerica.org, is stocked in university libraries around the world. EPI also produces numerous research papers and policy analyses; sponsors conferences and seminars; briefs policymakers at all levels of government; testifies before national, state, and local legislatures; and provides information and background to the media. EPI's policy center provides technical support to national, state, and local constituency and advocacy organizations.

EPI's founding scholars include Jeff Faux, former EPI president; Barry Bluestone, dean of the School of Public Policy and Urban Affairs and director of the Kitty and Michael Dukakis Center for Urban and Regional Policy, Northeastern University; Robert Kuttner, co-founder and co-editor of *The American Prospect*; Ray Marshall, former U.S. secretary of labor and professor emeritus at the LBJ School of Public Affairs, University of Texas-Austin; Robert Reich, former U.S. secretary of labor and professor at the Goldman School of Public Policy, University of California-Berkeley; and Lester Thurow, professor emeritus at the Sloan School of Management, Massachusetts Institute of Technology.

For more information about EPI, visit epi.org. You can contact us at 1333 H St. NW, Suite 300, East Tower, Washington, D.C. 20005, (202) 775-8810. You can also follow us on Twitter at epi.org/twitter and on Facebook at epi.org/facebook.

About the authors

LAWRENCE MISHEL has been president of the Economic Policy Institute since 2002. Prior to that he was EPI's first research director (starting in 1987) and later became vice president. He is the co-author of all previous editions of *The State of Working America*. He holds a Ph.D. in economics from the University of Wisconsin-Madison, and his articles have appeared in a variety of academic and non-academic journals. His areas of research are labor economics, wage and income distribution, industrial relations, productivity growth, and the economics of education.

JOSH BIVENS joined the Economic Policy Institute in 2002 and is currently the director of research and policy. His primary areas of research include macroeconomics, social insurance, and globalization. He has published two books while working at EPI, edited another, and has written numerous research papers, including for academic journals. He appears often in media outlets to offer economic commentary and has testified several times before the U.S. Congress. He earned his Ph.D. from The New School for Social Research.

ELISE GOULD joined the Economic Policy Institute in 2003. Her research areas include employer-sponsored health insurance, inequality and health, poverty, mobility, and the employer tax exclusion. She has published her research in a range of venues from academic journals to general audience periodicals, been quoted by various news sources, and testified before the U.S. Congress. Also, she teaches health economics and econometrics to graduate students at Johns Hopkins University and The George Washington University, respectively. She holds a master's in public affairs from the University of Texas-Austin and a Ph.D. in economics from the University of Wisconsin-Madison.

HEIDI SHIERHOLZ joined the Economic Policy Institute as an economist in 2007. She does research on employment, unemployment, and labor force participation; the wage, income, and wealth distributions; the labor market outcomes of young workers; unemployment insurance; the minimum wage; and the effect of immigration on wages in the U.S. labor market. She previously worked as an assistant professor of economics at the University of Toronto, and she holds a Ph.D. in economics from the University of Michigan-Ann Arbor.